THE CINEMA 4D XL HANDBOOK

LIMITED WARRANTY AND DISCLAIMER OF LIABILITY

THE CD WHICH ACCOMPANIES THE BOOK MAY BE USED ON A SINGLE PC ONLY. THE LICENSE DOES NOT PERMIT THE USE ON A NETWORK (OF ANY KIND). YOU FURTHER AGREE THAT THIS LICENSE GRANTS PERMISSION TO USE THE PRODUCTS CONTAINED HEREIN, BUT DOES NOT GIVE YOU RIGHT OF OWNERSHIP TO ANY OF THE CONTENT OR PRODUCT CONTAINED ON THIS CD. USE OF THIRD PARTY SOFTWARE CONTAINED ON THIS CD IS LIMITED TO AND SUBJECT TO LICENSING TERMS FOR THE RESPECTIVE PRODUCTS.

CHARLES RIVER MEDIA, INC. ("CRM") AND/OR ANYONE WHO HAS BEEN INVOLVED IN THE WRITING, CREATION OR PRODUCTION OF THE ACCOMPANYING CODE ("THE SOFTWARE") OR THE THIRD PARTY PRODUCTS CONTAINED ON THE CD OR TEXTUAL MATERIAL IN THE BOOK, CANNOT AND DO NOT WARRANT THE PERFORMANCE OR RESULTS THAT MAY BE OBTAINED BY USING THE SOFTWARE OR CONTENTS OF THE BOOK. THE AUTHOR AND PUBLISHER HAVE USED THEIR BEST EFFORTS TO ENSURE THE ACCURACY AND FUNCTIONALITY OF THE TEXTUAL MATERIAL AND PROGRAMS CONTAINED HEREIN; WE HOWEVER, MAKE NO WARRANTY OF ANY KIND, EXPRESS OR IMPLIED, REGARDING THE PERFORMANCE OF THESE PROGRAMS OR CONTENTS. THE SOFTWARE IS SOLD "AS IS " WITHOUT WARRANTY (EXCEPT FOR DEFECTIVE MATERIALS USED IN MANUFACTURING THE DISK OR DUE TO FAULTY WORKMANSHIP);

THE AUTHOR, THE PUBLISHER, DEVELOPERS OF THIRD PARTY SOFTWARE, AND ANYONE INVOLVED IN THE PRODUCTION AND MANUFACTURING OF THIS WORK SHALL NOT BE LIABLE FOR DAMAGES OF ANY KIND ARISING OUT OF THE USE OF(OR THE INABILITY TO USE) THE PROGRAMS, SOURCE CODE, OR TEXTUAL MATERIAL CONTAINED IN THIS PUBLICATION. THIS INCLUDES , BUT IS NOT LIMITED TO, LOSS OF REVENUE OR PROFIT, OR OTHER INCIDENTAL OR CONSEQUENTIAL DAMAGES ARISING OUT OF THE USE OF THE PRODUCT.

THE SOLE REMEDY IN THE EVENT OF A CLAIM OF ANY KIND IS EXPRESSLY LIMITED TO REPLACEMENT OF THE BOOK AND/OR CD-ROM, AND ONLY AT THE DISCRETION OF CRM.

THE USE OF "IMPLIED WARRANTY" AND CERTAIN "EXCLUSIONS" VARY FROM STATE TO STATE, AND MAY NOT APPLY TO THE PURCHASER OF THIS PRODUCT.

THE CINEMA 4D XL HANDBOOK

Adam Watkins

CHARLES RIVER MEDIA, INC.
Hingham, Massachusetts

Copyright 2001 by CHARLES RIVER MEDIA, INC.
All rights reserved.

No part of this publication may be reproduced in any way, stored in a retrieval system of any type, or transmitted by any means or media, electronic or mechanical, including, but not limited to, photocopy, recording, or scanning, without prior permission in writing from the publisher.

Publisher: Jenifer L. Niles
Production: ElectroPublishing, Inc.
Printer: InterCity Press, Rockland, Massachusetts
Cover Design: The Printed Image
Cover Image: Adam Watkins

CHARLES RIVER MEDIA, INC.
20 Downer Avenue, Suite 3
Hingham, Massachusetts 02043
781-740-0400
781-740-8816 (FAX)
info@charlesriver.com
www.charlesriver.com

This book is printed on acid-free paper.

Adam Watkins. The Cinema 4D XL Handbook.
ISBN: 1-58450-039-5

All brand names and product names mentioned in this book are trademarks or service marks of their respective companies. Any omission or misuse (of any kind) of service marks or trademarks should not be regarded as intent to infringe on the property of others. The publisher recognizes and respects all marks used by companies, manufacturers, and developers as a means to distinguish their products.

Printed in the United States of America
01 02 7 6 5 4 3 2 First Edition

   Library of Congress Cataloging-in-Publication Data
Watkins, Adam.
   The Cinema 4D XL handbook / Adam Watkins.-- 1st ed.
     p. cm.
   ISBN 1-58450-039-5 (pbk. : alk. paper)
   1. Computer graphics. 2. Computer animation. 3. Three-dimensional
display systems. 4. Cinema 4D XL. I. Title.
   T385 .W3763 2001
   006.6'96--dc21
                           2001003416

CHARLES RIVER MEDIA titles are available for site license or bulk purchase by institutions, user groups, corporations, etc. For additional information, please contact the Special Sales Department at 781-740-0400.

Requests for replacement of a defective CD must be accompanied by the original disc, your mailing address, telephone number, date of purchase and purchase price. Please state the nature of the problem, and send the information to CHARLES RIVER MEDIA, INC., 20 Downer Avenue, Suite 3, Hingham, Massachusetts 02043. CRM's sole obligation to the purchaser is to replace the disc, based on defective materials or faulty workmanship, but not on the operation or functionality of the product.

Acknowledgments

Thanks to Jenifer, once again, for your patience and help in the process.

Lots of thanks to the Maxon crew for creating such a great product and helping me as I developed this text. Keep going as we spread the word of your ever-advancing software.

Thanks to Dr. Pat Burr for her support of me and the work that I do. Without it, I would never be able to undertake such a book as this.

Tons of thanks to the C4D community. Especially the Post-forum Posse; the dialog there keeps things interesting and my mind racing.

Incredible gratitude to the contributing authors of this project. Your added knowledge and style gives this book depth and I learn much from you.

Special thanks to William E. and Ruth Mae Watkins and J.L. and Helen Allen for their exquisite examples of hard work and class. Your example has meant a lot to me my entire life.

Special thanks to my folks, Dr. Will Watkins and Kaye Watkins for their support, advice and wisdom.

Dedication

As always, Kirsten, your clever feedback, engaging debates, interesting ideas and beautiful eyes make every day worth living.

Contents

CHAPTER ONE: INTERFACE   1
- THE MAIN WINDOW   2
  - MANAGERS   2
  - CUSTOMIZING MANAGER SIZE AND LOCATION   3
  - UNDOCKING MANAGER WINDOWS   4
- COMMAND PALETTES   6
  - DOCKING AND UNDOCKING COMMAND PALETTES   7
  - CREATING COMMAND PALETTES FROM SCRATCH   7
  - ADDING COMMANDS TO COMMAND PALETTES   8
  - THE COMMAND MANAGER   9
  - ADDITIONAL COMMAND MANAGER CAPABILITIES   10
  - BACK TO THE COMMAND PALETTES   13
  - MENU MANAGER   13
  - GENERAL SETTINGS   14
  - VIEWS   15
  - OPENGL   17
  - COLOR   17
- CLOSING NOTES ON INTERFACE   17
- VIEW PANEL   19

CHAPTER TWO: BEGINNING MODELING   25
- 3D CONSTRUCTION THEORY   26
  - THE CONCEPT OF POLY-COUNT   28

NURBS	28
SPLINES	31
PRIMITIVES	32
PUTTING THE THEORY INTO PRACTICE	32
CREATING PRIMITIVES	32
ALTERING PARAMETRIC PRIMITIVES	34
PARAMETRIC PRIMITIVES AND THE OBJECT MANAGER	34
FILLETS	37
OTHER PRIMITIVES	38
CHAPTER THREE: PLAYING WITH PRIMITIVES	**41**
TUTORIAL 3.1 CREATING AN INTERIOR - STEP ONE: PRIMITIVES	42
SNAP SETTINGS	45
X-, Y-, AND Z-AXIS LOCK/UNLOCK AND USE WORLD COORDINATE SYSTEM	49
THE POWER OF GROUPS	50
USE OBJECT AXIS TOOL	52
VISIBILITY	54
TABLE CONSTRUCTION	55
DEFORMATION OBJECTS	57
LAMPS	61
CHAPTER FOUR: GENERATORS (NURBS)	**63**
NON-DESTRUCTIVE MODELING	64
NURBS	64
SPLINES	65
CIRCLE SPLINE PRIMITIVE	66
CREATING SPLINE (CURVES)	68
DRAW FREEHAND SPLINE	68
BEZIER SPLINE CURVE	69
B-SPLINE CURVE	69
CUBIC AND AKIMA SPLINE CURVES	70
EDITING SPLINES	70
WORKING IN POINTS MODE	73
BEZIER SPLINE ALTERATION	75
GENERAL SPLINE NOTES	76
NURBS	76
EXTRUDE NURBS	77
GENERAL NURBS INPUT FIELDS	78

Contents

Caps and Details	78
Rounding	82
HyperNURBS and NURBS in Practice	**83**
HyperNURBS Methods	88
Vital HyperNURBS Tools	**89**
Add Points	89
Bridge and Create Polygons	89
Extrude	91
Extrude Inner	92
Knife	92
Tutorial 4.1 NURBS and the Dining Room	**95**
Arrays and Instances	105
Boolean Objects	111

Chapter Five: Modeling a Car with HyperNURBS
By Jeff Carlson — **119**

Tutorial 5.1 Car Body	**121**
Modeling the Basic Shape	121
Modeling More Detailed Shape	**127**
Subdividing for the Future	127
Shaping the Results	**132**
Trunk Slope	132
Shaping the Windows	134
Splitting the Body	137
Panel Thickness	139
Window Thickness	144
Frame	146
Fenders	150
The Grill	159
Bumpers	161
Headlights	164
Taillights	166
Door Handles	167
Mirrors	168
Wheels	169
Epilogue: A Note on Hierarchy Structure and axis Placement	**173**
A Final Word	174

Chapter Six: Utilizing the Power of HyperNURBS: Modeling Organic Forms from Primitives — 175
- Tutorial 6.1 Primitive Based HyperNURBS Modeling of a Human Head By Anson Call — 176
- Tutorial 6.2 Character Head Tutorial By Desiree Maher — 183

Chapter Seven: Modeling a Human Face and Head
By Nicholas Woolridge — 191
- Tutorial 7.1 Modeling a Human Face and Head: Introduction — 192
  - Approaches — 192
- Head Anatomy — 193
  - The Skull — 193
  - Soft Tissue — 194
  - The Eye — 194
- Using Reference Pictures — 195
  - Getting the Necessary Views — 195
  - Using Drawings — 195
  - Using Photographs — 196
  - Adjusting your Reference Images — 196
- Setting Up your Reference in Cinema 4D — 197
  - Setting Up Your Workspace — 199
- Creating Polygons in Cinema 4D — 199
- Modeling the Eye — 200
  - Texturing the Eye — 202
  - Texturing the Globe — 203
  - Texturing the Iris — 203
  - Creating a "Look-at" Target for the Eyes — 204
- Starting the Face—Hierarchy — 205
- Creating the Eyelids — 205
  - Adding the Eyes — 210
- Building the Area Around The Eyes — 210
- Building the Nose — 213
- Building the Mouth — 217
- Filling in the Face — 220
- Fleshing out the Face — 222
- Building the Ears — 224
- The Rest — 230

Contents

Chapter Eight: Textures — 231
- Materials — 232
- Shaders — 233
  - Color Parameter — 235
  - Seamless Maps — 237
- Tutorial 8.1 Getting Started with Texturing a Room — 239
- Advanced Texturing of the Dining Room — 246

Chapter Nine: Texturing Characters — 253
- Tutorial 9.1 C4D and the Grid System for Texturing Characters (or anything, Really) — 254
  - Photoshop Work — 257
- Tutorial 9.2 Hippo UV Mapping By Kevin Aguirre, Jason Goldsmith, Chad Hofteig and Chris Villa — 264
  - UV Editing — 264
  - Arms, Legs, Tail — 266
  - Belly — 279
  - Head — 282
  - Ears — 282
  - Jaw — 284
  - Inner Mouth — 285
  - Head — 286
  - Nasal Passages — 287

Chapter Ten: Lighting and Camera Tools — 289
- Lighting in Action — 290
- Tutorial 10.1 Nighttime Lighting for the Dining Room — 290
- Tutorial 10.2 Daytime Lighting for the Dining Room — 300
- Tutorial 10.3 Romantic Lighting for the Dining Room — 304
- Tutorial 10.4 Global Illumination By Neil Vaughan — 310

Chapter Eleven: Animation Basics — 317
- Getting to it — 318
  - AutoKeying — 319
  - Non-AutoKeying Animation — 323
  - Timeline — 324
  - Animating within the Timeline — 325
- Tutorial 11.1 Animating a Bee's Wings — 328
- Tutorial 11.2 Camera Animation — 334
- Tutorial 11.3 Animated Flythrough — 336

Chapter Twelve: Advanced Animation and Character Animation — 339
- Segmented Characters — 340
- Kinematics — 342
- FK Walk — 345
- Inverse Kinematics — 348
  - IK Expressions — 349
  - Multiple Target IK (MTIK) — 351
  - IK Tags — 352
  - IK Walks — 355
  - Interpolation Issues — 355
- Bones — 359
  - Restriction Tags — 364
  - Selection Sets — 364
  - Vertex Maps — 366

Chapter Thirteen: Character Animation in Action — 371
- Tutorial 13.1 Rigging the Ant for Animation by Desiree Maher — 372
  - Gimbal Lock — 380
  - Back to IK — 381
- Upper Body and FK — 381
- Tutorial 13.2 Simulating Soft Body Dynamics By Chad Griffiths — 384
- Tutorial 13.3 Strategies of Facial Animation — 391
- PLA (Points Level Animation) — 391
- Facial Boning — 394

Chapter Fourteen: Rendering — 401
- Rendering Tools — 402
- Raytracer Options — 403
  - Transparency, Reflection, and Shadow — 405
  - Raytracing and the Effects Tab — 406
  - Raytracing and the Options Tab — 408
- CAL Rendering Options — 412
- Output and Save Tabs — 413
- Running Through the Tabs — 414
- Tutorial 14.1 C4D Cel-Rendered and Flash — 416
  - Cel-Rendered B&W Project — 417
  - Cel-Rendered Color Project — 419

Chapter Fifteen: An Overview of 3D Real-Time Content Creation
By Ian Mankowski — **421**

- Why Games? — 422
- Cinema 4D for Gaming Content Creation — 422
- Sprite Animation vs. 3D Real-Time Content — 423
- The Requirements of 3D Real-Time Content Creation — What You Need to Know — **424**
  - Game Animation Is a Team Effort — 424
  - Game Animation Requirements — 425
- Game Animation Is About Limitations — 425
  - Modeling Limitations — 425
  - Texturing Limitations — 426
  - Animation Limitations — 426
  - Palette Limitations — 428
  - End User as the Defining Limitation — 428
- Modeling for Games — 428
  - Setting Up the Workspace — 429
  - Defining the Poly-Count of your Model — 429
  - Starting Your Character — 430
  - Setting the Background Views — 431
  - Beginning Your Model — 432
- Extruding the Torso — **433**
- Creating the Legs — **435**
  - Creating the Arms — 436
  - Shoulders and Collarbone Area — 437
- Modeling the Head — **438**
  - Creating the Tail — 439
  - Refining and Optimizing the Mesh — 439
- Welcome to the World of Triangles — **440**
- The Tools to Use — **440**
  - Using the Knife Tool — 440
  - Welding Tool — 440
  - Move Selected Up, Move Selected Down Sequence — 441
  - Refining the Mesh — 442
- Texturing — **443**
- Ripping Apart the Mesh — **444**
  - Matters of Critical Importance — 444
  - Special Bits — 445

DISTORTING THE MESH	446
SCALING AND OPTIMIZING THE TEXTURE AREA	448
HOW TO SCALE FOR MAXIMUM OPTIMIZATION	449
GROUPING YOUR MESH	449
CREATING UVW COORDINATES	449
COPYING THE UVW COORDINATES	450
BODY PAINT	451

CHAPTER SIXTEEN: C.O.F.F.E.E.: A COMPREHENSIVE INTRODUCTION By DONOVAN KEITH — 457

WHAT IS PROGRAMMING?	458
GETTING READY TO PROGRAM	458
HELLO WORLD	459
A FEW WORDS ABOUT COMMENTING YOUR CODE	460
VARIABLES	461
VARIABLE TYPES	464
NUMERICAL OPERATIONS	466
LOGICAL OPERATIONS	467
CONDITIONALS	469
LOOPING	473
FUNCTIONS	475
A BRIEF OVERVIEW OF OOP	478
PREDEFINED CLASSES	482
PROGRAMMING EXERCISES	487
EXERCISE 1: COPY ROTATION	487
EXERCISE 2: BOUNCING BALL	489
EXERCISE 3: IN THE MIDDLE	492
EXERCISE 4: AUTO DOF	492
WHERE TO GO FROM HERE	493
THE C.O.F.F.E.E. SDK	493
GENERAL PROGRAMMING BOOKS	493
PLUGINCAFE	493

CHAPTER SEVENTEEN: LEARNING FROM THE MASTERS — 495

SIMON WICKER	496
ART BACKGROUND	497
C4D	498
WORKFLOW	499

Contents

Phil Captain 3D McNally — 501
- C4D — 502
- Success of "Pump-Action" — 503
- Modeling — 505
- Lighting — 506
- Character Animation — 507
- Camera Work — 508

Alec Syme — 510
- Background — 510
- C4D — 511
- Workflow — 512
- Employment — 513

Inspiration Gallery — 515
- Andreas Calmach — 515
- Christian Rambow — 515
- Dave Taylor — 516
- Dean Baker — 516
- Gareth Lockett — 517
- Gray Ginther — 517
- Janine Pauke — 518
- Laurent Heiderscheid — 518
- Martin Kay — 519
- Mark Mathieson — 520
- Micheal Ambjörn — 520
- Micheal Vance — 521
- Neil Vaughan — 521
- Onur Pekdemir — 522
- Jérome Pastorello — 523
- Philip Nicholson — 524
- Rai — 525
- Robert Boehm — 525
- Simon Knowles — 526
- Steve Townrow — 527
- Suon-Oon Lim — 527

Appendix A: About the CD-ROM — 529

Index — 531

Preface

WHY THIS BOOK?

In any software package, there are a number of benefits that arise from a fresh perspective on the tool and its uses. Maxon's Cinema4D XL version 6 and version 7 (C4D v6 and v7) are no exception. Despite its overall ease of use, C4D is also an incredibly powerful and diverse package. As such, the uses and methods of using it are diverse. Not that any one method is the "right" way; in fact the flexibility of being able to achieve powerful projects in a variety of ways is part of the strength of C4D.

Exploring these paths is the primary function of this book. Included with your copy of C4D software is a set of manuals that provide a useful reference filled with definitions of all the tools. These manuals are great to have and this book is not intended to replace the manuals. Instead, the book provides hands-on methods for analyzing the functions of C4D's many tools. The book takes a project-based approach that allows you to create impressive projects as you learn C4D's array of tools and functions.

In this book, all of the major areas of C4D and its uses are covered. Some light is also shed on many of the little understood and under-explored corners of the program. Beginning with the general tools and tool layout, you learn how to customize these tools so that you can create a work environment conducive to your workflow. However, it's important to note, this book doesn't attempt to cover every nook and cranny of this truly diverse package. There just isn't enough space to get to every part of the program; however, great care has been taken to explore the majority of the most powerful and most used aspects.

Standard C4D workflow is also covered; where to start, how to start, and when to finish. Then the real fun begins — the modeling tools within C4D.

Modeling is covered, from primitive methods and *NURBS*, to object creation, polygon creation, and NURBS editing. Manufacturing modeling techniques and methods to model human forms are covered in detail along with the various other modeling methods (there are nearly as many modeling methods as there are 3D artists). Often a specific method really "clicks" with certain people so with that in mind, some of the best modelers were invited to contribute a tutorial or two on their modeling paradigm. Thus, not only do we cover the modeling tools, but we analyze a variety of ways to use them, giving you a wide scope of potential methods to try and perfect.

After creating the shapes of our dreams, we put C4D's powerful texture capabilities to work. How do they work? When should they be used? What sorts of effects can be created with simple textures? How can we optimize textures to aid in quick renderings? Everything from creating textures from scratch, stylizing textures, and creating photorealistic textures, to using textures to denote geometry, and utilizing third-party textures to create truly dazzling effects is covered. We'll also look at the possibilities of procedural and bitmapped textures. Next we learn how to create maps from photos or from scratch, and investigate mapping textures to surfaces and how to make them stick. Perhaps most exciting, though, is the coverage of the new *BodyPaint* and how you can use this intuitive tool to paint a look on an object in previously unheard of ways.

After creating and texturing objects and projects, the all-important issues of cinematography and how to control the camera within C4D are explored. Stylized, realistic camera movement is covered as we review the tools included in C4D's camera capabilities. In the same chapter we take a very careful look at the too often ignored area of lighting and lighting theory by using lessons from the areas of photography and theatre. There is even a special section on the important role of lighting in creating photo-realistic or stylized scenes.

Moving along we get into the complex and powerful animation tools contained in C4D. This section covers the timeline, space curves, tangents, and *Beziers* (oh my!). C4D v6/v7 has new improved tools to utilize within the timeline, so we explore how to use these tools and when, where, and why to use them. How to organize projects is also explained, as it can make the difference between a project nightmare and an enjoyable time.

Also included is an extensive section on character animation. C4D is not often recognized as a character animation powerhouse but with the new tools present, the possibilities have skyrocketed. In this section we delve deeply into bones and the theory of movement, and explore how forward and inverse kinematics function, how to set Forward Kinematics (FK) and Inverse Kinematics (IK) chains up, and how to use them to create a desired motion.

Toward the end of the book, we look at areas that truly lift C4D above the level of a mere 3D animation package: creating custom expressions, and analyzing ways to program small scripts to optimize and streamline the creation process. Through C.O.F.F.E.E. tutorials, you learn how to change the simple GUI interface of C4D into an under-the-hood custom-built power machine.

Also included are looks at who is using C4D in the industry and how they are using it. Examples of how talented artists have used C4D to land their dream jobs and their suggestions for blossoming artists are included. You might be surprised at all of the places C4D has been and is being used in the entertainment industry.

WHAT IS IN IT FOR YOU?

This book is great for beginners. It reviews all of the tools within C4D and explains how best to use them. Through intensive tutorials you can learn ideas and techniques not covered in the manuals. You also learn about the theory and why things work the way they do — not so you can write your own 3D application, but because if you understand the theory behind the tool, you can better utilize the ideas within the tool. There was originally so much information in the early drafts of the book that beginners will find extra information in supplemental chapters contained on the CD. Can't get enough about the details of a particular NURBS? Check out the CD. Much of the information contained on the CD is very closely related to what is contained in the manual — just covered with a slightly different twist.

This book is also great for intermediate users. There are lots of folks out there who have been using C4D for awhile now. You have probably already gone through the tutorials contained within the manuals and have a fairly good grasp on how the tools work. This book will put new spins on the same tools, giving you a chance to see how the tool is used in ways you may not have tried. The tutorials in the latter half of the book are intense enough that they provide an excellent learning challenge if you have not mastered complex 3D ideas like modeling and animating human forms.

Additionally, this book is great for advanced users. Those of you who are C4D experts and have delved deep into the depths of digital domains will still find excellent information here. Have you ever thought it would be great if C4D just had a tool that would allow you to do X? Well, included here are tutorials on writing your own expressions with C.O.F.F.E.E as well as some in-depth analysis of making your own plug-ins. Even if you are not interested in programming as an advanced user, you can find out about some of the tricks various artists throughout the world have tweaked and mastered. And if you are comfortable and effective in C4D, hopefully, this volume will provide some further enhancing techniques. As icing on the cake, this book includes extensive instruction on the new *BodyPaint*. This could be a valuable first look at an incredible new tool from the masters at Maxon.

So young or old, novice or experienced, amateur or professional; enjoy this book. Hopefully it will provide you with tools, techniques, and tricks that will increase your C4D productivity, workflow, and the love and/or cash received thereof.

CHAPTER 1
Interface

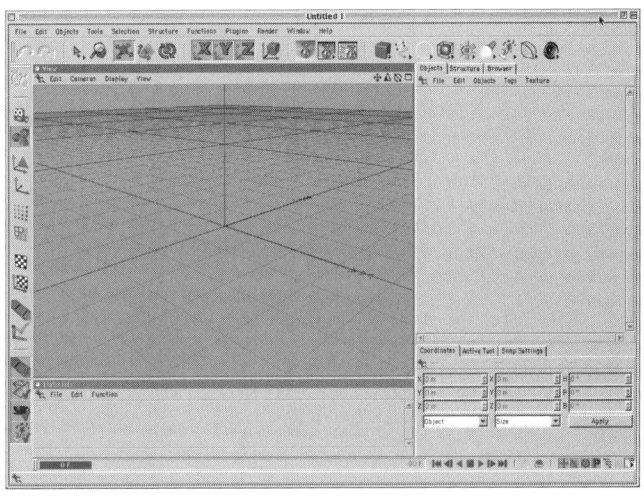

Interestingly enough, the interface of Cinema4D XL version 6 and 7 (v6 and v7) has a subjective mode to it to. Completely customizable, the interface can be modified and optimized to fit you and your style of working. Before we learn how to customize the interface, let's look at how the default interface is organized.

Upon opening C4D, you are presented with an interface that incorporates all major areas of the 3D creation process: modeling, texturing, lighting, cinematography, animation, and rendering.

THE MAIN WINDOW

Cinema4D has a powerful collection of tools organized in a fairly intuitive format for general use. In this chapter, rather than go through the laundry list of powerful tools, we will look at groups of tools. The focus is on how tools are organized rather than on how the tools work. Later, we'll be looking at how each tool works in the context of a tutorial that teaches both the practical and theoretical applications of the tools in C4D.

The C4D interface, cleverly called the *Main window* (Figure 1.1), is organized into palettes on three sides (top, left, and bottom) containing clusters of tools. These tool palettes live most happily on a screen that is running at least 1024x768; however, if you have a smaller screen, you can still get to all the tools on a given palette. By moving your mouse up to the divider line separating palettes that contain tools out of the range of your screen, your mouse pointer will change to a small white pan hand (Figure 1.2). Click and drag (click-drag) to the left and right (for command palettes along the top) or up and down for command palettes along the side to scroll through the tools visible in the palettes. These visible tools are completely customizable, but more on this later.

MANAGERS

These command palettes surround the view panels and several *managers*. Managers are actually windows that represent program elements within C4D. Each of these separate managers are actually parallel to the other managers running at the same time. The idea is that each manager can run independently; yet, the changes made in one manager are quickly transferred to the other managers running at the same time. There are actually quite a few managers within C4D; so many in fact, that there is simply not enough room to display all of them at once. As such, some of them are placed *beneath* other managers (Figure 1.3). These "buried" managers can be easily accessed by simply clicking on the corresponding tab. When a tab is clicked, that manager is brought to the foreground. There are even managers that aren't seen at all in the default main window — but more on these a little later.

Chapter 1 Interface

3

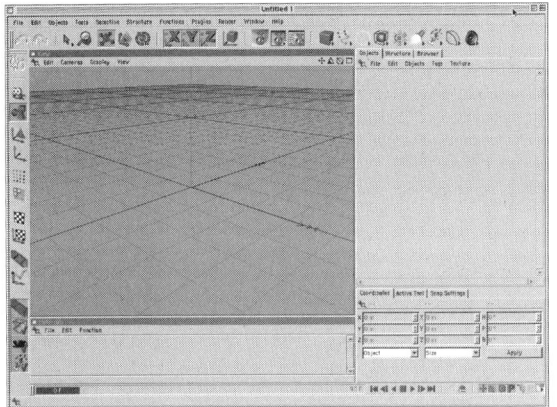

FIGURE 1.1 *C4D Main window.*

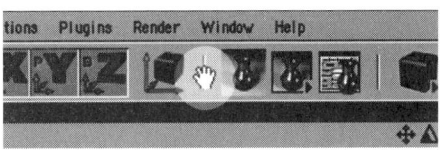

FIGURE 1.2 *Pan band.*

Customizing Manager Size and Location

The managers share screen space with the view panel and the command palettes. The location and size of the managers is customizable. By moving your mouse to the edge of a manager (Figure 1.4), you can resize the manager to fit your needs. In some cases this may be smaller (i.e. if you need more space for the view panels), while sometimes (i.e. if many tags are attached to objects within the Object Manager) you'll need more space for the manager. When the mouse pointer is over the edge of a manager it changes to a double arrow, indicating that C4D is ready to resize a window. Click-drag the double arrow, and you can resize the windows within certain parameters.

The windows and managers within the interface are said to be "docked". Notice that in the corner of the view panels and the various managers is a small Pin icon. This represents that this window (or manager) is temporarily pinned (or docked) at this place in the interface. If you don't like it there, simply click on the Pin icon and drag the window to a more appropriate place (Figure 1.5). As you drag, you'll notice that a dark line appears near to your mouse pointer, indicating possible new locations to dock the window you are moving.

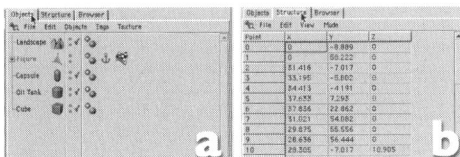

FIGURE 1.3 *To conserve space some managers are nested (a). In this case the Object Manager is visible while the Structure Manager and Browser Manager are nested beneath. By clicking on one of the tabs of nested managers, that manager is then brought to the front (b).*

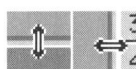

FIGURE 1.4 *Resizing windows arrows; these allow you to give more screen space to a given manager or window.*

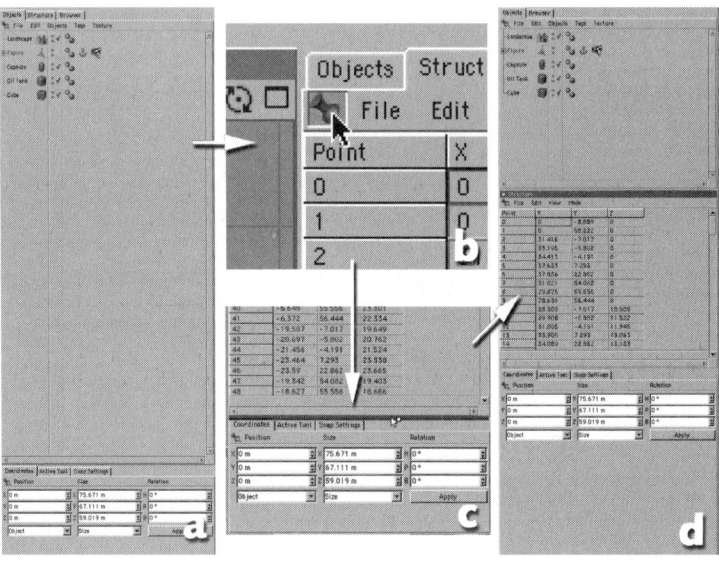

FIGURE 1.5 *(a) If you no longer wish a manager to be tabbed or don't need to have a dedicated window to view a manager, you can grab the manager by clicking the Pin icon (b) and drag it to where you wish it to be (c); upon release, other managers will move to accommodate the new manager's position (d).*

Remember that by moving windows around in this way, you still maintain one monolithic single overall windowed interface.

UNDOCKING MANAGER WINDOWS

But wait, there's more. Perhaps, you prefer to work with multiple floating windows (similar to previous versions of C4D). You can "undock" windows or managers so that they float along the top of your interface. To do this, click and release the Pin icon and select Undock from the resultant pull-down menu (Figure 1.6). The result will be a new window that appears separate from the main interface.

There are several important things to remember about undocking. First of all, after a window is undocked it can always be "docked" again. To do so, simply click-drag the Pin icon on the now undocked window to the place where you wish to dock it (Figure 1.7 a). A dark line will appear indicating the locations at which it can be docked. When the window is redocked, the windows around it will resize to fit (Figure 1.7 b). Note that you can also dock directly to a group of managers represented by tabs. When you are click-dragging the Pin icon, simply move your mouse pointer over the Pin icon of a manager grouped with others in tabs. Your mouse pointer will change to a pointing hand (Figure 1.8 a). Upon mouse release, the window will be docked and tabbed in the group you've selected (Figure 1.8 b).

CHAPTER 1   INTERFACE

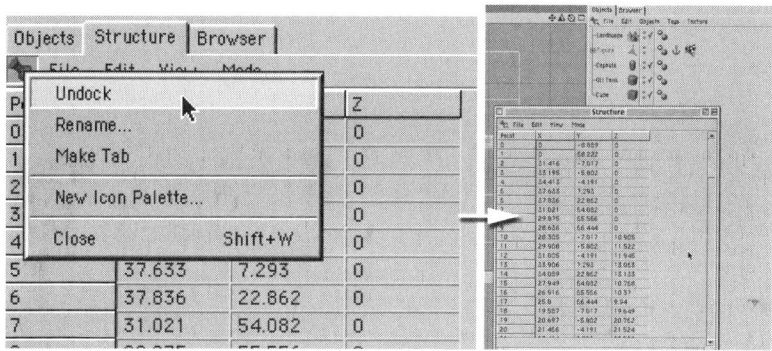

FIGURE 1.6 *Undocking window or manager.*

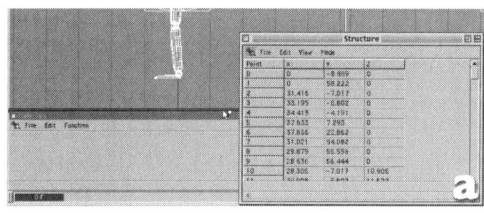
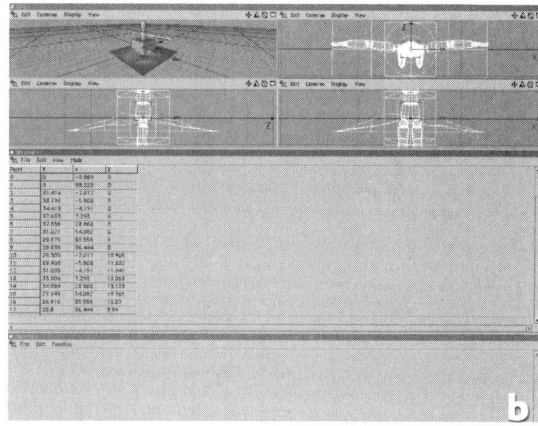

FIGURE 1.7 *(a) Docking process (dark line indicates possible docking locations. (b) Redocked window with resized surrounding windows.*

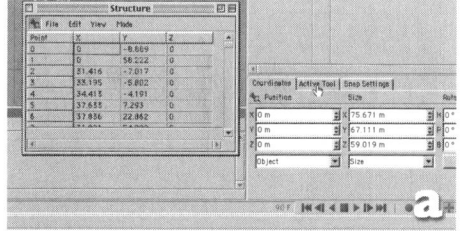

FIGURE 1.8 *(a) Altered mouse pointer to indicate that you are docking into a tabbed group of windows. (b) Docked manager placed within tabs.*

While we're at it, let's look at the other options that are part of the Pin pull down menu.

Rename — Self-explanatory method of renaming a manager if you so desire.

Make Tab — When a manager is undocked, you can add other windows to the floating window. You can choose to tab this manager from the beginning.

New Icon Palette — Using this tool you can create a new floating window (which can be docked later) that contains a custom set of tools. To actually place tools in this new palette, you must use the Command Manager which we'll talk about later in this chapter.

Close — Closes the window or manager.

Depending on your working style, the managers you want available and prevalent will differ greatly. Some artists work with two monitors and have managers open everywhere because they have the room. Other artists working with more restricted space may choose to group into tabs a large group of their managers or hide some completely.

COMMAND PALETTES

In C4D, the pull-down menus are said to contain *commands*. Each of these commands perform different functions that allow you to work in and manipulate the digital 3D space. Along the top, left side, and bottom of the default C4D interface are *command palettes* (Figure 1.9). These palettes are set up to allow you to quickly reach often used commands.

We'll not look at what the default command palettes contain. We'll be looking at all the tools over the course of the book — at this point we will look at how to organize, alter, add, and subtract commands from the command palettes.

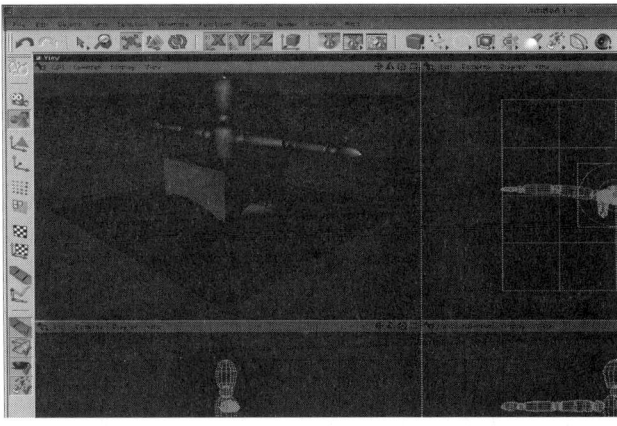

FIGURE *Command palettes in default interface.*
1.9

This information goes well in this chapter but may be useless to you this early in the reading. After you have read additional chapters and have found a working pace and style that you like, you may wish to come back to this chapter to learn how to customize your workspace to accommodate your workflow.

DOCKING AND UNDOCKING COMMAND PALETTES

The command palettes that C4D has set up by default are docked within the interface. Command palettes can be either docked or undocked. To undock a palette, simply right-click (COMMAND-click on a Mac) and select Undock (Figure 1.10).

Once these command palettes are undocked, you may dock them again. To do this, grab the command palette by clicking on the double line at the top of a vertical palette or the left end of a horizontal palette (Figure 1.11 a) and drag it to where you wish it docked (Figure 1.11 b). Similar to docking managers, a heavy black line will appear, indicating the possible docking positions as you near one (Figure 1.11 c).

CREATING COMMAND PALETTES FROM SCRATCH

By default there is only so much room available for the default command palettes. C4D seems to assume that you have a monitor that displays at least 1024x768. At that resolution, all the default command palettes are completely visible. However, you may have a bigger monitor or two monitors and would like to create additional palettes that contain your most often used commands or commands that aren't available by default. There are three ways to create a new command palette: 1) Select Window>Layout>New Icon Palette 2) In any extant

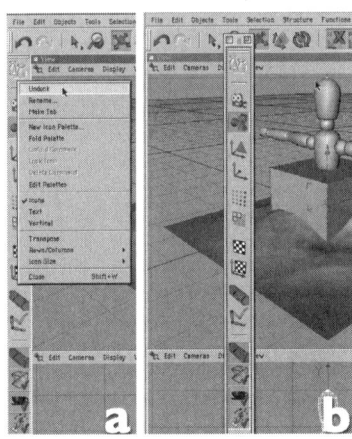

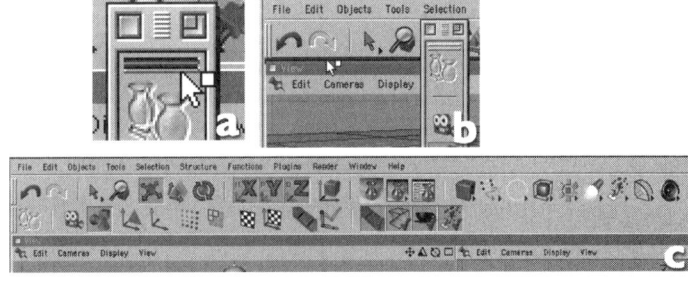

FIGURE 1.11 *(a) "Docking handle" for vertical palettes. (b) Dark lines indicate potential docking locations. (c) The result of the redocked command palette.*

FIGURE 1.10 *(a) Undock from right-clicked pull-down menu on command palette. (b) Undocked command palette.*

command palette or manager, click on the Pin icon and select New Icon Palette from the resultant pull-down menu (Figure 1.12 a) 3) Right-mouse click (COMMAND-click on a single-button Mac mouse) anywhere within an extant palette and select New Icon Palette from the menu (Figure 1.12 b).

ADDING COMMANDS TO COMMAND PALETTES

Notice that this new command palette is undocked and empty. To add commands to this newly born palette you must first activate the *Command Manager*. There are two ways to invoke the Command Manager. The first is to select Window>Layout>Edit Palettes. When this is selected, a big change comes over your interface. The Command Manager appears in the foreground and all the existing commands in existing command palettes are surrounded with blue boxes (Figure 1.13). C4D is letting you know it's ready to move tools.

Now, you can grab command icons from existing command palettes and place them into the new palette. When you attempt to place commands in a new command palette, note that the location to which you click-drag the command palette is very important. In the empty palette, the words "Empty Palette" appear within a sunken region (Figure 1.14). When you move new commands into this palette, the commands must be dropped within this sunken

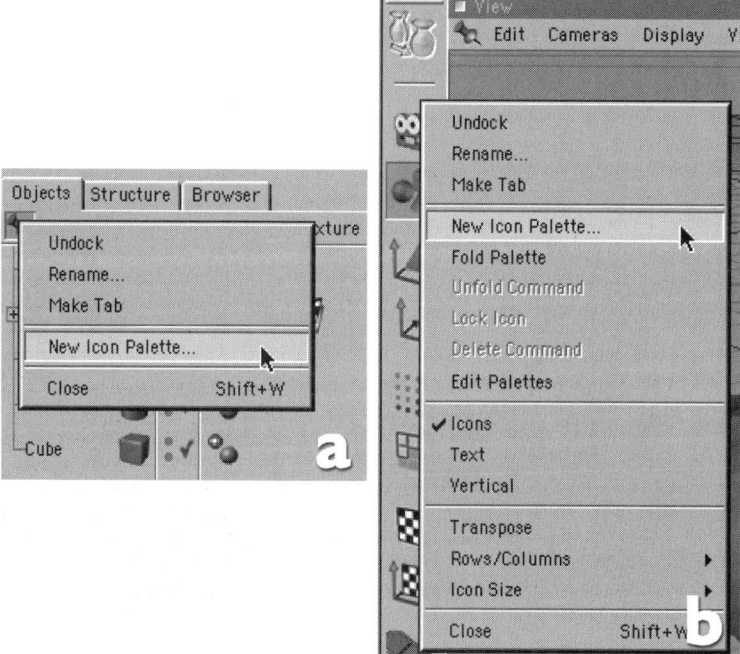

FIGURE **1.12** (a) Creating New command palette via the Pin pull-down menu. (b) Creating New command palette through existing command palette.

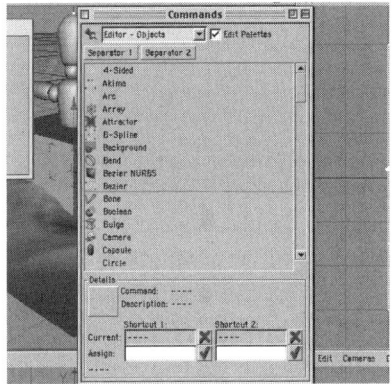
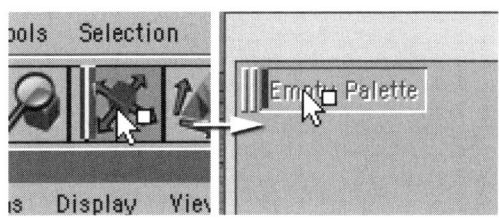

FIGURE 1.14 *The "hot" drop zone of new command palettes.*

FIGURE 1.13 *Activating the Command Manager and the resultant interface change.*

region. Trying to place them anywhere else will result in your mouse icon being substituted by the international forbidden symbol. After the first command is placed within a new palette, subsequent commands can just be dropped next to existing commands (Figure 1.15).

There is another way to invoke the Command Manager: select Window> Command Manager. When the Command Manager emerges this way, note that the command palettes aren't automatically ready to be altered. If the Command Manager is called up this way, you must click the Edit Palettes button at the top right corner of the Command Manager (Figure 1.16).

THE COMMAND MANAGER

The Command Manager is actually an incredibly versatile and powerful tool. We've already seen how activating it allows for the shifting of commands. However, note that within the Command Manager is a large list of commands that may not even be listed in existing command palettes. The Command Manager actually contains all the commands available in C4D. The Command Manager organizes the commands within C4D according to their primary function. An embedded pull-down menu next to the Pin icon allows you to display groups

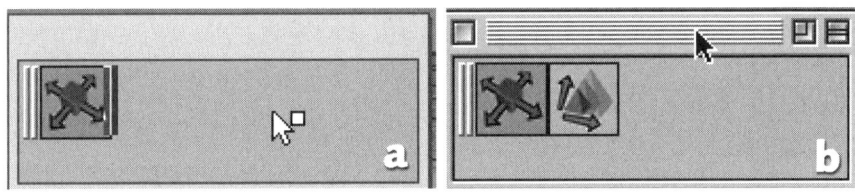

FIGURE 1.15 *Once a new command has been placed others can simply be placed next to it (a). And the tool's command is placed (b).*

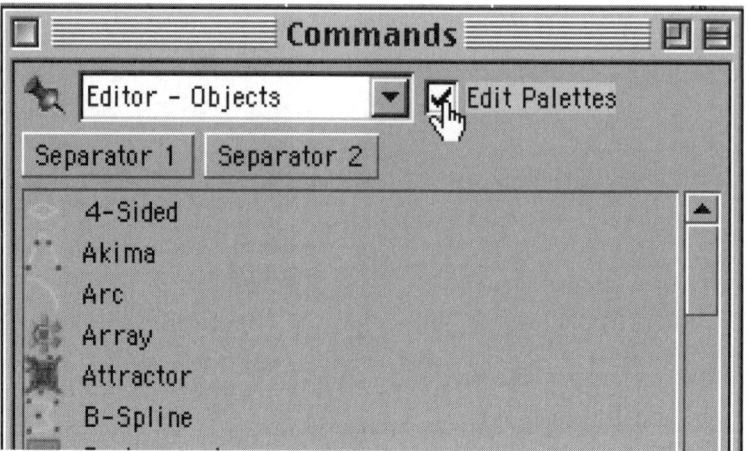

FIGURE 1.16 *Edit Palettes option must be checked to alter palettes.*

of commands (Figure 1.17 a). This includes the choice—All Commands—(Figure 1.17 b).

No matter what groups of commands the Command Manager is displaying, you can add a command to any command palette. To do so, make sure that Edit Palettes is activated, and then simply click-drag the command from the Command Manager to the command palette of choice (Figure 1.18). Again, a dark line will indicate where C4D is planning to place the new command.

ADDITIONAL COMMAND MANAGER CAPABILITIES

There is another function for the Command Manager: namely, the ability to alter keyboard shortcuts for any given command. When any command is clicked within the Command Manager, it will appear in the bottom section of the Command Manager in the Details section. If the command has a keyboard shortcut assigned to it, the shortcut will appear here under the Current input field (Figure 1.19 a). If you wish to change the keyboard shortcut for the command, click the "x" button next to the shortcut and it will be erased (Figure 1.19 b).

To assign a keyboard shortcut, click in the Assign input field. You can now enter any keystroke or combination of keystrokes that will appear in the Current input field (Figure 1.20 a). If this keystroke is assigned already to another command, you will be alerted immediately below the input field with an error that tells you what the conflicting command is (Figure 1.20 b). If you still wish to use that key combination for your tool rather than the default setting, first make sure that you erase it from the default command. To change the keyboard shortcut to something else, click again in the Assign input field and enter a new keystroke. When you are happy with the keyboard shortcut you have entered,

CHAPTER 1 INTERFACE

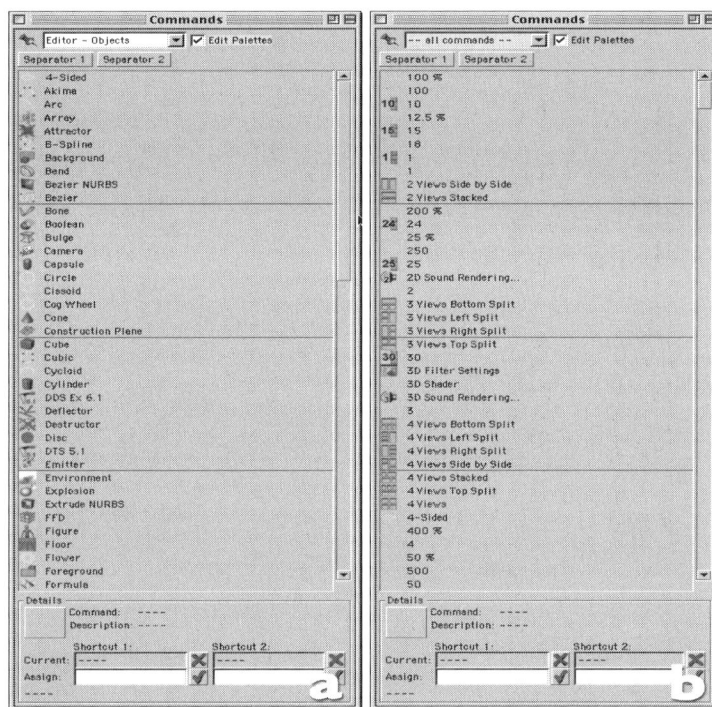

FIGURE 1.17 *(a) Groups of commands. (b) All Commands and the resultant list.*

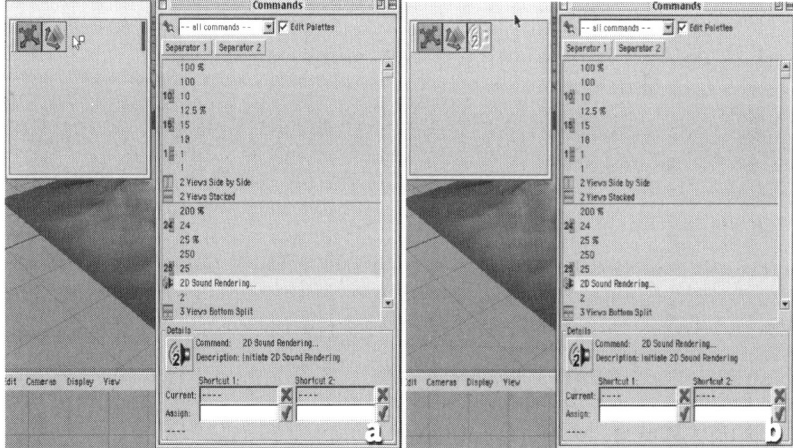

FIGURE 1.18 *Adding commands from the Command Manager by selecting the desired command and click-dragging to the desired palette (a). The result is shown in (b).*

FIGURE 1.19 *(a) If a command already has a keyboard shortcut, the Command Manager will display it. (b) Erasing assigned keyboard shortcuts.*

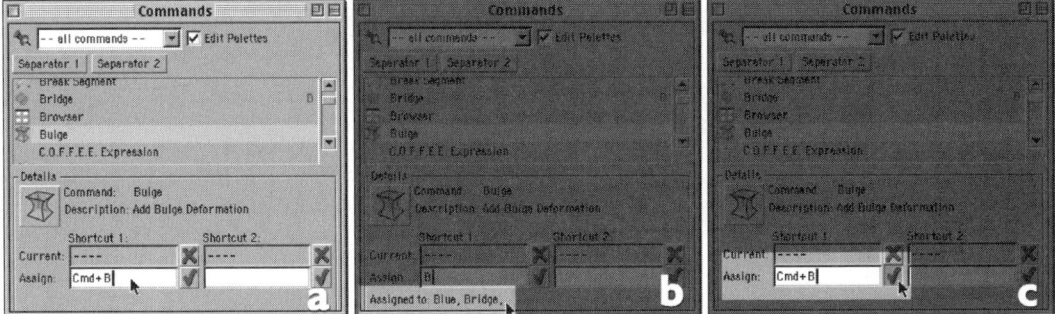

FIGURE 1.20 *(a) To add a keyboard shortcut, select the Assign input field and enter the keystrokes to assign. (b) Error indicates conflict of keyboard shortcuts. (c) Green checkmark indicates C4D will remember the new keystroke assigned to a command.*

click the green checkmark button next to the input field (Figure 1.20 c). The keystroke will then appear in the Current input field.

Notice that there are two sets of input fields within the Details section. You can enter more than one set of keystrokes for any one command. Also note that when a new keyboard shortcut has been assigned, it not only shows up in the Current input field, it also shows up within the Command Manager above and also in the pull-down menus of the general C4D interface (Figure 1.21). This is a perfect example of how C4D's managers are all intertwined.

C4D only allows certain combinations of keystrokes to be shortcuts. These combinations include a single key, CTRL-key, SHIFT-key, and CTRL-SHIFT-key. There are also certain default keys (for example, "1" for the Camera Move tool). These default keyboard shortcuts are called C4D's *hotkeys*. These hotkeys are very powerful in their flexibility (they override all other tools that may be active). However, these hotkeys are off limits to any other keyboard shortcut. It's also noteworthy that the manual suggests strongly that you do not attempt to assign a shortcut that is typically used by your operating system (like CTRL-ALT-DELETE on a PC or OPTION-COMMAND-ESC on a Mac).

CHAPTER 1   INTERFACE

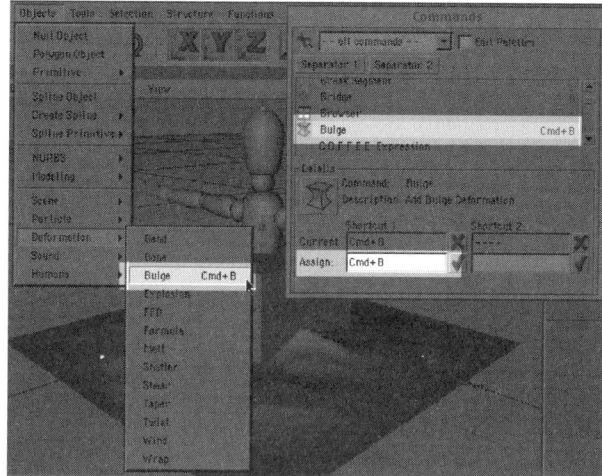

FIGURE 1.21 *All the places that C4D incorporates changes made within the Command Manager.*

BACK TO THE COMMAND PALETTES

Within your newly created palette, there is a slew of further customization that can be done. Right-mouse click (COMMAND-click) within any of the commands in the command palette and you'll be given a new pull-down collection of functions to optimize the look and function of the palette. These options include ways to fold or unfold commands (make nested groups of commands), make your commands appear as simple text, make your commands appear as text and icons, make your commands appear in rows or columns, change the number of rows or columns, delete commands, and change the size of the icons within the palette. Because these are effectively described in the manual, we won't repeat them here.

MENU MANAGER

Besides being able to alter the command palettes, C4D allows you to even alter the pull-down menu's organization of commands. This allows you to create new menus and submenus. The Menu Manager works much the same way as the Command Manager does. With simple drag and drop methods you can move commands from one manager to another. Pull-down menus are the least efficient way of accessing commands so we won't spend much time here discussing how to alter the extant menus. It's strongly suggested that you organize your most used tools into appropriate command palettes and assign good, easy-to-remember keystrokes.

GENERAL SETTINGS

There is one other location within C4D that allows for further customization of the interface's look and feel. This is within the General Settings dialog box. To access General Settings, select Edit>General Settings or use the keyboard shortcut of CTRL-E (COMMAND-E on a Mac). Most of the available settings within this dialog box are beyond what we need to alter and this area is covered extensively in the manual; however, there are a few areas that we should cover.

When General Settings is first selected, you are given a dialog box with five tabs (Figure 1.22). The first tab, General. contains a lot of very specialized settings that are beyond the scope of this chapter. However, it is important to note the ability to check the Save Layout at Program End option. When you alter your layout within C4D, whether it be new palettes, or altered manager organization of keyboard shortcuts, C4D saves these changes into a temporary "layout file". If this layout is not saved, when you close C4D, the new settings are lost. With Save Layout at Program End selected, you will maintain the changes made the next time you enter C4D.

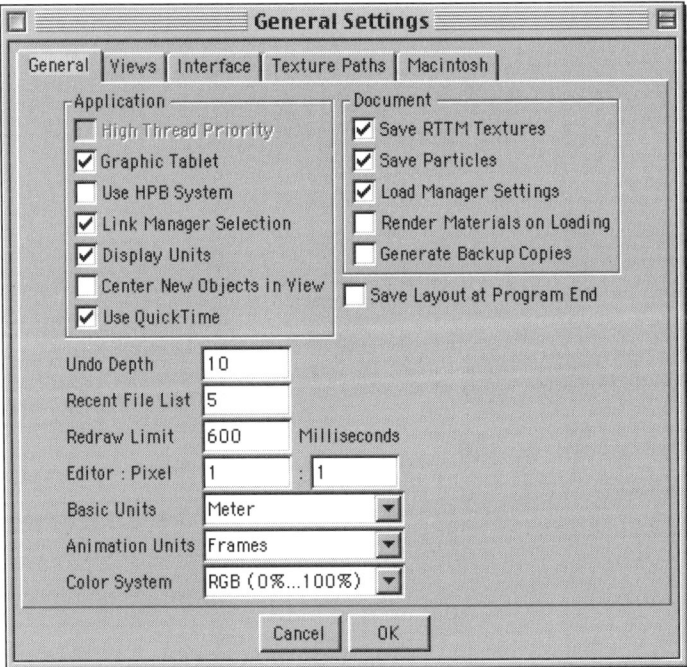

FIGURE 1.22 *General Settings dialog box.*

VIEWS

Clicking the Views tab provides some very useful tools. Within the Views tab is a Views section that allows you to customize what sorts of visual interactivity and guides are included in your interface (Figure 1.23).

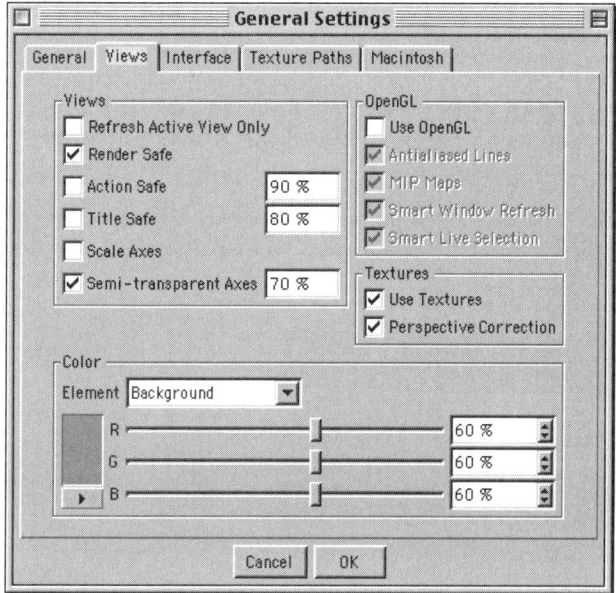

FIGURE 1.23 *Views tab within the General Settings dialog box.*

Refresh Active View Only - When you have toggled views to more than one view panel, you can move an object in one view panel and instantly see it moved in the other view panels. This is because the Refresh Active View Only option is turned off by default. In most cases it's important to be able to see how things are being positioned, rotated, and scaled within other views. However, when your projects get very large, this extra effort of drawing the changes immediately in four windows instead of one can contribute to a significant slowdown in your interface speed. If Refresh Active View Only is selected (as you may need to do with big scenes), C4D will wait to redraw the other view panels until after you have finished whatever function you are performing in the active window.

Render Safe - The Render Safe guides will never render, but they can help you in your workflow as you deal with issues of staging, framing, and virtual cinematography. What you see in the Editor or a view panel is not necessarily what will be seen in your final rendering. You may have your view panels set up to display very long or very tall windows. With Render Safe activated, you will be given some gray lines defining what will actually be shown when you render to the Picture Viewer (Figure 1.24).

Action Safe, Title Safe - What you see on a computer screen is often not what is seen on a television screen. TV screens often expand an image slightly and cut off the outside edge. By selecting the Action and/or Title Safe buttons, C4D will provide guides within the view panel to indicate the areas that you can be sure will be seen on a TV screen. See the Cinematography chapter (Chapter 10 – Lighting and Camera Tools) for more information about these settings and their valuable uses.

Scale Axis, Semi-Transparent Axis – Scale Axis and Semi-Transparent Axis options will make much more sense when we begin modeling; however, suffice it to say that each object is displayed with a set of axes. These axes help you move an object along a given axis, and allow you to know how the object is oriented in digital space. With these two options, you can choose how the axes of objects are displayed when the object is selected, or when you are zooming in closer or farther away from the object.

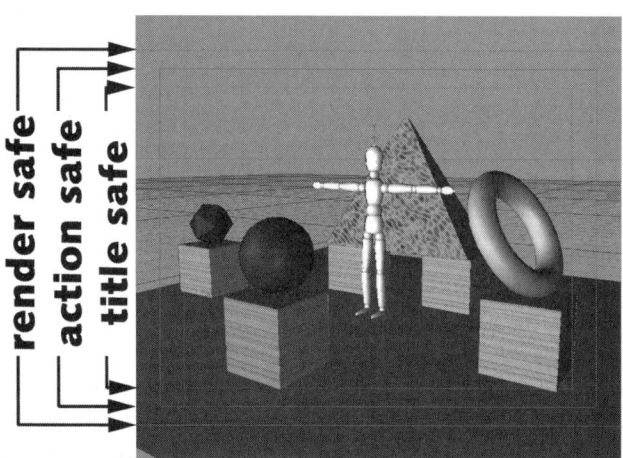

FIGURE 1.24 *Action Safe and Title Safe guides.*

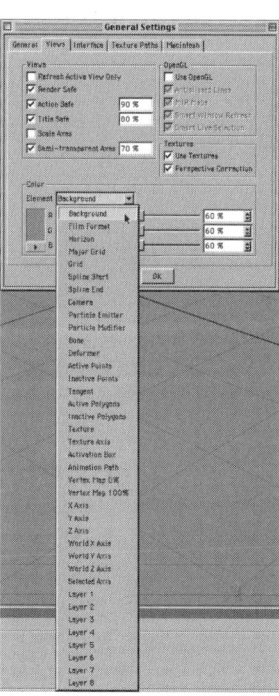

FIGURE 1.25 *You can alter any appearance of the interface you wish.*

OpenGL

OpenGL is a technology that has been developed specifically to assist in quick rendering of 3D worlds. It is used heavily in games and can be of great benefit in 3D animation. OpenGL can be software- or hardware-driven. Hardware-driven OpenGL (driven by the video card) is by far faster than software-driven. Most upper-end computers have video cards that utilize hardware-driven OpenGL acceleration. However, few actually have big enough acceleration to gain a significant speed up. With OpenGL selected, your C4D relies on its OpenGL routines, and taps into any available hardware acceleration to attempt to speed up the interface. If you are on a machine with a card with 16mb of Video RAM or less, you probably will not see a significant increase in speed with OpenGL selected. Not to worry, though. C4D's Real Time Texture Mapping (RTTM) is an elegant and speedy form of display.

If you are lucky enough to have significant hardware acceleration, the rest of the settings can assist in defining how you wish to use the extra horsepower. You'll need to read carefully the information included with your hardware to see if it actually supports the options listed in the OpenGL section of the Views tab.

Color

Some people just don't like gray. Some people don't like the color scheme defined by C4D's default. If you'd rather work in a default Editor window that displays the digital world as a black void, you can change that in the Color section of the Views tab. If you don't like Red, Green, and Blue as the defining colors for the X-, Y-, and Z-axes, you can change it here. Basically, any visual element of the interface of C4D can be changed in this area. Simply select the aspect of the interface you wish to change (Figure 1.25), and then change the color value using the sliders (Figure 1.26 a) or by clicking on the block of color, which will open a new Color Picker dialog box (Figure 1.26 b). You can change the settings and colors to your heart's content (Figure 1.27).

Closing Notes on Interface

As we've seen here, there are a multitude of changes that can be made in C4D to make the interface an environment you feel comfortable with. You can change colors, reorganize tools and commands, reorganize pull-down menus, and assign keyboard shortcuts. We've looked briefly at how to save the layout changes. Note that the alternate way of saving a layout is by going to Window>Layout>Save Layout As.... This will allow you to save a layout that can be called up later if need be.

Note that this Window>Layout> pull-down menu also has the options to Load Layouts and Save as Default Layouts. The combination of these two options

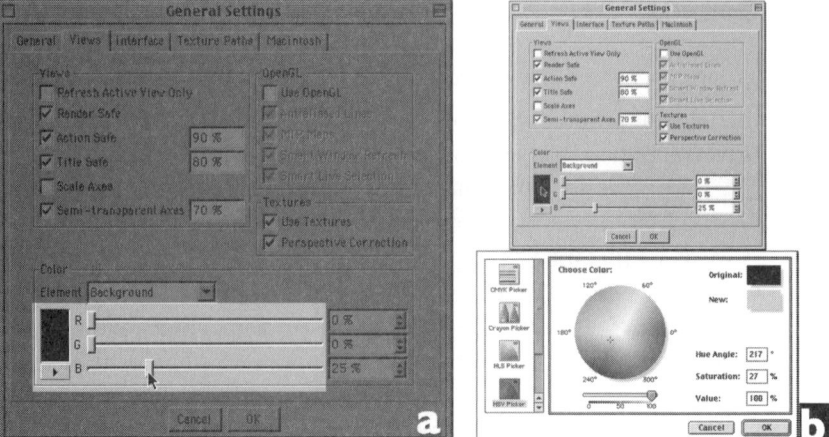

FIGURE 1.26 *(a) You can change the color of the interface by shifting the color sliders. (b) Another way to select a new color for an interface element is to click on the color swatch and then, using the Color Picker, select a new color.*

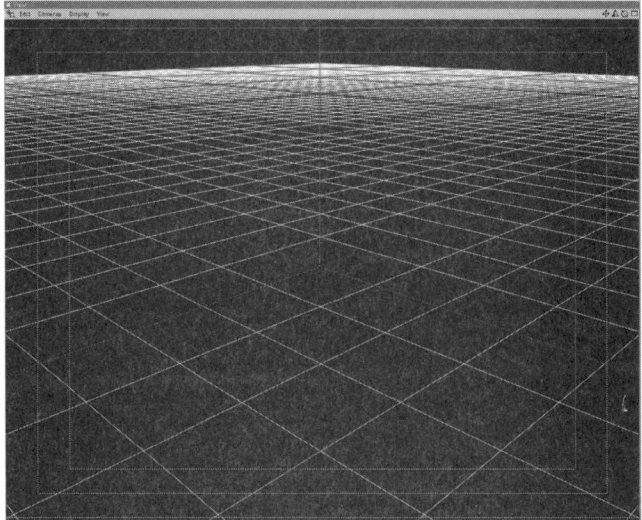

FIGURE 1.27 *The results carry through the interface.*

allows you to customize a collection of layouts to match differing needs. You may have one interface layout for modeling, another for animating. You may have one layout with a collection of tools that you use for creating game models, while you use another collection of tools for broadcast work. You can swap layouts within the same project. The power over layout is incredibly important for creating a smooth workflow.

Chapter 1 Interface

Also note that there is a Reset Layout option. Many of my students in the beginning are very afraid to experiment with altering the layout because they find it hard to get things back to where they want them if they make a mistake. With Reset Layout, there really isn't any reason to not experiment with adjusting the layout to fit your needs. As your 3D style changes and evolves, take time to experiment with layouts and custom organization of commands and managers. As a 3D artist, your time is money. Streamlined layouts can save all sorts of resources including energy, time, and money.

View Panel

The space that takes up the most visual real estate is the large view panel (Figure 1.28). The view panel is your window into the digital world. Objects that you model will appear within this space. A good way to think of this window is the viewfinder of a camera that allows you to view objects and their relationships to other objects. As it is a camera, there are several ways to adjust how this camera works.

Remember those early math classes where you were given series of *coordinates* to allow you to plot points in a graph where *x* represented the horizontal and *y* represented the vertical? Well, a computer thinks of digital space in much the same way. However, since we are dealing in 3D, there are more than just two directions.

Using the *Euclidean Geometry Model*, the computer keeps track of digital space along three axis – the X-axis (horizontal), the Y-axis (vertical), and the

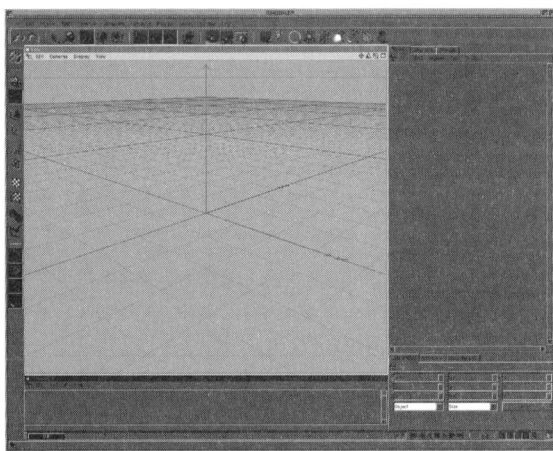

Figure 1.28 *View panel window.*

Figure 1.29 *Axis defining symbol present with new files.*

Z-axis (depth). Therefore, the computer thinks of an object's location as a defined point within these three axes. This is an important thing to remember as we begin looking at maneuvering within the space and moving objects within the view panels. Whenever you start up C4D or open a new document, you'll see a guide in the middle of your view panel defining these three axes (Figure 1.29).

Notice that the view panel has its own collection of pull-down menus, as well as a set of four tools within the upper right corner. These four tools are important tools, allowing you (the camera person) to control where the virtual camera is, where it is pointing, and what "lens" you are using (Figure 1.30 a).

These four tools function a bit differently than any other tools in C4D. For most tools in C4D, you select or activate the tool and then work with it within the view panels. However, to use these four tools, you must click-drag right on the tool symbol itself.

The first of these four tools (Figure 1.30 b), which looks like a cross with arrows on it, allows you to move the camera. Click-drag on that symbol and the camera will move up and down and right to left. Try it.

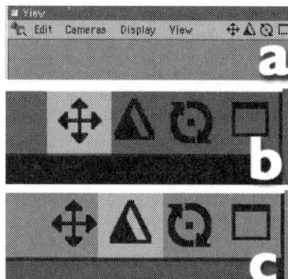

FIGURE 1.30 (a) View panel pull-down menus and tools. (b) Camera Move tool. c) Camera Scale tool.

By simply click-dragging on this Camera Move tool, you are able to move in two directions (*x* and *y*, or up and down). If you are on a Mac, hold down the COMMAND button and click-drag on this tool and you will move the camera closer or further away. On a PC, CTRL-click-drag or right-mouse-click-drag to get the same effect. By holding the "1" key down on your keyboard, you can also use this tool without having to click on the tool symbol itself. In other words, "1" is the keyboard shortcut for the Camera Move tool. When you hold the "1" down, the same rules apply – click-dragging moves the virtual camera up and down, and CTRL-click or right-click (COMMAND-click on a Mac) moves the camera in or out. Remember that this is always the tool to use when you wish to physically move the virtual camera you are looking through.

The second tool shown that is often misunderstood (Figure 1.30 c). It's often referred to as the Camera Scale tool – however, this is misleading. This tool is strictly a lens-zoom tool. Using this tool changes the focal length of the virtual lens. It does not actually move the camera any closer or farther away from the object. The keyboard shortcut for this tool is "2."

Below is an example of this. Figure 1.31 (a) shows a cube at the default camera setting. Figure 1.31 (b) shows the same cube when the Camera Scale tool has been click-dragged to the left. To get this kind of effect in the real world you would need a very short focal length, giving you a very fisheye view, or a view where the ideas of perspective are amplified and over exaggerated.

Conversely, Figure 1.31 (c) shows the same cube with an extremely long focal length. To do this, the Camera Scale tool was click-dragged to the right. This is analogous to using an extreme telephoto lens. The result is an image with shallow, nearly non-existent perspective.

The secret here is to remember that typically, while you work within the view panels during the modeling or animation process, you probably want to use a right-click-Camera Move tool (COMMAND-click-Camera Move tool on a Mac) to actually move the camera closer to your model, rather than the Camera Scale tool to change your style of lens. By moving the camera closer, you can maintain a constant focal length and work more accurately.

The next tool is called the Rotate Camera tool (Figure 1.32 a). As the name implies, this tool allows you to rotate the camera around a given point. This "given point" is usually the center of whatever object is selected. When a new file is opened and an object does not exist, the camera stays focused on the (0,0,0) point, or the center of the digital universe.

This tool is accessible through the "3" key on your keyboard. Remember this key must be held as you click-drag within the view panel. The Camera Rotate tool by default rotates the camera while it keeps the camera upright. However, by right-clicking (or COMMAND-clicking on a Mac) when you use this tool, you can give your virtual camera a "Dutch tilt" (Figure 1.32 b).

The right-most tool within the view panel is called the Toggle Active View tool (Figure 1.33 a).

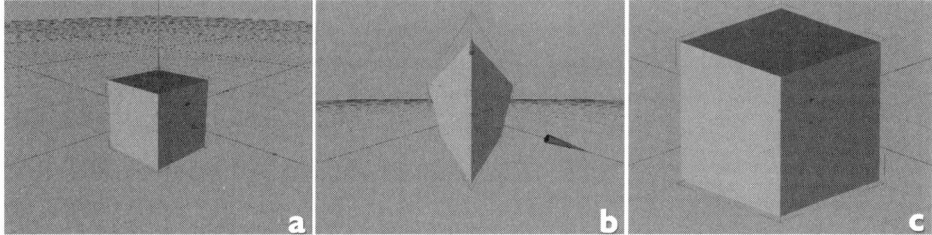

FIGURE 1.31 *(a) Cube at default setting. (b) Fisheye result of very short focal length from using the Camera Scale tool. (c) Telephoto lens effect of using Camera Scale tool.*

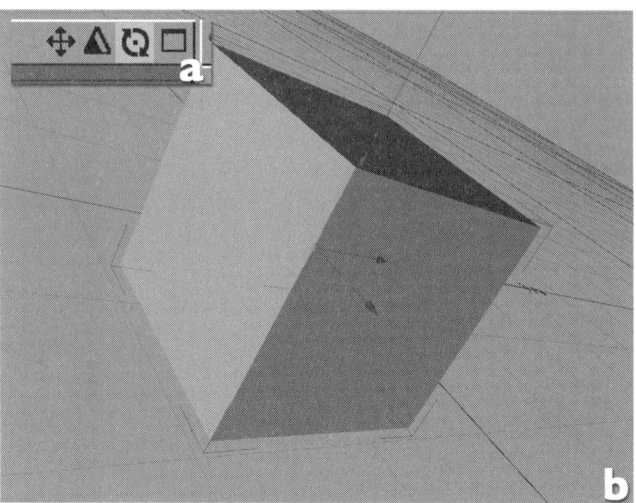

FIGURE 1.32 *(a) Camera Rotate tool. (b) Dutch tilt result of right-clicking with Camera Rotate tool.*

The default view that you get when you open a new document in C4D is one large view panel through which you are able to see the virtual world in perspective. Perspective is how our minds comprehend three-dimensional space on a two-dimensional plane. Real cameras capture reality in perspective and artists usually use perspective to portray reality in their works. However, this is not the only way to display the virtual digital space.

When the Toggle Active View tool is selected, the single view panel is suddenly divided into four panels that show the same space through four different cameras. This state of four views is called the *All-Views mode*. (Figure 1.33 b).

Note that while you are in All-Views mode, each view panel has its own set of camera control tools and pull-down menus. Within each of these four view panels, you can use the Camera Move, Camera Scale, and Camera Rotate tools to move the camera through which you are viewing the scene in that view panel around. Note also that each view panel has its own Toggle Active View tool which when it is clicked, expands that view to be the only view panel visible.

With any newly expanded view panel, you can again toggle back to All-Views mode by clicking the Toggle Active View tool (the keyboard shortcuts are PageUp and PageDown).

While you are in All-Views mode, only one view is "active" at a time. The other view panels will still refresh; however, when you do test renderings it's important to know which view panel is active. A view panel is active when you can see a thin blue line around it (Figure 1.34). Whenever you click inside a view panel or click along the upper area of the view panel (where the pull-down menus appear), you are activating that view panel. In essence, you are telling C4D, "Hey, I'm working in this window now."

Now that we know how C4D is laid out and how its general tools are organized (and how to change this organization if we wish), let's look at how to make things happen in this newly understood view panel.

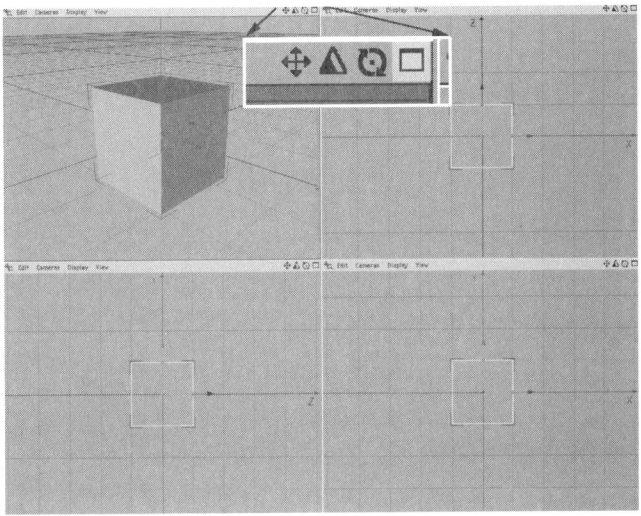

FIGURE 1.33 (a) Toggle Active View tool. (b) All-Views mode of the Toggle Active View tool.

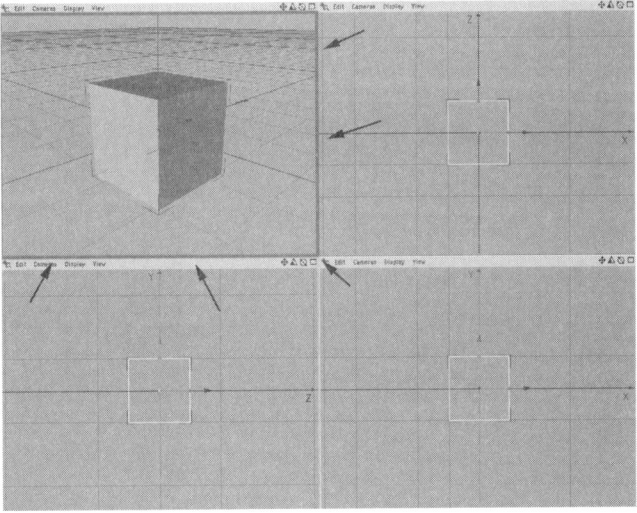

FIGURE 1.34 Active view panel as seen by exaggerated blue line.

CHAPTER 2
Beginning Modeling

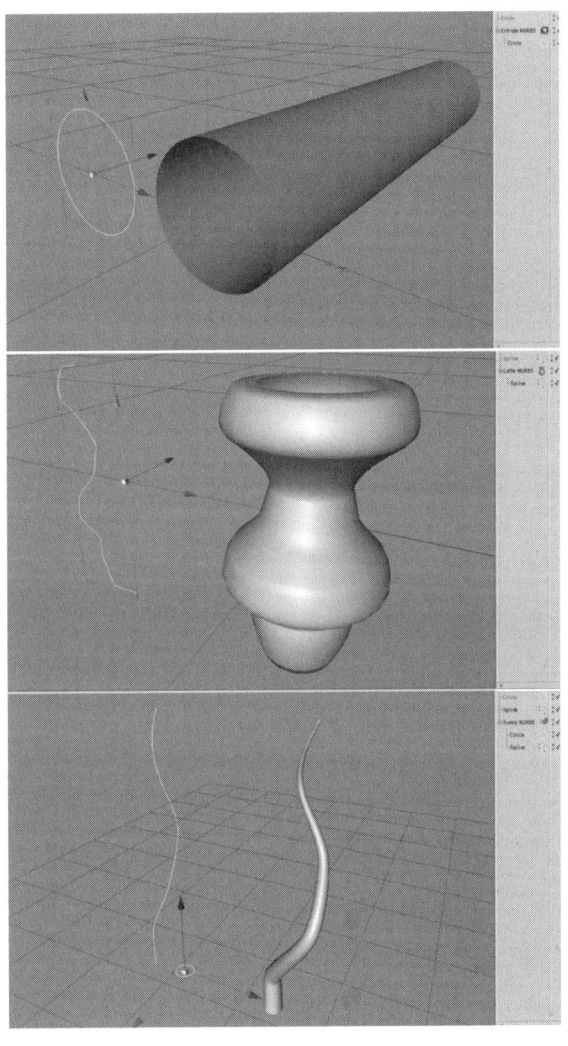

We've already looked at ways to manipulate our view in the 3D world. We've looked at perspective views and how to view the 3D world in the flat, non-interpretive formats of top, right, and front views using forms of parallel projection. Now that we know how to look at the world, it's time to look at how to create within it.

3D, although technically heavy and challenging, does include quite a bit of theory that is necessary to understand. Because of this, the first section of this chapter is dedicated to covering some of the basic ideas behind 3D object construction. Don't lose heart as you read through the ethereal, abstract theory analysis, however. The second section of the chapter looks in depth at how to realize the theory covered. The last part of the chapter takes all the theory, all the elementary how-to, and combines it to actually create.

3D Construction Theory

The most basic building block of 3D objects is the *point*. A point is analogous to the atom of our world. A point in 3D is visible in the Editor environment yet it never renders (Figures 2.1 a+b). When a group of three or four points are joined together, they create a *polygon*. One way to think of a polygon — this collection of points (atoms) that now have a new structure as a group — is as the molecule of 3D objects. Polygons (polys) are either triangular or square (quadrangle) two-dimensional objects that are seen both in the Editor and in the *Renderer* (Figures 2.1 c+d). These polygons are paper thin and rigid; that is, a polygon can be altered in shape by moving the points that make it, but the polygon itself cannot be "bent." When a large number of these rigid polygons are connected one to another and placed at small angles to one another, a curved shape can be created (Figures 2.2 a-c).

When points are used to create a polygon, they are also referred to as a *vertex*. These vertices can be altered (pushed and pulled in any direction) to change the shape of a polygon. Polygons may "share" points. For example, four or six points can create two polygons (Figure 2.3 a). When two polygons share points, the result is a solid surface. If two adjacent polygons do not share two common points, there is technically no solid surface. The result can be shears, or holes in a surface (Figure 2.3 b).

When several polygons are connected and enclose a three-dimensional space, they form a three-dimensional shape. For instance, Figure 2.4 (a) shows a pyramid created with six triangular polygons placed together. Figure 2.4 (b) shows a cube created with six square (quadrangle) polygons connected together.

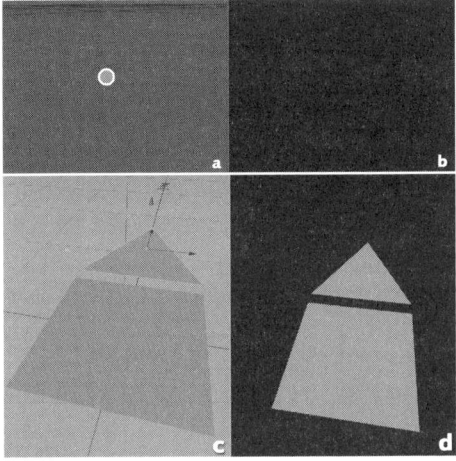

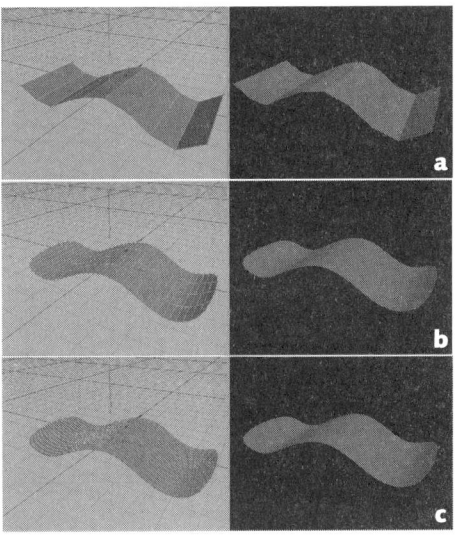

FIGURE 2.1 *Point in Editor (a) and Renderer (b). Polygons can be three- or four-sided (c) and visible in the Renderer (d).*

FIGURE 2.2 *String of polygons collected to create a curve. The more polygons, the smaller the angles and the smoother the curves. Figure 2.2 (a) shows the least number of polys and Figure 2.2 (c) shows the most.*

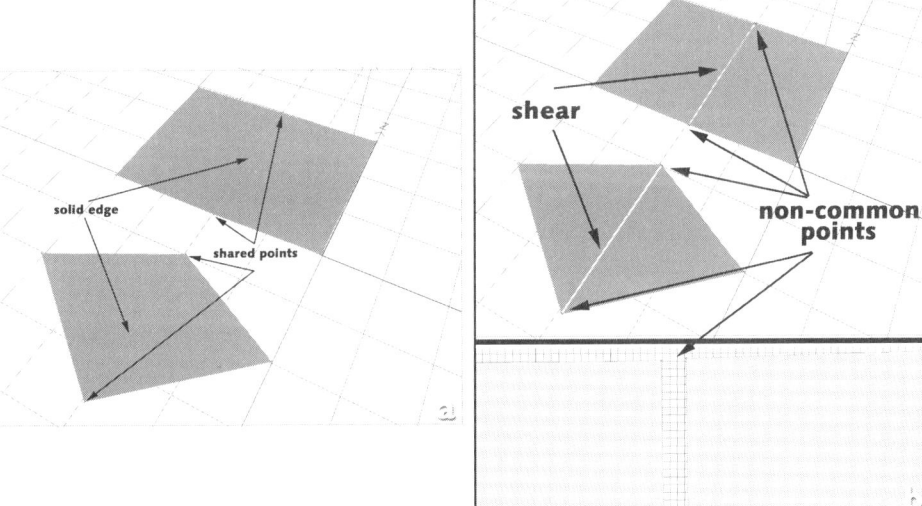

FIGURE 2.3 *(a) Shared points to create a polygon. (b) If points are not common and are actually two closely-placed points, the result is two polygons that have a hole or shear down the middle.*

Three-dimensional shapes can contain both square (quadrangle) and triangular polygons. As discussed earlier, only collections of polygons can give the effect of a curved shape. The more polygons a curvilinear shape contains, the "smoother" the curves. For an example of this see Figures 2.5 (a-c). Figure 2.5 (a) shows a circular shape created with a small number of polygons. The result: an angular looking ball that would be a killer in a game of dodgeball. Figure 2.5 (b) shows a similar spherical shape only using slightly more polygons to create the shape – notice a much smoother form. Figure 2.5 (c) shows a very high number of polygons creating the spherical form – this of course, is the smoothest of the three.

THE CONCEPT OF POLY-COUNT

The idea of polygons is central to almost all 3D modeling. As illustrated above, higher polygon counts (*poly-counts*) create smoother forms that are more pleasing and organic. However, the higher the polygon count, the more information your computer must keep track of. In a perfect world, your computer would not be limited or slowed by the number of polygons in your model or scene. However, as projects emerge and deal more and more with organic forms, the necessity of producing very rounded shapes becomes increasingly important. As these rounded shapes become more and more rounded, the poly-count becomes so high, your computer simply cannot handle all the calculations fast enough to display them for you in Editor format. Your *screen redraw* (the time it takes your screen to "redraw" the information visible while you are in Editor mode) can become painfully slow. In addition, C4D's usually speedy Renderer can be crippled when it must contend with huge amounts of polygons (Figure 2.6). We'll talk much more about this later (especially in the Games section Chapter 15); however, it is important to note that even if you are working on broadcast-quality projects, keeping an eye on your poly-count will help maintain a snappy interface and smooth workflow.

NURBS

Besides polygonal modeling, C4D also provides a form of modeling that allows for tremendous flexibility: *NURBS*. NURBS (an acronym (singular and plural)) stands for Non-Uniform Rational B-Spline. NURBS objects are objects created by object generators. That is, they themselves have no inherent geometry; rather, they use other objects to create (or generate) a new object. A true team player, NURBS can make a pipe out of a circle, a vase out of a squiggle, a vine from a line and a profile, and a head from a cube (Figure 2.7).

FIGURE 2.4 *(a) Polygonal pyramid shown at left in Wireframe mode to see the polygon collection. The image at right shows the pyramid rendered. (b) Polygonal cube shown at left in Wireframe mode to see the polygon collection. The image at right shows the pyramid rendered.*

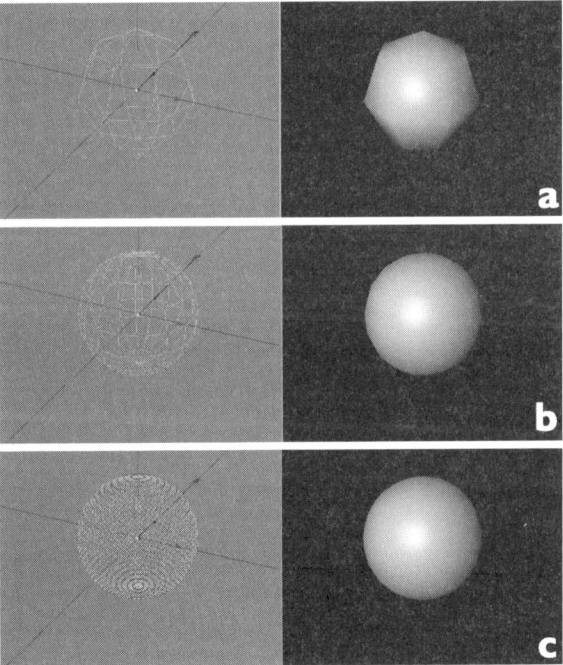

FIGURE 2.5 *(a) A minimum number of polygons creates very angular shapes. (b) Increase the number of polygons in a shape and increase the curves. (c) The highest polygon counts create the smoothest shapes.*

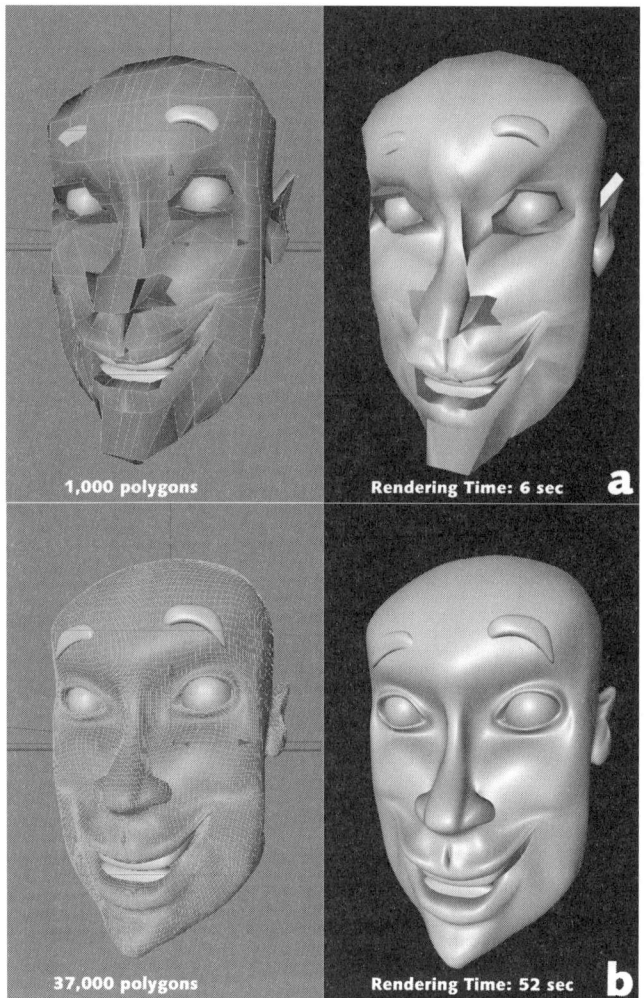

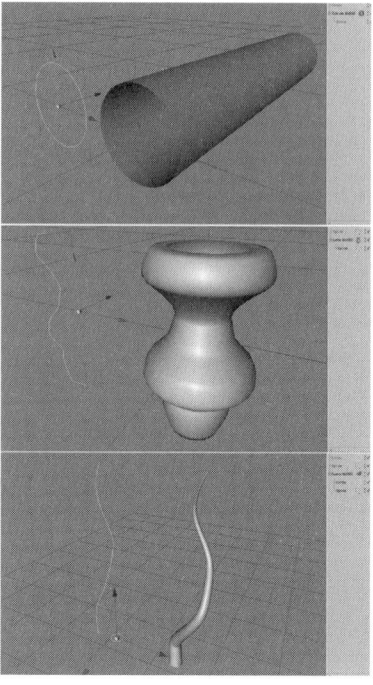

FIGURE 2.7 *A look at NURBS-based objects.*

FIGURE 2.6 *The top image (a), using about 1,000 polygons renders in less than 6 seconds. However, the smooth (and consequently high poly-count) image (b), although better looking, takes 52 seconds to render.*

In polygonal modeling you actually work with the building blocks of 3D shapes – polygons. In NURBS objects, you alter the source objects that create the final NURBS object and C4D automatically calculates the final effect of the polygons that make up the NURBS object. This allows for a tremendous amount of flexibility. By quickly altering a few parts of a constituent object, C4D can reorganize a large amount of polygons in the final NURBS object. This dynamic ability to change dramatically the shape of a 3D form is one of the huge benefits to NURBS-based modeling.

However, there are some drawbacks to this form of modeling. When you are using NURBS modeling, you rely heavily on C4D's interpretation of how the NURBS algorithms are functioning. If you are in control of the parameters of the NURBS object, this can be to your advantage. However, while an object is part of a NURBS object, you do not have control over the object on a polygon by polygon basis. This can be frustrating if you need to make minute changes to the model. This is not a fatal flaw, however, as NURBS objects can be changed into polygonal objects if need be. We'll look much more at the power of NURBS in the upcoming tutorials.

SPLINES

The primary building tools of most NURBS objects are *splines*. Splines contain points (or vertices) that still have no geometry of their own. These points define the shape (linear, curvy) of the lines between the points (Figure 2.8). Further, the lines that connect these points together also have no inherent geometry; the manual describes them as "infinitely thin." The idea is that splines will never render. They are simply a collection of points connected by lines that exist within three-dimensional space. The lines that connect these varying points in space create a shape through a process referred to in C4D as *interpolation*. Although splines themselves have no geometry, they can be used to create a wide variety of geometry. C4D has a nice diverse toolbox of spline creation operations. We'll talk much more about this later.

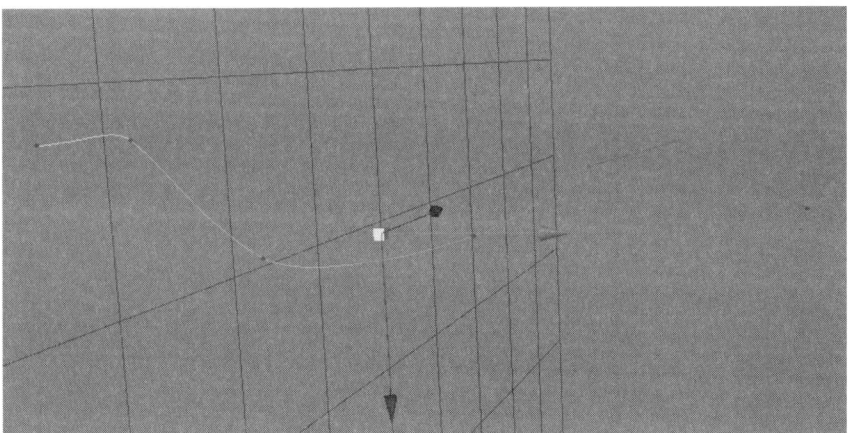

FIGURE 2.8 *Splines, which are used to create curves, NURBS, and paths, are collections of points with connecting lines.*

PRIMITIVES

The last type of object we'll discuss is the collection of objects that C4D makes really well. These objects are *primitives*. Primitives are objects that C4D creates via mathematical formulas that create a shape based on determined values. Because of this dynamic mathematical nature, most primitives in C4D are said to be *parametric*, meaning the parameters of these primitive objects can be easily changed. What this means is that although C4D actually uses polygons to display the objects in the Editor, primitives don't actually have any polygons of their own until rendered. The benefit of this is similar to NURBS objects: by altering the parameters, you can quickly get new shapes without having to alter the object at the polygonal level. The drawback is that you can only alter the shape according to C4D's parameter variables. There is a surprisingly large amount of possibilities in primitives. The best way to explore them is to create some and talk of the possibilities......

PUTTING THE THEORY INTO PRACTICE

CREATING PRIMITIVES

Before we get too far into the intricacies of primitives, it's worthwhile to mention one of the animators' best friends – the Undo function. If your interface is still set up in the default setting, you have a command palette across the top of your screen. This palette is broken up into five sections. These sections simply group the commands into groups of similar tools. The first section with the two curved arrows contains the *Undo* and *Redo* commands. C4D has what is called a *non-destructive* workflow, meaning that multiple undos are possible. With non-destructive workflows, C4D keeps information on parts of models and the method used to create shapes as you work. By default, you have 10 undo steps; you can change this by going to Edit>General Settings and then changing the Undo Depth setting listed in the General tab to your desired levels of undo. Remember that all of these undos must be stored in your computer's memory – so if you're memory challenged, keep this Undo Depth setting low.

The Undo and Redo commands are two of the most used commands in all of 3D-dom. Every artist, no matter how accomplished, works through series of refining and retrying. Keep the Undo and Redo buttons handy and know that there's no shame in undoing something just done. Indeed, many artists begin to develop a cramp in their hand as it sits ready to press the keyboard shortcuts for Undo (CTRL-Z or Command-Z) and Redo (CTRL-Y or Command-Y). Through the course of the steps we'll look at, we won't look at how to undo and redo as it's a fairly common concept to all of computer work; however, don't forget that this tool is there.

Let's continue to explore the tools. In the fifth section of the command palette on the top of your default screen is an icon of a cube (Figure 2.9 a). This Cube icon is the command function to create a cube primitive. To use it, simply click it once. Immediately, a box will appear in the middle of your view panel (Figure 2.9 b).

Immediately, there are several important things to notice about the C4D interface upon the creation of the cube. The first, of course, is the existence of a cube in the middle of the Editor window. However, the placement of this cube is also very important to note. Notice that the cube has been placed at exactly the center of known 3D space (Figure 2.10); that is, the center of the cube is at (0,0,0) in the *xyz* Cartesian coordinate grids. This is an important idea to remember in C4D. *When you are placing any new objects, the default location is at (0,0,0).*

On the cube itself, notice the many visible tools available. The first visual tool is the red "corner pieces." These red corner pieces define the space which the 3D object takes up within digital space. These red corner pieces are not interactive; meaning that they are not functional tools to grab or alter. They are simply a visual communication tool between C4D and you.

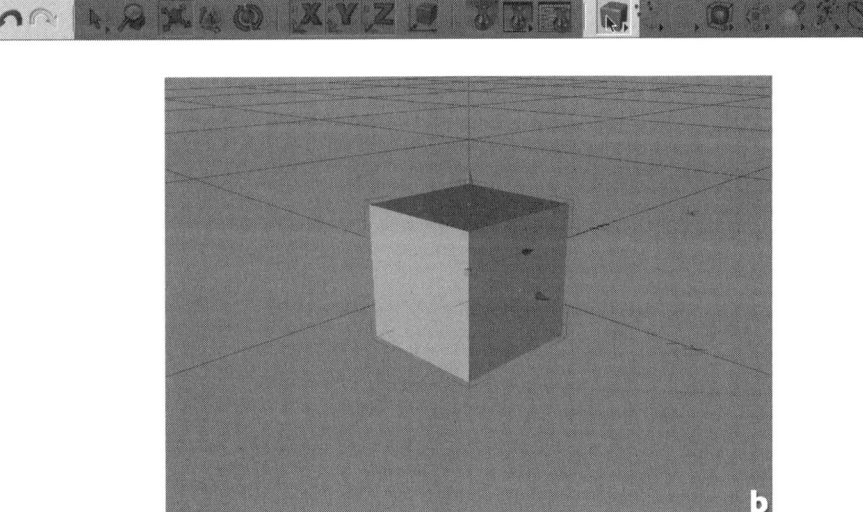

FIGURE 2.9 *(a) Primitive Cube icon – just click to use. Also notice the Undo/Redo tools at the far left. (b) Resultant primitive cube.*

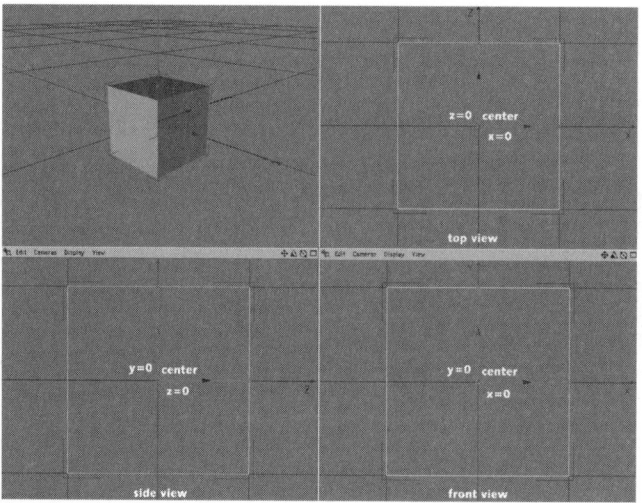

FIGURE 2.10 *New objects placed at the center of digital space.*

ALTERING PARAMETRIC PRIMITIVES

The next things to notice are the orange dots on the top and two sides of the cube (Figure 2.11 a). These are interactive, functioning tools that allow you to adjust the parameters of this Parametric primitive. These orange dots are only present on parametric Primitives – you won't see them on NURBS- or polygonal-based objects. These parametric handles allow you to interactively change physical characteristics of the objects. This is actually a visual form of altering the mathematical variables described earlier that create the shape. To use these interactive handles, simply click-drag them. For instance, if you wish to make a cube wider, simply click on the orange dot on the side of the cube and drag out to the desired size (Figure 2.11 b).

A little later we'll discuss different ways of altering an object including Object, Polygon and Tool modes. The real power of these parametric handles is that you can click-drag these handles no matter what mode or tool you actually have selected.

PARAMETRIC PRIMITIVES AND THE OBJECT MANAGER

While we're talking of parametric handles, notice what has appeared in the Object Manager (Figure 2.12 a). When you created the Parametric cube, an icon with the word "Cube" appeared in the Object Manager. The Object Manager is a visual list of *all* the objects present in a given scene. A lot of work can actually be done in the Object Manager and we'll be continually revisiting this manager.

Chapter 2 Beginning Modeling

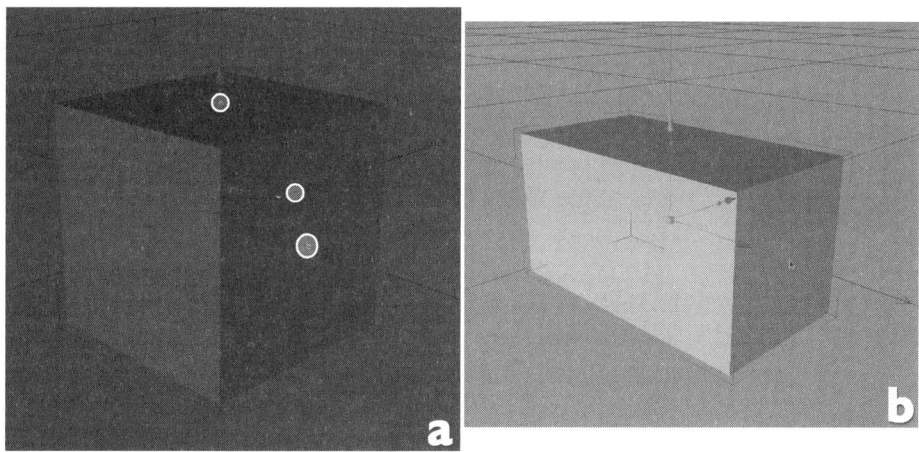

FIGURE 2.11 *(a) Parametric handles. (b) Altering parametric handles.*

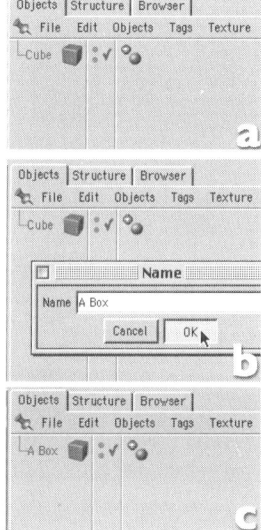

FIGURE 2.12 *(a) Object Manager. (b) By double-clicking on the name of the object within the Object Manager, you can rename your objects as you go. This becomes important as projects get more complex.*

Within the Object Manager you can change the names of objects. If you double-click on the word "Cube," you'll be presented with a new dialog box allowing you to rename this object if so desired (Figure 2.12 b). In simple cases like this, it may seem unnecessary. However, as your projects become increasingly complex and the list of objects grows, having appropriately named objects becomes not only a nice help but a necessity. It's suggested that you indeed spend good time re-labeling your objects as you go.

Besides changing the name in the Object Manager, you can alter the parameters of Parametric primitives. Double-click on the Cube icon and a new dialog box will appear (Figure 2.13 a). For a cube, the parameters available to edit are quite limited. The first column is set up to allow you to change the size of the cube in each direction. The second column allows you to change the *segments* of the Parametric primitive cube. The number of segments for a primitive cube is actually fairly unimportant while the cube is still a primitive. However, the number of segments becomes very important in other functions that may be built off of the cube.

The idea behind segments is that a primitive cube is constructed of six square (quadrangle) polygons. Each side is one polygon or one segment (Figure 2.13 b). If the segment number is increased, then the number of polygons used to create one face of the cube is increased (Figure 2.13 c). Note that while a Parametric cube is a primitive, you can't see the number of segments along each side while you are in it. The primitive always renders as a simple flat side. However, if you change your Display setting for the view panel to Wireframe, you can see the segments created. Larger numbers of segments allow for greater flexibility in future operations, but also begin to slow your computer down as it attempts to keep track of the larger amount of polys.

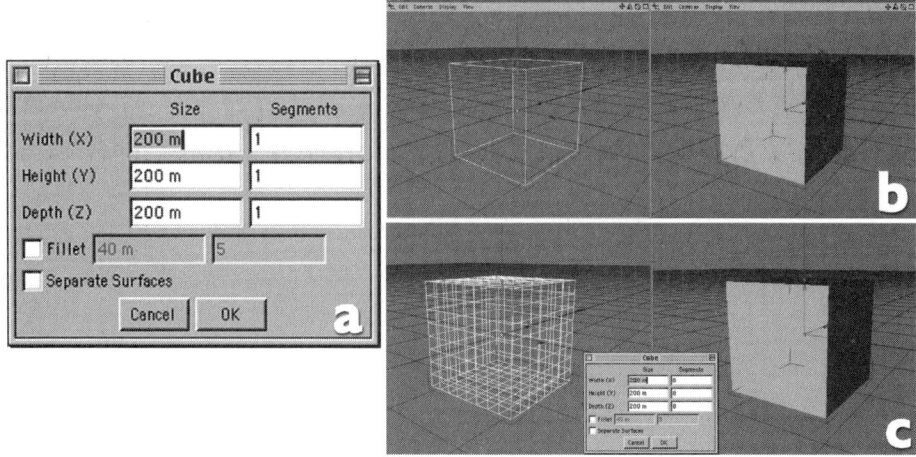

FIGURE 2.13 *(a) Parameter editing for Parametric Primitive Cube. (b) One segment = one polygon. (c) Multiple segments eventually lead to multiple polygons per face.*

FILLETS

Fillets are rounded sections or corners of shapes. Almost all of the primitives allow you to activate the Fillets option to make primitive forms less blocky and hard-edged (Figure 2.14 a). This is where some of the power of primitives really begins to emerge. To create the rounded edges shown in Figure 2.14 (a), you would need to manually shift an awful lot of polygons to create this rounded shape. However, with parametric primitives, you simply double-click on the blue Primitive icon (Figure 2.14 b) and activate the Fillet button within the dialog box and then edit the values set in the input fields to change the depth of the rounded edge (Figure 2.14 c).

Notice that as soon as you activate the Fillet option in the Primitive Cube dialog box, new orange parameter-altering handles appear on the object (Figure 2.15 a). These handles can again be dynamically altered to effect the depth of the fillet on the corner (Figure 2.15 b). Up to now, altering the orange parameter handles was something that could not be done by scaling the object. However, with the addition of these Fillet parameter handles, you can see how parametric handles *reshape* a primitive rather than resize it.

One other note about the primitive cube: there is also a checkbox to create a cube with Separate Surfaces. While your cube is still a primitive, this really doesn't have much bearing on your project in the Editor view or in a rendering. However, part of the idea behind primitives is that you can "tell" an object to no longer be a primitive and simply be a collection of polygons (a form made of polygonal shapes rather than formed by a calculation). This is done by making

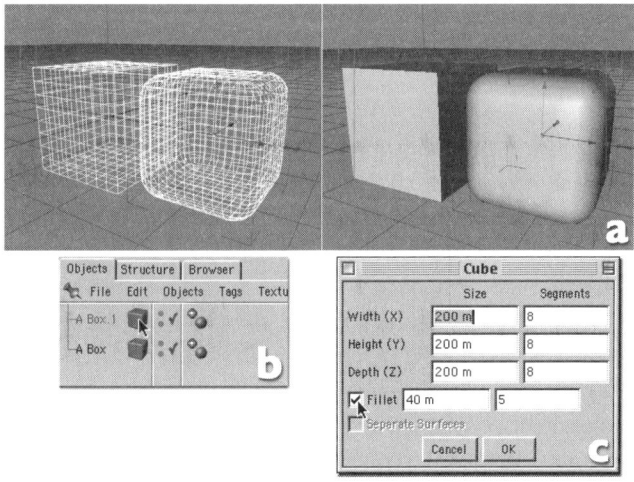

FIGURE 2.14 *(a) Non-filleted and filleted primitive forms. (b) Activate the Fillet functions by double-clicking the blue Primitive icon. (c) Fillet button and input fields activated to create the rounded shapes.*

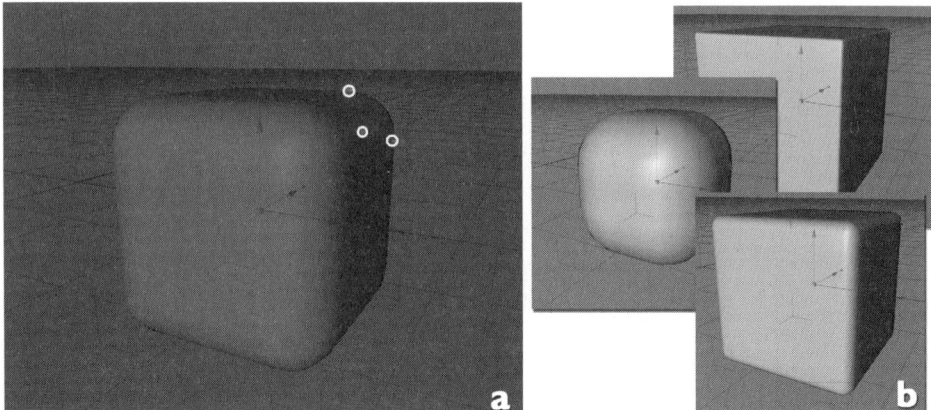

FIGURE 2.15 *(a) New parameter altering handles. (b) Various Fillet depths altered quickly with parameter altering handles.*

the object *editable* (Select Structure>Make Editable or use the keyboard shortcut "C"). If a cube without the Separate Surfaces box checked is made editable, the result is one shape where C4D understands all the segments to be connected together (Figure 2.16 a). However, if the Separate Surfaces option is checked and then the cube is made editable, C4D understands this primitive to now be six (or however many segments you have enabled) separate polygons – it sees the cube as a group of unconnected polygons (Figure 2.16 b).

OTHER PRIMITIVES

Some tools within command palettes contain other tools that are *folded* into the button. You can tell when other commands are folded by the small black triangle that appears at the bottom right hand of the command button (Figure 2.17). The collection of primitive shapes that C4D creates is one example. These primitive shapes are actually nested (or folded) within the Primitive Cube command on the top command palette. If you click and hold on the Primitive Cube command button, a small subset of selections will appear showing you the other available primitives in C4D (Figure 2.18). To select a primitive, and thus place it within your scene (placed at (0,0,0) and listed in your Object Manager), keep your mouse button clicked and move it over the desired form before releasing. Upon release, the primitive is placed.

It is also noteworthy that the primitive shapes available in C4D can also be accessed through the pull-down menu path of Objects>Primitives (Figure 2.19). The order in which they are listed is different than the order in which they are presented in the command palette.

Each of the remaining primitives have important differences and personalities that when you understand them, make them powerful building blocks. However, since this isn't a manual, each primitive isn't covered in print. Please take a look at the supplemental chapters on the CD for more information on each of the additional primitives.

ON THE CD

FIGURE 2.16 *(a) Without the Separate Surfaces option selected, C4D understands editable cubes as a solid (although hollow) polygonal shape. (b) With the Separate Surfaces option selected, C4D makes a primitive cube editable into separate independent polygons.*

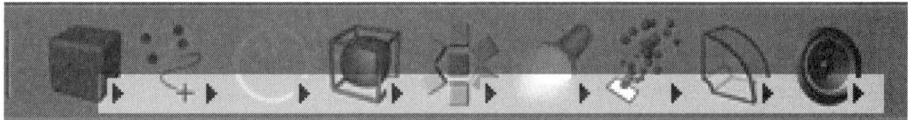

FIGURE 2.17 *Folded commands.*

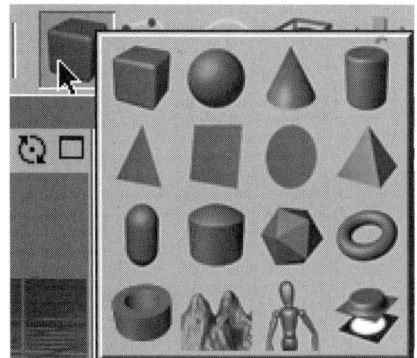

FIGURE 2.18 *Collections of primitives that C4D Creates.*

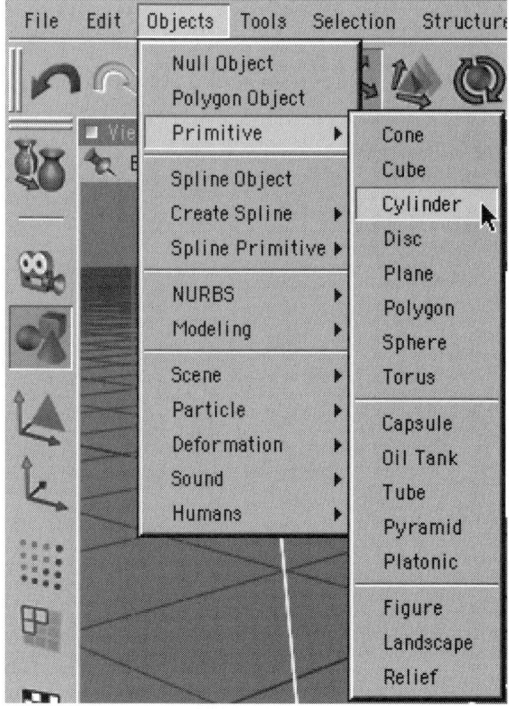

FIGURE 2.19 *Accessing primitive shapes with pull-down menus.*

CHAPTER 3

Playing with Primitives

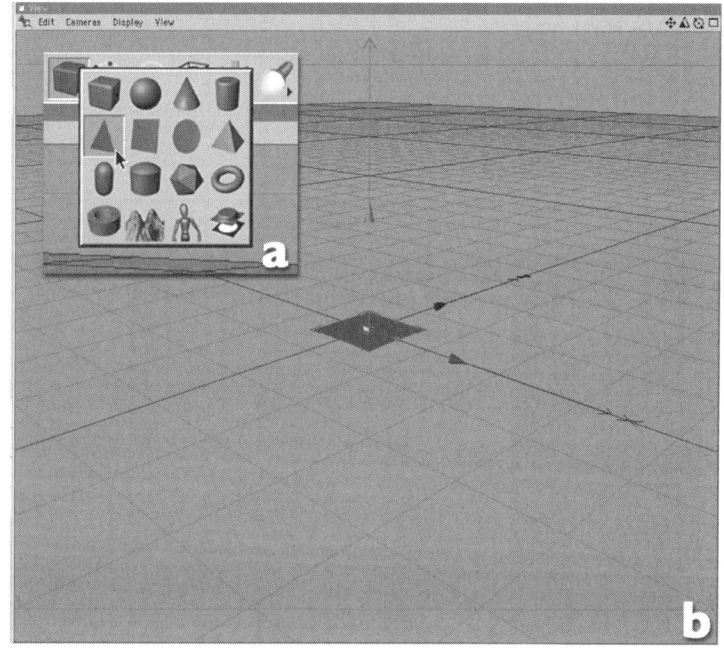

3.1 Creating an Interior – Step One: Primitives

TUTORIAL

To begin with, let's create the floor of the room. To do this, we'll use the most basic solid building block of 3D – the Polygon Primitive. Note that we could also use the Plane Primitive, but by default Plane Primitives are higher in poly-count, and since this floor is always simply going to lay flat, there really is no need to unnecessarily add polygons. Add a Polygon Primitive to the scene by selecting the Add Polygon Object from the command palette at the top (Figure 3.1 a). The result should be a small square in the middle of the scene (Figure 3.1 b).

The placement of this Polygon Object is fine – it's sitting directly on the Z- and X-axes. However, the size seems fairly small. Select the Scale Active Element tool and click-drag anywhere in the scene to increase the size of the polygon. Watch your Coordinates Manager (bottom right hand corner of the interface) as you drag to see how large you are making this polygon shape. Although shape is completely relative in this case, make this Polygon Object about 1000m x 1000m. You may wish to simply enter these dimensions manually in the Coordinates Manager by entering 1000 in the X and Z input fields.

Press "H" on your keyboard to have your view panel display all objects present in your scene (which in this case is just the polygon).

For the walls, we could use a Plane, Polygon or Cube Primitive. However, since we'll eventually be having windows in the scene and will be able to see the relief of the window sill, a Cube Primitive would work best. Place a Cube Primitive in the scene by selecting the Add Cube Object. Immediately a cube will be placed in the scene that looks really short – the reason for this is that half of the cube is actually sitting below the floor. Confirm this by toggling your view

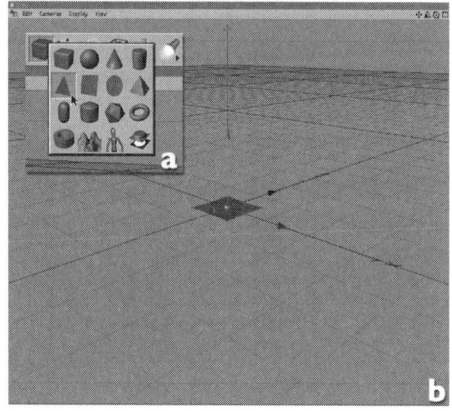

FIGURE 3.1 *(a) Add Polygon Object. (b) Placed Polygon Primitive.*

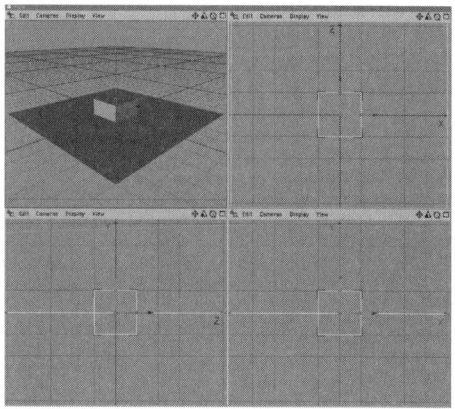

FIGURE 3.2 *Toggled views reveal that the cube is actually sitting halfway above and halfway below the floor.*

Chapter 3 Playing With Primitives

panels (Figure 3.2). In the bottom two view panels (right and front) you'll notice a square (the Cube Object) dissected by a white line (the Polygon Object).

The first order of business then should be to move this cube so that it rests on the floor. Activate the Move Active Element tool by clicking it in the top command palette. Now ensure that the Cube is the active object by checking your Object Manager to see if it is in red. If so, simply click-drag anywhere within your bottom two view panels and move the cube up so that it sits level with the floor (Figure 3.3 a).

Now we need to change this cube into a more suitable shape. With the Cube still the active object, activate the Scale Active Element tool and click-drag on the red (X) directional handle of the cube until it is much thinner (Figure 3.3 b). Scale it down in the x direction until the Coordinates Manager indicates it's about 20m thick (much too thick for a real wall, I know; the unit of measurement is actually of no import). Then we need to scale the wall so it's as long as the room. This time, instead of using the Scale Active Element tool, we'll use the Coordinates Manager. We know that the floor (and thus the room) is 1000m long in both the x and z directions. As we look at our cube, we can see that this is most likely to become the wall that runs along the z direction (blue). So, simply enter 1000m in the Z input field under the Size column and the cube will jump to that exact size (Figure 3.3 c).

Now, we need to move the wall from the center of the room to the edge of the floor. We can do this in one of two ways: 1) Use the Move Active Element tool in the view panel that shows the top view (top right hand view panel) and click-drag the red (x) directional handle until the wall is in place. Or 2) we know that the room floor is 1000m long since we entered that in the input field and we know that the floor's center is sitting at (0,0,0) since we haven't moved it. We then know that from the center of our digital universe to the edge of the floor in each direction is 500m. Now, we can use the Coordinates Manager to place the wall appropriately. It just so happens that the back end of the room is in the $-x$ direction, so, under the Position column, enter -500 in the X input field

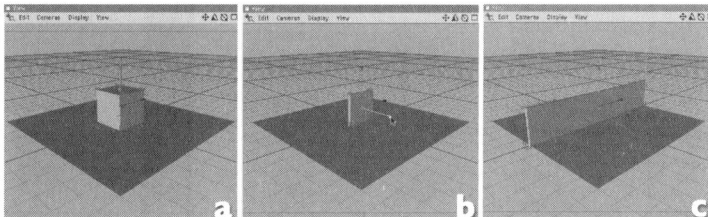

FIGURE 3.3 *(a) Using the Move Active Element tool, you can quickly move the cube (soon to be a wall) level with the floor. (b) Using the Scale Active Element tool, we can turn a block into the beginning of a wall. (c) By using the Coordinates Manager, we can quickly alter the size of the wall to match the floor.*

(Figure 3.4 a). The wall will jump back and be aligned just as you need it within your view panel (Figure 3.4 b).

To create the other walls we could repeat a similar process. Or, we could simply make copies of the wall already created and save ourselves several steps. With the cube selected, go to Edit>Copy, or press CTRL/COMMAND-C. Then go to Edit>Paste or press CTRL/COMMAND-V. Just like a word processing application copies and pastes collections of words, C4D copies and pastes collections of polygons. Now you may not be able to tell that an object has been copied and pasted by just looking at the view panel — in fact, the scene should look just the same as it did before the copy/paste operation. The reason for this is that C4D pastes copied elements right back in the same location as it was copied from. This is so that you don't have to go chasing around 3D space trying to track down what happened to your newly pasted element.

However, notice in the Object Manager that a new Cube has appeared. To keep it from being confused with the first Cube, C4D has renamed it "Cube.1" (Figure 3.5 a). Let's further refine the names by changing the labels for all the shapes thus far; to do this, simply double-click on the *name* of each object within the Object Manager. A small dialog box will appear, allowing you to change the name of the object you selected. Let's change the name of the Polygon Object to "Floor," the name of the first Cube to "Side Wall" and the newly created Cube to "Back Wall" (Figure 3.5 b).

Now we need to rotate the new wall into position at the back of the room. You can do this with the Rotate Active Element tool or again with the Coordinates Manager. For this back wall, we'll first need to rotate the object 90° around its Y-axis or 90° of its heading. If you are using the Rotate Active Element tool,

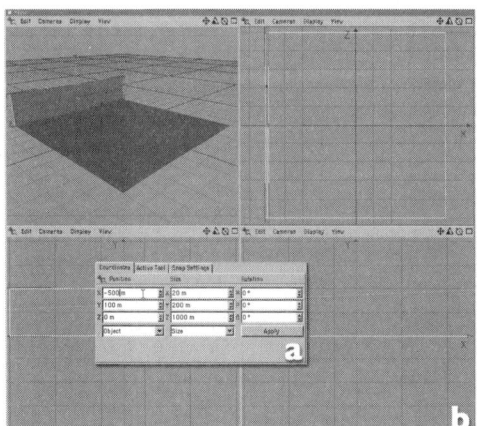

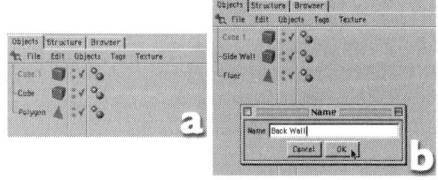

FIGURE 3.5 *(a) C4D will rename an object if an object with that name already exists at the same hierarchal level. (b) Renamed objects.*

FIGURE 3.4 *(a) Enter the coordinates of a direction in the Coordinates Manager. (b) Result of Coordinates Manager alteration.*

simply click-drag on the green directional handle (*y*) until the wall is rotated. If you are using the Coordinates Manager, enter 90 in the H input field of the Rotation column. The result should look something like Figure 3.6.

Now, you can use the Coordinates Manager to move the wall into place along the back wall by entering 0 in the X input field of the Position column and 500 in the Z input field (moves the wall back to 0 along the X-axis, and moves it back 500m along the Z-axis), or you can use the Move Active Element tool to manually move it back into position. Let's use the Move Active Element tool, but first let's look at some ways to enhance the use of this tool.

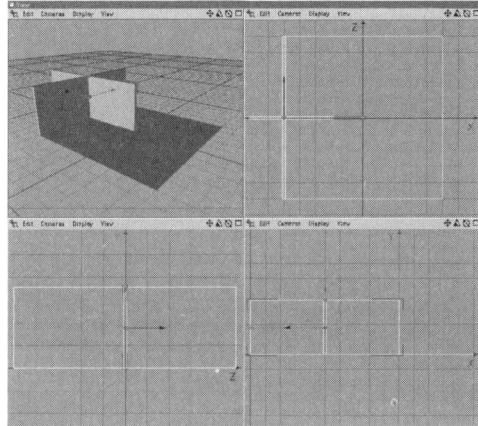

FIGURE 3.6 *Rotated new wall.*

SNAP SETTINGS

At the bottom right hand corner of the interface is the Coordinates Manager. Additionally, there are two other tabs (Active Tool and Snap Settings) that indicate managers that reside beneath the Coordinates Manager. The Snap Settings tab is of particular interest in this case. If you've ever dealt with CAD or even used guides in Illustrator or Photoshop, you'll appreciate the value of this area. Snap Settings allows you to activate settings within C4D that allow objects to snap to centers, edges, points, or polygons. By default, this is turned off to allow for free movement without hindrance. However, in this case, where we are building an interior in which things need to line up, this ability to snap into position is heaven sent.

Snap Settings is actually a very complex set of tools that luckily is explained in depth in the manual. However, for our purposes here it's important to mention a few things. 1) You must click the Enable Snapping checkbox to get things started. 2) If you are working in parallel projection view panels (top, front, right), then the Type is best set to Snap 2.5D. This allows objects to snap if they line up in the two dimensions present in that particular view and don't necessarily line up in the third dimension. 3) The Radius setting helps you determine the tolerance of the snap. Do you want things to snap if you are within an eighth of an inch on your screen or if you are within one half of an inch? This can be adjusted interactively. 4) All the other settings within this set of tools allow you to determine what sorts of things the object you are moving will snap to. In our case, we'll leave the settings as default, but make sure to check the Edge setting (Figure 3.7). 5) Be aware that, although we won't talk much about them here, there are snap settings under the Quantize tab that allow you to establish snap parameters for rotations and scale.

So now, in the top right hand corner view panel (top view), use the Move Active Element tool and move the wall approximately to the middle edge of the floor. You should notice that the wall "snaps" into place indicating that the center of the wall has found the edge of the floor as well as the gridline that defines 0 along the X-axis. If you flip back to the Coordinates Manager, you'll find that the settings displayed are just as they should be. Be careful as you do this that you don't end up aligning the edge of the wall to the edge of the floor. Although this wouldn't be all bad, the side wall is set up with the center of the wall on the edge of the floor – so for consistency's sake, let's do the same for the back wall. You may need to use the Camera Move tool and right-click-drag or COMMAND-click-drag to zoom in a bit to ensure your wall is placed appropriately. Your scene thus far should appear similar to Figure 3.8.

Now that we've spent all this time placing this wall, let's shorten it a bit so that we can place the nook in the wall later. You can do this in one of three ways. The first is to simply grab the orange *parameter handle* on the edge and

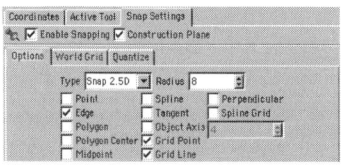

FIGURE 3.7 *Snap Settings activated and set for this tutorial.*

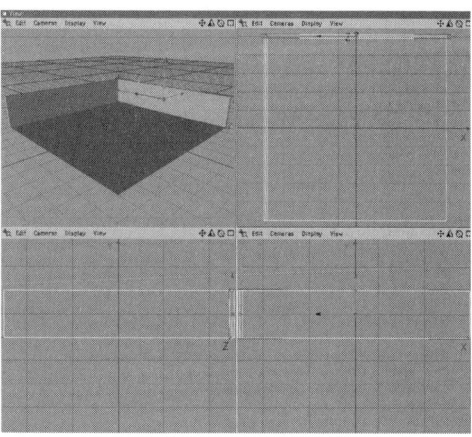

FIGURE 3.8 *Scene with two walls, one placed via the Coordinates Manager, one placed with Snap Settings.*

reshape the cube to be shorter. The other is to use the Scale Active Element tool and grab the blue *z*-directional handle and drag it smaller. The third way is to simply enter the new size into the Coordinates Manager. Notice that at this point the object's axis is different than the digital world's axis. We need to shorten the wall in the world's *x* dimension. However, when the wall is active, note that it is the object's *z* dimension that is vital to us at this point. This occurred because we rotated the first wall. So, alter the side wall's length by entering 400 into the Z input field of the Size column (Figure 3.9).

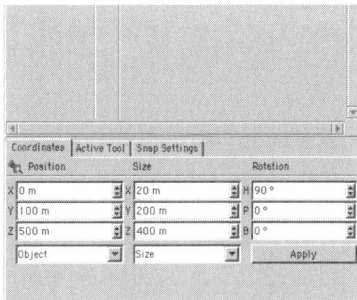

FIGURE 3.9 *Input 400m to the Z field to shorten wall.*

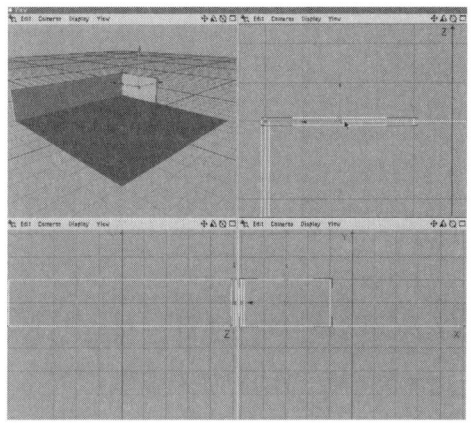

FIGURE 3.10 *With Snap Settings still enabled, quick arrangement of walls becomes possible.*

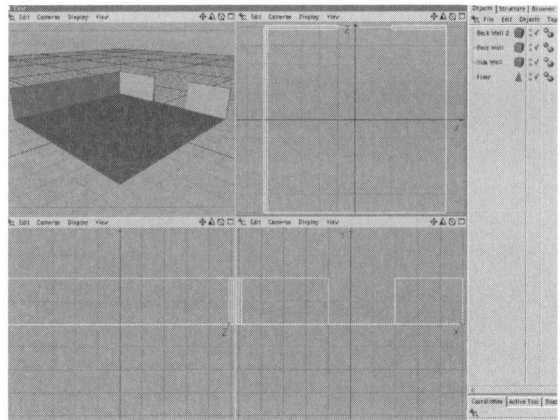

FIGURE 3.11 *Second back wall copied and pasted and moved into position.*

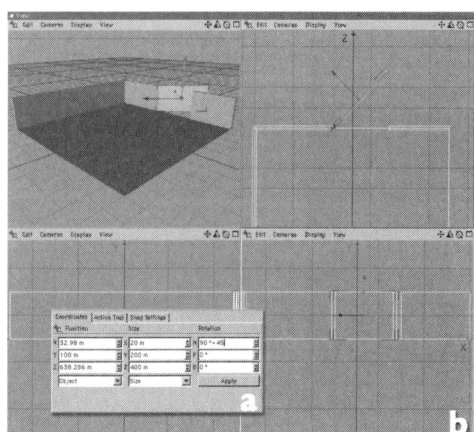

FIGURE 3.12 *(a) The Coordinates Manager allows for the dynamic use of formulae to calculate any value. (b) Our situation thus far.*

Use the Move Active Element tool to move this new shortened wall to the corner. The best view to do this is within the top view. With your Snap Settings still turned on, your wall should easily snap into place as shown in Figure 3.10. Zoom in to ensure that it is so. When you build architectural digital models, it becomes very important that joints are made cleanly to avoid light leaks later.

Copy and paste this new wall and rename it "Wall 2." Resize its Z size to 300m. Now move it to the other corner of the room. This should leave you with a gap in which we'll put a small niche in the room (Figure 3.11).

Now for the niche. This little area of the room will still require walls that are the same thickness as the other walls. So, to ensure consistency, simply copy and paste either of the back walls and rename it "Niche Wall 1." This time, we need to rotate the wall into a 45° angle. To do this, we'll explore some more benefits of the Coordinates Manager. If you copied one of the back walls, the H (heading) setting in the Rotation column should read 90°. C4D allows input fields to include mathematical formulae. In this case, we're going to want to rotate this new wall 45° from its current rotation state. Click on the H input field and simply enter "+ 45" and press Enter (Figure 3.12 a). The input field will instantly calculate this equation and Niche Wall 1 will add 45° to its current rotation value (Figure 3.12 b).

Now of course this wall is far too large for this nook. If you were designing this room, you could use the Scale Active Element tool to interactively find the appropriate length. For time's sake, let us assume you've already figured that out a good size would be 125m long. Enter "125" in the Z input field of the Size column for this Niche Wall 1. Zoom in on the top view so you're sure that you are getting clean joints, then using the Move Active Element tool, move the wall into position so the corners line up. Your Snap Settings should still be active so it should be fairly easy to find where the corners meet (Figure 3.13 a).

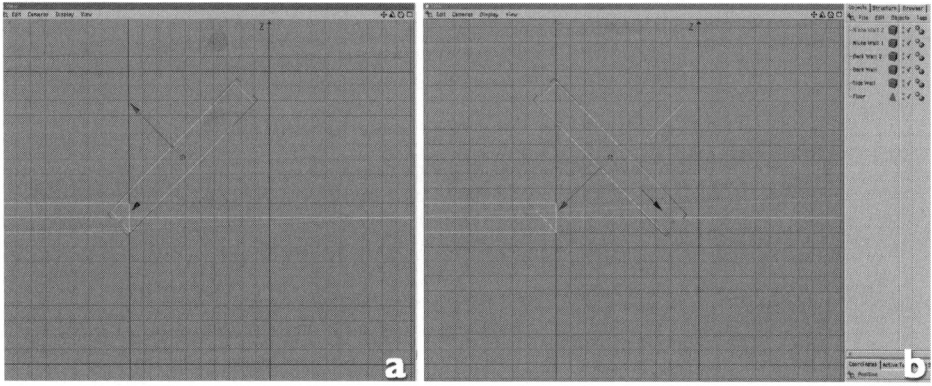

FIGURE 3.13 *(a) Resized wall snapped into position. (b) Copied and rotated Niche Wall 2.*

Note that as these walls are moved, all movement should really be done in the top view. Use the perspective view to take a look at what the model looks like, but to begin with, it's often more accurate to do movement from the one view. This way you make sure that all the walls stay rooted to the floor as they don't move at all in the *y* direction when you work in top view.

Copy and paste this wall and rename the new copy Niche Wall 2. In the H input field of the Rotation column enter +90 as the value to rotate the object into a mirror form of Niche Wall 1. The result will be an "X" of walls (Figure 3.13 b).

Now we need to move this wall over to the other side of the "hole" in the wall. It's important that this wall stays even (along the digital world's Y-axis) with the original wall. To do this we'll look at some important tools.

X-, Y-, AND Z-AXIS LOCK/UNLOCK AND USE WORLD COORDINATE SYSTEM

Next to the Move, Scale, and Rotate Active Element tools are four buttons with an X,Y,Z and a cube with directional handles on them (Figure 3.14 a). The first three buttons are called the X-, Y-, and Z-Axis Lock/Unlock tools. They are there so that you can define along which directions changes are allowed to be made. For instance, with the Move Active Element tool active, if you click (and thus lock) the X and Z buttons (Figure 3.14 a), you will only be able to move the object up and down along the Y-axis when you move the object. The notable exception to this is the use of the directional handles which override the X- ,Y-, and Z-Axis Lock/Unlock tools.

The same thing happens for the Scale Active Element and the Rotate Active Element tools. Remember that the settings of these Lock/Unlock tools are relative to the Move/Scale/Rotate Active Element tool that is active. So you can set only the Y to be unlocked in the Move Active Element tool, but when you switch to the Rotate Active Element tool, all three axes will be unlocked. However, when you return to the Move Active Element tool, only the Y-axis will be unlocked. Each of the tools remembers which axes are editable.

The Use World Coordinate System button allows you to define whether you are locking changes along the *object's* axis or the *world's* axis. Our wall here is a perfect example. By default, Use World Coordinate System is not depressed/selected. So if you lock the Y- and Z-axes with the idea that you'll move the new wall and keep it even with the first wall, you'll be frustrated. Upon click-dragging the wall, the Y-Y and Z-Zaxes will be locked, but the wall will move in the direction of the wall's X-axis (in a diagonal (Figure 3.14 b)).

However, if you click the Use World Coordinate System button (thus activating it), when you click-drag Niche Wall 2, it will remain even with the first wall as it will only be able to move along the *world's* X-axis (Figure 3.14 b). Move the wall along the world's axis over into position on the other side of the hole.

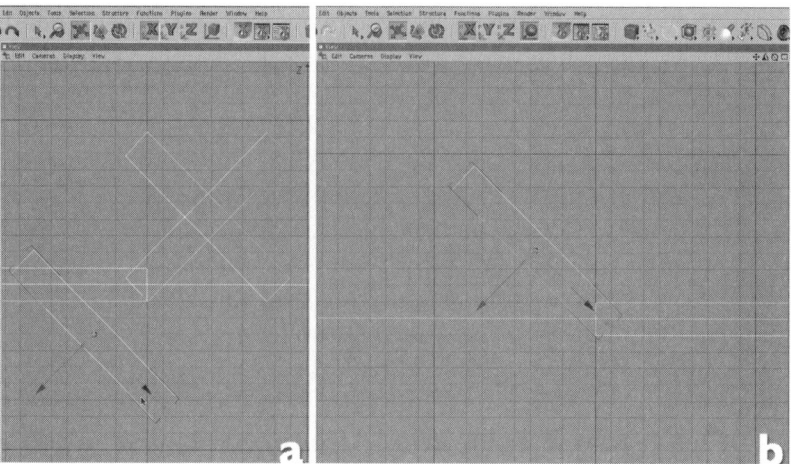

FIGURE 3.14 *(a) When the X-, Y-, or Z-axis Lock/Unlock buttons are depressed, an axis is editable; when the buttons are raised, the axes are not editable. When you use the object's coordinate system (Use World Coordinate System is deactivated) the object moves along the object's axis. (b) With Use World Coordinate System activated, objects will constrain according to the world's axis rather than an individual object's axis.*

Copy and paste either of the niche walls and re-label this new wall "Niche Wall 3." Rotate it so it runs parallel with the other non-niche wall segments on this wall (use the Rotate Object Axis tool or enter 90 in the H input field of the Rotation column in the Coordinates Manager). Move the wall up so that it approximates the position in Figure 3.15 and increase the size (only along the object's Z-axis) to also match the figure. We want to make sure that both the inside and outside corners of this niche are "clean" so that we can use the outside later if desired.

THE POWER OF GROUPS

Now that we've created several walls (in fact all the walls we'll create for this exercise), let's look at how to collectively alter them. C4D allows for a powerful method of organizing objects that is a little different than most other 3D applications. Almost all applications offer a "group" function, but C4D's method doesn't simply group objects — rather, it creates a Null Object (an object with no geometry of its own) to become a parent of all the objects you've selected. Let's look at how this works.

As discussed earlier, many managers have their own collection of pull-down menus. The Object Manager has an especially vital collection of tools located in the nested pull-down menus. Within the Object Manager, go to Objects>Group. Initially it will seem as though nothing is happening; however, notice that your mouse pointer has turned into a small cross. This is C4D telling you that it's ready for you to show it what objects are to be grouped together. Just marquee (click-drag) around the objects you wish to group (in this case the niche walls and a new object called Null Object will be created in your Object Manager.

Next to the Null Object in your Object Manager is now a small box with a plus in it. This box indicates that this object has *children*. The idea behind the parent-child paradigm in C4D is that whatever change you make to a parent object it is transferred down to all the children of that object. However, the children also maintain some autonomy in that they can be altered independently of the other children of the parent. In this way, this parent-child method of grouping is much more powerful than traditional grouping strategies in other applications. If you click on the box with the plus sign, the parent will expand to show the children it contains. Notice that the children are indented and visually shown as children by the gray line showing which object they are connected to.

It should be noted that you needn't use the group function to make any object a child of another. In the Object Manager, all you need to do is move (click-drag) an object over another object and release. You'll notice that when you do so, your mouse pointer will change to indicate that C4D knows you are trying to place an object as a child of another (Figure 3.16 a). Children can become the parents of other objects and multi-leveled objects are possible (Figure 3.16 b).

This Null Object (the parent of the newly grouped niche walls) can be renamed by double-clicking on the name. Rename this group "Niche." Notice in the view panels that a Null Object has its own directional handles (Figure 3.17). This means that the group (under the auspices of the parent object "Niche") can be moved, rotated, or resized. Try it. Use the Move Active Element tool and

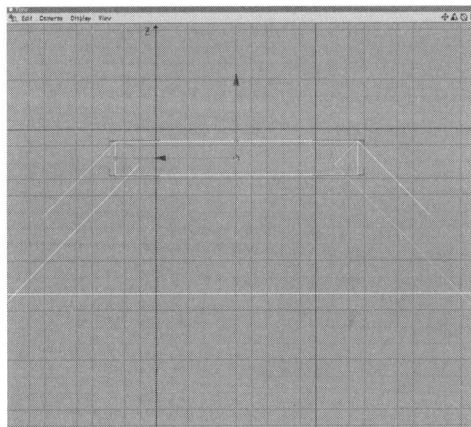

FIGURE 3.15 *Last section of the niche created, rotated, and resized into place.*

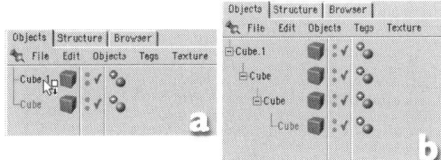

FIGURE 3.16 *(a) When you make one object a child of another, C4D will let you know when it understands your intention by a change in the mouse pointer. (b) Children can become parents of other objects.*

click-drag any of the directional handles. You'll notice that all of the Niche walls move together.

Continue with this grouping strategy by grouping the other walls into a new group that you rename "Straight Walls." Now, you should have three objects in the Object Manager – Niche, Straight Walls, and Floor. A nice power of grouping is that you can group groups. Press "G" on your keyboard (the keyboard shortcut for Object>Group Objects) and marquee around Niche and Straight Walls and rename the new group "Walls."

USE OBJECT AXIS TOOL

As we've seen, each group has its own directional handles by virtue of the Null Object acting as a parent. You've probably noticed by now that these directional handles actually have more use than providing simple handles for altering objects. These handles are part of what is called the *object's axis*. The object axis is the point around which all alteration of the object takes place. Objects rotate around this axis, objects grow out or shrink in around this point. Up to now in our tutorials the default object axis (usually the center) has been fine and acceptable. However, there are situations where it is not only convenient but necessary to have the object's axis in a different location than the default center.

Consider this example. Figure 3.18 (a) shows an arm modeled with all Cube primitives. The object axis for the group is situated somewhere near the geometric center of the collection of cubes – which in this case is near the elbow. This means that when the arm is rotated, it rotates around the elbow! Needless to say, this would make for one goofy moving character. To get the object axis at the elbow as it needs to be, we need to move the object's axis. Up to this point we have been moving objects with the use of the Object tool (Figure 3.18 b). The Object tool is by default activated when a new C4D file is open, as C4D assumes you'll want to be altering objects early in the process. But now, we want to alter the object axis; as such, use the Use Object Axis tool located a few tools below the Object tool along the left hand vertical command palette (Figure 3.18 c).

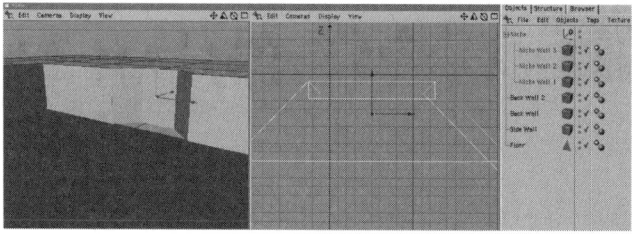

FIGURE 3.17 *Grouped objects have their own directional handles through the Null Object containing the objects.*

CHAPTER 3   PLAYING WITH PRIMITIVES

Besides having the Use Object Axis tool depressed in the command palette along the left, there won't be any difference in the appearance of the interface. The only difference is that now when you use the Move, Scale, or Rotate Active Element tools, the object's axis will move, scale or rotate, but the geometry itself will not. When you alter the object's axis, all the same rules apply as we discussed earlier when you moved objects – movement can be restrained and snapped. In the case of the arm, you would use the Move Active Element tool to move the object's axis to the shoulder joint. After this adjustment, if you selected the Object tool again, then the arm would rotate appropriately (Figure 3.18 d).

This is an important tool to be able to use even when you are not dealing with limbs – for instance doors rotate around hinges on the edge of the door – not in the center. In our scene created thus far, we have a collection of walls that seem a bit short. The walls have all been grouped, and so we can alter the size of the group "Walls" and have all the walls resize together; however, the default object axis for this group is floating in air above the ground. The result is that when we click-drag the *y* directional handle for the group, the walls not only increase in height above the floor, they also drop farther through the floor. Now this isn't the end of the world, as the group could simply be raised to meet the floor. However, we spent such careful attention to keeping the walls on the floor, it'd be silly to get sloppy now.

So, use the Use Object Axis tool and use the Move Active Element tools to move the object axis down towards the floor. Or, you can simply enter 0 in the Y input field of the Position column in the Coordinates Manager. The result will be the axis lying right on the floor. Now select the Object tool again and when the Scale Active Element tool is used to resize this wall group, all the walls "grow" from the ground.

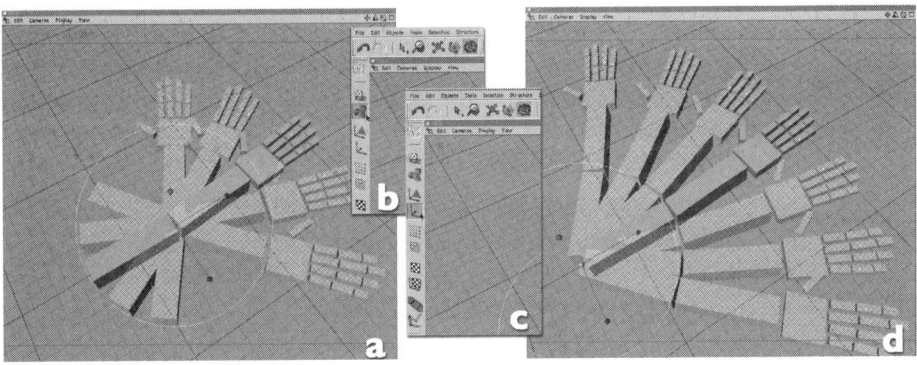

FIGURE 3.18 *(a) Arm with inappropriately placed object axis results in objects rotating in ways they oughtn't. (b) The Object tool that is activated by default upon opening C4D. (c) To alter the point of rotation or the point of alteration (the object axis) use the Use the Object Axis tool. (d) When an object axis is placed appropriately, objects can be rotated or otherwise altered in better ways.*

Visibility

Next, let's create a small table that will sit in the nook of the room that we've created. To do this, let's "hide" all unnecessary objects in the scene for now. To hide objects, simply click on the gray dots located under the second column beside the objects within the Object Manager. There are two dots for each object — the top dot represents whether or not the object is visible in the Editor. The bottom dot is to determine whether the object is visible in the Renderer.

Note that when you click on the dot multiple times, there are actually three states: gray, green, and red. The default gray means that the object is visible. When you click the dot once it turns green; which also means that it is visible but it goes one step further. When the top dot is red, the object is not visible in the Editor window. Further, if you assign a parent object to not be visible, this translates down to the children of that parent except when green dots are present. When the dot is green it indicates that the Visibility setting is to override the Visibility settings of parent objects. So, for example, click twice on the group Walls (turning the dot red). Suddenly your Editor window will only have the floor visible. For the table, it would be nice to see the niche walls for size reference, so expand the Walls group by using the Scale Active Element tool and click on the Niche group so that the dot appears green (Figure 3.19). The Niche group will be visible now, even though it is the child of a hidden object.

Being able to hide objects helps not only in cutting out unnecessary visual clutter as you work, but as you work, your projects can become fairly large. If you don't have the biggest, fastest, baddest machine, it can quickly be reduced to a crawl as it attempts to draw all the objects present. By being able to hide objects (especially those with a high poly-count), you can speed your screen redraw speed and thus streamline your workflow.

Table Construction

Alright, on to the table. For the tabletop, create a Cylinder Object (click on Add Cylinder Object in the top command palette nested below Add Cube Object). This will create a tall Cylinder in the middle of the room halfway through the floor. Press "O" on your keyboard to zoom in immediately to frame the active object (in this case our newly created Cylinder) in the center of our view panel. You may want to activate various views and zoom in with the "O" key to get a variety of close-up viewpoints of the object. Before we worry too much about the placement or size, let's round the corners off on this tabletop.

Double-click on the Cylinder icon within the Object Manager. In the resultant dialog box, click on the Fillet checkbox. Don't worry about any of the values within this dialog box as we'll alter them visually and interactively. Click OK to exit the dialog box. The Cylinder should now appear rounded at the edges (Figure 3.20 a).

CHAPTER 3 PLAYING WITH PRIMITIVES

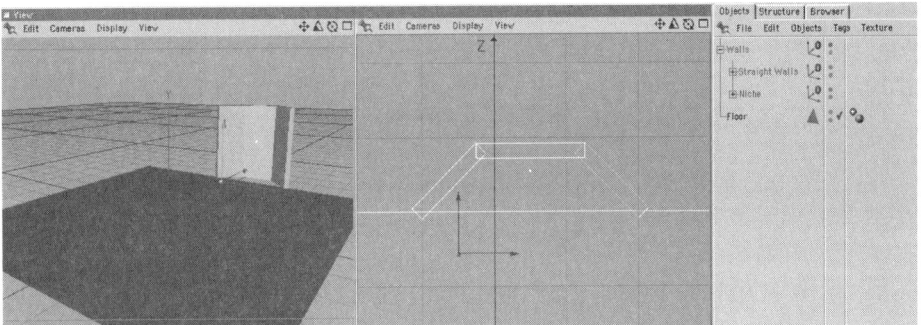

FIGURE 3.19 *When objects have green dots activated, they override any parent Visibility settings.*

This may actually be too round. So, click-drag on the orange primitive control handle that sits on the side of the Cylinder where the curvature meets the side (Figure 3.20 b). Click-drag this control handle until you have a slightly curved edge that looks good for a small round table.

Now click-drag the orange control handle located at the top center of the shape to make the Cylinder shorter. It's often a good idea to actually click-drag in one window (such as the perspective window) but determine the appropriate amount of alteration by looking in the other windows. Now that you have the tabletop thin enough, it still is sitting cut in half by the floor. This, of course, is due to the object axis being located at the default (0,0,0) when the new primitive was created. Move the Cylinder up off the floor to inspect that the shape and relative size are right for the room. Make sure you take plenty of time to view the shape and relationships from lots of angles by rotating your point of view in the perspective

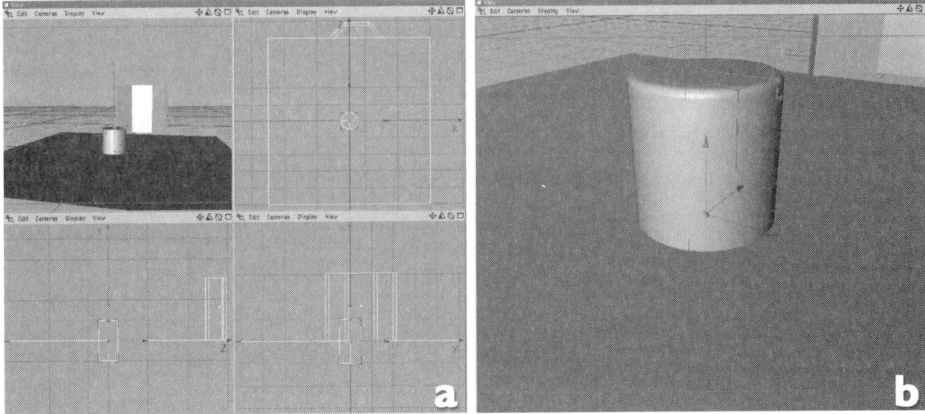

FIGURE 3.20 *(a) Fillet enabled cylinder. (b) Orange control handles allow for easy alteration of fillet radius.*

view panel and keeping the other view panels toggled open. Also take a minute to rename this Cylinder to "Tabletop" in the Object Manager.

Usually there would be some underpinning structures. However, since it's under the table, we'll use an old theatre adage, "If it ain't seen, don't build it." On a theatre set the most amazing sets seen by the audience often are a weird collection of wood and steel left raw with measurements, stage notes, and chewing gum on the back side. The reason is that since the audience never sees the backside, there's no need to spend any time making it beautiful. In 3D, this is equally important; so often 3D artists spend incredible time creating objects in exquisite detail when half of the object is never seen, or the object is quickly panned by in the course of the animation. 3D is much too time intensive to spend any on non-essential model elements.

So, we'll skip directly to the wood skirt under the tabletop. Let's use a Tool Object. After it is placed (Figure 3.21 a) it will be much too large for our taste. In addition, the shape is really wrong. Begin by widening the hole in the middle by click-dragging on the orange control handle that controls the inner radius (Figure 3.21 a). Resize the overall size of the object with the Scale Active Element tool and place it below the tabletop. You'll want to be sure that the Tabletop and this new shape line up in the *x* and *z* directions. If your Snap Settings are still enabled, this will snap into place. Another trick is to select the tabletop object, and highlight and copy (CTRL/COMMAND-C) the value in the X Position input field and then select the Tube object and paste this value into the X Position input field for that shape. Repeat the process for the Y Position input field. This ensures that the centers of these two objects are in the same place. Notice that when you resize the entire object in all directions, the relative proportions of the shape remain the same. Rename it "Table Skirt" (Figure 3.21 b).

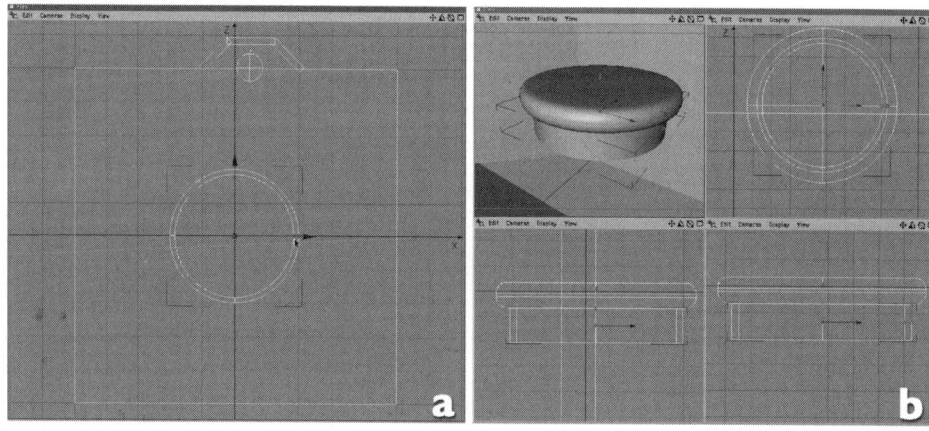

FIGURE 3.21 *(a) Large tube object quickly altered with the interactive primitive control handles. (b) Resized and replaced table skirt.*

DEFORMATION OBJECTS

To finish off the basic shape of the table all we need are legs. We could create graceful tapered legs in a variety of ways, but we'll use this opportunity to explore C4D's use of *Deformation Objects*. Along the top command palette, in the far right are a group of tools that are essentially there to create elements (including objects, lights, cameras, environments). One group of tools are those which appear orange. The orange tools are all Deformation Objects; that is, objects that deform some other shapes. These Deformation Objects have no geometry of their own, but when they are the child of an object, they deform the polygons of their parent. A good example will be the legs of the table.

First, create the geometry needed to deform by adding a Cube Object. Resize the object so that it is tall and thin like a leg would be (Figure 3.22). For the proportions used in this tutorial, a cube that is 12m wide and 12m deep and 94m tall works out to be about the right size. Be sure to leave the leg in the middle of the room for now, although you'll need to raise it so that it is sitting on the floor of the room to get a good idea of its length in comparison to the table.

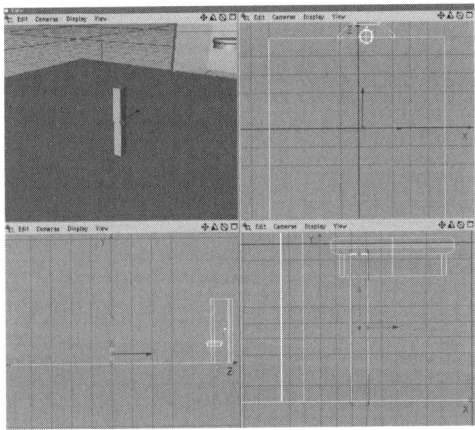

FIGURE 3.22 *Resized leg ready for Deformation Objects.*

Now create a Taper Deformation by selecting Add Taper Deformation from the collection of Deformation Objects in the top command palette (Figure 3.23 a) or by going to Objects>Deformation>Taper. In the middle of the scene will now appear a teal blue hollow box with orange control handles on it. Each Deformation Object works a little differently, although most operate on this same visual convention to allow you to adjust the size and visually alter the settings of the Deformation Object (some Deformation Objects such as Shatter and Explode have no such visual clues, though; we'll look at how to alter these in a bit). In order for a Deformation Object to actually affect a group of polygons or any shape, it must be the child (or on the same hierarchal level) as the polygons it is to affect. So for the leg, place the Taper Deformation Object beneath the Cube Object by dragging and dropping it on the Cube Object (Figure 3.23 b and c).

Deformation objects can actually alter shapes in all sorts of ways in relation to this teal box. You can limit the power of the Deformation Object with the Within the Box option (Figure 3.24 a), where the Deformation Object disregards polygons outside of the box. The Limited option affects polygons within the box and the other polygons outside the box move to accommodate the movement of the polys within (Figure 3.24 b). This is different, though, than the Unlimited option in which the polygons act as though the Deformation Object indeed surrounds the entire form (Figure 3.24 c). All of these modes are available when the Deformation Object's icon is double-clicked in the Object Manager (Figure 3.24 d).

The default setting for Deformation Objects is Limited. Most people find it almost intuitive to resize the Deformation Object so that it is slightly larger than the affected object. However, there are certainly cases where the other modes would be handy like Figure 3.25 which shows a cube with two Deformation Objects (one upside down) set in Within the Box mode to create a balustrade.

Now click-drag on the top orange dot of the Deformation Object and make the top of the shape bigger so it tapers to the bottom (Figure 3.26). Now an interesting thing can be observed here; notice that although the Deformation Object is actually tapered in a curved line, the Cube Object it is affecting still maintains straight edges. The reason for this is the nature of the segments or polygons that make up the Cube Object. Double-click on the Cube icon in the Object Manager and the resultant dialog box will display that the Cube Object (by default) has one segment in the x, y, and z directions. Indeed, if the scene thus far were displayed in Wireframe mode, we could see that each side of the Cube Object is just one segment (Figure 3.27 a).

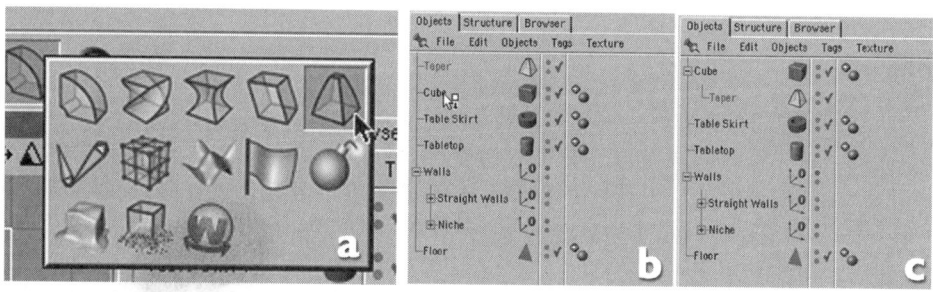

FIGURE 3.23 *(a) Create a Taper Deformation Object to taper the leg of the table. (b and c) To make the new Taper Deformation object have an effect on the cube, it must be placed as a child of the cube.*

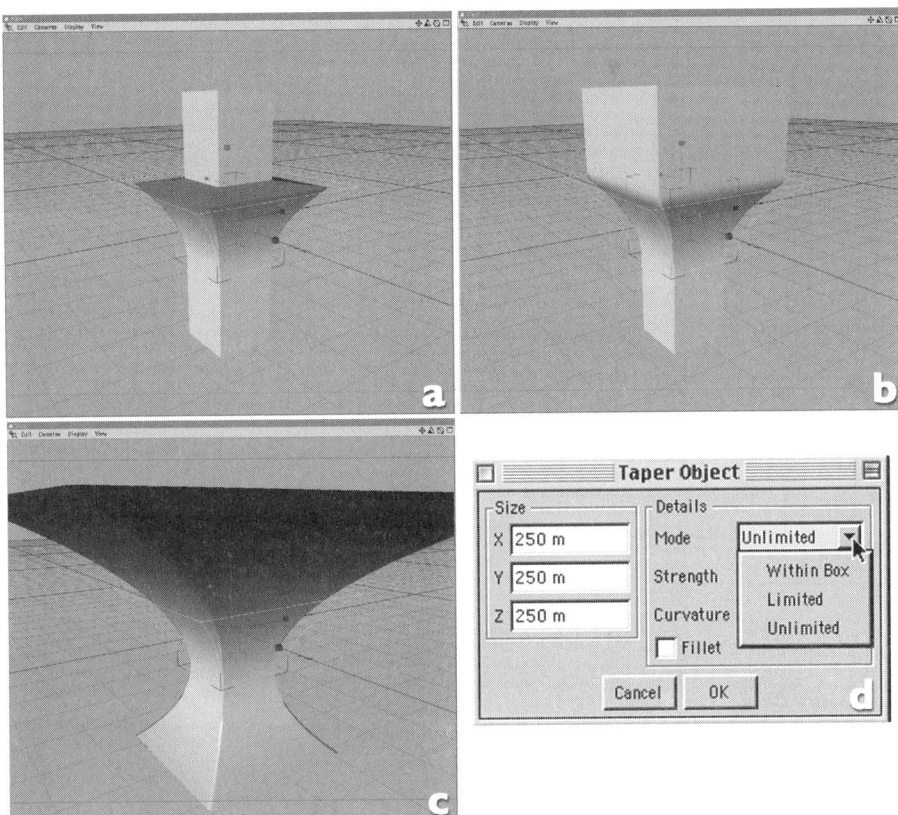

FIGURE 3.24 *(a) Within the Box mode limits the Deformation Object's influence to the polygons contained within the Deformation Object. (b) Limited mode directly affects the polys within the box, but the other polys in the affected object move to accommodate the changes. (c) Unlimited mode affects all the polys of an affected shape as though the Deformation Object were much larger than the affected object. (d) When the Deformation Object's icon is double-clicked, a dialog box appears allowing you to define the mode.*

In order to get a curved taper for this leg, we need to allow the leg to have more polygons, and thus more places to bend. Change the Y setting from 0 to 20. The resultant Wireframe mode shows that the increased polys along the Y-axis result in a rounded taper (Figure 3.27 b). This is an important concept to remember for all Deformation Objects. They are only as effective as the polygon topology they are affecting. Changes will still occur in low poly-count objects — they just won't be as smooth or rounded as in higher poly-count objects. Remember that the drawback to smoother, rounder Deformation Objects is that these high poly-counts begin to slow your machine down. The smoother your shapes, the slower your screen redraw. Sometimes it is worth

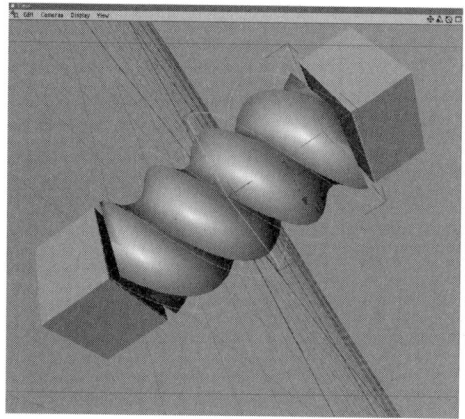

FIGURE 3.25 Two Deformation Objects used together in Within the Box mode to create a complex shape.

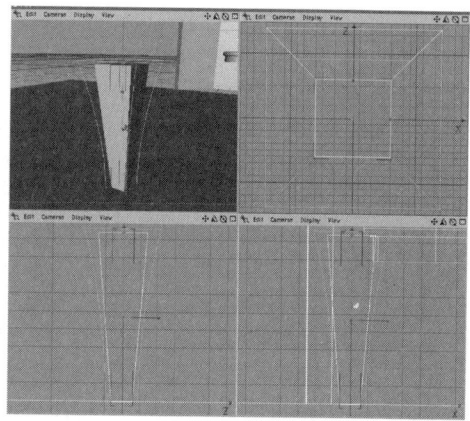

FIGURE 3.26 To actually enable changes in the Deformation Object, and thus deforming the Deformed Object click-and drag the orange control handle.

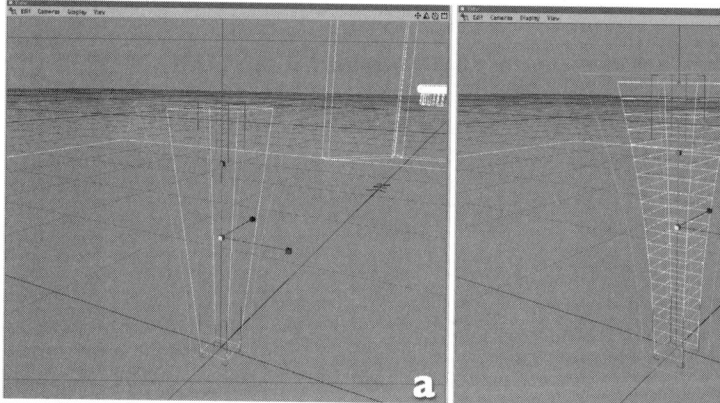

FIGURE 3.27 (a) Wireframe mode displays show the single segment sides of the Cube Object that is to become our leg; as such, the taper remains linear. (b) Increased segments along the Y-axis creates more curvilinear tapers in our leg.

your time to experiment and adjust your poly-counts to give you the best look with the least number of polygons.

One of the most powerful parts of Deformation Objects is the ability to apply more than one Deformation Object to one shape. Add a Twist Deformation Object (Figure 3.28 a) and resize it so that it is slightly larger than the leg thus far created. Make it a child of the Cube Object and then click-drag the orange control handle to twist our already tapered leg (Figure 3.28 b).

Now move this newly tapered and twisted leg so that it sits beneath the tabletop as we've made it so far. Figure 3.29 shows the bottom of the table constructed of a Torus Object, and several cylinders. Design the bottom as you'd like, but keep it all simple and made from primitives for now. When you have all the shapes built and laid into place, group (keystroke "G") all the shapes used to make this table together and call it "Table." Notice also in Figure 3.29 that the floor has been increased in size so that the floor lies beneath the table within the niche.

LAMPS

One last thing to model before we leave the realm of primitives. The sconces on the walls contain shades that are made of primitive forms as well. These are made of one Cone Object and two Torus Objects (Figure 3.30). The Cone Object is hollow because in the dialog box accessed by double-clicking on the Cone icon in the Object Manager, Caps was unchecked. In this same dialog box, the Top Radius input field was changed to a non-zero value. Then by simply adjusting the control handles, the hollow Cone Object can be altered to find an aesthetically pleasing shape. The Torus shapes were simply created and adjusted using the orange control handles to give a nice edge. When the shape is complete, group the Cone Object and the two Torus shapes together and call it "Sconce Shade." For now, just place one Sconce Shade up on the wall. We'll be looking at other ways to duplicate forms later.

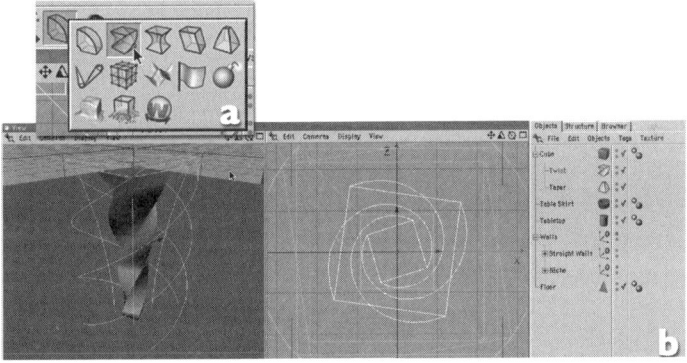

FIGURE 3.28 *(a) Add a Twist Deformation Object. (b)After making a child of the Cube Object, twist away at the orange control handle to create a twisted leg.*

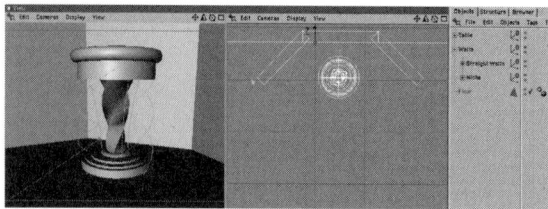

FIGURE 3.29 *Completed table.*

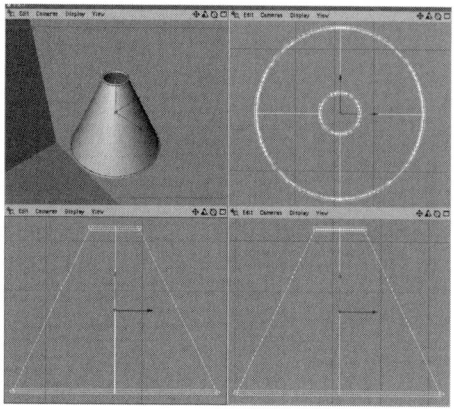

FIGURE 3.30 *Lamp shades made of simple Cone object with Caps disabled and a top radius enabled.*

CHAPTER 4

Generators (NURBS)

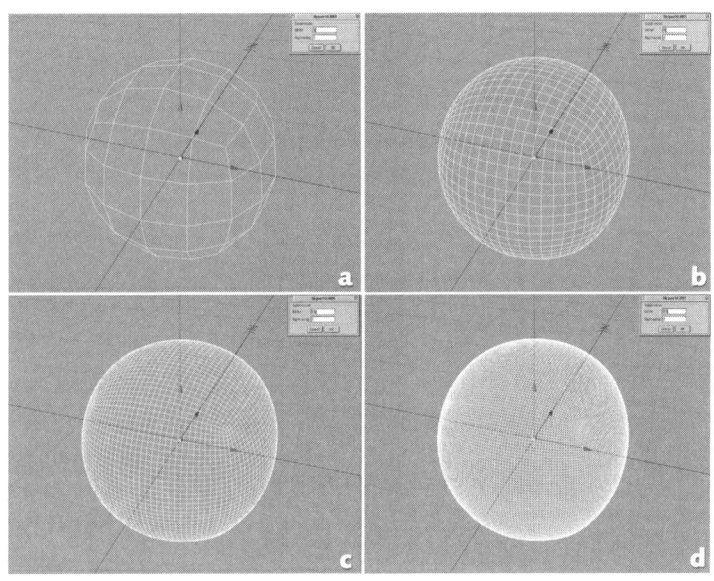

Non-Destructive Modeling

In the previous chapter we covered modeling techniques for creating objects, including a wide variety of primitives. These primitives are created quickly, and immediately placed within the scene. This is a very intuitive form of modeling, but in some ways very limiting. C4D includes a great collection of other modeling tools that expand the types of shapes possible and the freedom to continue to adjust these new shapes.

C4D has several techniques that make use of the idea of *generators*. Generators are objects that are created only through using other shapes or objects to create a new object with new geometry. The beauty of generators is that the objects used to create new forms via the generators still maintain their autonomy, and so they can be altered when necessary to change the form of the generator-based shape. This sort of freedom allows for smooth creation knowing that changes are always possible.

We touched in the last chapter upon one form of generator objects: deformation objects. When we used the twist deformer for the pedestal of the table, the deformation object itself had no geometry of its own; it was only able to manipulate the cube we placed within it. Such is the nature of almost all generator objects.

NURBS

The most common type of generator objects are NURBS. *NURBS* (singular or plural) actually is an acronym that stands for Non-Uniform Rational B-splines. The actual theory behind what this means exactly is complex and not particularly important except to note that its original conception was to find ways to accurately create curved surfaces. Although certainly not limited to curvilinear forms, NURBS do excel at making organic forms.

NURBS do not actually "contain" polygons. The idea is that through a collection of splines, an animator can quickly create a variety of forms that are calculations of forms rather than actual groups of polygons. Usually modeling is classified into polygon modeling and NURBS modeling. However, to assume that NURBS are polygon-independent is not entirely accurate either. For although the forms are calculated free of polygonal information, when C4D gets ready to render a NURBS (or take the information you've given it and "paint" the picture), it must place polygons instead of the NURBS in order to "see" the forms. Luckily, this all happens seamlessly behind the scenes and thus generally has no effect on your workflow. However, this bit of theory can become important in some advanced modeling or high memory requirement projects.

Chapter 4 Generators (NURBS)

Splines

The key building element of creating most NURBS objects are *splines*. Splines are not limited strictly to NURBS creation; in fact, they can be used for all sorts of things including animation paths and object organization within digital space. However, in this section we'll be focusing on splines' power as construction objects.

Splines have some interesting characteristics that are important to understand before they can be fully exploited as powerful modeling tools. First, splines are infinitely thin, appearing as lines that although they are visible in the Editor, do not render; they are construction objects. The manual describes splines as "a sequence of vertices connected by lines, lying in 3D space." The idea being, splines are a collection of points that you, the user, can alter to affect the line that joins these points together. These points are analogous to anchor points in vector based applications such as Illustrator. They are always editable and thus, the line is always changeable.

The nature of the line between the points can be straight or curved. The nature of the line is defined by the type of spline and the nature of the points that compose it. C4D provides for several ways to create splines. Mastery of how these splines are created and altered is key to creating effective NURBS objects.

There are actually two methods of creating splines within C4D. The first method is the ability to create an "empty spline" (Objects>Spline Object) and then fill this spline object with the spline information. The second is to use one of the two nested collections of spline creation tools located in the top command palette (Figure 4.1 a). Since the nested spline creation tools shown in Figure 4.1 (a) can do almost all the same things creating an empty spline would do, we'll focus our attention on the nested tools.

Let's talk first of the collection of tools to the right (Figure 4.1 b). This collection of tools allows for the creation of Spline Primitives. Spline Primitives are similar to the primitives we talked of in the last chapter; they are all splines that C4D makes very well and very quickly. They also all have collections of parameters that can be altered to dynamically and quickly change the shape of the Spline Primitive, as the spline is based upon a mathematical equation. A big difference between Spline Primitives and other primitives discussed in Chapter 5 is that there are no interactive parametric handles for Spline Primitives. That is, in order to alter the Spline Primitives' parameters, you must double click on the spline icon within the Object Manager (Figure 4.1 c).

Each of these Spline Primitives have characteristics particular to their general shape. Some editable parameters are as simple as changing the radii of a circle while others become more complex, including things like differences in number of pedals or cogs, thus changing the entire shape. Others become complex enough to take into account issues of three dimensions and don't get trapped in

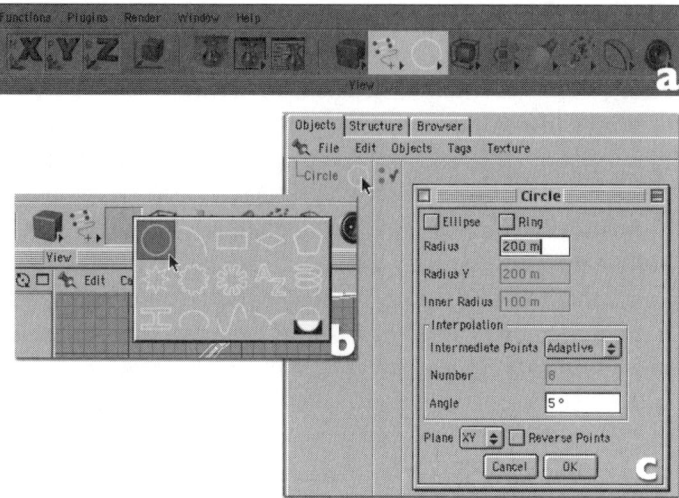

FIGURE 4.1 *(a) Nested spline creation tools in the top command palette. (b) Spline Primitive collections of tools. (c) In order to alter the parameters of Spline Primitives, you must double-click the Spline icon within the Object Manager.*

just two. Still others are complex enough to allow you to provide a mathematical formula to graph or even allow you to create a collection of text splines. The beauty of all of them is that they are so flexible, you can change their settings at any time.

We'll look briefly at how each of the splines function and how their different parameters can be used to create the spline shape you want. As we look at these individual Spline Primitives, there is one constant that we'll not talk much about: interpolation. Interpolation is how C4D divides up the spline and how it connects the lines between the vertices. However, the change is not noticeable when you are just viewing the spline by itself; only in context of a spline being used within a generator object (such as a NURBS object) do changes in the interpolation really come into play (except for the notable exception of using the setting of None). So we'll hold off on discussion of the interpolation settings for Spline Primitives until we get to a more in-depth discussion of these splines in a construction sense.

CIRCLE SPLINE PRIMITIVE

The Circle Spline Primitive is actually a much more diverse shape than a simple circle. Besides creating perfect circles (Figure 4.2 a), the Circle Spline Primitive dialog box also allows for the creation of ellipses (Figure 4.2 b) which allows you to define the differing width or height, and rings (Figure 4.2 c) which give you the power to shift the size of the "hole" of the ring. You can even make an ellipse with a hole in the middle (Figure 4.2 d).

CHAPTER 4   GENERATORS (NURBS)   67

As is the case with all Spine Primitives, when you create a Circle Spline Primitive (done by clicking the Circle Spline Primitive tool (Figure 4.3)), C4D will place the circle facing the view that is active. So if the top view is active, placing a Circle Spline Primitive will place a circle along the XZ plane (Figure 4.3 a). If the front view is active, then the circle will be created along the XY plane (Figure 4.3 b). Besides rotating the circle into another orientation (if desired) you can also change the Plane setting within the dialog box for the Circle Spline Primitive to change what plane it is lying along (Figure 4.3 c). The difference between these two methods is that rotating the Circle Spline Primitive would cause the circle's X,Y, and Z axes to then not be lined up with the digital world, but changing the plane leaves the object's axes in alignment with the world's axis.

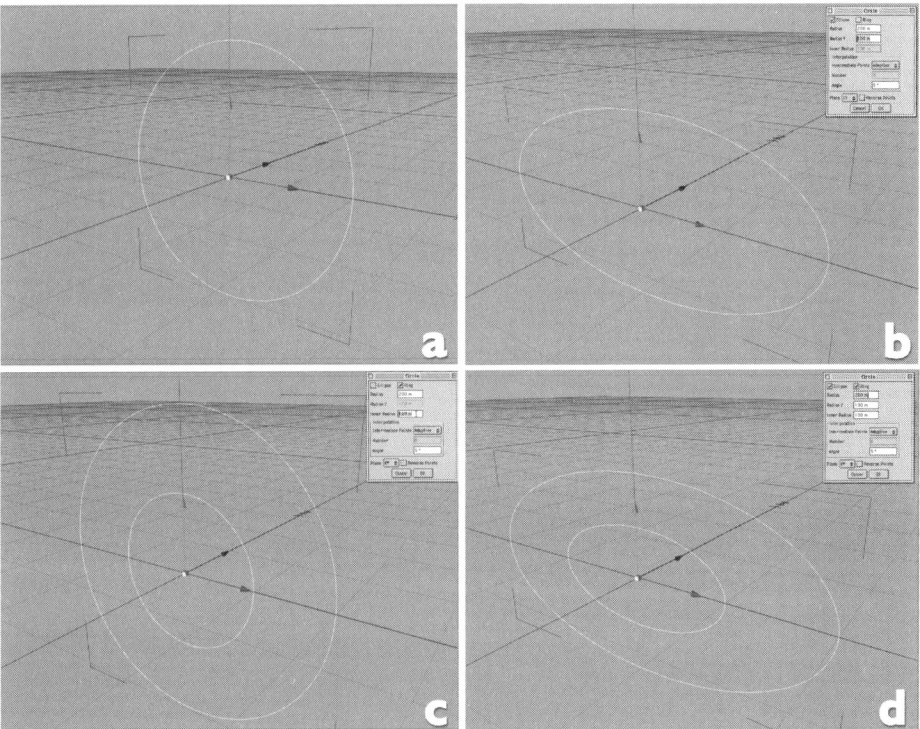

FIGURE *Figure 4.2 (a) A Circle Spline Primitive. (b) The Circle Spline Primitive also allows*
4.2   *for the creation of ellipses. (c) Rings are quick and easy to create with the Circle*
          Primitive Spline. (d) By activating both the Ring and Ellipse functions of the Circle
          Spline Primitive, you can create a flattened ring.

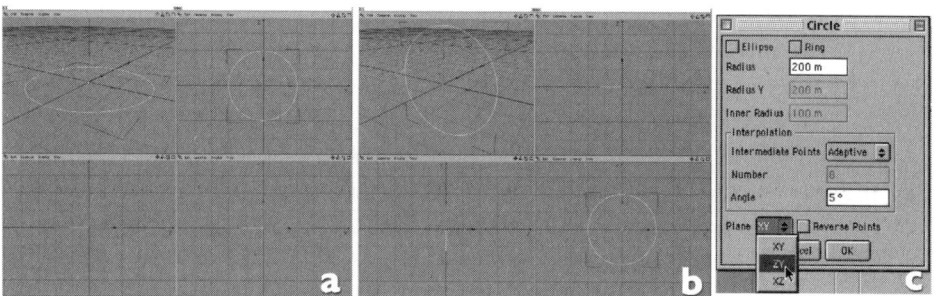

FIGURE 4.3 *(a) When the top view is active, creating a Circle Spline Primitive places the circle lying along the XZ plane or facing the top view plane. (b) When the view is front, the Circle Spline Primitive is created along the XY axis or facing the front view plane. (c) If you create a Circle Spline Primitive and find that it is lying along the wrong plane, you could rotate it into place, or simply change the Plane setting in the dialog box.*

CREATING SPLINE (CURVES)

Although C4D's collection of spline primitives are indeed diverse and powerful, they don't make every shape you'd possibly need. Luckily, there is a second collection of tools (Figure 4.4), that allows you to create any curve you'd like. Notice in Figure 4.4 that there are five different tools to create custom curves. All of these tools create spline curves as per your definition; however, they each use a slightly different methodology for creation. Each of these methods are simply ways of creating the spline using different interpolation or methods of joining vertices.

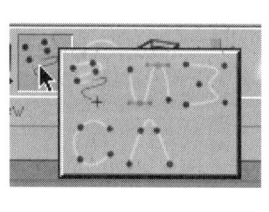

FIGURE 4.4 *Create Spline (Curves) tools.*

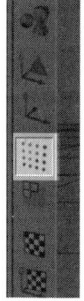

FIGURE 4.5 *After creating a spline, you will automatically be placed in Points mode allowing you to alter the spline just created.*

DRAW FREEHAND SPLINE

The first tool gives you the most freedom, but the least control. The Draw Freehand Spline tool allows you to simply click and draw in one motion any curve you wish. As soon as you release your mouse button with this tool, you are bumped out of the tool, a spline object appears in the Object Manager, and C4D interprets your sketch by placing vertices.

The freedom comes from being able to simply "draw" the shape you want; the limitation in control comes from C4D deciding where to place your vertices. This may not seem like a big issue but revision is an important part of the 3D animation game, and you want to maintain all the control you can.

Notice that after drawing the shape, you don't have a simple white line defining the spline as we did with the primitives. Further, if you were to use the Move Active Element tool and try to move things, you'd be annoyed to find that nothing moves. This is because, after drawing a spline, you are automatically placed within Points mode. You can tell you're in Points mode by checking out the command palette along the left side of the screen (Figure 4.5).

The next four spline curve creation tools are all forms of creating curves that give you the ability to define each vertex as you see fit. Each uses a slightly different method.

BEZIER SPLINE CURVE

If you come from a traditionally 2D graphic design background, this will be the most familiar. It functions very similar to Adobe Illustrator's Pen tool. When the Draw Bezier Spline tool is selected, your mouse pointer changes to a symbol like (Figure 4.6 a). Unlike the Draw Freehand Spline tool which is exited as soon as the mouse button is released, the Draw Bezier Spline tool stays active until you select another tool, or "close" the spline by clicking on the initial point where the spline was started. Each time you click and release the mouse, a new vertex is placed.

While you are in the Draw Bezier Spline tool, if you simply click and immediately release, a vertex is placed with no visible Bezier handles. By simply clicking and releasing several times, a jagged line can be created (Figure 4.6 b). If you click-drag while you are in this tool, you'll be given a vertex, but the dragging part of the action will create Bezier handles making the curves easy to alter in the future (Figure 4.6 c).

Note that closing a spline means that after creating a series of points, you return to the first point. When this is done, you are exited out of the Draw Bezier Spline tool. However, if you don't close the spline and don't select another tool you'll remain within the tool; thus, if you press the DELETE button on your keyboard, the last point drawn will be deleted rather than the entire spline. In order to delete the spline, you must exit Points mode and enter Model mode or Object mode (Figure 4.7) and then press DELETE.

B-SPLINE CURVE

The Draw B-Spline tool is a way of creating very curvilinear forms. It's different from any of the other spline curve creation tools in that you are creating a set of vertices that the spline runs *between* rather than *through*. While you are within

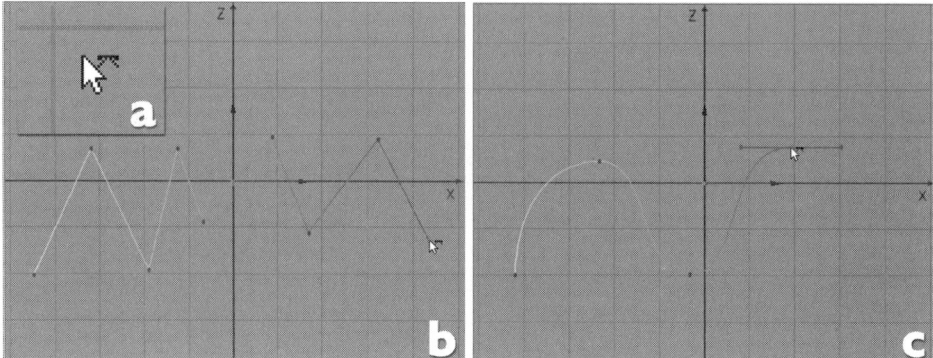

FIGURE 4.6 *Figure 4.6 (a) When you are within any Creating Spline tool, the mouse pointer will indicate it by appearing like this. (b) Clicking and immediately releasing creates vertexes without curvilinear interpolation, thus giving you a straight line. (c) By click-dragging in the Draw Bezier Spline tool, you create vertices with Bezier handles.*

the Draw B-Spline tool, each time you click and release the mouse the spline thus far will be drawn to that point (Figure 4.8 a). When you click on the next position, however, the spline shifts from running through to the last point, to running beside it (Figure 4.8 b). If the spline is open, the first point and last point will actually be on the spline's path (Figure 4.8 c); but if the spline is closed, none of the spline will run through the points (Figure 4.8 d). This is a great tool to use if you don't need exact curves, but are interested in making sure you have an extra smooth spline.

CUBIC AND AKIMA SPLINE CURVES

When you use the Cubic or Akima Spline Curves tools, you simply click and release at points you wish the spline to pass through. The spline passes through these points, rounding out the spline as it goes based upon the new information given. Both attempt to make a smooth spline. The biggest difference is that cubic splines will "overshoot" points in order to make a nice rounded curve (Figure 4.9 a). The Draw Akima tool at times is more accurate, but sometimes creates undesirable effects (Figure 4.9 b).

EDITING SPLINES

The beauty of splines is that you're never locked into any part of them. What happens if you draw a spline with the Draw Akima Spline tool, but you don't like the sharp corners it gives you? What if you draw an open spline and later need it closed? What if you simply don't like the positions of the vertices created? What if the entire spline is simply too big? All of these things can be controlled with relative ease.

Chapter 4 Generators (NURBS) 71

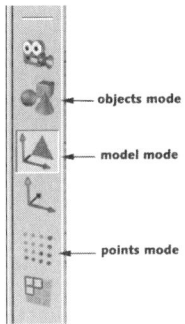

FIGURE 4.7 *Exit out of the default Points mode you are in to delete an entire spline. Select Object mode or Model mode.*

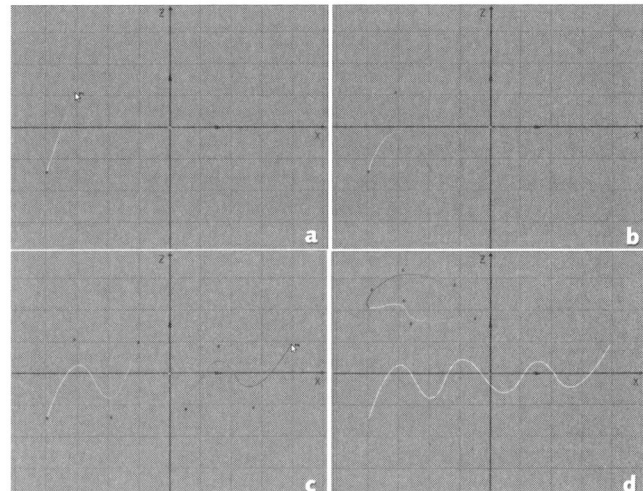

FIGURE 4.8 *Creating B-Splines is different than other methods, as this tool creates vertices that the spline runs between rather than through. Still it is a very powerful tool to create nice smooth lines.*

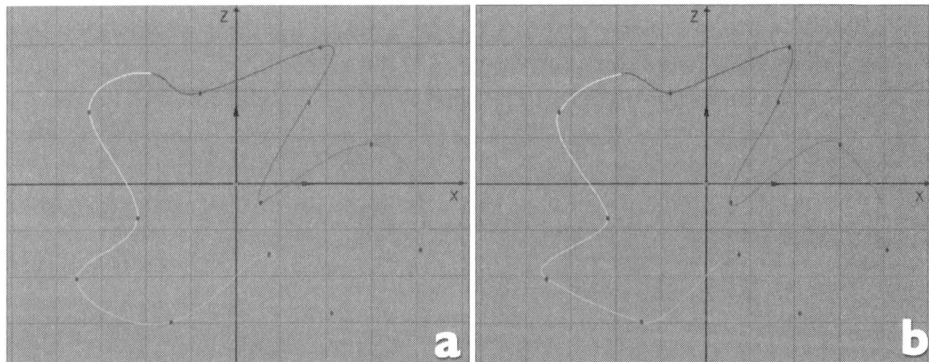

FIGURE 4.9 *(a) The Draw Cubic Spline tool creates nice rounded splines that emphasize round curves. (b) Akima splines are often a bit more accurate, but you can end up with sharper corners.*

When a spline is created, a Spline object immediately appears in the Object Manager. This spline can be renamed to whatever you'd like by double-clicking on the word "Spline." However, you can also change a variety of other settings by double-clicking the yellow "squiggly" located next to the word which opens the Spline dialog box (Figure 4.10 a).

The first noticeable power is the ability to change the style of interpolation labeled under the Type setting (Figure 4.10 b). You can change the way the vertices are interpolated into a style as though you drew it with a different Draw

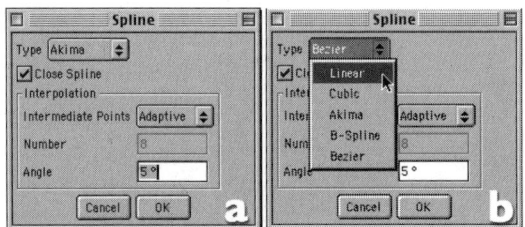

FIGURE 4.10 *(a) The Spline dialog box allows for a host of options to be changed. (b) The Type setting allows you to alter the type of interpolation for already created splines, regardless of the Draw Spline tool that was used to create them.*

Spline tool. Figure 4.11 shows the same curve with different types and the resultant splines.

Immediately below the Type setting is the ability to make the spline closed. So if you create an open spline, by activating the Close Spline selection, C4D will close the spline off.

When you create a spline, you are automatically defaulted into Points mode. This is no accident. Notice that when in Object, Model, or Polygon modes the spline (whether active or not) appears as a white line. It is only when you are in Points mode that you have the power to select the points or vertices that compose the spline and alter their position, rotation, or distance from one another. Further, if there is more than one spline within your scene, only the active spline will show its vertices, and thus only the active spline can be altered. To "activate" another spline for editing while you are still in Points mode, click on its name in the Object Manager.

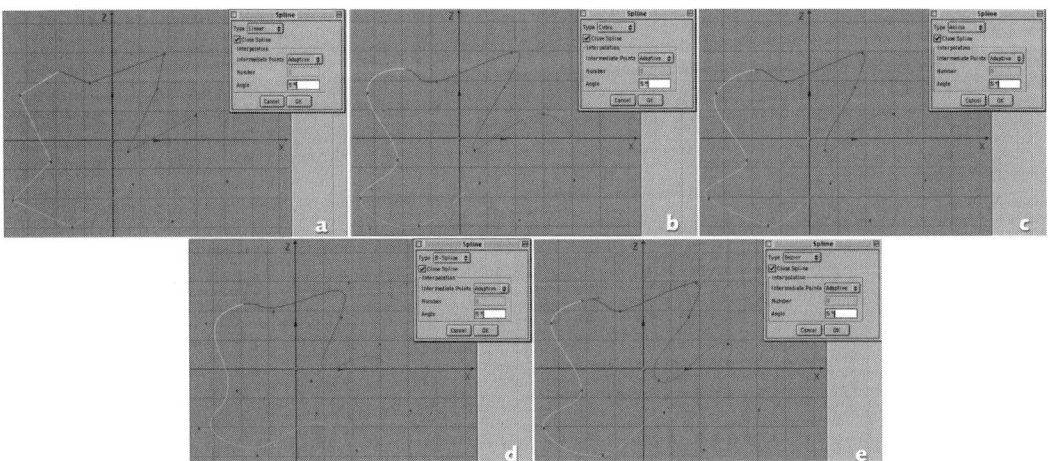

FIGURE 4.11 *An identical collection of points can yield a variety of splines. (a) Linear (b) Cubic (c) Akima (d) B-Spline (e) Bezier.*

WORKING IN POINTS MODE

By being in Points mode, you can see all the points that make up the curve you've just drawn. To work with the points within Points mode, think of all alterations as two steps. First, click and release on the point you wish to alter (it will turn from brown to orange). Second, alter the point (move, rotate, scale). This may seem counter-intuitive, but it is the way C4D works. The benefit to this is that you can select a point and then click anywhere within your view panel and affect the point. Points can be moved, scaled, or rotated, although usually most points are simply moved.

Remember that you can select more than one point. While you are in Points mode and with Move, Scale, or Rotate Active Element tools active, you can select more than one point at a time by holding the SHIFT key down and selecting the additional point. Similarly, you can drop a point from a selection by continuing to hold the SHIFT button down and clicking an already selected point. There is another notable way to select points: using the collection of Selection tools (Figure 4.12 a).

This is actually a nested collection of four tools. The first is called the Live Selection tool and it allows you to "paint" a selection. Click (the mouse pointer

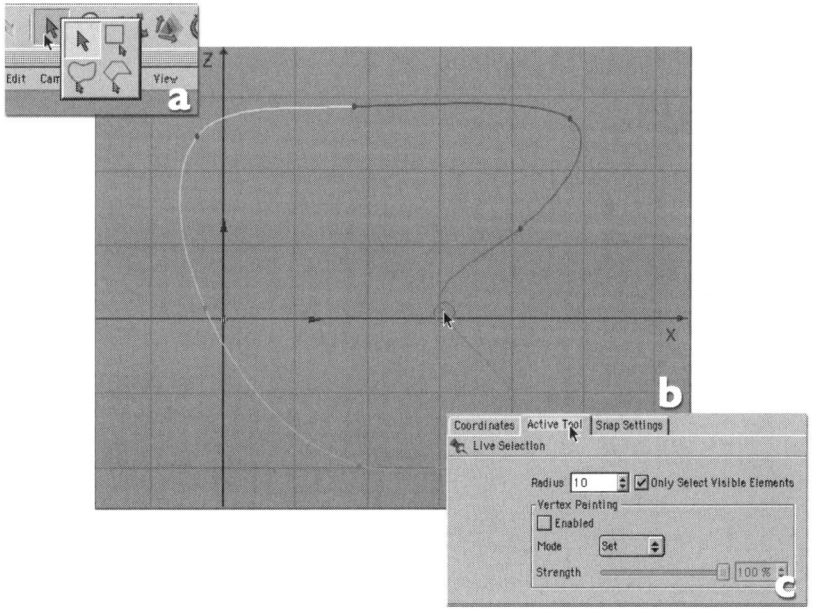

FIGURE 4.12 *(a) Selection tools (b) Using the Live Selection tool is an intuitive process of painting a selection. (c) Active Tool Manager allows you to change the size of the Live Selection brush.*

will turn to a circle indicating the size of your brush) and drag over the points you wish to select. The selected points change color when they are selected (Figure 4.12 b). You can add points of the active spline to the selection by holding the SHIFT key down and "painting" over the desired points or remove points from the selection by holding the CTRL (or COMMAND) key and painting over the tools you wish to remove.

You can control the size of the Live Selection brush in the Active Tool Manager (located beneath the Coordinates Manager) at the bottom right hand corner of the default C4D interface (Figure 4.12 c). By increasing or decreasing the radius, the size of the circle indicating the Live Selection brush will increase or decrease accordingly. We'll talk much more about this Active Tool Manager later, as it is extremely useful in a variety of situations.

The other three tools — the Rectangle Selection, Free Selection, and Polygon Selection — are all other ways to select collections of points (and later polygons) by marqueeing (Figure 4.13 a), drawing around (Figure 4.13 b), or

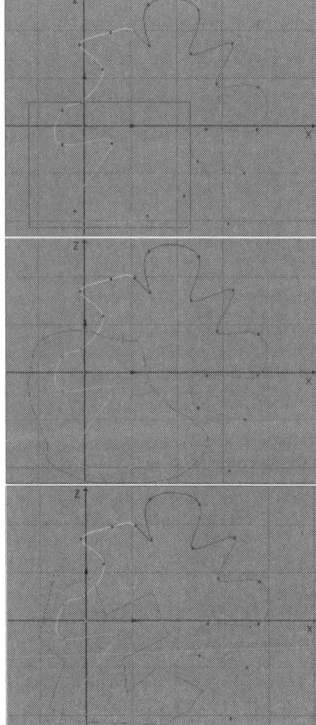

FIGURE 4.13 *The other Selection tools are handy ways to select points with squares (a), freehand selections (b), or polygon shapes encompassing selections (c).*

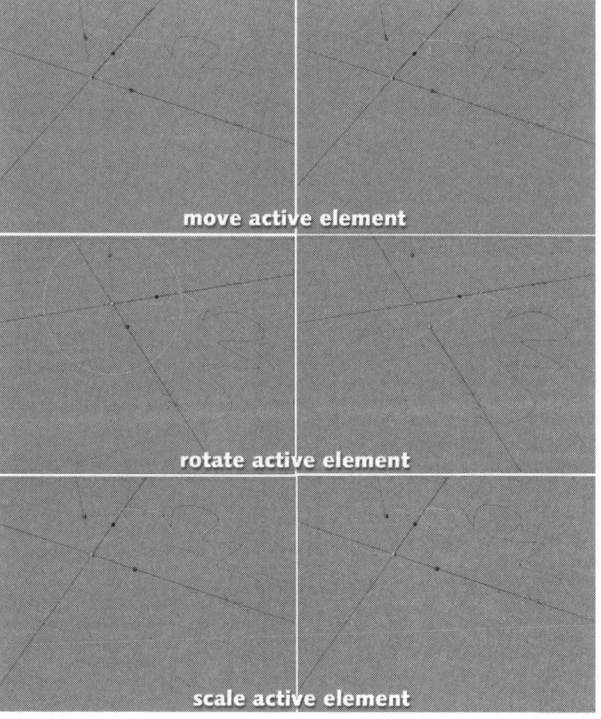

FIGURE 4.14 *Once points are selected, they can be moved (a), rotated (b), or scaled (c) independently of the other points on the spline.*

creating a selection by defining a shape by clicking on the corners of that shape (Figure 4.13 c). Again, when you are finished with each of these Selection tools, selected points will appear orange.

Once these points are selected, you can use the Move Active Element tool to move them around and the spline will reshape accordingly (Figure 4.14 a). Similarly, you can use the Rotate Active Element tool to rotate a group of points around the spline's axis (Figure 4.14 b) or the Scale Active Element tool to scale the points out or in from the spline's axis (Figure 4.14 c).

BEZIER SPLINE ALTERATION

Now an important thing to note here is that selecting any one point with a spline using Type Linear, Cubic, Akima, or B-Spline, activates a vertex by showing the orange dot in place of the brown. You can move this point directly and the spline will readjust according to the Interpolation settings given it. However, Bezier splines have a noticeable difference. As we mentioned before, when you create a Bezier spline, you could create a Linear spline by clicking and releasing on a spline with vertices that have Bezier handles. You can still directly move the vertex, but these Bezier handles (presented in purple) allow some extra control over the shape of your spline.

While you are in Points mode, you can select a point by clicking and releasing on it. If the spline is indeed a Bezier spline, purple handles will appear. If you grab either of these Bezier handles (the manual calls them tangent handles) by click-dragging, you'll notice that the Bezier handle opposite it will move as well. If you pull the handle outward your curve will become "longer." If you move the handles closer together, the curve becomes "shorter." You can even click-drag a handle so short that it begins to lengthen in the opposite direction. When this happens the spline develops a loop.

Bezier

One of the big benefits to Bezier Splines is the ability to create non-round vertices. By holding the SHIFT key down when you click-drag a handle, you can move one handle independently of the other. The result is an immediate shift from a smooth corner to a sharp corner. So, you could create a curve that was longer on one side of the vertex than the other. By SHIFT-dragging points you can create sharp corners as they would appear in teardrops or waves. Literally you can create any shape with Bezier splines. They are so powerful, in fact, that C4D uses these curves when it works with animation paths; but we'll talk more of this later.

GENERAL SPLINE NOTES

There are a few important things to remember when you work with splines. The first is that nothing is permanent; you can change any point or any Interpolation setting of a spline – so don't sweat it when you rough out a shape. The second is that splines, although they exist in 3D space, are still drawn in the limitations of your two-dimensional monitor. As such, it's very important that, in order to maintain control over the spline, you draw the spline in *any view* **but** the perspective view. When you draw and work with a spline while you are viewing a scene with a perspective camera, it becomes impossible (without spinning the object around repeatedly) to tell where the points are in relation to each other in all directions. If you draw in the perspective view, a seemingly good-looking spline is actually a mess of points in all sorts of directions (Figure 4.15). Draw splines in front, top, or side views, then — if need be — move the points around, viewing their relative position in the perspective view.

NURBS

ON THE CD

C4D's NURBS tools are shown in Figure 4.16 (a+b). This collection of six tools are perhaps the most powerful modeling tools within the package. The first one shown there, HyperNURBS, is so powerful, in fact, that we'll be devoting all of the next chapter to it. The remaining NURBS tools shown are Extrude, Lathe, Loft, Sweep, and Bezier. Because much of this is covered in the manual, we'll look first at the Extrude NURBS tool. There are descriptions of the other NURBS Objects in the supplemental material on the CD. Please refer to that for specific questions on other NURBS Objects.

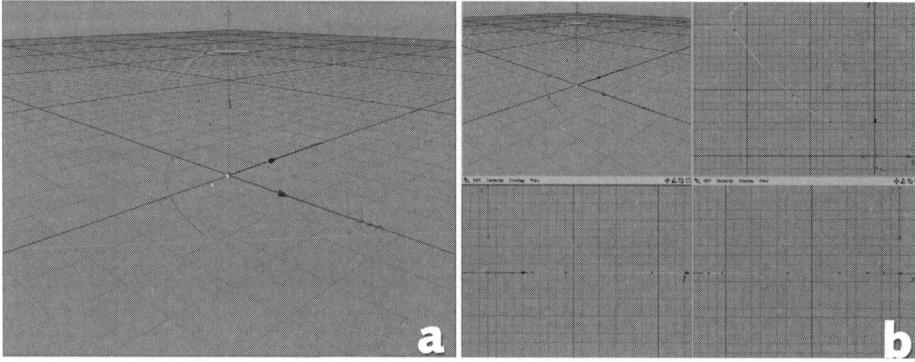

FIGURE 4.15 *If you are drawing a spline in perspective view (a), the vase outline that you think you're drawing could actually end up being an elongated line lying along one place (b). Always initially draw splines from non-perspective views.*

CHAPTER 4 GENERATORS (NURBS)

The key to NURBS tools is that, with the exception of the Bezier NURBS Object, none have their own geometry. They are object generators, meaning that they create forms from other objects within C4D – namely, splines. When any NURBS is created it will show up in the Object Manager, but there will be nothing but an object axis in the view panel to show that the NURBS object even exists. To give the NURBS object forms, you must tell it what splines it is allowed to use. This is done by making splines children of NURBS objects. To do this, in the Object Manager, take a spline and "drop" it into a NURBS object (Figure 4.16 b). We'll look at the specifics in the following explanations.

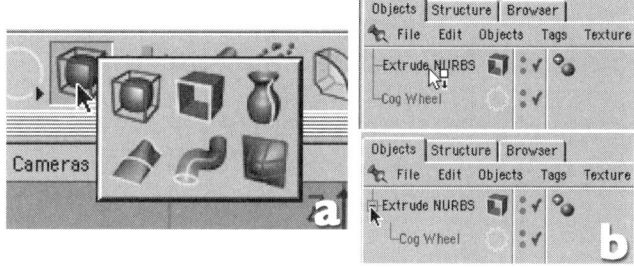

FIGURE 4.16 (a) The NURBS collection of tools. (b) To allow a NURBS object to know what splines it should use to build its forms, drop the spline into the NURBS object.

EXTRUDE NURBS

Aptly named, the Extrude NURBS object allows you to extrude a profile along any direction. Imagine this tool as the simplest way to give three dimensions to two-dimensional splines. As an example, create a Text Spline Primitive and change the text it creates to your name (Figure 4.17 a).

If this were rendered, you would be left with a black screen, as splines themselves have no geometry to render. Now create an Extrude NURBS object by selecting it from the top command palette, or by selecting Object>NURBS> Extrud NURBS. Again, if you were to render this scene at this point, you would still get a black screen as all you have are two objects with no relation to each other. Give them a relationship by dropping the Text Spline Primitive into the Extrude NURBS Object (Figure 4.17 b).

Immediately, your text should have depth. Notice that in Figure 4.18 the dialog box for the Extrude NURBS object is open (double-clicked in the Object Manager). The direction the Extrude NURBS Object Extrudes by default is along the Z-axis. In the case of the text, you can see that the blue object axis handle (Z) is indeed facing backwards and this is just what you want. However, it should be noted that if you have a spline facing the X- or Y-axes, remember that you can change the direction along which the Extrude NURBS Extrudes to match.

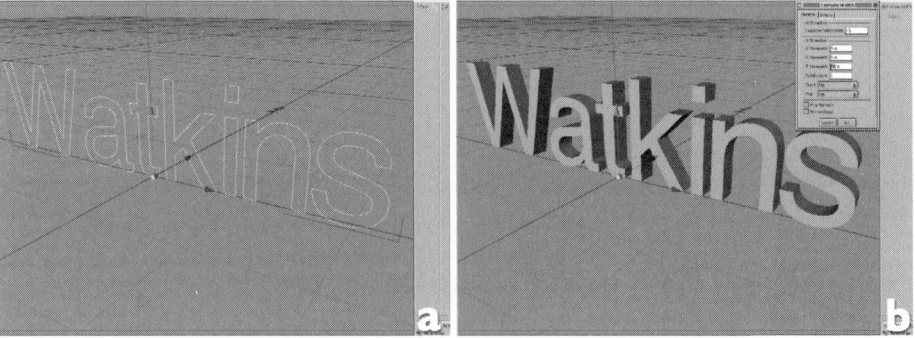

FIGURE 4.17 *(a) Simple Text Spline Primitive with your name. (b) As soon as a spline is placed within an Extrude NURBS, the spline is given depth, dimension, and geometry.*

GENERAL NURBS INPUT FIELDS

Other important functions of this dialog box include the Isoparm Subdivision input field which allows you to define how many subdivisions will be shown when you are viewing your scene with Isoparm display. The Isoparm Subdivision input box allows you to determine how many segments C4D includes as it Extrudes the spline (Figure 4.18).

CAPS AND DETAILS

The Cap settings determine whether you have a hollow or solid extrusion. Selecting No Cap for both Start and End gives a hollow extrusion, while setting just one to No Cap and leaving the other with Cap on, obviously leaves an interesting shaped Jell-O mold (Figure 4.19 a+b).

The Start and End settings also allow for much more diverse settings. Note that you can also set the Start and/or End to Rounding. This provides a bevel without a cap to the extrusion. This gives you much more refined forms than simple straight back extrusions. To explore the idea of rounding, let's place the Start setting at Cap and Rounding and leave the End setting with just Caps (Figure 4.20).

All of a sudden you'll have a beveled collection of text. There are actually a wide variety of parameters that can be altered in this beveled look. The settings that allow you to do this are located under the Details tab of the Extrude NURBS dialog box (Figure 4.21).

To discuss the Details tab, let's actually start at the bottom half with all the checkboxes. Further, to get a better idea of the changes we're going to make, the screen shots be taken from a much closer angle. Notice that by default the Hull Inwards setting has been activated. The hull refers to the outermost area of the extruded splines. With this activated, the Extruded NURBS (or any NURBS using Caps, for that matter) provides the bevel you'd expect (Figure 4.22 a) as

Chapter 4 Generators (NURBS)

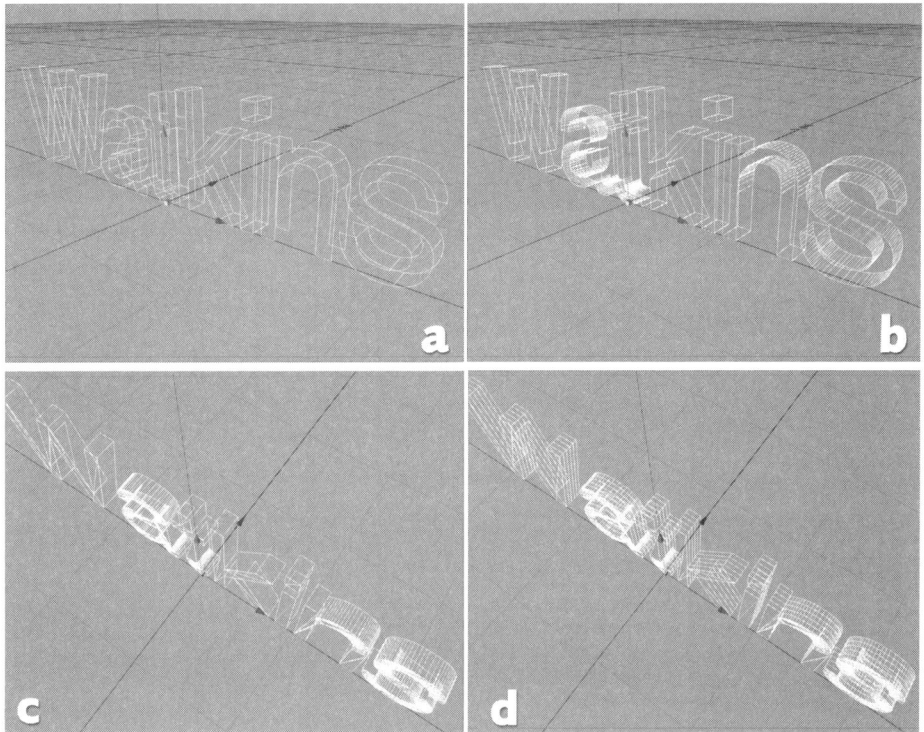

FIGURE 4.18 *There is no visual difference over different Isoparm Subdivision settings in any display mode but Isoparm. (a) Shows the text with an Isoparm Subdivision setting of 10 while (b) shows a setting of 200. A setting of 1 subdivision (c) vs. a setting of 4 (d).*

FIGURE 4.19 *Cap settings can determine whether you have a solid, hollow, (a) or "empty" extrusion. (b) has No Cap for Start with Cap set for End.*

FIGURE 4.20 *Our text thus far with Start settings of Cap and Rounding and End setting of Caps.*

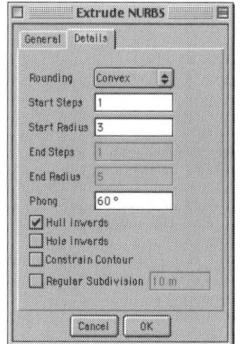

FIGURE 4.21 *The Details tab within the Extrude NURBS dialog box.*

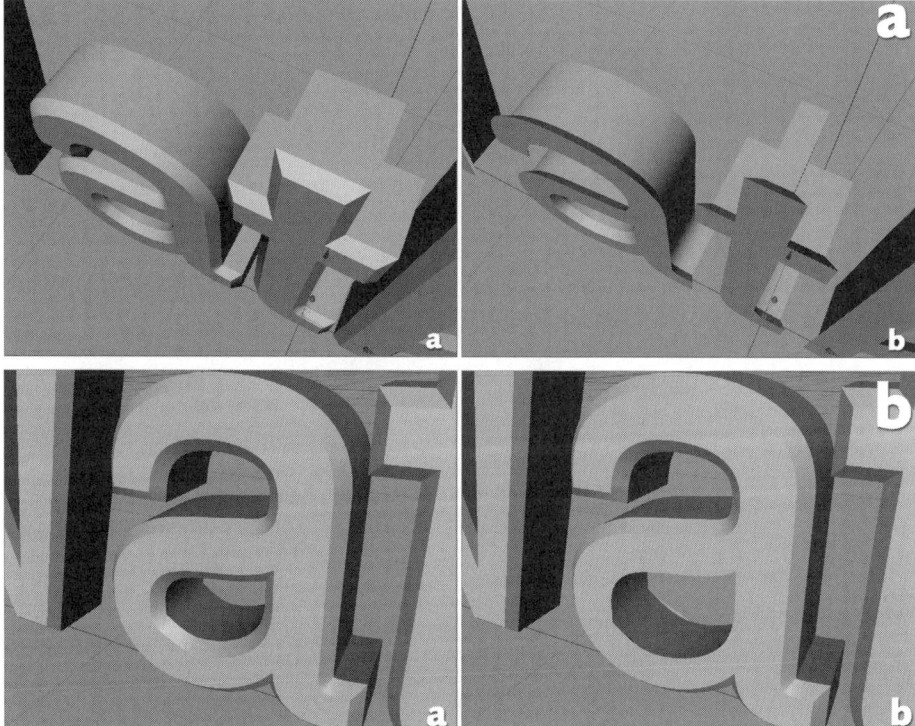

FIGURE 4.22 *With Hull Inwards activated, the rounded (or beveled) cap Extrudes inward from the face of the extrusion (a-a). With this deactivated, the extrusion increases in size off the face of the extrusion (a-b). Turning the Hole Inwards option on (b-b) or off (b-a) makes a big difference with splines that have a "hole."*

the rounding comes outward and inward off the front of the extrusion. With Hull Inwards turned off, you get an interesting but odd extrusion and cap combination (Figure 4.22 b).

The "Hole" Inwards setting only refers to splines that actually have "holes." For instance, in the word "Watkins" the only hole is the hole in the "a." With this deactivated, the holes act as the rest of the hull; when it is activated, C4D pulls the rounding inward which can create some odd effects (Figure 4.22 b).

When a spline is first extruded with regular caps, the extrusion goes straight back leaving the overall look of the text and font the same (Figure 4.23 a). However, sometimes confusingly, when Cap and Rounding is selected, all of a sudden the spline seems to get "fatter;" almost as if someone turned on the "Bold" button for text (Figure 4.23 b). The manual calls this "inflating." This inflation can be eliminated by activating the Constrain Contour setting.

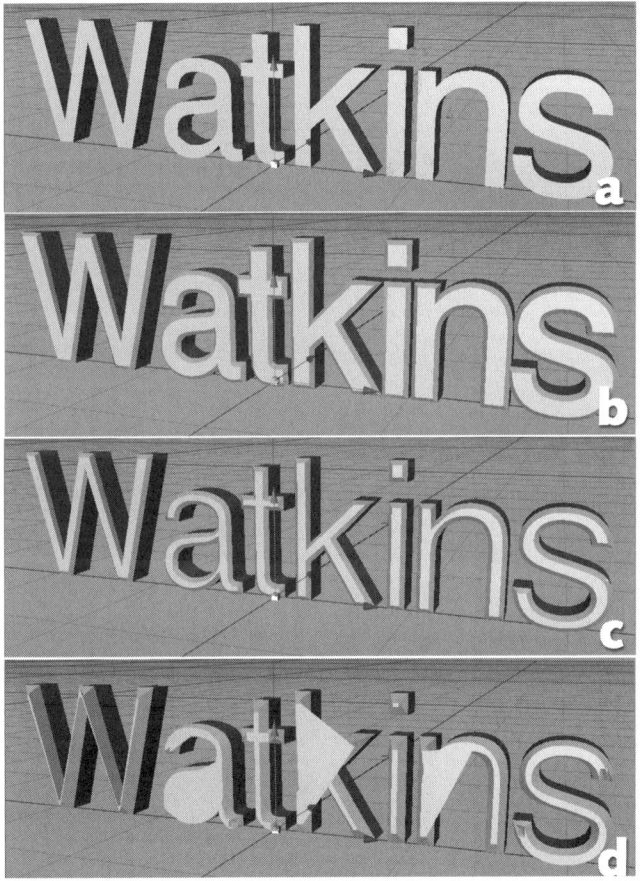

FIGURE 4.23 *The Constrain Contour checkbox allows you to maintain the size of your outer hull.*

This keeps the overall hull the same size (Figure 4.23 c). The drawback to using the Constrain Contour option is that if the radius of the rounding (we'll talk of this later) is too large, and the hull isn't allowed to expand, you can get some odd overlaps where the cap is bigger than the bevel (Figure 4.23 d).

The Regular Subdivision checkbox is really only applicable if you plan on bending, twisting, or otherwise distorting your text. The Regular Subdivision option has to do with establishing the polygon topology of the extrusions. By default, the extrusion is thought of in C4D as collections of triangular shapes. These work great unless the shape is bent all over the place. When this happens there sometimes appears to be some "shearing" or tearing where the triangles aren't able to bend appropriately in relationship to one another. By activating the Regular Subdivision checkbox, the extrusion is then built of quadrangles (rectangular shapes) with triangles only positioned on the edges. The higher the Subdivision setting, the less shearing you'll see in such deformation situations; however, the heavier your poly-count will be.

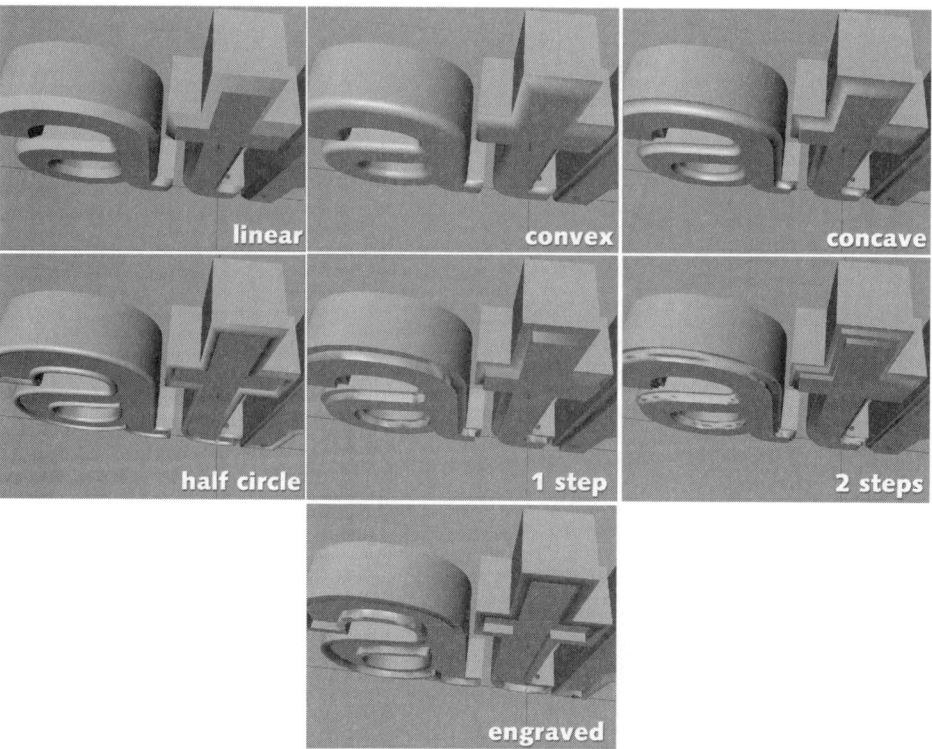

FIGURE 4.24 *Examples of the different Rounding settings. Note that all of these Rounding settings maintain constant Start Steps and Start Radius settings.*

ROUNDING

The Rounding settings allow you to determine what shape the rounded hull will appear. The easiest way to illustrate the different rounding options are pictures of the Rounding settings results (Figure 4.24). However, before we go into the rounding options we need to be sure that C4D has enough information to work with as it attempts to round the caps. Still within the Details tab of the Extrude NURBS dialog box are two input fields called Start Steps and End Steps. These let you determine how many steps C4D is to take to get from the edge of the extrusion to the edge of the rounding. With only one step, the beveling will always be in straight lines. If you increase the number of steps, you increase the smoothness possible in the rounding. In this example only the Start Steps setting is active.

Also note the Start Radius input field. Imagine the rounding profile. The Start Radius is the radius of the circle that would define the rounding if it were laid tangent to the spline being affected. Figure 4.25 shows two renderings of the extruded text with differing values for the Start Radius field and a superimposed circle to illustrate the idea.

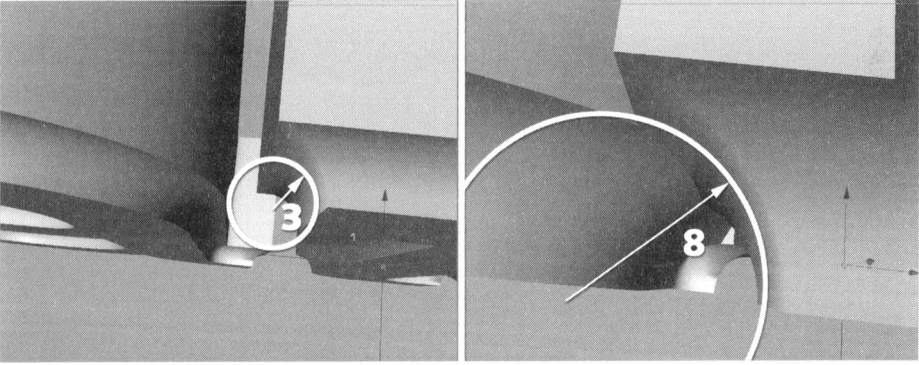

FIGURE 4.25 *(a) With a Start Radius setting of 3, the depth of the rounding is much less than if the Start Radius setting were 8 (b).*

HyperNURBS AND NURBS IN PRACTICE

A method of modeling quickly gaining popularity in the 3D world is that of *subdivision modeling*. Also referred to as cage modeling, the basic idea is that you, the modeler, create a low poly form which the 3D application subdivides into a more organic and high poly form. The low poly shape is called the cage, with the subdivided form being inside the cage. A simple example is shown in Figure 4.26 using HyperNURBS (C4D's version of subdivision). Here, a simple cube (which acts as the cage) made up of sixpolygons, is placed within a

HyperNURBS object by making the cube a child of the HyperNURBS object. Notice that the single polygon in each face is now subdivided to provide far more polygons, and hence more places to bend, ultimately creating a rounder shape.

There are several general rules about HyperNURBS that are important to remember. The first is that HyperNURBS can only affect one object or group of objects at a time. So in Figure 4.27 (a), even though all three cubes are children of the HyperNURBS object, only the first (the cube in the middle) has been subdivided. This problem is solved in Figure 4.27 (b) as the three cubes have been grouped together and the Null Object parent has been dropped into the HyperNURBS. C4D thinks of the Null Object group as one object and thus rounds all the shapes contained therein.

The second rule is that HyperNURBS has a dialog box (accessible by double-clicking the HyperNURBS object within the Object Manager) that allows you to define how many times to subdivide the contained polygons in both the Editor and the rendered (*Raytracing*) version (Figure 4.28). The benefit of this is that you can select a low number of subdivisions in the Editor to keep the interface snappy, but have a higher number of subdivisions (thus a smoother surface) when the object is rendered to the Picture Viewer (Figure 4.29).

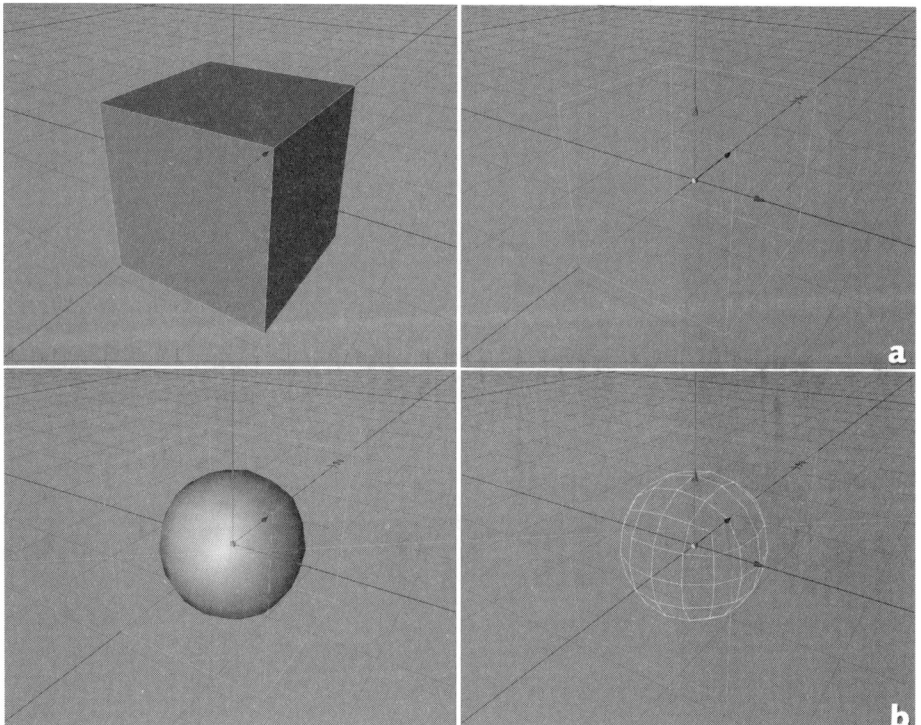

FIGURE 4.26 *Simple illustration of HyperNURBS. (a) Shows a simple six-sided cube that when it is placed within a HyperNURBS object, (b) each side is subdivided and rounded.*

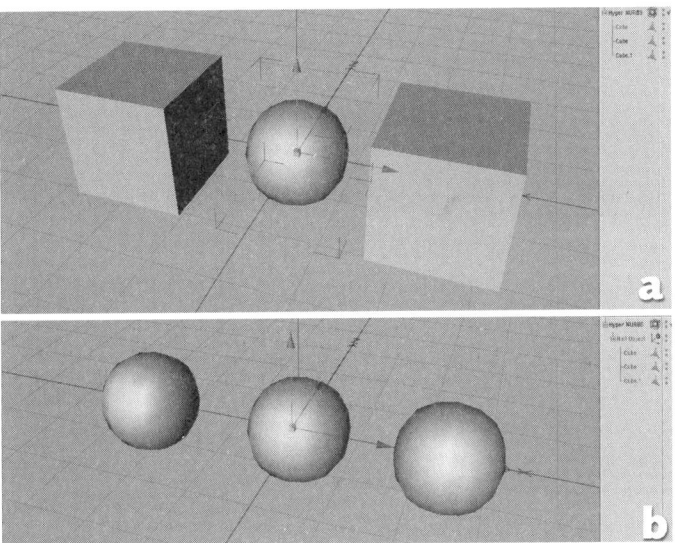

FIGURE 4.27 *HyperNURBS only affects one object or group at a time.*

 The Raytracing subdivision settings are only in effect for renderings done to the Picture Viewer; simply rendering the active view panel will reveal a rendering using the settings in the Editor input panel.

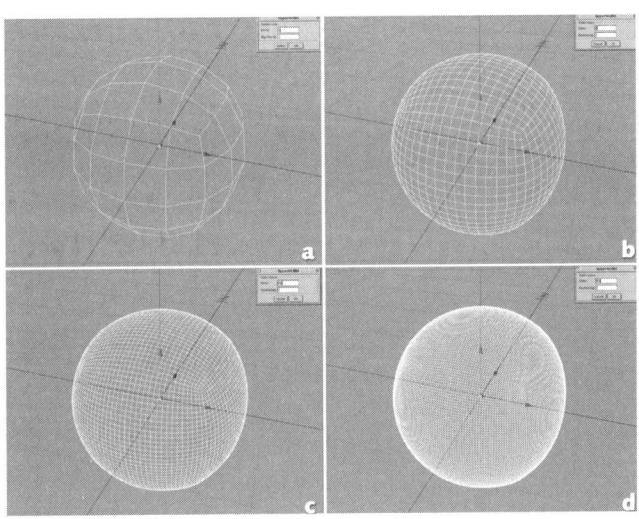

FIGURE 4.28 *These images all begin from the same six-sided cube but as the number of Editor subdivisions are increased, the number of polygons increases and so does the roundness of the object.*

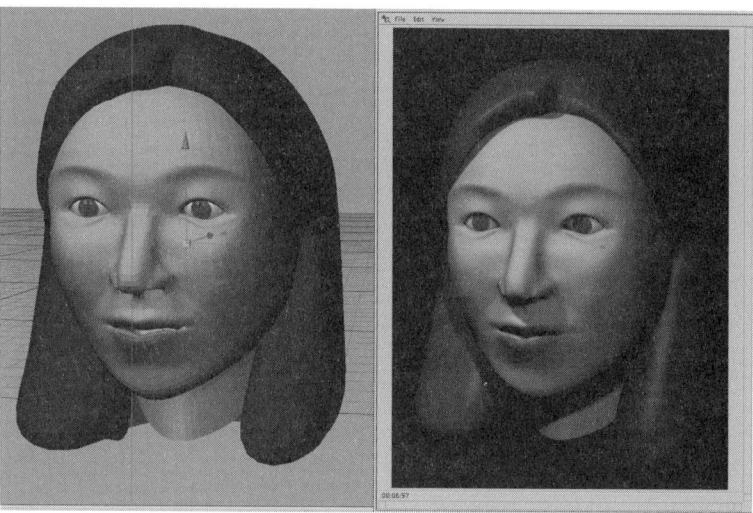

FIGURE 4.29 *In this example, the Editor setting is set to "2" revealing a very blocky looking model since the number of times C4D is subdividing each shape is fairly low. However, the Raytracing setting is set to 12, revealing a very smooth surface in the final rendering as there are many polygons where only a few were originally placed. Model by Ya-Tsun Yang.*

HyperNURBS rounds edges according to how large each polygon is in relation to a connected neighboring polygon at an angle to it. Thus a cube with an original segment setting of "1" will make for a very round HyperNURBS object (Figure 4.30 a). If you increase the number of segments the original form has, the angles will become sharper as the relative size of the polygons decreases (Figure 4.30 b and c). If polygons are resized (Figure 4.30 d), then the small polygons make for sharper corners as they are on the right of Figure 4.30 (d), than they do on the left where the segments are farther apart (larger relative polygons).

The fourth general rule that is important to understand is that only connected polygons are rounded. For example, Figure 4.31 shows a Cube Primitive that has Separate Surfaces activated. C4D sees each face of the cube as a separate object rather than seeing the collection of planes as connected parts of one object. So, the edge of each individual polygon is rounded, but not in relation to the other planes.

The last rule is that C4D works better with quadrangles than triangles. When you create low poly meshes, try to stick to 4-sided polygons rather than triangular polys.

Chapter 4 Generators (NURBS)

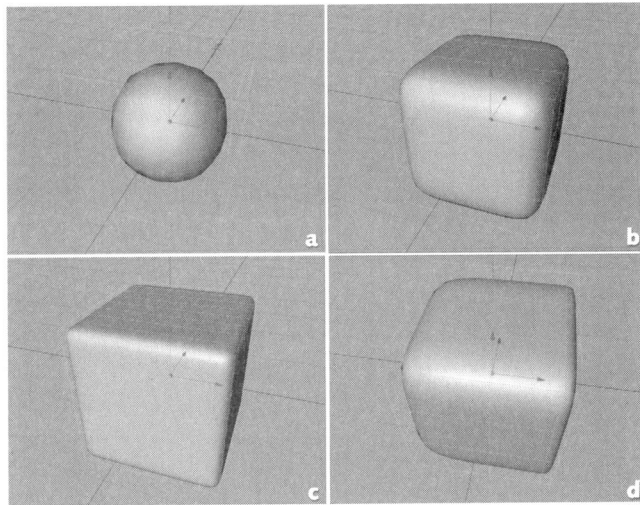

FIGURE 4.30 *The farther the segments are apart, the rounder the HyperNURBS.*

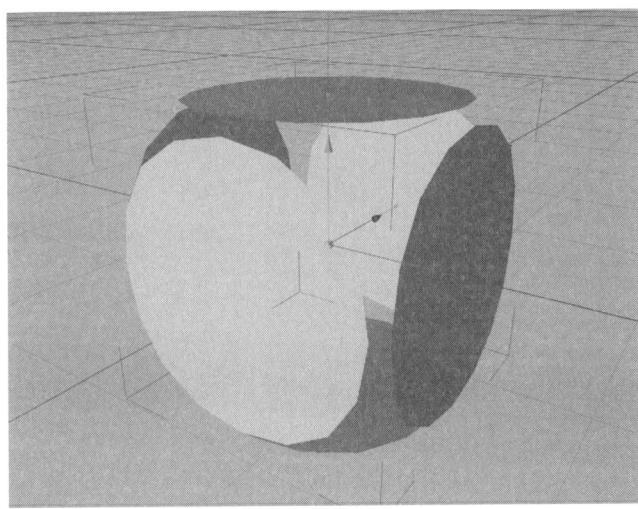

FIGURE 4.31 *Only conected polygons are rounded.*

HyperNURBS Methods

Generally, there are two main methods of creating the "cage" polygon form that you will later place within the HyperNURBS object. The first is altering a primitive form (see Chapter 5) that we'll refer to as the Primitive Cage method. This method involves creating a primitive shape like a cube or circle and extruding, twisting, or otherwise modifying the form to create a rough approximation of the desired form. When the form is placed within a HyperNURBS object, you are given a rounded version of the boxy approximation (Figure 4.32).

The benefit of this method is that the polygons are already connected to each other. And creating new polygons is easy using Extrudes and Inner Extrudes (discussed on pages 104-105).

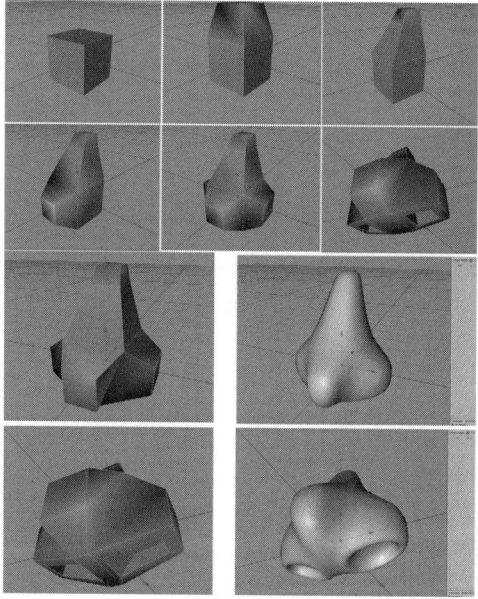

FIGURE 4.32 *One method of working with HyperNURBS is to create the cage form by altering a primitive form such as this cube. When the altered cube is placed within a HyperNURBS object it becomes a much more organic shaped nose.*

The second method is to manually build each polygon within a Polygon Object and then place this polygon form into a HyperNURBS object. We'll call this the Point Cage Creation method. This allows ultimate control over the polygon topology, but takes longer, as each point must be constructed and moved, then combined with other points to create a polygon. However, using this careful process reveals amazing results (see Chapter 7 by Nicholas Woolridge).

Vital HyperNURBS Tools

Beneath the Structure pull-down menu is a collection of incredibly powerful tools. Strictly speaking, these tools are not HyperNURBS tools; in actuality they are polygon manipulation tools. However, they are indeed vital when you are working with forms planned for placement with a HyperNURBS object, as most HyperNURBS objects are determined by polygon-based objects.

Add Points

The Add Points tool allows you to create the building blocks of polygons. You may add points to any polygon-based object, including an empty polygon object (Objects>Polygon Object). When a Polygon Object is first created it is completely empty without any polygons. When the Polygon Object is selected in the Object Manager, you can select the Add Points tool (your mouse pointer will change to indicate you are within the Add Points tool) and add points to the form by holding the CTRL (or COMMAND) button down and clicking where you desire points. Make sure that you are in Points mode to see where you are placing the points (Figure 4.33). Now these points are fairly useless by themselves; without connecting them, there is not geometry to see or even place within a HyperNURBS object. This is where the Bridge and Create Polygon tools come in.

Bridge and Create Polygons

The Bridge and Create Polygons tools, both located beneath the Structure pull-down menu, allow you to create polygons from extant points. The Bridge tool (also activated by pressing "B" on the keyboard) allows you to "bridge" points together to form polys. To use this tool, click on a point and drag to another and release. This defines an "edge" to bridge from. Then click-drag from a third to a fourth point to define the opposite edge to bridge to. Upon releasing your mouse, a polygon will be formed (Figure 4.34).

The Create Polygons tool works much the same way, except that using this tool, you want to click on each point (three or four) that you wish to make a polygon out of. You can click-drag from point to point or just click and release on a series of points, making sure that the last point clicked is the same as the first.

This seems like a long way to create a polygon when one could simply be created by selecting it from the Primitives list. The real power comes when you create a series of points which are then connected with either the Bridge or Create Polygons tools to make a form (Figure 4.35 a-f). When this form is dropped in a HyperNURBS object, your simple collection of points and polys becomes a complex form (Figure 4.35 g). This is the essence of the Point Cage Creation method of building HyperNURBS cages.

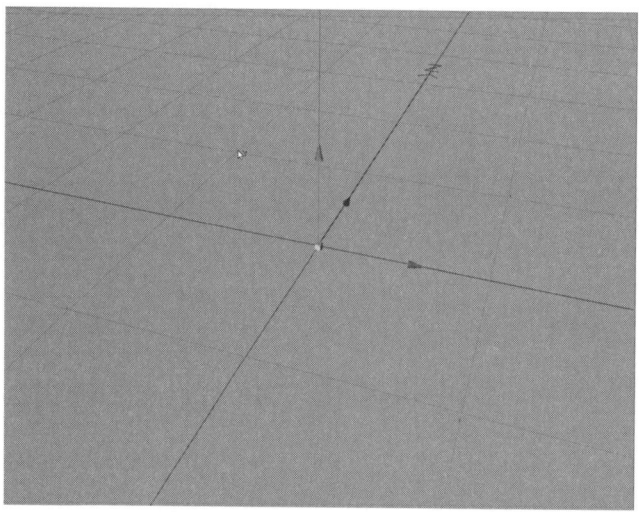

FIGURE 4.33 *After activating the Add Points tool, you can add points to an otherwise empty Polygon Object. You can also add points to other objects, but they must be selected in the Object Manager.*

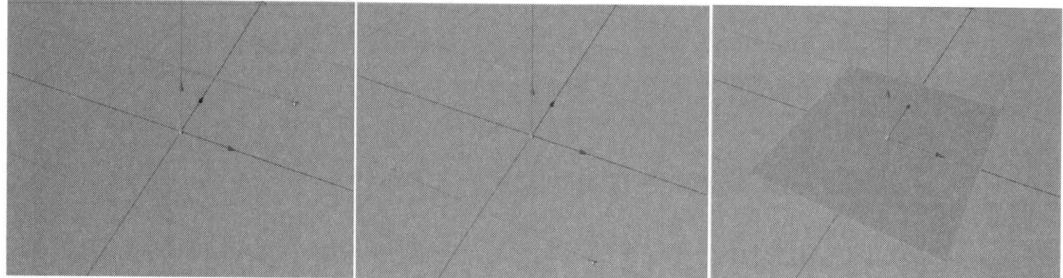

FIGURE 4.34 *The Bridge tool can be used to create new polygons.*

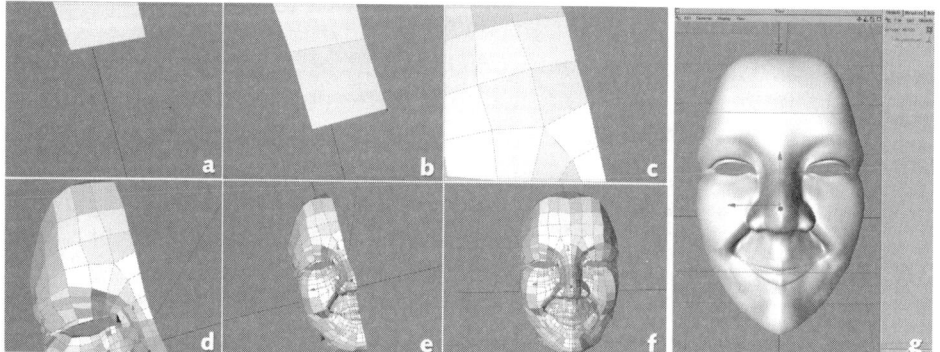

FIGURE 4.35 *When the Add Points, Bridge, or Create Polygon tools are mastered, incredible forms are possible by creating a very general cage. Model by Desiree Maher.*

Chapter 4 Generators (NURBS)

The other tools we're going to talk about within the Structure pull-down menu, Extrude, Extrude Inner, and Knife, are primarily tools for use with the Primitive Cage Creation method. This method starts with a primitive form that is made editable (Structure>Make Editable). Although a primitive form will work within a HyperNURBS object, the only way to alter the polygons to utilize the Primitive Cage Creation method is to have a polygon-based form, which primitives are not. All of the tool explanations below will be built upon the idea of having a Cube Primitive that has been made editable.

EXTRUDE

The Extrude tool only works while you are in Polygon mode and a polygon-based form is active in the Object Manager. What it does is take a selected polygon and extrude it away from the place it was in the direction of the polygon's normal. The key is, as it Extrudes, it creates new polygons to fill in the spaces that would have been left by simply moving the polygon away from the rest of the form (Figure 4.36). The key to using this tool is to remember that every time you click-drag (even a little) and release, a new collection of polygons is created. If no other tool is selected, the Extrude tool stays active and subsequent click-drags produce added extrusions. Often people end up with an intense group of extrusions because of errant mouse clicks. The best method is to use the Live Selection tool or the Move Active Element tool to select a polygon to extrude, and then switch to the Extrude tool to extrude that polygon.

Notice that when the Extrude tool is activated, the Active Tool palette displays a variety of editable settings in the bottom right hand corner of your screen. Perhaps the most important setting there is the last. The Preserve Groups setting allows you to determine if a group of polygons will be extruded as a group, and thus not create polygons between the extruded polys, or to extrude each separately (Figure 4.37). The Maximum Angle and Variance settings go hand in hand with the Preserve Groups option as they determine if groups of polygons

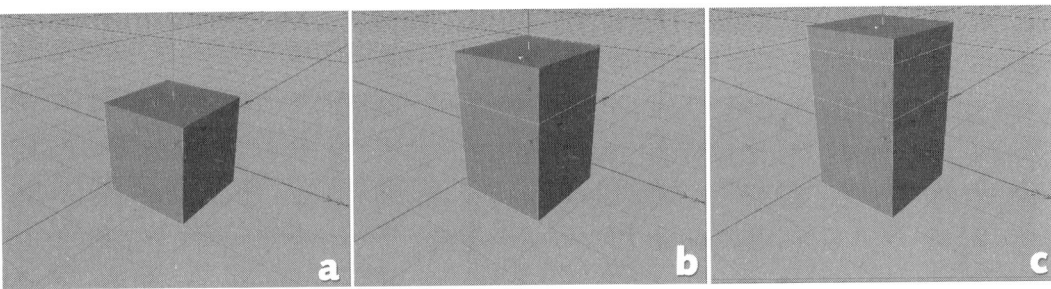

FIGURE 4.36 *Extrusion process. (a) Begin by selecting a polygon or polygons to be extruded. (b) With the Extrude tool activated, click-drag to extrude that polygon away from the object. (c) Subsequent click-drags will continue to extrude.*

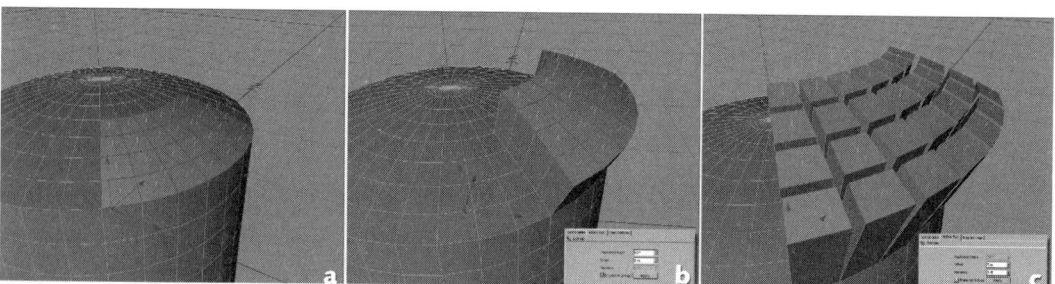

FIGURE 4.37 *With a group of polygons selected (a), you can extrude as a group (b), or separately (c), as determined by the Preserve Groups option in the Active Tool palette.*

are to be extruded together (if the relative angle to each adjoining polygon is less than the value entered) or if they are to be extruded separately (if the relative angle of each adjoining polygon is more than the value entered). The Variance setting allows you to quickly create a variety of extrusions (with Preserve Groups deactivated) in a short amount of time (Figure 4.38). The Offset setting allows you to numerically determine the distance the polygons are extruded.

EXTRUDE INNER

The Extrude Inner tool works much like the Extrude tool except that instead of extruding a selected polygon away from the object, it creates a new polygon that remains flat against the overall form (Figure 4.39). The same rules apply to the settings in the Active Tool palette. The real strength of this tool comes from the ability to use the Extrude Inner tool in combination with the Extrude tool. For instance, Figure 4.40 shows a cube which uses an Extrude Inner, followed immediately by an Extrude.

KNIFE

The Knife tool is a great way to "cut" a polygon or collection of polys. If you have a form, let's say a primitive cube, that has been made editable and now has had a series of Extrudes performed on it, you may find that you need an extra extrude that you forgot to insert. Or, perhaps you have a shape that is a good start, but you need more segments than you presently have. The Knife tool allows you to cut or subdivide polygons.

Figure 4.41 shows a simple editable cube. Note that each face of the cube is composed of one polygon. The Knife tool can change this very easily. The simplest form of using the Knife tool (while you are in Polygon mode) is to select a polygon with the Live Selection tool, and then activating the Knife tool, and click-dragging to define the "cut." Holding the SHIFT key down constrains the angle to whatever setting is listed in the Constrain Angle dialog box within the Active Tool palette. The results are shown in Figures 4.41 (a-c).

Chapter 4 Generators (NURBS)

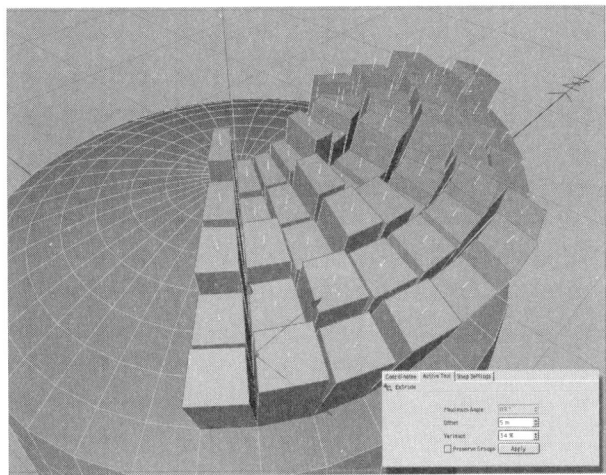

FIGURE 4.38 *The Variance setting allows for quick extrusions of varying lengths.*

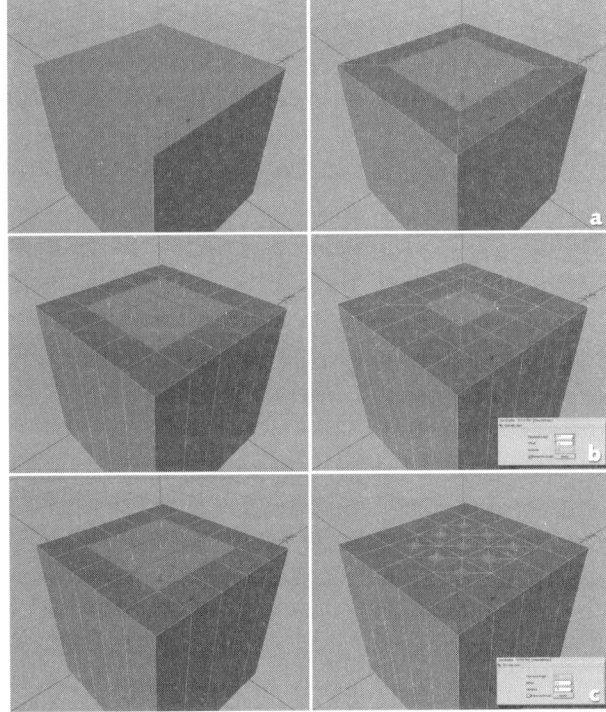

FIGURE 4.39 *Extrude Inner (a) with simple polygon. (b) With multiple polygons selected, a group of new polys can be created along the face of the object, or (c) individual polygons can be created.*

Aye, but here's the rub. Using the Knife tool as it is set up by default almost causes more problems than it solves. The first is that when it is only cutting one polygon, C4D must create triangles on the other faces to compensate for the split poly on one face. The second problem, is that while we are cutting in the perspective view, we've actually created a crooked cut that can be seen from a flat front view (Figure 4.42 a). The trick to the Knife tool then, is to 1) make sure that all cuts are done from a flat on view (front, back, right, left, top, bottom) and 2) make sure that the default Restrict to Selection option is turned OFF when you make cuts. This way, when a cut is made holding the SHIFT key down from an appropriate viewpoint, the Knife tool cuts completely through the object and keeps the cut straight (Figure 4.42 b).

These tools may all seem fine and dandy, but what do they have to do with HyperNURBS? Well, if you create a HyperNURBS object and then take the cube created as shown in Figure 4.40 and make it a child of the HyperNURBS object, you would get the organic form shown in Figure 4.43. The beauty of it all is, by selecting the cube within the HyperNURBS, you can continue to alter the blue cage form using the Extrude, Extrude Inner, and Knife tools and the Hyper-NURBS object will continue to recalculate the curve, creating a complex form based on your simple changes.

FIGURE 4.40 *By using Extrude Inner and then immediately using Extrude, hollowed out forms can be easily created.*

FIGURE 4.41 *The Knife tool in action.*

CHAPTER 4 GENERATORS (NURBS)

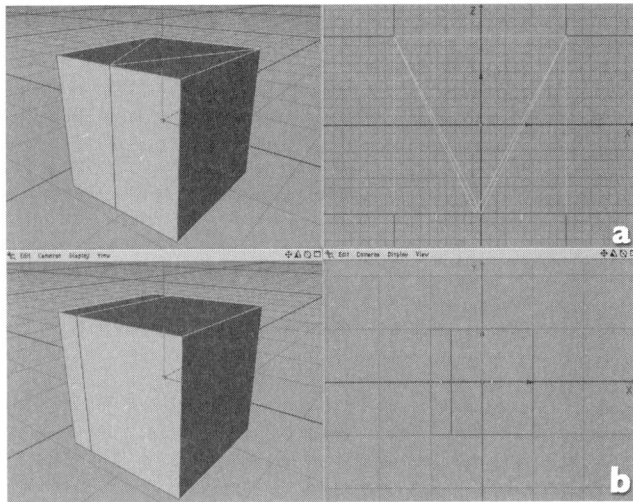

FIGURE 4.42 *(a) When the default Restrict to Selection option is activated and the Knife tool is used in a perspective view panel, the results are uneven cuts that create triangles. (b) When you cut from a non-perspective view while you hold the SHIFT key down, clean cuts that knife through the entire object can be made.*

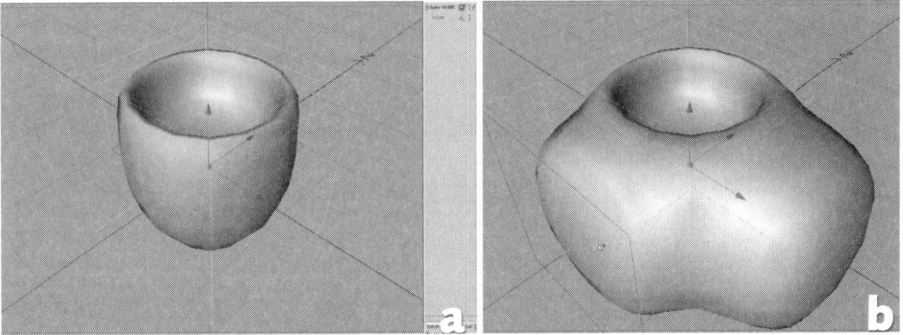

FIGURE 4.43 *(a) Figure 4.42 dropped in a HyperNURBS object creates a rounded form. (b) You can continue to alter the form by altering the cage that was the original shape.*

TUTORIAL

4.1 NURBS AND THE DINING ROOM

So now that we've talked for a long time about specific objects and some specific tools relating to NURBS, let's look at them in action. Open up the room that you created for Tutorial 3.1 (Figure 4.44). Notice that a few extra walls have been added since we looked at it last; do this on your version as well, using simple Cube Primitives.

As this room is going to be a dining room, let's start off with building a table. We could build the table all within the room setting, but it is often less confusing if you construct separate objects in separate files and merge them later. So for the table, make a new file (File>New). Notice that when you do this, your room file seemingly vanishes; it is actually still open and can be accessed from the Window pull-down menu, so don't worry.

To start, we'll create the top of the table using an Extrude NURBS object. The table is oval and is created by activating the top view panel and creating a Circle Spline Primitive. Double-click the circle's yellow icon and change the setting to create an ellipse that is only 100m wide for its Y radius (Figure 4.45).

Now create an Extrude NURBS object and make the circle a child of the Extrude NURBS object. The first thing C4D will do is extrude the circle in the default Z direction; unfortunately, this is equivalent to smearing the circle backwards rather than giving it any thickness upward. So, double-click the icon next to the Extrude NURBS and change the Y Movement setting to 7m (or whatever looks appropriate to you) and change the Z Movement setting to 0. While you're at it, create a bit of a lip to the top of the table by changing the End setting to Cap and Rounding, as the top of the table in this case will be the end of the extrusion. Now further define the lip we are creating in the Details tab by selecting Concave, changing the End Steps setting to 8 to allow for a good curvature, and reducing the End Radius setting to 2. Upon clicking OK, you should be presented with a form much like Figure 4.46 (b). Now, with the Extrude NURBS object selected you may resize the entire object to fit your preference.

To continue on with the style of the room, we'll use the same twisted pedestal legs we used for the niche table. To save time, jump to your Room file (via the Window pull-down menu) and select the cube (with the deformers as children) from the Object Manager and copy it (Edit>Copy). Then go back to

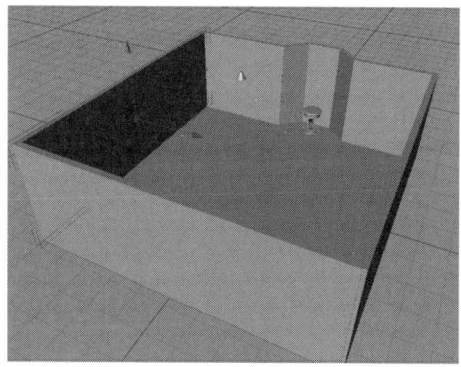

FIGURE 4.44 *Our room with a few extra walls.*

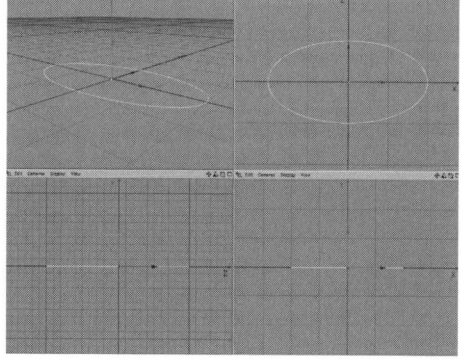

FIGURE 4.45 *Creating the tabletop begins with a Circle Spline shaped to an ellipse.*

CHAPTER 4   GENERATORS (NURBS)

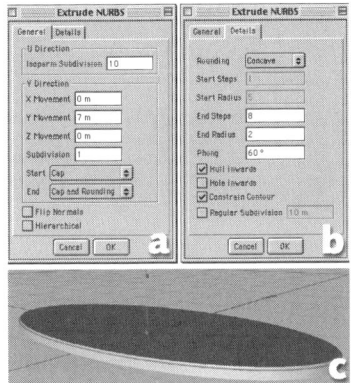

FIGURE 4.46 *The settings and results of the tabletop extrusion.*

your Table file via the Window pull-down menu and paste the cube (Edit>Paste) (Figure 4.47).

To give the pedestal a base from which the smaller legs will sprout, create a Cylinder Primitive (Figure 4.48 a + b). Open the Cylinder Primitive dialog box and change Height Segments to "1" as we don't need any more than that, and reduce Rotation Segments to "6" to create a six-sided block. Resize appropriately.

To create the legs at the bottom of the pedestal, we'll again use an Extrude NURBS object. First, we'll need to create the profile of the leg. To do so, make sure you are in a front or side view (non-perspective) and use one of the Draw Spline tools (the Draw Bezier Spline tool is used in Figure 4.49 a) and draw a rough outline of what you want your leg to look like (Figure 4.49 b). Remember to keep it rough since as soon as you are done drawing the spline, you'll still be in Points mode, allowing you to select points and adjust them or their Bezier

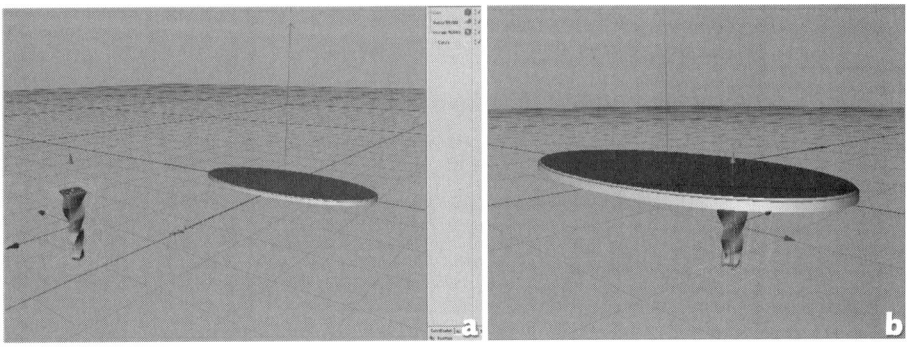

FIGURE 4.47 *Paste the twisted cube into the table scene. It obviously pastes out of place and will need to be placed more appropriately into the scene.*

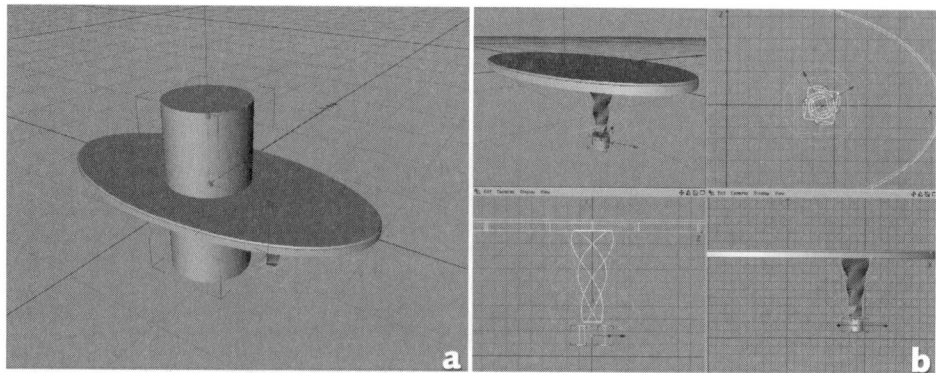

FIGURE 4.48 *We create the block at the bottom of the pedestal by creating a Cylinder Primitive and then changing the settings to provide a six-sided block.*

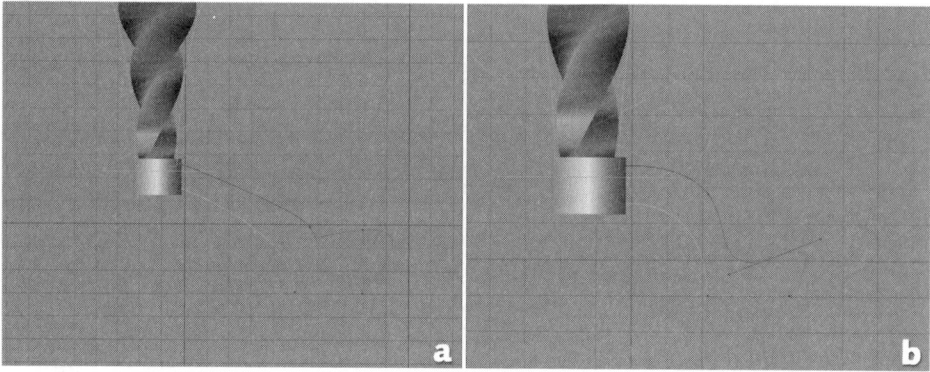

FIGURE 4.49 *Roughly sketch the form in and make adjustments as needed to create the spline that will be used to create the bottom legs.*

handles as needed. Remember the trick of holding the SHIFT key down to adjust one end of a Bezier handle, leaving the other end unaffected.

To give the new leg thickness, create an Extrude NURBS object that the spline you've just created will be dropped into. To give this leg a little detail, make sure that Rounding is turned on for both Start and End. Roughly match the settings to those shown in Figure 4.50.

Now as we've been building this leg, we haven't worried much about the location of any of the object axes. The problem is that when the Extrude NURBS was created, it was created it at (0,0,0), so that now, even though all the geometry is down at the bottom of the table, the leg's axis of rotation is up in the middle of the tabletop (Figure 4.51 a). To fix this, select the Object Axis tool and move the axis down with the Move Active Element tool so that it is at the edge of the leg (Figure 4.51 b). Placing it here makes it easy to rotate the leg into position around the block placed at the bottom of the table.

CHAPTER 4 GENERATORS (NURBS)

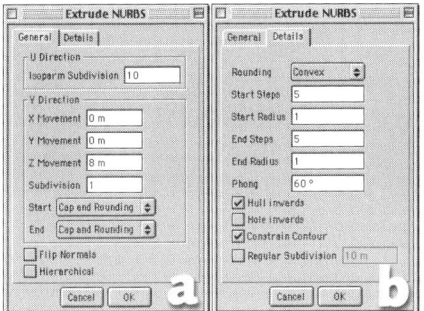

FIGURE 4.50 *Extrude NURBS settings for bottom legs.*

Rotate the leg into position at the bottom block (Figure 4.51 a). You may find that hiding the twisted pedestal (by clicking the top right gray dot next to the object in the Object Manager until it turns red), helps you to see the necessary information in the view panel. In Figure 4.51 (b), the leg is rotated exactly 30° as entered in the Coordinates Manager. Copy and paste this leg twice and rotate each of these legs into position around the pedestal block.

Now press "G" on your keyboard to group the three bottom legs, the block, and the twisted pedestal together. Copy and paste this and move it over into place on the other side of the table. Make sure that while you are moving it, you use the red X handle to ensure that the copy of the leg doesn't move up or down or in the Y direction. Lastly, make sure to group everything together and name it "Dinner Table."

Now select the Dinner Table object and copy it, and paste it into the Room file. The table will probably paste in below the floor and probably the wrong size. Visually, move the table and resize it so that it appears to fit in the room

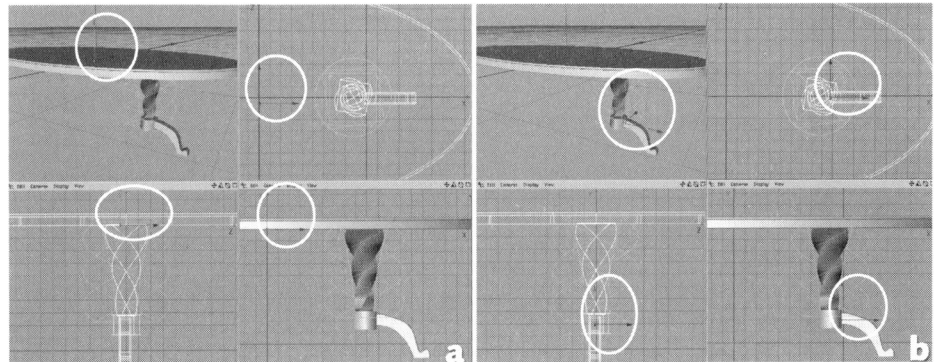

FIGURE 4.51 *Make sure to realign the object axis for the new Extrude NURBS to be at the inside edge of the leg.*

(Figure 4.52). At this point, you may want to make adjustments to your room as well so that it matches the table.

To explore some of the other NURBS objects, let's create a vase and flower to place on the table within the niche. Again, it is easier to create the vase in another file and then copy the new element into the room. Create a new file and create an outline for a vase in one of the non-perspective views (preferably right, left, front or back – not top) with one of the Draw Spline tools. Make sure that you create a closed spline so that the vase actually has some thickness. A single spline would make a paper-thin vase (Figure 4.53 a). Create a Lathe NURBS object and make the spline a child of it (Figure 4.53 b).

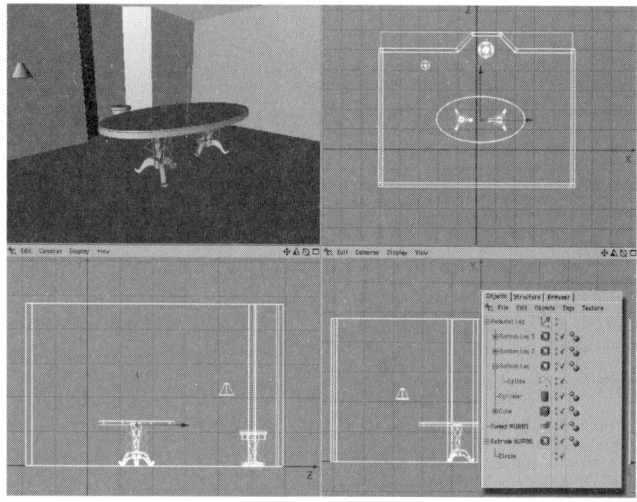

FIGURE 4.52 *Our room this far with the added table.*

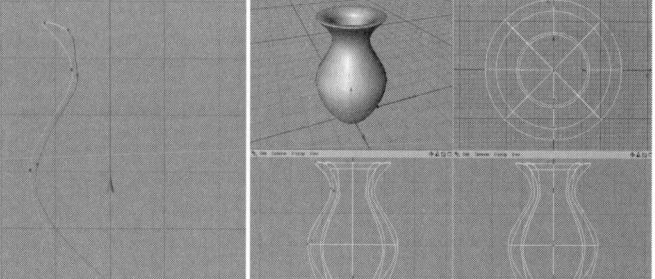

FIGURE 4.53 *(a) The simple spline created with the Draw Bezier Spline tool. (b) The spline placed within the Lathe NURBS object and resultant vase.*

Chapter 4 Generators (NURBS)

There are several important things that should be mentioned about this Lathe NURBS object. First, the spline that was used to create it is a closed spline, thus creating an object with thickness. Second, note that it was drawn with the understanding that the Y-axis would be the center of the lathe. So the bottom of the vase (where the vase is closed) sits right on the Y-axis, while the top (where the opening of the vase occurs) is placed away. The third issue is that the spline was not drawn in a perspective view panel; this is really a key to successfully creating splines for use in NURBS. By creating it in a side view, you can be sure that the spline is exactly flat, and thus will lathe appropriately. The beautiful thing about this now is that you can select the spline in the Object Manager and while you are in Points mode, shift the points of the spline to change the form of the vase. Take time to re-label the Lathe NURBS to "Vase."

To create a cartoonish flower, we'll use a Sweep NURBS object. So we'll need a path spline and a contour spline. Begin by using a Draw Spline tool to create a path for the flower stem (Figure 4.54 a). Again, make sure to initially draw the spline in a side front or backback view. Then after the spline is drawn, you can go back in other views and shift the points around (Figure 4.54 b).

Now that we have the path of the stem, we need to create the spline that will define the cross-section. Create a simple Circle Spline Primitive, and resize it to be about the size of the flower stem. Create a Sweep NURBS object and drop the path spline (probably called "Spline" at this point) and then the contour spline (Circle) into the Sweep NURBS. You should get a result similar to Figure 4.55 (a). If you have a result similar to Figure 4.55 (b), where the stem is flat, you will need to change the Plane setting for the Circle Spline so that the Circle Spline knows what axis to extrude along.

We'll further refine the Sweep NURBS object by making the contour spline (Circle) taper off. To do this, double-click the Sweep NURBS icon in the Object Manager and change the Scaling setting to 10%. This will cause the contour to be 10% of its original size when it reaches the end of the path (spline) (Figure 4.56).

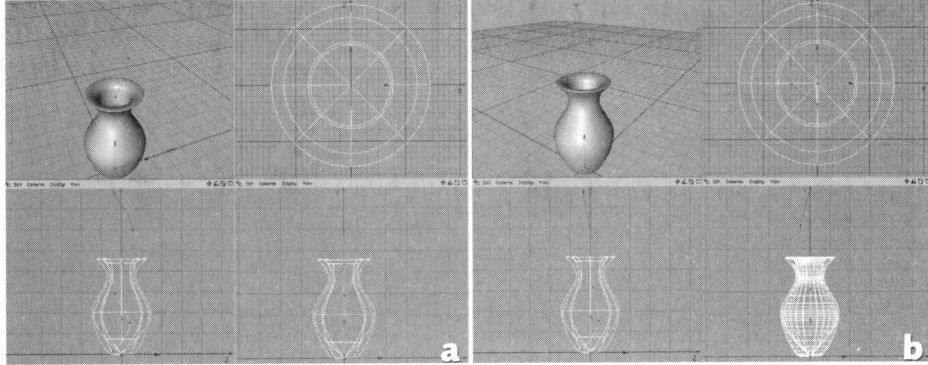

Figure 4.54 *a) Create the path for the flower stem with a spline, b) here the Draw Cubic Spline tool was used.*

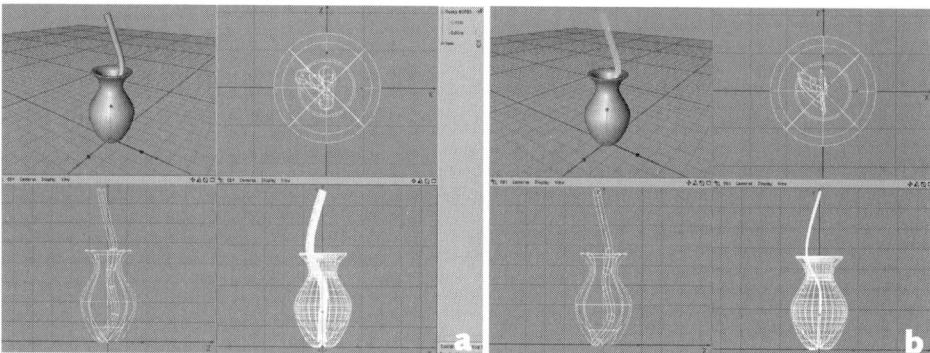

FIGURE 4.55 *Initial Sweep NURBS object; (a) is correct, the incorrect object (b) is a result of the Circle Spline being on an inappropriate plane.*

To create a couple of leaves, we'll use a Bezier NURBS object. Create a Bezier NURBS object and move it a bit away from the vase and stem for now. Press "O" on your keyboard to zoom in on the Bezier NURBS shape so that we can work with it. The leaf that we're going to build here will be gently curving overall, so we won't need a lot of subdivisions. However, down the middle of the leaf, we'll probably want a little crisper edge, so we'll need to adjust the Grid Points setting to allow for more rows of points. Double-click the Bezier NURBS icon in the Object Manager and change the X Grid Points setting to "5." In the perspective view, make sure that the Display pull-down menu is set to X-Ray so that you can easily see the grid points (Figure 4.57).

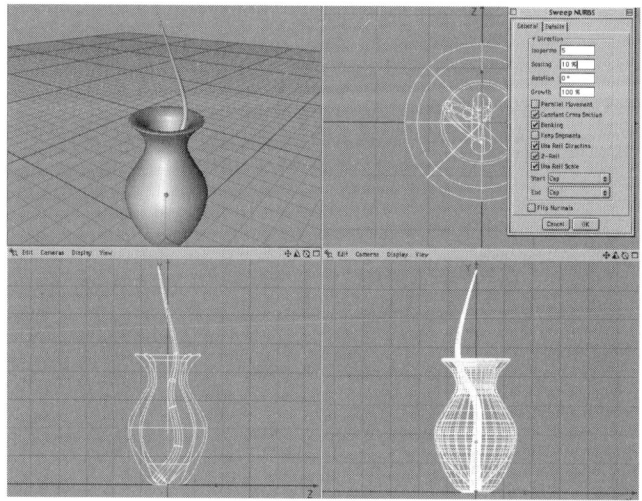

FIGURE 4.56 *Changing the Sweep NURBS object options to taper the shape.*

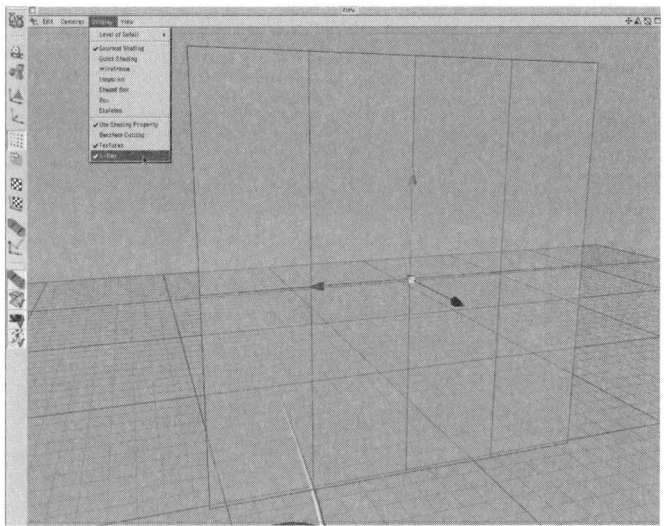

FIGURE 4.57 *Our 5x3 Grid Points Bezier NURBS viewed in the perspective window in Points mode with X-Ray turned on in the Display pull-down menu.*

Before we start shaping, we'll first want to organize our points to define areas of higher definition. Make sure that you are in Points mode and activate the Live Selection tool. "Paint" over each of the rows of points on either side of the center row. Then switch to the Scale Active Element tool and using the X restricted scale handle (the red box) click-drag to the left (Figure 4.58 a+b). Scaling like this brings the two rows of points closer toward the middle.

Now, use the Live Selection tool to select the row of points down the middle. Move these points backward using the Move Active Element tool. Again, make

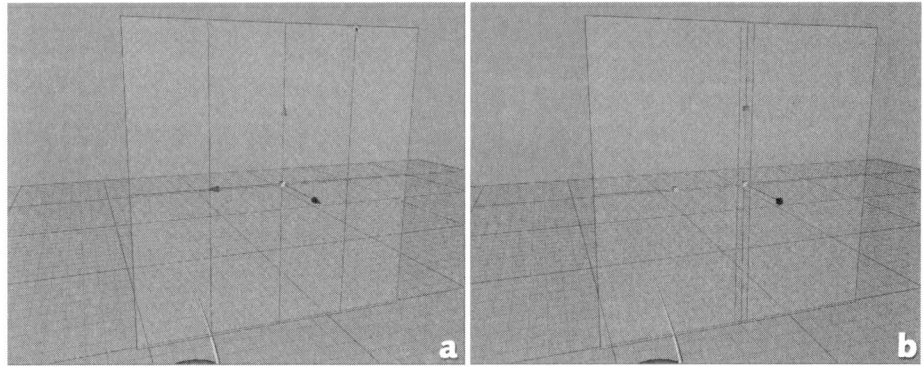

FIGURE 4.58 *Preparing for shape altering by properly organizing the points.*

sure to use the constrain movement handles (blue cone for the Y direction) (Figure 4.59). Now that we have a middle trough, we can select each of the other points to form the outer edge into a leaf (Figure 4.60).

Now use the Object Axis tool to move the leaf's object axis to the bottom, and then switching to Model mode or Object mode, move and scale the leaf into position on the stem. Copy and paste a few copies (Figure 4.61).

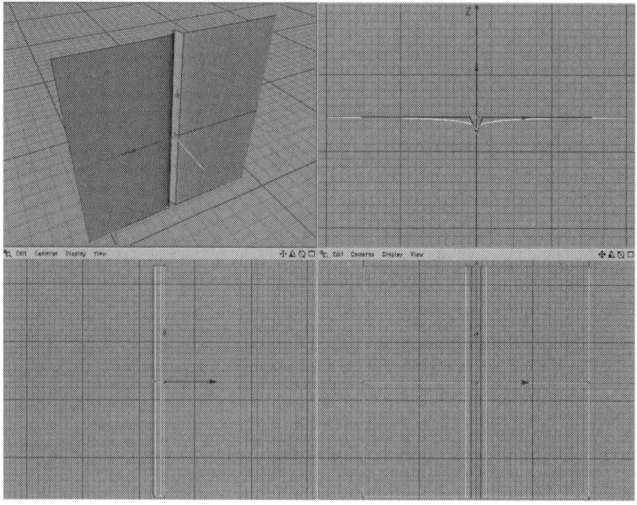

FIGURE 4.59 *Creating a trough in the middle of the leaf.*

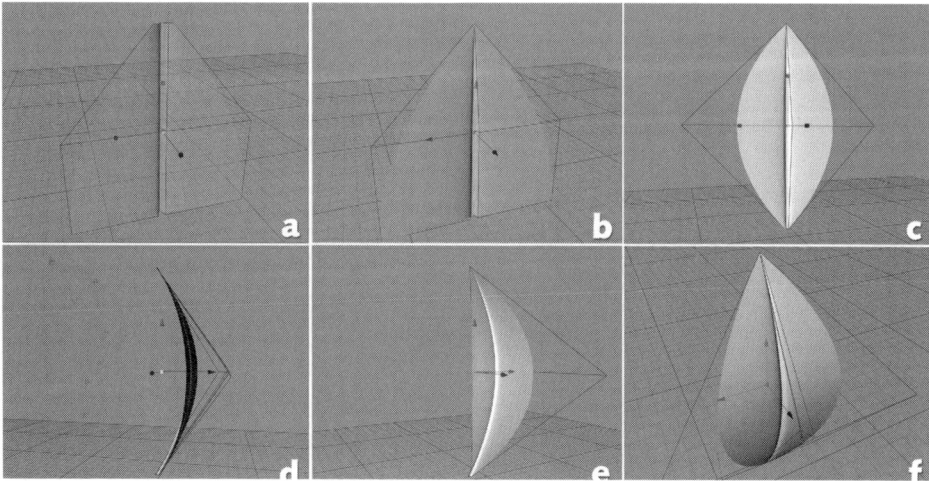

FIGURE 4.60 *The rest of the leaf is formed by selecting and moving the remaining points into position to form a leaf shape.*

Chapter 4 Generators (NURBS)

Repeat the same process for the daisy flower petal. The shape will be a bit different, but again make sure that the object axis for the Bezier NURBS is at the bottom center. This will become important as we create an array. Create a flattened Oil Tank Primitive and resize it so that it looks right for the center of the flower (Figure 4.62)

FIGURE 4.61 *Leaves in place.*

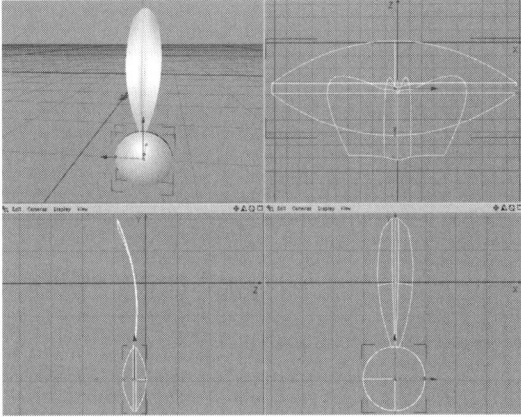

FIGURE 4.62 *New flower petal with flower center made from Oil Tank Primitive.*

Arrays and Instances

An Array Object is a tool that allows you to place one object within it, and C4D will duplicate and rotate *instances* of the object placed in the Array Object. An instance is a powerful tool with 3D. The idea, is that to save poly-counts, C4D can display the same object several times. This is different than a copy of an object. If you have 30 petals, C4D is displaying 30 petals; however if you have 30 instances of a petal, C4D is displaying one petal 30 times. This doesn't save you any rendering time, but does keep your poly-count low, and thus your file size stays smaller.

The petals of a flower are a perfect location to use an array. Create an Array Object by selecting it from the top command palette (Figure 4.63 a) or by going to Objects>Modeling>Array.

When an Array Object is created, it appears in the Object Manager, but no new geometry appears in the view panel. We are going to want our Array Object to center around the flower center (our Oil Tank Primitive), so use the Move Active Element tool to move the Array Object to the middle of the Oil Tank Primitive (Figure 4.63 b).

In order to let the Array Object know which shape to "array," place the petal as a child of the Array Object. The result will be somewhat weird (Figure 4.64 a), as an Array Object rotates and works with the object it is "arraying" by the object's Z-axis, which in this case is the backside of the petal. To remedy this situation, first select the Array Object and using the Rotate Active Element tool or the Coordinates Manager, rotate the object (90° in pitch) so that the petals are facing the correct direction (Figure 4.64 b). What we now need to do is change the object axis of the petal, so that its Y-axis is facing in towards the array. With the Object Axis tool, and with the Bezier NURBS Object that is your petal selected in the Object Manager, use the Rotate Active Element tool to rotate the petal's axis into position (Figure 4.64 c).

By double-clicking the Array icon within the Object Manager, you can shift the radius to bring the petals closer together. You can increase the number of copies to create a more dense collection of petals, or leave the number at 7 and instead copy and paste the Array Object and rotate the Bezier NURBS for this new Array Object so that the petals bend in at a slightly different angle. Repeat and you can get a fairly organic looking flower with 24 petals visible, with only 3 petals' worth of geometry. Group the Array Objects and Oil Tank together and name the group "Flower." Move it into position at the top of the flower stem.

Group the flower, stem, and vase together and copy and paste the new group into the room (Figure 4.65). Resize as needed.

One thing that is often forgotten when people model rooms is that many rooms have crown molding around the top of the room. Further, nearly every room has a floorboard that visually joins the floor to the wall. To create these pieces of trim around our room, we'll make use of a Loft NURBS object. The key

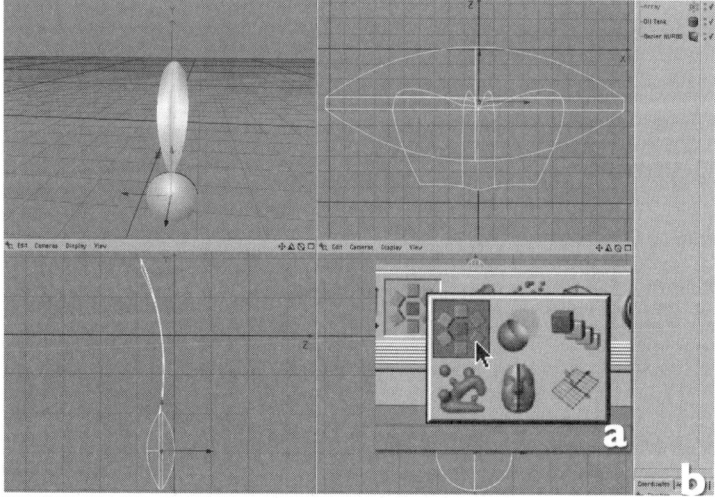

FIGURE 4.63 *(a) An Array Object. (b) Move the Array Object into position within the middle of the flower center.*

CHAPTER 4 GENERATORS (NURBS)

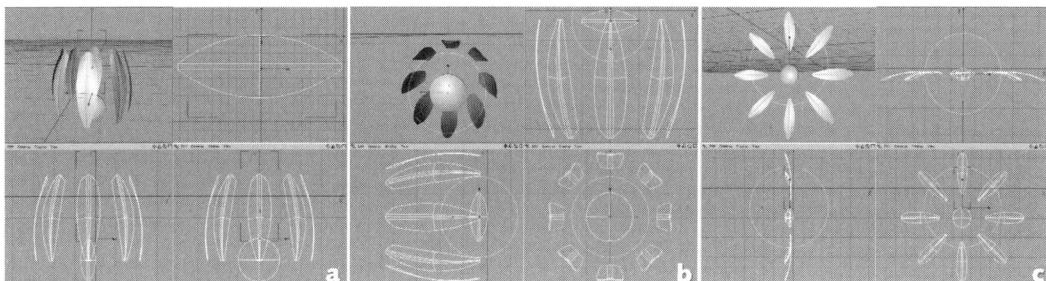

FIGURE 4.64 *Manipulating the array.*

here will be to create a cross-section of the trim that will act as a guiding "rib." Then we'll place each of these ribs at each corner of the room to guide the Loft NURBS in which direction it should be going.

Start out by drawing a spline in a non-perspective view (Figure 4.66 a). Use a corner of the wall as a reference to see that the scale and relative point placement is appropriate. Again, if you are using a combination of smooth and angular splines, a Bezier spline is often the best choice.

By using the wall as a guide, we've kept the spline even on one side, but have created another problem. Since the wall is not at (0,0,0), the newly created spline's center is far away from the actual spline (Figure 4.66 b). Correct the problem by using the Object Axis and Move Active Element tools to move the spline's axis so that it sits on the back end of the spline (Figure 4.66 b). This will

FIGURE 4.65 *Placed vase and flower.*

allow for easy placement and rotation of the spline later. Make sure that the axis is in line with the spline from a top view as well.

Once the spline's axis is properly aligned, and you're sure that the spline is at a proper height, switch your attention to a top view. To make sure that the molding is all a constant width around the room, we need to make spline guides in the corner that "respect" both walls. As such, we'll want to turn the spline 45° (Figure 4.67). This gives the soon to be created Loft NURBS a good guide in its travels as it "lofts" between guiding splines. Copy and paste this spline (the new copy will begin in the exact position as the old) and move this new spline into the next corner of the room (in this case we're moving clockwise). Make sure to once again rotate the spline to create a good corner guide.

Continue to copy and paste each spline and move it into position around the room (Figure 4.68 a). The order of these copied and pasted splines is important. When the Loft NURBS is created, it will move from spline to spline in the order they are placed as children to create the form. If one spline gets out of place,

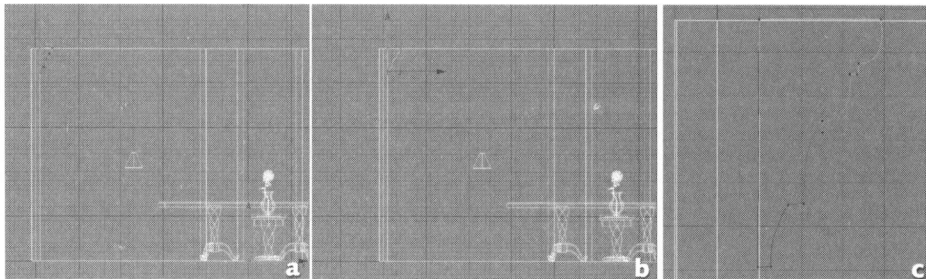

FIGURE 4.66 *(a) A simple cross-section drawn in a non-perspective view. (b) Make sure to move the spline's axis to sit on the back end to make for easy corner placement. (c) A close up of the spline.*

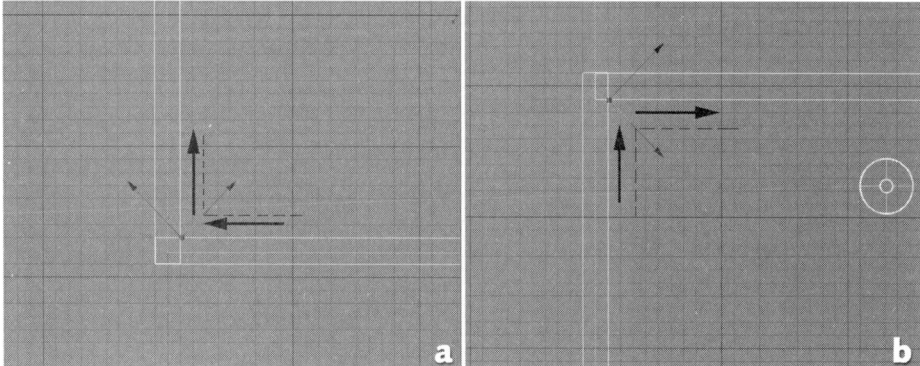

FIGURE 4.67 *Rotating the spline 45° ensures that the Loft NURBS (anticipated in black) will have a good corner to turn.*

you end up with the Loft NURBS jumping ahead to a spline, then doubling back to hit another. By copying, pasting, placing, rotating, then copying and pasting this new spline and repeating the process, you can ensure that your splines are all in the correct order. Continue to work around the room until you reach the last corner without a spline (Figure 4.68 b).

Now take each of these splines and place them one at a time as children of a Loft NURBS object. When they are all children, you'll find that the result is less than ideal (Figure 4.69 a). NURBS in general are great ways to create organic forms. As such, the default Loft NURBS tries to create nice organic interpolation between splines. To correct this, double-click the Loft NURBS icon and check the "Linear Interpolation" option to get rid of the rounded connections. While you're at it, click the Loop option so that the Loft NURBS will continue to connect the last spline back to the first (Figure 4.69 b).

Repeat this process for a floorboard (Figure 4.70).

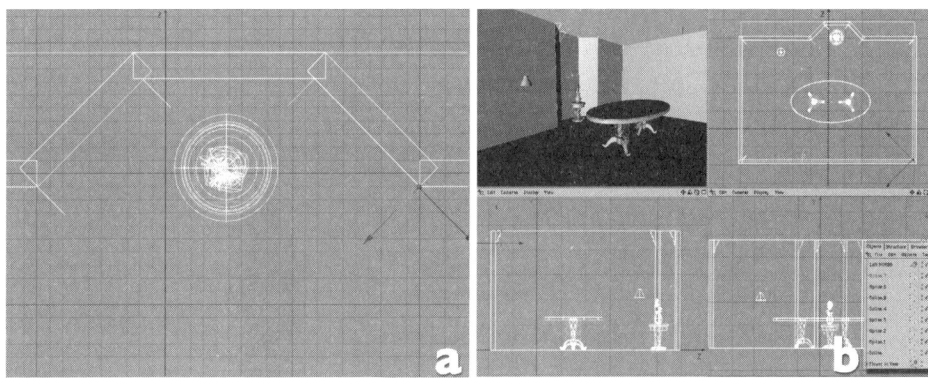

FIGURE 4.68 *(a) Make sure to place each pasted copy in the corner and rotate it appropriately. (b) Make sure every corner is covered by one spline.*

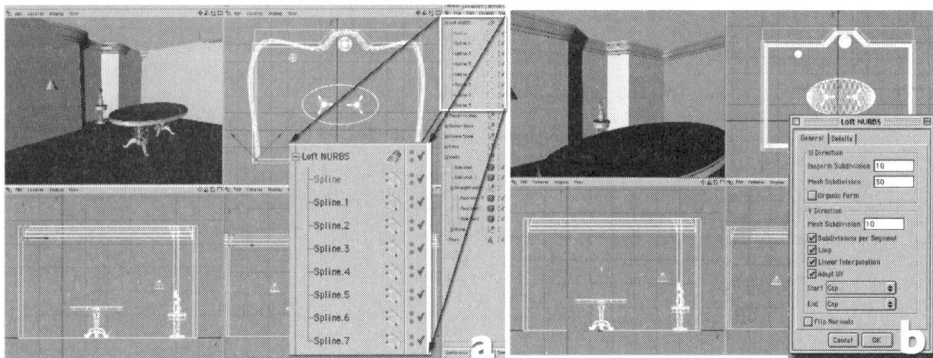

FIGURE 4.69 *(a) Problematic original Loft NURBS using non-linear interpolation. (b) The Loft NURBS dialog box with appropriate options checked.*

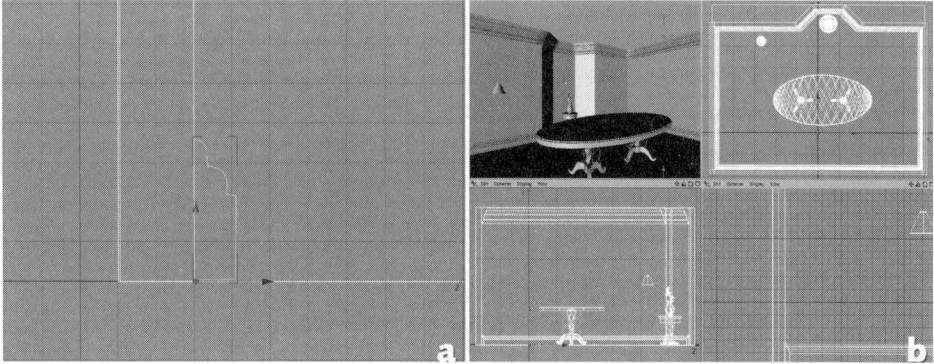

FIGURE 4.70 *Floorboard created in the same method.*

With these same techniques, doors (Figure 4.71 a) and windows (Figure 4.71 b) can be constructed. Make sure that the windows actually have a pane (Plane Object) of glass placed within it. The pane of glass will probably be a simple Polygon or Plane Primitive.

Copy, paste, scale, and place your door and window into place within the room. The biggest problem now is that there are doors and windows with no holes to place them in. To create the necessary holes, we will need to make use of Boolean modeling.

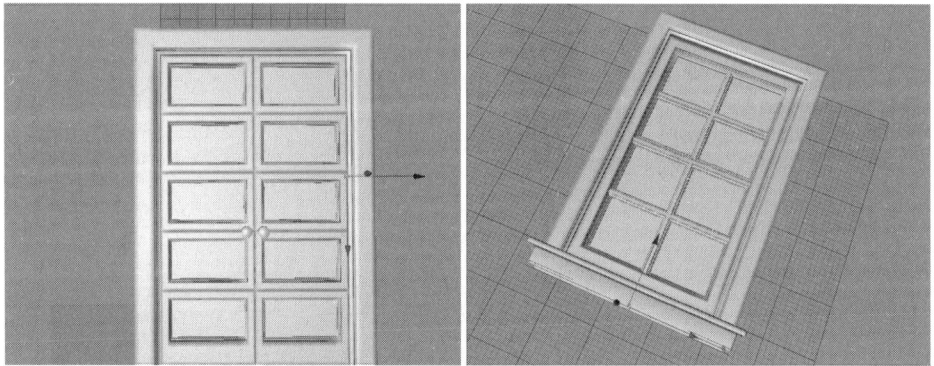

FIGURE 4.71 *Doors and windows created with Loft NURBS and extrusions.*

BOOLEAN OBJECTS

Most search engines today allow for you to search for cougar –car; or bear +teddy –roosevelt. Meaning in the first example, "find sites to do with cougars, but not the car." In the second, "find sites about bears and teddy, but none that deal with roosevelt." Boolean modeling works the same way. You get to define "take this wall, but not the block set within it, and show me the result."

Boolean Objects are created from the top command palette (Figure 4.72 a) or by going to Objects>Modeling>Boolean. The Boolean Object itself has no geometry, but rather generates forms from other objects placed as children within it. The first object is always referenced as "A" with the second being "B." If you double-click the Boolean icon in the Object Manager, you can change the function of the Boolean to perform the functions shown in Figure 4.72 (b).

For the holes where our windows and doors will go, the "A" will be the walls and the "B" will be cubes we create that are the same size as the door or window that will fill the hole. So for the window, first create a Cube Primitive that is the same width and height as the window and at least as deep as the wall it will be cutting a hole in. Move it into place so that it completely intersects the wall (Figure 4.73).

Make sure you have a Boolean Object created in your Object Manager, and drop the Cube Primitive you're using as the hole object (B). Then find the wall for the niche shown in Figure 4.74 and drop it into the Boolean Object as a child (A). Since A Subtract B is the default setting for Boolean Objects, as soon as both objects are children of the Boolean object, the Primitive Cube (B) will disappear and the result will be a clean hole in the wall (Figure 4.75). Note that now your

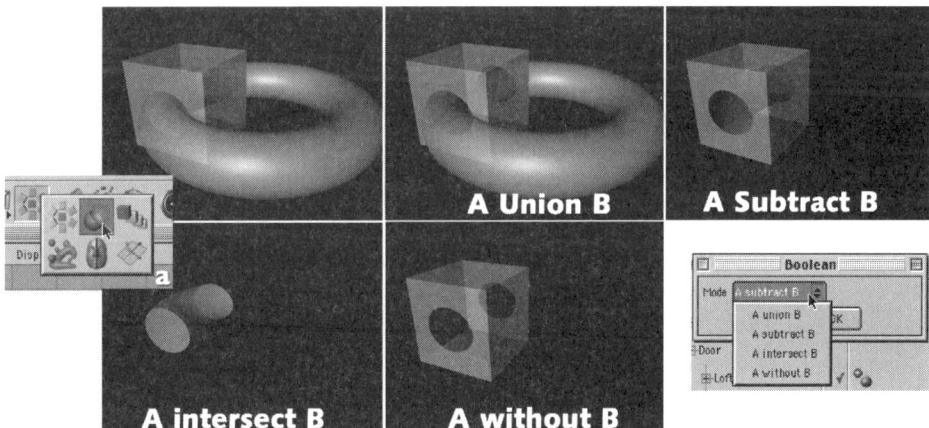

FIGURE 4.72 *(a) Creating a Boolean Object which itself contains no geometry. (b) The various functions of a Boolean Object. These are renderings with a semi-transparent texture applied to see what's happening on the inside of the object.*

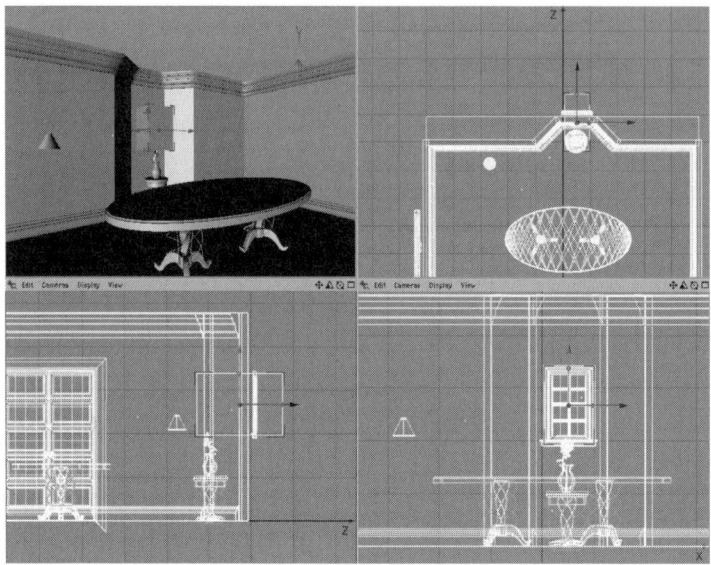

FIGURE 4.73 *To effectively use a Boolean function for A Subtract B, make sure that the shape you're using as the "hole" shape completely penetrates the wall, and is the same size as the object to be filling the hole.*

niche wall is part of a Boolean object, which you may want to rename something like "Niche Wall with Hole."

Repeat this process for the other niche walls and any other places that you'd like to place windows, and move pasted copies of the windows into the holes (Figure 4.75).

Now for the doorway it gets a bit more tricky. As before, create a Cube Primitive that is the appropriate size to cut a hole, however; this time we don't just need to cut a hold in the wall, but also in the floorboard. Boolean Objects only work with two objects or two groups. You might think that if the floorboard, the wall, and the Cube Primitive were put in a Boolean Object, all would be well. Unfortunately, the Boolean Object would subtract the second shape from the first and completely ignore the third. To solve this problem some grouping is needed.

The Cube Primitive will remain by itself; however, group the side wall where the door will be with the floorboard. Then create a Boolean Object, and make the Wall-Floorboard a group and the Cube Primitive children of it (Figure 4.76).

The next thing we'll do is create the openings in the remaining walls. To do this, we'll use an Extrude NURBS as the object that will cut the hole. Begin by creating a nice spline in the shape of the opening. Remember to draw it in a non-perspective view; preferably the one perpendicular to the wall you are to cut from (Figure 4.77 a). Create an Extrude NURBS object and make the newly drawn spline a child of it. Place the Extrude NURBS so that it intersects the appropriate wall (Figure 4.77 b).

Chapter 4 Generators (NURBS) 113

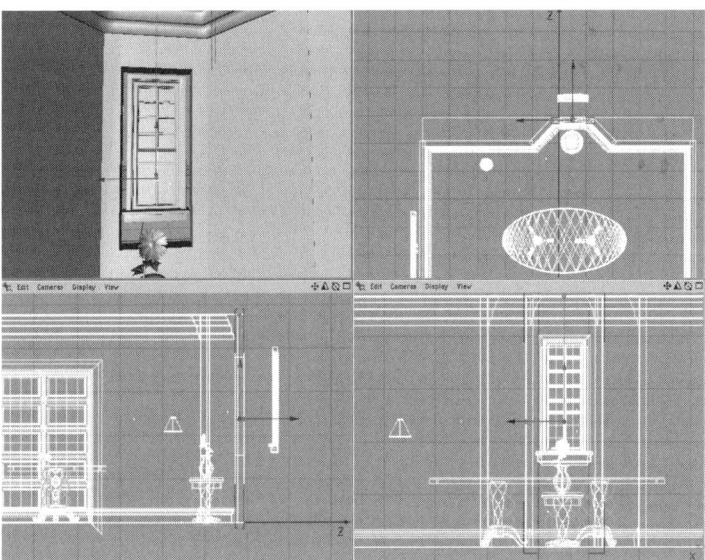

Figure 4.74 *The results of the Boolean operation. You can see right through the hole to see the window sitting outside.*

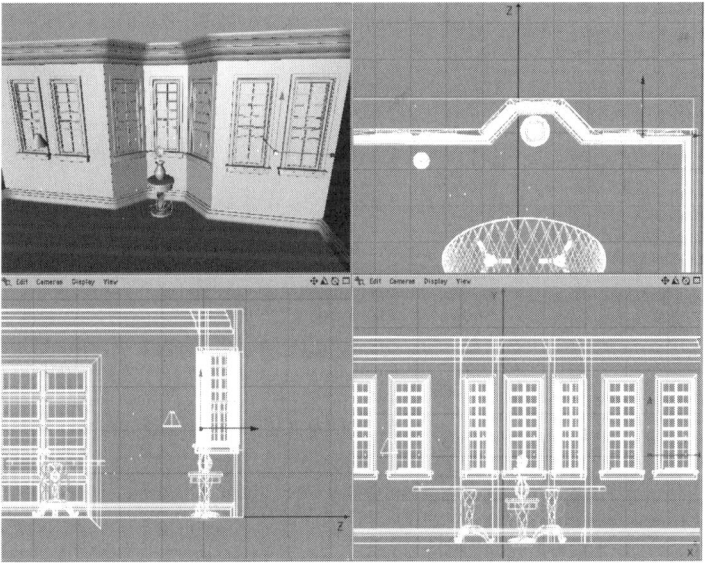

Figure 4.75 *All the windows in place set within holes.*

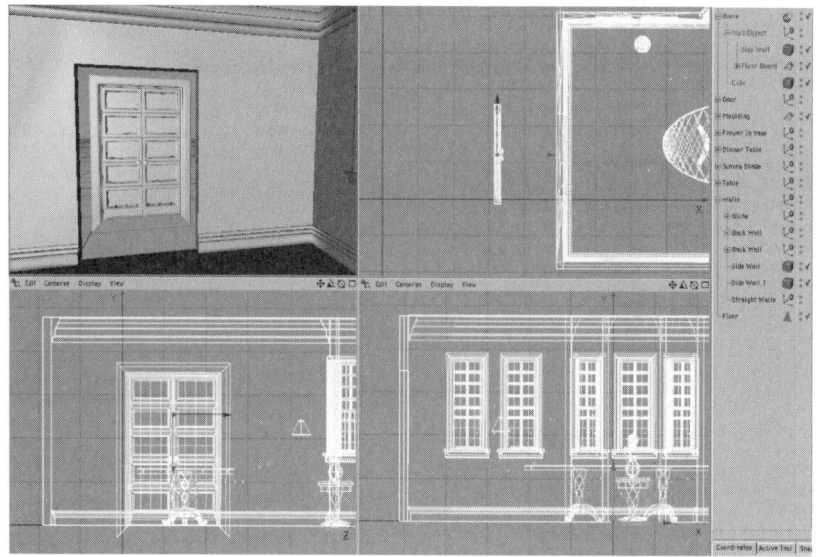

FIGURE 4.76 *Compound cut made by grouping the wall and floorboard together before placing into the Boolean Object.*

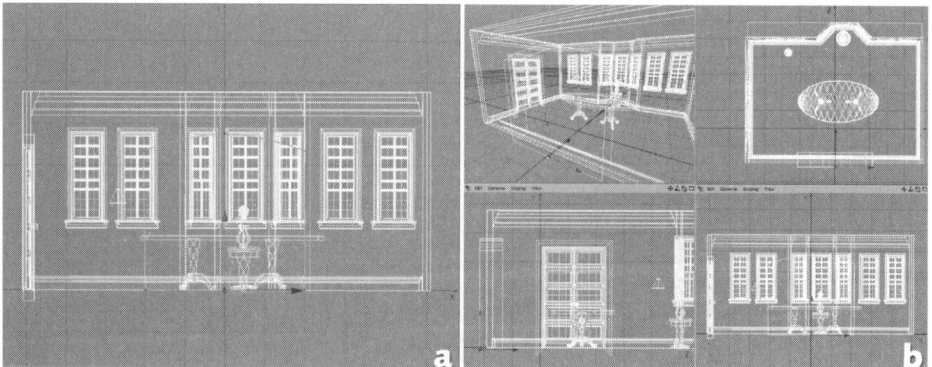

FIGURE 4.77 *Preparing for cutting archway from wall.*

Now, track down the wall you are going to cut from within your Object Manager and move it close to the Extrude NURBS object that is to be the archway hole. We're going to cut this Extrude NURBS from the wall, but we'll also need to cut it from the floorboard. But the floorboard is already tied up in another Boolean function. So what's to be done?

The trick is to use the already functioning Boolean Object. We've looked at using a group to cut from, now we need to make sure that the object we're cutting is actually a group as well. Remove the Cube Primitive that is acting as the hole for the door from the Boolean Object. Group the Cube Primitive and the Extrude NURBS together; you may want to label this new group "Holes." Now take this Holes group and replace it within the Boolean object, taking extreme care to maintain the proper order. Now, take the wall that the arch is being cut from and make it a member of the Wall-Floorboard group so C4D knows that it also should be subtracted from. Pretty complex — pay special attention to the Object Manager shown in Figure 4.78. The key is to remember, in the Boolean's eyes, there are only two objects: the group that contains all the shapes being cut from (including both walls and the floorboard), and the group of holes (including the doorway hole and the archway hole).

Copy and paste the Extrude NURBS that creates the archway and rotate it 90°. When the invisible Extrude NURBS is pasted, it will become visible as this new copy is not within the Boolean Object. Move this newly pasted Extrude NURBS into position inside the only unmolested wall. Resize it a bit smaller and then drop it into the "Holes" group of the Boolean Object we've been working with. It then will cut from the floorboard. When the last wall is placed within the Wall-Floorboard group, it too will be subtracted from — giving a result similar to Figure 4.79.

The remaining objects in the room are all built using techniques already described. Figure 4.80 shows the room from a couple of different angles. The chairs are built almost entirely out of Cube Primitives except for the seat cushion that is built with a Loft NURBS. The runner in the middle of the table is a simple

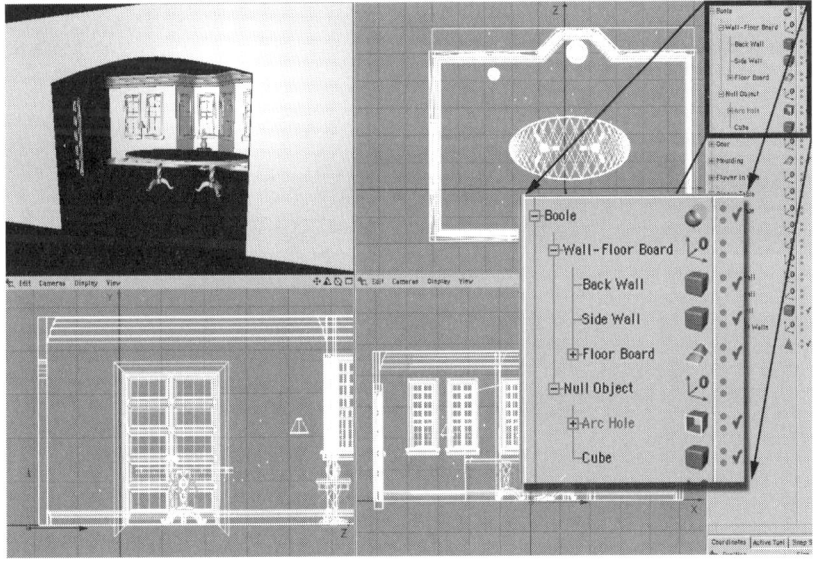

FIGURE 4.78 *The arch cut by using the already extant Boolean Object with appropriate grouping.*

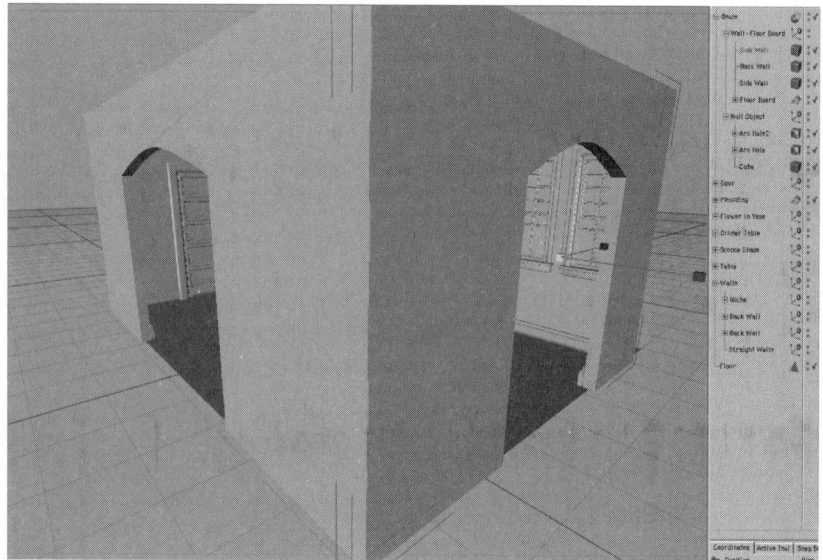

FIGURE 4.79 *Arches cut, doorways functional, and window ready.*

Bezier NURBS that was carefully edited at a points level to curve down at the edge of the tables. The bowls are Lathe NURBS.

One problem you may notice is that when we look out the arches, we see the grid of the digital world. This will be a problem later when we render and these arches open up into black voids. A common theatre trick is to place "backing flats" in holes like this. A backing flat is a simple wall that denotes the rest of the house although none of it is really built. Figure 4.81 shows the results of some carefully placed backing flats.

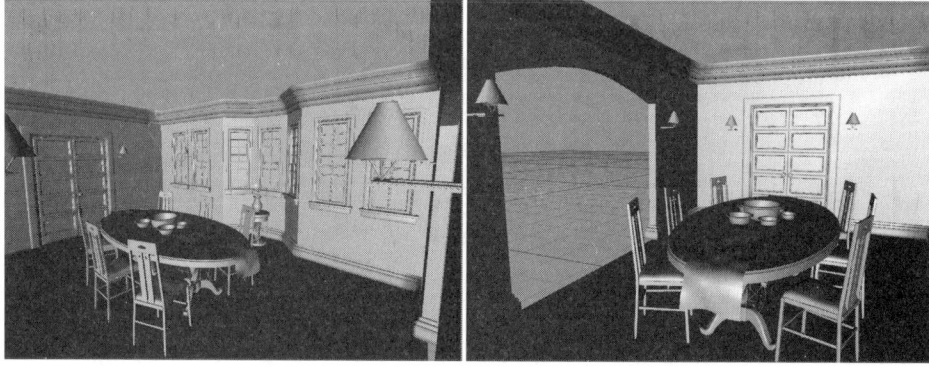

FIGURE 4.80 *The room thus far with added objects all built using techniques described thus far.*

CHAPTER 4 GENERATORS (NURBS)

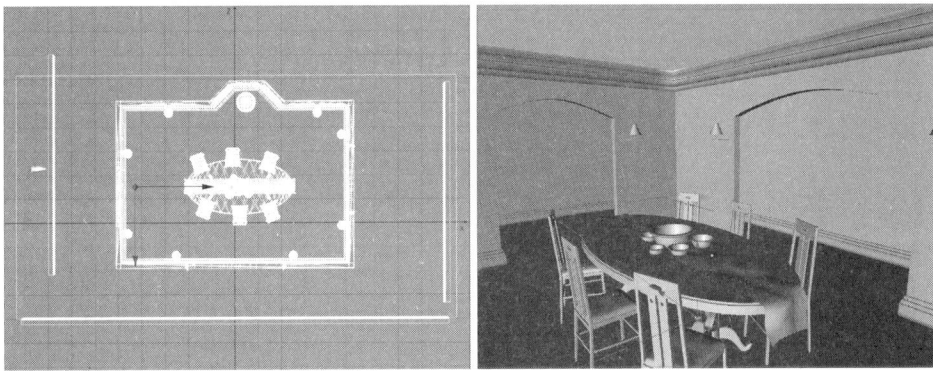

FIGURE 4.81 *Backing flats.*

And with that, we'll leave the realm of basic modeling. The coming chapters have some excellent tutorials on modeling organic forms such as human heads. There are other areas of C4D that enable other methods of modeling. However, if you master the techniques described here, you can create nearly every form imaginable.

CHAPTER 5
Modeling a Car with HyperNURBS

By Jeff Carlson

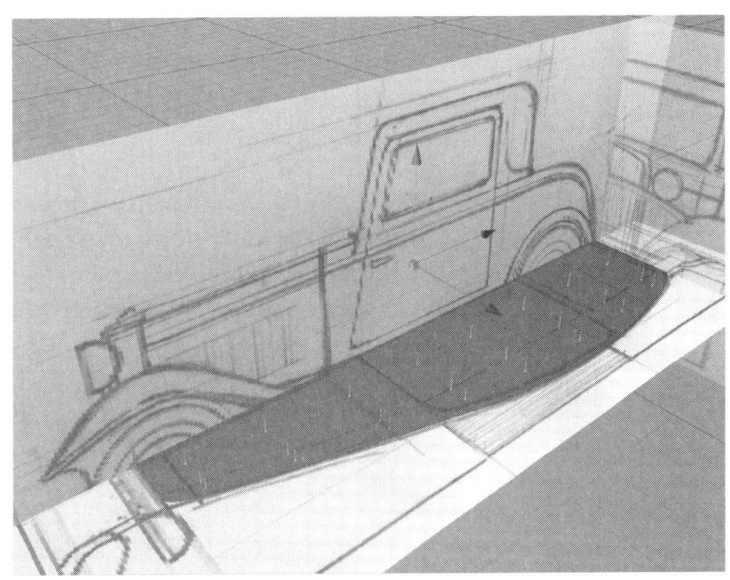

With Cinema 4D XL version 7, Maxon broadened the feature set of an already powerful 3D rendering and animation package to include a type of modeling based on subdivision surfaces. Typically, low detail meshes are affected to form much smoother and more organic models than their lack of polygons would otherwise lead to. In Cinema 4D XL, this subdivision surface modeling is implemented as HyperNURBS. HyperNURBS are used as parent objects in a hierarchy that affects the objects placed within that hierarchy to smooth them. Typically, this form of modeling is ideal for organic creations where edges and facets are undesirable. You don't see it being used for a lot of vehicles, but why not? It is one of the fastest and easiest ways to create objects once you get used to how to control the cage geometry to get the smoothed result you want. Sharper edges are possible, and fillets are automatic due to the smoothing action of the HyperNURBS parent object, so it would seem to be a great way to achieve the myriad of man-made objects that are mechanical in nature but organic in design.

To illustrate the point, I've chosen to show you how I would typically model a car. For interest sake, I've chosen an early 1930's model car that I've always been partial to. I won't bother putting an exact year and model name on it, since it is not my goal to achieve 100% accuracy to the original, but rather to merely depict the vehicle in question. Depending on your car modeling needs (whether you just need to "imply" a certain type of car or if you need to create an exact replica), you can add as much detail and accuracy to your own model as you require, using the same techniques. The accuracy of the model is limited only by the source material (be it detailed blueprints or your imagination) and, of course, the time and effort you spend on it.

Furthermore, I have gone to lengths to ensure that HyperNURBS is the main thrust of this tutorial, so much so that the car is almost entirely dependent on them. To suit your own situation though, you should never feel limited to using one technique to the exclusion of others, or to the detriment of the result. In fact, great modeling seems to come about best when you can combine a number of powerful techniques in the ideal situations for each of them. That being said, again I mention that I am only providing HyperNURBS insight to show that it can be a viable solution for a modeling a vehicle — a technique you may have otherwise not attempted.

When you start models like this, you'll probably find the amount of effort you put into planning the geometry has a direct correlation to the amount of effort you will end up spending FIXING the geometry.

While the planning stage never appeals to me (I'd just dive right in if I could), I REALLY don't like the fixing stage. When you model cars with HyperNURBS, it seems it's one or the other. I choose planning, and recommend it for you too. To begin with, I've prepared some reference pictures of the car I will model (Figure5.1 a). I have sketched a basic three-view drawing (not to any particular scale, but each view is relative to the others in dimensions), and applied them to three different planes as textures. This is a technique I personally favor over the standard background image implementation because it enables me to get right into the modeling and see in three dimensions how it relates to the reference material (Figure 5.1 b). Also, if these plane views are slid back and forth along their respective normals, you can move specific converging details together and see in 3D space where you should model these.

Cinema 4D XL doesn't allow for any direct variation of cage influence, (i.e. no point weighting to make some edges sharper than others) so you have to plan the topography of the model to control areas of varying curvatures. Areas of the cage that have a high density of polygons have a tighter influence over the underlying subdivision surface, while low density cage areas result in very loose influence over the underlying surface. It is just our luck that things like cars have a wide variety of shapes and curves to them, and furthermore, it seems that each make and model of a car brings its own unique problems to the table. The best medicine for the woes of model planning seems to be practice. Only through practice can you gain an appreciation for the numerous solutions available to you in modeling with HyperNURBS.

TUTORIAL 5.1 CAR BODY

MODELING THE BASIC SHAPE

The main thrust of modeling the car's body is going to start with the overall shape as seen from above the car, and then move into adding detail in the other views. It works smoothest to model from general to detailed with subdivision surfaces and in this car's case, the most general aspect of the body will be that it is pretty much an elongated bottle shape from above (Figure 5.2). The panel walls rise almost straight up from the outline of this basic shape. Therefore, it makes sense to begin with this first.

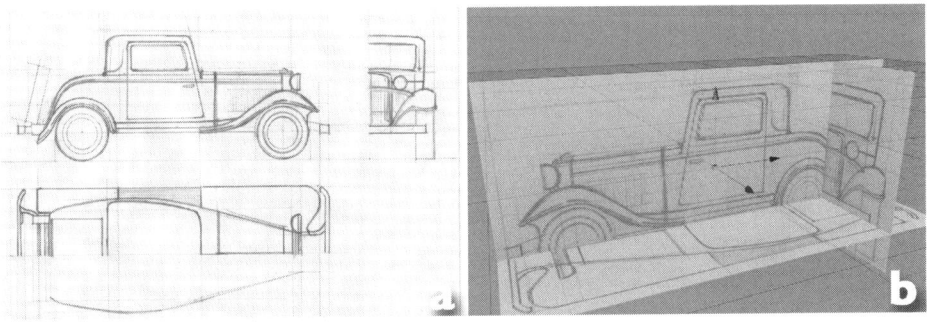

FIGURE 5.1 *(a) Planar sketches of the car to be modeled. (b) By creating three planes and applying planar drawings, you can get right into 3D space with your reference material.*

From the top view, we can lay out a simple plane that covers the area of the body (Figure 5.3). Through editing the plane's parameters, it can be made the correct maximum width and length (so as to completely cover the most outward edges of the car body), and with an appropriate segmentation. This plane is segmented eight times along the length so that the edge points may be edited to produce a sufficiently smooth curved shape that matches the top reference view. It is segmented twice along the width dimension so that one half may be deleted and the object placed within a symmetry object for ease of modeling.

Now make this plane editable. We're going to need to get right into the polygons and points, after all.

Select the half of the polygons that accounts for one side of the car (the one side that is not over the top of the reference image) and delete them. After deleting polygons, it is good practice to delete the unused points that get left behind (IF you know you aren't going to be using them again. There may be times when you will want to leave certain points in place to later use in the creation of other objects, but that is not the case here). Switch to Points mode and select all points. Run the Optimize command (Structure>Optimize) with the Unused Points checkbox selected. Since cars are symmetrical down the middle, we can reduce our workload by using a symmetry object to do half the work for us!

Drop the polygonal plane into a HyperNURBS>Symmetry>Plane hierarchy. You can see it is immediately affected by becoming smooth and rounded.

Keeping all of these polygons selected, grab the Knife tool and make some of the initial cuts that will be required in this view (Figure 5.4). The two knife cuts are based on a line that runs off the side of the rumbleseat compartment in the back. This double knife cut will allow for a hard edge with tightly rounded corners for several elements... namely, the rumbleseat cover and opening, and the side edges of the front and back windshields. Although these elements when they are completed may not all fall along this basic straight line, it is easier to

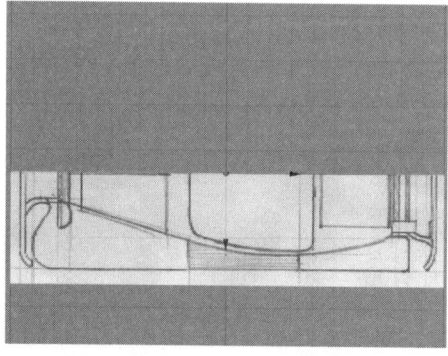

FIGURE 5.2 *This car is modeled along a general elongated bottle shape best seen from the top view.*

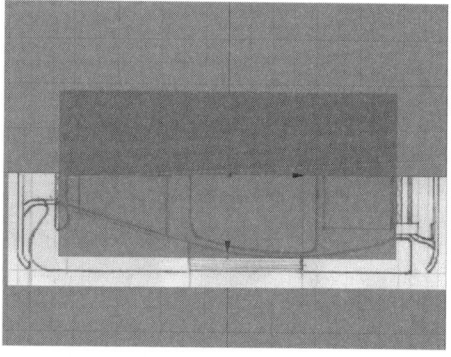

FIGURE 5.3 *Create a simple plane while you view the model through a top view.*

foresee the necessity of this cut and make it now. The reason being that in HyperNURBS modeling, it is desirable to avoid triangulation of the control cage whenever possible, and cuts like this can be made much easier straight through all polygons in a given direction before the shape of the car body disallows such modification.

Now that the structure (segmentation) is suitably handled for the one direction, we can manipulate the points to match the reference picture closely. In the first stage of this operation, I merely made the external points (along the outside edge of the plane) match up to the outer edge of the car body as per the reference picture. The interior rows of points (along the double knife cuts) are positioned in such a way that the thin polygon occurs along the points I will use to define the rumbleseat compartment edge, the rear window, and the front windshield. The remainder of this line is positioned in such a way as to merely follow the general flow of the car's outer edge (especially along the front) (Figure 5.5).

Then, two of the lines of points across the width of the car (two of the original eight segment divisions from when we made the plane) should be selected and repositioned so that they correspond to defining elements of the car in the top view — namely, being placed as the front and back edges of the cab exterior. This will be important when we begin to shape this object in other dimensions.

Switch to the side view. Make sure that the plane is positioned along the Y-axis so that it is even with the bottom of the body panels in the reference picture (Figure 5.6).

At this time, make a copy of this object hierarchy and paste it back into the scene. Then make this duplicate invisible so that we can use it later. The copy will be used for the lower car chassis and frame, which starts off from this basic shape also. I like to keep various copies of different stages of the model within the scene as I'm building it, but that's a personal modeling approach. You never

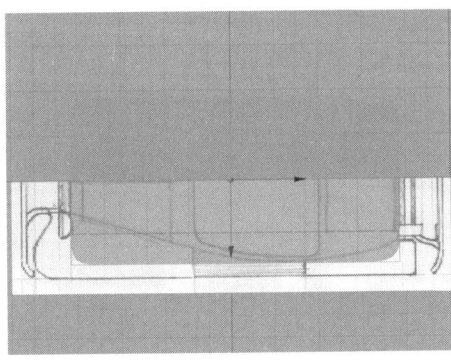

FIGURE 5.4 *Cuts made with the Knife tool.*

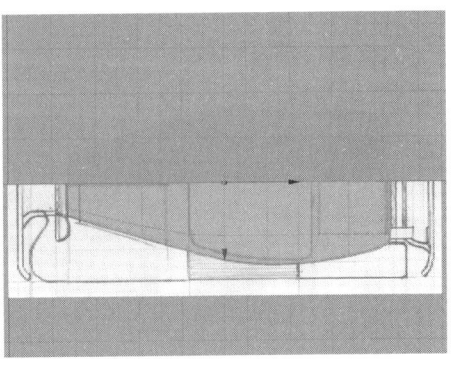

FIGURE 5.5 *Shape the remaining points into the general outline of the car body.*

know when you might need a portion of an earlier stage to go back and construct an adjoining piece, right? (Okay, I admit... I'm a digital packrat... but it works to my advantage this time!)

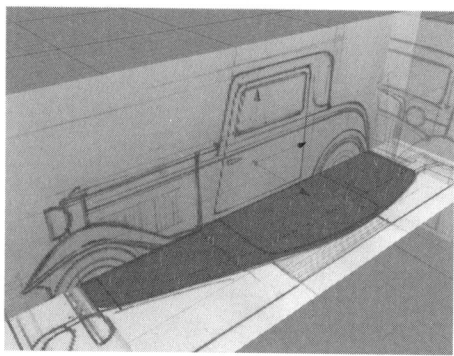

FIGURE 5.6 *Align your newly shaped plane along the Y-axis-even with the bottom of the body panels.*

Continuing on with the car body! Select all of the polygons on the plane and use the Extrude tool to extrude the polygons of the plane up along the Y-axis so that the height of the car body matches the reference picture. This will be done in two stages. For the first extrusion, the whole plane can be extruded up to the height of the top of the hood (Figure 5.7 a). From there, the polygons that make up the shape of the cab can be selected and then extruded to match the height of the car roof in the reference picture. It is a good idea to make the cab out of two extrusions initially... one extrusion that offsets the polygons just slightly from the surface of the top of the car, and the second extrusion that then extrudes the cab roof polygons the rest of the way up (Figure 5.7 b). The first thin

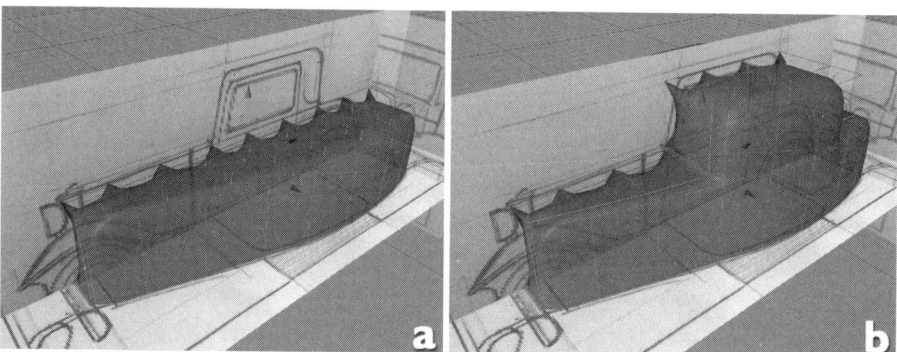

FIGURE 5.7 *(a)Extrude the plane initially to the height of the top of the hood. (b) Extrude the cab by making two extrusions to get a good "hard" transition from body to cab.*

row of polygons will keep the transition from the car body to the cab portion fairly tight and controlled; otherwise, the curvature between the two parts will be far too loose and organic.

Because the extrusion process creates "walls" along the outside of the polygons being extruded, there will be some unwanted polygons created along the plane of symmetry (Figure 5.8 a). This is just an unavoidable byproduct of working with geometry changes along the edge of a symmetrical object. You have to remember that certain tools will require some cleanup. Remembering is not hard though, as these extra polygons will cause a visible disturbance in the appearance of the HyperNURBS mesh. These polygons are unnecessary and should be selected and deleted. It is easiest to get at them by temporarily disabling the symmetry object (change the green checkmark in the Object Manager to a red "X"), hiding any reference material that may be in the way, and then selecting and deleting the offending polygons (Figure 5.8 b). Again, after deleting these polygons, it is a good idea to switch to Points mode, select all points, and then optimize them to get rid of unused points.

To complete the most basic of shaping for the car body now, some slope must be added to the front portion of the cab. A look at the line of the door also indicates that the same slope is adopted by this opening and continues down the side of the car (Figure 5.9 a). If the polygons in this area were to remain uniform and vertical, we would be at a loss for how to complete the door opening. Select the points that make the top front edge of the cab, and the corresponding points on the bottom edge of the car, and move them into place along the Z-axis so that the polygon edges are aligned with the slope of the cab and door edge (Figure 5.9 b).

As a result of changing the Z-axis position of those points when you add that slope, you'll find if you switch back to the top view that these points no longer are perfectly in line with the general shape of the car body (Figure 5.10 a).

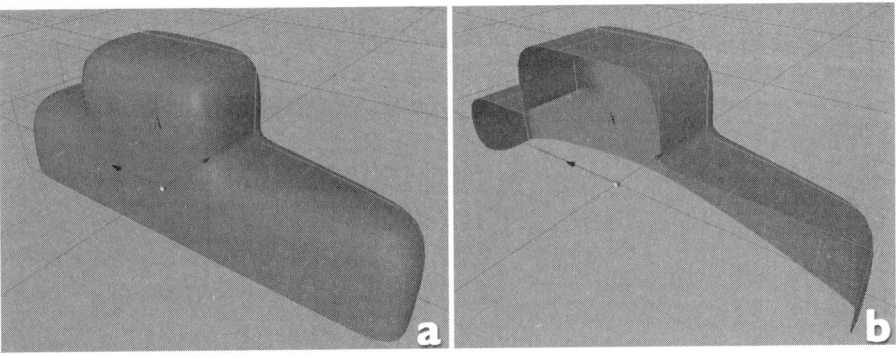

FIGURE 5.8 *(a) Unwanted polygons created through the extrusion process. (b) Delete the offending middle polygons.*

It is important after manipulation of points and polygons to make sure you check other views and make adjustments as necessary. In this case, the fix is simple; we just select each point and realign it to the curve of the car body as seen in the top view (Figure 5.10 b)

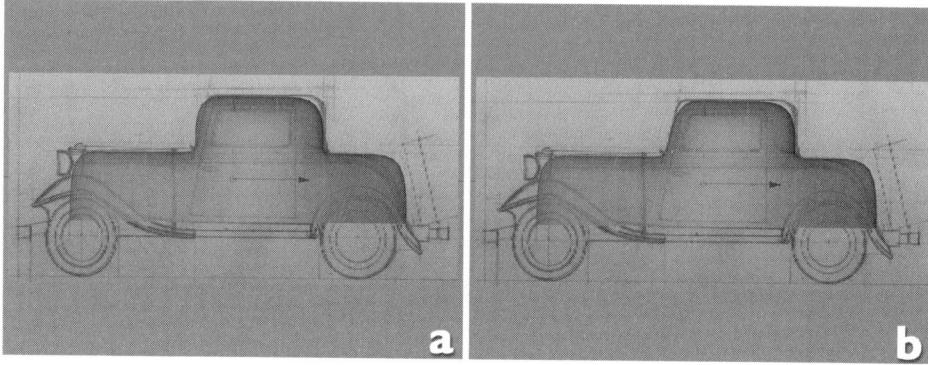

FIGURE 5.9 *(a) To create an effective cab, some additional adjustments must be made. Select the points at the front of the cab, and the point at the bottom of the car in the same vertical line as the cab points. (b) Arrange the points to allow for the slope of the cab front and prepare for the slope of the door.*

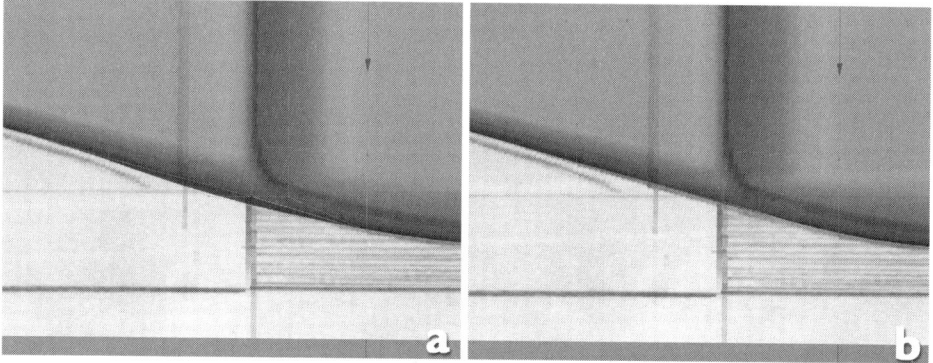

FIGURE 5.10 *(a) After adjusting the points, a view from the top reveals points out of position with the general curvature of the car. (b) Readjust these moved points to match curvature of the car body.*

MODELING MORE DETAILED SHAPE

SUBDIVIDING FOR THE FUTURE

So far we've managed to give ourselves the basic foundation of a car model. From here we can begin to analyze the car and continue to model in elements that will add more detail and begin to make it recognizable.

From the side view, we can systematically begin subdividing the low poly cage with the Knife tool to define these elements. Since the basic shape of the car was achieved, most of these knife cuts will not do much to affect the general shape other than sharpen certain areas. These areas can be softened up again later with some slight point manipulation. The main aspects we want to provide geometry for in this view are things such as the panel edges for doors (including windows) and the hood, and the rumbleseat opening.

This part becomes the most difficult to complete since it requires a level of planning and forethought that can only be achieved or understood with plenty of practice using HyperNURBS in these situations. It has been my experience that I almost always have to bang out a quick "test model" to check to see if my planning is adequate and what sort of pitfalls I may encounter and have to work around. Once you get the basic feel of when certain techniques work and what you need to keep in mind when you build certain common elements like sharp panel or door edges, this "test" phase becomes more of a formality. For our purposes, let's assume I have already tested my plan (I have), and for now I will simply explain the conclusions and reasoning behind my plan.

From the reference picture, the first areas to consider are elements that need clear definition. These are crucial to the success of the model, and include the doors and windows, and panel edges. These are areas that will likely be breaks in the mesh, as well as being areas that will provide starting points for operations such as extrudes, smooth shifts, extrude inners, etc. We need to look at areas which will require edges to be made to support hard changes in geometry in the model as we continue. For this reason knife cuts must be added in the following areas:

Top and Bottom Door Edges:

These door edges are defined by a double knife cut for each door edge, both top and bottom. The knife cuts are made straight across the entire selected body of the car and pass directly along the lines in the reference image that define the door edges (Figure 5.11).

NOTE

Knife cuts to subdivide meshes in this manner work best when they are made straight along the existing mesh in such a way as to avoid causing any triangulation. Triangulation is something to be avoided in a lot of cases when you deal with HyperNURBS, because it tends to make the subdivision surface beneath the low polygon cage somewhat messy. Quad polygons make for nice clean meshes... (This whole idea is difficult to explain, but if you'd like to see the difference firsthand, just drop a low polygon editable sphere into a HyperNURBS parent and view the subdivided mesh in Wireframe mode. Then select all polygons of the control cage and run the Triangulate command. Suddenly the underlying mesh is constructed much more strangely.) If knife cuts were made to just a few polygons, the surrounding unselected polygons would triangulate to accommodate the change in structure. For that reason, knife cuts are best planned and made straight through all polygons of a model.

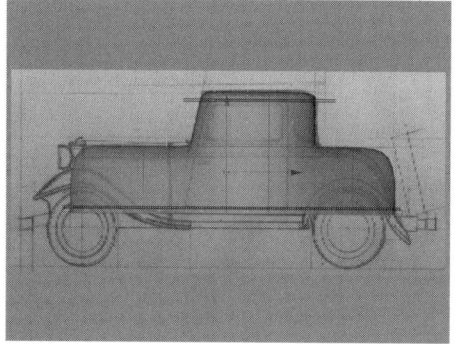

FIGURE 5.11 *Knife cuts to create door edges. Make sure to cut completely through the entire car body.*

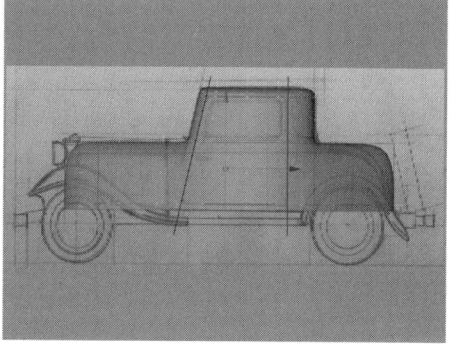

FIGURE 5.12 *Single knife cuts for door edges.*

The edges of the door will be used to split the geometry from the main body of the car so that doors are separate and can be constructed to open if you so choose. For that reason alone, we will need to define the door edges with one knife cut, so as to define the geometry that will make up the door. However, because the HyperNURBS smooth and round exposed corners when we split the object, it is important that we retain control of exactly where the edges and corners are positioned. The smoothing action of the HyperNURBS Object will completely disregard the accuracy of the edge defined with a single cut. If we were to separate the door from the body right now, we would find that the corners of the door opening would be very loose and organic, and completely inappropriate if we are attempting to match our reference images! The control cage of a HyperNURBS object has tighter influence over the underlying mesh when the polygons are smaller and the polygon edges closer together. With tighter, narrower polygons, much sharper edges and corners can be constructed. Basically, areas of greater detail in the low polygon cage allow for greater control of detail in the resultant surface. Following that reasoning, to make sharper corners on the door opening, we need some geometry that will tighten up the control cage's influence in that area, and that is why we go for the second knife cut very close to the first. When the door polygons are separated now, one knife cut essentially defines the door edge, and the other pins the corners tightly in place. It is possible to double cut ALL edges that define the opening, but I have found this is overkill for the extra control it offers. If the corner is tight enough in one direction, it allows control over the shape of the more gradual uncontrolled edge, and the result is that it is very difficult to find a reason why you wouldn't just keep it simple!

Front and Back Door Edges:
These again are cut in to define the points at which the door object will become separate from the car body object. They are based on the corresponding lines on the reference picture for these door edges, and pass right through all polygons of the car body object to avoid triangulation (Figure 5.12). These door edges will be fine as single cuts for the reason I mentioned above... that enough control over the sharpness of the door opening corners is gained by double cutting the top and bottom edges. There is no need to double cut these as well.

Main Window Edges:
For the side windows, the main edge can be defined by selecting the polygons on the upper half of the door between the top door edge and the double line that separates the lower car body and the cab (Figure 5.13 a). Then, an Extrude Inner performed on these polygons causes the polygon edges to be offset inwards toward the edges of the window as defined in our reference picture (Figure 5.13 b). It may be necessary to select certain points after making this inner extrusion to move them into proper positioning according to the reference picture.

Top and Bottom Window Edges:
A simple Extrude Inner provides only one line to define the window edge so when the window is split away from the door, the rounding on the corners would again be too organic and loose. To combat this, we can double up on the top and bottom edges of the window by making knife cuts through the door and window polygons (just make sure all polygons on the model are selected). These cuts need to be made to cross inside of the area of the window; other-

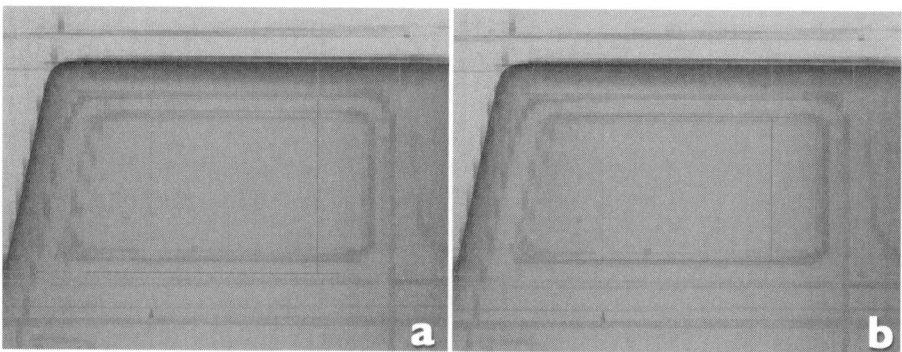

FIGURE 5.13 *(a) Side window edges are defined by first selecting the polygons that will make the window (b) 19 and using Extrude Inner to offset the polygon edges.*

wise, they will have no effect on the sharpness of the corners. When the cuts are properly made, we end up with a similar structure defining the window edge as we have defined the door edge (Figure 5.14).

Front and Back Hood Edges:

The hood, or engine cover, on this model of car is a gull-wing panel that starts just behind the chrome grill and terminates just in front of the cab front. Should we want to enable our model's engine cover to open (for instance to display the fine replica engine you may choose to model for it that I will NOT be showing you how to make) we will need the panels to be separate from the main car body. A single knife cut for each edge would be sufficient to separate the panels; however, we would run into the problem of the HyperNURBS rounding the corners of the separated panels. Furthermore, a double knife cut may sharpen these corners, as we planned with the door edges and windows, however, it

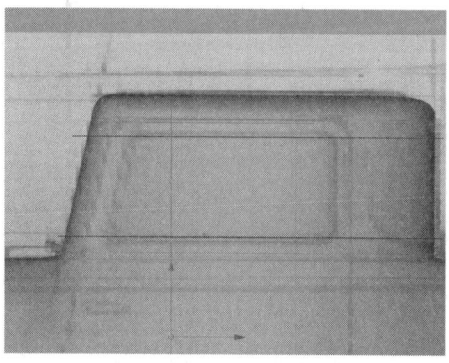

FIGURE 5.14 *Additional knife cuts made to keep corners tight and looking manufactured.*

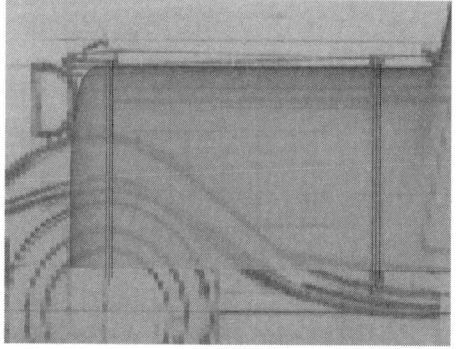

FIGURE 5.15 *Still further knife cuts allow for appropriate panel edges.*

would only sharpen the corners of either the car body or the engine cover, depending on which object the narrow polygons got included in.

The split is going to be going right through the front of the car from top to bottom, and we will need sharp edges on both sides of the separation point. Therefore, in this case, a triple knife cut is required for each panel edge. The middle knife cut is the separation point, while the outer two cuts sharpen the corners for each of the car body and engine cover edges (Figure 5.15).

Assorted Other Subdivisions:

A vertical cut can be made on the car body just behind the back wall of the cab. This will provide the top (forward) edge of the rumbleseat opening. This edge only needs to be a single knife cut since the double lines we added way back when we were first structuring the plane in the top view will provide the control over sharpening the corners we need.

Three subdivisions running the length of the car body provide the final cuts we make with the knife tool in the side view. The topmost cut runs along the horizontal joint of the engine cover, where the panel will further be separated to correctly create the gull-wing effect. The next knife cut runs horizontally along the body and achieves two things. One is that it will help shape the edge of the car body around the rear wheel well (it is important to position this cut just on the edge of the rear fender in the reference picture). The other is that it will provide the lower (rear) edge for the rumbleseat opening. The final knife cut is made along the body about midway between the previous one and the double knife cut that defines the lower door edge. This knife cut simply will help the back end of the car hold some of its shape when the rumbleseat panel is split from the rest of the car body (Figure 5.16).

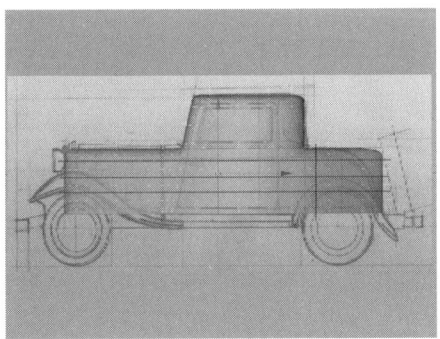

FIGURE 5.16 *Added subdivisions also created with the Knife tool.*

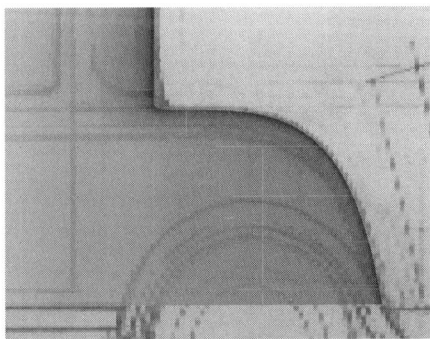

FIGURE 5.17 *Constrained (along the Z-axis) movement to create the appropriate trunk slope. Ensure that while doing this you are moving the points both on the outer side of the car and the inner plane.*

SHAPING THE RESULTS

TRUNK SLOPE

Now that we've effectively cut up our basic model into subdivisions that will facilitate further modeling, we can move on with the detailed shaping of the car body. The first portion I've concentrated on is to pull the shape of the trunk area into line. Looking at our side view reference picture, the trunk is very rounded. In Points mode, the points along the back edge of the trunk can be pulled into place over the top of the reference image to create this same slope.

Working strictly in the side view, disable the Only Select Visible Elements option in the Active Tool Manager for the Selection tool. Now select the points along the back edge of the trunk and move them constrained along the Z-axis until they line up with the reference image. One set of points near the top of the curve may need to be moved down on the Y-axis to match the curve (Figure 5.17).

The knife cuts we made give us enough subdivision on the back end that with the HyperNURBS rounding the mesh, we have enough control over the slope to accurately match our reference. So it looks as if that will be sufficient from this view.

But wait! This is 3D, and now that we've moved these points into place along the Z- and Y-axes, we shouldn't forget about the third axis! Switch to the top view and have a look. In moving the points forward on the Z-axis, we brought the edge points that were shaped to the overhead view out of alignment (Figure 5.18 a). These points along the outside edge of the trunk should actually follow the basic bottle shaped curvature of the car body as seen from the top view. In this case, the fix requires nothing more than selecting these points one at a time and moving them (constrained along the X-axis) back into alignment with the

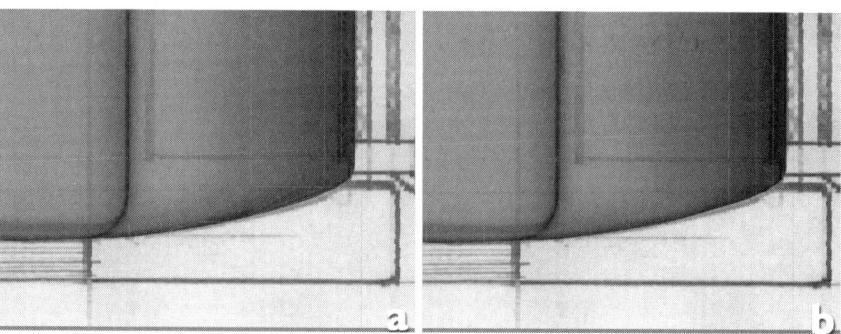

FIGURE 5.18 *(a) In moving our points in side view, some points have been misaligned. (b) Upon realignment, the trunk is complete.*

body's shape in the top view reference. Our trunk curvature should now be complete! (Figure 5.18 b).

Around the outside of the rear fender, there is a portion of this car body that is cut away that allows for the fender piece to connect to the car frame. This cut away portion must follow the curvature of the outside of the fender pretty well for two reasons: one being that we want it to look good, and the second more important one being that we are going to use the geometry from THIS part of the model to make THAT part of the model!

From the side view, select the polygons that roughly cover the portion of the wheel and fender visible in our reference image (Figure 5.19 a). Using the Extrude Inner tool, we create an inner "ring" of sorts, which will further allow us to modify the shape of the cut away section (Figure 5.19 b).

Delete the original polygons so that the ring of polygons created with the Extrude Inner operation lines an opening in the car body. Then delete the lower polygons of the ring. You should be left with a really rudimentary square cut away that only barely resembles what we want (Figure 5.20).

Now comes the fun part! Point manipulation!

Working strictly in the side view at first, select each point that lines the cut away opening and move it so that the round shape of the fender begins to be defined. You may need to move adjacent points on the mesh to accommodate these edge points, but the key thing to remember is just to try and make the transition from car body polygons to fender edge appear as natural and uniform as possible. Avoid any radically shaped polygons, and everything should work out easily enough (Figure 5.21).

Once the point placement has been solved for the side view, it is important to remember the placement of these points from the top view. Because they are positioned differently again with respect to the Z-axis, they will be out of line with the car body contour as seen from the top view.

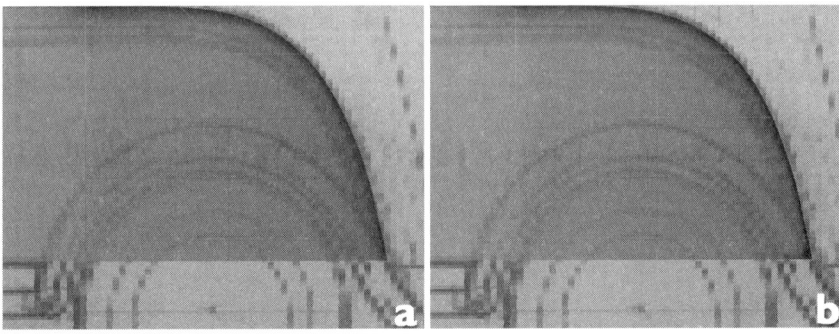

FIGURE 5.19 *(a) Select the polygons in the general area of the wheel and fender area. (b) Use the Extrude Inner tool to create an inset ring of necessary polygons.*

FIGURE 5.20 *By deleting the newly created polygons, we are left with an approximation of the wheel well.*

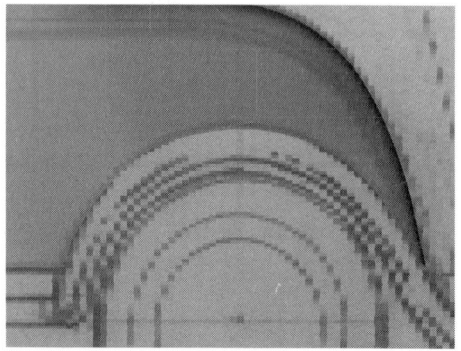

FIGURE 5.21 *With careful point manipulation, the fender area can be accurately modeled.*

It is best to select each point that was moved one by one and check it in the top view. Move it constrained along the X-axis back into alignment with the body shape in the top reference picture. This point manipulation may seem arduous at first, but when you think about it, when you get good at manipulating points and polygons, you've gotten good at the root elements that all 3D mesh modeling stems from! (Well, that's the thought that keeps me going anyway!)

The end result of aligning these edge points in the X-axis should leave you with a perfectly round cut away opening that closely matches our reference.

SHAPING THE WINDOWS

The rear window is smaller than the polygon edges we made with our knife cuts would dictate right now. We made those cuts, though, with the idea that generalized cuts could be used to define prominent features of common elements. From there, certain manipulations would have to be made to adapt the geometry to each element. The outside vertical edges of this rear window are defined by the same double cut that we used along the length of the car body from the top view that also defined the edges of the rumbleseat opening (which is wider) and the front windshield (which is wider still). However, to make our rear window, we need to adapt the polygon edges to fit more appropriately. In this case, the corner edge simply needs to be moved along the back wall of the cab inwards to make a shorter, narrower window opening. (Figure 5.22)

The side window should not require any modification like this, since it was defined directly with knife cuts made in the side view. The front windshield, however, needs the polygon edges surrounding it widened so that the window takes up most of the front of the cab surface. (Figure 5.23)

FIGURE 5.22 *Window forms can be refined by simply adjusting the points of the HyperNURBS cage.*

FIGURE 5.23 *Adjusting the front windshield.*

Curving the Hood:

To give the hood a slightly rounded appearance, select all polygons on the upper hood surface except for the ones along the outermost edge. Move these polygons upwards on the Y-axis to raise them a little over the level of the hood (Figure 5.24 a). Next, select the points in the middle of the hood that lie on the plane of symmetry and move them upwards on the Y-axis so that more slope is added to the hood (Figure 5.24 b).

Rounding the Cab:

There's no magic secret to this operation either. This is merely all point manipulation while you watch the Editor window for the visual feedback. Selecting various rows of points and individual points, start shaping the cab roof to the

FIGURE 5.24 *(a) To form the hood, select the polygons that would compose the hood and move them upwards slightly along the Y-axis. (b) Further refine the form by adjusting the middle points. Make sure to move them only along the Y-axis to avoid tears in the ultimate symmetry object.*

shape you want by moving the points into place. Try to work from general to specific, so that you can select the top row of edge points all at once, for example, and move them simultaneously (Figure 5.25 a). Then select some of the central polygons of the roof and raise them to provide a little bit of roundness to the top (Figure 5.25 b and Figure 5.26 a). After the general rounding is done, you can begin selecting individual points and tweak them to taste. Before long, the roof will look fairly natural and accurate (Figure 5.26 b and Figure 5.27).

Engine Cover Curvature:

Along the bottom edge of the engine cover panels, the panel curves slightly to sit over top of the front fenders. Where the front fenders meet the car frame, the curvature is much less than where the fenders flare overtop the wheels, but the curvature is visible nonetheless. From the side view, simply move selected points into position (constrained along the Y-axis) in Figure 5.28. Because they are only moved upwards on the Y-axis, there is no need to adjust them from the

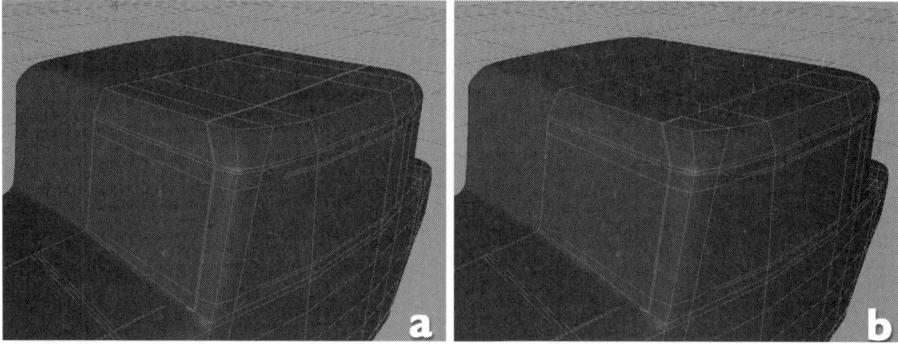

FIGURE 5.25 *(a) To round the cab begin generally, by moving entire collections of points. (b) Continue shaping by selecting large groups of polygons and adjusting their height.*

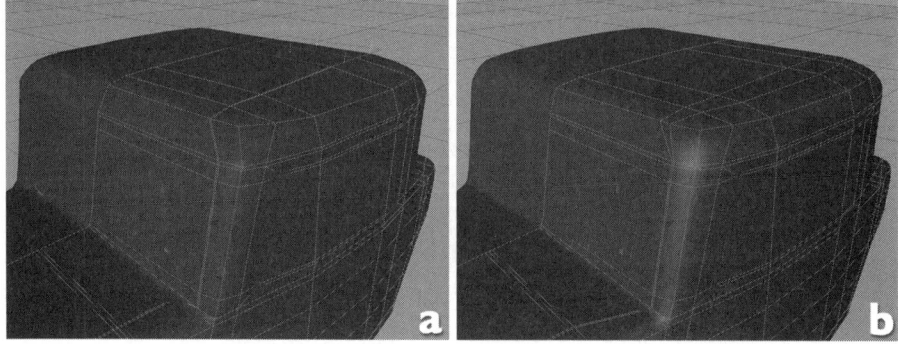

FIGURE 5.26 *(a) By selecting continually smaller collections of polygons, the adjusting can become more and more precise. (b) Finally, after general polygon editing is completed, get as detailed as needed by altering points.*

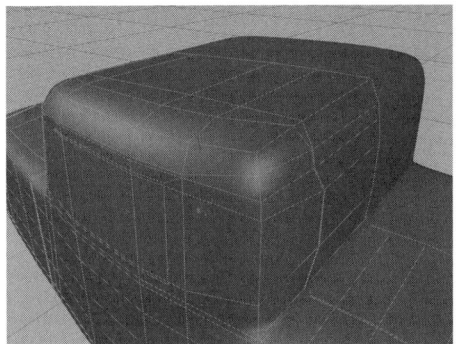 

FIGURE 5.27 *The final cab shape.* FIGURE 5.28 *Appropriate points to select to create engine cover curvature.*

top view to realign them to the body curvature… they will not have been affected in that direction.

And with that, the shaping of the car body is pretty much complete. There may be minor tweaks to take care of as the need arises further on, but for now, the shape of the car body is sufficient to begin splitting it up into the various panels.

SPLITTING THE BODY

The process involved in splitting for all of the various panels is to select the polygons that will form the new object, and use the Split command (in the Surface submenu of the Structure menu). The new object is formed out of duplicates of those polygons. It can then be organized under the car's hierarchy so that it also gets treated with the Symmetry and HyperNURBS parents (group multiple objects under Null Objects to have the Symmetry and HyperNURBS parents affect the whole group). Once the new object is made, you can return to the original object and delete the selected polygons that became the separate object. (Remember, after deleting polygons, you can switch to Points mode and optimize for unused points.)

That being said, you can apply this method to the following areas:

Rumbleseat:

Select the polygons that make up the surface of the rumbleseat compartment, including the narrow polygons on the side edges. These polygons are to be left on the compartment cover as they make corners of the compartment panel sharp and controlled; meanwhile, the double cut on the corners of the opening keeps those corners sharp. When this panel is split away from the main body, the shapes retain their fit even when the HyperNURBS rounding takes effect. Split these polygons from the car body and rename it "Rumbleseat". (Figure 5.29)

Rear Window:

The polygons for this split include the narrow one on the outside vertical edge. These polygons can be split away and renamed something like "Rear Window Trim". (Yes, we'll be using these window polygons later!) (See Figure 5.30.)

Door:

Select all polygons that make up the door, including the narrow polygons created by the double knife cuts on the top and bottom door edges. Make sure to include the window polygons as well. We will split those off the door object we create. Split these door polygons away from the car body and call the new object "Door" (or something equally descriptive!). (See Figure 5.31.)

Door Window:

Now select the polygons from the newly made door object that form the door window. These include the narrow polygons at the top and bottom edges of the window. Split these from the door object and rename the new window object "Door Window Trim" (Figure 5.32).

Front Windshield:

The polygons that make up the front window include the narrow vertical polygons on the side edges. Split these from the main car object and rename the new object "Windshield Trim".

Engine Cover:

Select the polygons that make up the engine cover, from the plane of symmetry right down to the bottom edge of the car body. These should include a row of narrow polygons on each side of the cover panel. Split this engine cover off from the main body and rename it "Engine Cover" (Figure 5.33 a).

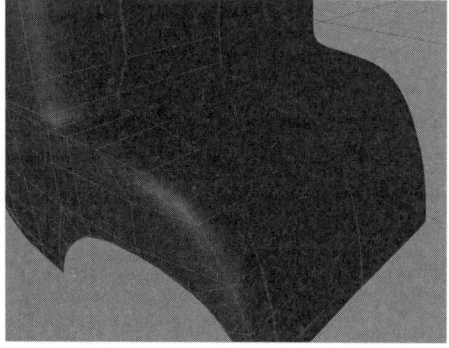

FIGURE 5.29 *Adjusting polygons needed for the rumbleseat.*

FIGURE 5.30 *Splitting polygons for the rear window.*

FIGURE 5.31 *Splitting door polygons.*

FIGURE 5.32 *Splitting door window selection.*

Lower Engine Cover:
Select the polygons that make up the side part of the engine cover (but leave one row of polygons at the top of the sidewall unselected), and split these from the engine cover object (Figure 5.33 b).

Front Grill Base:
This is the remaining piece at the front of the car that is now unattached to the main body of the car, but still a part of the car body object. It can be split to form its own object, just so that it will not act as part of the main body when you work with it (Figure 5.34).

PANEL THICKNESS
Thickening the panels is mainly for aesthetic value. You can see now that all the parts are separated into various objects, that the "paper thin" appearance

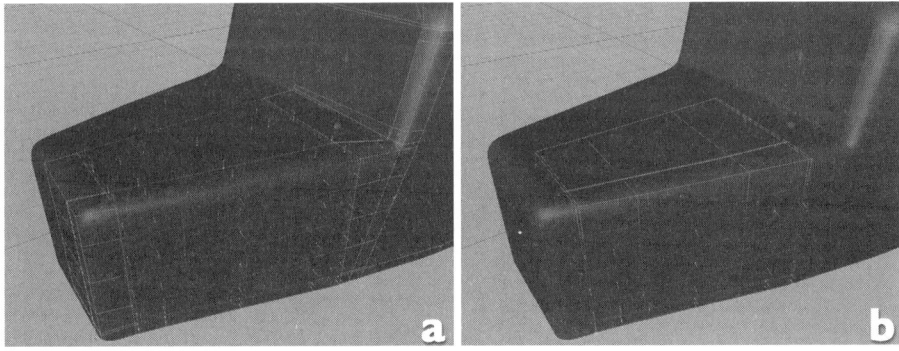
FIGURE 5.33 *Splitting engine cover polygons.*

detracts greatly from the look of the car. We need to give it some weight, some dimension!

The easiest way to add thickness to simple polygonal objects of this "shell" nature is to use the Extrude or Smooth Shift functions on duplicate polygons of the object to move them inwards towards the center of the model from the original. This works very well for simple objects like doors, trunks, hoods, windows, etc. but can get a little less useful for more complicated parts like the main body of a car. It generally works when the bends and curves of a model are not too extreme and there is plenty of room for the thickness to be generated without overlapping geometry and twisting normals.

This car body is simple enough that the Extrusion method will work well on all parts. Had it been a more complex car body with tighter polygon structure, some thickness may have had to be added with manual polygon creation. I'm glad I don't have to subject you to that right now!

To introduce the mechanics of this method, we'll start out with an easy piece and walk through that one. All other pieces will be similar in procedure.

Rumbleseat Cover:

With only the rumbleseat cover visible in the Editor window (it's just easier to see this way!), select all polygons. The normals of the selected polygons should all be facing outwards towards the exterior of the car (Figure 5.35). Try to imagine this shell as the outer surface of the car panel, and that what we are going to do is create a back surface and move it inwards towards the interior of the model. Using the Copy and Paste commands from the Structure Manager (in Polygon mode), make duplicates of these polygons. When these polygons are pasted, it is likely that the object in the Editor view will look extremely strange. This is due to two identical polygonal surfaces actually being part of the same

FIGURE 5.34 *Splitting grill base polygons.*

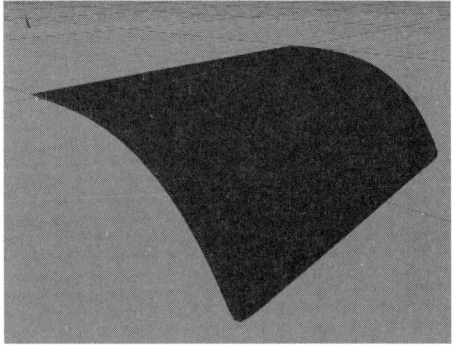

FIGURE 5.35 *Polygons with appropriately placed normals to be used for adding thickness to the rumbleseat cover.*

object but existing in the same space while they attempt to be smoothed by the HyperNURBS parent. I know I have difficulty fathoming that, and I'm not surprised that the computer has problems too! We don't need to be alarmed, though, since those polygons won't be staying there for long.

Without changing which polygons are selected, activate the Reverse Normals command. This flips the selected duplicate polygon normals over so they are now a surface facing the interior of the car (Figure 5.36 a). Now they just have to be offset from the originals. Using the Extrude tool with groups preserved (in the Active Tool tab), extrude these polygons inward towards the interior of the car three times, by just slivers each time (Figure 5.36 b). The total thickness of these three extrusions corresponds to the thickness of the panel. Why use three narrow extrusions rather than one thicker one? The thinner the polygons, the sharper the edge between the surfaces... and this being metal, we don't want it to look too pillowy!

This panel is nearly done, but there is one bit of cleaning up that needs to be done. Extrusion was carried out on an object being affected by a Symmetry Object, and now there are extra polygons on the plane of symmetry just making a mess of things. Switch off the symmetry object in the Objects Manager by clicking the green check changing it to a red 'x' and get in close so you can see them (Figure 5.37 a). Select all polygons that make this middle wall on the plane of symmetry and delete them. Enable the Symmetry Object once again, and the transition across the mirror plane should now be smooth (Figure 5.37 b).

Car Body:

The above method can be used for all of the panel thickness we will add on these parts we have split up from our initial car body. The doors, window trims, windows, engine covers, and rumbleseat compartment cover are all really simple in structure — they are almost flat, or rounded with just gradual curvature.

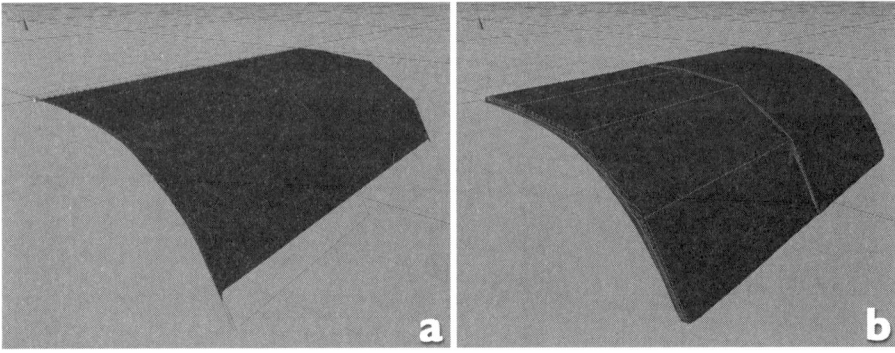

FIGURE *(a) Reversed normals. (b) Multiple extrudes to keep sharp edges.*
5.36

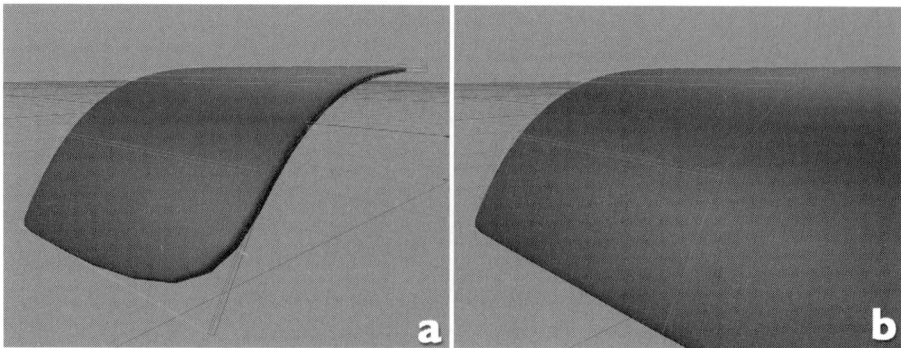

FIGURE 5.37 *(a) Disabled symmetry allows you to find offending polygons. (b) When the polygons that lie along the symmetry plane are deleted, the seam disappears.*

By far the most temperamental of the parts to add thickness to (as is usually the case), is the main car body. In every car I've modeled, after splitting apart the easy panels, there is inevitably one part that is more complex than the rest, and therefore less suited to the polygon "copy, paste, reverse, extrude" method. Usually these more complex parts have more demanding geometry or tighter structure that is less tolerant of extrusion of all polygons at once. Oftentimes, I have to fake the thickness on the visible portions of the main car body by manually adding the polygons in places such as door and trunk openings. Luckily for you, this car body is very simple and definitely able to be thickened in the Extrusion method. (I don't think anyone wanted to learn how to copy and paste hundreds of points and then bridge them did they? Thought not...)

So, we will proceed with the same method as before... with one caveat. There is an important setting to keep an eye on when you extrude complex surfaces such as this, and that's the Maximum Angle setting in the Active Tool Manager for the Extrude tool. By default in Cinema it is set to 89 degrees; thereby meaning that any polygons extruded that are greater than this angle in relation to each other will not extrude together, but will form a third polygon between them. While this may be good in some situations, in this case it is not. Some of the polygons where the side meets the top of the car body on the rear end of the car are 90 degrees to each other, and when they are extruded by our thickening method, they produce overlapping polygons that arc out of the surface of the car, and generally mess things up! To avoid having to fix the problem afterwards, we can force these polygon extrusions to behave by increasing the maximum angle they remain together at. I managed to eliminate the problem by setting this value to 100 degrees, just to be sure.

With that done, simply continue with the thickening process. Select all polygons, and copy and paste them within the Structure Manager. Reverse the normals and then extrude very slightly three times out to the thickness desired.

(You should try to keep the thickness fairly consistent between all of the panels you modify. It just makes sense!) Make sure to carefully clean up the extraneous polygons on the plane of symmetry, and the main car body should give you no more trouble than that!

The door and the two engine cover pieces should be very straightforward. Simply proceed with the thickening method as outlined previously (Figure 5.38 a). The top engine cover piece will surely need the maximum angle for the Extrude set above 90 degrees, due to the right angle between side and top polygons. Because the door and side engine cover panel do not touch the plane of symmetry, no cleanup of polygons will be required for those pieces. The top engine cover panel, however, does touch the plane of symmetry... but we will not delete the polygons on the plane of symmetry as we ordinarily would since this is a special case. We want this top engine cover to be jointed in the middle – right along the plane of symmetry. Therefore, it should retain that middle wall of polygons, but we should select them and move them over just slightly so that there is a split down the middle (Figure 5.38 b).

Now add the thickness to the front grill base piece of the car (Figure 5.38 b).

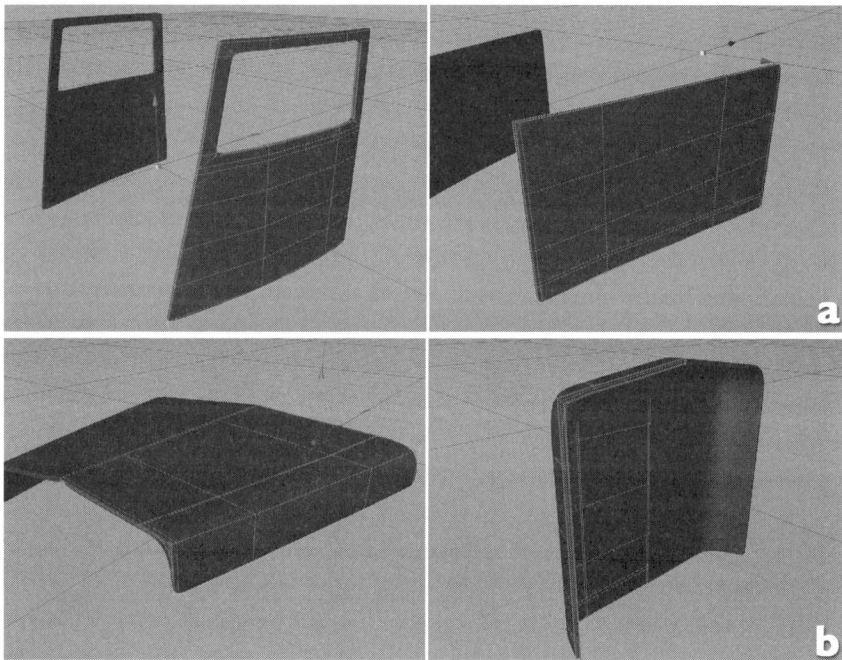

FIGURE 5.38 *(a) Adding thickness to the door and engine cover pieces. (b) Thickening the top engine cover and the front grill base.*

WINDOW THICKNESS

Now that the main surfaces of the body are thickened, we can go back and work with the window portions that were separated during the splitting stage. All windows are going to be thickened in the same way as the car panels, and won't present any problems as they are relatively simple structures that are pretty flat overall. However, as a bit of added detail, we are going to provide a bit of trim around what will be the glass portion of the window. How do we use the existing geometry to achieve this? It is the same in all cases, so let's walk through the process for one window.

Select all polygons on the object we called "Door Window Trim", and perform an Extrude Inner operation to create a thin border of polygons, as the selected polygons move inwards towards the center of the window surface. Now split these polygons to form a new object named "Door Window" (Figure 5.39).

Return to the "Door Window Trim" object and delete the inner polygons so that this object is constructed of the external ring of polygons. Select all of these and use the thickening method we've been practicing to add some volume to the trim. Make this trim relatively thin.

Now select the polygons of the object we called "Door Window", and thicken them. Select the whole object for both "Door Window Trim" and "Door Window" and move them slightly inwards towards the center of the car to place them in proper position. That should make for a visibly believable window (Figure 5.40)!

Now let's look at the rear window. Because this window crosses the plane of symmetry, there are a couple of special circumstances to be aware of when you are making the trim and window objects. First, let's proceed as before, by selecting all polygons and running the Extrude Inner to create the inner ring of

FIGURE 5.39 *Refine the windows, giving relief by splitting the window polygons, and forming an object named "Door Window."*

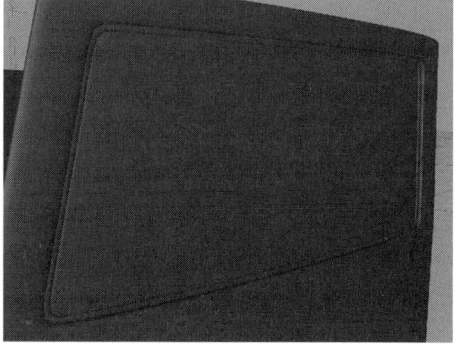

FIGURE 5.40 *Completed window.*

polygons that will define the trim. Some of these new inner points may have to be manually adjusted along the surface of the window to create a more substantial trim size (I had to move the corners upwards and inwards so that the trim was more significant in size) (Figure 5.41 a). Now, the first problem to notice is that the Extrude Inner has created a narrow polygon in the middle of the window where the window meets the plane of symmetry. We will have to eliminate this polygon, so select it and delete it (Figure 5.41 b). Now, to close the gap that was created from this deletion, select the two points that bordered the innermost side of that polygon and use the Set Value command (Structure>Edit Surface>Set Value) to set the X value of those points to zero. The points will return to x=0, slamming shut the gap seamlessly (Figure 5.41 c). Now we will have a trim object that can span the plane of symmetry perfectly.

Split the inner polygons away from the ring of polygons that will make the trim. Rename the split object as "Rear Window".

Return to the "Rear Window Trim" object and delete the inner polygons so that all that remains is the exterior ring of polygons that defines the trim (Figure 5.42 a). Use the thickening procedure to add volume to the trim. Once this trim is added, the second problem appears. Due to the extrusion of a symmetrical object, there are extra polygons lying on the plane of symmetry (Figure 5.42

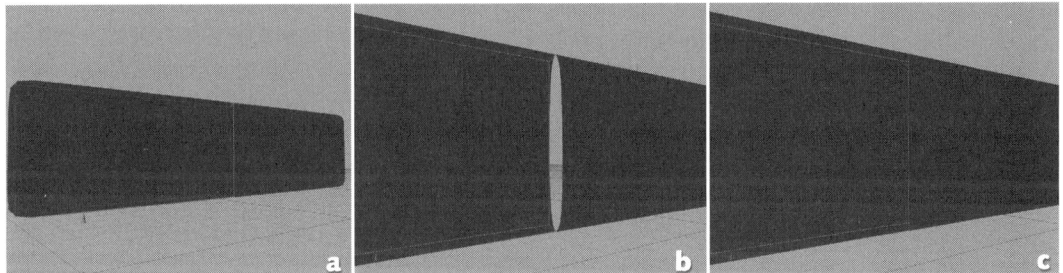

FIGURE 5.41 *Trimming the back window (a). Delete offending polygons along the plane of symmetry (b). Seamless finished window (c).*

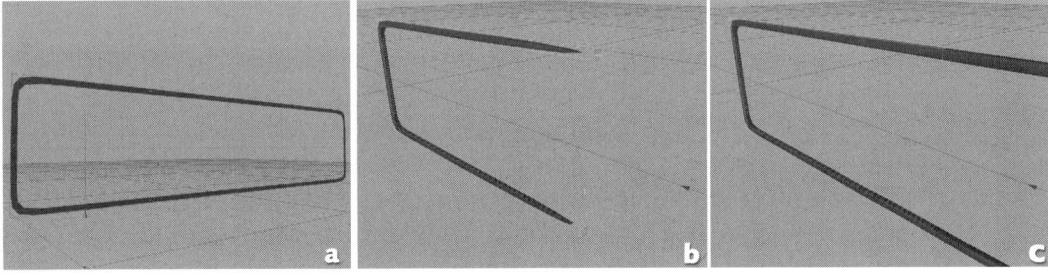

FIGURE 5.42 *(a) Rear window trim. (b) After extruding, the HyperNURBS object doesn't symmetry well. Simply select the polygons on the symmetry seam and delete. (c) The Rear Window Trim spanning the plane of symmetry.*

a and b). Turn off the symmetry object temporarily and delete this wall of polygons, so that the "Rear Window Trim" object spans smoothly across the plane of symmetry (Figure 5.42 c). Now move the window trim inwards towards the center of the car so it fits into position in the window opening.

Switching to the "Rear Window" object, select all polygons, copy and paste them, and then extrude them to create the thickened window. Select the extra polygons that appeared on the plane of symmetry from the extrusion operation and delete them. Now move the "Rear Window" object into position and the back window is complete.

Now simply repeat this procedure to complete the front windshield.

With that, the car exterior is largely done, and certainly the most difficult part is out of the way. Now the remainder consists of a frame, fenders, wheels, and all of the various bits of trim that will finish it off. Of course, some of the more die hard modelers may choose to continue and put an engine in or add an interior to the cab. Luckily for me, that's beyond the scope of this tutorial, but you shouldn't have many problems once you're competent with the rest of this!

FRAME

We can now move on to adding a frame for the car. I'm sure there's just a swarm of you thinking this is the worst order to approach things! Most would argue that you need the frame to model the exterior to and if you didn't have a good framework in place, how could you hope to build the outside accurately? That may work for some situations, but my logic for doing the exterior first is simple too…. The outside is what you see; so you have to put most of the effort into that — the frame in this case is mainly just to fill some gaps behind exterior elements. I certainly wouldn't want to bother modeling the frame perfectly and then cover it all up. Also, when you look at the reference pictures, it's pretty tough to tell what the frame looks like, isn't it? It would have been a very difficult starting point… maybe even counter productive! So, for all those reasons, I model my car's frame later rather than sooner.

You can unhide the copy of the original plane I had you make way back when we were first subdividing the original plane object and shaping it to the reference picture. (If you didn't make a copy, you can just begin to make it over again, and stop when you get to the point just before you extrude it). (See Figure 5.43.)

We have to make some modifications to the plane to put it in a useable state for our frame. The first and most noticeable is the deletion of polygons in the rear corner to make square insets for the fenders and wheels. Consequently, some knifing of the rear section was done to increase corner sharpness for these rectangular spaces. The even knifing is also done with a bit of an eye towards the future here. You see, the plan will be to extrude various polygons of this plane upwards to fill in as walls for the cab, wheel wells, rumbleseat compartment, and engine space. In particular in the back, we will run into the problem of wanting to keep the extruded walls within the confines of the exterior car shell, and the only way we will be able to do that in the back end of the car where the shape is so rounded, is to make several areas along the back where the walls will be height adjustable.

Also take the time to compare this plane and the subdivision placement with the elements of the car body we just made. You should make some knife cuts that outline certain places where we will be adding features. One will be a wall between the cab back and the rumbleseat compartment, and the other a wall between the cab front and the engine. Also, a wall will go up right in front of the engine space, and walls will be extruded to the sides of the rumbleseat opening. Furthermore, the subdivisions that run the length of the frame are moved in such a way as to facilitate the extrusion of braces in the front and rear of the car that will seat the bumpers. (It may help you if you skim ahead to see how all of these elements will be made so you can have a better idea of how to plan your geometry) (Figure 5.44).

Once the geometry for the plane is properly set up, select the plane object and move it so that it is placed as if it were at the height of the floor of the cab interior. You can check this in the side view with reference pictures turned on. The surface normals should be facing upwards so that this plane essentially makes the floor surface of the car (5.45 a).

This plane needs to be thickened so that it makes the basic frame of the car. In Polygon mode in the Structure Manager, copy and paste all of the polygons. Then reverse the normals so they face toward the underside of the car, and extrude the polygons downward. Remember that tight extrusions at the beginning and end of the thickened surface make for sharper corners. Check the thickness of the frame against what is visible in the reference picture. The final underside of the car is made from where this last extrusion stops (Figure 5.45 b).

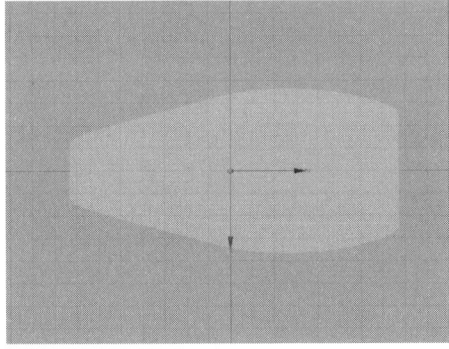

FIGURE 5.43 *Unhide original subdivided plane.*

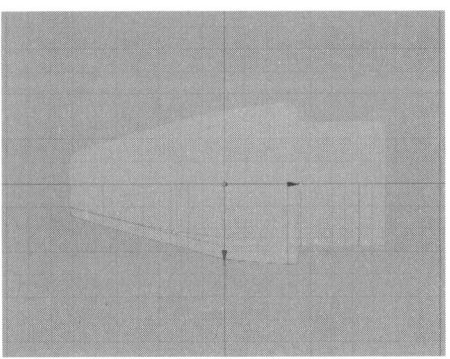

FIGURE 5.44 *Subdivide the plane to plan for the frame of the car. Planning ahead is the key here.*

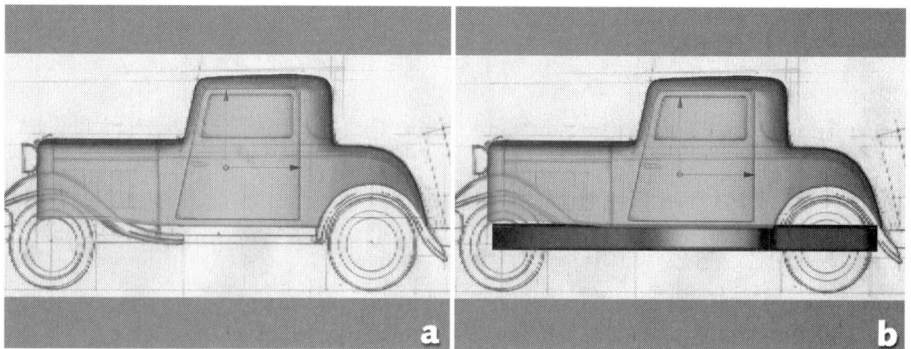

FIGURE 5.45 *Move the plane into position at the base of the car (a). Add thickness to the selected polygons (b).*

(If you want to model all of the workings of the car from beneath, you'll have to dream up your own approach! I'm stopping short at what can be seen normally!)

Select the polygons on the top of this frame surface that will make up the engine space for the car. This includes polygons that will form the starting point of the front and back walls, as well as the floor of the engine compartment. Raise it slightly with an Extrude function, so that any gap between the floor surface of this front area and the bottom of the engine cover's downward extent is eliminated (Figure 5.46). Check the side view to be sure this engine floor is high enough.

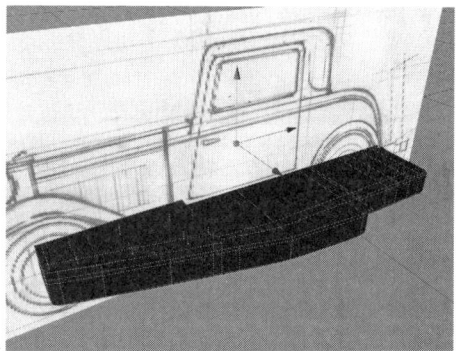

FIGURE 5.46 *Add height to the frame under the engine covers.*

Then deselect the middle polygons of this floor, so that only the polygons that serve as the base for walls on the front and back of the engine compartment are selected. Use the Extrude tool to extrude these polygons upwards into actual walls now. Examine the appearance of the walls against the exterior shell and see how close the fit can be made. It should be possible to get it fairly accurate in height in the middle, and then reduce the height of the walls on the side corners to account for the slope of the engine covers. The best thing to keep in mind is that close counts at this stage… you are unlikely to need this compartment to be modeled airtight (Figure 5.47 a)!

Next, select the polygons on the back part of the frame that will surround the rumbleseat compartment, to form the walls there as well as the back wall of the cab interior. Extrude these up to the maximum height of the car body shell (the same height as the engine compartment walls) (Figure 5.47 b). Then, selecting the points at the top of the rumbleseat wall subdivisions row by row, shape the walls to fit within the rounded confines of the outer shell (Figure 5.48 a).

Finally, extrude the posts from the front and back of the frame that will hold the bumpers (Figure 5.48 b). Check the length and positioning of them to the side reference picture. This completes the basic frame.

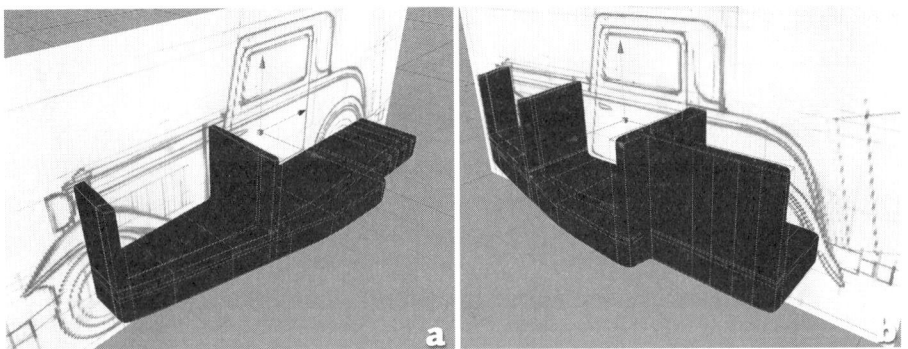

FIGURE 5.47 *Extruding walls of engine compartment (a). Extruding the middle compartment walls (b).*

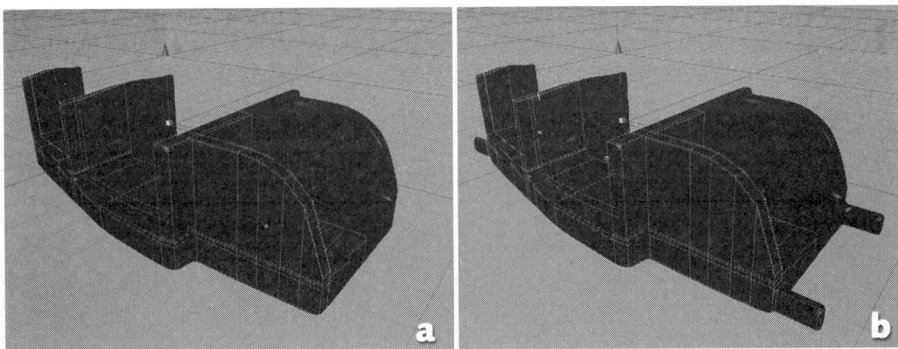

FIGURE 5.48 *Adjusting the rumbleseat with wall subdivisions (a). Adding bumpers (b).*

FENDERS

The fenders for this type of car offer an interesting challenge. They are not merely parts of the car body, so they can't be factored in to our original construction; they must be added on afterwards as separate pieces. But the problem we face with adding components on to existing model geometry is making them fit correctly. One technique I have learned to use is spline projection and subsequent point duplication. The basic idea is this: a spline defining the connection is drawn in a planar manner (from the side view for instance), and then projected onto the geometry that it will connect to. The points from this projected spline can then be copied and pasted into a polygon object and used as the basis for constructing the adjoining geometry. Incidentally, this technique works great for these fenders! So let's run through it with examples.

Front Fender:

From the side view, draw a linear spline (no rounding) that defines the general curve of the area where the fender will adjoin to the car frame (Figure 5.49). When you consider splines for projection, it is important that they have enough segments as to project well against the surfaces they are meant to. The points themselves project against the surface of the geometry, and the spline segments run between these points. The segments themselves are not bound to adhere to the target geometry but rather interpolate between the points. Therefore, a spline with a low number of segments projected against a fairly curved surface will have areas where the segments seem to travel underneath the target surface between points that rest on said surface.

The point I'm trying to make is that we need significant segmentation to make a clean projection but we also want to remember that these points are merely the basis for polygon construction later on(therefore, as few as possible to get acceptable projection).

Once we achieve the spline shape we like, make sure that this spline is positioned outside of the target surface geometry. The projection target is actually the ZY plane in this case, and whatever geometry gets between this spline and the target plane is the surface that the spline will end up on. Copy this spline object and paste it in place so that there are two identical spline objects. With all points of one of the splines selected, run the Projection command (Structure>Edit Spline>Project). One spline should now be molded to the exterior of the car frame object, and the other spline will remain in place (Figure 5.50). Select the spline that was not projected, and move it so that it defines the outer edge of the fender (as seen from the top reference view).

Create a new polygon object, (placing it under a HyperNURBS>Symmetry hierarchy), and using the Structure Manager, copy the points from the projected spline and paste them into the structure of the polygon object. Perform this point copy/paste procedure to copy the point of the straight outer fender edge spline into the polygon object as well.

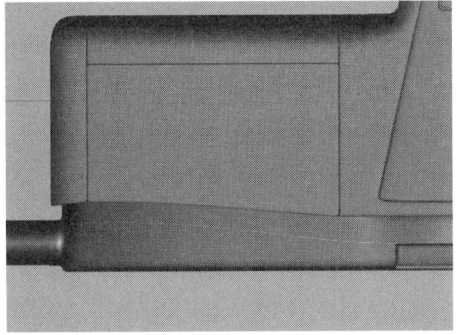 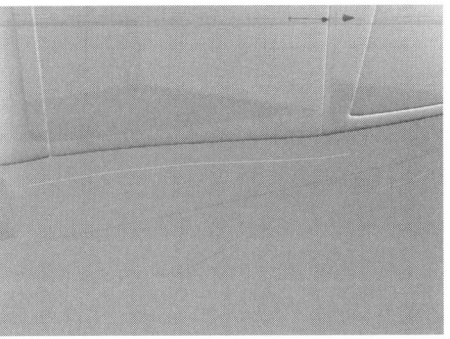

FIGURE 5.49 *Begin the front fender by drawing a linear spline from a side view.*

FIGURE 5.50 *Two splines (one molded to surface of the car).*

Now using the Bridge tool running between matching pairs of points, create polygons with these points so that a basic fender surface results (Figure 5.51 a). One problem that we faced with the front fender is the fact that not all of the fender adjoins to the car frame; the actual fender surface is much larger than what we can produce using this spline projection. (You may notice at some point that if the spline you project can't completely be intercepted by geometry, portions of it WILL make it to the target plane; in this case, if we had made a spline that defined the entire fender, some points would have projected onto the car frame; and the overhanging point in the front, where the fender does not adjoin to the car frame, would have wrapped around the front of the car frame and come to rest on the ZY plane. So we defined only the joint between fender and frame, and now compensate for the rest of the front fender surface area by creating extra polygons off the front of the basic fender surface (Figure 5.51 b). (The method I use is to copy and paste the leading edge points within the Structure Manager and then create the new polygons with the Bridge tool, but there are other methods including an edge extrusion type plug-in.)

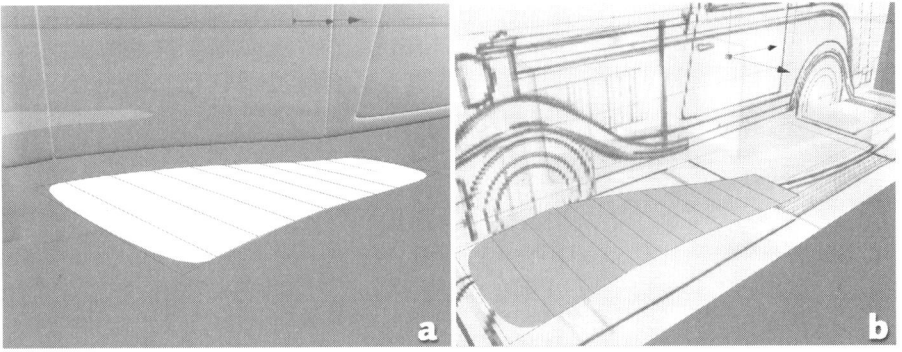

FIGURE 5.51 *Use the Bridge tool to join the points to create the necessary polygons. (a) Add extra polygons off the front of the fender surface (b).*

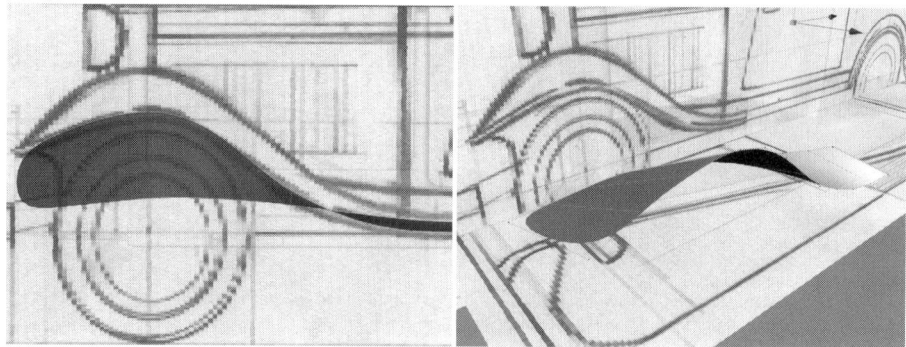

FIGURE 5.52 *Flare the fender by adjusting points.*

Now, using the Knife tool (with all polygons selected), make a cut right at the back of the surface (making a very narrow polygon that creates a sharp edge for the joint between front fender and the running board).

Switching between views, select each point along its outer edge and move it vertically on the Y-axis (make sure to constrain it to Y movement only for neatness), so that the edge of this surface along the outside now corresponds to the top outer edge of the fender in the reference picture. (This surface will be the top surface of the fender – we will be copying and moving these polygons downwards to make the bottom surface later). Once these points are in place, the surface will be flared rigidly between the joint to the frame and the outer edge of the fender (Figure 5.52). This is a starting point, but we will need more subdivision to shape the fender.

From the top view, with all polygons selected, make a knife cut that runs the length of the fender. This cut will be the crest of the bulge that sits atop the wheel on the fender piece, so it should be positioned where the bulge will be greatest on the fender surface (Figure 5.53).

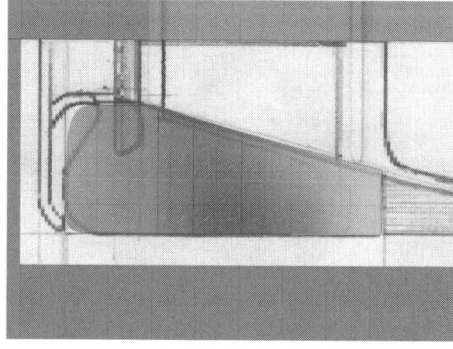

FIGURE 5.53 *To create the bulge over the top of the fender, use the Knife tool to split the polygons into two, thus providing an extra row of points.*

Next, select the points along the crest line and move them vertically along the Y-axis (use the constraints) so that they are positioned in such a way as to make the crest of the bulge match the profile of the fender in the side view reference picture. Now the flared shape of the fender resembles our intent much more closely (Figure 5.54).

Next, from the top view, make a knife cut that runs the length of the fender but is situated very tightly against the outer edge of the fender (Figure 5.55). Zoom in to the rear edge of the fender where it will butt up against the running board, and select some of these new points and move them vertically on the Y-axis to create a more square, "step-like" shape for this edge. The top surface of the fender should be horizontal, with a sharp square outer edge, and a steeply sloped outer face. This rear edge should finish in the same shape that we expect the running board to take so the transition is as smooth looking as possible (Figure 5.56). To sharpen the step edge between vertical and horizontal faces of

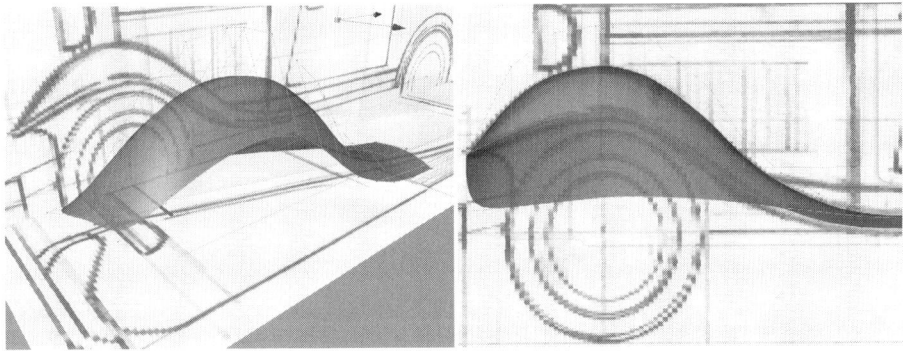

FIGURE 5.54 *Adjust the new points along the Y-axis to provide for fender bulge.*

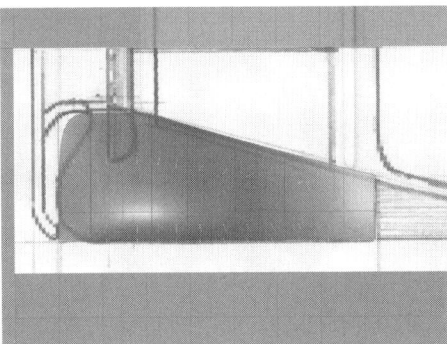

FIGURE 5.55 *Make an additional knife cut near the outer edge.*

FIGURE 5.56 *Finish the fender in the shape of the upcoming running board.*

this portion of the fender, another knife cut may be necessary just slightly further inwards toward the center of the car from the last one.

For added control over the shape of the fender bulge, more knife cuts can be made between the crest line and the inner edge of the fender. The points of these lines can then be moved into position to help represent the shape of the fender more accurately, or more to your taste (Figure 5.57).

Once the top surface of the fender is shaped to your liking, select all polygons and using the Structure Manager, copy and paste them within the object so there are two sets of identical polygons in identical locations. Only one set will remain selected, and you can reverse the normals on these polygons so that they will be the outer surface of the bottom of the fender.

The panel thickening method we used previously was based on the Extrude function, which is good for most purposes when we want the extrusion to be influenced by the normals of the source polygons, but for this object, we just want to move the bottom surface downwards on the Y-axis to offset it from the top surface. However, if we were to try and move the polygons selected right now, all polygons on the object would move. To circumvent this problem, use the Disconnect function (Structure>Edit Surface>Disconnect) with Preserve Groups enabled. This does not make these polygons into separate objects, but rather now they can be manipulated independently of other polygons. After having done this, move the bottom surface polygons downward along the Y-axis so that they are offset an appropriate distance to portray the thickness of the fender.

Once this is done, switch to Points mode and create the edge surface polygons by using the Bridge tool around the outer edge of the entire front fender (except for where it adjoins to the car frame – here it is unnecessary and counter-productive to create a rounded edge surface, as we need this joint to be fully against the car frame) (Figure 5.58 a).

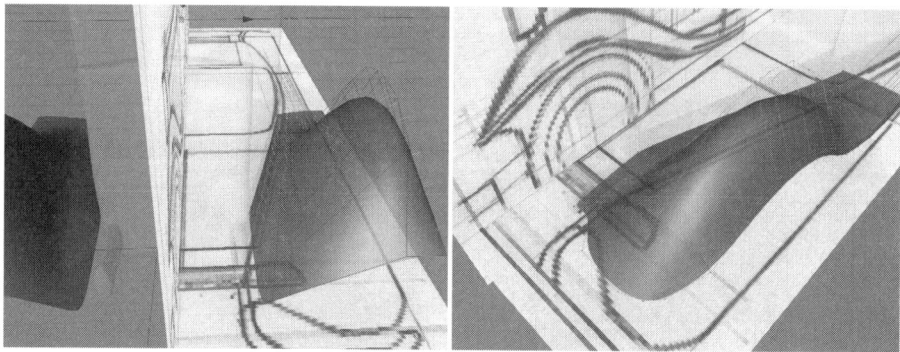

FIGURE 5.57 *Added knife cuts to allow for added shape control.*

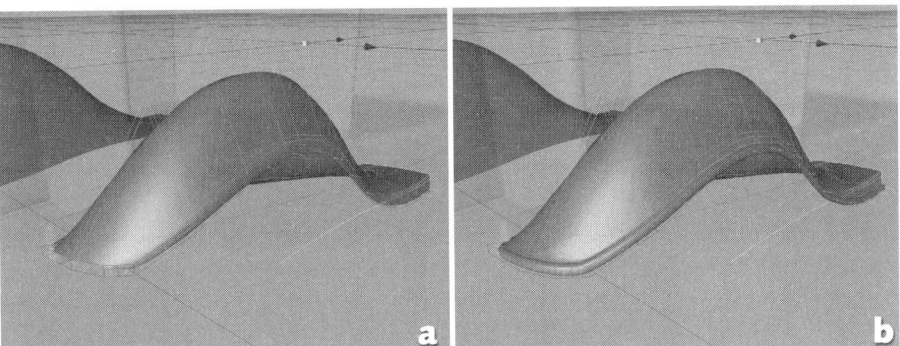

FIGURE 5.58 *(a) Create the outer edge with the Bridge tool. Rounding the lip (b).*

When all of these outer edge polygons are made, select all polygons and align the normals so that they all face outwards. Then select only the newly created outer edge surface polygons, and use the Extrude tool twice in small amounts to create a nice rounded "lip" around the edge of the fender (Figure 5.58 b). This should conclude work on the front fender, barring any tweaking you choose to do in the future!

Running Board:
The method for achieving this portion of the model is similar to the front fender, but far less complicated to shape, as it is in essence a flat step. We want to make the inner edge follow the curvature of the car frame again. (Ordinarily, you might just overlap this kind of geometry but that doesn't help you learn the uses of spline projection!!!) We can resort to our spline projection technique as outlined before, by drawing a linear spline in our side view that runs along the top edge of the running board from the rear of the front fender to the point where the rear fender will begin (Figure 5.59 a).

Copy and paste this spline so that there are two identical splines (they should be positioned in such a way as to be the outer edge of the running board). Next, select one spline and project it to the ZY plane. It will mold to the exterior of the car frame object (Figure 5.59 b).

Create a polygon object under a HyperNURBS>Symmetry hierarchy. Working via the Structure Manager, copy the points from the two edge splines into the polygon object. Then use the Bridge tool to create the polygons for the top surface of the running board (Figure 5.60).

Use the Knife tool to make sure the front and rear edges of the running board are sharp where they meet the front and rear fenders. Also, add a knife cut along the length of the running board in the middle (in line with the cut on the front fender that was the crest of the bulge over the tire), and two knife cuts along the outer edge. The cut in the middle of the board is merely to match the

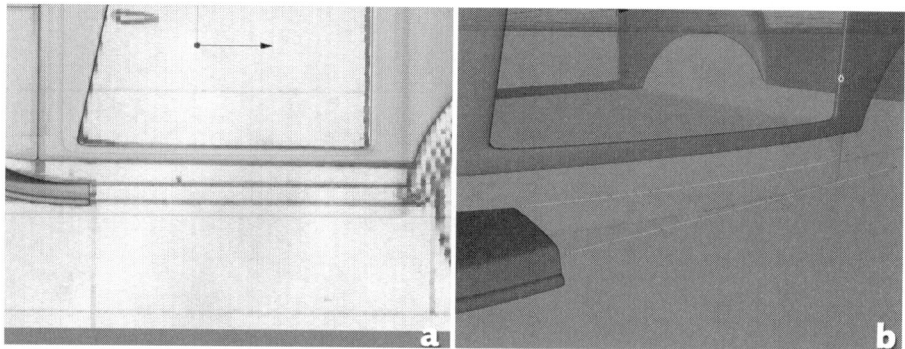

FIGURE 5.59 *Begin the running board by again creating a linear spline (a) and then copying and pasting that spline (b).*

structure of the front fender somewhat, in case adjustments need to be made along this line to blend the two pieces more aesthetically, and the cuts on the outside edge are to be used to produce the square step edge and steeply sloped outer face of the running board (Figure 5.61).

Select the outer edge points and move them down on the Y-axis so that they line up with the top of the lip of the front fender. The outer edge surface should remain slightly sloped from vertical so that when the polygons are copied, offset, and moved downwards, the copies do not intersect with the originals along the face (Figure 5.62).

Now we can thicken the object by selecting all polygons and copying and pasting them within the Structure Manager. Reverse the normals of the polygons, and use the Disconnect function with the Preserve Groups option enabled. Now simply move the duplicate polygons downward to form the bottom surface of the running board (Figure 5.63).

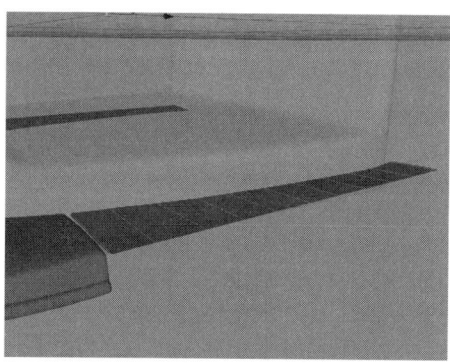

FIGURE 5.60 *Round the board by creating a HyperNURBS object and adding pasted points from the two edge splines.*

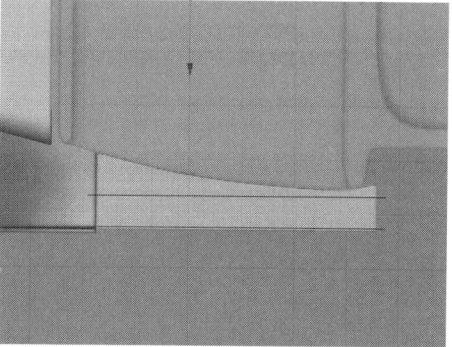

FIGURE 5.61 *Use the Knife tool to make added cuts to ensure sharp edges.*

Use the Bridge tool to create the outer surface of the running board by bridging between corresponding points on the top and bottom surfaces. Once again, don't be concerned with creating the surface that is situated along the car frame surface (Figure 5.64 a).

Next, select the outer edge surface polygons along the one side of the running board, and extrude them twice to form the rounded lip. The completed result should be visually continuous from the front fender. It likely won't need any tweaking since both objects were created with the same method, but if it does need some work, it should only be a matter of isolated point manipulation (Figure 5.64 b).

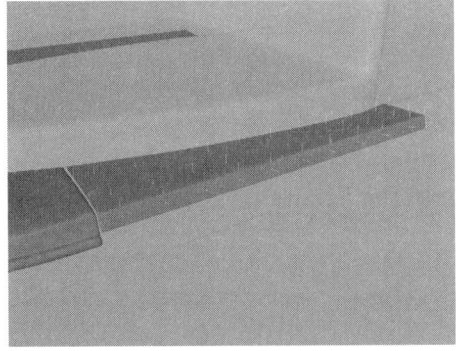

FIGURE 5.62 *Moving points so that they are closer to adjoining points creates the sharper lips of the areas needed.*

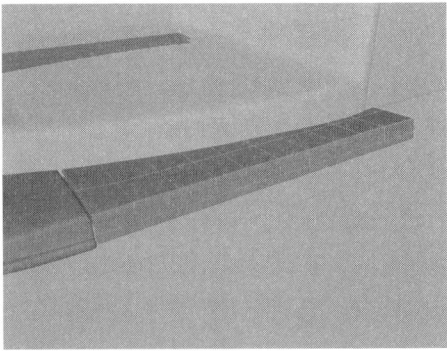

FIGURE 5.63 *Thickening the object to create the bottom surface of the running board.*

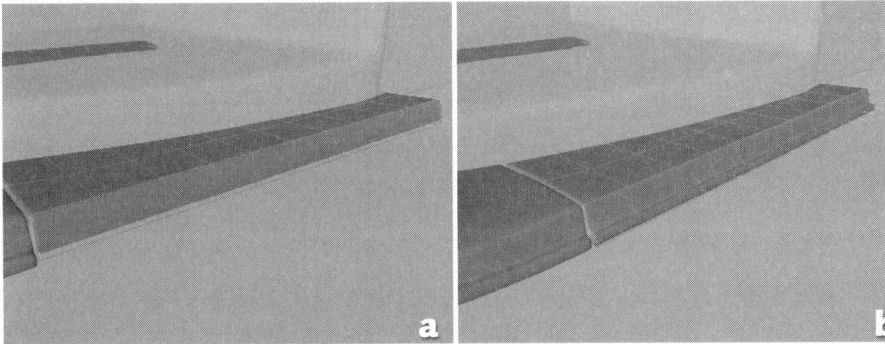

FIGURE 5.64 *Adding the outer edge with the Bridge tool (a). Giving the outer edge a lip (b).*

Rear Fender:

The rear fender will use a slightly different procedure to start the object off. We don't necessarily need to draw a spline to define the curvature of the fender, and also due to the flatness of the frame object in the rear wheel area, we don't need to project any points to this surface. In fact, we can get away from merely copying some existing points into a polygon object and moving the points within that polygon object to define the fender edges.

Create a polygon object under a HyperNURBS>Symmetry hierarchy. Next, select the original car body object where the curvature of the body was adapted to fit around the fender. Select the points on the outside edge of this wheel well and copy them from the Structure Manager. Paste the points into the Structure Manager of the rear fender polygon object.

With all points of the rear fender selected now, run the Set Value command to set all points at an equal X value. That way, they will fit flat against the side of the car frame object. You can move the points into position there now. With all of these points still selected, copy and paste them within the Structure Manager and move the new points into position as the outer fender edge. Finally, use the Bridge tool to create the polygons that make up the top fender surface defined by these points (Figure 5.65).

The points copied from the car body were a great start, but they didn't go all the way to define the shape of the top surface of the fender. If you look at the points, though, you can find where you can move some pairs of points along the front edge and rear edge of the fender into new locations so as to extend the surface of the fender more like what we have in our reference image. If not, it is still possible to copy and paste these edge points to create new polygons for the front and rear edges (like we needed to for the front fender). The method is not overly important, but the result should be to create a top surface that conforms to the reference picture as closely as possible (Figure 5.66).

Using the Knife tool, make a cut that sharpens the front edge of this fender where it will meet the running board. Then, make a cut that runs the length of the fender very near to the existing outer edge (Figure 5.67). Select the outermost points of the polygons and move them inwards so as to create the outward

FIGURE 5.65 *Creating the rear fender.*

FIGURE 5.66 *Further refinement of the fender shape.*

CHAPTER 5 MODELING A CAR WITH HYPERNURBS

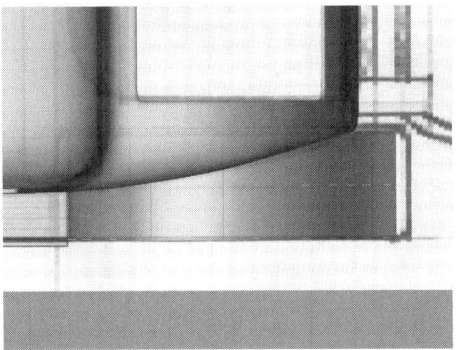 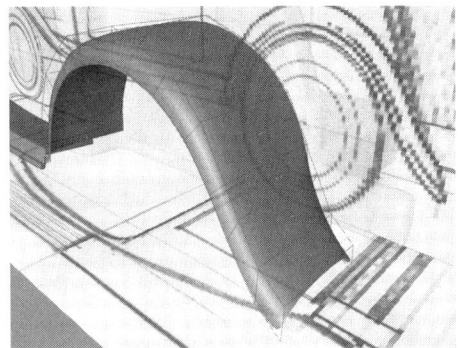

FIGURE 5.67 *Use the Knife tool to create cuts that provide for the additional polygons needed to create an accurate fender shape.*

FIGURE 5.68 *Adjusting the inner edge of the rear fender.*

facing portion of the top fender surface. Check the result against the reference image to make sure the points are being positioned adequately. Keep in mind there is an edge in the back of the fender that will be seen protruding from the back of the car beyond the car body. It will be necessary to make a knife cut and perform this procedure for at least the visible portion of the inner edge of the rear fender (Figure 5.68). Also, use the Bridge tool to create the polygon on the back of the rear fender so that the outer wall of the fender surface is continuous around the outer side, back, and visible inner side of the rear fender.

Copy and paste these polygons within the Structure Manager so that duplicate polygons exist within the rear fender object. Reverse the normals, then disconnect the polygon's and move them downward on the Y-axis to create the bottom surface of the rear fender. Use the Bridge tool to create the polygons between relevant portions of the rear fender (visible edges), and then select these polygons (Figure 5.69 a). Use the Extrude tool twice to create the visible lip around the fender and with any luck, the task is complete (Figure 5.69 b)!

THE GRILL

At this point, we can return to a place in the model that had basically been abandoned right after the detailed shaping of the car body was completed. The groundwork for the grill had been done, but none of the detail. We can begin to refine areas like this now.

First, selecting the points along the bottom of the grill object, move them downward on the Y-axis to round the bottom of this grill trim slightly (Figure 5.70).

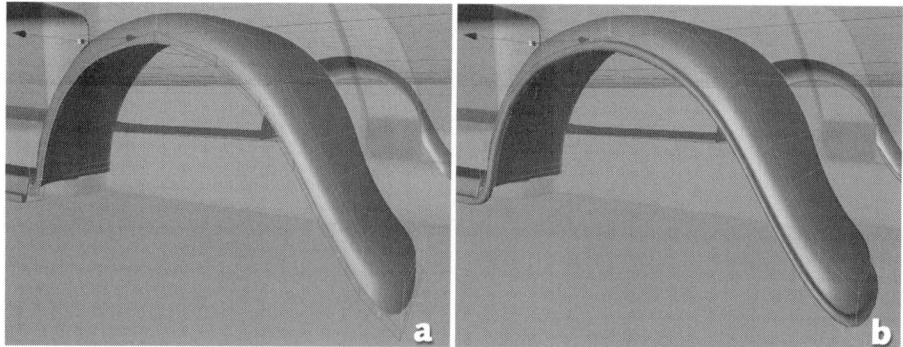

FIGURE 5.69 *Using the Bridge tool to create thickness to edge (a). Extruding out the lip (b).*

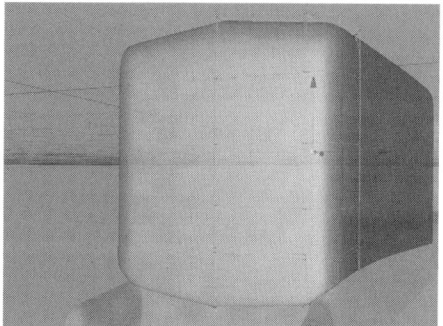

FIGURE 5.70 *Rounding the grill bottom.*

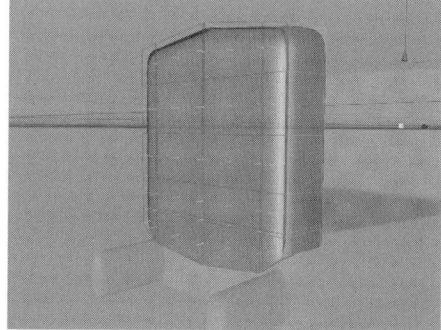

FIGURE 5.71 *Delete unnecessary back side polygons.*

Next, select the polygons that make up the back face of the grill object (the side facing inwards toward the engine compartment) and delete them. Make sure you are not deleting any of the polygons that form the side wall of the grill object — only those on the inside face of the middle back surface (Figure 5.71).

Next, select the polygons on the outside front face of the grill object, and use the Extrude Inner command to draw them inwards toward the center of the grill object's forward surface. This creates a clear border around polygons that will serve as the edge of the trim around the grill opening (Figure 5.72 a). Next, with these same polygons still selected, extrude them back inwards toward the engine compartment to create the inner surface of the grill opening (Figure 5.72 b).

Run the Split command to make a duplicate object of these selected polygons. Leaving it in place, use the Knife tool to cut the basis for the grill slats into it. Delete any extraneous polygons (Figure 5.73 a). Then, select the polygons that define the slats for the grill and extrude them back outwards toward the front of the grill opening to complete the grill (Figure 5.73 b).

CHAPTER 5 MODELING A CAR WITH HYPERNURBS

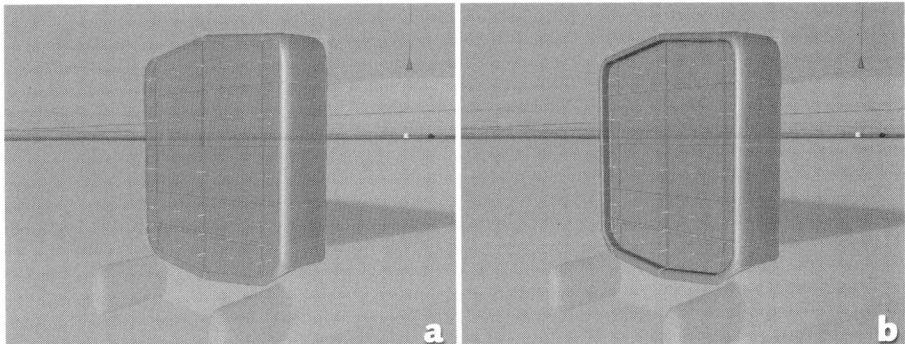

FIGURE 5.72 *Adding the inset area of the grill through the Extrude Inner command.*

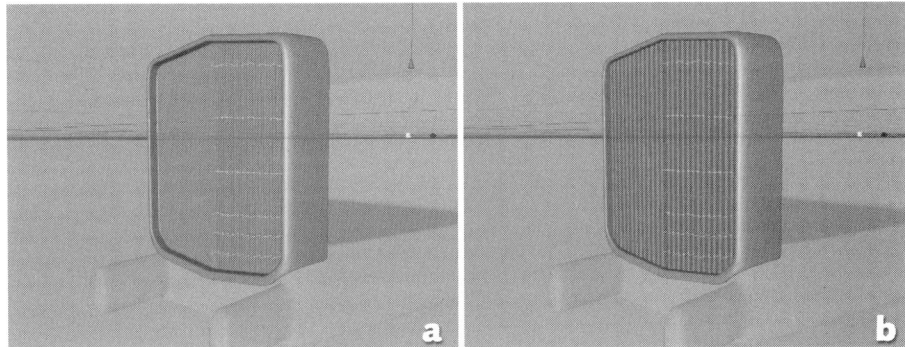

FIGURE 5.73 *Expanding and completing the grill through Split and Extrude.*

BUMPERS

The bumpers represent the part of modeling that I really love — reusability. Hey, I won't lie, nothing makes me happier than when you can model one component and use it multiple places. Now the bumper is simple enough that it wouldn't cause too much trouble to model all parts of it... but it's always nice to be aware of when to use the Copy and Paste functions to make life easier.

Front Bumper:

That being said, the main component to this type of bumper is along a metal plank that is curved on the ends. There are two of these planks per bumper — stacked one on top of the other — and the rear bumper and front bumpers are identical.

Start out by drawing a linear spline that is based on the rear edge of the bumper in the top view reference picture. We will again use HyperNURBS and Symmetry objects, so you only need to draw one half of the bumper (Figure 5.74 a).

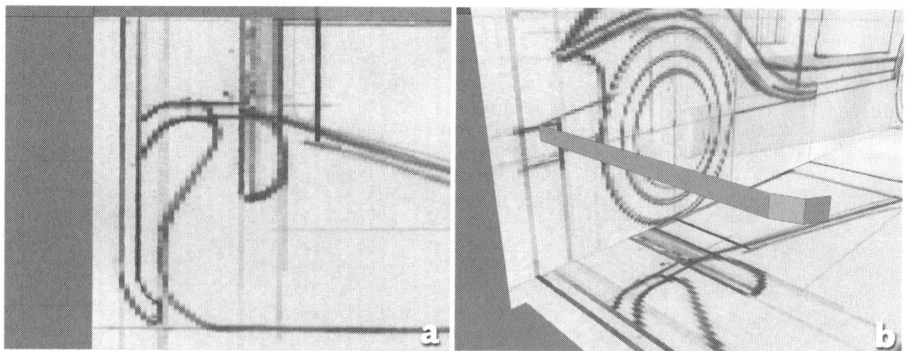

FIGURE 5.74 *Creating bumper via a new linear spline and extruding.*

Once this spline is done, extrude it to make a surface that is the height of one plank. Make it editable so that it is a polygon object, and make sure the normals face towards the car (Figure 5.74 b).

Select all polygons and copy and paste them within the Structure Manager. Reverse the normals of the selected polygons and use the Extrude tool two or three times to move these polygons forward into position as the front surface of the bumper. The narrower the extrusions, the sharper the edges of the Hyper-NURBS object become (Figure 5.75).

Once the bumper strip is shaped to your satisfaction, you can select all polygons and paste them again in the Structure Manager. Use the Disconnect function with Preserve Groups enabled, and then move the new polygons down on the Y-axis so they sit below the top strip (with a small space in between the strips) (Figure 5.76).

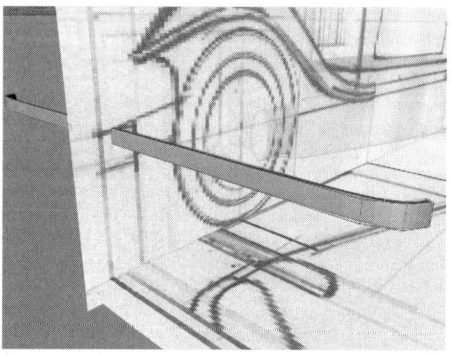

FIGURE 5.75 *Adding thickness to bumper.*

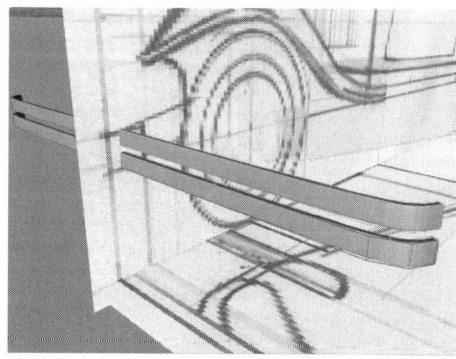

FIGURE 5.76 *Creating the second bumper.*

Next, select the protruding post on the front of the car frame object, and using the Extrude Inner function for varying the post width, and the Extrude function for controlling the post length, fashion an extension to the post that comes out to "support" the bumper object (Figure 5.77 a). If you'd like, you can also switch to top view and use knife cuts and point manipulation to shape bends into the post (Figure 5.77 b).

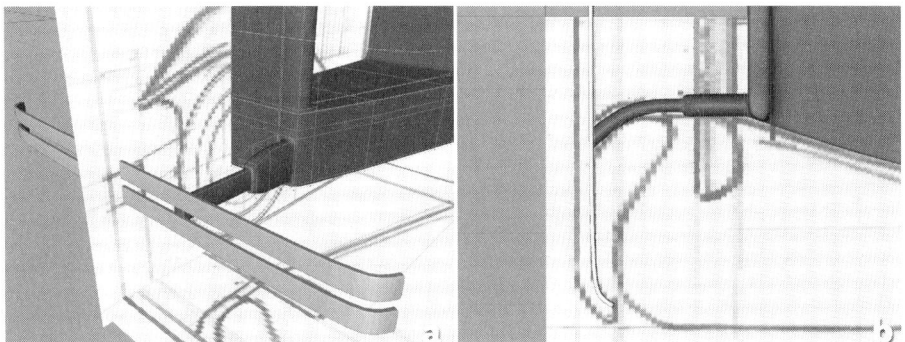

FIGURE 5.77 *Creating the connecting posts from bumper to car frame.*

Rear Bumper:

Select the bumper object, and copy and paste the object in the Object Manager (making sure it is still affected by HyperNURBS and Symmetry parents). Make a mirror image of this bumper along the XY plane so that it looks identical, but faces the rear of the car. Move this rear bumper object into position at the back end of the car (Figure 5.78 a). Next, shape the post protruding from the rear of the car frame object using Extrude and Extrude Inner commands so that it reaches the rear bumper object. From the top view, use the Knife tool and point manipulation to shape the post (Figure 5.78 b, c).

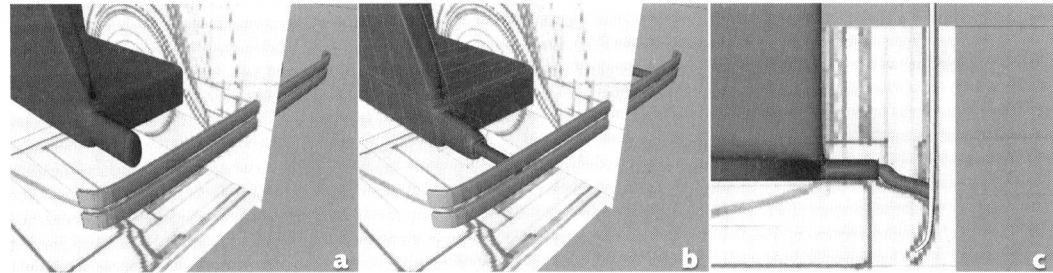

FIGURE 5.78 *Creating the rear bumper.*

HEADLIGHTS

The headlights on this car are simple little bowl-shaped objects that sit perched on top of a bar that stretches across in front of the grill between the front fenders. To begin, we can create this bar by projecting a box spline onto the fender from the top view (Figure 5.79 a). Copy and paste the corner points of this projected spline into a polygon object that has HyperNURBS and Symmetry parent objects. Then use the points to create the polygon (Figure 5.79 b).

Select the polygon and make sure the normals face outwards. Then, use the Extrude tool a small amount twice to create a base for the bar where it adjoins the fender. Use the Extrude Inner tool to narrow the polygon from the width of the base, and continue making the bar by using the Extrude tool. The aim is to extrude the bar in such a way that it will meet its symmetrical counterpart in the middle, along the plane of symmetry. Use point manipulation to keep it shaped acceptably and positioned so that the extrusion goes predictably. Then the last section of the bar is going to meet the plane of symmetry, so select all the points of the end polygon and use the Set Value command to set the points to an X value of zero. The end will be completely flat against the plane of symmetry at that point, and the end polygon can be deleted (Figure 5.80).

For the light itself, a standard cylinder primitive, when it is given fairly low subdivision (in this example three Height segments, two Cap segments, and eight Rotation segments) provides an excellent starting point. Position the cylinder approximately, and drop it into a HyperNURBS >Symmetry parent hierarchy (Figure 5.81 a). Make the cylinder editable so that we can alter the points and polygonal structure. Select all points on the rear face and rear edge of the cylinder and scale them inwards to taper the object into a rounded bowl or rounded cone shape. It may also help to scale the next row of points inwards just slightly for more refinement on the shape of the light (Figure 5.81 b).

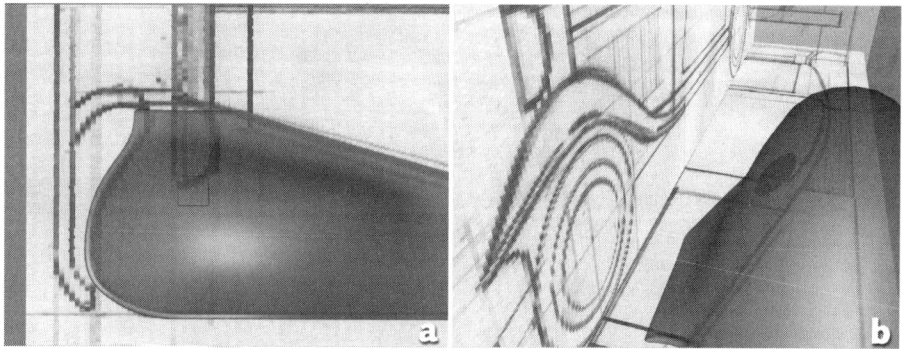

FIGURE 5.79 *Begin headlight construction by projecting a box spline upon the fender curvature.*

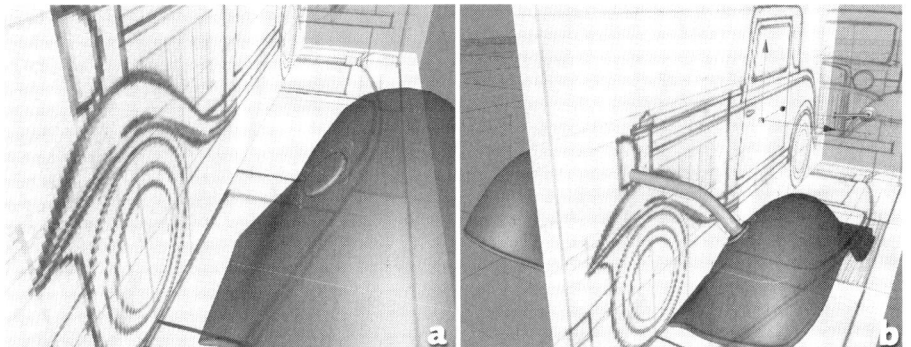

FIGURE 5.80 *Continuing the headlight base with multiple extrudees.*

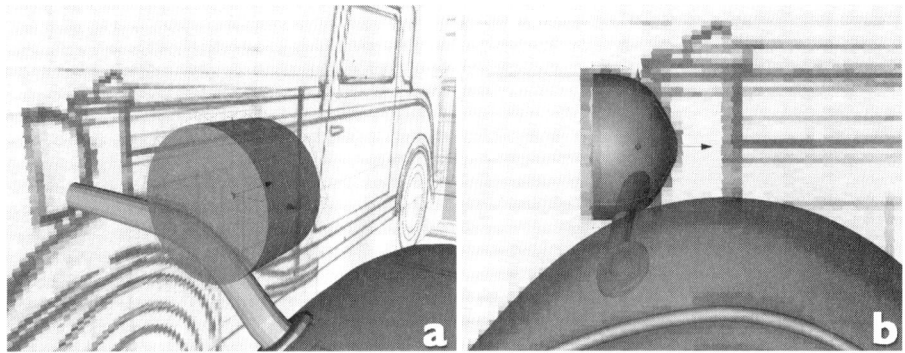

FIGURE 5.81 *(a) Create the light with a standard cylinder primitive. (b) Adjusting points to refine the light shape.*

Select the front face of the headlight object and use the Extrude Inner command to offset the polygon selection inwards and create an outer ring on the front face. Keep the same polygons selected, and run the Extrude tool to extrude these polygons toward the rear of the light so that the outer ring of polygons on the front face becomes a lip (Figure 5.82 a). Then use the Move tool to move the extruded polygons back toward the front of the car where they originated from, and the lens surface becomes rounded (Figure 5.82 b). Once the shape you desire is achieved, complete the positioning of the headlight object on the bar.

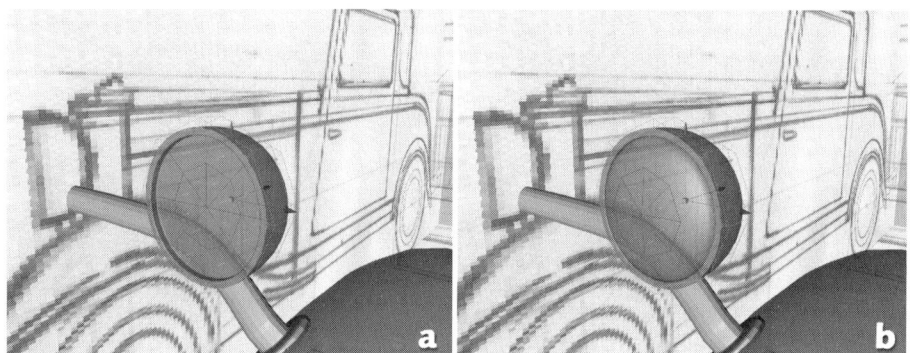

FIGURE 5.82 *Creating the roundness of the headlight.*

TAILLIGHTS

The taillight is nothing more than an exact copy of the headlight object, scaled down and repositioned to the back of the car (Figure 5.83). The only work to be done for this element is to create the supporting bar that runs between taillights and passes through the rear bumper posts. To do this, simply create a cube that is two segments in width along the X-axis and one segment in the Z- and Y-directions. Make the cube wide enough so that the ends sit beneath the taillights once they have been positioned. Delete half of the polygons and drop the cube into a HyperNURBS>Symmetry hierarchy (Figure 5.83 a). Select all polygons and use the Knife tool to make a cut on the end of the cube right beneath the taillight. Select the top-facing polygon on the end subdivision of this cube, and extrude it upwards toward the bottom of the light object. Remember, one small extrusion followed by a larger one will keep the corners of this bar tight and controlled (Figure 5.83 b).

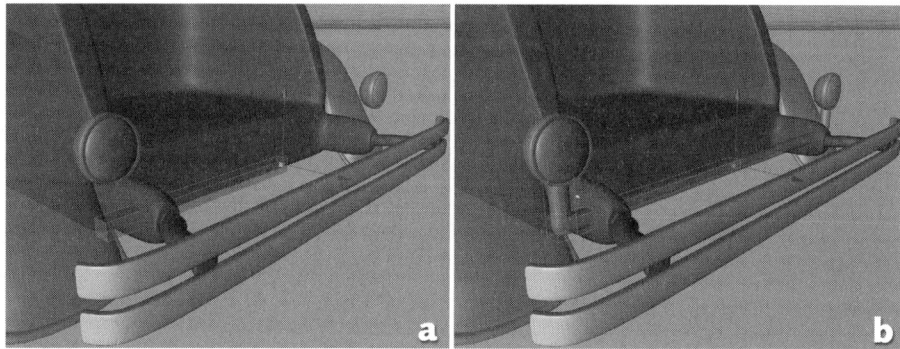

FIGURE 5.83 *Creating the support bar for the rear headlight, which is a resized duplicate of the front headlight.*

CHAPTER 5 MODELING A CAR WITH HYPERNURBS 167

Next, make two even knife cuts in the center of the bar between the two car frame posts (Figure 5.84 a). Selecting the polygons that make up the innermost section of the bar, move them up along the Y-axis. This will be used as a support for the spare wheel (Figure 5.84 b).

DOOR HANDLES

To place elements like door handles on the surface of the car, I resort to spline projection yet again. In this case the door handle connects to the car door surface in one spot, with a roughly oval shaped base. To achieve the base where the handle adjoins the car surface, we can create a spline in a box shape in our side view that defines where we want the base situated on the ZY plane. Make sure this is only a box with four corners, as we will use the points to make polygons and we can keep it simple by having to make only one quad polygon with four points. Under HyperNURBS subdivision, a single polygon smooths into an oval shape.

Next, move the spline so that it is outside the surface of the car door, and use the Projection command (project to the ZY plane). The points of the spline will come to rest on the car door surface (Figure 5.85 a). Copy and paste these points via the Structure Manager, into a new polygon object with a HyperNURBS and Symmetry parent. Create a polygon from these points, and you can see a round oval shape is created roughly on the surface of the car door. Make sure the polygon normals are facing outwards from the car surface (Figure 5.85 b).

Select this polygon, and extrude it just slightly to create a hard adjoining edge between the handle and the door surface. Extrude again to give some appreciable thickness to the handle base. Then, by using a combination of Extrude and Extrude Inner commands, fashion the handle outwards from the car surface (Figure 5.86 a). Finally, select the rear-facing polygon on the last outward extrusion and extrude that polygon towards the back of the car to complete the handles (Figure 5.85 b).

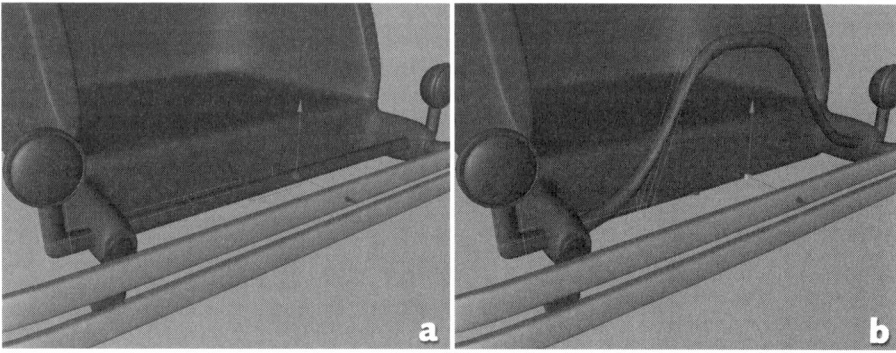

FIGURE *By adjusting the rear light support bar, the spare wheel support can be created.*
5.84

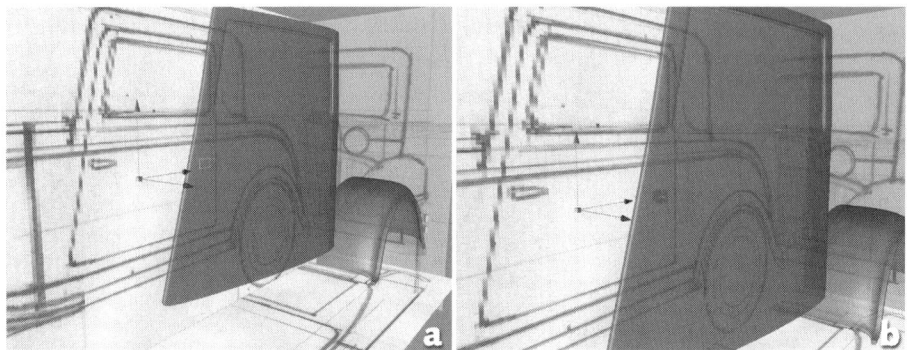

FIGURE 5.85 *Projecting the beginning of the door handles.*

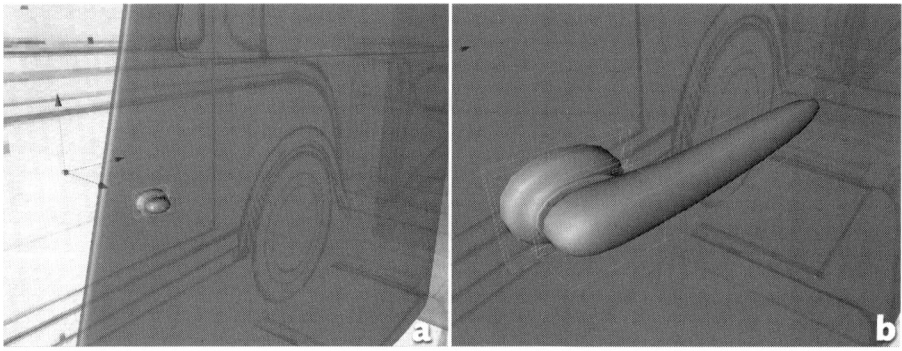

FIGURE 5.86 *Fashioning the door handles.*

MIRRORS

Mirrors are another element that can be started by projecting a box spline onto the side of the car surface. Draw the spline from the side view, project it, and then copy the points into a polygon object with HyperNURBS and Symmetry object parents. Then create a polygon from these points, making sure the polygon normals face outwards (Figure 5.87).

Extrude the polygon slightly to create a sharp edge where the mirror adjoins the car. Then, extrude again to create the base of the mirror. Use Extrude Inner to make the selected polygon shrink in size inward, and then extrude again to create the base. Make sure the face of the polygon is turned sufficiently in the direction that you want extrusion to occur (Figure 5.88 a). Extrude the end of the base out again to create the main pole of the mirror (Figure 5.88 b). Select all polygons and knife the end of this pole, so that there is a square polygon on the end of the pole facing the back of the car. Extrude this polygon slightly, and then use the Extrude Inner tool to flare the polygon into a wide, round mirror shape (Figure 5.88 (c and d)).

CHAPTER 5   MODELING A CAR WITH HYPERNURBS   169

FIGURE 5.87 *The beginning of the mirror creations.*

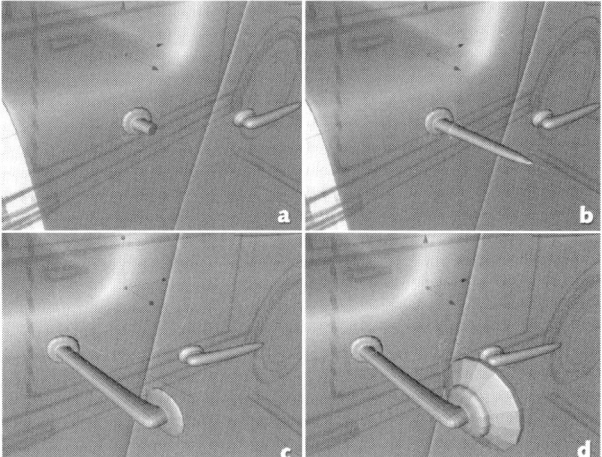

FIGURE 5.88 *Creating the mirror shapes off the surface of the car.*

Finally, when the mirror has been shaped to your satisfaction, extrude the mirror face back into the mirror object just slightly to create a small lip on the mirror edge (Figure 5.89).

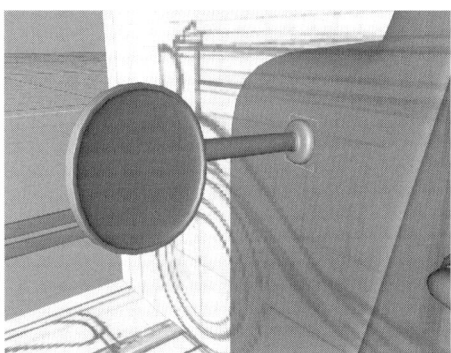

FIGURE 5.89 *Adding a lip to the mirror edge.*

WHEELS

The wheels of a car are based on simple primitives with slight point and polygon manipulation. There are numerous tutorials all over the Internet about how to model tires, or hubcaps, or alloy wheels, but they mostly involve styles that would be inappropriate for this car! So in the interest of dressing this car up right, I'll demonstrate a quick spoked wheel with a slightly more antique flavor that is suitable for our model.

Tire:

Begin by creating a tube primitive that conforms to the shape of the tire in your reference image. We can keep the geometry fairly light — maybe 12 Rotation segments, 3 Cap segments, and 3 Height segments. Make this primitive editable and place it under a HyperNURBS parent object (Figure 5.90).

Use the Optimize command to make the Cap and Height portions welded at their edge points (before optimization, the edge points of Cap and Height sections are multiple). The tube will immediately round off significantly under the influence of the HyperNURBS parent. Select the inner surface of the tube and scale it inwards, so that it becomes narrower and the outer surface of the tire tapers towards it. This will make the tire wall more rounded and natural looking.

The outer tread surface can be selected and tapered inwards in the same manner, but to a much lesser degree — just enough to slightly round the edges of the tread surface, but not so much as to make the tire wall appear affected (Figure 5.91).

Once this is done, you can apply a bump map cylindrically around the outer surface to simulate the tread of the tire to quite good effect. But then, this is a modeling tutorial, so I'll leave the joy of discovery up to you!

FIGURE 5.90 *Create a tube primitive with 12 rotation segments, 3 Cap segments, and 3 Height segments to begin tires. Place appropriately in relationship to car.*

FIGURE 5.91 *Tapering the outer tread.*

Hub:

The hub for this wheel consists of an inner "hub", and an outer ring, connected with interwoven spokes. The whole thing is about half of the width of the tire, and mirrored through the center of the tire, so it is duplicated for the outside and inside of the wheel.

To create the outer ring, make a tube object with one segment in each of the Cap and Height values, and once again use 12 Rotation segments. Make the object editable and place it in a HyperNURBS parent object. Use the Optimize command to consolidate the tube side and Cap portions into one object. The HyperNURBS object will then have a visible effect on the smoothing of the tube object.

Position the tube so that it approximates the rim of the hub. Select the polygons on the inside surface and outward facing cap of this tube object, and use Extrude Inner to sharpen the edges and create an inner row of polygons on these surfaces (Figure 5.92 a). Without changing the selection, use the Extrude function to cause the newly created polygon rows to indent from the rest of the surface. This step adds some aesthetic detail to the front of the hub, as well as creates a groove around the interior of the rim for seating the ends of the spokes we will be making (Figure 5.92 b).

Next, select the inner surface polygons of the rim and the immediately adjacent row of polygons on the side surfaces (Figure 5.92 c). Move these polygons towards the middle of the tire to slope the whole rim inward along the front surface, and move the spoke groove further back (Figure 5.92 d).

Create a cylinder in the middle of the wheel to represent the hub center. This cylinder can be of similar structure to the tube objects we were creating previously. Use 12 Rotation segments, 3 Height segments, and 2 Cap segments. Make this object editable and place it in a HyperNURBS parent and use Optimize to

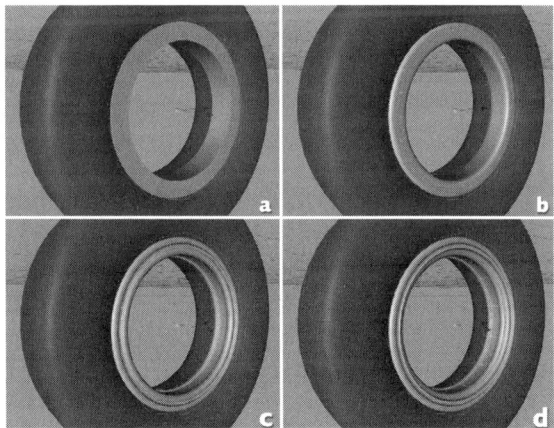

FIGURE 5.92 *Creating the hub by giving initial roundness and continuing construction of the inner ring.*

weld the edges of the cap and side portions of the cylinder. The cylinder becomes rounded on the edges (Figure 5.93 a). Select the inner polygons of the outward facing surface of the hub object and move them away from the cylinder along the X-axis to round the hub center. Then extrude them minutely to create a raised lip. Now select the outer ring of polygons on the outward facing surface of the cylinder, and use Extrude Inner to create a row of polygons within these polygons. Extrude these new polygons into the hub center to create a little indentation for aesthetic value (Figure 5.93 b).

Now, select the polygons that make up the rear portion of this hub center (furthest in along the X-axis towards the center of the wheel), and scale them down in the Z- and Y-directions so the diameter of this portion of the hub center decreases. This area will seat the inner ends of the spokes we create.

To fashion the spokes, merely create two cylinders (they don't need to be editable or HyperNURBS, or anything, but simple cylinders!) and position them in a crossed manner at the top of the hub center (Figure 5.94 a). The ends of both sides of both spokes should be placed within the respective seatings we made for them on the hub objects. Make sure the axis for this spoke group is in the center of the wheel, and then use the Array command to create the rest of the spokes around the wheel center (Figure 5.94 b).

Mirror this entire hub assembly down the middle of the tire and place a copy in the back of the tire so that there is a hub object on either side of the tire (Figure 5.95).

Finally, make sure that all axes for the tire group are in the wheel center so that you can rotate the wheel predictably for animation or scene set up. Use the Object Axis tool to move the axis without moving the corresponding object out of position.

Copy and paste enough wheels (including a spare on the back of the vehicle mounted on the support we made in the taillight step), and if desired, run cylinders between them for axles. That should be more than adequate detail for most purposes, as the axles remain hidden from normal view.

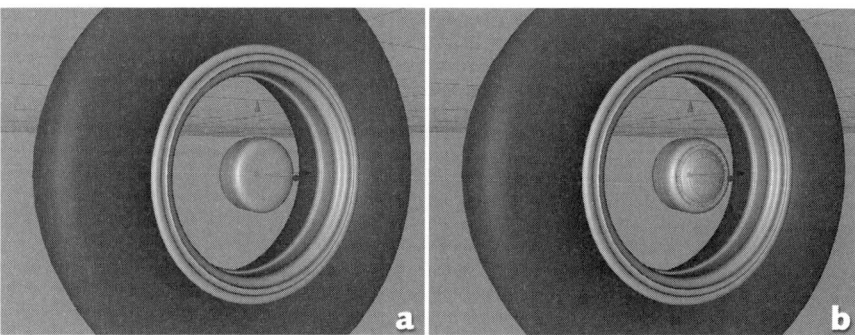

FIGURE *Preparing the hub.*
5.93

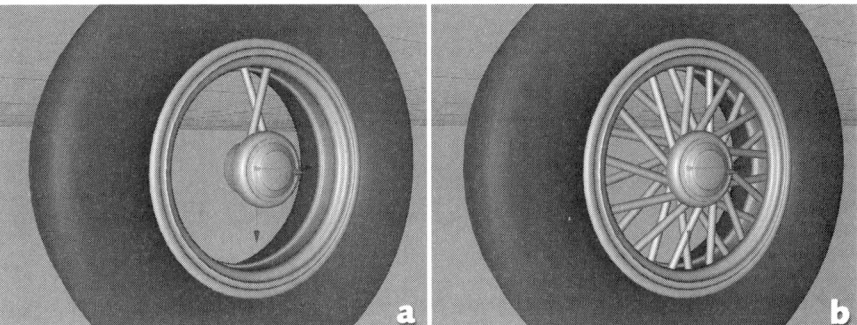

FIGURE 5.94 *Creating the spokes with simple primitives.*

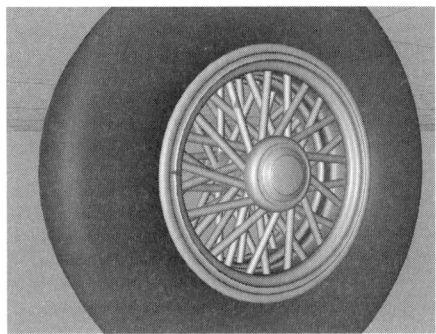

FIGURE 5.95 *Mirrored hub to add density to spoke collection.*

EPILOGUE

A NOTE ON HIERARCHY STRUCTURE AND AXIS PLACEMENT

So now that the car is modeled (interiors and engines and mechanics are up to you!), how should it be set up so that it can be manipulated like a car? How can it also be optimized so that the object hierarchy is most efficient?

When objects were split off from the main body object, the default axis position was always central; that is, inherited from the axis position of the car body. The positioning of the parts are correct, but you couldn't pivot a door open at this point because the axis is in the center of the car and wouldn't act as a hinge for rotation purposes. We will have to use the Object Axis tool to position the axes for our movable parts into place to act as hinges would. We should then concentrate on setting up the hierarchy so that the car is finalized.

The first thing I do once the object is finalized is to make objects under Symmetry parents editable so that both sides become represented by tangible geometry. There are most likely arguments against doing this, mainly that it eliminates the advantage of having half the geometry, but I tend to disregard this. I tend to view the Symmetry object as a modeling aid mostly, and once my modeling is done, I like to have both halves of the model made of polygons. I also like that by making the object editable I can get rid of concerns over what needs to be under Symmetry hierarchies, and what needs not be. Furthermore, before I make symmetrical objects editable, I take objects that I want to act independently across different sides of the model out of the symmetry parents (a good example of this would be the car doors and engine covers – they should be independent of each other). I then copy and paste these objects and mirror them so that I have individual doors on each side.

Take the time to set the car up with doors that can open independently (separate objects, with properly positioned object axes), and structure the hierarchy logically. You may have noticed by now that a HyperNURBS and Symmetry parent object has the limitation of only affecting one object underneath it, but rather than having one HyperNURBS object for each child object you want to affect, try placing everything within a Null Object underneath the HyperNURBS parent, and instantly you have the solution.

A Final Word

Hopefully, at the end of this all you have something that looks like a car (Figure 5.96 a and 5.96 b)! But whether you do or not, more importantly you should have spent considerable time practicing all the skills that make for successful HyperNURBS modeling. Everything that gets taken into consideration, from the planning stages, to the object shaping, to the detailed modeling, is all strengthened with experience more than tutelage. If this car didn't turn out satisfactorily, take comfort in the fact that the next one will be easier with the knowledge you've gained about what works with HyperNURBS and what doesn't. And if you were one of the lucky ones who got a good-looking car straight away, congratulations! You are off to a better start than I ever was! Happy modeling!

FIGURE 5.96 *Hopefully the result of your hard work. The final, finished, untextured car.*

CHAPTER 6

Utilizing the Power of Hyper-NURBS: Modeling Organic Forms from Primitives

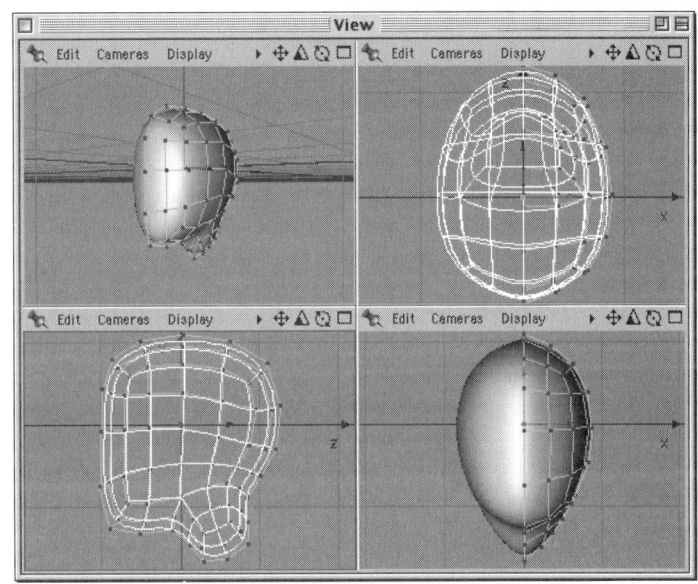

In Chapter 4 we looked at a lot of various modeling techniques dealing with NURBS. In Jeff Carlson's tutorial in Chapter 5, a slew of innovative modeling techniques were explored within the realms of HyperNURBS. As discussed earlier, there are two major types of HyperNURBS modeling — the first deals with altering a primitive form within a HyperNURBS to create a much more complex shape. This chapter deals with this technique. See Chapter 7 for more information on building an effective HyperNURBS object from scratch by building the shape up point by point, polygon by polygon.

PRIMITIVE BASED HYPERNURBS MODELING OF A HUMAN HEAD

TUTORIAL *By Anson Call*

The following tutorial will show you how to make a head using HyperNURBS and related tools. Please remember that this example isn't the only right way to model a head, and that along the way there can be many deviations that you could take depending on your wants and needs. There are just some things we won't delve into, like individual discretion on what particular features of the head should look like. That's up to you. Also, this tutorial assumes that you have some experience with C4D and its interface. If you don't understand what a HyperNURBS is, then you should first analyze Chapter 4 of this book or read through the HyperNURBS sections of the manual first. With that said, let's get started.

First, let's set up our HyperNURBS by creating a Cube Primitive (name it "Face") and a HyperNURBS object and placing the "Face" object as a child of the HyperNURBS. Make sure that you make the "Face" object editable (Structure>Make Editable). Secondly, perform a subdivision on the cube (Structure>Subdivide) (Figure 6.1). Then change to Points mode. Your project should look something like Figure 6.2.

Notice that there aren't many points on the HyperNURBS. There'll be a lot more later, but remember that less is more in this case, and keep it as simple as possible. The next thing you need to do is to get a basic shape of the head you want. Do this while you alternate between Points mode and Polygon mode by selecting the Points tool and the Polygon tool. It would also be a good idea to import front and side profiles into the corresponding modeling window to use as a guide. Remember this is just a basic shape (Figure 6.3).

Next, select one half of the model using either the Points or Polygon tool and delete it, leaving the other half intact as shown in Figure 6.4 (a) and (b). Then take the half of the face still visible and place it as a child of a Symmetry Object (Figure 6.4 c).

Chapter 6 Utilizing the Power of HyperNURBS   177

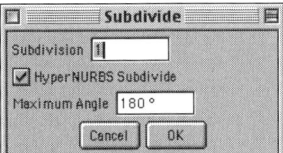

FIGURE 6.1 *After creating a Primitive Cube object, be sure to make it editable and subdivide it.*

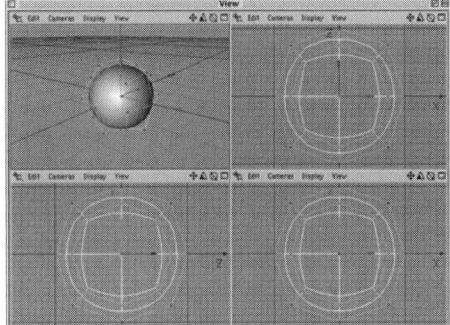

FIGURE 6.2 *The basic form of the soon-to-be head.*

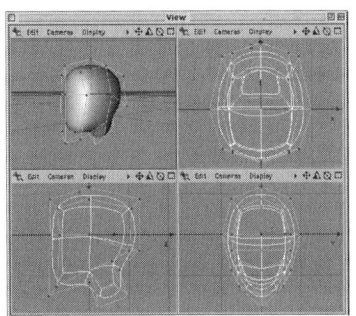

FIGURE 6.3 *Basic head shape created by altering extant points and polygons.*

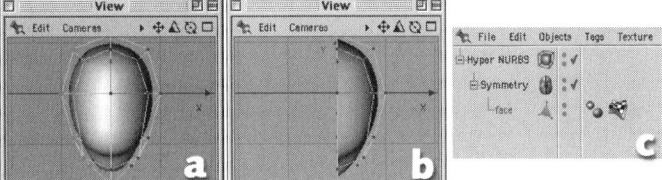

FIGURE 6.4 *Deleting one half of the model will save time as you only need to model one half of the face.*

Now we'll need more points to work with. So repeat the subdivision step listed above with the same settings. This should give you enough points to proceed (Figure 6.5).

At this point you can do some more tweaking to the basic shape, before we go on. Don't be afraid to turn the Symmetry Object off and on by clicking the green checkmark next to it as you need it. It will help you see your model better. It is important that you try to keep the points as evenly spaced as possible (avoid bunching them up) because this will help you avoid wrinkles.

Now let's perform a few knife cuts on our model to add points that will later assist us. Figure 6.6 shows the results of the knife cuts with highlighted points. Repeat the process once more using similar cuts to those shown in Figure 6.7.

With these added knife cuts, we should have enough polygons to begin creating details of the face. Let's start with the nose. Select the polygons shown in Figure 6.8 and use the Extrude tool to extrude them twice.

Up to this point, the shape that we have has worked well within a Symmetry Object. This is because the middle plane that the object is mirrored along has been devoid of polygons, thus it has no puckers as the HyperNURBS attempts to round the form. The problem with these recent extrusions is that they have created new polygons along the face of the mirrored plane. To solve the problem, select the polys along the inside of the nose and delete them (Figure 6.9).

You will have some points that have wandered off the X-axis. Let's put them back. Select a point and enter zero for the X-axis. Do it for any point on the nose that needs it. You can tell by turning on symmetry and locating any rips. If it has a rip, it's because a point or points does not have a value of zero for its X-axis (Figure 6.10).

Next, take some time to push and pull the points of the new extrusions into a more nose-like shape. Remember to activate the HyperNURBS object often so you can see what the rounded version of the nose appears as. When you are happy with the overall shape of the nose, start on the nostril. To form the nostril, switch to Polygon mode and we'll use several Extrude Inners (done with the Extrude Inners tool) so that we have enough points to work with to get a clean edge to the nostril (Figure 6.11). Once you have around three or four Extrude

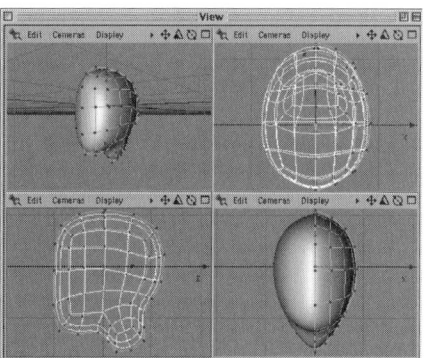

FIGURE 6.5 *Our face thus far after being subdivided within a Symmetry object.*

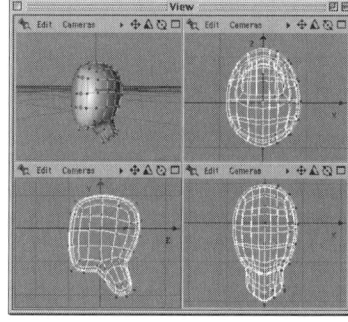

FIGURE 6.6 *Create some more subdivisions for high polygon areas of the face using the Knife tool.*

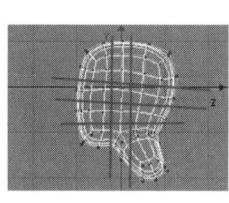
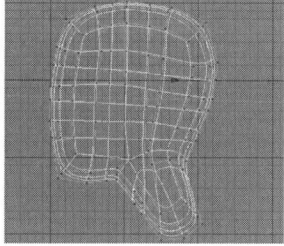

FIGURE 6.7 *Continue with the Knife tool from a side view to further create necessary subdivisions.*

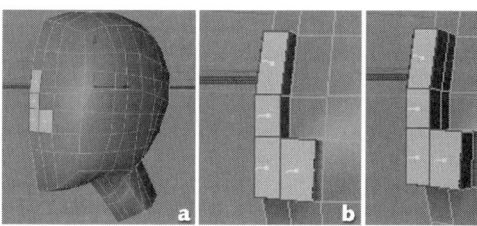

FIGURE 6.8 *To begin creating the nose, select the polygons shown and extrude them twice.*

Inners, realign the points to make sure you have a good-sized innermost polygon, and then extrude upward into the nose.

Let's move on to the mouth. In order to create the necessary geometry for this region, we'll need a few more knife operations. You may need to adjust the position of some of the points to make room for these new cuts (Figure 6.12).

Again, from this point, we'll create the added geometry for the mouth through a series of Extrude Inners (Figure 6.13). And just like before, the Extrude process will create some polygons close to the symmetry plane that need to be deleted.

In the process of deleting all of these polygons, you may notice that when you switch back to Points mode, there are extra points floating around. The simplest way to get rid of this extra garbage is to just select the errant points and delete them. This sort of housekeeping is highly recommended, as it keeps the visual workspace clean. After you have deleted the polygons, take care to move all the points on the innermost area of the mouth to the X-axis (Figure 6.14).

Now that we have all the geometry we need to create the mouth we can begin to form the oral cavity. An oral cavity is important to have later if the model is ever to be animated. Select the innermost four polygons (Figure 6.15 a) and using the Move Active Element tool, move them straight back into the head

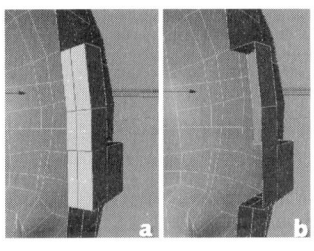

FIGURE 6.9 *Deleting the inner polygons created by the recent extrusion will keep the Symmetry Object clean.*

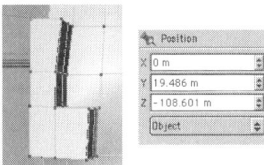

FIGURE 6.10 *Through the extrusion process, some of the points along the symmetry plane may have strayed. Clean up by looking for tears with the Symmetry Object activated and then zeroing out the stray points' X value in the Coordinates Manager.*

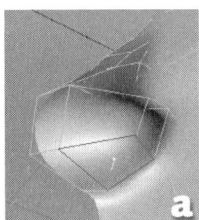 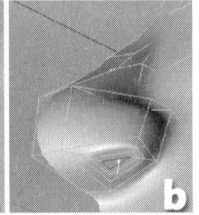 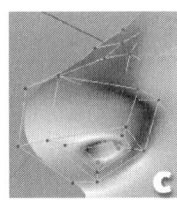

FIGURE 6.11 *The nostril is formed by first creating several Extrude Inners followed lastly by a regular Extrude to create the nostril.*

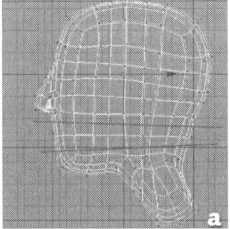 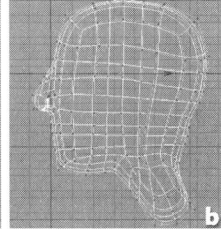

FIGURE 6.12 *After carefully arranging the extant points to allow for some added subdivisions, cut the entire model in these places to add some new subdivisions to create the mouth.*

(Figure 6.15 b). Then resize these polygons to give a more cavernous shape to the mouth (Figure 6.15 c).

With the oral cavity created, we can turn our attention to the lips. Since we've done a series of Extrude Inners already, we have the polygons necessary to create the lip shapes. To do this, shift to Points mode and adjust the points to better form the lips. This is still a rough interpretation, so feel free to make any additional changes (Figure 6.16).

Let's move onto the eyes. Again, we'll need some added polygons to accurately form this region. To get this added geometry, we'll use a series of Extrude Inners (Figure 6.17).

When you have sufficient Extrude Inners, pull the last set of created polygons into the head to form the eye cavity. This process is very similar to the one done to form the mouth. However, the eye is probably the most complex part of the head (other than the ear) so you'll need more points in order to get enough geometry to give you the appropriate amount of control (Figure 6.18).

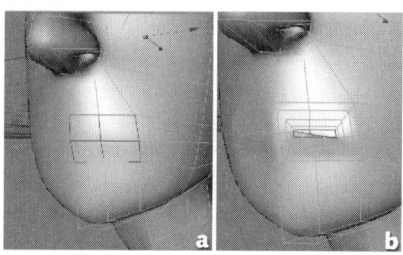

FIGURE 6.13 *Create needed geometry with a series of Extrude Inners.*

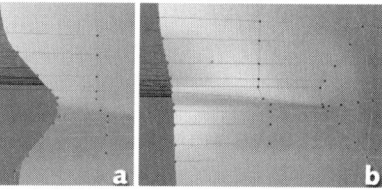

FIGURE 6.14 *Further clean up the area by selecting the points on the innermost edge of the remaining polygons and moving them to X=0.*

FIGURE 6.15 *Creating the oral cavity.*

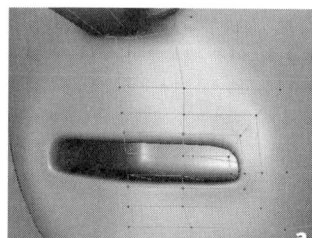 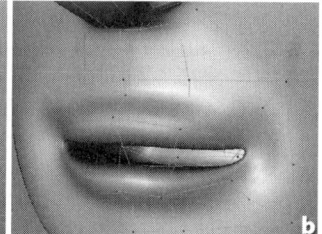

FIGURE 6.16 *Continue to form the lips, using the already present points.*

At this point, it is a good idea to bring a sphere in to use as an eye (Figure 6.19 a). Create a Sphere Primitive to help you get the shape you want as you form the eye. After the sphere is placed, continue to refine the eye by pushing and pulling the points around the eye into place (Figure 6.19 b).

On to the ears. Switch back to Polygon Mode and select the polygons that are in the general area of the ears. Once these are selected, go to Selection>Hide Unselected to hide the rest of the head. This way you can work unencumbered with the delicate and intricate parts of the ear (Figure 6.20).

To create the general shape of the ear, extrude the polygons, rotate them, and extrude them again. This produces a very nice starting collection of polygons in a very general shape of the ear (Figure 6.21).

Take the polygons thus far and rough out a general shape of the ear (Figure 6.22).

The inner areas of the ear is a complex collection of curves. In order to model this, we need more geometry. Select the polygons for the inner section of the ear and create lots of Extrude Inners (Figure 6.23 a). Then select the polygons that form the overall inner ear area and use the Extrude tool to extrude inward (Figure 6.23 b).

Now to refine the ear a bit, switch to Points mode and manipulate the existing points to get a bit more detailed ear (Figure 6.24).

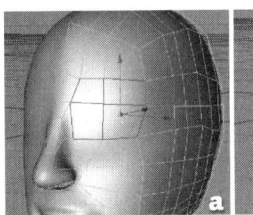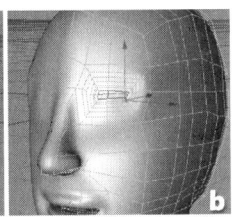

FIGURE 6.17 *Adding necessary polygons for the eye area through a series of Extrude Inners.*

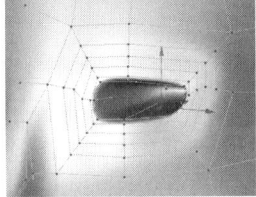

FIGURE 6.18 *Pull the last extrusion into the head to create a cavity for the eye.*

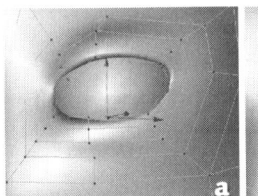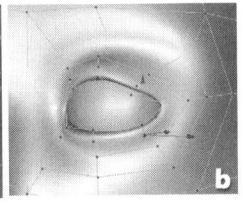

FIGURE 6.19 *Create a sphere to model around for the eye. Adjust the extant points to better form the eye.*

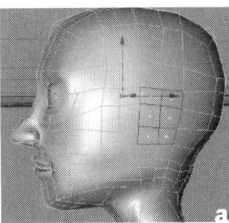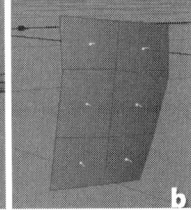

FIGURE 6.20 *To work with the ear, first select the polygons that will create the ear and hide the rest of the head.*

Unhide the hidden polygons and you're left with a fairly general looking head (Figure 6.25). We've really done minimal work on the eyes, ears, mouth, and nose, and much work should still be done in those areas. However, the hard work has been done and you can go ahead (pun intended) to refine those areas to get the shape you want (Figure 6.26).

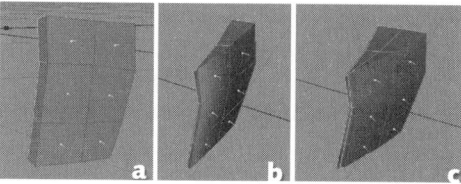

FIGURE 6.21 *Create the rough shape of the ear with extrusions, rotations, and more extrusions.*

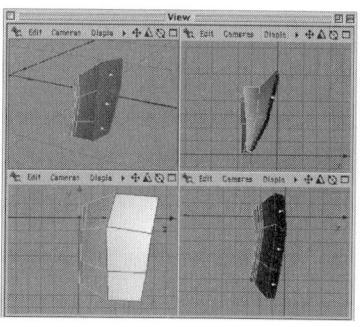

FIGURE 6.22 *General ear formed from extant polygons.*

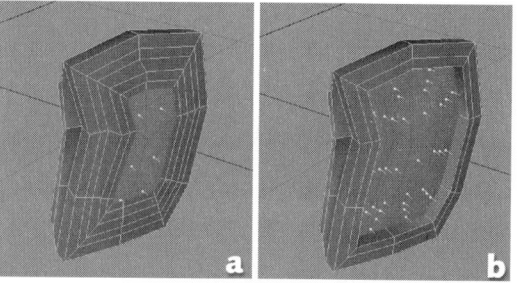

FIGURE 6.23 *Creating the general shape of the ear through inner extrusions to create added geometry, and a final extrusion of a collection of polygons to create the shape.*

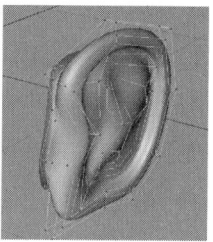

FIGURE 6.24 *Manipulating points to create more detailed ear.*

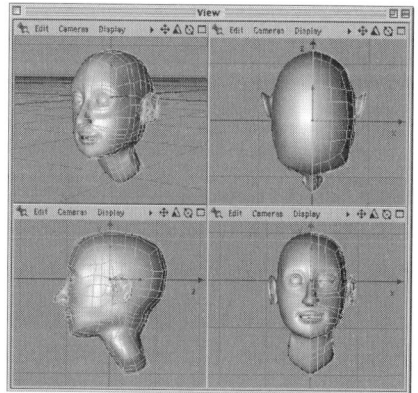

FIGURE 6.25 *Generic head.*

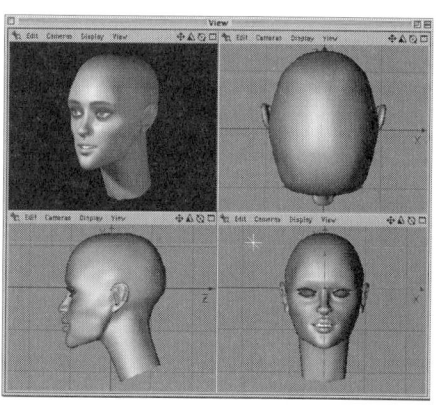

FIGURE 6.26 *More refined version after refining general shape.*

6.2 CHARACTER HEAD TUTORIAL

By Desiree Maher

TUTORIAL

The method of HyperNURBS modeling in the tutorials in this chapter makes use of creating all the subdivisions needed for the entire head before ever beginning to move points or polygons around. The character head shown in Figure 6.27 is the outcome of this tutorial.

Before any actual modeling takes place, take the time to create several sketches. This step saves a lot of time and is very important in the overall planning process of modeling a character in 3D. Sketch the model from at least two viewpoints — the front and profile. Make sure the main features on each sketch are proportional and line up with each other by placing them in the same file within Photoshop and using guides to ensure that they are aligned. Most importantly, pay attention to the bottom of the chin, the nose, the center of the eye, and the top of the head (Figure 6.28).

FIGURE 6.28 *It's vitally important to make sure that all the basic features of the face are lined up. Do this in Photoshop or some other imaging editing program before ever importing into C4D.*

FIGURE 6.27 *The results of our modeling labors.*

When the guides have been placed, and you are sure that all major features are aligned, copy and paste each view point into a different Photoshop file and save them separately for later use in a material. After adjustments have been made accordingly, carefully plan out how many subdivisions the character head will have. At the most basic level, at least three lines of division are needed to form a rounded area such as a lip. The number of subdivisions depends on how round, elaborate, or detailed a feature is. The more subdivisions a feature encompasses, the more points are available to shape it, and thus the more detailed it can be. However, it is ideal to determine the least amount of essential subdivisions first in sketch form. This is accomplished first by drawing vertical lines on the frontal sketch at the edges of the major parts of the features on the face such as the corners of the eyes, the sides of the nose, the corners of the mouth, and anywhere else where you will need to have points available to help with modeling. Then using the same sketch, draw horizontal lines in the same fashion to mark key areas. Repeat this method using the profile sketch as well. This process is recommended to ensure that there is a plentiful amount of points available so that each feature can be formed adequately. Of course, there are several key areas beyond what was mentioned, but basically in this model there are at least three lines of subdivisions for the eyes, tip of the nose, and mouth areas. More can be created later as needed with extrusions. Create a Cube Primitive and change the Segments setting to correspond to the number of subdivisions determined in your sketching process. Make the cube editable.

In Cinema 4D, we'll need to create a couple of planes to guide us as we model. Insert two planes, one along the X-axis and one along the Z-axis. Create a new material with the sketch of the frontal study of the character as the color map and apply it to the plane that lies along the X-axis. Make a second material using the profile study of the character and apply this one to the plane along the Z-axis. Make sure the size of the plane and original image are proportional by adjusting the plane's size in meters to the front and side images used as color maps. Although these are two different units (meters vs. pixels), this ensures the proportions of the plane are accurate to the size of the material you are going to place on it. Make these adjustments in the corresponding section of the Coordinates tab.

To model the character head, begin by creating a Cube Primitive and subdivide so that is it is 11 segments high, 11 segments wide, and 12 segments deep as figured by the discussion above (Figure 6.29).

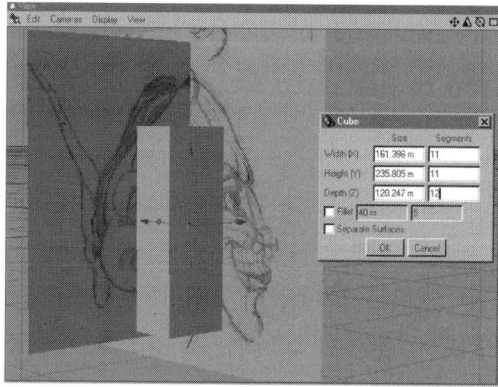

FIGURE 6.29 *Create two planes to allow for the creation of guide objects to help guide the modeling process. Pay special attention to the size and proportion to avoid stretching the image, and thus distorting your modeling reference.*

To keep the workflow swift, we'll be using a Symmetry object so we only need to model one half of the face. In Polygon mode, select one half of the polygons of the Cube Primitive and delete them. Switch to Points mode to deal with the points left behind by selecting them and deleting them or use Structure>Optimize to delete all the unused points. Then place the cube into a symmetry object to create the other half and place the symmetry object into a HyperNURBS object to create a smooth collection of features.

While you are in Points mode, use the images of the frontal and profile of the character face, select points where needed, and position them so that a simple overall rounded form is created (Figure 6.30). There is no need to add any great detail at this point, such as cheeks or the chin, because this will be modeled later after the main features of the face have been created.

To facilitate the look of a natural eye socket, move the outer points making up the four polygons that are to be used for the eye, so that a more rounded shape is formed. Once this is done, switch to Polygon mode and select the four polygons forming the eye, then Extrude Inner slightly to create a slightly smaller set of polys. Then Extrude these polygons inward so that the eye socket is formed. With the same polygons selected, Extrude Inner again and then Extrude these polys out to form the outer section of the eyelids (Figure 6.31).

To create the inner portion of the eyelids, Extrude Inner slightly and then Extrude these polys inward once more toward the inside of the head. Finally, delete the four original polygons to create the eye opening.

Now that the eyelids have been constructed, move the points of the eyelids and eye socket so that they take a more rounded shape (Figure 6.32). At this point it is helpful to place the eyeball, made from a sphere primitive, in the

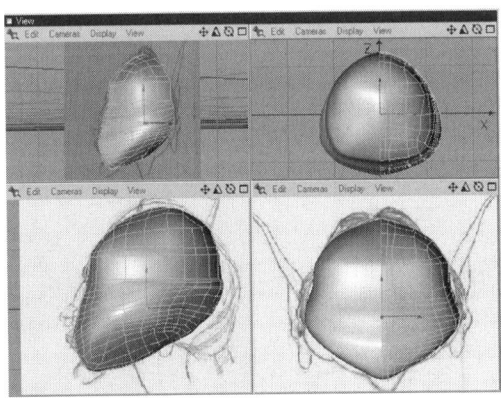

FIGURE 6.30 *Create an overall shape of the head by moving points around to roughly match your model.*

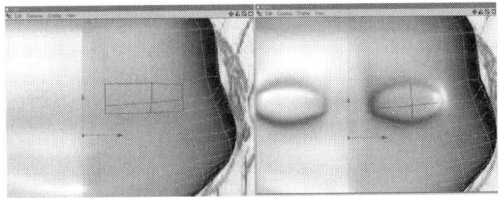

FIGURE 6.31 *Create the eye sockets through a series of Extrude Inner – Extrude combinations.*

opening so that the lid can be rounded around it. Take time to refine the points around the newly placed sphere so that you have a "tight fit."

To create the nose, jump back into Polygon mode and select the polygon that will become the tip of the nose and Extrude out. For the bridge of the nose, select the polygons in that area and Extrude them as well (Figure 6.33). We'll want all of these polygons to Extrude out together, which they won't do if they are not lying relatively flat. So, to keep the relevant bridge polys as one unit, make sure the Preserve Group box is checked in the Active Tool dialog box while the Extrude tool is active. You may also need to further adjust the values of the Maximum Angle, Offset, and Variation settings to ensure that the polys Extrude out together and don't form polygons between the extruding facets. Make sure to take time to delete any polygons that form during the Extrude process along the plane of symmetry.

Select the polygon that lies on the side of the tip of the nose and Extrude out to form the nostril. The nostril cavity is formed by selecting the polygon on the bottom of the nostril, Extruding Inner, and then Extruding again, but Extruding inward into the nostril (Figure 6.34).

Elongate the chin by selecting the polygons or points and using the Magnet tool to click-drag and form the chin and sides of the face (Figure 6.35).

To create the mouth, first select the polygons that are going to be used to form this region, and Extrude them in toward the center of the head. It may be necessary to adjust the polygons so that they lie flat to each other and Extrude correctly. One such method is selecting the polygons and going to Structure>Edit Surface>Set Value and aligning the polygons along the appropriate plane. In this example, the polygons were aligned along the z plane at a certain value. They were then Extruded, and the residual polygons created along the center of the model in the extruded area were selected and deleted (Figure 6.36).

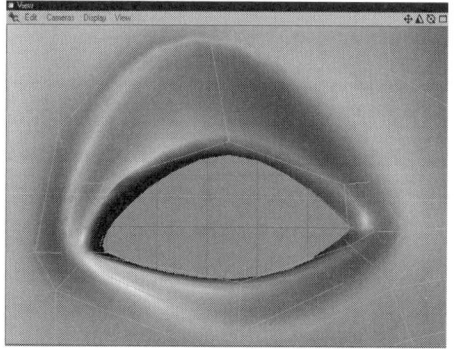

FIGURE 6.32 *Refine the eye at the Points level.*

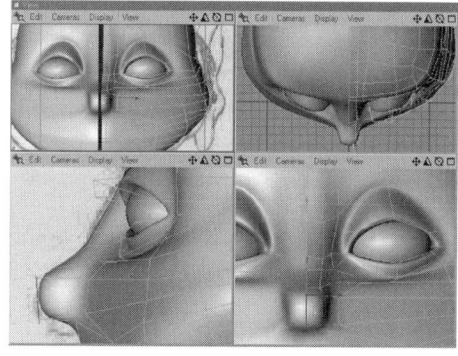

FIGURE 6.33 *Create the nose tip and bridge with simple extrusions.*

Chapter 6 Utilizing the Power of HyperNURBS

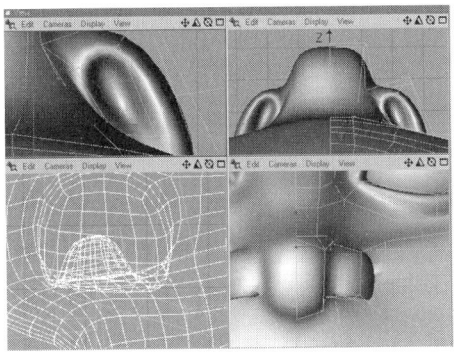

FIGURE 6.34 *Nostrils are forms through Inner Extrudes – Extrude combinations.*

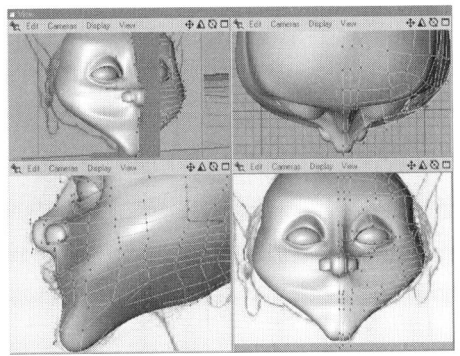

FIGURE 6.35 *Elongating the chin through Extrusions.*

Form the lips by selecting points and moving them, using the drawings as guidelines (Figure 6.37). Be careful when using the Selection tool that the Select Visible Elements box is checked in the Active Tool dialog box. This ensures that only the desired polygons or points will be selected and manipulated, and that you aren't accidentally selecting points or polys on the back side of the head.

Begin modeling the ear with a new Cube Primitive. Subdivide the box into six segments wide, one segment deep, and four segments high. Make the object editable and begin to move the points of the box so that it forms the general shape of the character's ear (Figure 6.38). Place the object in a HyperNURBS object. Round the edges of the ear by shifting polygons and points.

Select the polygons that make up the lobe of the ear and using the Scale Active Element tool, enlarge the area until it looks suitable (Figure 6.39).

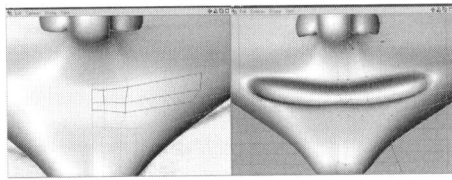

FIGURE 6.36 *Creating the mouth through extrusions. Make sure to delete unwelcome polygons formed along the symmetry Y-axis.*

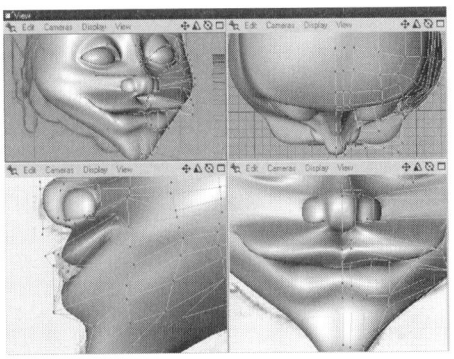

FIGURE 6.37 *Refine the lips according to your sketches. Make sure to work on the Points level at this point.*

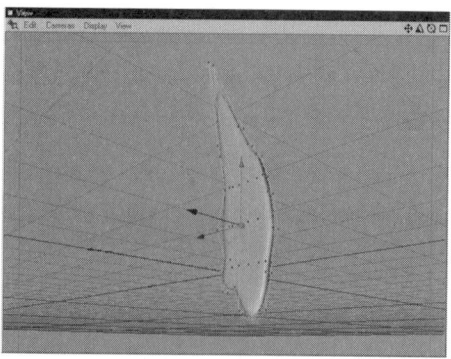

FIGURE 6.38 Create the ears with a separate Cube Primitive placed in a HyperNURBS object.

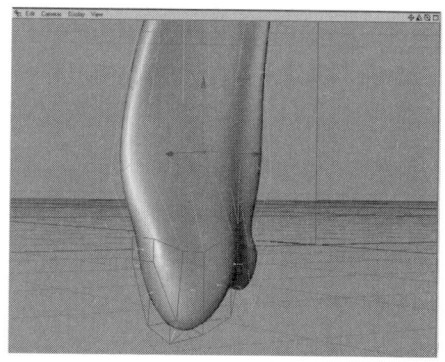

FIGURE 6.39 To give lobes with mass, select the polygons composing that area of the ear and scale them outward.

On the portion of the ear that faces the head, select the points that make up the inner region of the ear shape, and round the overall shape made by the polys by moving the outer points. Then select these polygons and Extrude out, making the terminal end smaller than at the beginning of the extrusion (Figure 6.40). Slightly angle the extrusion outward and toward the earlobe of the ear.

To create the inside of the ear, begin with an Extrude Inner of the inner polygons and a slight Extrude towards the center of the head to form the outer folds of the ear. Extrude Inner again with these same polygons and arrange the outer points into more of a rounded shape, followed by another Extrude again towards the center of the head (Figure 6.41).

To create the cheeks, select three of the polygons in the cheek area, and Extrude outward to give the cheek area more volume (Figure 6.42). Fine-tune the area by positioning the points of the cheek to create a round cheek (Figure 6.43).

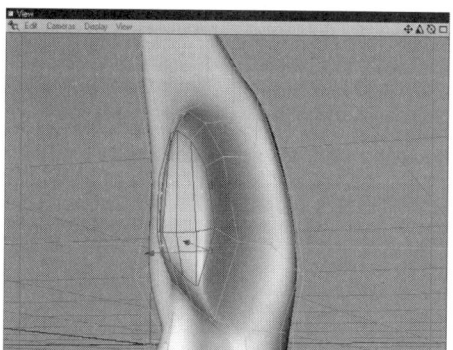

FIGURE 6.40 Create the part of the ear extending to the head with extrusions and moving the inner polys.

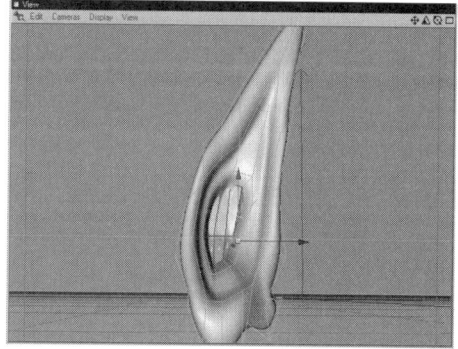

FIGURE 6.41 Continue to refine the inner ear with more Extrude Inners and Points level manipulation.

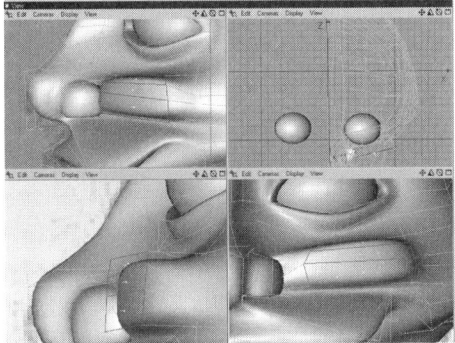

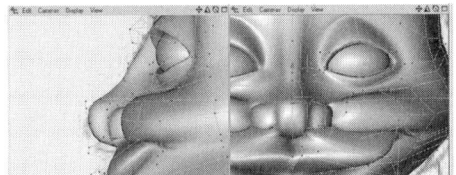

FIGURE 6.42 To give the cheeks the necessary volume displayed in the sketch, add polygons by extruding the cheek polys outward.

FIGURE 6.43 Refine the cheeks on a Points level, using the newly created points.

The eyebrows are created in a similar fashion. Select a row of polygons about the eye area and Extrude out to form the basic shape (Figure 6.44). Manipulate the points of the extrusion to form the eyebrow. Pull the eyebrow down just over the eye socket to give it more depth (Figure 6.45).

Lastly, position one ear on the character head using the Rotation tool to rotate it slightly forward. Then place the ear object in a symmetry object, giving the character two ears (Figure 6.46). Add any other details you find necessary to further define the character.

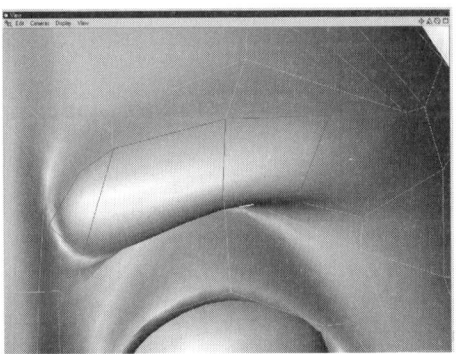

FIGURE 6.44 Eyebrows are given appropriate mass in the same fashion. Select polys in the eyebrow area and Extrude out.

FIGURE 6.45 Then refine the shape at the Points level.

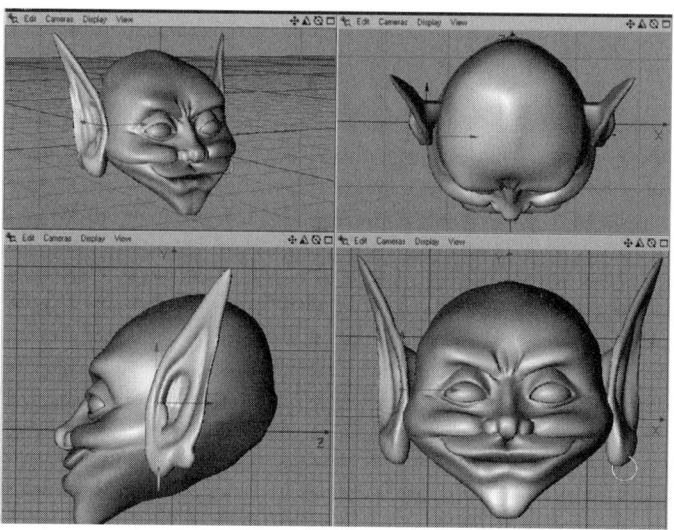

FIGURE 6.46 *Rotate the ear and place it in a symmetry object to finish the character.*

CHAPTER 7
Modeling a Human Face and Head

By Nicholas Woolridge
(Assistant Professor, Biomedical Communications, University of Toronto)

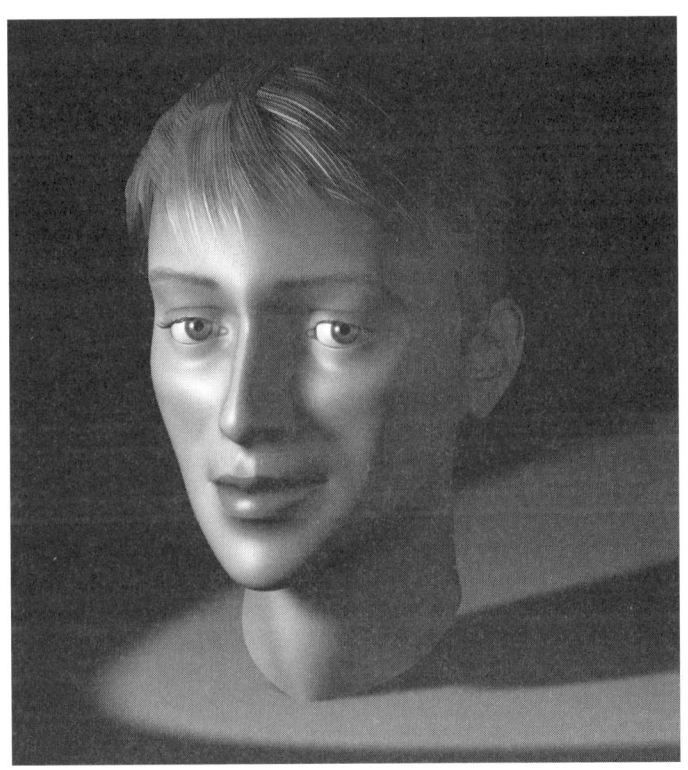

7.1 Modeling the Human Face and Head: Introduction

TUTORIAL

Creating a realistic three-dimensional head in a 3D program is a great challenge, and an even greater learning experience. Planning is required, but the payoff to that planning will be a piece of geometry that can be textured, animated, and rendered in a very gratifying way.

Creating a convincing realistic face is especially difficult. The human visual-perceptual system devotes a large part of its resources to the recognition, understanding, and memory of faces. Human beings can be very critical of artificial faces when they are "off." Relatively minor flaws in proportion or symmetry can render a face implausible.

The flip side of this concentration of perceptual power on facial recognition means that we try to see faces everywhere; the "smiley" face is an example of an extremely simplified face that humans have no trouble recognizing and understanding. Sometimes it is hard to look at a power outlet without seeing a startled blockhead! This means that "cartoony", simplified, or caricatured faces are often easier for viewers to accept than a poor attempt at realism.

Having said that, this chapter will be about creating a realistic human face and head, but the basic techniques presented here could be applied to the creation of exaggerated or non-realistic heads, or, indeed, to any complex organic shape. This tutorial is pretty detailed, but there is still a lot of room for the kind of tweaking that will test your spatial abilities. The basic structure presented in this tutorial can be adapted to many heads; finessing the model can make it a truly individual work.

Approaches

There are several different approaches to modeling a head. Some people like to start out with a polygon primitive like a sphere or cube, and use various modeling techniques (subdividing polygons, extruding, smooth shifting) to refine the basic shape into a head. Others like to build up a head shape from a complex of metaballs. Still others like to use swept or lofted splines or deformed NURB spheres to create the head shape.

We are going to use a more basic approach, and build most of the polygons we need from scratch. This has the advantage of allowing us total control over the arrangement and placement of our polygons; we can put few very large polygons at the back of the head, for instance, where the need for detail is not great, and many small polygons around the eye, where we want to have fine detail. We will create one half of the head, and let Cinema 4D's symmetry object

Chapter 7 Modeling a Human Face and Head

create the other half. The symmetry object will be placed inside a HyperNURBS object, which will take our relatively low-resolution polygon cage and dynamically subdivide it, smoothing over harsh edges, and creating a rounded and organic-looking surface.

The instructions I will provide will be fairly specific, but there is always room for tweaks that will change or improve upon my results. Consider my steps a rough guide; your judgment, observation, and eye will determine what ultimately emerges from this tutorial.

Head Anatomy

Modeling a head well requires an understanding of the bony and soft tissue anatomy that underlies the skin. The two major components that create the distinctive look of each face are the skull and the soft tissues.

The Skull

The skull provides the hard under structure that defines the architecture of the face. It is a complex of 22 bones, consisting of two major components: the cranial skeleton, which encloses the brain; and the facial skeleton, which underlies the face. A drawing of a standard anterior, or frontal, view of the skull can be seen in Figure 7.1.

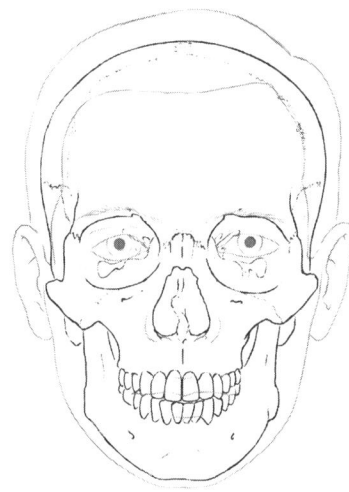

Figure 7.1 *An anterior view of a typical human skull, with external features overlaid.*

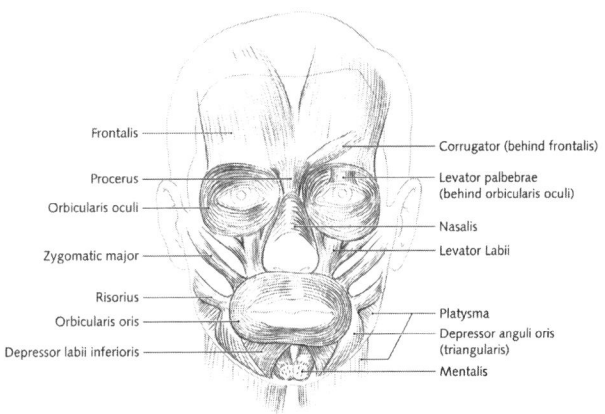

Figure 7.2 *An anterior view of the muscles of facial expression. Note the concentric arrangement of the muscles around the eye and mouth.*

SOFT TISSUES

The skin, muscles, fat, connective tissues, blood vessels, and other soft tissues round off the sharp edges of the skull, and determine the surface appearance of the face. The facial musculature serves to mobilize the mandible, assist in phonation (creating speech sounds), and creates the expressions that allow us to display emotion. Figure 7.2 shows some of the important muscles underlying facial expression. Note especially the concentric orientation of the muscles surrounding the eyes and mouth (the "orbicularis oculi" and "orbicularis oris" muscles, respectively). Keeping this arrangement of muscles in mind will help us plan the construction of our head so that it is optimized for animation.

THE EYE

The shape of the human eye could be described as two spheres – one smaller, one larger – superimposed on one another. The forward part of the smaller sphere (the cornea) sits just forward of the larger sphere.

In reality, the globe of the eye is rarely perfectly spherical (which, along with variations in the shape and deformability of the lens, often accounts for visual impairments and the need for corrective lenses). Figure 7.3 shows an accurate transverse (horizontally, from front to back) profile of the eye that can be lathed into a correct globe.

The other component of the eye that we need to be concerned with is the iris, a radially arranged complex of muscles and blood vessels covered with a pigmented epithelium that regulates the size of the pupil, and thus varies the amount of light that enters the eye. Its profile can also be seen in Figure 7.3. It is the pigmentation of the iris, of course, which lends the distinctive color to an eye. (On the CD, in the directory for this chapter, you will find illustrator files of the globe and iris profiles, which can be imported into Cinema 4D and dropped into a lathe nurbs object to create the geometry of the eye.)

ON THE CD

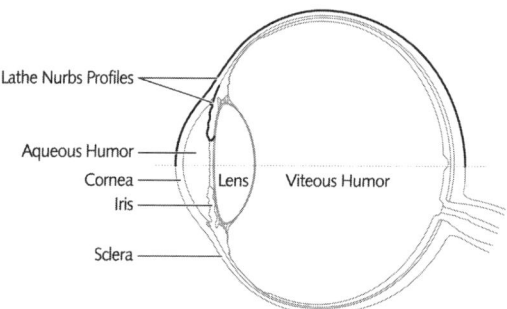

FIGURE 7.3   *A cutaway view of the eye (in this transverse section, it is interesting to note that the optic nerve does not exit at the rear "pole" of the eye). The profiles necessary for constructing the eye in Cinema 4D are indicated by the dark lines.*

USING REFERENCE PICTURES

Creating or obtaining good reference images will make modeling the head much easier. If you are scanning drawings or photographs, do so at a fairly high resolution. Ultimately, you will have to scale them down in your image editor, but that is always better than scaling up images that were scanned too small.

GETTING THE NECESSARY VIEWS

The most important views are the front and side (usually right) views. A top view can be helpful as well, but is not strictly necessary.

USING DRAWINGS

ON THE CD

The example I will be using in this tutorial is a hand-drawn face, scanned into the computer (see Figure 7.4). You can use the face I've drawn [file on the CD], or draw one yourself. If you choose to draw one yourself, here are a few things to keep in mind:

- There are a number of good "Anatomy for Artists" style books available that can be useful in helping you maintain realistic proportions in your drawings. One of my favorites is *The Artist's Complete Guide to Facial Expressions* by Gary Faigin. This book is also enormously useful as a reference in creating believable facial expressions.
- Using graph paper, or a ruler-drawn grid, can be useful in maintaining consistent eye, nose, ear, and mouth levels between your views.
- Even the most carefully drawn face will still have inconsistencies between the front and side views. Look at your reference images as a general guide, and feel free to adjust and improvise once you are modeling in C4D.

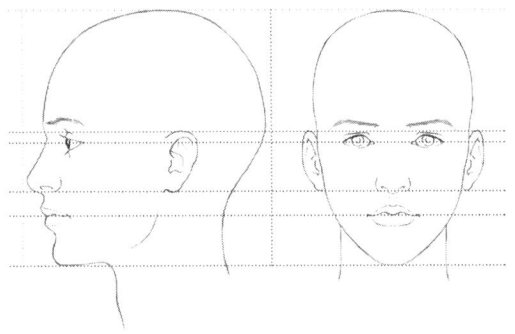

FIGURE 7.4 *The face reference we will use in this chapter. Notice the approximately square shape of the head from the side, and the location of the eyes halfway up the head.*

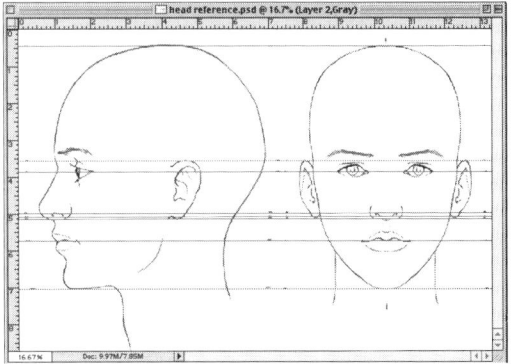

FIGURE 7.5 *Lining up vital facial characteristics within Photoshop to ensure accurate reference within C4D.*

Using Photographs

Another good option is to photograph someone in the requisite views. If you choose this option, keep these things in mind:

- Set up the camera at about the height of the subject's eye. Use a tripod for a nice stable image, and to maintain the camera's elevation between shots.
- Make sure your subject takes up most of the frame (i.e. a portrait shot from the shoulders up).
- Do not shoot in harsh sunlight. Shadows can obscure detail, and if you are planning to use the images as the basis for a texture map, you will have to spend a lot of time laboriously retouching the image to eliminate them.
- Use a long, or telephoto, lens to shoot your subject. At the very least, do not use a wide-angle or "short" lens. In other words, try to position yourself relatively far away from your subject, and zoom in to frame them within the viewfinder. Wide-angle lenses exaggerate foreshortening, and can distort parts of your subject so that they do not match well between views.

Optionally, you can draw reference "polygons" on your subject. Choose an eyeliner pencil or some other fine, easily removable makeup to draw on one half of your subject's face. Look ahead in this chapter to get hints on the placement of polygons, and carefully adapt them to follow the contours and changes in the planar surfaces of your subject's face and head. This technique allows for easier "triangulation" of the location of specific vertices on the modeled face.

Adjusting your Reference Images

Using an image editor, you will now need to adjust your reference images so that they will appear at the correct size in C4D. For the purposes of this tutorial, I will assume you are using Photoshop, but most pixel-based image editing programs should work.

Open the scanned drawings or photographs in Photoshop. If you have scanned your images separately, combine them into one document as seen in Figure 7.5.

Use Photoshop's guides feature to help you align the two images and check that the features line up. If, for instance, the ears are larger in the side view than in the front view, you could use Photoshop's tools to scale the ears down somewhat in the side view. If you are using photographs, you may discover that you need to rotate the side view slightly in order to make the features line up with the front view (especially if you were unable to position the camera at the subject's eye level).

In these drawings, you may also need to use Photoshop's tools to make the front view symmetrical by selecting and copying the left half of the face, then pasting and horizontally flipping it so that it covers the right half that I had originally drawn. You may find that you have drawn a somewhat asymmetrical face, and, while most people do not possess perfectly symmetrical faces, our construction process will involve mirroring one half of the face to make the other, and it is important to make sure that the face still looks OK.

You may find it helpful to replace the white background in your drawing with a light gray. This makes it much easier to see inactive polygons, splines, and HyperNURBS hulls, which are colored white by default in C4D. I did this by adding a Levels adjustment layer in Photoshop. Slide the bottom right output slider to position 170. This makes the drawing easy to read, but darkens the background enough to allow structures on top of it to stand out.

Once you are happy with the alignment and orientation of your images, front and side views need to be copied individually from the master file and saved separately into their own files. Make sure that the front view is centered in its file; this will ensure that the center of the face falls on the Y-axis in C4D. Scale both images to a size appropriate for use as a modeling reference; make sure you maintain the same pixel dimension and offset in each file, so that they match when placed in C4D. I tend to use pixel dimensions that are easy to remember (in this case 600 pixels horizontally by 800 pixels vertically), since you will need these dimensions when setting up your views in C4D. C4D relies on your knowledge of the image's dimensions to display it at the proper aspect ratio.

SETTING UP YOUR REFERENCE IN CINEMA 4D

To display your reference images in C4D, switch to the right view in the view panel and look under the view's Edit menu for the Configure... menu item. In the Configure Viewpoint dialog box (Figure 7.6), you will see an option for setting the background at the bottom of the dialog box. Clicking on the Path button will bring up an Open dialog box that will allow you to locate the lateral reference file (the Path field on your computer will obviously differ from that shown in the screenshot). Check the Show Picture option, and, most importantly, fill in the Horizontal Size and Vertical Size fields to reflect the pixel dimensions at which you saved the reference files (600 x 800, if you are using the supplied images. Note that C4D inserts default values here of 800 x 600, opposite to that of our tutorial files.). Switch to the front view and repeat with the front reference image (Figure 7.7).

Setting up our picture this way means that we are modeling a head that is almost 800 meters tall (about half a mile) as far as Cinema 4D is concerned! Does this matter? Well, no, luckily. The units used in most 3D applications are more or less arbitrary, and you can always scale down your finished work to the "correct" size. It can be convenient, however, to model to scale, or to the same scale factor, when you are working on a large project or with a number of collaborators. This will allow you to integrate various components of your models without having to resize elements that do not match.

Save your new file even though there is no geometry yet; the reference image setup will be saved with the file. It is a good idea to create a folder just for this project and to store the project files, and any reference images or texture files within that directory (or within another directory in the main project directory). This way, if you move the project directory to another computer, C4D will have no trouble finding the necessary files.

It is a good idea to save multiple versions of your files incrementally. For instance, initially save your file as "myfile1.c4d", then periodically, as you make major changes to the project, save it as "myfile2.c4d", "myfile3.c4d" etc. This protects you to some extent from potential file or disk corruption, and allows you to revert to earlier states of your project if you make any large, irreversible mistakes.

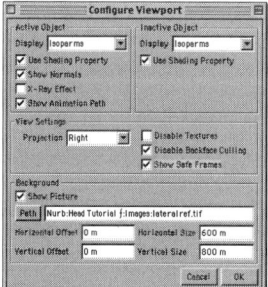

FIGURE 7.6 *The Configure Viewport dialog box.*

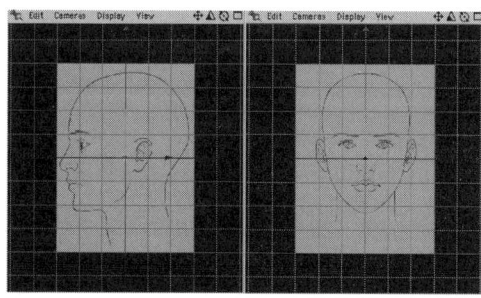

FIGURE 7.7 *How the reference images will appear in the right and front viewports.*

Chapter 7 Modeling a Human Face and Head

Setting Up Your Workspace

The customizability of Cinema 4D allows you extensive freedom to set-up the environment to suit your working habits. At the least, you might consider temporarily hiding palettes that are not relevant to the modeling task, such as materials.

7.2 Creating Polygons in Cinema 4D

TUTORIAL

Cinema 4D allows polygon modeling with three-sided or four-sided polygons; higher numbers of sides are not allowed. In order for HyperNURBS to predictably smooth your polygonal model, all the polygons in the mesh should be quads, or four-sided polygons. The easiest way to ensure this is to carefully build the polygons yourself, or to start from a primitive composed of quads.

Sometimes it will seem impossible at first to build and join different parts of your mesh using quads. Many structures and joints will seem easier to build with three-sided polygons (tris), but you must resist the urge. With persistence and planning, you should be able to restrict yourself to quad-based construction.

Let's try making some polys, just to see how it's done:

1. Open a new file in C4D, and insert an empty polygon object in the world space (Objects>Polygon Object). All that will appear is an object axis at 0,0,0.
2. Click on the Points mode button, and choose Add Points from the Structure menu.
3. Switch to the front view. Hold down the CTRL/COMMAND key and click to add three horizontal rows of five points in the workspace. The Add Points tool usually adds points to existing geometry; in order to add points in empty space, you must hold down the CTRL/COMMAND key.
4. Choose the Bridge tool from the Structure menu. (Pressing the "B" key will also switch to this tool.)

NOTE

But wait, Cinema 4D also has a Create Poly tool in the Structure menu. This tool requires that you click in order on each of the points along the perimeter of your poly. This takes more pointing and clicking than the Bridge tool, and is especially inefficient when you are creating a contiguous strip of polygons. Its advantage is that you can create three-sided polygons, and that the direction in which you click the points controls the way the poly's normals points (clockwise = normals point towards you; counter-clockwise = normals point away from you).

5. Click-drag from the upper left point to the point just below it. Cinema 4D will try to find the nearest eligible point for you, so if your points are relatively widely spaced, you will not have to click-drag all the way to the second point. Then move to the next point in the top row and click-drag to the point below it (Figure 7.8). You've just created your first poly!
6. Move to the next point in the top row and click-drag to the point below it. Continue in this fashion until you reach the end of the top row. Cinema 4D will make a contiguous strip of polygons.

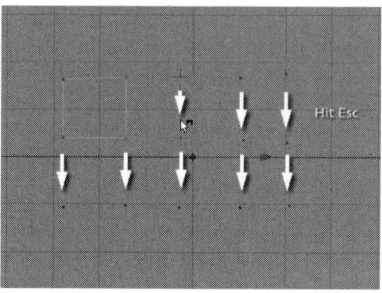

FIGURE 7.8 *Creating two rows of polygons. This screenshot was taken after joining two points to create the second polygon. The arrows indicate the order (top row, left to right, then bottom row, left to right) and direction that should be used when using the Bridge tool to create polygons.*

7. Now, to make the second row of polygons, you must rest the Bridge tool by pressing the Escape (ESC) key. This is necessary because Cinema 4D is attempting to be helpful by joining each new polygon to the last one made. If you do not do this, C4D will create a new poly between the last vertical edge of the first row and the first vertical edge of the second row. Try it to see; then click Undo. Whenever you want to break the continuity of your poly building with the Bridge tool, you must press the ESC key, or switch to another tool, and switch back to the Bridge tool.

MODELING THE EYE

ON THE CD

We will start by modeling the eye; fortunately, the shape of the eye makes it fairly simple to create. We are starting with the eye because they are important guides when modeling the eyelids and the areas of the face around the eye. On the CD there is a file, "eye profile.c4d", which contains correctly scaled (for the purposes of this tutorial), anatomically accurate splines representing the globe and the iris. Feel free to modify them, or create your own in a vector graphics

Chapter 7   Modeling a Human Face and Head   201

program like Illustrator, save them as Illustrator files (in any version below 9), and open them in C4D.

To begin, open the "eye profile.c4d" file in C4D. You should see two spline objects in the Object Manager, "Globe Spline" and "Iris Spline" (Figure 7.9).

Insert a Lathe NURBS object (Objects>NURBS>Lathe NURBS). By default the Lathe NURBS object will lathe an object around a vertical (Y) axis. We must rotate the Lathe NURBS object 90° on the X-axis. The easiest way to accomplish this is to type "90" into the P (Pitch) field of the Coordinates Manager, then press Enter (or click the "Apply" button).

Now, duplicate the Lathe NURBS object by CTRL/COMMAND-dragging a copy in the Object Manager. Click-drag the "Iris Spline" object into one of the Lathe NURBS objects. You should see a disc appear with a hole in the middle (the pupil). Double-click on the Lathe NURBS object to rename it "Iris" (Figure 7.10).

Click-drag the "Globe Spline" object into the remaining Lathe NURBS object. The globe shape should appear. Double-click on the Lathe NURBS object to rename it "Globe" (Figure 7.11).

Apart from texturing, the eye is essentially complete. Unfortunately, in some lighting situations, C4D will render the eye as if it is lit from within, so we need something to block the light from entering through the pupil. Create a disc primitive (Objects>Primitives>Disc, or select the flat disc shape from the Primitives pop-up menu). Double-click the Disc icon in the Object Manager, and enter "15 m" in the Outer Radius field. Rotate the disc as we did the Lathe NURBS objects, by 90° in the P direction. In the right view, slide it into place just behind the iris.

In the Object Manager, choose Group Objects from the Objects menu (or press the "G" key). The mouse pointer will change to a "+" sign; click-drag a

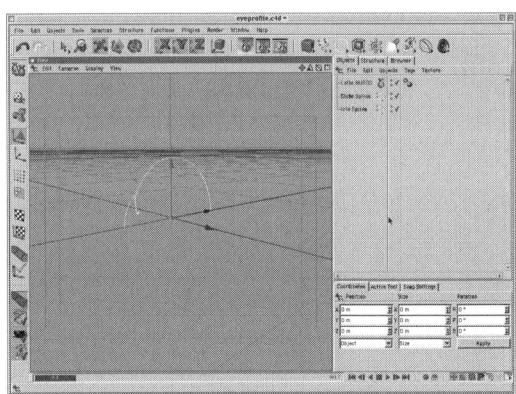

FIGURE 7.9   *The file eye profile.c4d as included on the CD provides two splines for creation of the necessary eye shapes.*

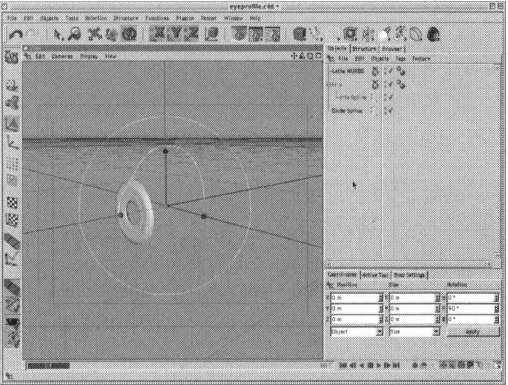

FIGURE 7.10   *Use the Lathe NURBS function to create the iris.*

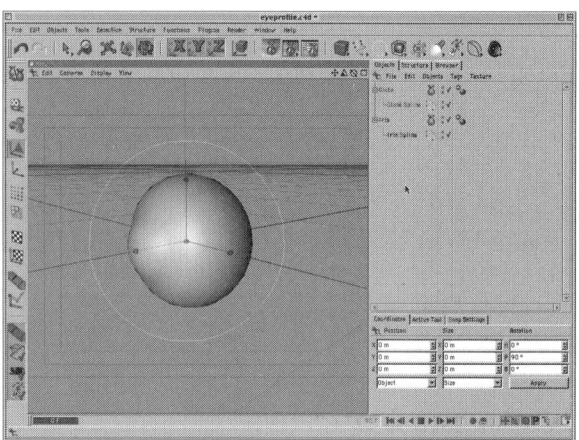

FIGURE 7.11 *Another Lathe NURBS object creates the general shape of the eye.*

marquee over everything in the Object Manager. C4D will create a new Null Object and insert the "Globe", "Iris" and disc objects into it. Now the eye can be moved, copied, and pasted as a unit. Double-click on the Null Object to rename it "Eye".

One last adjustment: later on, we will add a target expression for the eye. This will allow us to animate the eye's tracking behavior easily by having it automatically point to an animated Null or other object. Target expressions work by pointing the object's positive Z-axis at a particular target object; right now, the eye's positive Z-axis points out the back of the eye, so if we were to use a target expression, the eyes would point away from the target. This will not do! Select the "Eye" object in the Object Manager, and choose the Object Axis tool. Rotate the Eye's axis 180° along the Y-axis, or 180° in the H (Heading) direction in the Coordinates Manager.

Save your work. This eye can ultimately be used and adapted in many projects.

TEXTURING THE EYE

We haven't talked much of texture in the book yet. However, consider this a powerful preview to the ideas of texturing. Please see Chapter 8 for more information on C4D's texturing capabilities.

CHAPTER 7 MODELING A HUMAN FACE AND HEAD

ON THE CD

We are going to proceed with texturing the eye because I find it helpful when I am modeling to have a very good idea of the eye's appearance within the developing face. Several image files are included on the CD for you to use or adapt to your own purposes. The files on the CD are fairly large (512 x 512 pixels); this size is unnecessary if the eyes of your character will be small when ultimately rendered. You can scale them down in a program like Photoshop if their memory usage becomes a concern. The size of file I have included will stand up to very close renderings of the eye at broadcast resolutions.

The disc that sits behind the pupil should be textured a simple flat black with no specular highlight.

TEXTURING THE GLOBE

ON THE CD

The globe requires three image maps: a color map (Figure 7.12 (a) "eyecolor.tif" on the CD) to give the surface an off-white color with blood vessels; a transparency map (Figure 7.12 (b) "eyetrans.tif" on the CD) to create a clear cornea and opaque sclera; and a bump map (Figure 7.12 (c) "eyebump.tif" on the CD) to subtly elevate the blood vessels. I found I had to set the bump amplitude at about –30 to look correct.

If you look closely at someone's eye from the side, you will see that the iris seems to bend around and fill the contours of the cornea. This is due to the important, and unintuitive, refractive behavior of the cornea and the aqueous humor in the anterior chamber of the eye. Fortunately, this effect is easy to achieve: set the index of refraction on the Transparency tab of your globe texture to between 1.1 and 1.3.

Set the specular highlights of the globe to be a tall narrow spike; the healthy eye is always glossy and wet, and specular highlights are essential to achieving that look.

Once you've created the texture, apply it to your globe object by click-dragging the texture's icon from the Materials Manager to the globe object in the Object Manager. Choose a "Flat" projection in the Texture tag dialog box. You will then need to choose the Texture Axis tool, and rotate the texture 90° in the P direction (using the Coordinates Manager). Then choose Texture>Fit to Object in the Object Manager (if C4D asks you if you want to "include sub-objects", click on "Yes"). Do a test rendering to see whether the transparent section of the texture is properly positioned over the cornea.

TEXTURING THE IRIS

ON THE CD

The iris requires two image maps: a color map (Figure 7.13 (a) "iriscolor.tif" on the CD) to give the iris its distinctive color and radial striations; and a bump map (Figure 7.13 (b) "irisbump.tif" on the CD) to emphasize its texture.

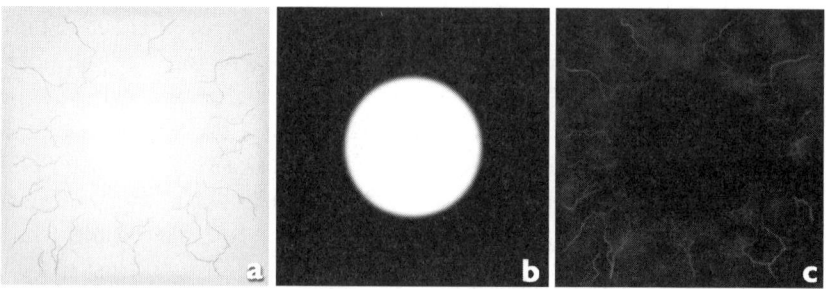

FIGURE 7.12 *(a) Color map for the eye (eyecolor.tif). (b) transparency map for eye (eyetrans.tif). (c) bump map for eye (eyebump.tif).*

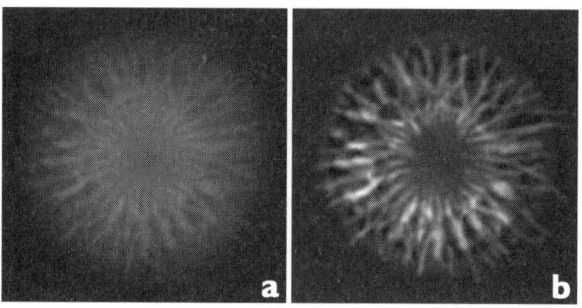

FIGURE 7.13 *(a) Color map for the iris color. (b) bump map for the iris to assist in emphasizing the texture.*

The specular highlights for the iris can either be set to nothing, or to a rather wide flat hump, in contrast to the tight, wet highlights of the globe and cornea.

To apply your iris texture to the iris object, follow the steps outlined above for the globe.

ON THE CD

Save your textured eye. There is a completed version of the eye on the CD; the file is named "eyetextured.c4d".

CREATING A "LOOK-AT" TARGET FOR THE EYES

If you want to play with the targeting of the eyes before we start modeling the face, here are the steps to follow:

1. Create a new Null Object. Rename it "Eyetarget". Position it somewhere out in front of the eye.
2. Select the "Eye" object, and in the Object Manager's File menu, choose New Expression>Target Expression.
3. A dialog box will appear; enter "Eyetarget" (without the quotation marks) in the "Search for" field.
4. Move the "Eyetarget" object around in 3D space; the eye will follow it as you do.

STARTING THE FACE—HIERARCHY

OK, let's start building the face. Open the saved file with reference images in C4D. First, we will create the object hierarchy necessary for this project. Begin by creating a new polygon object (Objects>Polyon Object) in which to create the face. To ensure that you only have to build one side of the face, next create a new Symmetry Object (Objects>Modeling>Symmetry). Now, within the Object Manager, make the Polygon Object a child of the Symmetry Object. Lastly, create a HyperNURBS object and place the Symmetry Object as a child of it (Figure 7.14 a). Interestingly enough, after all of this, you won't see anything new in your view panel but a new set of constrained handles. This is because we have not given any geometry to any of our present objects.

Double-click on the Polygon object to rename it "Head mesh" (Figure 7.14 b).

Click on the checkmarks next to the HyperNURBS and symmetry objects to "switch them off". This will allow you to build and edit your face quickly without the overhead and distraction of displaying the HyperNURBS smoothed mesh and the reflected side of the symmetry object. You can toggle these objects back on when you want to see your progress. Your Object Manager should look something like Figure 7.14 (c).

Now we are ready to start building polys!

CREATING THE EYELIDS

The eyelids and other areas around the eye are crucial to creating a convincing and expressive face. But do not be alarmed; they are pretty easy to build. We will first ring the eye with polygons, then use the Extrude and Bevel tools to create the inner portion of the eyelids. Here's how:

Switch to the front view. Zoom in on the eye. Make sure that you are in Points mode and choose Structure>Add Points. This will allow you to begin placing the points that will later be used to create the polys forming the eye. Remembering to hold down the CTRL/COMMAND key, click to add points along the boundary of the eyelids. I find that about six points will adequately describe the upper lid, and five for the lower, with four extra points to describe the lacrimal caruncle at the inner corner of the eye (Figure 7.15). Notice that two points are placed adjacent to one another, one above and one below, at the outside corner of the eye. This is to sharpen that corner, which, if described with only one point, would be unnaturally rounded by the HyperNURBS smoothing process.

Although the points are currently in the correct position in the XY plane, they are probably sitting exactly on that plane. In other words, their Z position hasn't

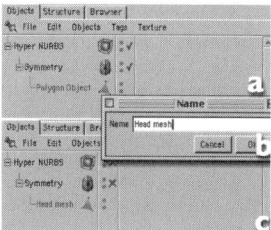 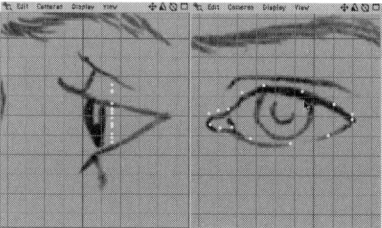

FIGURE 7.14 *(a) An important key to effectively building the face is to set up an appropriate hierarchy early in the process. (b) Renamed Polygon Object. (c) Hierarchy aligned, named, and ready to go.*

FIGURE 7.15 *Place points initially in the general shape of the eye, making sure to give plenty of points to define this fine area of the face.*

been properly set yet. In the side view you can see that the points you have just made need to be set into position in that view. I usually keep the front and side views open next to one another, and switch back and forth, selecting in one view, moving in another. Select a point in the front view, then move it into correct position in the side view.

When you add points in the front view, you control their placement in the XY plane, but what determines where they are placed in the Z direction? Usually, C4D will place the new point at the Z coordinate of the last selected point. If there is no last selected point, it will probably set its Z coordinate to 0. This also applies to the other views, with their respective perpendicular axes. If you do not want C4D to surprise you with the placement of points, before you add a point, select one that is close in position in the Z direction (if you are adding points in the front view) to the point you want to add.

Some of the points, such as those at the inner part of the eye, will be difficult to place in the side view, since they are not visible there. Keeping the three-dimensional shape of the eye in mind, you can estimate their location, since much of your initial placement will have to be tweaked, anyway.

Add another ring of the same number of points farther out from the first set. Place the points so that they more or less radiate out from the middle of where the eye will sit (Figure 7.16).

Make polys from the two concentric rings of points around the eye using the Bridge tool (see "Creating Polygons in Cinema 4D" earlier in this chapter) (Figure 7.17).

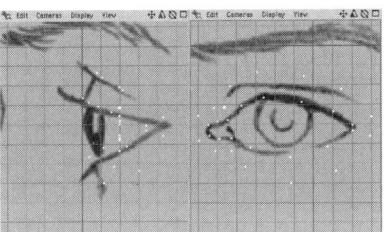

FIGURE 7.16 *A new ring of points, making sure to radiate out of the middle of the eye.*

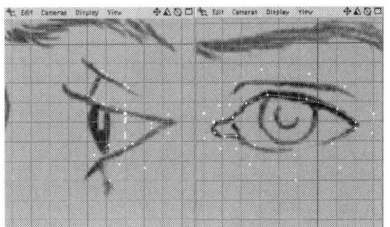

FIGURE 7.17 *The first set of eye polys are made by bridging the points already created.*

Create a second ring of points around the eye in the front view, position them in the side view, and use the Bridge tool to make polys from them (Figure 7.18).

Now, we are going to fill in the eye. Huh? Why are we filling in the eye? Well, it makes modeling the edge of the eyelids and the details at the inner corner of the eye much easier. Select the Bridge tool and, starting at the inner corner of the eye, build polys across the eye opening. If you have followed my arrangement of points, the last poly will be a triangle, which you will have to build with the Create Polygon tool. Do not worry; these polygons are necessary for the next few modeling steps, but will then be deleted, so your mesh will not be polluted with a triangular polygon (Figure 7.19). In order to make the normals' directions on these new polygons consistent, select Structure>Align Normals; if the surface normals (visible in the perspective view) do not point out from the head, choose Structure>Reverse Normals.

Switch to Polygon mode, choose the Selection tool, and "paint" a selection of the polygons you made in the last step (the ones covering the opening of the eye) (Figure 7.20 a). Choose the Structure>Extrude tool, and extrude those polygons back slightly; the perspective view can often help you judge this. The depth of the extrusion should be about the relative depth of the eyelid on a real eye (Figure 7.20 b).

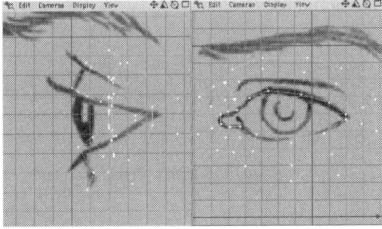

FIGURE 7.18 *Continue to use the Bridge tool to build the necessary polygons.*

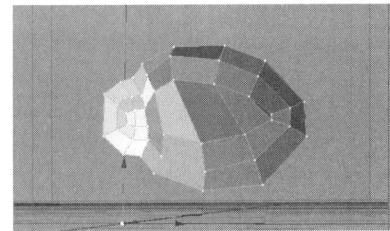

FIGURE 7.19 *You'll be left with a triangular polygon – not to worry, we'll be rid of it shortly.*

Choose the Selection tool again, and select the same polygons you did in the last step, minus the two polys at the inner corner of the eye that define the lacrimal caruncle (Figure 7.21 a). Choose the Extrude tool again and extrude the polys again slightly (Figure 7.21 b). Then choose the Move Active Element tool and move the polys in the positive Z direction so that they sit behind the outside corner of the eye when viewed from the side. This unrealistic "eyelid depth" will allow some flexibility in your placement of the eyes later on (Figure 7.22 a). We are finished with the polygons we just extruded, so press the DELETE key to remove them (Figure 7.22 b).

In the front view, select the two polygons that lie over the lacrimal caruncle (Figure 7.23 a). Choose the Structur >Bevel tool (make sure Preserve Groups is enabled in the Active Tool palette), and create a small hump (Figure 7.23 b).

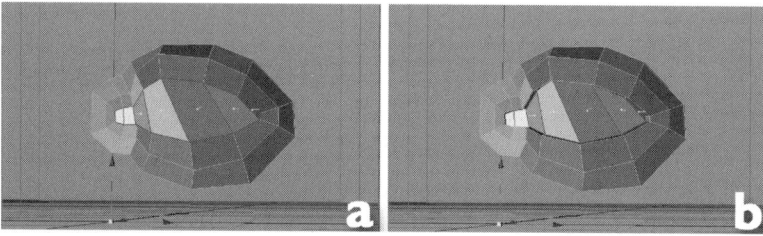

FIGURE 7.20 *(a) In Polygon mode, select the newly created eye covering polygons. (b) Extrude them back to the relative depth of the eyelid on a real eye.*

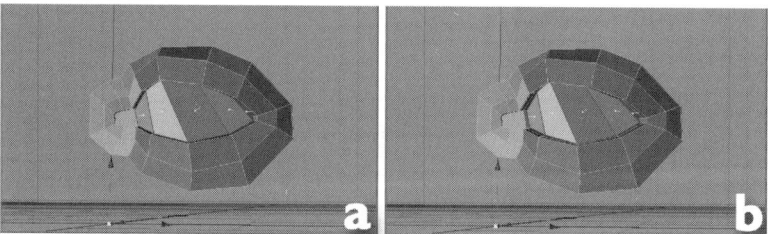

FIGURE 7.21 *(a) Select all the polys of the eye "covering" except the innermost. (b) Extrude these polygons again very slightly to allow for another fold of skin.*

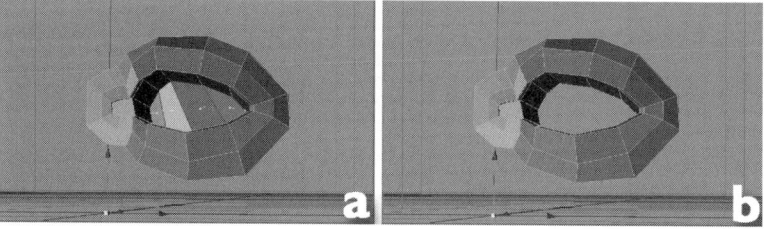

FIGURE 7.22 *(a) This may look a bit unrealistic, but will allow for real flexibility when it comes time to place the eyes. (b) Remove the newly extruded polygons as they are no longer needed.*

CHAPTER 7 MODELING A HUMAN FACE AND HEAD   209

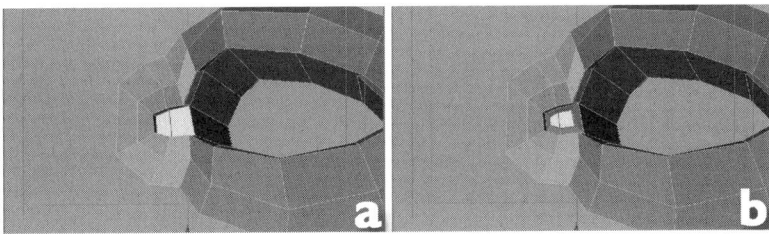

FIGURE 7.23 *(a) Select the lacrimal caruncle polygons. (b) Use the Bevel tool to create the necessary bump.*

Switch to a perspective view, and "switch on" the HyperNURBS and Symmetry objects to check your progress by clicking on the red Xs in the Object Manager. You can tweak the position of your mesh points in this view, or in the orthogonal views while you watch updates in the perspective view (Figure 7.24).

 *You may wonder why your model is rendering in a faceted way. When you create a polygon object from scratch, as we have, it comes with no tags assigned to it. In order for any polygonal object to appear smooth, it must have a Smoothing Tag associated with it. To add a smoothing tag to your head mesh, choose Add Tags>Smoothing Tag under the Object Manager's File menu.*

The smoothing tag can interfere with modeling tasks, since it attempts to smooth the mesh, and makes it difficult to tell the boundaries of polygons, in the interactive Quick Shading and Gouraud Shading modes. Often, deleting smoothing tags when you model, or just click-dragging them to another piece of geometry (or even a light) is a good idea. Then you can click-drag them back onto your mesh when you want to get a high-quality preview or rendering of your model.

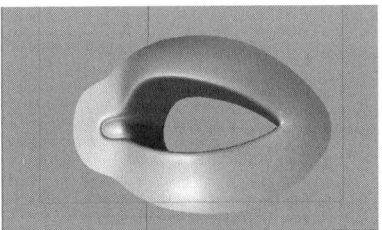

FIGURE 7.24 *Check your progress by switching the HyperNURBS on to see the eye in its smoothed state.*

ADDING THE EYES

At this point, you may want to add the eyes we created earlier to ensure that the eyelids we have just created will conform to an actual (rather, virtual) eyeball. You can do this by choosing File>Merge and selecting your eye model file or the "eyetextured.c4d" file from the CD. Merge imports the contents of one file into the file you currently have open.

ON THE CD

Once the eye has appeared in your workspace, switch to the front and side orthogonal views to position it appropriately in space. The eye may appear small to you, since many people imagine the globe of the eye to be larger than it really is. The diameter of the eye is approximately the same as the width of the eye opening. Position it so that the front of the eye and cornea is comfortably behind the upper lid. In a normal resting eye looking forward, the upper lid covers about half of the portion of the iris above the pupil, and the bottom of the iris touches or just dips below the lower lid.

If you've pushed and pulled the points the way I did, you'll see something like the eye in Figure 7.25 (a).

Looks like we have to do some adjusting. The inner portion of the eye looks fine, but the outer upper and lower lids recede too quickly, so those points will need to be pulled forward and outward somewhat. Switch to the orthogonal views (front and side), and select the two points defining the outer part (not the corner) of the upper lid. Move them away from the face slightly in the side view, and somewhat away from the center of the face in the front view. Repeat for the two points on the lower lid (Figure 7.25 b).

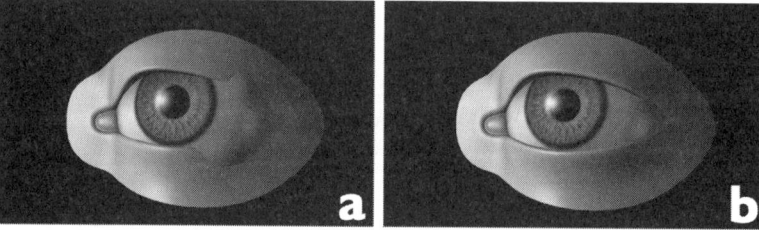

FIGURE 7.25 *(a) Merged eye. Oops. (b) Adjusted points around the eye to match eye shape.*

BUILDING THE AREA AROUND THE EYES

Now that we have the eyelids done, we can start to expand our mesh to the area around the eyes. We will be tackling a difficult and often overlooked part of the upper eyelid, the area where the open upper lid folds up underneath the overhanging brow (known as the "superior palbebral sulcus"). We will generally be building concentric rings of polygons that echo the orientation of the orbicularis oculi muscle underlying the area.

"Switch off" the symmetry and HyperNURBS objects in the Object Manager. Switch to Points mode, and select one of the points along the edge of your existing structure (this will ensure that the points you create next will be created at that level in Z-depth). Choose the Add Points tool. In the front view, add a ring of points outside the perimeter of your eyelids (Figure 7.26); be sure to use the same number of points as your existing ring of polys. Choose the Bridge tool and make polys from your new points and the points on the perimeter of the existing mesh.

Choose the Move tool and select points in the front view and move them in the side view to better define their Z-depth. The points toward the bridge of the nose, the brow, and the cheek should start to move forward; those toward the ear should start to move back (Figure 7.27).

Add another ring of points and make polys from them as we've done earlier. (Figure 7.28).

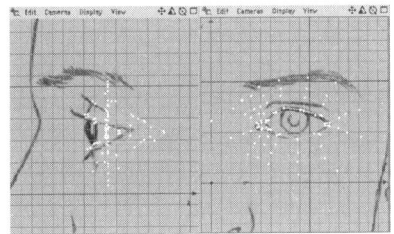

FIGURE 7.26 Add new points around the eye.

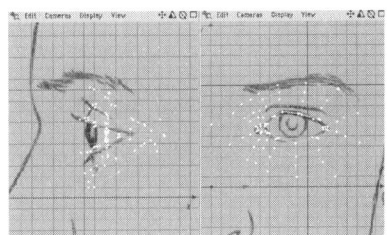

FIGURE 7.27 Move the newly created points and move them into position along the Z-axis.

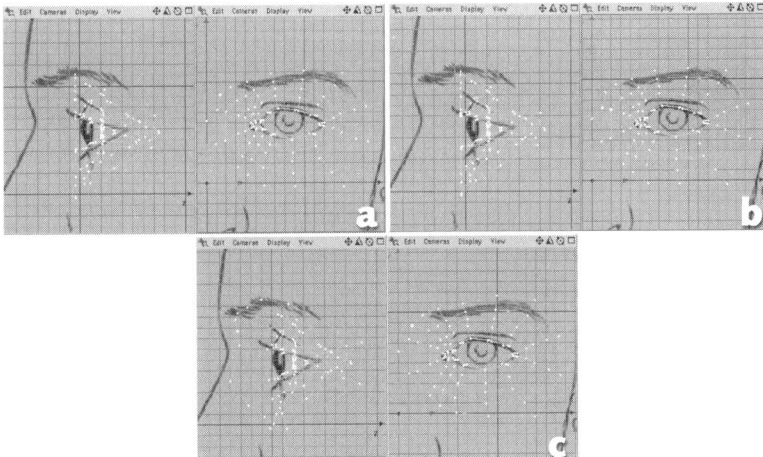

FIGURE 7.28 Additional ring created by another ring of points which are bridged and then aligned into position.

Now we have to move some of the brow points around to create the fold above the eye. Select the four points in the arch above the eye (Figure 7.29). Move the points downward and outward individually. The perspective screenshots below (first with the HyperNURBS off, then with it on) give a sense of the result you should get (Figure 7.30). You may have to exaggerate the position of the points since, as you can see in the screenshot with HyperNURBS on, the rounded HyperNURBS surface will "pull in" from the extremity of your point placement, especially on sharp corners. Tweaking the points in the perspective view can be very helpful at this stage.

Reposition the top row of points (along the brow) to be closer to the line of the fold.

Add another partial ring of points around the eye, and reposition them to fit the contours of the face. The points along the center seam may need to be precisely positioned along the X-axis so that a seam does not develop in the symmetry object (see note below) (Figure 7.31).

"Switch on" the symmetry and HyperNURBS objects to get a sense of our progress (Figure 7.32 a). Even though you clicked on the Y-axis when you were creating the points along the center of the face, they are probably not *exactly* on the Y-axis (in other words, their X coordinate is not *exactly* zero). As you may have noticed, this will create an unsightly seam when you "switch on" the symmetry and HyperNURBS objects. There are two solutions to this problem. The easiest is to double-click on the symmetry object and set its Weld

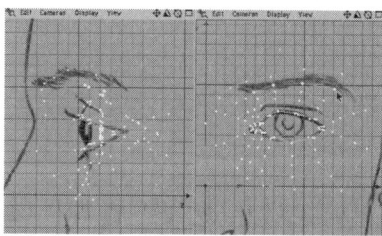

FIGURE 7.29 *To really create the fold over the eye, select several points over the eye.*

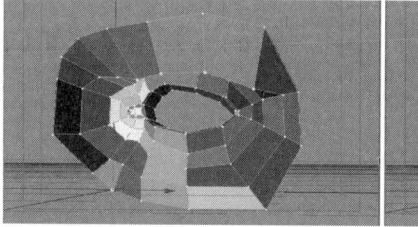

FIGURE 7.30 *The result is a nice fold of skin.*

Chapter 7 Modeling a Human Face and Head

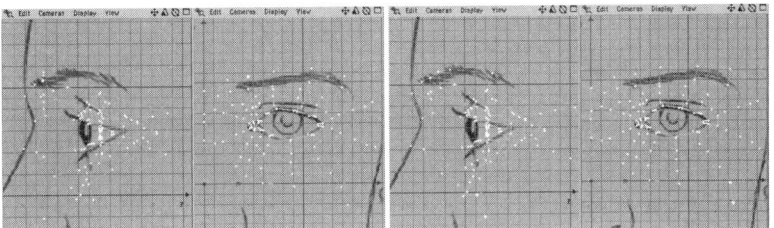

FIGURE 7.31 *Build outward from the eye following the contours of the face.*

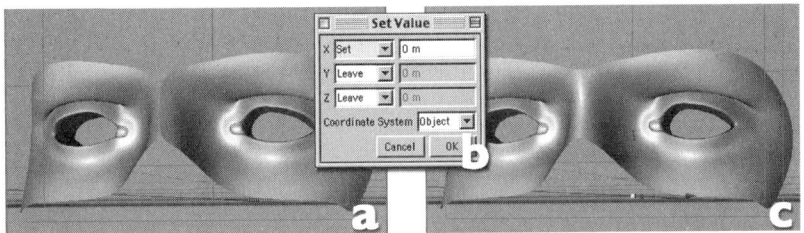

FIGURE 7.32 *(a) The face thus far; notice the gap in the middle. (b) Using the Set Value command. (c) After setting values for the points along the symmetry plane, we have an accurate start to the face.*

Points Tolerance setting to a higher value. This will expand the range of points that the symmetry object will consider close enough to the center to create a seamless joint. The other option is to select the points that should be on the seam, and use the Structure>Edit Surface>Set Value command, with 0 in the X field (Figure 7.32 b). You can edit the coordinate of a single point more easily by setting the value in the Coordinates Manager, but this will not work for multiple points at once, since the Coordinates Manager will just move the average position of all the points to zero. We have successfully built a Halloween mask (Figure 7.32 c)! Let's move on to the nose.

Building the Nose

The human nose is another extraordinarily variable form, capable of many characteristic variations, but built upon a common structure. As the following construction progresses, you can periodically turn on the HyperNURBS and symmetry objects and check out the nature of your model in the perspective view. Spin around the developing model to get a sense of its 3D form, and tweak the point positions as you see fit to refine the model.

Begin by adding three more or less parallel lines of points along the length of the nose, and use the Bridge tool to make them into polys (Figure 7.33).

The arrangement of polys along the side of the nose near the eye is not optimal, so we are going to do some reconfiguring. Switch to Polygon mode and choose the Selection tool. In the perspective view, select the polys. Press the DELETE key to delete those polys; notice, however, when you switch to Points mode that the points that defined those polys are still there (Figure 7.34).

Now switch back to the front and side views to build a new poly arrangement for the area. Add a point as indicated in the Figure 7.35, and delete the lowest lone point. Use the Bridge tool to build a new set of polys (Figure 7.36).

Now we will start filling in the area between the nose and the cheek. Add and reposition 6 points to the mesh in the gap and make polys as shown in Figure 7.37.

Add another 7 points as shown in Figure 7.38, and make polys from them with the Bridge tool. Here we are increasing the amount of detail as we prepare

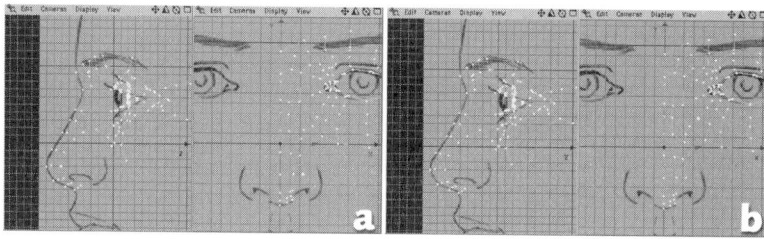

FIGURE 7.33 *Creating the first collection of polys to form the nose.*

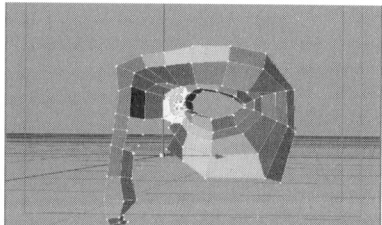

FIGURE 7.34 *Delete these polys; but notice that in Points mode the points which made the polygons are still there.*

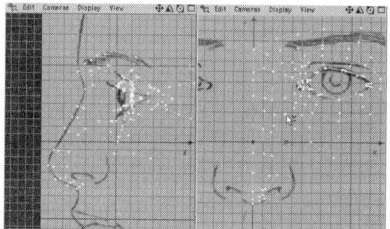

FIGURE 7.35 *Add a point and delete the lowest point.*

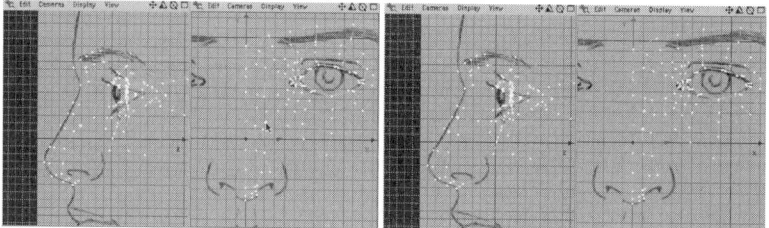

FIGURE 7.36 *Bridge the points to create new polygons similar to this.*

for modeling the nostrils and the crease that typically runs diagonally downward across the cheek from the edge of the nose.

Now we will zoom in even more and add 6 points that will help define the edge of the nostril. Build polys from the points (Figure 7.39).

Add 4 points defining the outer edge of the nostril, and build polys as seen below (Figure 7.40).

Now comes a tricky part, since the points start to overlie one another in the orthogonal views and make it difficult to see how the polys should be built. Add 7 points around the nostril's edge as seen in Figure 7.41. In the next three screenshots, you can see the progression of poly building from these points. This complex modeling is necessary to create the sculptural qualities of the nose, and to avoid the "flat-bottomed pyramid" look some modeling techniques create.

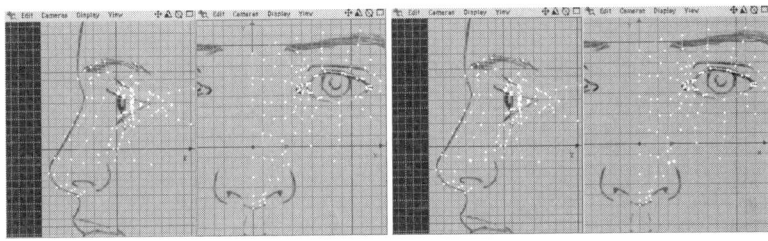

FIGURE 7.37 *Fill the area in between the nose and cheek with a topology similar to that shown here.*

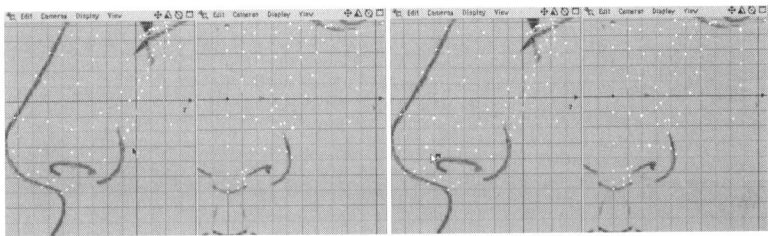

FIGURE 7.38 *Prepare for the creation of the nose by adding denser points and polygons.*

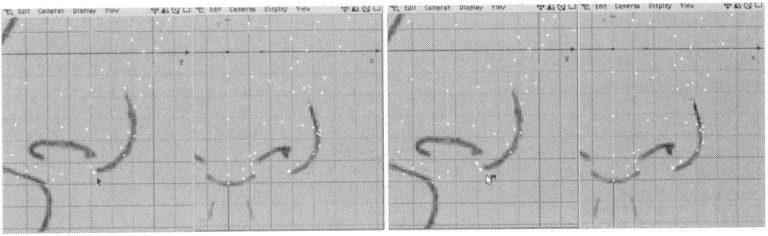

FIGURE 7.39 *Continue to add detail for the nostrils. Make sure to zoom in sufficiently to accurately place the polygons.*

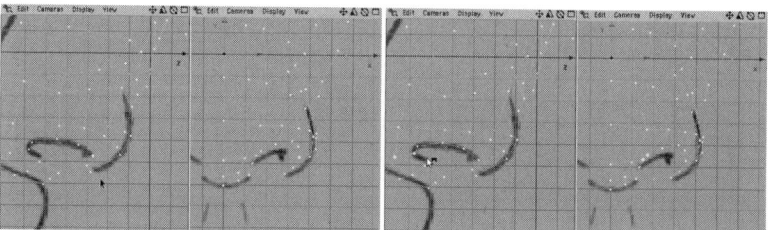

FIGURE 7.40   *Begin construction on the outer nostril.*

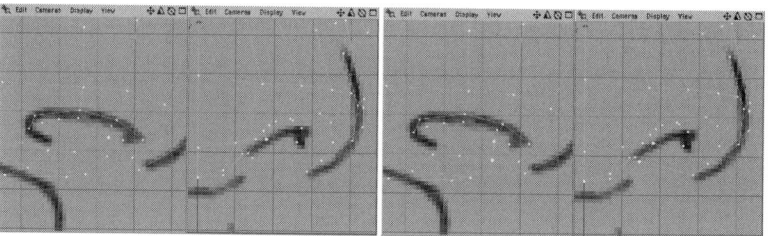

FIGURE 7.41   *Begin by adding 7 points and bridging them to create the edge of the nostril.*

Now, as we did in the eye, we will close the hole we have created with polys, and then extrude those polys to create the depression of the nostril (Figure 7.42).

Switch to the perspective view, and move your viewpoint around until the bottom of the nose is easy to see, and then switch to Polygon mode. Select the polys covering the nostril (Figure 7.43 a). Extrude them slightly into the nose (Figure 7.43 b), and after switching to the Move tool, move them upward within the nose to create a suitably deep nostril (Figure 7.44).

Now, switch on the HyperNURBS and symmetry objects to see what you've done. Choose Structure>Align Normals if there are any display anomalies on the surface. There is still plenty of room for refinement, but the basic structure is starting to take on a good form (Figure 7.45).

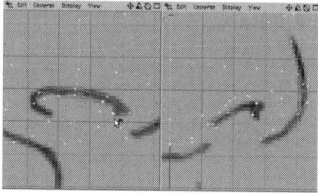

FIGURE 7.42   *Closing up the nostril to prepare for extrusion technique.*

CHAPTER 7 MODELING A HUMAN FACE AND HEAD   217

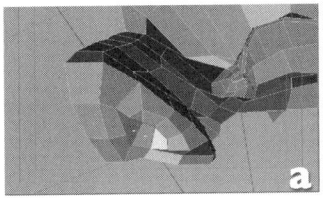 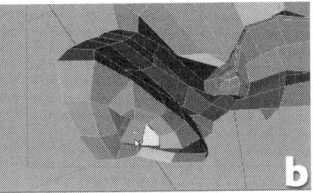 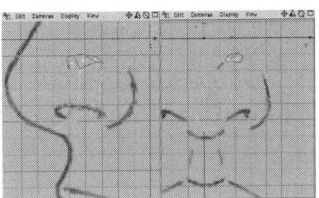

FIGURE 7.43 *(a) Select the polygons covering the nostril. (b) Extrude the nostril polygons slightly into the nostril cavity.*

FIGURE 7.44 *Use the Move tool to move the newly extruded polygons up.*

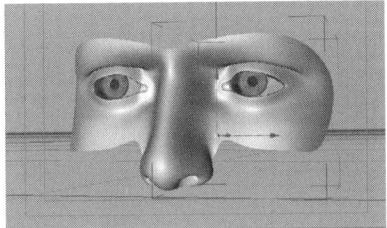

FIGURE 7.45 *Our face with eyes and nose thus far.*

BUILDING THE MOUTH

The mouth will not take long to model. It is important to be able to define enough geometry to give us sharp edges when we want them, but soft or no edges in other places. A common mistake in modeling the mouth (and, indeed, in drawing it) is to create a definite outline around the lips. Most lips have "sharp edges" only near the "filtrum" (the trough in the upper lip just beneath the nose) and sometimes at the bottom of the lip; what defines the edge of the lip most distinctly is the change in color and texture from the skin surrounding the mouth to the well-vascularized vermillion of the lips themselves.

Make sure you are in Points mode. In the front view, add a series of points defining the contours of the mouth. Notice the closely placed points at the point of the filtrum and at the corner of the mouth. Make polygons across the mouth with the Bridge tool. Notice the oddly shaped four-sided polygon at the middle of the mouth (Figure 7.46).

Switch to Polygon mode, and select the polys you just created (Figure 7.47 a). Choose the Extrude Inner tool and click-drag on the selected polys to scale them down slightly (Figure 7.47 b). Then do it again, so that there are two concentric rings of polys, and the selected polys are in the middle (Figure 7.48 a). The Extrude Inners will have created two polygons which we do not need on the inner side of the mouth — select them and delete them (Figure 7.48 b).

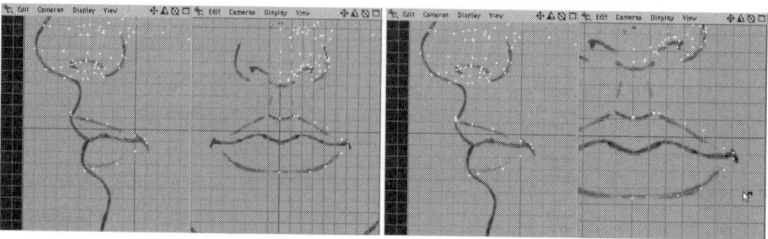

FIGURE 7.46 *Create the mouth by blocking out the general points and bridging to create polygons.*

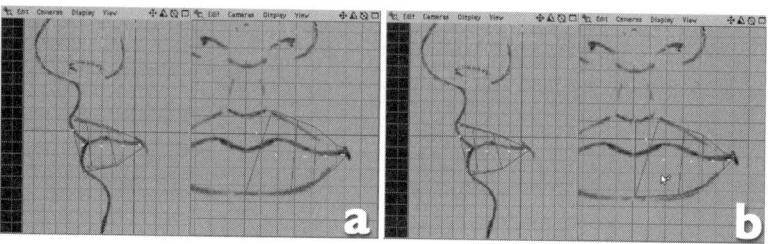

FIGURE 7.47 *(a) Select the newly created polygons. (b) Use the Extrude Inners tool to create a new set of polygons slightly smaller.*

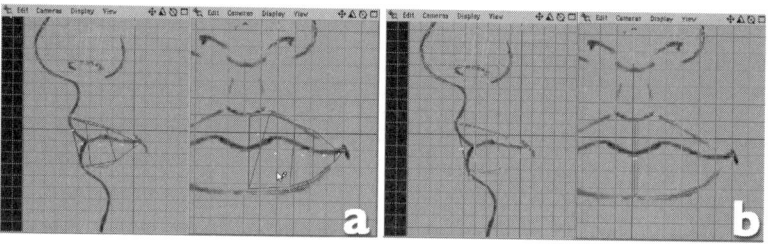

FIGURE 7.48 *(a) Repeat with the Extrude Inners tool to create yet another set of smaller polygons. (b) Select and delete the unnecessary polygons at the center of the lips.*

Switch to Points mode, and rearrange the points resulting from the two extrusions to follow the contours of the lips. The points near the Y-axis along the edge of the polygons we deleted in the last step should be set to 0 on the X-axis. You may need to zoom in on the corner of the mouth to straighten out the points there, which may have "overlapped" during the extrusions.

Switch to Polygon mode and select the central polygons again and Extrude Inner slightly again (Figure 7.49).

Select the spare polygon near the center line and delete it (Figure 7.50 a). Switch to Points mode and rearrange the new points to create a narrow opening for the mouth (Figure 7.50 b).

CHAPTER 7 MODELING A HUMAN FACE AND HEAD 219

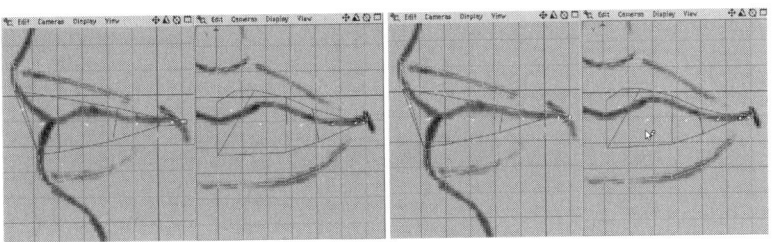

FIGURE 7.49 *In anticipation of modeling the mouth opening, again select the inner polygons and use the Extrude Inners tool.*

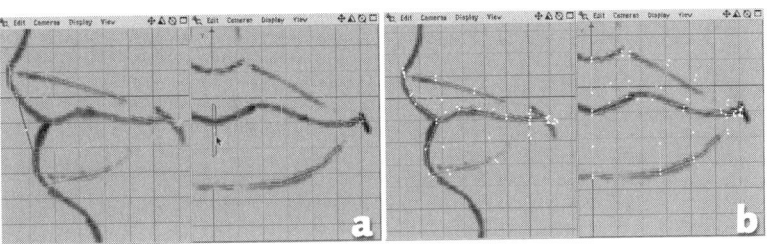

FIGURE 7.50 *Delete unnecessary polygons (a) and arrange points to prepare for mouth opening (b).*

Switch to Polygon mode and select the central polygons again (Figure 7.51). Extrude them back slightly (Figure 7.52 a), and then choose the Move tool and click-drag them rearward in the side view (Figure 7.52 b).

The external lips are complete, except for the inevitable tweaking. The interior of the mouth can be created quite quickly by continued extrusions and reshaping of the polygons we started with.

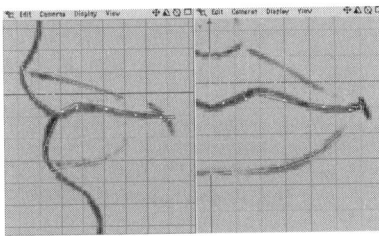

FIGURE 7.51 *For the mouth opening, select the center mouth polygons carefully.*

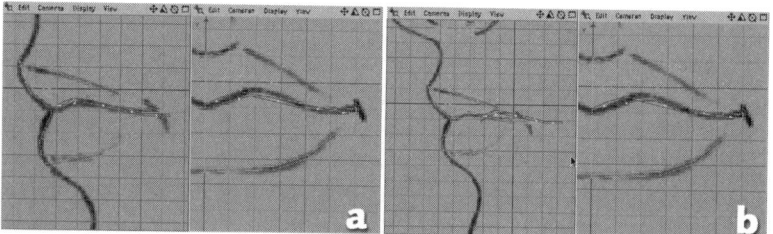

FIGURE 7.52 *Extrude the center mouth polygons back (a), and then move the newly extruded polys back into the mouth (b).*

FILLING IN THE FACE

Now we will start filling in the face around the mouth. As we get farther and farther from centers of interest like the mouth, our polygons should become bigger and less dense.

Create a concentric ring of points around the lips, and reposition them to follow the contours of the face. Use the *Bridge* tool to build polys from them (Figure 7.53).

Create polys between the bottom of the nose and the polygons connected to the top of the mouth. Notice how the points that are close together at the edge of the filtrum and the lip (creating a defined edge) spread farther apart as they work up toward the nose, smoothing out the boundary of the filtrum (Figure 7.54).

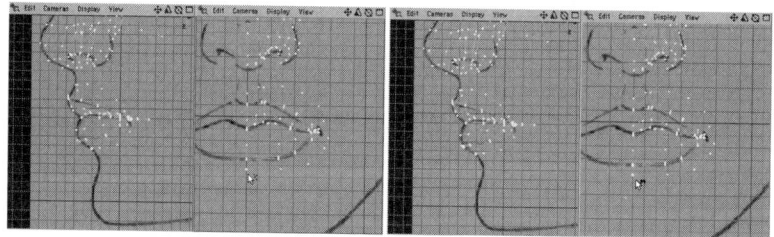

FIGURE 7.53 *Begin building out from our eyes, nose, and mouth, by creating slightly less dense collections of polygons.*

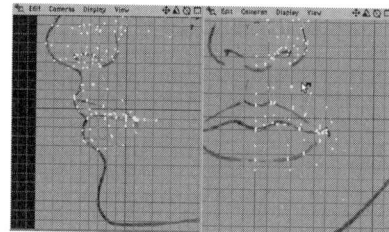

FIGURE 7.54 *Connect the nose and mouth with new polygons. Take extreme care to make the density of polys higher nearer the middle of the face.*

Create another concentric ring of points around the lips, and reposition them to follow the contours of the face. Use the Bridge tool to build polys from them. Set the X position of the seam points to 0 if necessary (Figure 7.55).

Create yet another set of concentric points, and build polys from them as in the previous steps. Also create the four extra polygons necessary to create the crease beside the nose. Notice the oddly oriented four-sided polygons which join the outer edge of the nose to the crease, and terminate the crease above and to the side of the mouth (Figure 7.56).

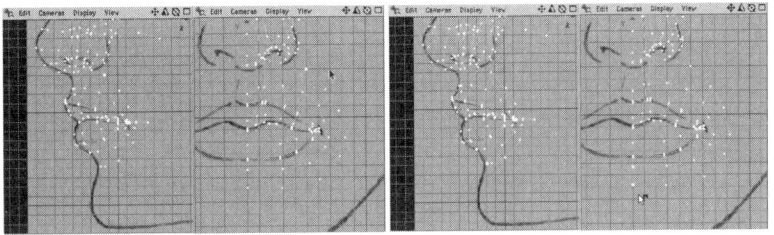

FIGURE 7.55 *Continue to build out from the extant mouth polygons.*

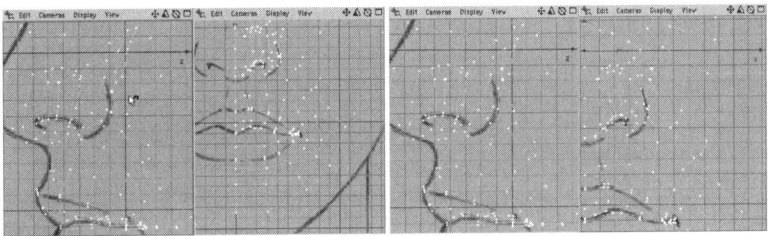

FIGURE 7.56 *Build out towards the chin from the mouth.*

Use the existing points to create three large polygons, bridging the area beneath the eye with the area near the mouth and nose (Figure 7.57).

Now let's once again "switch on" the HyperNURBS and symmetry object and see how our model is looking. Hmm, getting there. She is somewhat androgynous, and perhaps a little angry-looking right now, but we should be able to refine her facial qualities later into just about any expression, and emphasize or de-emphasize various facial characteristics at will (Figure 7.58).

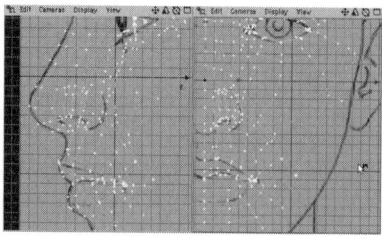
FIGURE 7.57 *Complete the missing areas between eye, mouth, and nose.*

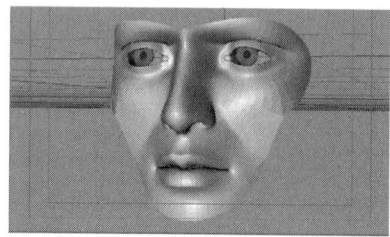
FIGURE 7.58 *Progress thus far.*

FLESHING OUT THE FACE

Now, having completed some of the most difficult sections of the face, we can proceed rapidly to fill in the forehead, chin, and cheeks. To start, let's look at the inner brow. Switch to Polygon mode and select the poly indicated in Figure 7.59, and delete it (Figure 7.59).

Switch to Points mode, and add a series of points as indicated in the screenshot below. Essentially, you will be extending the concentric rings of polygons surrounding the eye. Choose the Bridge tool and make polys from the points you just created (Figure 7.60).

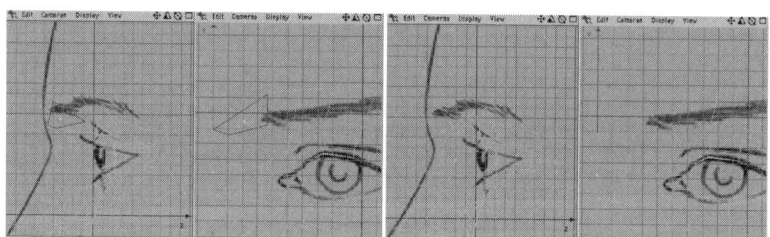
FIGURE 7.59 *To allow for more accurate polygon placement, delete the existing polyons at the inner brow.*

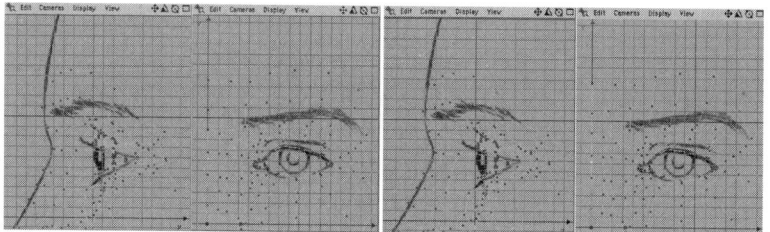
FIGURE 7.60 *Continue with the idea of concentric rings to add new detail to the brow.*

Add more points as indicated below, and create polys from them. Note the lowermost new polygon; its shape is necessary (in the arrangement of points and polygons I have chosen) to bridge an area of higher detail, the brow, with one of lower detail, the cheek (Figure 7.61).

Now we move to the chin. Create a row of points following the profile of the chin in the side view. Then create three more rows of points that follow the contours of the chin. Make them into polys. As always, if your initial arrangement of points does not look good in the perspective view, they can easily be tweaked in the perspective or orthogonal views (Figure 7.62).

Now add a series of points over the cheek to "flesh out" that area, and create polys from them with the Bridge tool. Notice how sparing we are with polygons in this area of low detail. Of course, there may be characters you might want to model where more detail is necessary in the cheek; for instance an older

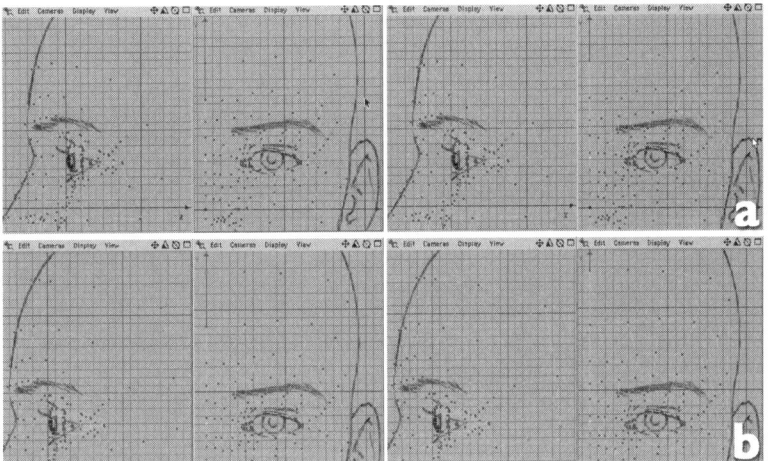

FIGURE 7.61 *(a) Continue to build out with new points and polygons. (b) Building further out to complete the forehead.*

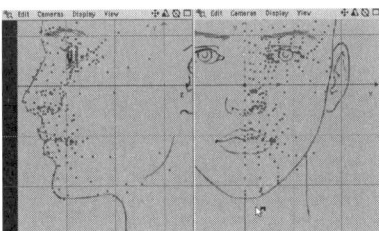

FIGURE 7.62 *Bridge the chin points and take time to carefully align these new polygons to make the appropriate shape.*

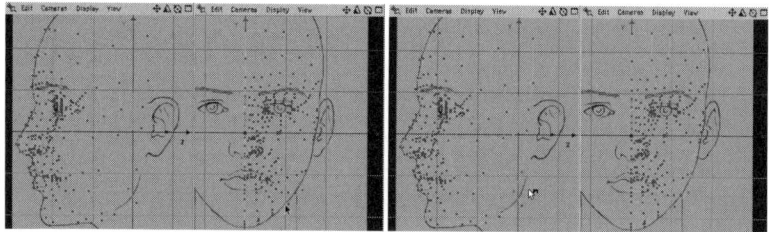

FIGURE 7.63 *Create the chin by continuing the process of new points that are later bridged. Be sure to allow these polygons to get bigger and bigger as there is less detail across the cheek region.*

character might have deep wrinkles that you would include in the geometry (although small wrinkles and other surface features are better handled in a texture map). (See Figure 7.63.)

BUILDING THE EARS

The external ear is a very complex three-dimensional structure; it is easily as variable and almost as intricate as the human face! Ears are not an easy modeling task. Shown here will be a framework that should provide adequate geometry for the ear, but modeling the exact ear you are looking for will take close observation and a lot of tweaking.

ON THE CD

To get a good idea of what we're building, we'll again work off a drawing. Load the alternate side view "lateralrefear.tif" from the CD into your side viewport (choose Configure... under the view panel's File menu). This includes a schematic view of the initial polys needed to model the ear.

Switch to Points mode. In the side view, zoom in on the ear, and place new points on the dots in the reference picture (the screen captures shown do not use the "lateralrefear.tif" image). Select all of these points, and in the front view, move them along the X-axis so that they are more or less flush with the side of the head. Create polygons from the new points using the Bridge tool (Figure 7.64). Try to follow the poly arrangement in the reference material. In order to make the normals' directions on these new polygons consistent, select Structure>Align Normals; if the surface normals (visible in the perspective view) do not point out from the head, choose Structure>Reverse Normals. (Once you have created the polygons, you can switch back to the regular "lateralrefear.tif" file as the background of the right viewport (Figure 7.65).

In order to create some depth in the ear, we will switch to Polygon mode and select all of the polys, and then extrude them out a short way. Judge the depth in the side view; approximate is OK, since just about every point will need to be individually tweaked (Figure 7.66).

Chapter 7 Modeling a Human Face and Head   225

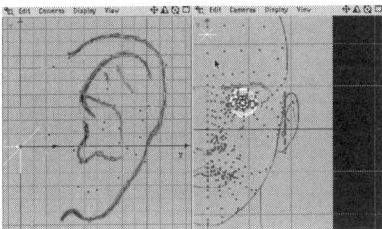

FIGURE 7.64 *Create the ear by first creating in the side view all necessary points and polygons as designated by the reference material.*

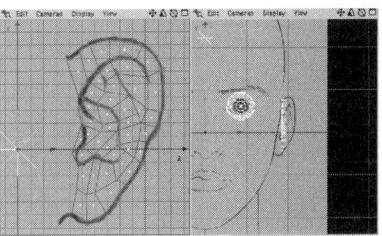

FIGURE 7.65 *Ensure that all of your newly created polygons have the correct normals' directions.*

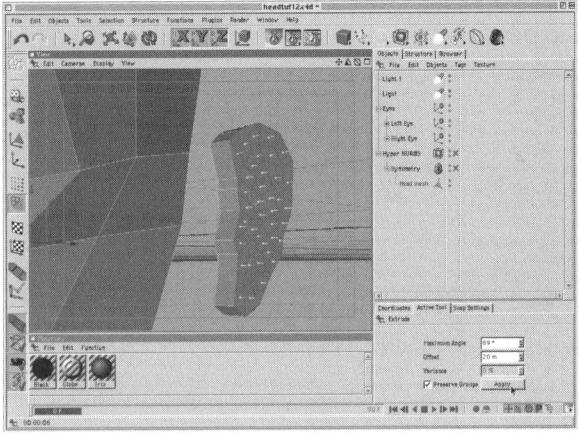

FIGURE 7.66 *Give the flatly created polygons the third dimension by extruding them all out.*

Switch to the Selection tool, and select the polys indicated in the screenshot, and delete them.

Select the group of polygons indicated in Figure 7.67, and extrude them inward by about half the distance of the extrusion in the last step.

Select the group of polygons indicated in Figure 7.68, and again extrude them inward by about the same distance as the extrusion in the last step.

"Switching on" the HyperNURBS object will reveal the essential geometry of our new ear, minus all the necessary tweaks to make it look plausible (Figure 7.69).

Choose the Selection tool, and make sure that Only Select Visible Elements is unchecked in the Active Tool palette. Select the two points where the ear lobe would join the rest of the face, and in the front view, slide them toward the side of the face. Try to triangulate the part of the ear you have selected in the side view with its position in the front view (Figure 7.70).

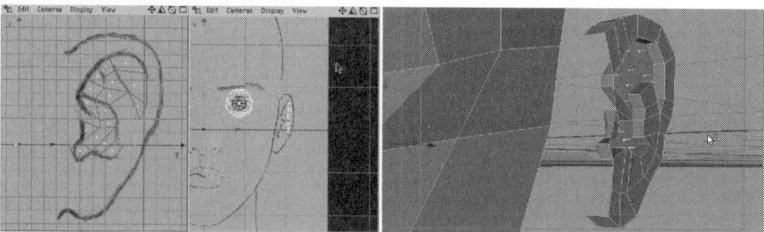

FIGURE 7.67 *Carefully select the polygons shown here and extrude inward towards the head.*

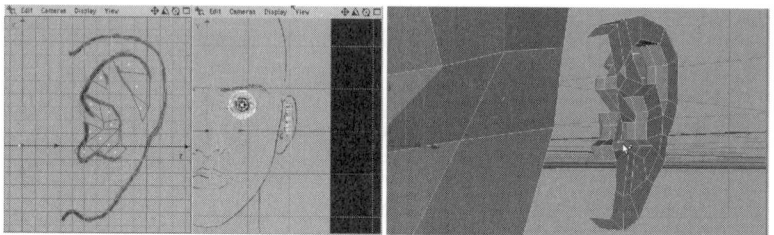

FIGURE 7.68 *Again, a careful extrusion as dictated by this screenshot, gives further dimension to the ear.*

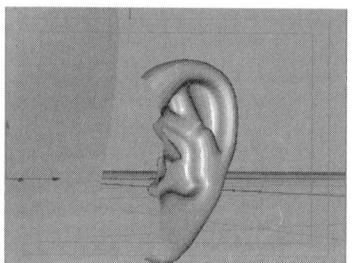

FIGURE 7.69 *The ear thus far. Turning the HyperNURBS on allows us a more accurate view of the work thus far.*

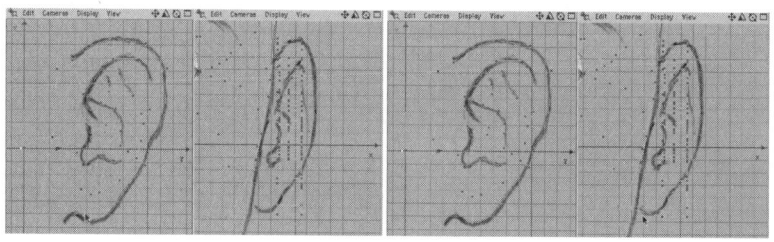

FIGURE 7.70 *Fine tune the ear lobe into position by starting at the bottom of the lobe and aligning to the side of the head.*

As you can see in Figure 7.71, continue to select points in the side view and slide them into position in the front view. This will require frequent cross-checks with the perspective view to keep the growing confusion of points correctly positioned.

Eventually, you will have a much more organic basic structure for the ear (Figure 7.72).

But there is still tweaking to be done! Select the points inside the curling rim of the upper part of the ear (known to anatomists as the "helix") as shown in Figure 7.73 a. Choose the Scale tool and click-drag to the right in the workspace to scale the points up in size, until they just disappear behind the overlapping points. This will create a realistically curled rim (Figure 7.73 b).

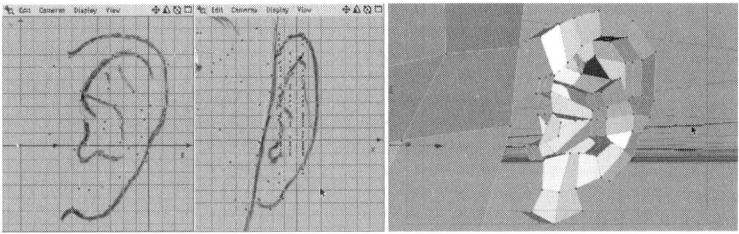

FIGURE 7.71 *Further refine the ear, working up from the bottom.*

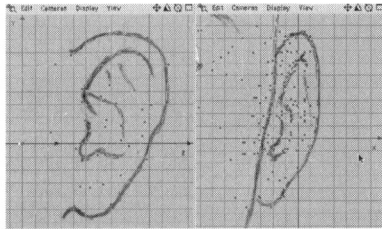

FIGURE 7.72 *Roughly attached ear.*

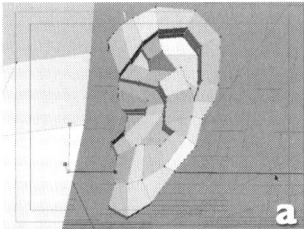 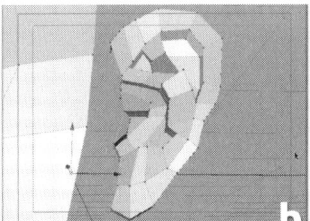 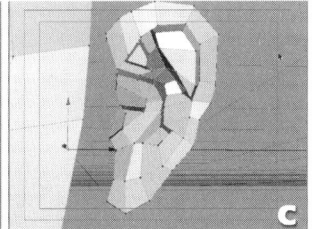

FIGURE 7.73 *(a) Begin to create the "rim" of the ear by selecting the points in the middle of the upper ledge. (b) Use the Scale tool to scale the points up in size so that they disappear, creating the rim. (c) Refining the antihelix.*

Now we can start to do some serious tweaking. The first area most needing work is the curving "Y"-shaped structure known as the "antihelix". There is a hard step-like transition in the current model between the outermost part and the "lower" parts which can be smoothed out by carefully rearranging points (this can be done in the perspective view, but just remember that the points move in the plane parallel to your "view plane"). The outer portion of the antihelix can also have its width narrowed.

The crus of the helix is the structure below the antihelix. It should transition gently from the "surface" level of the ear near the front to the deeper areas below the antihelix toward the back. This, too, can be accomplished by rearranging points in the perspective and orthogonal views (Figure 7.73 c).

Select the poly indicated in Figure 7.74 and Extrude Inner it a small distance (Figure 7.75 a). Then switch to Points mode, and rearrange the points to create a somewhat rounder form (Figure 7.75 b). Then switch back to Polygon mode and Extrude it inward a small distance (Figure 7.75 c). Then choose the Move tool and click-drag it inward a good distance, as judged in the front view. This is the actual ear opening (or "external auditory meatus").

Now we will move on to modeling the back side of the ear, and joining it initially to the cheek. Switch to Polygon mode and choose the Selection tool. In the Active Tool palette, make sure that Only Select Visible Elements is unchecked. Select all the polygons visible in the side view, being sure not to select the edge polygons that ring the ear. Choose Selection>Hide Selection to hide the polygons (Figure 7.76).

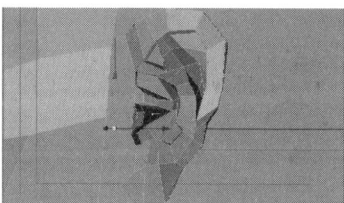

FIGURE 7.74 *Select this polygon to create the ear opening.*

FIGURE 7.75 *(a) Extrude Inner it slightly. (b) Use the Points mode to create a rounder polygon. (c) Extrude.*

Switch to Points mode, and select the points on the outer edge of the visible ear polygons. Choose Selection>Hide Selection to hide those points. This will allow you to more easily create new polygons for the back of the ear (Figure 7.77).

Add new points (shown in Figure 7.78 are 14 points) and make polygons from them to fill in the back of the ear.

Now we can connect the polygons on the cheek to the ear. Joining two sets of polys that have very different numbers of points would at first blush seem very difficult, but it's a cinch. In Figure 7.79 you can see that we want to connect two cheek points to eight ear points. Fortunately, we do not have to make polys with two points on each side of this divide. All but one of the eight polys you see in the second screenshot below have three points on the ear, and one on the cheek. Feel free to experiment with other arrangements (Figure 7.80).

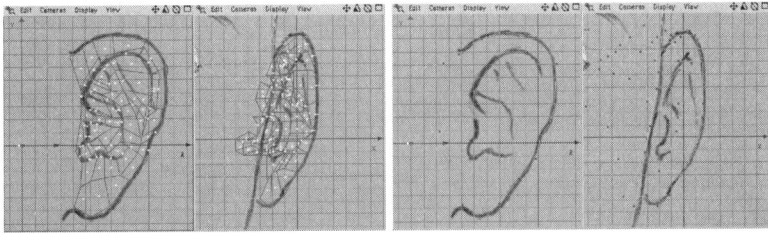

FIGURE 7.76 *To construct the back of the ear appropriately, first hide the polygons that make up the front of the ear.*

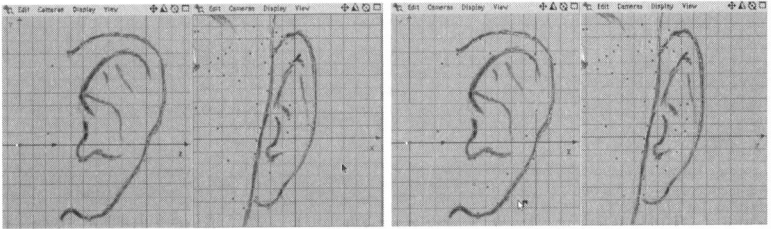

FIGURE 7.77 *Again, to facilitate easy construction of the back of the ear, hide unnecessary ear segments.*

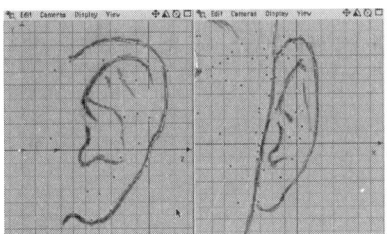

FIGURE 7.78 *New points appropriately bridged create the back of the ear.*

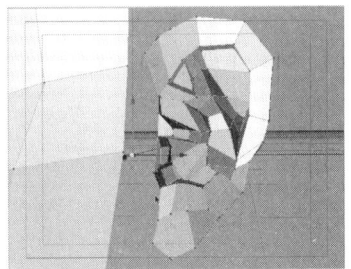

FIGURE 7.79 *This shows the eight ear points needed to connect.*

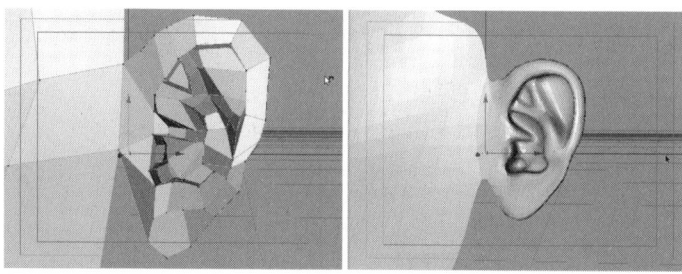

FIGURE 7.80 *Connecting the eight ear points to two on the head can come by creating new collections of polygons to ultimately reduce the number of connecting points as you move closer to the ear.*

THE REST

Well what comes after the ear? Well the rest of the head, of course. I've run out of space to detail the construction of the neck and the back of the head, but I think the techniques I've detailed in the preceding pages will stand you in good stead as you fill in the gaps. As a guide to my approach to these areas, I've included on the CD several image files of the polygon placement on the finished version of the head that can be substituted for the reference drawings in the front, side, and back viewports.

ON THE CD

Below you can see a test rendering of our character with a preliminary texture map, eyelashes, and polygonal hair textured with Bhodinut's *Smells Like Almonds* shaders (Figure 7.81).

In a later chapter I will detail some of the techniques you can use to animate the head, including bones, vertex weight maps, and point-level-animation.

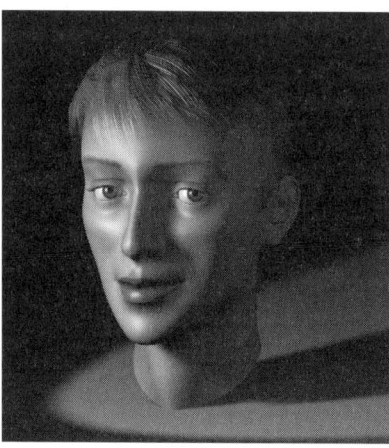

FIGURE 7.81 *Finished product.*

CHAPTER 8
Textures

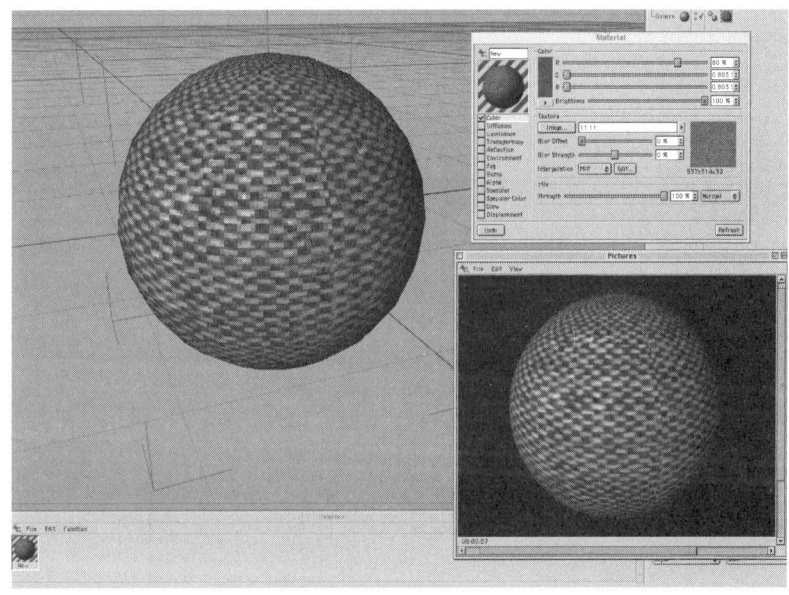

231

Materials

When the ball is not in motion, there is only one thing that visually differentiates a bowling ball from a tennis ball from a pea from a beach ball from a wicker ball from a....you get the idea... texture. Textures are the visual clues that reference the tactile and visual qualities of a surface. Texture is everywhere and without it our real world would be a drab existence indeed.

3D is no different. If you've been following the tutorials, you're probably tired of looking at the same gray plastic-looking models. In this chapter we're going to look at ways to spruce up our models, to give them color, dimension, tactile surfaces, reflective qualities, and even define the geometry of objects through texturing.

An important thing to note before we dive into things is that although "Texture" is the general catch phrase for surface qualities in 3D, each program handles the actual nomenclature a little differently. C4D uses the term "Material." A material is a collection of instructions that define a surface. These materials are kept track of in the Materials Manager at the bottom of the interface (Figure 8.1). A new material can be created by selecting File>New Material within this Materials Manager.

Each of the instructions that define the material are called "Parameters." When you double-click a material within the Materials Manager, a window called the Materials Editor will open, allowing you to alter these parameters (Figure 8.2). There are parameters that define the color, other parameters define how reflective the surface is, etc....By clicking on the name of a parameter, the Materials Editor will change to display the options available for editing that parameter. Each parameter can be defined separately from the other parameters; however, a material takes into account all *active* parameters to create a final surface quality. An active parameter is checked within this Materials Editor. Now here's

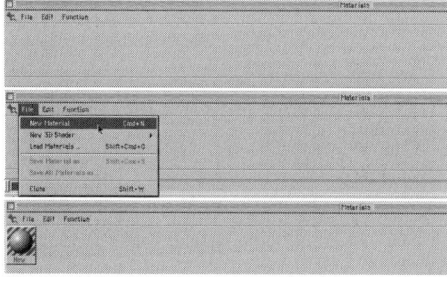

FIGURE 8.1 *Materials Manager.*

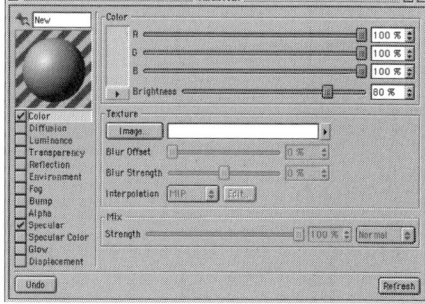

FIGURE 8.2 *Materials Editor.*

the tricky part: often a parameter will have two sections, a "Color" section and a "Texture" section. The idea here is that you can define a flat color in the Color section, or you can import a bit-mapped image or a procedural shader into the Texture section. The images brought into the Texture input fields are often referred to as "maps" as they tell C4D what to do where.

The best way to see how textures function is to see a texture built from scratch and see how the different parameters interact with each other. But before that, let us take a brief divergence into the realm of "Shaders."

SHADERS

Shaders are procedural textures, and thus are independent of pixel-based images. There are two different types of shaders: 3D and 2D. 3D shaders are incredibly powerful in that they are able to take into account the actual shape and mass of an object. Within the Materials Manager you can create a new shader through File>New 3D Shader and then pick from a variety of 3D shaders that C4D makes very well (Figure 8.3 a). When you've selected a 3D shader, it will show up in the Materials Manager like any other material. If you double-click on the shader in the Materials Manager, you'll be presented with a box different than typical Materials dialog boxes (Figure 8.3 b). For a detailed description of how each of these 3D shaders work, take a look starting on page 508 of the manual. We won't cover them here, as 3D shaders tend to fall into the "canned texture" look very easily. A canned texture is a texture someone else made and that everyone else is using. Typically, canned material on a reel is bad news and a real turn off for employers. So, although many folks are masters at altering the procedural shaders included in C4D, we'll not talk much of them here.

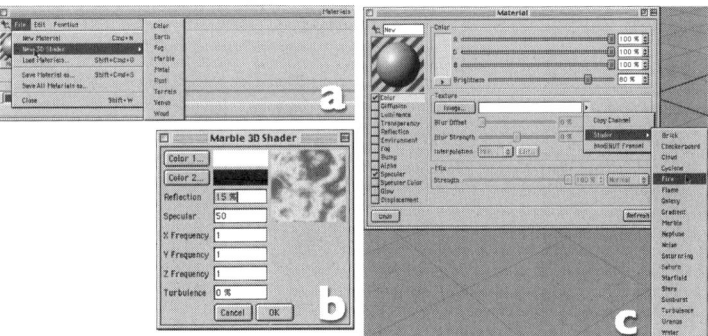

FIGURE 8.3 *(a) Creating a new 3D shader. (b) The Marble 3D Shader dialog box; very different than the default Materials Editor. (c) Accessing 2D shaders.*

There is another kind of shader, the 2D shader. These shaders are procedural maps that can be imported into the Texture input field within a material. They are accessed through the little triangle just to the right of the Texture input field (Figure 8.3 c). You can edit most 2D procedural textures by clicking the Edit...button within the Texture subset of tools. Again, if you are interested in the specifics or how to control these 2D Shaders see page 508 in the manual.

To explore the true power of materials let's make one. Create a Sphere Primitive in an empty scene and create a new material by going to File>New Material within the Materials Manager.. Now immediately save this file into its own folder somewhere on your hard drive; you'll see why this is important in a minute. To apply a material to an object in C4D, you can either click-drag the material from the Materials Manager to the object within the view panel or onto the name of an object in the Object Manager (Figure 8.4 a). When you do this, the Texture dialog box (Figure 8.4 b) will open to allow you to scale or change the mapping of the material on the object. For now just click OK, as we'll be discussing a lot of the options available here later. Once this is done, the Object Manager will show a material has been applied, as a material icon will appear next to the object. Also, the view panel will attempt to make a rough approximation of the texture (depending on what interface settings you have established) (Figure 8.4 c). Notice that the default settings of a new material are identical to the gray plastic; so there doesn't appear to be any immediate change in the view panel.

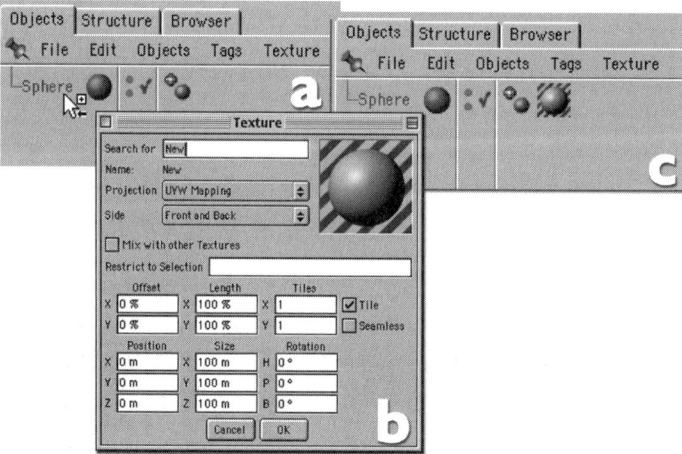

FIGURE 8.4 *(a) Apply a texture by click-dragging it from the Materials Manager to the object you wish to apply it to in the Object Manager. (b) The Texture dialog box that opens upon application of a material. (c) You can tell a material has been applied by the icon next to the object in the Object Manager.*

Double-click the new material within the Materials Manager to open the Materials Editor. This Materials Editor is non-modal, which means you don't have to close it down every time you make a change to a material; simply hit the Refresh button and your changes are made. Also notice that this Materials Editor can be "pinned" into position if you have the screen real estate with the Pin icon at the top left corner. Next to that is an input field allowing you to define the name of your texture.

By default, a new material is set to the same gray plastic that objects appear by default in. As such, the Color parameter and the Specular parameter are activated. This gives it the gray color selected in the Color section of the Color parameter and a bit of a sheen or highlight, which is what the Specular parameter activates. Just for an exercise, deactivate both the Color and Specular parameters so that there are no parameters active. The result is a pitch-black material. It's so black, in fact, that it completely obliterates any form we were once able to see (Figure 8.5 a).

COLOR PARAMETER

Now activate the Color parameter by checking the checkbox. Make certain that you are working with the Color parameter by making sure it is highlighted in the list of parameters. The most basic power of colors is the ability to simply select a color using the sliders (R=Red, G=Green, B=Blue) or click the rectangular swatch and pick a color using your system's color picking system. As soon as you pick a color, you will see the color change in the "preview sphere" within the Materials Editor, the preview sphere for the material in the Materials Manager, the material tag in the Object Manager and finally, the red sphere in the view panel (Figure 8.5 b).

But there's much more that can be done with this Color parameter. Besides simply altering the overall color, you can place an image within the Texture input channel. Simply click the Image…button within the Texture section of the

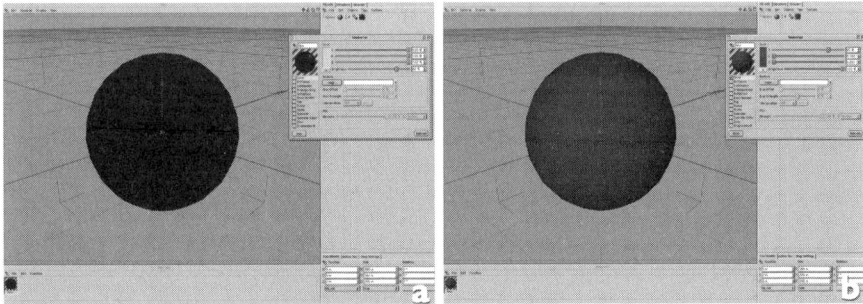

FIGURE 8.5 *(a) No parameters activated. (b) Color parameter activated with a simple color.*

Materials Editor. C4D will then prompt you to tell it what image to use. C4D is very open in acceptable formats, it will accept, .jpg, .iff, .tiff, .tga, .bmp, .pict, and Photoshop .PSD. You can even import a .mov or .avi file as a moving texture. For this, we'll use a swatch of fabric scanned on a scanner (Figure 8.6 a). When you select an image, C4D will immediately prompt you with the message shown in Figure 8.6 (b), telling you that the image is not in the appropriate "search path." The reason this appears is that C4D does not import the image file into the C4D file. Instead, it simply links to that particular image which it will access when it comes time to render. C4D looks for these images at the same level directory as the C4D file is saved at. If it does not find the file there, it looks for a folder called "Tex," and looks in there. So, when you attempt to import a file from some other directory, C4D recognizes it is not in its "search path" and politely asks if you'd like it to copy the image file there.

This has drawbacks and advantages. The advantage is that you can easily update the image outside of C4D and when the C4D file using that image map is opened, all the materials using that image map will be updated. The drawback is that you must carefully keep track of these images. Don't throw them away once you've imported them into C4D.

If you click "Yes" on the message, you'll find that the folder your C4D file is saved in all of a sudden has a new visitor – the image file you've imported. You can keep it there or create a folder called "Tex" and store the image map there. This is really the best way to do it as you can then anticipate C4D and drop all your image maps into this folder to import later.

Once a bit-mapped image is selected, the name will appear in the Image...input field and all the preview spheres will show the result. There are two sliders that allow you to soften the imported image if you wish. Below that is a setting called Interpolation which we'll discuss in the next chapter. Notice that in Figure 8.7 the Picture Viewer is open. This is a rendering created by selecting the Render in Picture Viewer button from the top command palette.

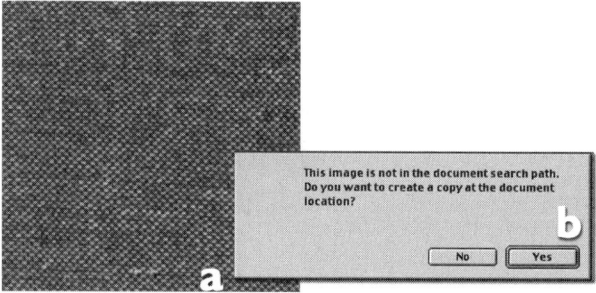

FIGURE 8.6 *(a) Swatch to be used as a color image map. (b) Error message when you import an image file from an unexpected location.*

Notice that when an image map is imported, it overrides the setting in the Color section of the parameter. The Mix section of the Color parameter allows you to mix the Color and Texture information. Assume that the Texture setting is the top layer of the material. If the Mix setting is set at Normal and 100%, then the top texture completely covers the bottom color. If you reduce the strength, the bottom color will be allowed to show through (Figure 8.8 a). This setting can also be set to "Add" the Color information's RGB values to the Texture setting (Figure 8.8 b), "Subtract" the Color information's RGB values from the Texture setting (Figure 8.8 c), or "Multiply" the values (Figure 8.8 d).

SEAMLESS MAPS

Notice that in all of the renderings where an image map has been used thus far, there is an ugly seam down the side of the sphere where the left edge and the right edge of the map are meeting up. These seams are very common when you are building materials from scratch. Luckily, with a little Photoshop help, these seams can quickly and easily be taken care of.

Begin by opening the image map up in Photoshop. Activate the Offset filter (Filter>Other>Offset). What this filter does is move the entire image off to the side or up and down. The real power comes from being able to wrap around. This takes the part of the image that has been offset off the edge of the canvas and brings it in on the other side. What this means is that the edges of the

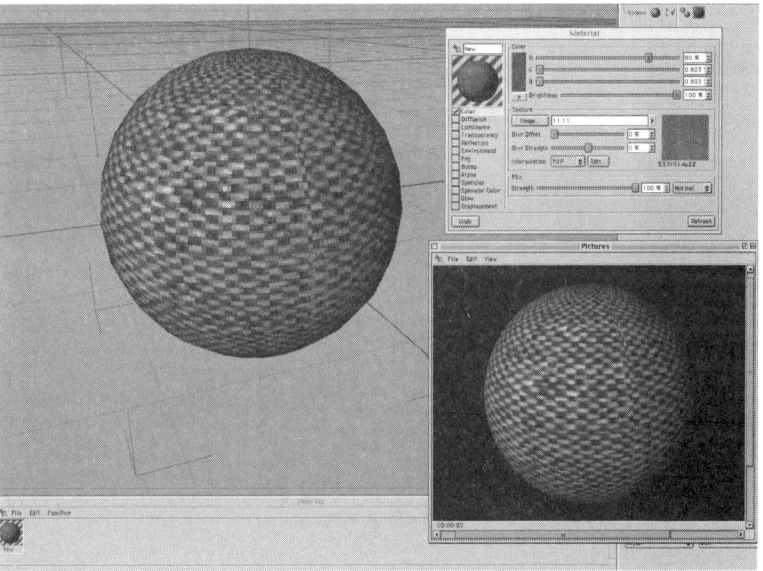

FIGURE *Image map imported to the Color parameter.*
8.7

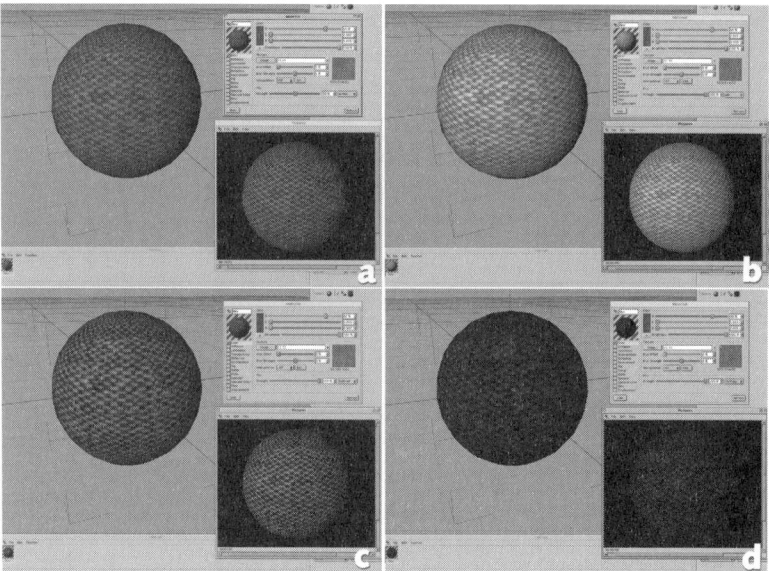

FIGURE 8.8 *(a) Normal setting at 50%. (b) Add (c) Subtract (d) Multiply. Make sure to check out the color versions of these images on the CD.*

canvas match perfectly and the seams are then in the middle where you can get at them (Figure 8.9 a). The amount you offset the image largely depends on the size of the image and is completely arbitrary. Just make sure that it is offset a good amount so that the seams are clearly in the middle and easy to alter.

The trick then is to use the Rubber Stamp tool to work out the seams that are running down the middle of the map (Figure 8.9 b). Once you've worked them

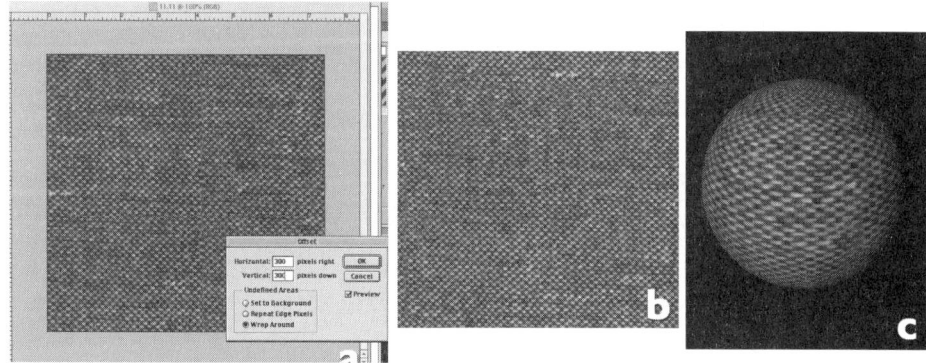

FIGURE 8.9 *The Offset filter puts the seams in the middle of the scene to work out. (b) Seamless map created with Offset and Rubber Stamp tools in Photoshop. (c) The rendered result of a seamless map.*

out, make sure to run the Offset filter once more to make sure you didn't inadvertently create new seams. Now your old seamed image map is replaced with your new and improved seamless map with no more lines. (Figure 8.9 c).

It's important to make your color image map seamless early on. As we work through the chapter, we're actually going to build a lot of the other maps from this color map; so if the color map is seamed, the rest are seamed as well. It just makes sense to do it right to begin with.

8.1 Getting Started with Texturing a Room

TUTORIAL

Open the room we've been working on in past tutorials. Using the basic parameters we've been discussing, we'll begin to put some color and life into our room.

Let's begin by putting some color on the walls. In the Materials Manager create a new material (File>New Material). Double-click the material within Materials Manager. Make sure the Color parameter is activated: enter the Color parameter window by clicking on the word Color in the list of parameters. Let's make the walls of this dining room a light khaki color. Click on the rectangular color swatch and pick a nice tan (something around R=90%, G=83%, B=75%). For now leave the other settings as is. Label this material "Tan Walls" (Figure 8.10). Now find the walls to your room within the Object Manager; don't worry about the backing flats, just the walls. You may have them grouped together as part of a Boolean object, or they may be a list of walls grouped with other objects like floorboards as they are in Figure 8.10 (a). Apply this texture to all the walls by click-dragging the texture from the Materials Manager to the object in the Object Manager (8.10 a). For now, just click OK for the Texture window that pops up after material application.

Make sure that as you are applying these materials, that you don't apply them to too general a group. Turns out that a material will be transferred down to include objects that are the children of any object. You probably don't want tan windows with tan glass. Take some time to track down each wall and place the texture accordingly. Another shortcut you might want to use to save your mouse miles of travel is the ability to copy a material from one object to another. By holding the CTRL (COMMAND) key down and click-dragging a material tag, you can copy the material to another object. After you have all the wall materials in place, take a moment to do a quick test rendering by clicking the Render Active View button (Figure 8.10 b).

Now there are obviously a lot of weird things in this room: no ceiling, no lighting except for the floodlight that sits above the camera view we're looking through, etc. But still, a scene should never look as flat as it is appearing here.

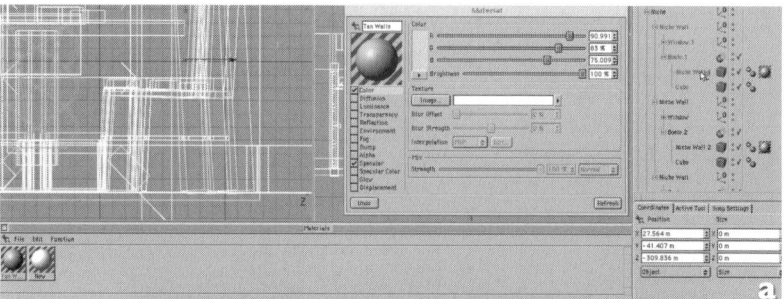

FIGURE 8.10 *(a) Placing a simple texture on multiple walls. (b) Test rendering for the room.*

To fix this problem, we'll need to adjust the bump of the material to give the walls a bit more interest.

Activate the Bump parameter and using the right triangular button at the end of the input field, select Turbulence from the list of 2D shaders. Turbulence is one of the best ways to give a slight variation to a surface. The Strength setting of the Bump parameter needn't be very high and shouldn't be very high; somewhere around 5-7% is fine (Figure 8.11 a). This gives the material just enough tactile properties so that the walls don't look so plastic-like. The next thing to do is adjust the Specular parameter to be more in line with a painted wall. The default setting for materials is a very plastic setting for the Specular parameter. A latex or oil painted wall would have a wide, flat specular. Increase the Width setting, and decrease the Height setting (Figure 8.11b). Click Refresh and do a test rendering.

The great thing about this texturing system is that when we make a change in the Materials Editor and click Refresh, the changes are communicated out to every place the material has been applied. If we wanted to make the room bright red, we only need to change the Color parameter of the material, and all the walls with that material applied would then be red.

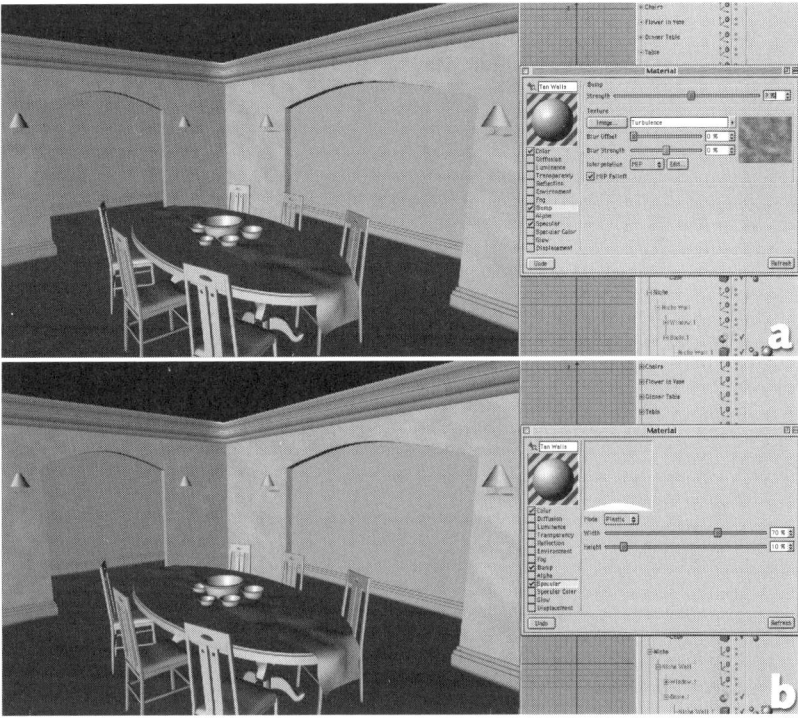

FIGURE 8.11 *Adjusting the Bump and Specular parameters to give a bit of character to the walls.*

Now that the material is looking better for the walls, let's place a material into the hall walls and make it a different color. Instead of having to worry about making a material from scratch and trying to match all the settings but the color, we'll duplicate this "Tan Walls" material. Make sure the Materials Manager is active by clicking on the material "Tan Walls". Using the Edit pull-down menu *within the Materials Manager*, select Copy and then Paste. A new material will appear called "Tan Walls.1". If your Materials Editor is still open, that will become the material currently available for editing. Change the name of this new material to "Burgundy Walls" and change the Color parameter setting to a burgundy color. Now apply this new material to the backing flats; making the walls in the hall a dark burgundy (Figure 8.12 a).

You may notice at this point that there are some problems with the scene as we've set it up. The materials on the walls seem to be different scales (they are) and the insides of the arches are white, rather than the tan of the rest of the wall. Not to worry, we'll fix these issues shortly.

Let's move on to the trim (floorboard and molding) in the room. Assuming that this is a painted wood, create a new material, call it "Trim", and change the Color parameter from the default gray to a white. Again, activate the Bump

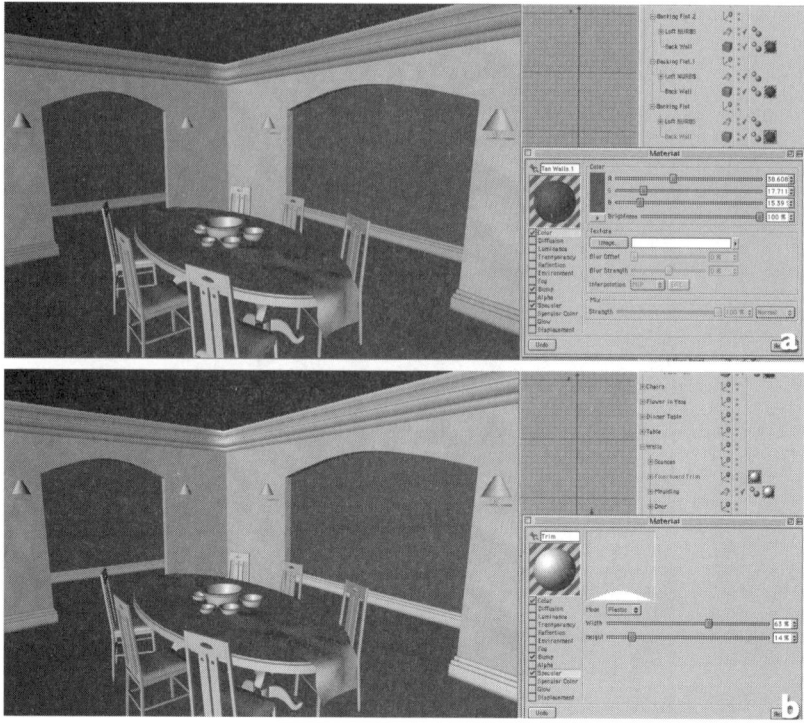

FIGURE 8.12 *(a) Burgundy backing flats. (b) White trim. Even smooth painted wood should have a bit of bump to it.*

parameter and use Turbulence or Noise (one of the Shaders located under the triangle at the end of the Image input field) at a very low strength to give a bit of tactile quality to the surface. Also, increase the Width, and reduce the Height of the Specular parameter. Find all the trim in your scene and apply the material to it (Figure 8.12 b).

Let's turn our attention to the windows for a minute. We'll want the trim on the windows to match the molding and floorboard. But let's take a minute and look at how the parent-children relationship works with materials. Assuming you have each window grouped together, click-drag the "Trim" material onto each window group (Figure 8.13 a). This will make the entire window (including the glass) have the wood trim. Create a new material and name it "Glass." Glass is a really complex material and is largely a subjective call; however, almost all glass should have the Color, Transparency, Reflection, and Specular parameters activated. The Color and Transparency parameters often have a little bit of a gray-blue selected as the color. The Transparency setting can have 100% transparency, or you may wish to limit the Transparency setting a little lower so you can see the pane better. The Reflection channel, largely

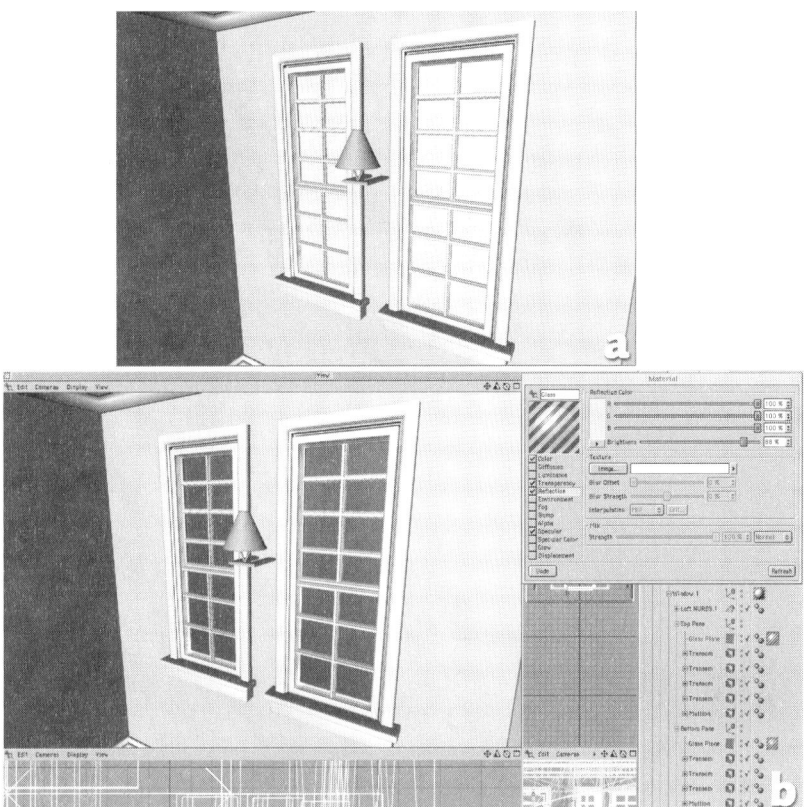

FIGURE 8.13 *Applying glass to the windows and trim to the window trim.*

depends on what time of day you plan your scene in. During the day, glass has a fairly low amount of reflection on the inside of a house as the most powerful light source is outside (the sun). However, at night, when the most powerful light in the house is your lamp on the table, the inside of the glass is highly reflective making it difficult to see outside. Let's assume this scene is in the evening, so we will leave the reflective qualities quite high (80%). Finally, glass specular qualities are very broad and actually quite high. Some folks (if you are designing an older house where the glass has begun to wave) like to place Turbulence in the Bump channel. This is all up to you.

Now, apply this material to the object (within your window group) representing the glass (Figure 8.13 b). Notice that in Figure 8.13 (b), the "Trim" material is applied to the window as a whole and the rendering shows every object that is part of the window being that white trim – except the glass. This is because if a child has a material applied (as the glass planes do) this texture overrides any parent object's texture. This saves lots of time, as you only need to drop trim on 7 windows, and 14 paanes of glass, rather than dropping trim on each piece of window trim, each transom, and each mullion.

Now let's focus in on a sconce. This sconce will be mostly metallic and will present an interesting group of challenges. For the base, let's create a chrome-like silver material. Create a new material and activate the Color, Reflection, Specular, and Specular parameters. Often chrome has a slight blue color with high (90%+) reflection. The key to making this metal believable will be in the Specular parameter. First, change the mode to Metal. Then, make the Width setting very thin (10%) but make the Height setting extremely high (150%). This gives our metal an intense, thin highlight. Change the Specular Colorparameter to something with a little blue and you'll be set.

For the bars holding the shade up, let's use a brushed brass effect. For this effect, create a bump map in Photoshop that is a grayscale image. A simple method is to create Noise (Filter>Noise>Add Noise) (Figure 8.14 a), then use extreme Motion Blur (Filter>Blur>Motion Blur) to smear the noise to the side (Figure 8.14b). Use the Offset technique to work out any seams and increase the contrast a bit (Figure 8.14 c). Make sure to save it in a "Tex" folder within the same directory as your Room.c4d file. Create a new texture and activate the Color, Reflection, Bump, Specular, and Specular Glow parameters. Give the material a goldish-brown color, make the Reflection color a yellow color, import the just-created bump map, and turn the yellow Specular parameter to Metal mode with a low Width setting and very high Height setting. After application, the appearance should be something like Figure 8.14 (d).

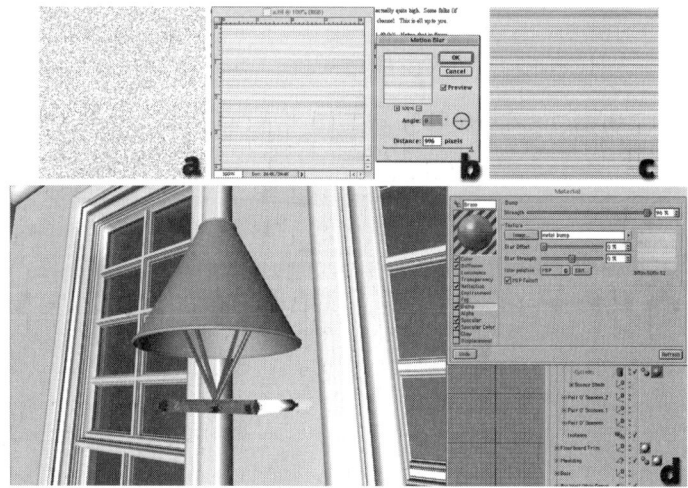

FIGURE *Creating a brass texture.*
8.14

For the shade we'll make a pierced steel look. This way there will be interesting shadows and light cast immediately around the area when a light is put within it. Again, as a metal, this should have a slight color (light blue for stainless steel) and a very high, thin Specular parameter with a bit of color in the Specular Color parameter. Again, the Reflection parameter should be activated and kept at a fairly high setting. However, for this texture there will be a couple of specialties. The first specialty we'll activate is the Alpha parameter so that we can place an image map of the pierced pattern we wish to use (Figure 8.15 a). Also, as this would be hot from a light source, we'll use the Diffusion channel heavily to dirty up the steel a bit (Figure 8.15 b). Figure 8.15 (c) gives a quick look at what the light shade would do if a light were placed within the sconce (more on lighting in Chapter 10).

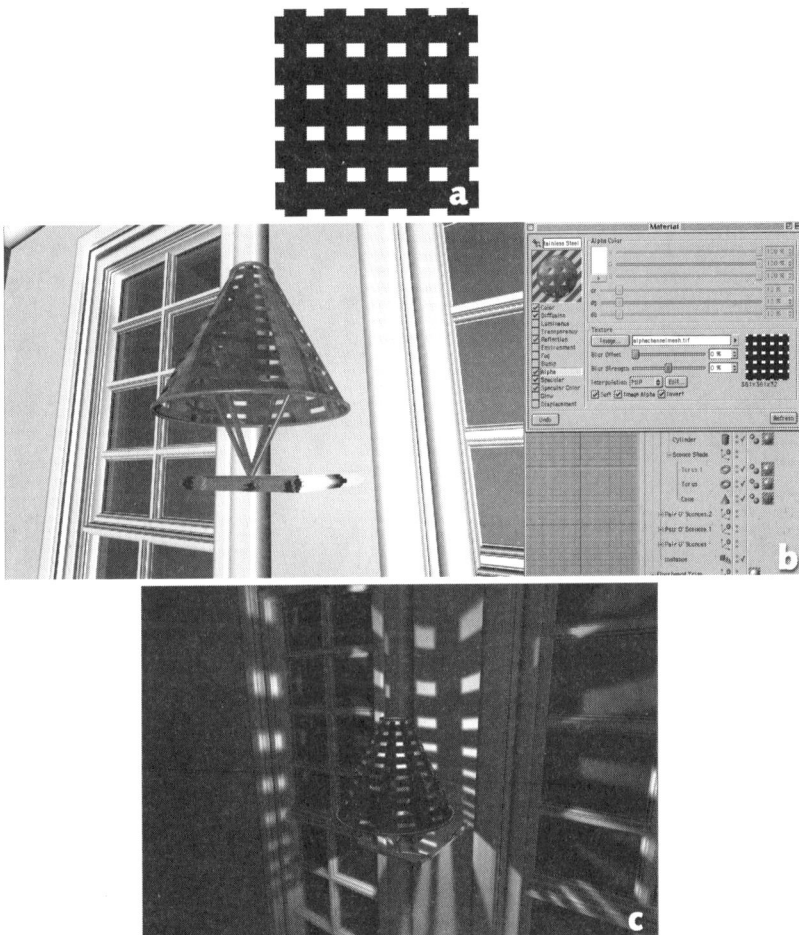

FIGURE 8.15 *Texturing the sconce.*

Make sure to place these metal textures on all sconces in the room.

The last set of materials include a simple Color and Specular parameter enabled material for the runner on the table. A plain green color for the flower stem and some simple flat colors for the flower. The only tricky part here was that a bump map was applied to the flower center, and instead of importing a bit-mapped image, a Checkerboard 2D shader was selected with a very high rate of repeat (Figure 8.16). Also in this last rendering are the doorknobs, textured with the brass material we built for the lamp (Figure 8.17).

There's still much to be textured here. However, much of good texturing has to do with mapping. In the next chapter we'll look at how C4D thinks of materials, how it applies the materials, and how we can further define how materials are placed across image surfaces. We'll look at other sources for texture maps and C4D built materials and we'll finish texturing this room.

ADVANCED TEXTURING OF THE DINING ROOM

In the last section we looked at how to create our own materials using some simple shaders and how to create our own materials based upon scanned objects (including photographs). On the web there are numerous resources for textures. Just enter "Textures" in any search engine and a multitude of entries will appear. One great source is http://www.3dcafe.com, which stores large collections of freely downloadable models and some images for use in materials (Figure 8.18).

Make sure you explore these images and grab the largest version of the image that you can. Once you have an image, you can use the image as a guide to build up your various maps. First make sure that the downloaded image is seamless, using the Offset/Rubber Stamp technique described earlier in this

FIGURE 8.16 *Flower center using Checkerboard 2D shader as a bump map.*

FIGURE 8.17 *Remaining simple textures.*

chapter. This first seamless version will probably become your color map. Then, you can create new layers within Photoshop to begin building up other image maps. The process shown in Figure 8.19 is building a final bump map by, drawing over the color map, and then deleting the color layer.

In this case, we'll want to build the floor for our room from the color and bump map shown in Figure 8.20. Open your room file within C4D and create a new material called "Floor." Activate the Color, Diffusion, Reflection, Bump, and Specular/Specular Color parameters. Import the color and bump maps you prepared into these parameters. Within the Diffusion setting, use a low intensity setting for Turbulence to give just a hint of dust. Keep the Reflection setting low (around 20%). Now apply this material to your floor object (Figure 8.20 a).

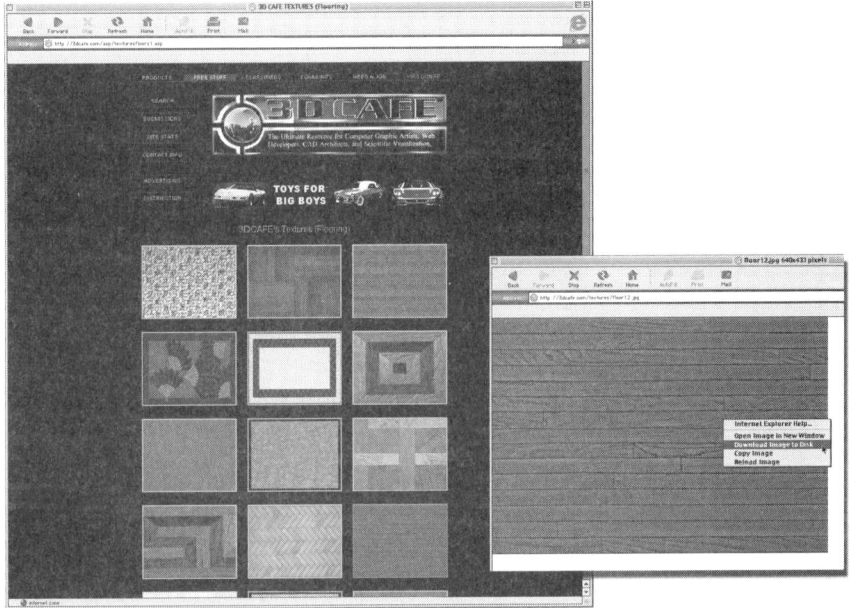

FIGURE 8.18 *3D Café is one of many online sources of images for use in creating materials.*

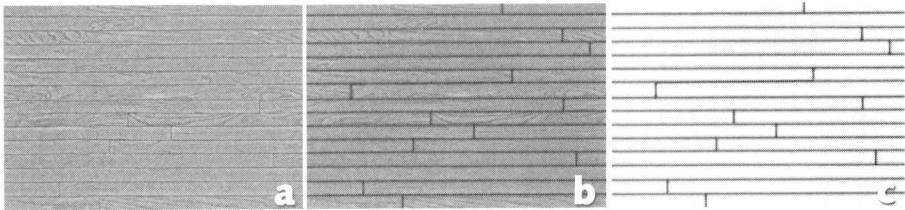

FIGURE 8.19 *Building custom maps from stock images off the web.*

The problem is that as it looks now, the slats of the floor are about two feet wide. This is because of C4D's assumption that by default one copy of the material should cover the entire object. This is often a problem with floors. Luckily, this is very easy to correct. If you double-click the Texture tag within the Object Manager, you can change the Length setting to make the scale of the texture more appropriate. Often, it is a matter of trial and error to find the right size (or you can use the Texture tool to manually resize the material), but for this project, it turns out that 20% is about right (Figure 8.20 b).

Besides sites like 3D Café, there is a fantastic resource on the web to get materials made especially for C4D to use or to study. *Deepshade* has a fantastic collection of materials created by many of the C4D masters around the world, that are free to download. The address is http://www.maxon.net/deepshade. Once you get into the "shaders," you can click on any material you are interested in to get a close up look (Figure 8.21). If you find one you like, you simply download the file (which downloads in a .sit format – you'll need Aladdin System's Stuffit Expander (also available at *Deepshade*)). When the file has been downloaded and unstuffed, you'll notice that it is actually a C4D file and often in a "Tex" folder. To use these textures, simply take the entire folder (usually labeled by a number), including the C4D file and its "Tex" file, and put it in the "Tex" file for your project.

To actually use the material that you've downloaded, use the File>Load Materials pull-down menu within your Materials Manager. Select the C4D file of the material. C4D will then import all the materials connected to that file. Sometimes projects from *Deepshade* are one material, while other times the actual appearance is a result of several layers of materials. For the table and the wood on the chairs, we'll download and import *044 Dark Wood* submitted by *Phil 3D*.

Once this material has been loaded, try and place this "Dark Wood" material on the Dinner Table group. This would make sense as the entire table is made

FIGURE *(a) Newly placed floor material. (b) Fixed floor with correct scale.*
8.20

CHAPTER 8 TEXTURES 249

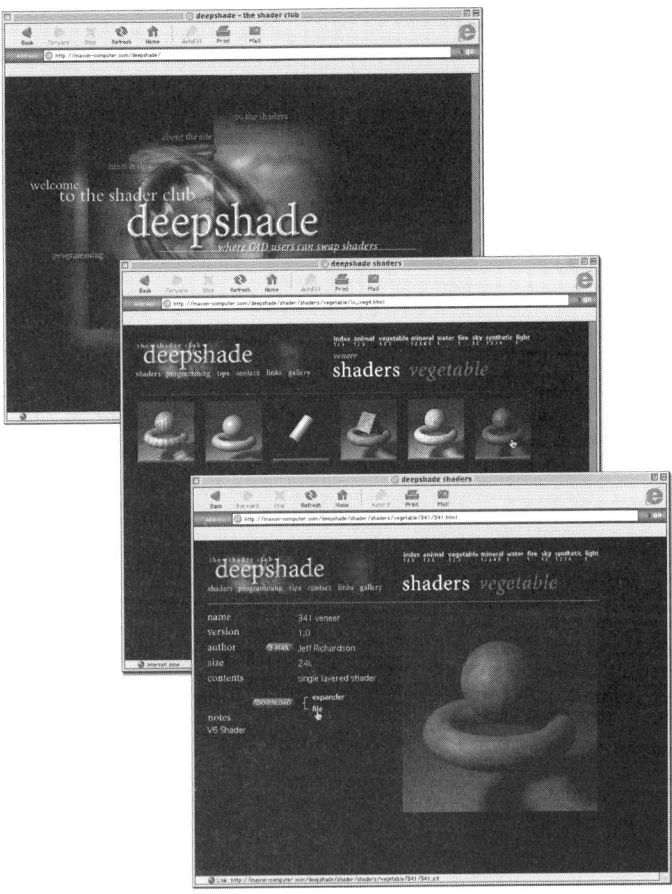

FIGURE 8.21 Deepshade *is one of the best resources for Cinema 4D information and materials.*

of the same wood; however, because the polygon topology is so different over different parts of the table (very dense in the high curve areas, very few polygons in places like the top of the table), the textured results are less than desirable (Figure 8.22). The *UVW* mapping has attempted to wrap around the edge, while the top appears flat and painted. In situations like this, it is important to texture each part of the table separately.

Let's start on the top. As the table has this huge surface area on the top, we need to pick a projection method that doesn't bunch up at the poles. The textures that do that best are Flat and Cubic. Move the Texture tag from the Dinner Table group and move it to the Extrude NURBS form that composes the tabletop and change the Projection setting to Flat (Figure 8.23 a).

There's a problem here. The material is being projected alright, but it's as though the projector is sitting on our window rather than from above. We need to rotate the texture to project downward. This sort of rotation from side projection to top projection is a rotation of pitch. Open the Texture tag by double clicking it in the Objects Manager and enter 90° in the P input field (Figure 8.23 b).

Ah, that's looking better. However, there is still a problem; as the material is being projected downward, it ends up leaving streaks of color down the side of the tabletop. Therefore, a more appropriate projection would be Cubic so that these sides of the tabletop would appear as wood as well (Figure 8.23 c). Change the Texture tag to Cubic for the tabletop.

For everything under the table a different projection method will be needed for each part. The twisted cube that is the pedestal part works best with Cylindrical Projection. The short legs (Extrude NURBS forms) are closest to a cube and so Cubic Projection works for them (Figure 8.24).

Next, we'll turn our attention to the chairs. Repeat the same process for the wood parts of the chairs. Again, applying one material to the entire object will not produce the desired results, so you'll need to get specific. Luckily, most of the chairs are cubic based, so the projection choices are easy (Figure 8.25). The seat of the chair can be textured completely with 2D shaders. Activate the color

FIGURE 8.22 *Putting the "Dark Wood" material on the whole table produces undesirable results.*

FIGURE 8.23 *(a) Flat projection on just the tabletop. (b) Rotated Flat projection. (c) Cubic Projection ends up being most appropriate for the tabletop.*

and bump maps and select a 2D Checkerboard shader for the Bump parameter. Edit the shader and select a high number of U and V Frequency settings. This creates a nice weaved material look. Lastly, add the same "Dark Wood" to the niche table.

You may want to take some quick test renderings to see how your woods are working together. You want your floor and table to still look good together even if they are different types of wood (Figure 8.26). If you find that you need to change the characteristic of one material or the other, simply open the material from the Materials Manager and make the adjustment there; everyplace the material is used will automatically be updated.

The door is a painted door and so it can be created entirely within C4D's Materials Editor, no image map is required.

Let us finish the room off by working with the vase. To do this, create a new file in Photoshop and paint the design and color you would like to see on the vase. Remember that this map is going to wrap around the vase to paint accordingly. Since the vase is going to have a very porcelain feel, you don't need any image maps beyond the color map (Figure 8.27 a).

Once your color maps are complete, create a new material and bring this color map into the Color parameter. Adjust the Specular and Reflection channels to create a nice smooth surface and apply the texture to the vase. Make sure that the Projection is Cylindrical so that the map will truly wrap around the vase (Figure 8.27 b). You will also need to resize and move the material into position so that it "fits" the form it is designed to cover.

The possibilities of refining and creating textures and materials are nearly infinite. There are layers and layers of techniques that could be applied to these objects. One of the trickiest areas to texture are the skin textures of characters. In the next chapter we'll look at ways to texture character forms.

FIGURE *Completed textured table.*
8.24

FIGURE *Textured chairs and table.*
8.25

FIGURE 8.26 *Variety of renderings finding the right color for woods.*

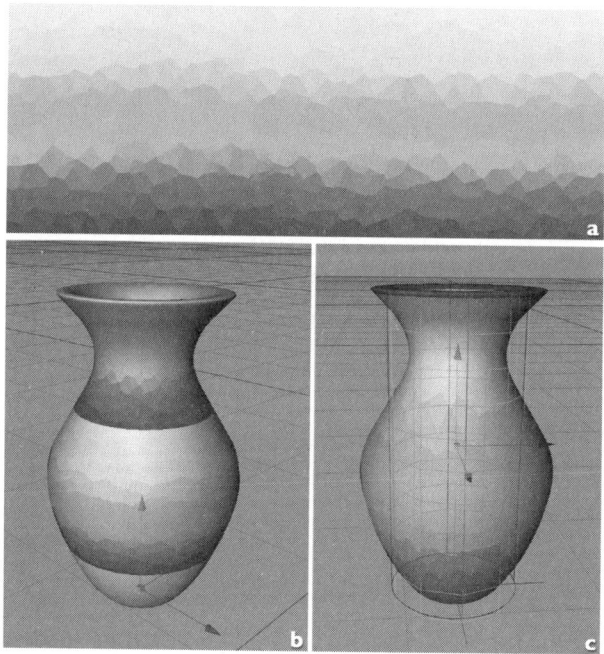

FIGURE 8.27 *(a) Vase color map. (b) Final vase.*

CHAPTER 9

Texturing Characters

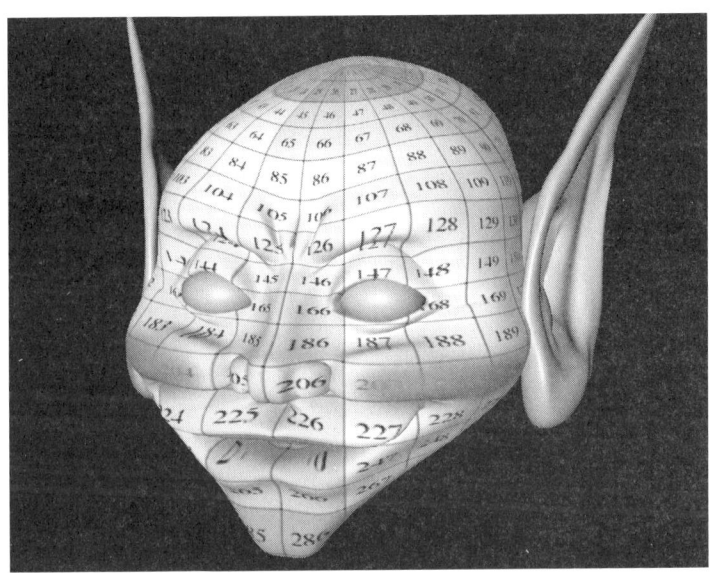

So we've looked at how to texture a room. We've analyzed ways to make materials define a visual geometry. We've looked at ways to make materials project across surfaces appropriately, and how to make textures from scratch. All of that is great to know, but the challenge of texturing really emerges when we begin dealing with character forms. The problem is that the face has great variations in color, hue, and bump as you move from one area to another. This may not seem like a problem, as you can create any texture you want, right? Well, the problem isn't creating a texture or color map to place on a face, it's making sure that the red of the cheeks lines up with the cheeks while the brown of the stubble lines up with the jaw line.

9.1 C4D AND THE GRID SYSTEM FOR TEXTURING CHARACTERS (OR ANYTHING, REALLY)

TUTORIAL

C4D's texturing capabilities are robust and fairly easy to use. However, the challenge is always knowing exactly where textures are going to lie when we work with a complex form. Characters are amongst the most complex of models, especially since they are typically all one mesh. With a character face (perhaps one modeled using HyperNURBS techniques), you don't have the luxury of creating one texture for the mouth, another for the nose, and still another for the cheeks. The most effective method is to create one material that incorporates all these areas. The trick then is making this texture work with all parts of the face; to do this, we must know where the material will end up.

Figure 9.1 shows the model by Desireé Maher created as a result of a tutorial in Chapter 6. In this tutorial, we will be looking at ways to bring life to the surface of this creepy creature.

The process of this technique will be to apply one texture to the face. Originally, this one material will be the grid shown in Figure 9.2. But after we've placed the grid on the face, we can use it as a guide in Photoshop to know what parts of the material are falling where. Then we can paint over the grid in Photoshop with assurance, as we know where each number falls across the face. The grid is a simple numbered and colored grid. Sometimes just using numbers can be easier, but the colors provide a quicker visual reference when it comes time to painting over the character.

Now in Desiree's model, the ears are a separate object than the head. So we'll worry about them separately. For now, open the model, ModelbyDesireeMaher.c4d and create a new material. In this material, activate the Color and Luminance parameters. Import the grid into both these parameters and reduce the intensity of the Luminance parameter to about 30%. We want the Luminance parameter activated, so that even if we need information on the dark side of the object, we'll still be able to see the numbers and colors.

Chapter 9 Texturing Characters

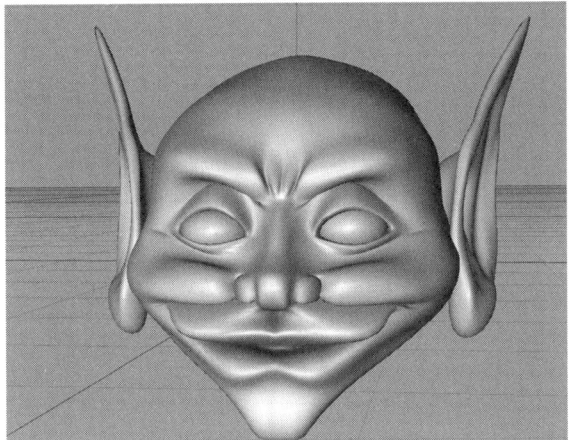

FIGURE 9.1 *Model by Desiree Maher.*

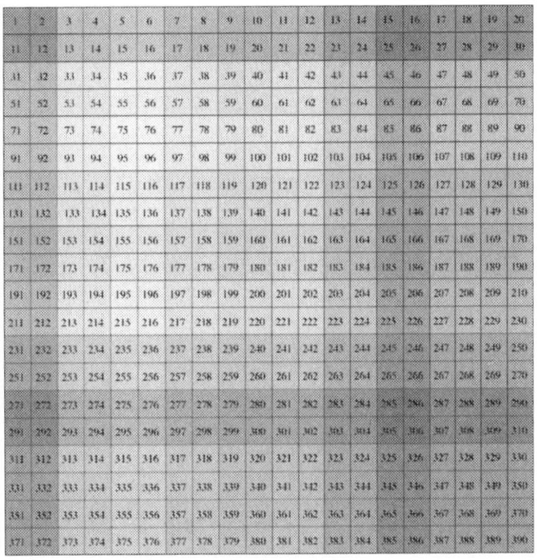

FIGURE 9.2 *Colored grid for guide in texturing.*

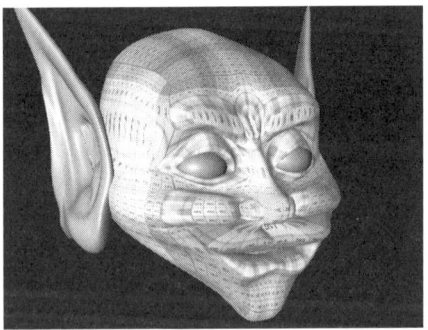

FIGURE 9.3 *Applying the material with UVW projection creates an interesting but useless projection situation.*

Upon applying the material to the head, a rendering will reveal an odd image indeed (Figure 9.3). As we discussed earlier, UVW projection works hard to analyze the polygons that exist and stretches and squeezes the material to match the density of polygons. Unfortunately, this means that we have many copies of the grid across the face. For this technique, we must be able to have one copy of the texture cover the entire object. If we didn't then, as we painted a blush in the cheek, we'd end up with little blushes all over the face.

The best projection method for this technique is Spherical. Spherical projection does bunch the texture up at the poles; however, for characters, the bottom of the neck and top of the head (the poles) are typically less important. Besides, at the tend of this tutorial we'll look at ways of correcting this bunching. Make sure also, that if you are using a HyperNURBS and Symmetry object, that you apply the texture to the HyperNURBS object and not to the Cube or Symmetry Object. The key after you have changed the Texture tag to use Spherical Projection is to take lots of renderings and save each of them. You need to be able to see everywhere this texture is. How does it fall across the lips? What numbers of the grid make up each eyelid? Etc.... Figure 9.4 and 9.5 show a variety of renderings for this character.

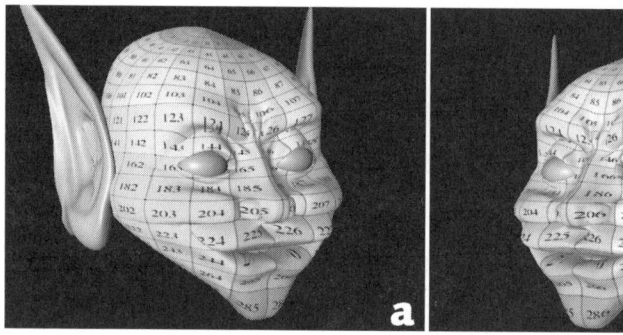

FIGURE 9.4 *The more renderings the better.*

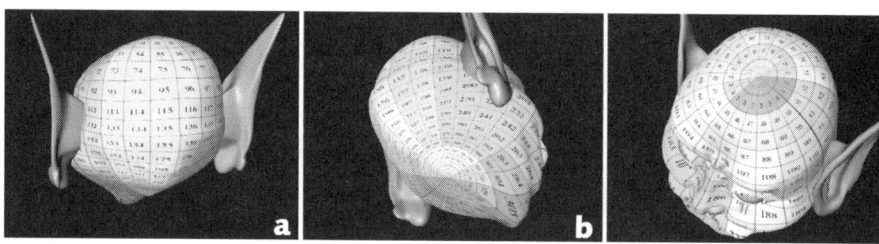

FIGURE 9.5 *Make sure you get the tops and bottoms and back sides of the head.*

Multiple views are so important, in fact, that this would be a great place to create a QTVR Object movie. We talk much more on rendering in Chapter 14, but as a quick preview, a QTVR movie is an interactive movie in which the viewer can rotate around in a space or rotate an object. C4D makes QTVR movies very well. To set one up, click on the Edit Rendering Settings button and edit the tabs as follows. Leave the General tab as is (make sure it is set to Raytracing so you can see accurately how the grid falls across the surface). In the Output tab, enter whatever size you are willing to wait for; the larger the better (640x480 is nice), but the rendering takes a while so you may want to settle for something around 320x240. In the Save tab, select QTVR Object in the Format selection (Figure 9.6). Make sure that you enter a path (place to save the file) so

CHAPTER 9 TEXTURING CHARACTERS

ON THE CD

that the movie can be saved for later viewing. The default settings in the QTVR tab are good, as they give you a nice view from everywhere (Figure 9.7). See the QTVR movie included with the CD.

All of these movies or renderings are there to provide information. The more information you have about where the numbers are, the better equipped you are paint in the right places.

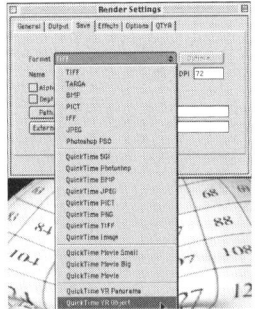

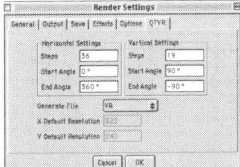

FIGURE 9.7 *The QTVR settings allow us to have a movie that will show from the top to the bottom, from the front to the back.*

FIGURE 9.6 *Creating a QTVR movie within Edit Render Settings.*

PHOTOSHOP WORK

Once you have plenty of renderings, open the grid within Photoshop. Save it as a file called "Face Color." Make sure that you save both of these images in the "Tex" folder at the same level of the model.

You'll want to make extensive use of Photoshop's Layers capabilities. So make sure your Layers palette is active. Generally, you don't ever want to paint directly on the layer with the grid, you want to always preserve this layer so you can always see where you're painting.

Within the Face Color file, create a new layer (Layer>New Layer). This can be our base layer of green gray. Fill the entire layer (Figure 9.8).

Now the big problem is, as soon as we filled this layer, we could no longer see the grid to paint anything else. As such, hide this skin layer (Figure 9.9). Remember that it's there though, it'll be important to select colors as you go that jive with the colors of this general skin.

Let's start out by giving the little creature some color in her cheeks. If we look at our renderings (Figure 9.10), we can see that the cheeks are in grid cells 202,203,204 and 207,208,209. Knowing this, we can find those cells on our grid and *in a new layer* paint over these areas. Since we're working on a character, we don't want any sharp edges of color. So the Airbrush is often the best tool to use to build color up gradually (Figure 9.11). Save the file; note that there is no need to flatten the image; in fact, we want to keep all the layers. C4D works very well with Photoshop PSD files.

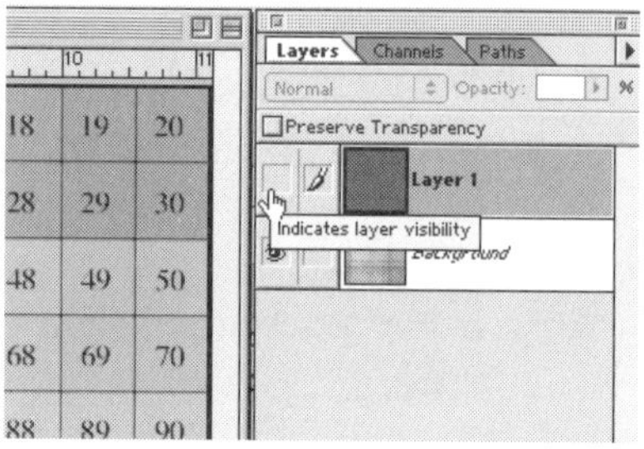

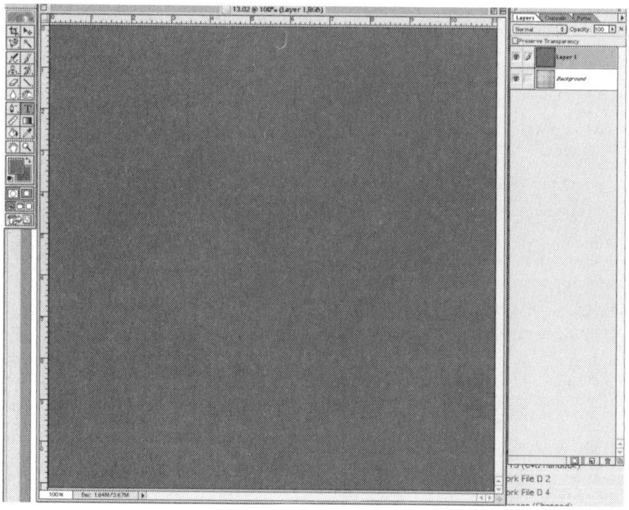

FIGURE 9.9 *Just after you've built it, you need to hide the new layer so you can continue to see the grid beneath.*

FIGURE 9.8 *Fill the entire new layer as this will be the skin.*

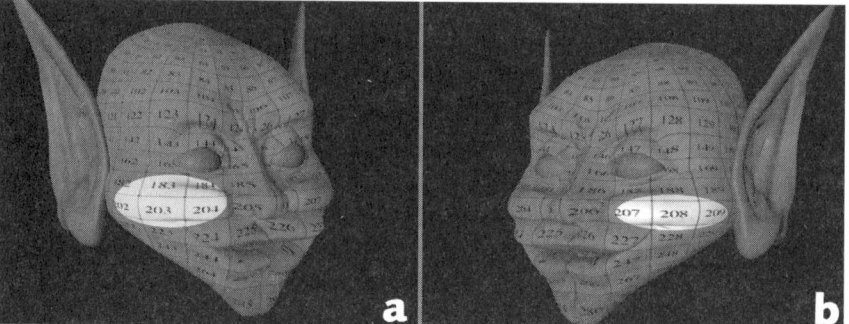

FIGURE 9.10 *Starting with the cheeks, we just need to know where to start painting.*

Now, we need to replace the color image map from the original grid with this new file (which includes the grid, but also our new colors that we've painted on). Just open the material in C4D, and relink the Color Texture input field to our new Face Color file by clicking the Image input field button and re-selecting the file. From now on, you won't need to relink, as C4D will simply look at the Face Color image whenever it needs to render; thus as you update, C4D will update. You should note, though, that it will only update when you render. After you save changes in Photoshop, you won't be able to see the changes in the Editor window of C4D unless you have relinked. Typically there's no need to relink, as you want to make sure you're rendering often to make sure your placement is really in the right spot. Once your new Face Color has been imported into the material to replace the old, re-render (Figure 9.12).

Chapter 9 Texturing Characters

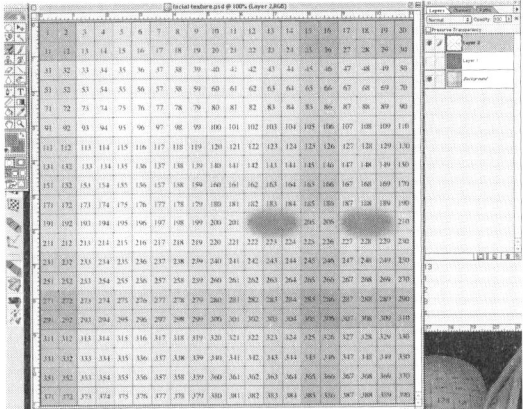

FIGURE 9.11 *Knowing which grids to paint over allows us to get started painting our texture.*

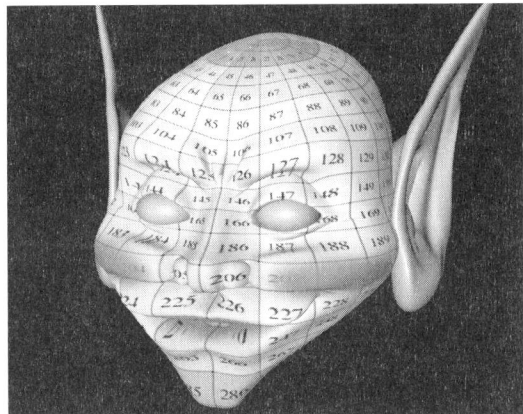

FIGURE 9.12 *Render often to see how your updates in Photoshop are shaping up.*

Create a new layer and select a little darker color and paint in around the eye socket. Again, pay special attention to which grids need color and then use a very soft Airbrush (10%-15%) opacity to layer colors down (Figure 9.13). You may find it to be a timesaver to do one eye, save in Photoshop, render in C4D, adjust, save, render, and when you're satisfied that you have a good idea of what shape you need, start in on the other eye (Figure 9.14).

Occasionally, you'll also want to activate the general skin layer to get an idea of how all your colors are working together (Figure 9.15). Because C4D works so well with Photoshop files, you can activate one layer and hide another, save, and then immediately render in C4D to see the results (Figure 9.16).

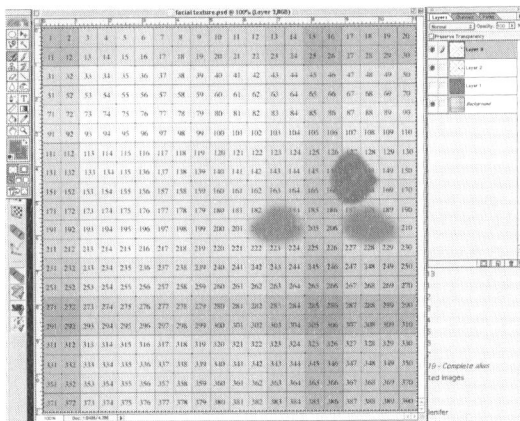

FIGURE 9.13 *Work out the rough shape of the eye with a soft Airbrush.*

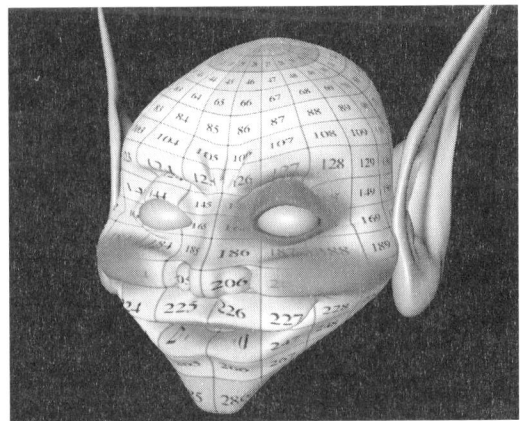

FIGURE 9.14 *Rendering of the rough eye.*

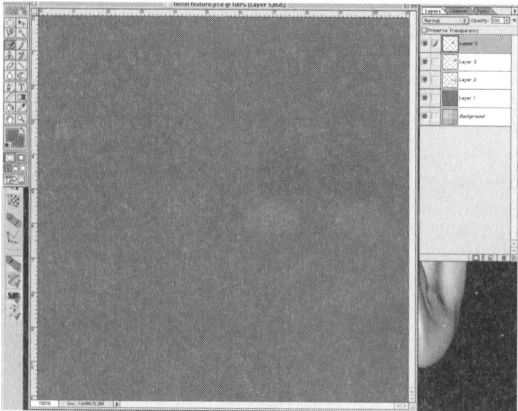

FIGURE 9.15 *Activated skin layer to get an idea of color cohesion.*

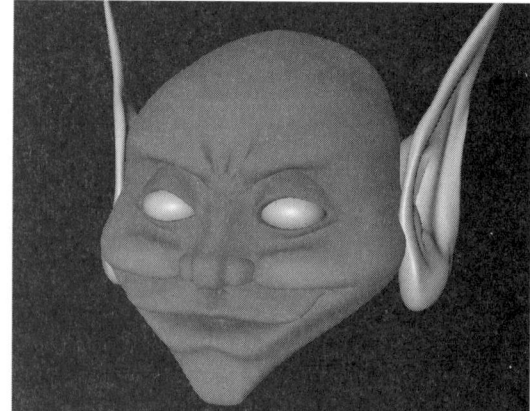

FIGURE 9.16 *Rendering of eyes, cheeks, and color thus far.*

Back in Photoshop, hide the skin layer again and build the lips up with a bit of color (Figure 9.17) on their own layer. This will probably take several times of painting, saving, rendering, and painting again to get it right. The process of refining is an important part of this technique as it's difficult to get the placement right the first time every time (Figure 9.18).

There's a lot of interpretation still left to do on the color. Simply look for things you'd like to see on the face (maybe a mole here or there, or abnormalities to the skin) and paint them in. Remember that faces really oughtn't have any fields of colors with hard edges unless they are painted there artificially as in lipstick or clown makeup (Figure 9.19). When you're finally happy with the overall color map, make sure that your Luminance parameter is off from earlier, and take a test rendering. (Figure 9.20).

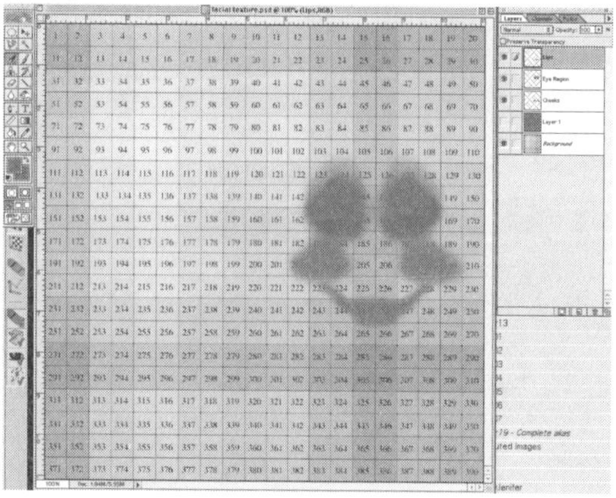

FIGURE 9.17 *Building the lips up.*

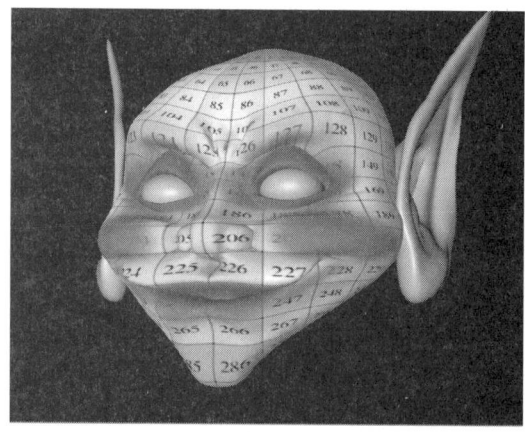

FIGURE 9.18 *Rough rendering of lips.*

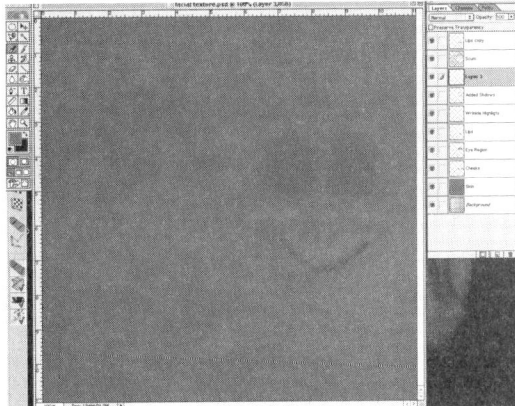

FIGURE 9.19 *Completed color map.*

FIGURE 9.20 *Rendering with color map.*

It's looking good, but still has a bit of a plastic-like look. In C4D make sure your Specular parameter is deactivated. Now the key is to build up a bit of bump to further augment the material. To do this, we'll build directly off the Face Color map. In Photoshop, save a copy of this Face Color to a file named Face Bump and open that new file. Be sure you don't overwrite your Face Color map with the steps we're about to execute.

With the Face Bump map open in Photoshop, convert the image to Grayscale (Image>Mode>Grayscale). This will give you a rough idea of where the bumps are. Make sure you hide the layers that include your lips, cheeks, and eye color as you don't want them to affect the bump. Further, you'll want to make some adjustments to this map. For instance, the moles will need to rise off the surface, so they need to be painted white (Figure 9.21). You may also want some of the rough texture painted in to rise off the surface of the skin instead of falling back; black areas would need to be inverted to white. Save the file.

Within C4D, open the Materials Editor for the face material. This time, activate the Bump parameter and import our Face Bump image into the Image dialog box and take a rendering (Figure 9.22).

To further refine this bump map, we'll add some crows feet around the eyes and wrinkles on the nose. In Photoshop (still working with Face Bump), make the layer with your eye color visible again to get an idea of where the eyes and nose are. This time, paint in some dark black thin lines to define where the surface of the skin should render as though it is receding (Figure 9.23). Save again and render (Figure 9.24).

A little while ago, we turned the Specular parameter off to not have that plastic look. However, there are probably a couple of places on this model — like the lips and the moles — where a Specular highlight would be appropriate.

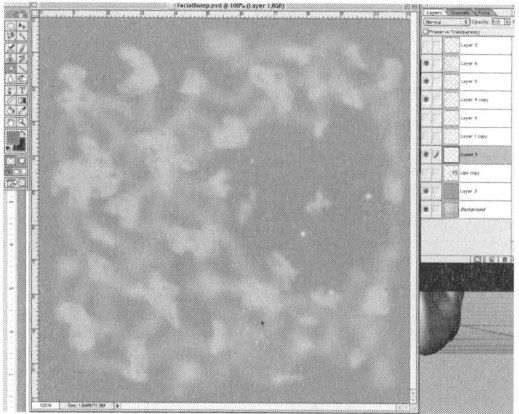

FIGURE 9.21 *The first bump map, altered a bit to allow the moles to be rendered as though they rise off the surface, and allowing skin abnormalities to rise as well.*

FIGURE 9.22 *A first rendering with simple bump map.*

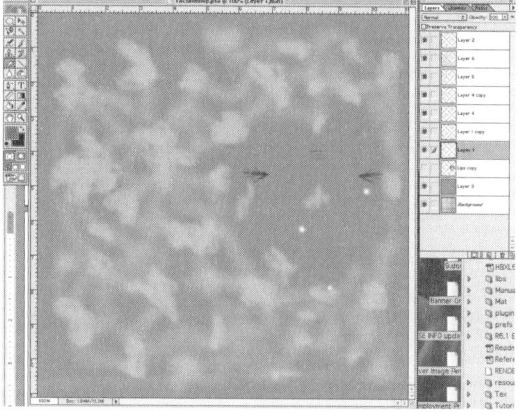

FIGURE 9.23 *Augmented bump map with crows feet and nose wrinkles.*

FIGURE 9.24 *Rendering with new bump map.*

Luckily, we have the bump map in grayscale already that would be easy to convert to a Specular map. Open your Face Bump and save a copy as "Face Specular." When this file is open, adjust the gray layer to black as we don't want any Specular highlight overall, and change the lips and mole areas to white with most everything else black (Figure 9.25). In C4D once again open the Materials Editor and activate the Specular and Specular Color parameters. Import the Face Specular map into the Specular Color parameter. This will tell C4D to give the lips and moles highlights, but nothing else (Figure 9.26).

Chapter 9 Texturing Characters

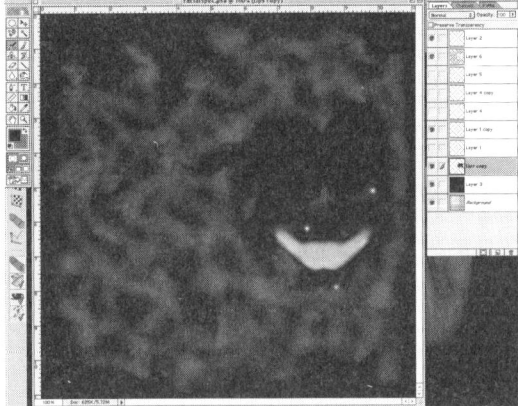

Figure 9.25 *A Specular map built off of a bump map.*

Figure 9.26 *Rendering of Specular map. Notice matte skin everywhere but the moles and mouth.*

It's starting to really come along; however, it still looks a little plastic-like. Some additional bump would help a lot, but you noticed how the grid was stretched awkwardly. If we were to create an additional bump that covered the entire surface in the material we are using thus far, we would get the same unsightly stretches. The solution is to create another material with nothing activated but the Bump parameter, establish a bump here, and then place this material so that it lays atop our Face material. Then we would be free to alter that bump independently of the material below it; thus minimizing the bump distortion.

When you create this new material (call it "Skin Bump"), only activate the Bump parameter. It turns out that the Marble 2D shader makes for quite a nice skin bump (Figure 9.27). This texture can be confusing to work with since it appears black in all the preview settings, just remember it's only there for bump. Click-drag this Skin Bump material onto the face and make sure to also check the Mix with Other Textures option. Reduce the size to somewhere around 10% in both X and Y input fields so that the adjustment is just enough to give the illusion of small pores (Figure 9.28).

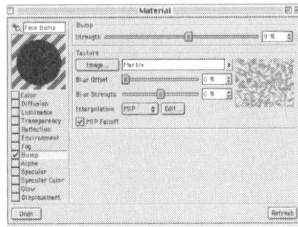

Figure 9.27 *Use the Marble 2D shader to create the bump for the independent bump map "Skin Bump."*

The rest of the face is fairly basic. You could repeat the process with the ears or simply create a green texture that roughly matched the face. Texture the eyes and you're ready to go (Figure 9.29).

FIGURE 9.28 *After applying the second material to the face as well, we have an independent bump to affect the quality of the skin.*

FIGURE 9.29 *Finished face.*

9.2 HIPPO UV MAPPING

TUTORIAL

**By Kevin Aguirre
Jason Goldsmith
Chad Hofteig
Chris Villa**

UV EDITING

ON THE CD

In this project, we're going to set up the UVs (UV Texture coordinates, not light frequency) for the Hippo included on the CD called ModelbyChadGriffiths.c4d. This is a relatively straightforward process, if you understand UVs. If you don't understand UVs, the BodyPaint 3D manual has a good introduction to them.

Before we start editing UVs, it will help to have some understanding of the different issues we'll face. So let's start by talking about an ideal world.

The ideal world for UVs is a regular grid of polygons that are all co-planar. In English this means a flat plane where every polygon is a square of the same size. This is all well and good, but not much use in the real world.

So, why did we bother looking at an ideal world? Well, we can get some clues about how to make the real world less painful by looking at the ideal world. If the ideal world is a flat plane with equal sized, square polygons, then the closer we can make our model to that, or at least portions of it, the better.

One other important thing to note about our ideal world is that it is not a solid. In other words, this object has edges that don't connect to each other, providing a natural seam. The fewer of these there are, the more challenging the task of getting the UVs just right.

So, now that we have a little foundation, let's build on it. The next obvious question is, what do we do when our model deviates from the ideal? Well, then it's time to start balancing our different options.

If you look in the BodyPaint 3D manual, in the Tutorial section, it begins with a discussion of UV. In the section on editing the UVs of a cube, there are five different things you can balance when you decide how to work with your UVs: correspondence of UV mesh to actual geometry, number of disconnected surfaces or seams, number of overlapping surfaces, ability to paint in the 2D texture view, and recognizability of major geometric surfaces. These are described in detail in the BodyPaint 3D manual, so you can look there for more information.

Let's look at our Hippo and see what we have to work with (Figure 9.30). The first thing we'll notice is that our geometry is not very regular; we have lots of different sized polygons. Secondly, its not very grid-like; we have polygons connecting all over the place. Thirdly, we have almost no opened edges, this little Hippo is pretty solid. Welcome to the real world.

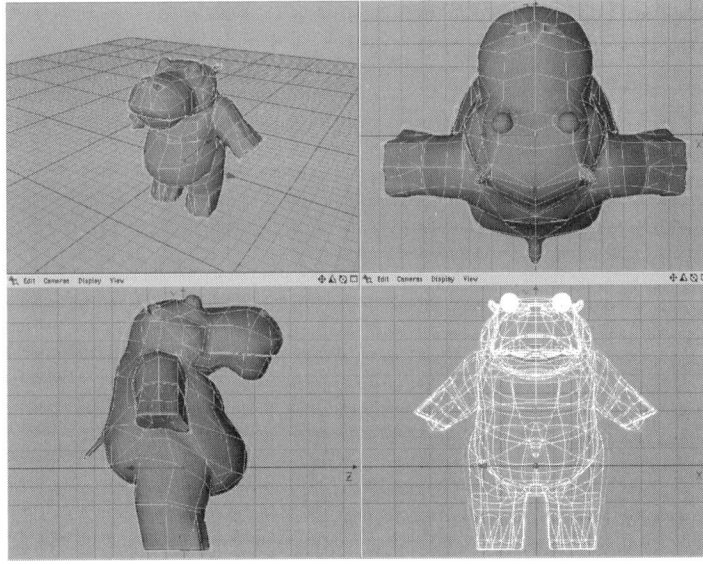

FIGURE 9.30 *Our Hippo. Model by Chad Griffiths.*

So here's how we decided to approach this:

1. We decided we didn't care how many seams we had.in the UV mesh. Why? Because this little guy is going to run about jiggling all over the place. The seams should be pretty well hidden by that. Also, we placed the seams in places like the underarm or along an edge that almost looks like a seam anyway. With BodyPaint 3D's painting tools, we can hide these pretty well anyway.
2. We decided that we would paint the Hippo mostly in the 3D view. This way we don't have to worry too much about how the UVs look in the 2D view. They actually don't end up too bad, as you'll see, but we didn't care too much either way.
3. We decided that we're probably not going to paint a photo-realistic texture on this Hippo. You could if you wanted to, but that wasn't our goal. We wanted this guy to be paintable, but we're not too concerned about having fine control on how it's done. If we can paint some blush on its cheeks and lay down some detail, great.
4. Since this IS a character, we knew we couldn't have overlapping surfaces. You don't want to be painting the Hippo's nose and have spots appearing on his backside. So, we made sure that our UVs were laid out cleanly in the 2D view.

So, with all this in mind, let's dig in and tear this Hippo to bits, and hopefully put him back together again. We're going to do most of the work in this tutorial by using interactive mapping. Since we're not too concerned with seams, it is an ideal choice for getting the Hippo worked into shape. Interactive mapping lets us select UVs and then use the different projection types to rearrange them. So, if we select some UVs and choose a Flat mapping for them, they are flattened out nicely for us.

Let's get started with the hands and feet. Then we'll move onto the arms, legs, and tail. After that, we'll do the Hippo's belly. Then we'll go on to the most complex part, the head.

ARMS, LEGS, TAIL:

Create Selection tags for the hands and feet by switching to Polygon mode (Tools>Polygons). Activate the HippoPoly by selecting it in the Object Manager. Then use the Live Selection tool (Selection>Live Selection) to select the end polygons of the left arm. With these polygons selected, create a Selection tag (Selection>Set Selection).

A new red triangle will appear next to the HippoPoly in the Object Manager; double-click on it and rename it "Left Hand Skin" (Figure 9.31).

While you are still in Polygon mode, and with the Live Selection tool still active, select the polygons on the right hand. Make a Selection tag for this as well. In order to create a new Selection tag and not overwrite the previous tag, we must deselect the tag in the Object Manager. Create the Selection set (Selection>Set Selection). Double-click on the new tag in the Object Manager and rename it "Right Hand Skin", then click OK (Figure 9.32).

Repeat the last step for creating Selection tags for the right and left foot naming them accordingly, "Left Foot Skin" and "Right Foot Skin" (Figure 9.33 and 9.34).

Create a new material in the Materials Manager (File>New). Click-drag the material onto the HippoPoly object in the Object Manager. A Texture dialog box will appear. Leave the settings as default and click OK. Switch to the Layers Manager — by default it is located in the lower right corner of the screen. Then activate the Color channel (Channels>Color). A dialog box will appear. Leave

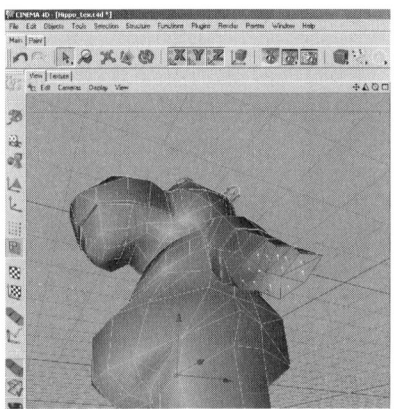

FIGURE 9.31 *Creating the Left Hand Skin selection set.*

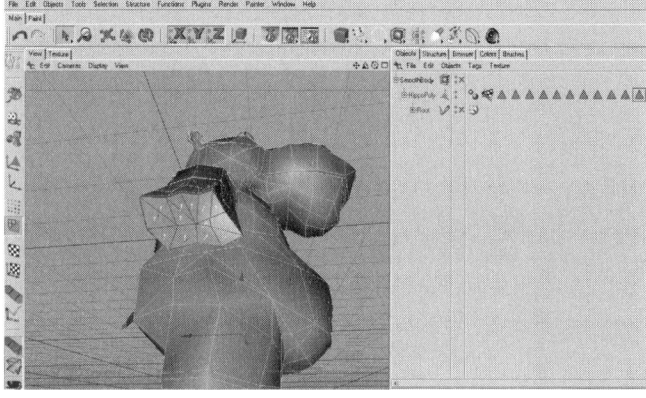

FIGURE 9.32 *Creating the Right Hand Skin Selection set.*

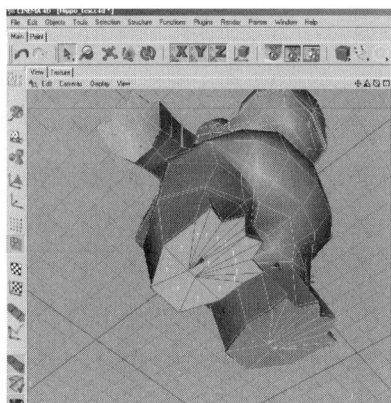

FIGURE 9.33 *Left Foot Skin Selection set.*

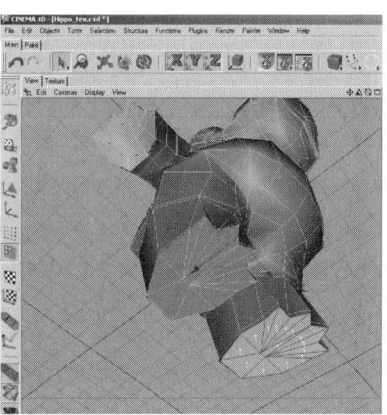

FIGURE 9.34 *Right Foot Skin Selection set.*

the settings as the default and click OK. Double-click on the texture to activate it in the Texture view.

Switch to Polygon mode (Tools>Polygons) if you are not in that mode already. Make sure no polygons are selected on the model. Locate the "Right Hand Skin" Selection tag to the right of the HippoPoly object in the Object Manager. Double-click on it, and in the dialog box choose Select Polygons (Figure 9.35).

Switch to the Texture view. In order to view the UV you must go to (Tools>Show UV Mesh). Once the mesh is visible, start interactive mapping (Functions>Start Interactive Mapping). In the dialog box that appears choose Flat for the projection. Click OK.

Switch back to the view panel. The Texture tool is now activated, and you can then move (Tools>Move), scale (Tools>Scale), and rotate (Tools>Rotate) your texture until it fits the selected hand polygons. The following values can be input into the Coordinates Manager as well:

Position: X = -595, Y = 240, Z = 120;
Size: X = 95, Y = 140, Z = 100; and
Rotation: H = 85, P = -60, B = -90 (Figure 9.36).

In order to see the polygons being worked on more clearly, select the Polygon tool (Tools>Polygons), then hide the unselected polygons(Selection>Hide-Unselected).

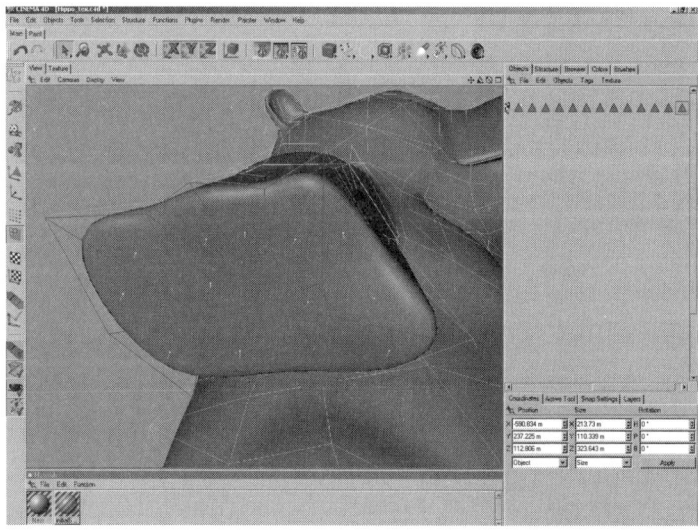

FIGURE 9.35 *The Right Hand Skin Selection set after choosing Select Polygons.*

Chapter 9 Texturing Characters

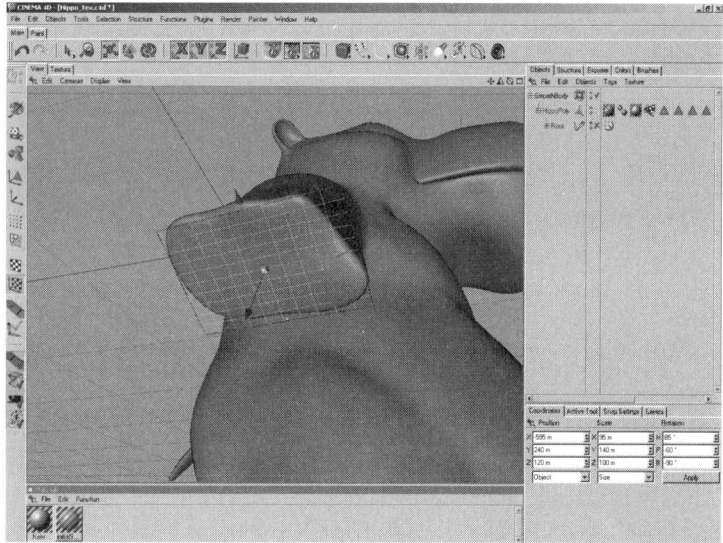

FIGURE 9.36 *Positioning the texture for the Right Hand Skin Selection set using interactive mapping.*

Switch back to the Texture view panel and stop interactive mapping (Functions>Stop Interactive Mapping). Your UVs are now set up for the hand. You will need to scale them down to have room for the other UVs on the texture bitmap. Use the UV Uniform Scale tool (Tools>Uniform Scale) and click-drag the UVs down, and with the Move tool (Tools>Move), place them in the upper right corner of the texture map (Figure 9.37).

Making sure you are in Polygon mode, deselect the right hand polygons. Then, locate the "Left Hand Skin" selection tag to the right of the HippoPoly object in the Object Manager. Once you have found the "Left Hand Skin" tag, double-click on it and from the dialog box select Select and Hide Others. You are going to be using the same basic method here for getting the left hand UVs as was done for the right hand UVs (Figure 9.38).

Switch to the Texture View and start interactive mapping (Functions> Start Interactive Mapping) again and choose Flat for the projection once again.

Switch back to the view panel; all you need to do is adjust the H rotation to get the texture axis in the correct place. In the Coordinates Manager, change the H rotation from 85 degrees to -85 degrees. Click Apply (Figure 9.39).

Go back to the Texture View and stop interactive mapping (Functions>Stop Interactive Mapping). The UVs may not appear on the texture bitmap. If this happens, zoom out from the texture until you see the UVs. Select the Move tool (Tools>Move) and move the UVs so they are visible on the texture. Next, scale them down and move them into the corner with the other hand UVs (Figure 9.40).

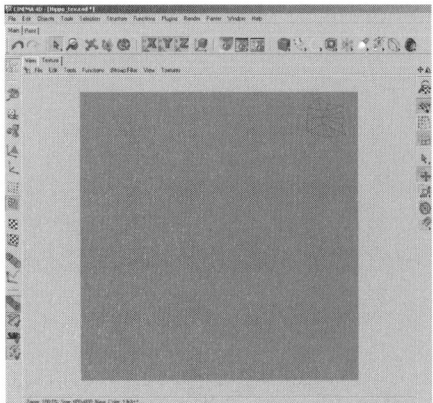

FIGURE 9.37 *Scaled UVs placed within the Texture view panel to allow for other Polygon selections.*

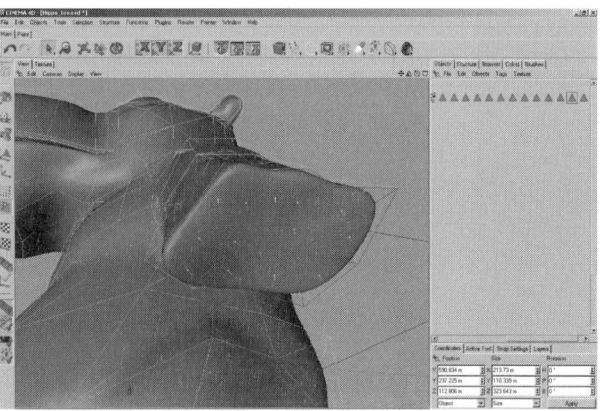

FIGURE 9.38 *Repeating the above steps, only this time starting with the Left Hand Skin.*

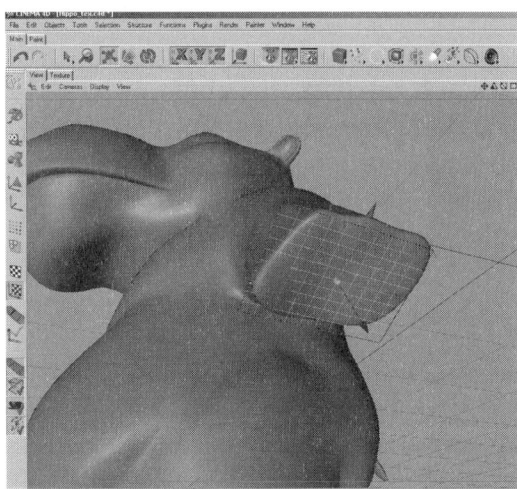

FIGURE 9.39 *Texture placed for the Left Hand Skin selection set with interactive mapping.*

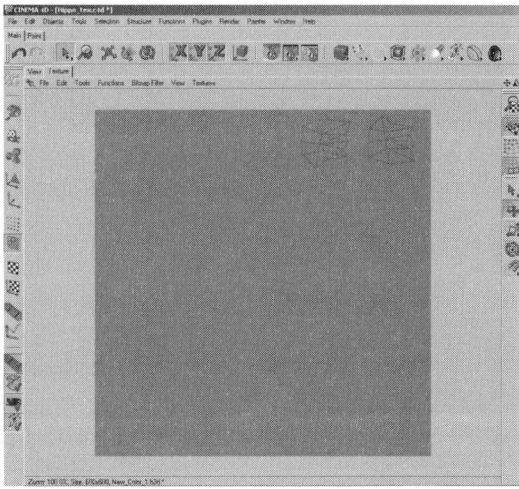

FIGURE 9.40 *Placing the UVs for the Left Hand Skin in the Texture View.*

Continuing on with similar techniques, we'll move to the feet. With the Polygon tool active (Tools>Polygons), unhide all the polygons (Selection>Unhide All). Deselect the Left Hand polygons. Then select the "Left Foot Skin" polygons by locating the Selection tag and double-clicking on it in the Object Manager. In the dialog box, click on Select and Hide Others. Then, start interactive mapping again by going to the Texture view and selecting (Functions>Start Interactive Mapping) and again use Flat Projection. Click OK (Figure 9.41 a).

Switch back to the view panel. You only need to make a couple of slight adjustments to get the texture axis lined up. Change the P rotation to -90 degrees, the X size to 120m, and the Y size to 175m (Figure 9.41 b).

Switch back to the Texture View, stop interactive mapping (Functions>Stop Interactive Mapping). Scale (Tools>Scale) the UVs down and place them in the corner with the hand UVs (Figure 9.42).

One more time, switch back to the view panel and unhide all (Selection> Unhide All). Deselect the Left Foot polygons and select the Right Foot polygons with the help of the Right Foot Skin selection tag (Figure 9.43 a).

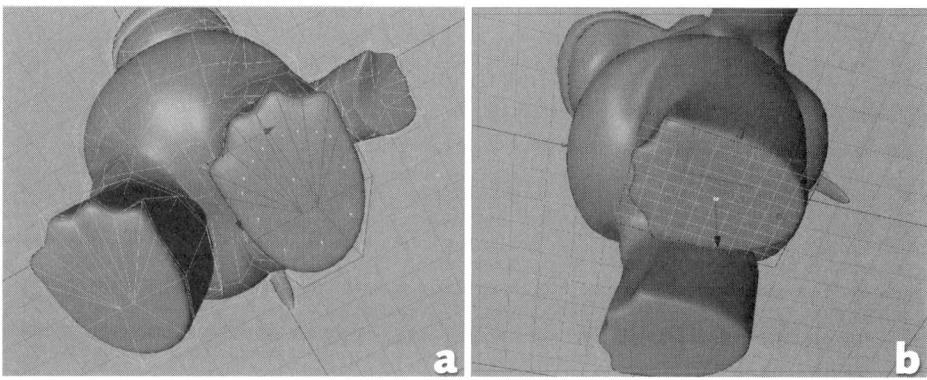

FIGURE 9.41 *Interactively mapping the feet bottom by selecting the Selection sets and adjusting the map.*

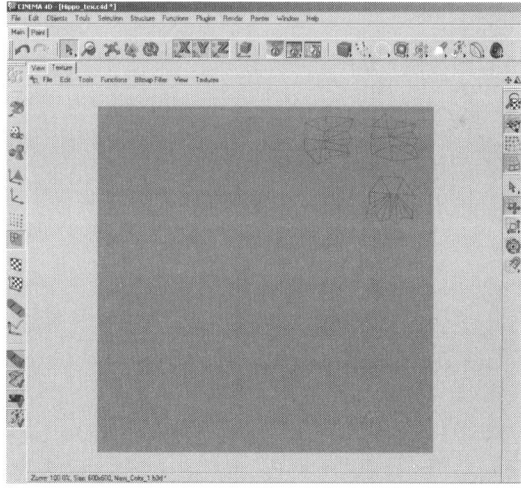

FIGURE 9.42 *In the Texture View, scale and move the new UVs into place.*

Switch to the Texture View and start interactive mapping (Functions> Start Interactive Mapping) again and choose Flat for the projection once again.

As you can see in the view panel, you should not need to make any changes for the texture axis to line up properly with the foot. All you need to do now is go back into the Texture view panel and stop interactive mapping (Functions> Stop Interactive Mapping) (Figure 9.43 b).

Scale (Tools>Scale) the Right Foot UVs down and move them into the corner with the other hand and foot UVs (Figure 9.44).

Deselect the "Right Foot Skin" polygons, and then select the "Right Leg Skin" polygons using the Right Leg Skin Selection tag in the Object Manager. Using the Selection tool (Selection>Live Selection), deselect the foot polygons we mapped earlier by holding down the CTRL/ key and deselecting. Then make sure the tag in the Object Manager is selected for the "Right Leg Skin," and go to Selection>Set Selection. This overwrites the previous selection on this tag.

With these new polygons selected, start interactive mapping in the Texture View (Functions>Start Interactive Mapping), select Cylindrical for the Projection, and click OK (Figure 9.45).

Switch to the view panel, then move (Tools>Move) and rotate (Tools>Rotate) the cylindrical texture axis so that it wraps around the right leg. The settings are as follows:

Position: X = -205, Y = -105, Z = 65
Size: X = 200, Y = 350, Z = 150
Rotation: H = 70, P = 0, B = 0

Switch back to the Texture View and stop interactive mapping (Functions>Stop Interactive Mapping). Scale down the Right Leg UVs (Tools>Scale) and move (Tools>Move) them under the hands and feet on the texture map (Figure 9.46).

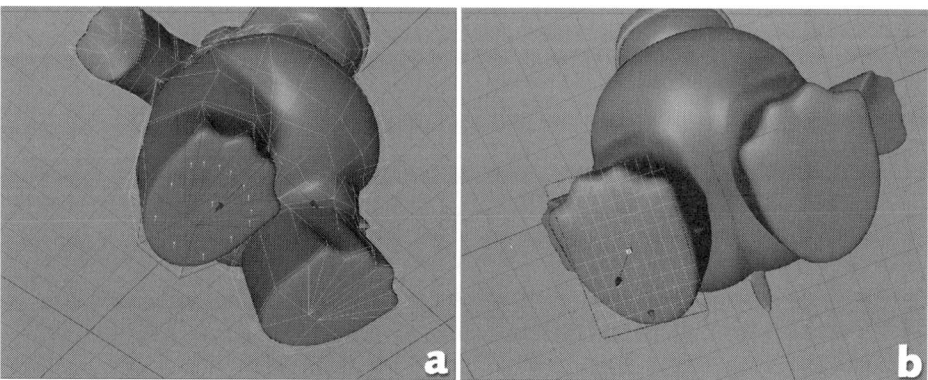

FIGURE 9.43 *Creating UVs for the Right Foot Skin Selection set.*

CHAPTER 9 TEXTURING CHARACTERS

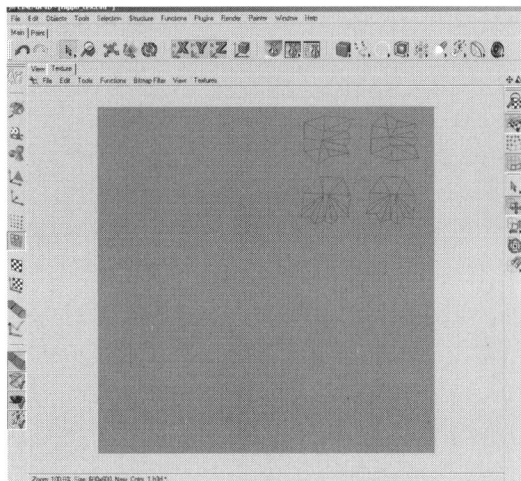

FIGURE 9.44 *Placing the Right Foot Skin UV in the Texture View.*

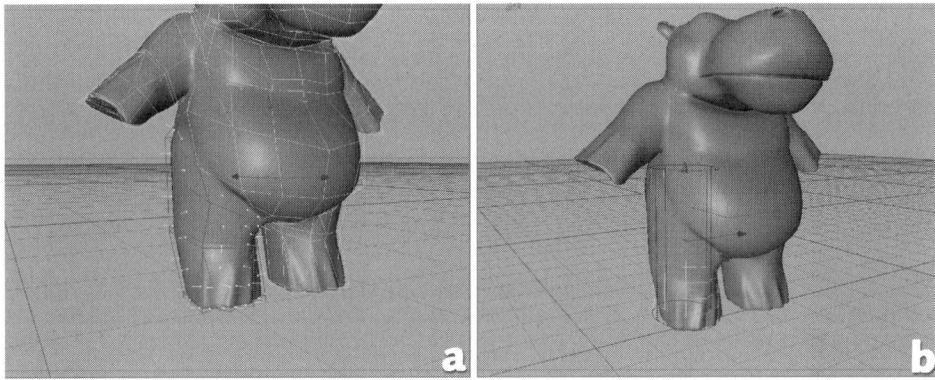

FIGURE 9.45 *Interactively mapping the Right Leg Skin selection set.*

Deselect the "Right Leg Skin" polygons, and then select the "Left Leg Skin" polygons using the Left Leg Skin Selection tag in the Object Manager. Using the Selection tool (Selection>Live Selection), deselect the foot polygons we mapped earlier by holding down the CTRL/COMMAND key and deselecting. Then make sure the tag in the Object Manager is selected for the "Left Leg Skin" and go to Selection>Set Selection. This overwrites the previous selection on this tag (Figure 9.47 a).

With these new polygons selected, start interactive mapping in the Texture View (Functions>Start Interactive Mapping), select Cylindrical for the Projection, and click OK.

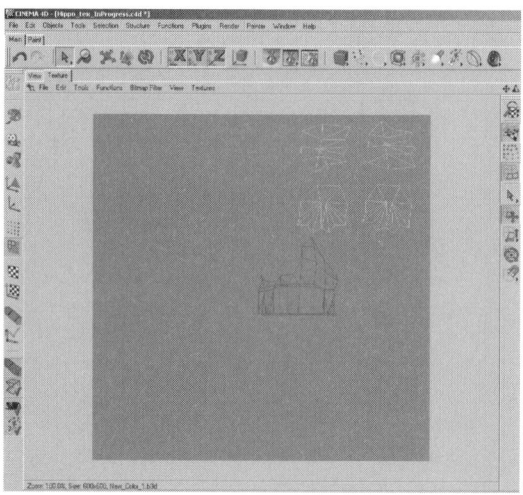

FIGURE 9.46 *Position the Right Leg Skin UVs in the Texture view panel.*

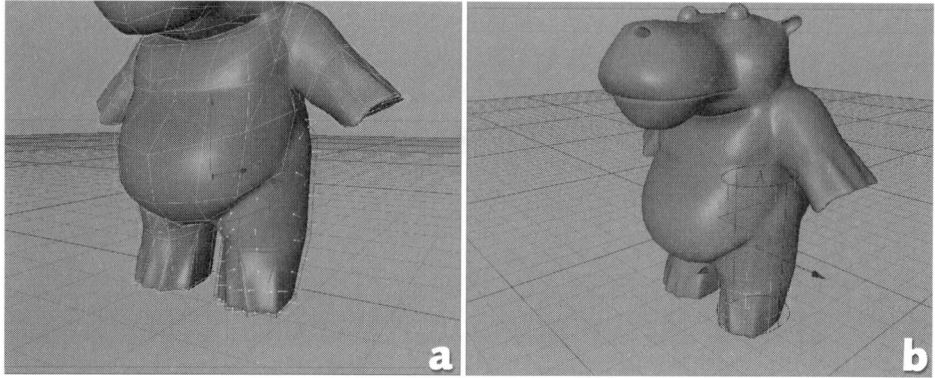

FIGURE 9.47 *Left Leg Skin Selection set and interactive mapping.*

You just need to make minor adjustments to the position of the texture axis in the view panel, it's already pretty much in place. Change the Position settings to X = 205, Y = -105, Z = 65. Change the H rotation to -90 degrees (Figure 9.47 b).

Go back to the Texture View and stop interactive mapping. Scale down the Left Leg UVs, and move them in place under the hands and feet, and next to the Right Leg UVs on the texture map (Figure 9.48).

Deselect the "Left Leg Skin" polygons, and then select the "Right Arm Skin" polygons using the "Right Arm Skin" Selection tag in the Object Manager. Using the Selection tool (Selection>Live Selection), deselect the hand polygons we mapped earlier by holding the CTRL/COMMAND key and deselecting. Then

CHAPTER 9   TEXTURING CHARACTERS

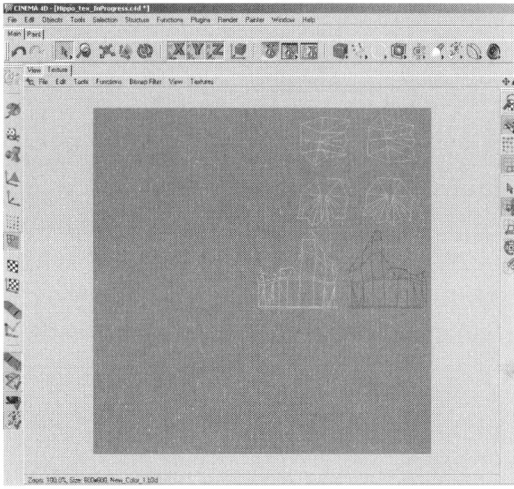

FIGURE 9.48 *Positioning Left Leg UVs in the Texture view panel.*

make sure the tag in the Object Manager is selected for the "Right Arm Skin" and go to Selection>Set Selection. This overwrites the previous selection on this tag (Figure 9.49 a).

Start interactive mapping (Functions>Start Interactive Mapping). Choose Cylindrical for the projection. Click OK.

Switch to the view panel, and adjust the texture axis so that it wraps around the right arm (Figure 9.49 b). The settings are as follows:

Size: X = 150, Y = 250, Z = 150
Rotation: H = 12.5, P = 11, B = 52

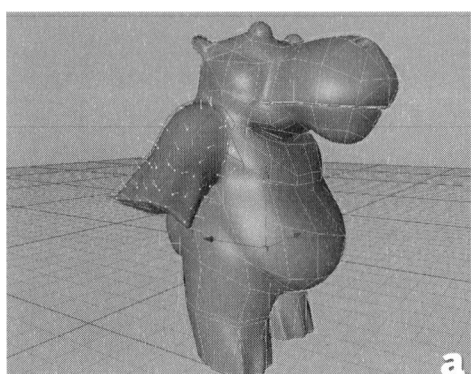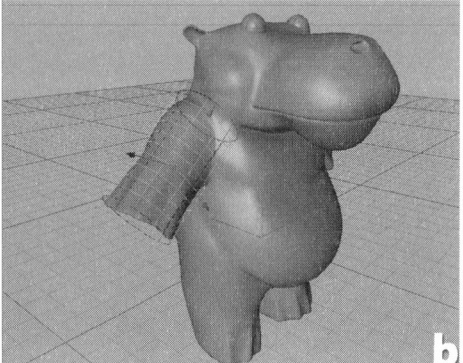

FIGURE 9.49 *Interactively mapping the Right Arm Skin.*

Go back to the Texture View and stop interactive mapping (Functions>Stop Interactive Mapping). Scale down the UVs for the Right Arm and move them below the rest of the UVs you've already done (Figure 9.50).

Deselect the "Right Arm Skin" polygons and then select the "Left Arm Skin" polygons using the "Left Arm Skin" Selection tag in the Object Manager. Using the Selection tool (Selection>Live Selection), deselect the hand polygons we mapped earlier by holding the CTRL/COMMAND key and deselecting. Then make sure the tag in the Object Manager is selected for the "Left Arm Skin" and go to Selection>Set Selection. This overwrites the previous selection on this tag.

In the Texture View, start interactive mapping (Functions>Start Interactive Mapping). Choose Cylindrical for the projection. Click OK.

Input the following coordinates in the Coordinates Manager to change the alignment of the texture axis (Figure 9.51).

H = -165, P = 18, B = 47.

Switch back to the Texture View and stop interactive mapping (Functions>Stop Interactive Mapping). Scale (Tools>Scale) down the UVs and place them next to the UVs of the other arm (Figure 9.52).

Deselect the Left Arm polygons and use the Tail Skin Selection tag to select the Tail polygons. Start interactive mapping (Functions>Interactive Mapping). Choose Cylindrical for the projection. Click OK.

Switch to the view panel and input the following settings into the Coordinates Manager:

Position: X = 0, Y = 125, Z = 490
Size: X = 20, Y = 100, Z = 20
Rotation: H = -45, P = 35, B = 30

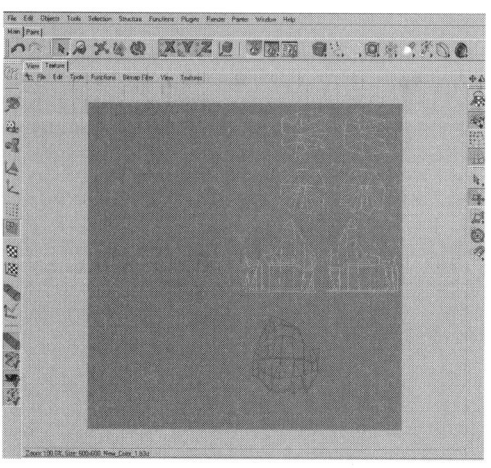

FIGURE 9.50 *Placing the Right Arm UVs in Texture view panel.*

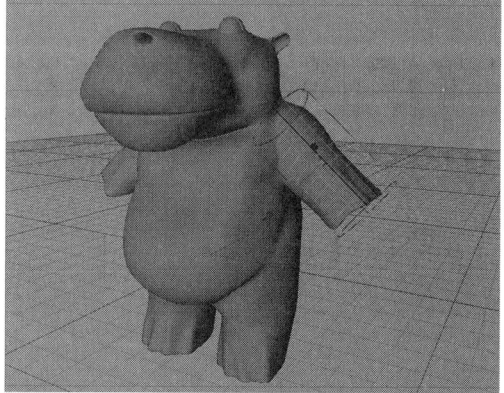

FIGURE 9.51 *Interactively mapping the Left Arm Skin.*

FIGURE 9.52   *Placing the Left Arm UVs.*

Switch back to the Texture View, and stop interactive mapping (Functions>Stop Interactive Mapping). Scale down the Tail UVs, and move them to a proper place on the texture map, out of the way of other UVs. Deselect the Tail polygons and use the Back Skin selection tag to select the back polygons. Deselect all of the polygons except for the bottom ones as shown in Figure 9.53.

You are going to create a separate Selection tag for these polygons so you can map them differently than the rest of the back polygons. If there are any tags selected in the Object Manager, deselect them; we don't want to overwrite

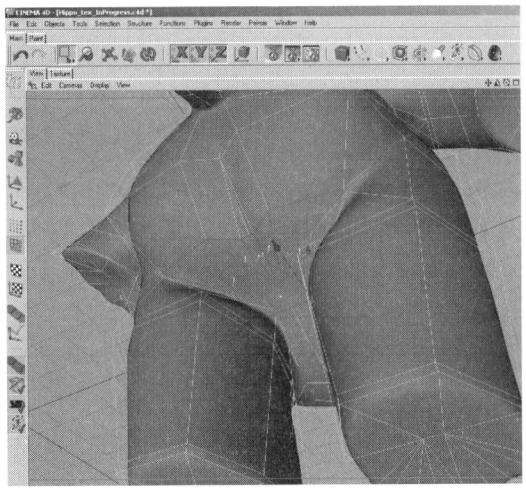

FIGURE 9.53   *Polygons to be a separate Selection set.*

our previous tags. Create a tag for these polygons by going to Selection>Set Selection. Double-click on this new tag and call it "Bottom Skin".

Reselect the Back polygons and deselect the Bottom polygons. Now with the Selection tag highlighted for the Back polygons, go to Selection>Set Selection. This will overwrite the tag, creating Back Skin without the bottom polys.

Now switch to Texture View and choose Start Interactive Mapping (Functions>Start Interactive Mapping). Choose Cylindrical for the projection and click OK. In the Coordinates Manager, change the values of the texture axis to the following:

Position: X = 0, Y = 270, Z = 175
Size: X = 375, Y = 600, Z = 300
Rotation H, P, B = 0

Go back to the Texture View and stop interactive mapping (Functions>Stop Interactive Mapping). Scale the Back UVs down and move them into the upper left corner of the texture map.

Deselect the Back polygons, and then use the Bottom Skin Selection tag to select the bottom polygons.

In the Texture View, start interactive mapping (Functions>Start Interactive Mapping) and choose Flat for the projection. Click OK.

In the view panel, move and resize the texture axis to fit into position on the bottom. The settings are as follows:

Position: X = 0, Y = -95, Z = 220
Size X = 200, Y = 200, Z = 100
Rotation H = 0, P = -80, B = 0

In the Texture View, stop interactive mapping (Functions>Stop Interactive Mapping), and then scale down the Bottom UVs and position them in place on the texture map.

Deselect the Bottom polygons and use the Chest Skin selection tag to select the Chest polygons. Switch to the Texture View and Start Interactive Mapping (Functions>Interactive Mapping). Choose Spherical for the projection. Click OK.

In the view panel, enter these settings in the Coordinates Manager to position the texture axis in place.

Position: X = 0, Y = 240, Z = 20
Size: X = 400, Y = 350, Z = 300
Rotation: H, P, B = 0

Stop interactive mapping in the Texture view panel and then scale down the Chest UVs and position them in place on the texture map under the Back UVs.

These are the easier parts of the Hippo to map. Why? Because they all are pretty well defined. The hands and feet are nice and flat. The arms and legs are just cylinders. The only somewhat challenging part was the tail. From here on out, things might get a little more difficult. Let's keep going with the Belly.

BELLY:

Deselect any polygons that are selected . In the Object Manager select the "Belly Skin" Selection tag and click on Select and Hide Others. After you select the polygons, hide all the unused polygons to see the others better (Figure 9.54).

In the Texture View, start interactive mapping. Set the Projection to Spherical and click OK.

Adjust the texture map so that it encompasses the entire belly, but remaining as tight as possible. Use the following settings:

Position: X= 0, Y= 80, Z= -105
Size: X= 275, Y= 275, Z= 275
Rotation: H= 0, P= 0, B= 0

Once the map looks correct, go back to the Texture View and stop interactive mapping (Function>Stop Interactive Mapping) (Figure 9.55.)

There is a small group that did not connect. Select the small group of polygons in the upper left. These need to be reattached to the rest of the UVs. Select the Move tool (Tools>Move) and move them over to the right of the larger portion of the UV (Figure 9.56).

You should be able to see the area in which these UVs fit. In the Active tool tab, turn on Snapping then activate Points Mode. Select the UV Point tool and click-drag the points to their appropriate locations. Use the opposite side for reference (Figure 9.57).

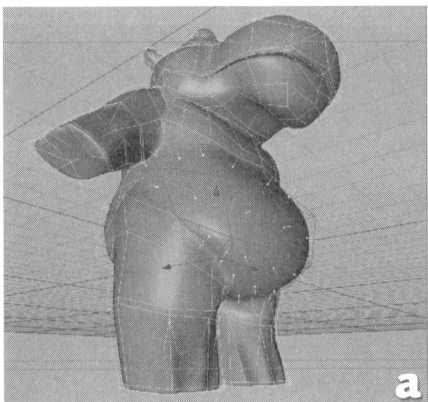 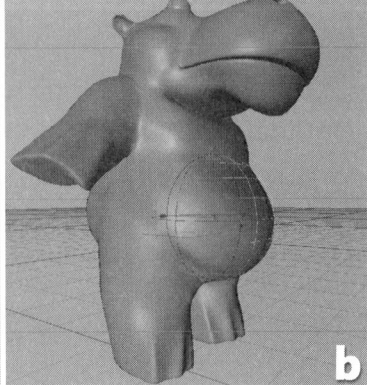

FIGURE 9.54 *Interactive mapping for the belly.*

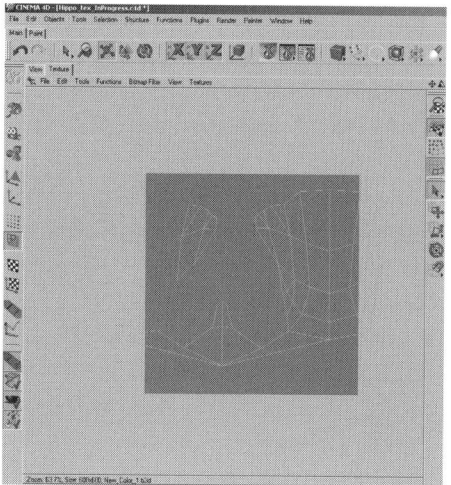

FIGURE 9.55 *Placing the Belly UVs.*

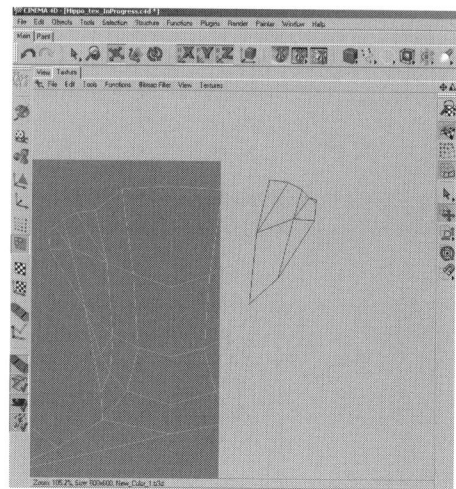

FIGURE 9.56 *Finding the disconnected belly UVs.*

Switch back over to the UV Polygon tool and select the group of UVs to the left. They need to be rotated 180 degrees while they are also being reshaped (Figure 9.58).

Go to Functions>Transform and enter 180 in the Angle field. This will flip the UVs over (Figure 9.59).

Switch back to the UV Points tool and select the one point that is off to the extreme right. Move it to meet the lowest corner of the large mesh (Figure 9.60).

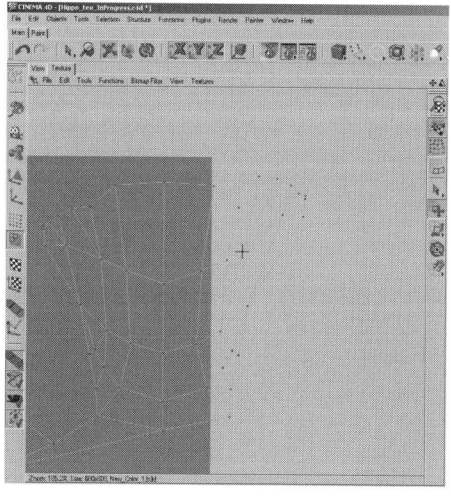

FIGURE 9.57 *Connecting the stray belly UVs.*

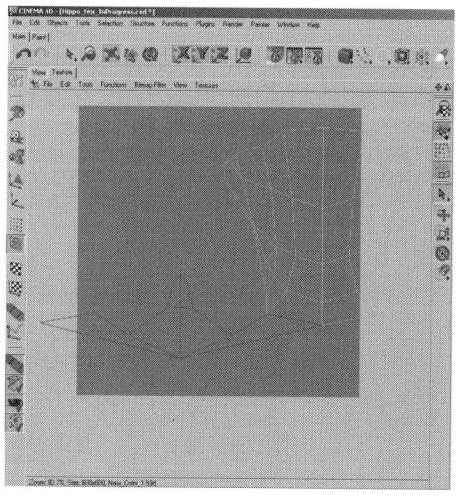

FIGURE 9.58 *Continuing to refine the belly UV.*

CHAPTER 9 TEXTURING CHARACTERS

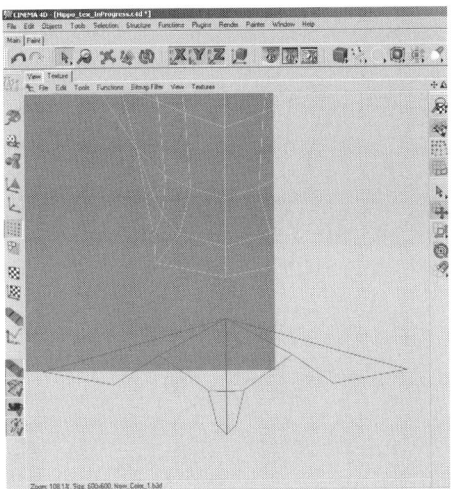

FIGURE 9.59 *Flipping UVs.*

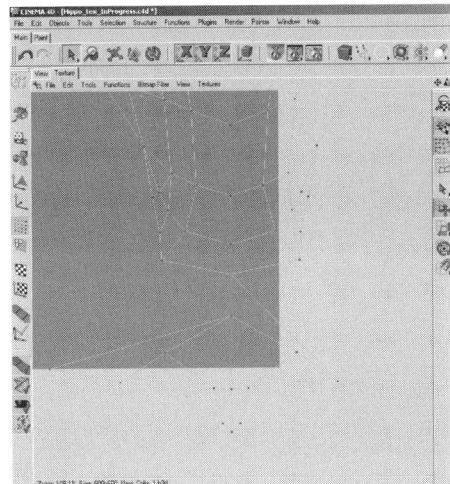

FIGURE 9.60 *Tightening up the belly UVs.*

Select the next farthest point to the right and move it to the right corner of the large mesh (Figure 9.61).

Now, move the points on the opposite side so that the sides match up.

Select all of the lower points and move them up. You will also need to select and move the outer points of the lower mesh inwards. Use the image to get the locations (Figure 9.62).

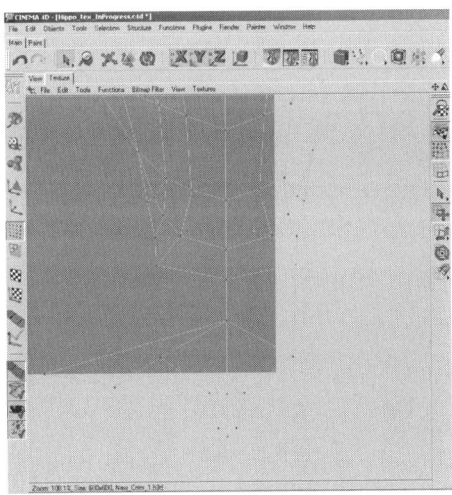

FIGURE 9.61 *Continuing to tighten the UVs.*

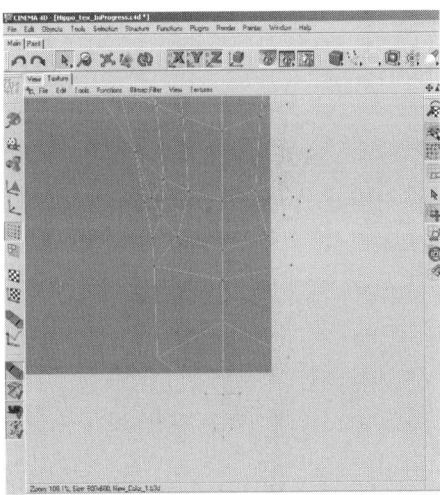

FIGURE 9.62 *Finishing up the tightening of the belly.*

Switch to the UV Polygon tool and move the entire selection to the bottom left corner of the Texture View.

Now the Belly is done. We'll do the Back. After that, all you have left to do is the Head.

HEAD:

Now for the hardest part. Don't worry, though, we're using the same techniques as last time. This is really going to go smoothly. Let's jump in and look at the ears.

EARS:

Select all of the polygons that make up the ears and create its own Selection set (Selection>Set Selection). Select the Head Selection tag and click Restore Selection. Hide all the unselected polygons (Selection>Hide Unselected). Then click on the Ears Selection tag and click Deselect Polygons. Click on the Head Selection tag so that it is highlighted. Once it is highlighted, go to Selection>Set Selection. This will overwrite the previous Head Selection tag (Figure 9.63 a).

Deselect any polygons you have selected. Highlight all of the polygons on the inside of the right ear. Do not select the outside or the edge of the ear.

Switch to the Texture View and start interactive mapping (Functions>Start Interactive Mapping). Set the Projection to Flat Mapping. Click OK.

Input the following coordinates into the Coordinates Manager (Figure 9.63 b).

Position: X= -235, Y= 865, Z= 160
Size: X= 55, Y= 45, Z= 45
Rotation: H= -50, P= 20, B= 0

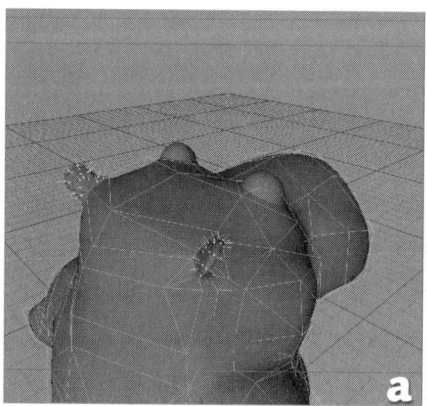 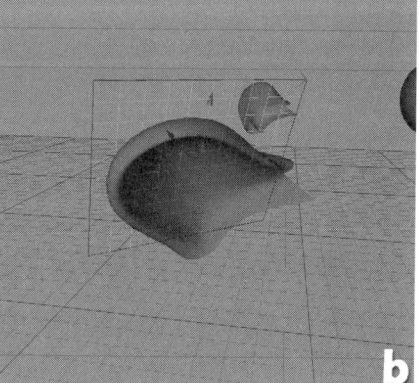

FIGURE 9.63 *Interactively mapping the ears.*

Stop interactive mapping. In the Texture View, you should see the UVs that resemble the ear. Scale them down and move them off to the side for now (Figure 9.64).

Deselect any polygons you have selected. Highlight all of the polygons on the inside of the left ear. Do not select the outside or the edge of the ear. Switch to the Texture View and start interactive mapping (Functions>Start Interactive Mapping). Set the projection to Flat Mapping. Click OK.

Input the following coordinates into the Coordinates Manager.

Position: X= 235, Y= 865, Z= 160
Size: X= 55, Y= 45, Z= 45
Rotation: H= 50, P= 20, B= 0

Stop interactive mapping. In the Texture View, you should see the UV that resemble the ear. Move them off to the side for now (Figure 9.65).

Select the outside of the right ear. The operation is the same as before.

Start interactive mapping (Function>Start Interactive Mapping. Choose Flat Mapping, and use the following settings:

Position: X= -220, Y= 880, Z= 180
Size: X= 55, Y= 45, Z= 45
Rotation: H= -50, P= 20, B= 0

Stop interactive mapping. In the Texture View, you should see the UV that resemble the ear. Move them off to the side for now.

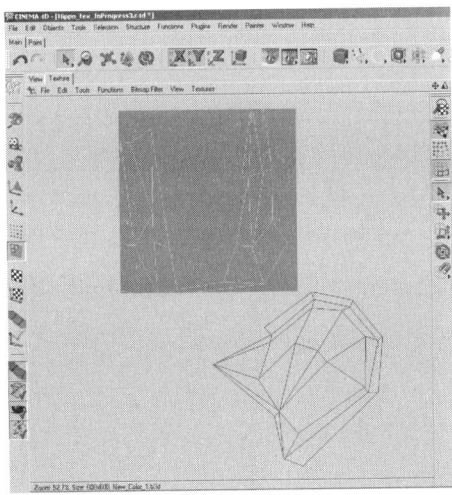

FIGURE 9.64 *The Ear UVs.*

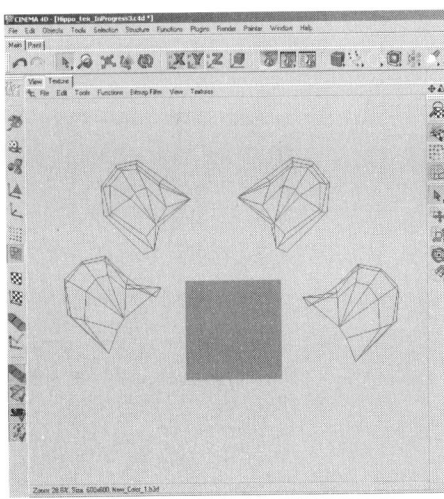

FIGURE 9.65 *Continuing with Ear UVs.*

On the rear selections, you may notice that some of the UVs are overlapping. To fix this, switch to the UV Points tool (Tool>Edit Points) so we can edit the points. Make the Rear Ear UVs match the image (Figure 9.66).

Scale down all of the UVs in a uniform fashion (Tool>Uniform Scale) and place them in the texture along with the rest of the meshes.

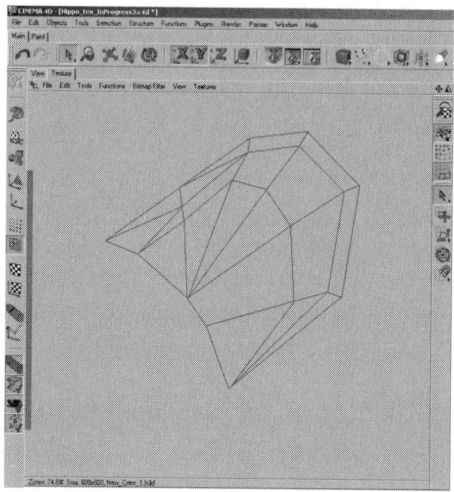

FIGURE 9.66 *Editing UVs so they won't overlap.*

Jaw:

Deselect all the polygons, double-click on the Head selection tag and restore the selection (Figure 9.67 a).

Select all of the Lower Jaw polygons. You may want to set a Selection tag for these polygons to easily select them later. Set this selection aside as you did with Ears. This will make it much easier to work with.

Select the Lower Jaw Selection tag and start interactive mapping (Function>Start Interactive Mapping).

Input the following coordinates into the Coordinates Manager (Figure 9.67 b).

Position: X= 10, Y= 660, Z= -270
Size: X= 325, = 240, Z= 30
Rotation: H= 0, P= 90, B= 0

Stop interactive mapping (Functions>Stop Interactive Mapping). You'll notice that some of the UVs are overlapping. To fix this, choose the Points tool and make the changes to your UV mesh so that it matches Figure 9.68.

Shrink the UVs down and place them in the texture with the rest of the mesh.

CHAPTER 9 TEXTURING CHARACTERS   285

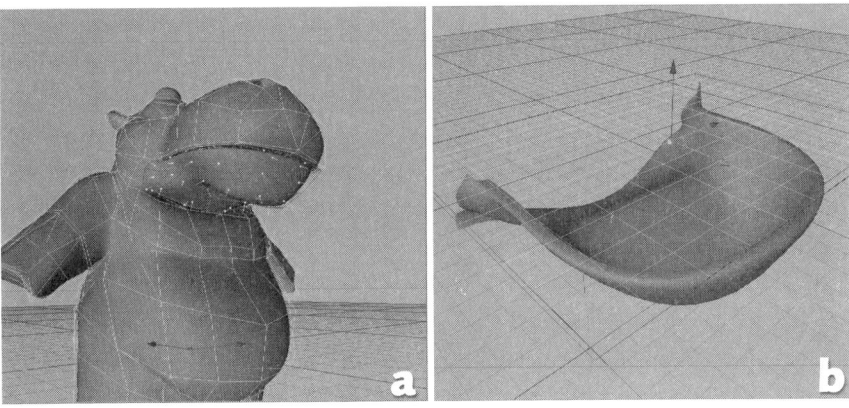

FIGURE *Interactive mapping of the lower jaw.*
9.67

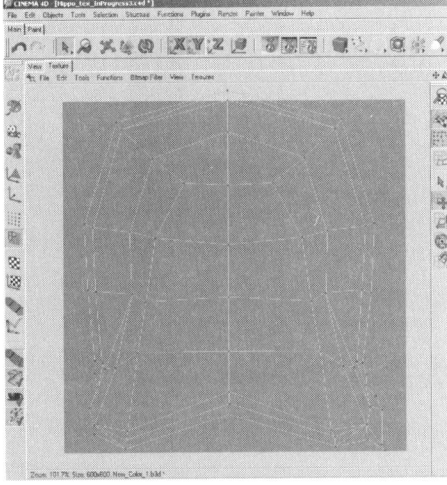

FIGURE *Fixing overlapping UVs.*
9.68

INNER MOUTH:

Select all of the polygons that make up the inner mouth and create its own Selection tag; name it "Inner Mouth". To make it easier to select these polygons, select the polygons on the top of the mouth and hide them (Selection>Hide Selection). Do the same thing for the bottom. Create the Selection tag .Unhide all of the head, so now you have a Selection tag for all of the polygons in the inner mouth (Figure 9.69 a).

Select the Head Selection tag and click Restore Selection. Then go to the Inner Mouth Selection tag and click on Deselect Polygons. Click on the Head Selection tag again so it is highlighted. Go to Selection>Set Selection.

Select the Inner Mouth Selection tag while you select only the top polygons. Start interactive mapping. Use Flat Mapping with these settings (Figure 9.69 b).

Position: X= 0, Y= 650, Z= -285
Size: X= 300, Y= 250, Z= 110
Rotation: H= 0, P= 90, B=0

Stop interactive mapping. Scale and move the UVs off to the side for now.

Invert the selection so the bottom of the inner mouth is selected. Start interactive mapping again. Use the same settings as before.

Stop interactive mapping and select all of the UVs. Scale them down and place them in the texture with the rest of the mesh (Figure 9.70).

HEAD:

Select the Head Skin Selection tag. Start interactive mapping. Choose Cylindrical Mapping along with the following settings (Figure 9.71):

Position: X= 0, Y= 675, Z= -115
Size: X= 335, Y= 490, Z= 300
Rotation: H= 0, P= 90, B= 0

Stop interactive mapping. Most of the UVs will come out OK, but there might be a few that are out of place. Select these UVs, and move them to the opposite side of the model. Choose the Points tool and turn Snapping on to "lock" the points into place. You may also want to zoom in. This will make things much easier on the eyes. Match your UVs as close to Figure 9.72 (a, b, and c) as possible.

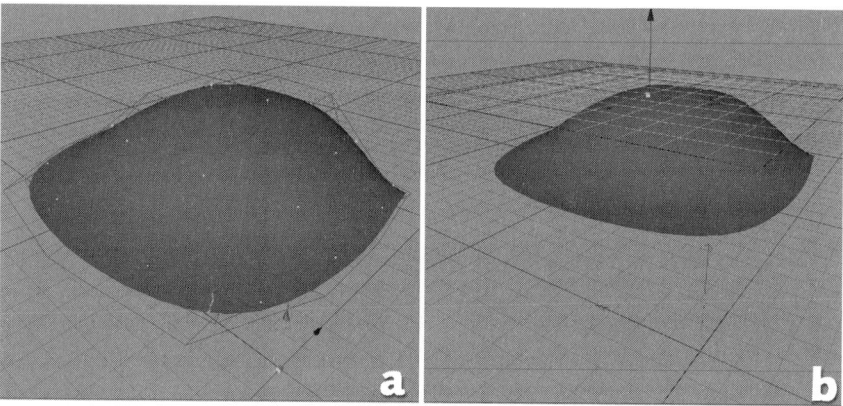

FIGURE 9.69 *Interactive mapping for the inner mouth.*

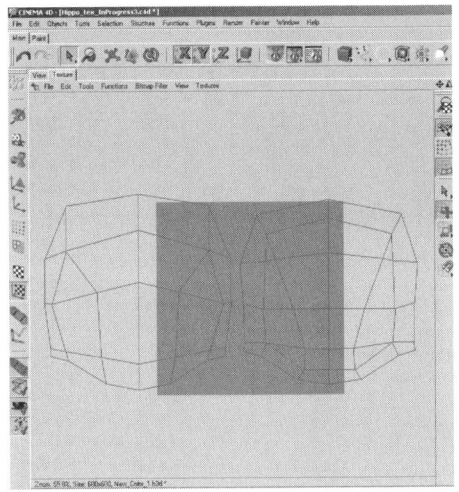

FIGURE 9.70 Scaled inner mouth within the Texture view panel.

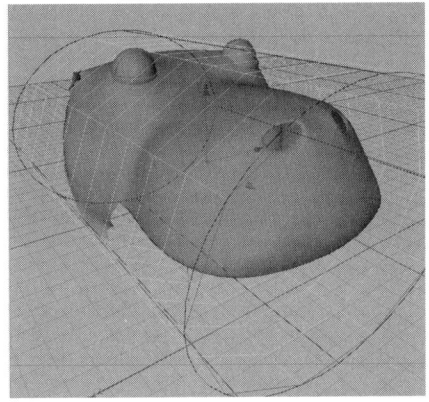

FIGURE 9.71 Interactively mapping the head.

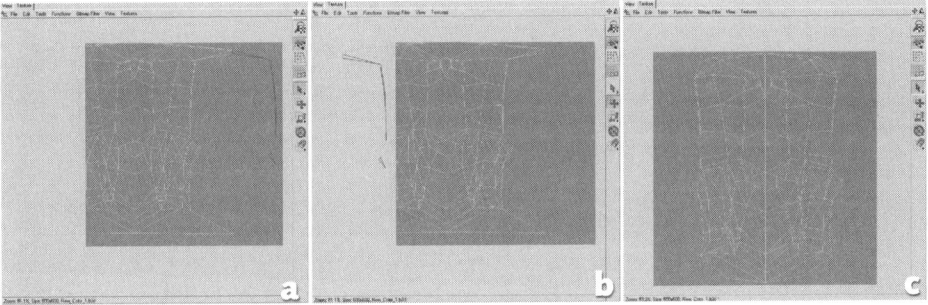

FIGURE 9.72 Shifting UVs for the head.

NASAL PASSAGES:

Select all of the polygons that make up the nasal regions and create its own Selection tag. Also remove the set out of the Head Selection tag by selecting just the nasal passage polys. Invert the selection so that all of the head polys are lit, minus the nose. Save over the Head Selection tag (Figure 9.73 a).

Select the right nasal passage and start interactive mapping.

Select Cylindrical Mapping along with these settings (Figure 9.73 b):

Position: X= -55, Y= 840, Z= -400
Size: X= 45, Y= 80, Z= 30
Rotation: H=0, P= 90, B= -15

Stop interactive mapping. Set the UVs off to the side for now (Figure 9.74).

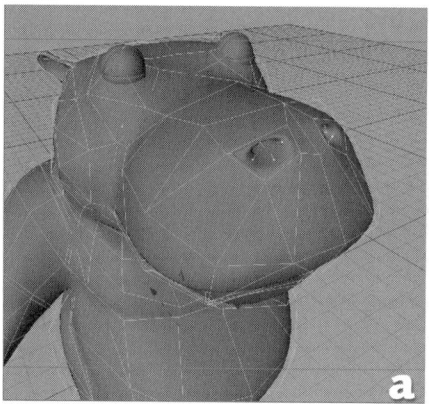 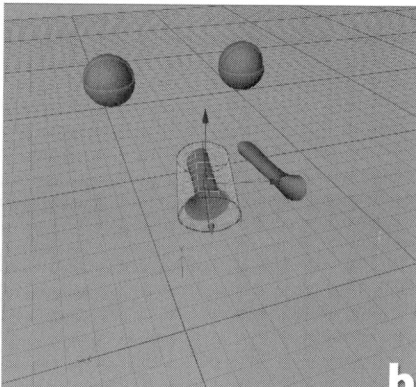

FIGURE 9.73 *Interactively mapping the nostrils.*

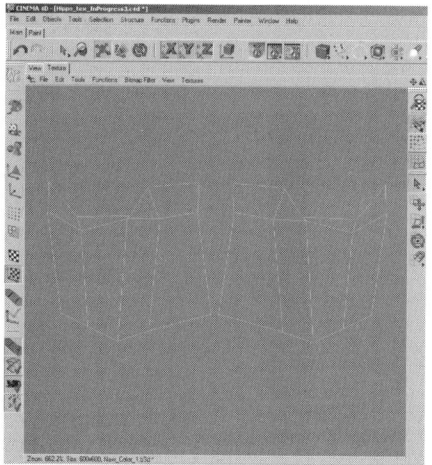 

FIGURE 9.74 *Nostrils within the Texture view panel.*

FIGURE 9.75 *Completed UVs for the entire Hippo.*

Select the left nasal passage and start interactive mapping. Select Cylindrical Mapping along with these settings:

Position: X= 55, Y= 840, Z= -400
Size: X= 45, Y= 80, Z= 30
Rotation: H=0, P= 90, B= 15

Stop interactive mapping. Select all Nasal UVs and scale down. Place within the texture (See Figure 9.75).

Now, with all the UVs created, you can use BodyPaint or any painting software package to paint the color, bump, and other parameter maps. With this UV map so well defined, you will know where your colors will intersect the model.

CHAPTER 10
Lighting and Camera Tools

So why would Lighting and Camera tools be in the same chapter? Well, because they are both ideas of how to best present the work you have created. Interestingly enough, the right lighting and the right camera can hide poor work, make mediocre work look good, and make good work look great. Conversely, the wrong lighting and camera work can reduce the best 3D modeling and texturing to shambles.

Like most of 3D, lighting and camera work have two distinct sides. One is the technical issue of understanding how the tools within C4D work. The other is knowing how to utilize those technical issues to create an aesthetic result. The aesthetics of good lighting will be touched on in this chapter and covered more in depth in the next. However, first we must understand how lighting and cameras work. If you are unfamiliar with the Lighting and Camera tools within C4D, please be sure to see Chapter 10 Supplemental on the CD for details on lighting instruments and camera specifics.

ON THE CD

LIGHTING IN ACTION

There are lots of theories to good lighting. There are theories that photographers use which are different than what theatre set designers use, which are different than an interior designer's techniques. The overall solution is that there is no set formula for creating lighting. Every situation offers unique challenges and new solutions to different problems. In this chapter, we'll analyze a few lighting problems and look at some ways to go about solving them. These aren't the end all answers of lighting, but they are a good place to start.

TUTORIAL

10.1 NIGHTTIME LIGHTING FOR THE DINING ROOM

When you light a fairly complex model like the room we've been modeling, it is often a good idea to do a few tests of your settings and lamp instruments somewhere besides within your model. Once you begin placing a lot of light sources in a model (especially if they are casting shadows or have any visible effects) your computer can become painfully slow as it tries to calculate all the new information. When you try to render, even with C4D's speedy renderer, you might as well go for a drink while you wait. So, to create the chandeliers that sit in this room, let's create them in a new C4D file.

Figure 10.1 shows the chandelier modeled. There are no textures, as an interesting part of the lighting for this project will actually be the material. Sounds odd, but C4D (out of the box as of version 6) does not calculate true translucency. You would think that by placing a Light Object within this lamp and giving the glass part of the object a transparent material, the material would light up. However, the rendering engine is just not that sophisticated. There are some third party solutions to this problem. BhodiNuts's *Smells Like Almonds* have shaders that do illuminate if a light is set behind it; however, if you don't have SLA we need to fake the look of translucency.

First, before we dive into the translucency issue, add a floor and a ceiling to this scene, so you can get a rough idea of what will be going on as we work with the light. The distance doesn't need to be exact; we just need to have surfaces to see how the light is working within the chandelier. Also, create a simple black metallic texture and place it on all the rods or non-glass parts (Figure 10.2).

What we'll do now is first, make a texture for the glass parts of the object that makes it look as though there is a light within it, and *then* actually add the Light Object. Create a new material and apply it to the glass part of the chandelier. Activate the Color, Luminance and Glow parameters. Making this glass shade look as though there is really a light behind it will be a combination of effective Luminance and Glow parameters manipulation.

Let us assume that the light source is a regular tungsten bulb. Let's also assume that it has a bit of a yellow tint to it (as most tungsten bulbs do). Within the Luminance and Color parameters, select a color that is a very unsaturated cream (R=100, G = 96, B = 82, Brightness = 87). The Luminance parameter will give this glass its own light regardless of what lights are around it. In the Glow parameter, leave Use Material Color checked, but change the Inner Strength setting to 200% and set the Outer Strength setting to 150%. The radius is up to

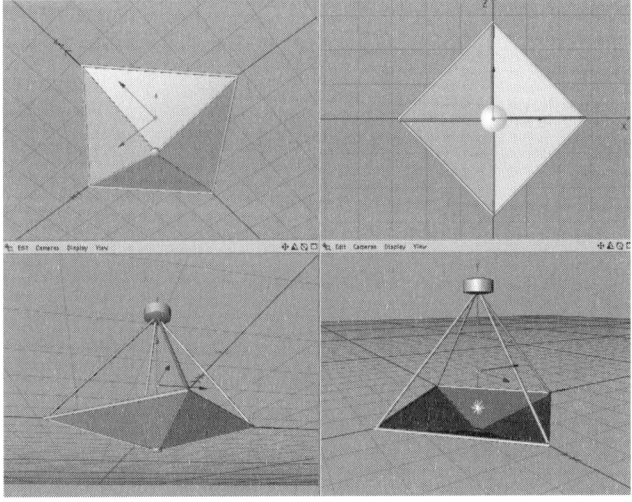

FIGURE *The Lamp model with one light.*
10.1

how big your lamp is at this point, but take some renderings to find out. The idea here is that you want a little bit of glow off the face of the glass, but not so much that the shade becomes a flaming ball. Apply this new material to the glass section of your lamp and take some test renderings at a variety of distances to see what you've got (Figure 10.3).

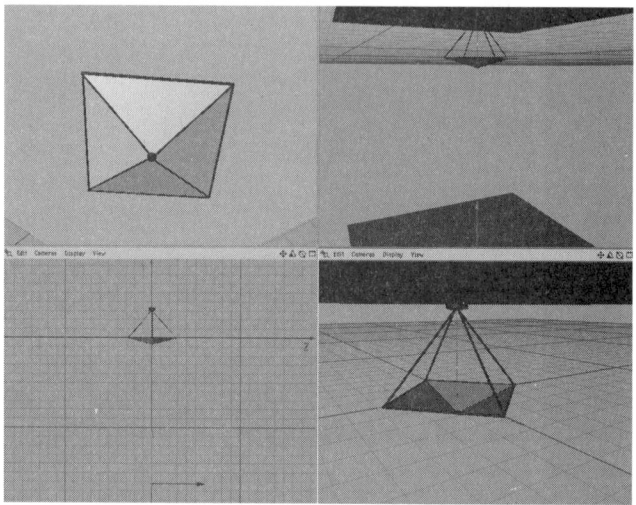

FIGURE 10.2 *Added floor and metallic texture.*

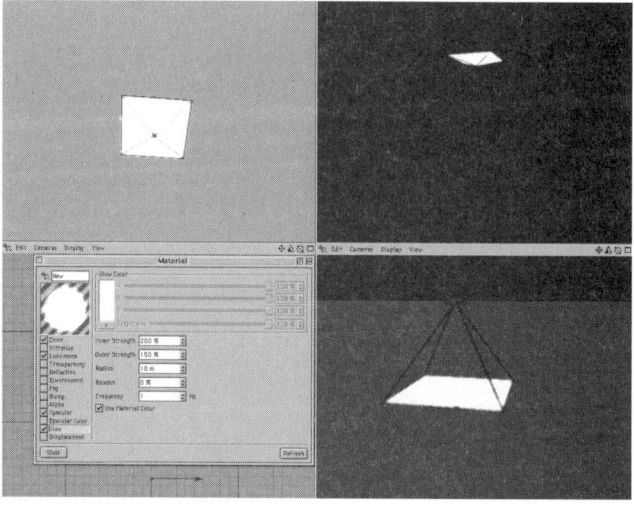

FIGURE 10.3 *The Lamp Object with a translucent material.*

When you're happy with the translucency effect, it's time to add some actual light to the scene. It's a bit unsettling to see the renderings in Figure 10.3 and see this glowing lamp with no evidence of any light radiation on the floor or ceiling. Add a Light Object to the scene and position it so that it sits within the shade. Since we probably will never be viewing this light source with our heads against the ceilings, we don't need to build anything else into the lamp geometry to "'support"' this new Light Object. Also add a couple of simple primitives on the floor to provide something for shadows. When you first apply the light and render (Figure 10.4) you can see that this is not a bad start. The ceiling is lit and so is the floor. Unfortunately, there are no shadows anywhere. Open the Light dialog box by double-clicking the Flashlight icon in the Object Manager and change the color of the light to a light cream and activate Soft Shadows (Figure 10.5).

Upon rendering, the ceiling looks great. The metal parts are casting shadows and the lamp truly appears to be hooked to the ceiling. However, the objects on the floor have disappeared. The reason is that the shade is blocking all the light; there's a huge shadow across all of the floor. To fix this, we're going to add a Render Tag to our glass.

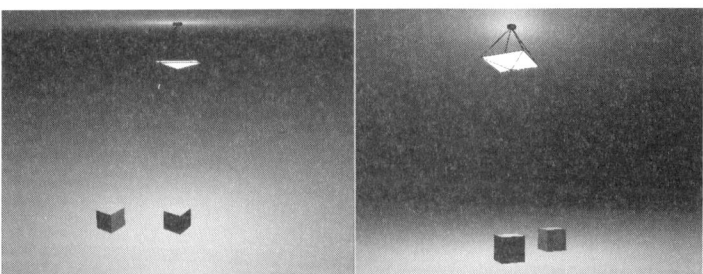

FIGURE 10.4 *Placed light with no shadows.*

FIGURE 10.5 *Once shadows are activated for the light source, the ceiling looks better but there are problems with the floor.*

Render Tags are added to objects by right-clicking (or COMMAND-clicking) on an object and selecting New Tag>Render Tag from the resultant pull-down menu (Figure 10.6). Immediately a dialog box will appear, allowing you to define some characteristics for the object that affect how it is rendered. In this case, we want to deactivate the Cast Shadows option. This will allow light to pass unobstructed through the glass. Take some test renderings to see how well this has worked (Figure 10.7).

Getting closer, however, the metal underpinnings of this shape are casting way too heavy a shadow on the floor. In reality, the light would be much diffused and would never cast that kind of a shadow. So, to keep these bottom metal underpinnings from casting shadows, repeat the process of adding a Render tag to those objects or copy the Render tag from the glass to these underpinnings by CTRL-click-dragging (or COMMAND-click-dragging) the tag. Take another rendering to make sure all's well (Figure 10.8).

Now that there is a fairly good lamp with a light here, group all the chandelier parts and the light together and name the group "Chandelier." Since we are going to have two of these in the room and they'll be the same, we'll create an instance of this Chandelier Object instead of just copying and pasting the group. By creating instances of the chandelier, we are simply displaying the same chandelier more than once. So if we make alterations to the original, the instances will reflect those changes. This way if we need to make adjustments to the

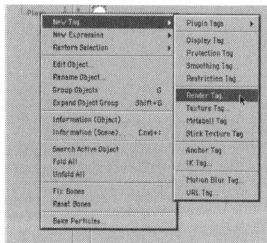

FIGURE 10.6 *Adding a Render tag.*

FIGURE 10.7 *Renderings with shade no longer casting shadows.*

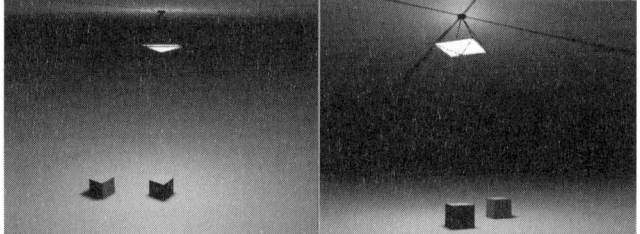

FIGURE 10.8 *All shadows as they ought to be.*

intensity of the light or anything else, we only need to do it once (to the original) and the changes will automatically be updated to each instance. Create an instance from the top command palette by selecting the Add Instance Object or by going to Objects>Modeling>Instance. Double-click on the Instance Object icon and make sure that the object it is instancing is Chandelier. When the Instance Object is first created, it may not be properly aligned with the ceiling or the original Chandelier. Rename the Instance Object to "Chandelier Instance" and move the instance into position, then copy and paste this instance and place it as well. Take a test rendering (Figure 10.9).

The renderings in Figure 10.9 show that we have three Chandeliers, and thus three light sources. Since we left the Light Object's Falloff and Intensity settings at their defaults, we now have three Light objects in the scene at full intensity. The result is '"overexposed"' areas everywhere. The floor is so washed out, you'd think it was in heaven somewhere. We need to adjust the light Brightness and Falloff settings. Within the original Chandelier object, open the Light dialog box and within the Details tab, reduce the Brightness setting to 20%. Take a rendering to see the results (Figure 10.10).

This seems a bit dark for three lights. The reason this seems dark is that with chandeliers like this, there would not only be light from the light chandelier going down, but there would also be quite a bit of soft, diffused bounced light coming off the ceiling. Using v7 you could simply activate Radiosity in the

FIGURE 10.9 *Three chandeliers, one the real thing, and two Instance Objects.*

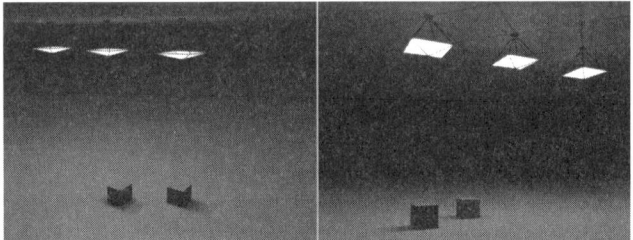

FIGURE 10.10 *Three light sources at 20%.*

Render Settings, but this adds considerable rendering time; further, v6 does not support Radiosity (the rendering engine that calculates bounced light). However, there are ways around this. One way is through the use of "Light Arrays."

When a light source is near something like a light colored ceiling, there exists quite a bit of wrapped, bounced light. Light radiation comes from more directions than just the light source, as the radiation bounces off the other surfaces. So, the key then is to create light sources around the main light source that produces enough light to appear as though it were bounced. A light array is a collection of lights entered around a main light source that produces this non-intense bounced light. An easy way to create a light array is to create an Array Object (Objects>Modeling>Array). Copy and paste the main light and place this light within the array. Open the Array dialog box, and tell the array to create 12 copies. You'll need to find the best settings for the radius as dictated by your scene. The instances should be a little ways away from the main light source to provide that "wrap-around" quality (Figure 10.11). Now this light array needn't be shadow casting or very intense; open the Light dialog box for the Light Object within the array, change the Brightness setting to around 3%, and turn off the shadows. Place this Array Object in the Chandelier group so that there is an array present in all of the instances (Figure 10.12). Take a couple of renderings.

There are a lot of nice things happening in Figure 10.12. First, there is more light overall. Second, the shadows everywhere are softer, as though the bounced light were softening them all up. It gives us a much nicer feel overall. But there's still a problem. The ground is lighter than the ceiling. Add a couple more planes to act as walls (Figure 10.13) and you'll see that the farther away the objects are from these lights, the brighter they are. Not how it works in the real world.

The problem is with our Falloff setting. All the lights we have in our scene have no Falloff setting in the Details tab. Which means that with Omni Lights created, the further from the light source we get, the wider the light radiation. So, as we move further from the light, these radiation rings begin to overlap more and more. The result is further and further, we get more and more overlap, and thus more and more light. Of course, this is just opposite of what should be happening. In the real world, light should be most intense on the ceiling, as it's the closest to the light sources, and the other walls and floor should be lighter the closer they are to the light and darker in the corners that are furthest from the light.

So how do we correct this? Well, C4D, as we discussed earlier, has settings that will allow you to define a falloff. That is, as the light radiation moves further from the light source, more and more of the radiation is "'absorbed"' into the objects in the scene. Of course C4D doesn't calculate this for you; rather, you get to manually define these regions. In both the main Light Object and the Light Object in the Array, change the Falloff setting in the Detail tab to "Inv" (Inverse).

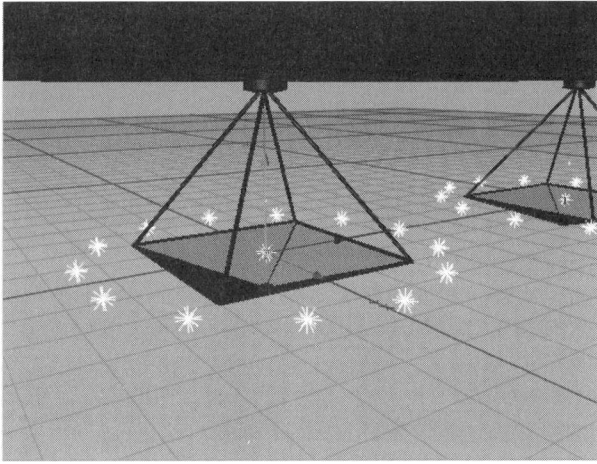

FIGURE 10.11 *Create a light array with an Array Object. Set the Radius setting of the Array Object to spread the lights out just a bit from the center light.*

FIGURE 10.12 *Rendering using the Light Array.*

FIGURE 10.13 *Brighter objects showing up farther from the light sources.*

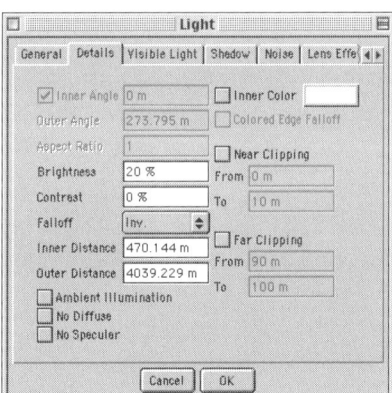

FIGURE 10.14 *To get the light radiation to work more like it does in the real world, activate Falloff for both the main Light Object and the Light Object for the Array Object.*

While you're there, change the Inner Distance setting to something besides "0" (Figure 10.14). Since we know that the room is oblong as well, change the light Type for the main light to Tube (no need to do this for the Array).

Back in the Editor window, visually adjust the Inner Distance setting so that it clearly intersects the ceiling. This tells C4D that the light is to be at full intensity (whatever Brightness setting is assigned to the light) at this distance. So the ceiling is well lit. Then click-drag the Outer Distance setting out quite a ways (Figure 10.15). We do want to make sure that there is light cast all over the room; we just want to be sure that it is getting less intense as it travels. Make the Outer Distance setting further than the confines of the room. Repeat this process for the Array light; keep the Inner Distance setting tight, but really let the Outer Distance setting out quite a ways. Render to see what you've got (Figure 10.16).

To further emphasize the hotspot of the ceiling, add one more Light Object. This time, make the Light Type "Spot" and place it so that it faces up towards the ceiling. Only use about 40% intensity for this light. It's there to augment, not to control the lighting setup (Figure 10.17).

Once you've got things working right in this mock room, group all the chandeliers together and copy and paste them into the Dining Room. You'll need to resize the group to match the Dining Room, and you'll need to position them as they need to be. Take an initial rendering to see what you've got (Figure 10.18).

We're getting closer, but we're not quite there yet. The Light Array does a good job at keeping shadows soft in a way consistent with bounced light, but that is almost exclusively from the ceiling. We need to remember that the walls

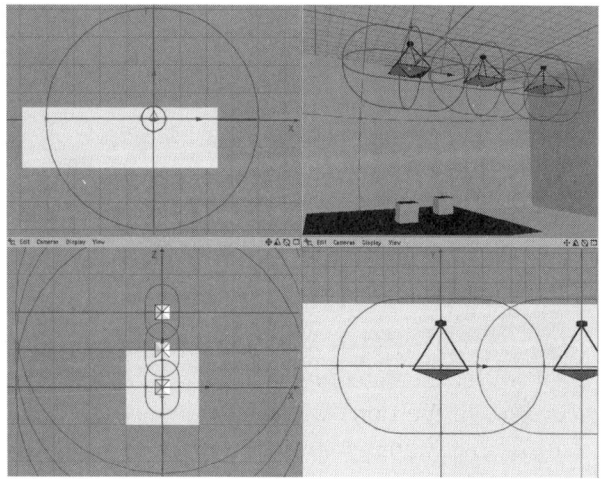

FIGURE 10.15 *Defining the Inner and Outer Distance settings so that the light radiation is bright close to the light source, and steadily dissipating as it moves away from the light source.*

FIGURE 10.16 *Rendering reveals the light acting as it should. The darkest spots are the corners of the room and the areas furthest from the light. The lightest areas are right next to the light source.*

CHAPTER 10   LIGHTING AND CAMERA TOOLS   299

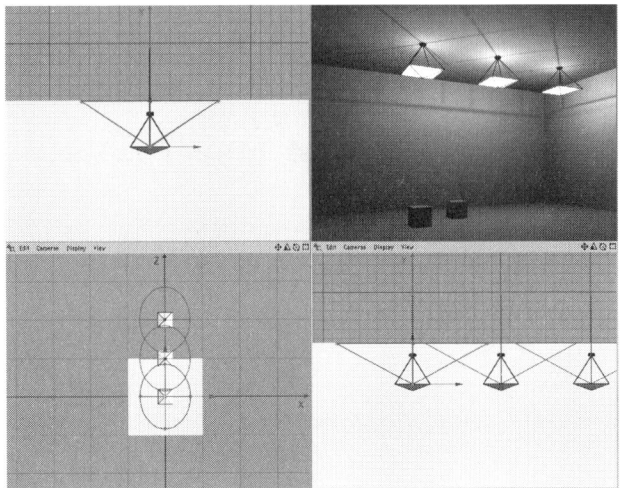

FIGURE 10.17 *One last Spot Light to augment the hot ceiling.*

FIGURE 10.18 *Chandeliers placed within the Dining Room scene.*

and windows would bounce light as well. To fake this kind of bounced light over such a large distance, we'll use area lights.

Create a Light Object and change its Type to Area. Area lights are big walls of light. Take this wall of light and put it just in front of one of the walls of geometry in the Dining Room (Figure 10.19). You will want to make the wall of light slightly smaller than the real wall so that the edges of the area light can help illuminate the corners. This means that you'll probably need to change the Aspect Ratio within the Details tab of the Light dialog box to get the area light longer than it is tall.

The idea here is that the wall of light is emitting the radiation that would be bouncing off the walls. Make sure the color of the area light is the same, or close to the same, as your walls. Repeat the process for all the walls in the room. You needn't activate shadows for these area lights, as their primary job will be to soften shadows in the room and brighten corners and dark spots (Figure 10.20).

For the final touches, put small Omni Lights in the sconces by adding light objects. Make sure that the Shadows option is turned on so we can see the result of the pierced steel material we have created. Make sure also to make the Falloff setting for the sconces very small. We don't want these sconces to make a great deal of difference in the overall illumination; we just want to see that they are on (Figure 10.21).

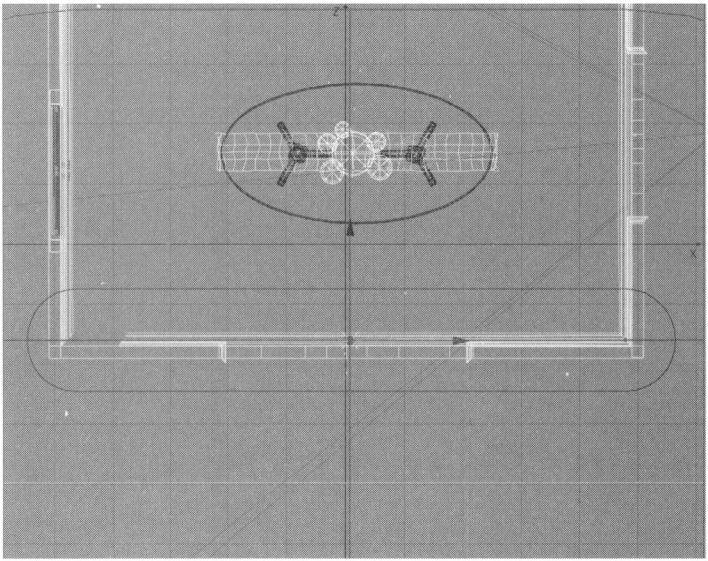

FIGURE 10.19 *To further produce the image of bounced light, create area lights and place them just in front of the walls.*

FIGURE 10.20 *Rendering with area lights.*

FIGURE 10.21 *Final rendering complete with bounced light.*

10.2 DAYTIME LIGHTING FOR THE DINING ROOM

TUTORIAL

In the last tutorial we lit the scene as though it were late at night, the sun was down, and the light sources were all artificial. Daytime lighting will use some of the same techniques we've just described, but some new ones as well.

If this were during the daytime, the lights would probably not be on. Therefore, make sure that your Glow parameter is turned off for the chandeliers. Similarly, make sure to hide all the chandelier lights in both the Editor and the

Figure 01 - © Copyright Suon-Oon Lim, 2001.

Figure 02 - © EUROSPORT/Jérôme Pastorello.

Figure 03 - Laurent Heiderscheid, NiceLTD.com. © Copyright Nicosia Creative Expresso, 2001.

Figure 04 - © 2001 Alec Syme.

Figure 05 - © 2001 Alec Syme.

Figure 06 - © 2001 Alec Syme.

Figure 07 - © 2001 Phil McNally.

Figure 08 - © 2001 Simon Wicker.

Figure 09 - © Copyright Neil Vaughan, 2001.

Figure 10 - © 2001 Simon Wicker.

Figure 11 - © Copyright Philip Nicholson, 2001.

Figure 12 - © Copyright Robert Boehm, 2001.

Figure 13 - © Copyright Steve Townrow, 2000.

Figure 14 - Results of Chapter 9's character texture tutorial.

Figure 15 - Results of Chapter 10's nighttime lighting tutorial

Figure 16 - Results of Chapter 10's daylight lighting tutorial.

Renderer (make sure both gray dots are clicked and turned red in the Object Manager). Similarly, delete all area lights used as bounce from the last tutorial as well. The bounce for this daytime scene will be totally different, and we'll want a clean lighting palette.

So if everything is turned off now, you should actually have a fairly dark room. Let's light the scene as a midmorning scene and assume that the windows are facing towards the east. This will allow us to work with volumetric light as it streams into the room. Since we are going to use volumetric light, we can't use the logical choice of a Distant Light setting to work as the sun. So, we'll use a Parallel (Square) Light Object to create the sun just outside the window.

After you have the Parallel Light Object created, make sure that you have Hard Shadows and Volumetric settings selected, and that the Inner Distance setting is more than 0 for both the Details tab and the Visible Light tab. Since this is the sun, also make the Brightness 200% in the Details tab and the Brightness in the Visible Light tab 150% (Figure 10.22). With the assumption that this is mid morning, the light would still have a little bit of a yellow-orange tinge. Make sure this is set in the General tab under the Color setting.

With all that light at all that intensity, you'd think the room would just be completely full of light. Turns out, the rendering actually looks like Figure 10.23. The reason is that we only have the Parallel Light Object as a light source. Since C4D doesn't calculate bounced light (as of version 6), we get to fake it again. If you are using v7 and are familiar with the Radiosity functions, you can skip this section, although the method covered here will often cut down on rendering time.

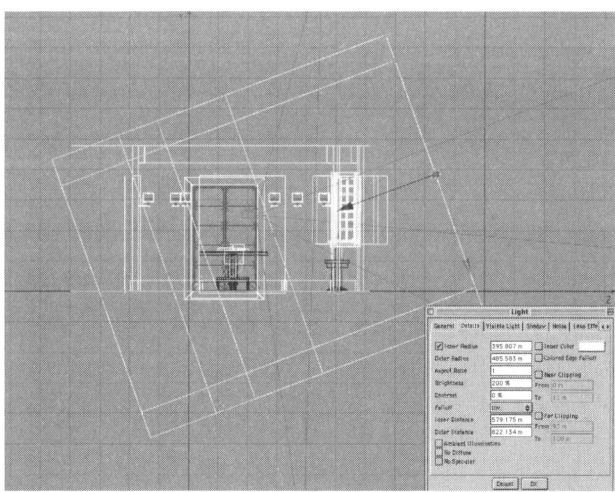

FIGURE *Set up a Parallel Light Object to act as the sun.*
10.22

FIGURE *Despite having a bright light with*
10.23 *high intensity visible light, the result is still a dark room. This is because we have no bounced light.*

At a time like this, where there are no other lights on in the room, the bounced light is incredibly important. It's actually more important than the light streaming into the room. This parallel light that we've built is a slow renderer (volumetric lights always are), so for now, hide it in both the Editor and the Renderer. Further, to move quicker, hide all the furniture as well so you don't have to wait for your computer to redraw it, and you don't need it to render.

Now with just your empty room, you can more quickly begin to plot out how the bounced light would behave and where it would illuminate. The first place the majority of the light streaming through the window would hit is the floor. To create this reflected light, create a Light Object and make sure that it is an Area Light Object; rename it "Floor Bounce". Because the floor is a polished wood, it would reflect light quite well, so make the Brightness of this bounced light quite high – around 200%. Make sure to activate Soft Shadows (as this bounced light would create very diffuse shadows). Make sure that this Floor Bounce light has an Inner Distance setting, so that you can control where this light is at full intensity. Remember that these bounce lights are going to be the only true illumination in the room. Once the light is created, lay it a ways off the floor. Notice in test renderings that if the area light is too close to the floor, it won't produce much radiation on it. You actually need to keep it off the floor a little bit so that it also illuminates the floor (Figure 10.24). Take lots of test renderings until you get a good image indicating bounced light (Figure 10.25).

The next largest source of bounced light would be the walls opposite the window. For the walls in this Dining Room, we need to actually make three area lights — two for either side of the arch — and one for the backing flat. The trick

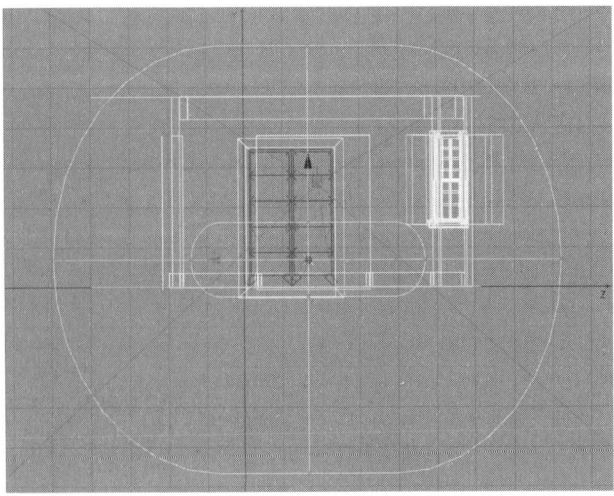

FIGURE 10.24 *To create the Floor Bounce Object, make sure your area light is actually a ways off the floor.*

FIGURE 10.25 *Leave the distance between the Inner and Outer Distance settings large as the bounce would be a very soft, very diffuse light.*

this time is that since the backing flat is a dark burgundy, we need to make sure that the area light providing that bounced light is producing a red/pink color. Create three new area lights and name two of them "OppWall Bounce." Set the Brightness settings to only about 35% for both as these walls are further from the light and are not as glossy – therefore, there is not as much bounce. Again, make sure that there is an Inner and Outer Distance setting. Maneuver the Inner Distance setting so that it barely kisses the wall, and make the Outer Distance setting large to provide soft light to the scene. Since the light from the window is streaming in and down, these area lights needn't cover the whole wall. Chances are they would only cover the bottom part. So keep these a bit shorter overall. The third area light should be a bit higher because of its red color; about 60%, and it should have the same Inner and Outer Distance settings; however, this time, change the color of the area light to a pink color. Rename this light Red Bounce (Figure 10.26). Take a rendering to see how the bounce buildup is going (Figure 10.27).

To finish the room up, we need to make some very weak area lights on the ceiling and the two side walls. The Brightness setting should only be around 15 percent and these really have no need to cast shadows (Figure 10.28). If you're really brave, you could create a special area light for the blue door that of course would be blue.

When all the bounced light is in place, turn the Volumetric Parallel Light Object back on to get the sun streaming through the windows again (Figure 10.29). If everything is set up right, the scene should actually appear as though there were only one light — the streaming sunlight. All the bounce area lights we've

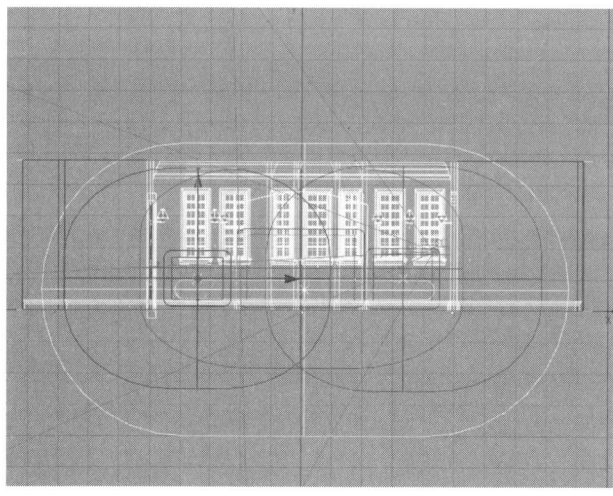

FIGURE *Creating back wall bounces.*
10.26

FIGURE *Rendering with back wall bounce.*
10.27

inserted should simply be reinforcing the idea that an extremely bright light is coming into the room. Unhide your furniture and give this daytime scene a final rendering (Figure 10.30).

FIGURE 10.28 *Completed bounced light.*

FIGURE 10.29 *Final lighting all set together.*

FIGURE 10.30 *Rendered with Furniture unhid.*

10.3 ROMANTIC LIGHTING FOR THE DINING ROOM

TUTORIAL

We've looked at night and day. In both of the previous tutorials we've been looking at ways to make the scene believable, using area lights to establish bounced light and light arrays to soften shadows. Now, we can have a little fun. Lighting for a romantic evening is always a favorite of students since there is so much that can be done. The real key to this type of lighting? Props.

Seems odd, but oftentimes, the best lighting isn't necessarily all in the lighting. Much of lighting is making sure the objects are present that make us believe the lighting layout. For this romantic setting, props are everything. Begin by creating some candlesticks (Figure 10.31). Then make sure to model the flame for the candle as well (Figure 10.32). Although we'll be looking at ways to trick the camera into thinking there's much more here than we are building, it's important that you actually have some geometry for the flame. Again, because the Dining Room is so large and cumbersome at this point, create your candles in a separate file. Your Editor will stay snappy and you'll be able to do test renderings much faster.

Although we may not ever see this candle flame close up, we can make a low memory material that will help keep the flame realistic. Light a candle and take a look at what's happening in the flame. The bottom of the flame (the hottest area) is blue. The flame then moves to a yellow white as you move up the flame. To do this, activate the Color, Luminance, and Transparency parameters. In the Image…input channel in all of those parameters, select Gradient from the list of 2D shaders. Click the Edit…button within each parameter and edit this gradient so that it is axial at 270° from a dark blue to a light yellow. So , in other words, you should have this gradient in all three channels. Apply this new Flame texture to the flame objects. Activate the Texture mode so that you can scale and move the texture so that it is appropriate on the face of the candle (Figure 10.33). Later, we're going to put a lens effect on this flame that covers up most of what we've done here; however, since lens effects are post-rendering effects, they won't show up in any reflections in the scene. Since we have a reflective table and reflective bowls, we need to have a working texture on the object.

Now that we have a good texture on the flame object, we need to make the scene look as though it is actually emitting light. Unless you are using v7's radiosity functions, no matter what material you put on the object, by itself it will never put forth any light radiation. Only Light Objects will do this. A candle flame casts light in all directions. So the best choice would be an Omni Light. Create a Light Object and leave it's Type as Omni. If we were only going to have

FIGURE *Modeled candlesticks.*
10.31

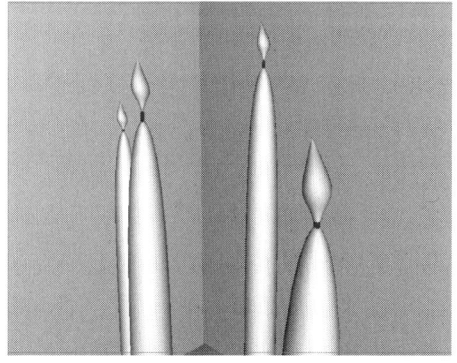

FIGURE *Modeled flame.*
10.32

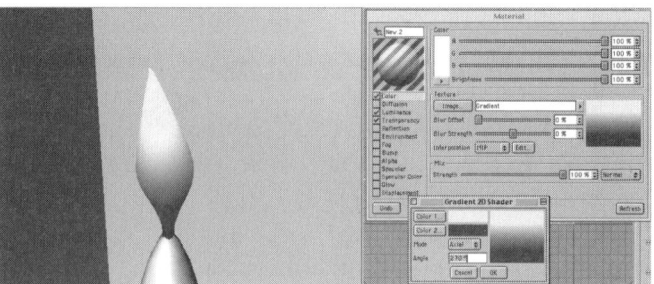

FIGURE 10.33 *A roughed out flame texture.*

one candle we'd want the shadows to be hard, but since we're going to have multiple candles and thus multiple light sources, the shadows should have a less hard edge – set the shadows to soft. Candles have a soft orange light to them so set the color to an amber-orange color (R=98.8%, G=75.7%, B=21%).

In the Details tab, set the brightness to about 60%. Set your Falloff setting to Inv. and make sure that your Inner Distance setting is more than 0. Back in the Editor, you want to make sure that your Inner Distance setting is very small, probably no bigger than the flame itself. However, the Outer Distance setting should be very large. We want this light to degrade very slowly but have a fairly wide range. As a finishing touch, go to the Lens Effect tab and activate a Manual Glow setting. Deactivate "Use Light Parameters", as we want to define this glow manually. In the Glow Editor tab, set the Glow settings to Element 1, Type 4, Size 20%, R-2 and select a creamy yellow for the color. Leave the Ring setting inactive, but set the Beams setting to Element 1, Type 2, Size 30% (Figure 10.34). Hide all the other candlesticks so that you just have one candle with this new point light and take a test rendering.

FIGURE 10.34 *The point light at the top of the flame can help give off the orange light of the scene, and the lens effect can help soften our flame object.*

This isn't a bad start; however, there are some problems. Because a Point Light Object starts at a point, it is easy to quickly block its light radiation. This is just such a situation. First, make sure that the Flame Object has a Render tag that makes it not Cast or Accept shadows. Secondly, even if it the flame object doesn't cast shadows, since the light is so close to the top of the candle, the candle blocks the light downward. Thus, the entire bottom of the scene is totally dark. To get around this problem, we'll create another Light Object. Make this object a Spot Light Object with Soft Shadows. Give it a light yellow color. In the Details tab, leave the Inner Angle setting at 0, but make the Outer Angle setting 175°. Make the Brightness setting only about 45%. Again, activate Inv. Falloff and make sure the Inner Distance setting is more than 0 so you can control it. Make sure the Spot Light Object is pointing downward and move it a little bit above the top of the flame (Figure 10.35).

Getting very close; but we still need to deal with issues of bounce. With v7, activate Radiosity in the Render Settings if you have not done so, or continue following along to fake it. For these candles, we'll want to make sure that whatever surface they are sitting on exudes a bit of light bounce. So create another Light Object and make it an Area Light Object. Hold off on making any color changes until we figure exactly where they're going to sit. In the Details tab we want this bounce to be very soft, so assign Inv. Falloff, but leave the Inner Distance setting at 0. Visually adjust the Outer Distance setting in the Editor to give off a slight bounce from the floor (Figure 10.36).

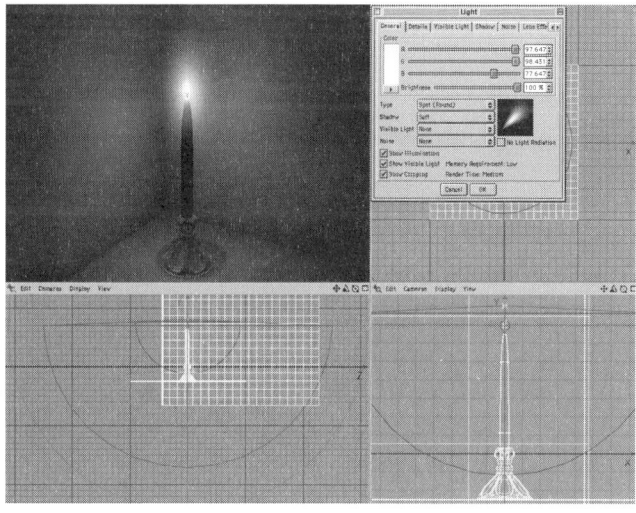

FIGURE 10.35 *A Spot Light Object overcomes the problem with the Point Light Object's radiation being blocked by the top of the candle.*

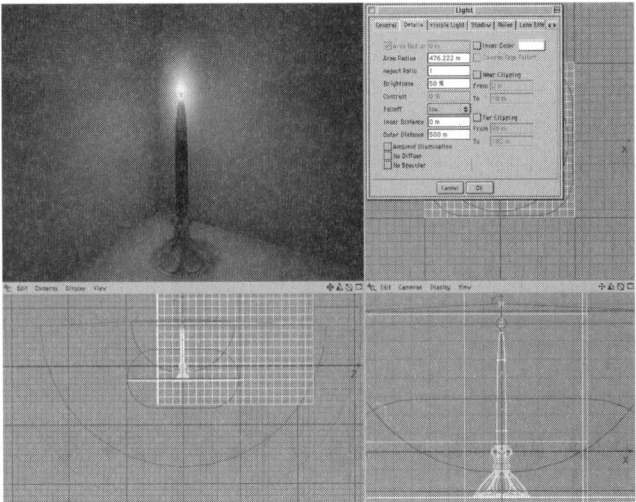

FIGURE 10.36 *Finished candle lighting.*

Group all three of these lights together and call it Flame. Make several instances of this flame and put them within each copy of the candles. This way, if there needs to be adjustments when the group is rendered it's a simple task. Show all your candles and take a rendering to see how all of the candles work together (Figure 10.37).

Once you're happy with the effect of the candles, copy and paste them into the Room scene. At this point, make sure that these candles are the only light source. Undoubtedly, you'll need to resize the group of candles so that they fit in with the scale of the room (Figure 10.38). Further, you'll probably need to increase the main light source for the candle so that it extends past the walls. We want this light to give very soft light to almost every corner of the room (Figure 10.39).

Although, in theory, most of these walls would probably be giving off a little bit of bounced light, the amount would be almost negligible. The closest plane that would be providing bounced light is the table, but we've taken care of that with the area lights at the bottom of the candle. Since they are sitting on the table, simply give a little bit of a red color to that area bounce light and you're set. The only other area that would cause any noticeable bounce would be the ceiling. Create a Area Light Object of very low Brightness (10%), and align it with the ceiling as we have done in the past (Figure 10.40). Make sure that it's color is a slight amber color. Activate your sconces at a low brightness to give some more texture to the room (Figure 10.41). Add any other props (wine glasses, roses, etc...), render, and you're done (Figure 10.42).

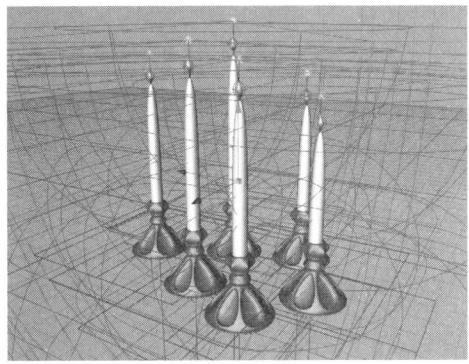

FIGURE 10.37 *Group of candles.*

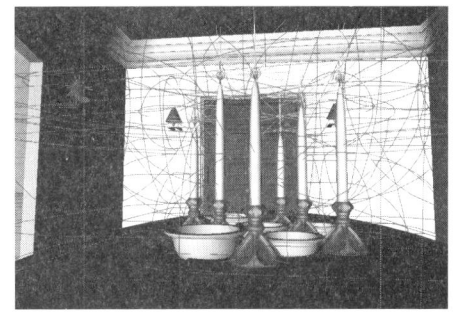

FIGURE 10.38 *Scaled candles.*

FIGURE 10.39 *Extended light source to give the room nice orange glow.*

FIGURE 10.40 *Area light on the ceiling for bounced light. Area light at the base of candles tinted red.*

FIGURE 10.41 *Sconces turned on for added depth and texture.*

FIGURE 10.42 *Added props and the seduction is complete.*

10.4 GLOBAL ILLUMINATION

By Neil Vaughan

TUTORIAL

Global illumination is illumination that takes into account light from the environment other than a direct light source. What this means is that global illumination calculates not only light from a direct source, such as a spotlight, but also reflected light from other objects. Most renderers and raytacers work with local illumination, in which only direct light is taken into account.

To illustrate, imagine a darkened room. A table lamp is switched on. Not only is the table beneath the lamp illuminated but other parts of the room become visible too. What causes the parts of the room out of the beam cast by the lamp to be illuminated is light that has bounced off those surfaces that are directly illuminated by the light beam.

At present, Cinema 4D XL v6 does not support GI: we have to simulate it using the tools currently available. Even so, this will yield results comparable to a dedicated GI rendering.

To begin, we start with a simple, unlit scene that we intend to light with global illumination. What we are going to create is what many people term as a "skydome." This is a hemispherical array of lights, fully encompassing our scene, which simulates indirect lighting.

To start to create the skydome, we have to ensure that our lights sit hemispherically within our scene, with each light sitting equidistantly from its neighboring lights. To do this we place a sphere, as in Figure 10.43, making sure it is of sufficient size to encompass the entire scene. This sphere is going to act as a template for the GI sphere placement. Don't panic, we're not going to place them all by hand!

You'll notice, too, that the bottom section of the sphere has been removed. because none of our lights are being placed below the floor!

Now, going into the Object menu, select Create Spline>Bezier and trace a profile around the right hand edge of the sphere (Figure 10.44). This spline will be used as the master guide for placing the first row of lights. Next, we'll add one single spotlight with the values indicated in Figure 10.45. You'll notice in the dialog box that the value has been dropped down to just 1%. This may seem hardly worthwhile but what we are striving for is a scene incorporating exactly one hundred lights. With each light emitting just 1% of bright light, that'll be 100% of illumination overall. Perfect. Any more lights or a greater value in the Brightness dialog box would result in a stark, bleached-out image. Make sure your Shadow tab has the values indicated here in Figure 10.46.

One final point, make sure the light has a Target Expression setting with your model being the target. We want all of our lights to point at one specific point in space.

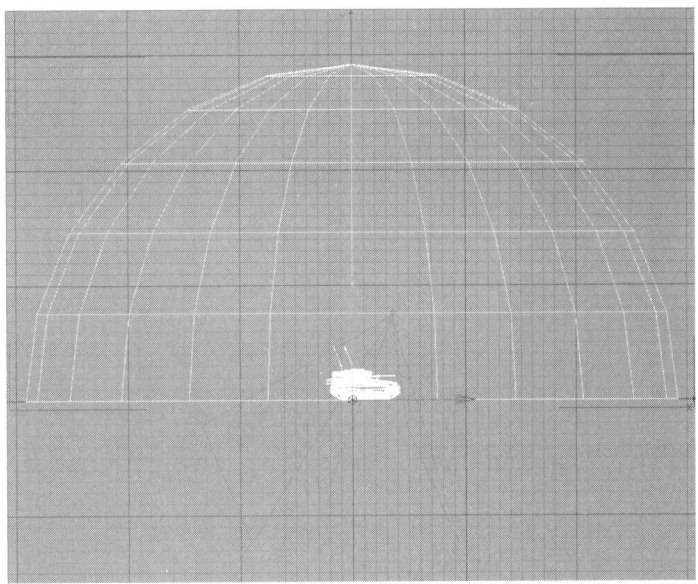

FIGURE 10.43 *Start the skydome by creating a sphere encompassing the entire scene.*

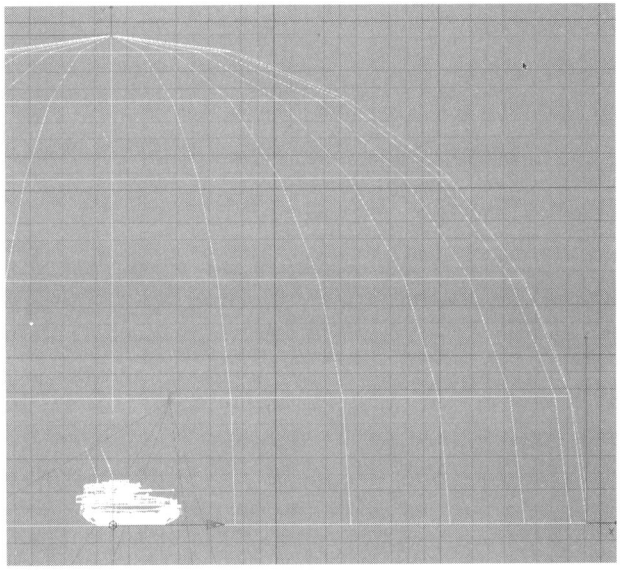

FIGURE 10.44 *Create a profile using one of the Draw Spline tools to approximate the shape of the sphere.*

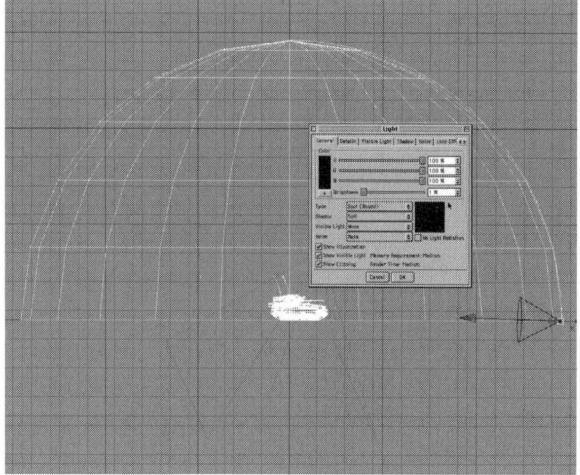

FIGURE 10.45 *Adding one spotlight with an extremely low Brightness setting.*

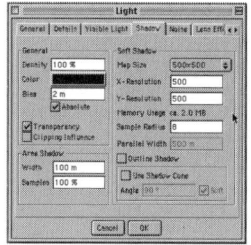

FIGURE 10.46 *Shadow settings for GI skydome light.*

So we have our first light. Next we're going to make an instance of this light. Not only does this save on memory, it also has another fabulous benefit. If we need to alter our lighting, we simply amend our first spotlight and all other lighting is altered accordingly. This is a real boon when you're dealing with a scene with a hundred lights!

Move this instance to a position where it sits on our spline next to our first light (Figure 10.47). Repeat this process of adding instances (you can hold the CTRL/COMMAND key on your keyboard while you click-drag the spotlight in the Object Manager) until you have an array of ten lights spaced equidistantly along the spline (Figure 10.48).

You'll notice, too, in the Coordinates Manager that these lights have been grouped for convenience and to save many a headache later on. If this isn't done at an early stage, you'll soon find yourself in all kinds of a mess with so many lights to wrestle with. Also, ensure that each of these lights sits neatly on the Z-axis at position 0 in the Coordinates Manager. This confirms that they are all sitting perfectly in a straight line.

We need to group these lights for convenience but also for another very important reason. Now that they are grouped, you'll notice that the group axes lie at position 0,0,0. This is precisely what we want because we are now going to duplicate this group (again, hold CTRL/COMMAND and click-drag in the Object Manager) and rotate it 36° around the heading. Why 36°? Well now it all becomes clear. As we have ten lights in our original array and we want one hundred lights to illuminate our scene, we need ten groups of lights. As this is a spherical array, we divide the total number of degrees in a circle by the number of arrays we desire: 360° / 10 = 36°.

Chapter 10 Lighting and Camera Tools

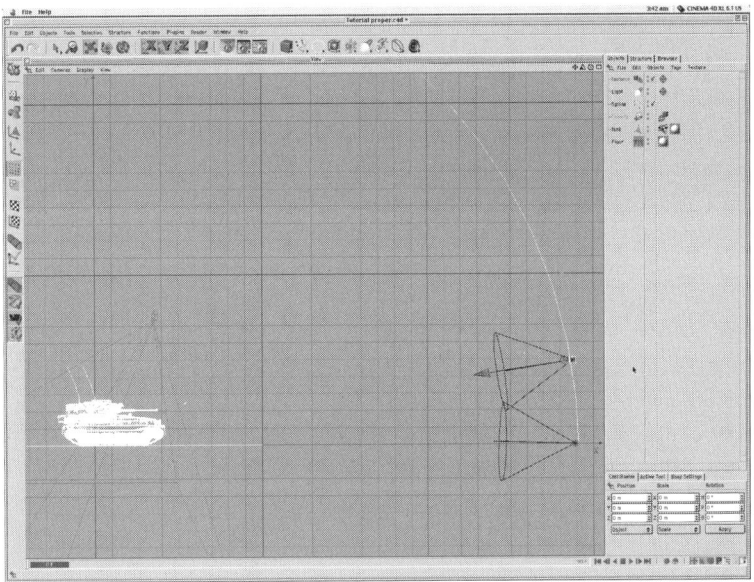

Figure 10.47 *Place your first instance on the spline.*

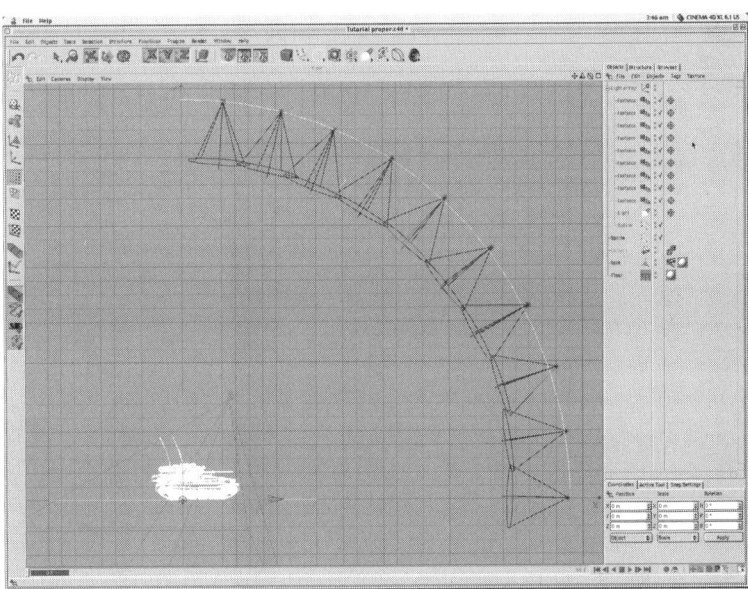

Figure 10.48 *Continue to organize light instances along the spline arch.*

By consecutively duplicating our light group and rotating it 36° at a time, we'll end up with one hundred lights arranged geometrically around our model (Figure 10.49 and 10.50).

A quick test rendering reveals that our model is starting to look as if it is lit with global illumination (Figure 10.51).

But, to be honest, it's still looking a little monochromatic and lifeless. This is where a Distant Light setting comes in. This light is paramount to your scene's overall look and mood. It also helps to bring out those little nuances of subtle detail that can really make or break a scene. In this tutorial, we've gone for a cool, steely blue, but a warmer color such as an orange would have worked equally well. You need to choose a color that compliments your scene: a deep red for a sunset, a bright yellow for a summer morning, whatever works best. Use the settings in Figure 10.52 and Figure 10.53, but make sure your Distant Light setting does not cast shadows.

The reason for this is that sometimes a shadow generated from a Distant Light setting can produce unwanted results, and a shadow is especially undesirable in a simple scene with only one model. We need to have more control over the shadow, as it needs to really accentuate the model's form and also enhance where it sits in the scene. For this, choose a Shadow Only light. Now this isn't an inherent feature of Cinema 4DXL and is found only in some high-end 3D graphics applications. But again, using the built-in tools, we can fake it. Place a new spotlight into the scene targeted at the tank, above and slightly in front, so

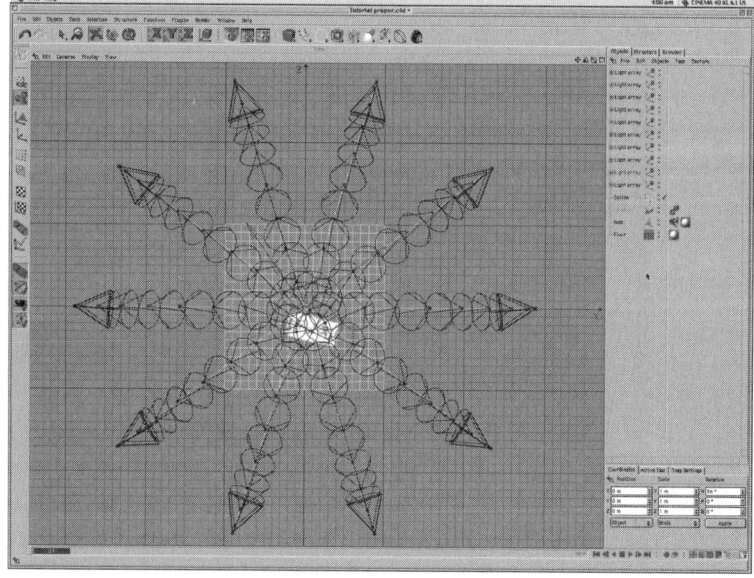

FIGURE *Rotated groups of lights.*
10.49

Chapter 10 Lighting and Camera Tools

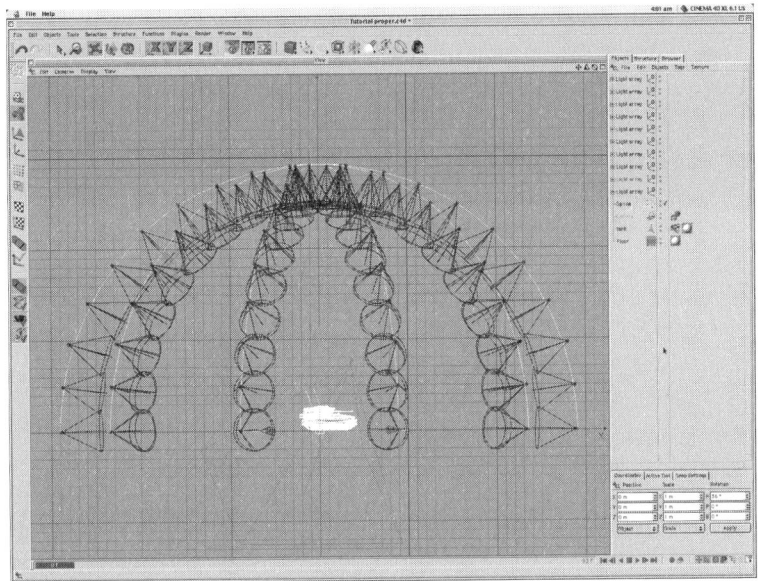

Figure 10.50 *Completed layout of light sources.*

Figure 10.51 *Quick test rendering of the skydome to this point.*

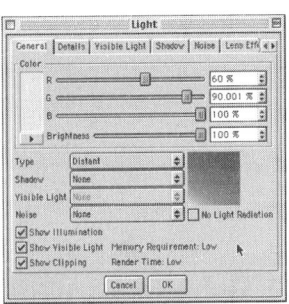

Figure 10.52 *Settings for Distant Light.*

that the shadows pass over the near side of the model (Figure 10.54). This will also help to boost the shadow beneath the model itself. Adding another light like this will only add to the overall illumination of the scene — something we don't want, as the look of the scene now is very washed out. However, we probably do want to add another shadow. So duplicate this light, making absolutely sure it is sitting in the same position as the first light (the one just added). Disable Shadows and in the Details tab, set your Brightness at -100%. This light then negates the illumination of the first light while it still enables it to cast a shadow. Clever. You now have full control over this shadow without the fear of it disturbing your carefully crafted lighting.

So now we're finally ready to render. As the model has no reflective or transparent surfaces, disable these in the Render Settings menu. Render, sit back, and wait for the complete, globally illuminated scene to be rendered (Figure 10.55).

A final note: Arrays can be great fun and can yield some great results, but they do have limitations. In almost all of your lighting experience, you'll tend to need to use more dramatic effects. The classic three-point lighting will serve almost any given situation. Generally, only outdoor scenes and product shots will need to use global illumination. There is much more to lighting a scene than just adding an array. Use them sparingly.

Play around with global illumination but do not rely on it solely as a means to an easy lighting setup.

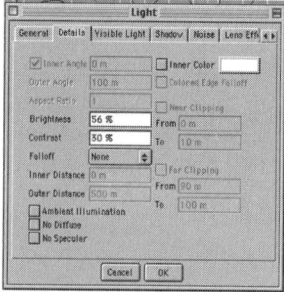

FIGURE 10.53 *More Distant Light settings.*

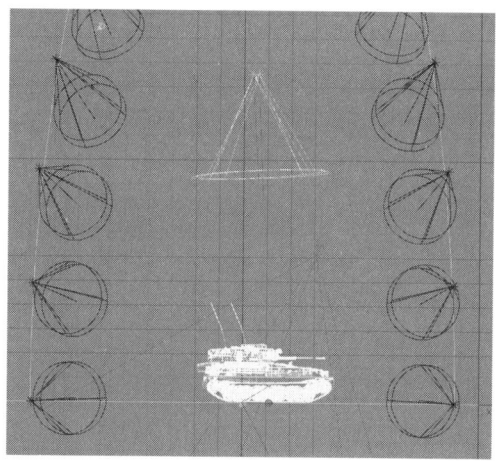

FIGURE 10.54 *Shadow manipulation for GI.*

FIGURE 10.55 *Final rendering.*

CHAPTER 11

Animation Basics

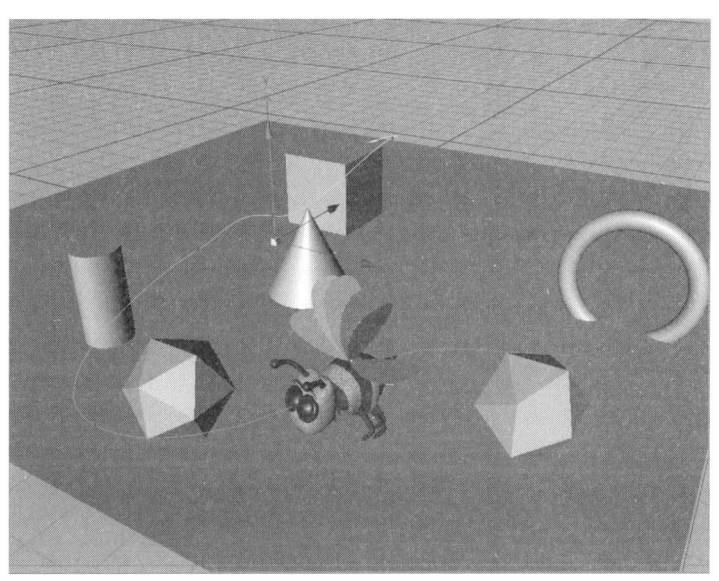

Animation is a relatively young art form, yet it still has a history. The art of drawing individual cells to create the illusion of motion continues to evolve and continues to excite. However, even with the continuing evolution, the basic tenets of animation have remained the same. Animation is composed of a series of still images, each slightly different than the last. When these are viewed in rapid succession (several each second) it gives the illusion of movement.

This movement is hard to capture. Most animation runs between 24 and 30 frames per second; which means that even a short 2-minute animation has anywhere from 2800 to 3600 frames. So, as animation evolved and animation teams began to emerge, an artistic production line began to form. The master animator would draw the most important frames — the keyframes — of an animation (i.e. the character at the bottom of a jump, the top of a jump, and the landing) to sketch out the movement and the moments of most important action. Then, the more junior animators would come in and draw all the "in-between" frames. These less experienced animators ironically ended up drawing most of the frames of an animation. You can still see this process at the end of many animations as the credits will display a group of "In-betweeners."

3D animation runs along this same idea. You are the master animator and establish the keyframes of the animation. The computer acts as the in-betweener, and fills in all the frames in between. Animation then becomes the process of giving your computer enough information so that it knows how to accurately fill in the frames in between. C4D works at a standard 30 frames per second (fps); so establishing a simple move over 3 seconds could mean as few as two keyframes, while C4D creates the other 87 frames.

GETTING TO IT

Along the very bottom of the default interface are some simple, but powerful tools for animation within C4D (Figure 11.1) called the Time Manager tool palette. The blue bar is the time slider. That is, this shows you where in your animation you are. The number on the bar shows you what frame number you are on. This time slider is a time machine of sorts. Whatever frame is displayed on the time slider is portrayed in the view panel above. If you scrub (click-drag) this time slider back and forth, your animation will play back and forth above. The other number at the end of the time slider track indicates the total number of frames in the project.

The next seven tools are familiar to everyone who has used a VCR. These allow you to maneuver through your animation. The two tools after that are the tools allowing you, the master animator, to establish those keyframes we've talked about. The first, Record, allows you to manually record a keyframe. The

Chapter 11 Animation Basics

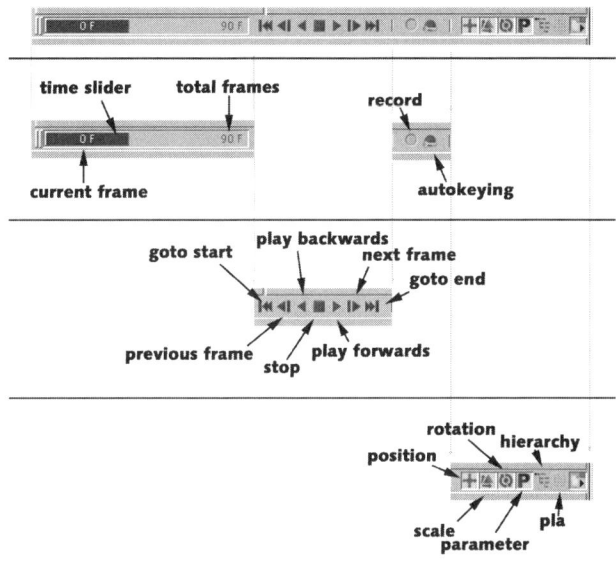

FIGURE 11.1 *The Time Manager tool palette.*

FIGURE 11.2 *With only the Position track activated, we will only be recording keyframes along the Position track.*

second, AutoKeying, is more of a "state of being" tool; when it is depressed, C4D will automatically record keyframes anytime you make a change in your view panel. The next four tools allow you to define what "tracks" you wish to actually record keyframes for (much more on this later). The Hierarchy tool allows you to choose whether or not you want to record keyframes down to children of a parent who has recorded a keyframe. PLA stands for Points Level Animation. We'll talk more of this later, but the basic idea is that you can actually animate any object at a Points level.

Let's see how all this works. To start out with, let's explore the simplest form of animation: AutoKeying.

AutoKeying

To enable AutoKeying, click the AutoKeying button in the Time Manager tool palette. Create a simple Cube Primitive. To start out with, let's just animate the position of this object. To do this, deactivate all the other tracks in the bottom right corner by clicking them (Figure 11.2). The reason we're doing this is to make sure that we aren't creating keyframes unnecessarily. Although extra keyframes won't necessarily hurt you, they can really get in the way if you need to do some editing; so it's a good habit to get into to not record any keyframes that are not needed.

Now, even though we have AutoKeying activated, click the Record button once. This just gives C4D a reference point – in essence you've just told C4D,

"At 0 frames, you are to be right here." It's important to remember that all motion consists of at least two keyframes; the first tells C4D where to start, and the second tells it where to end. Recording this first keyframe manually just lets C4D know that it's to start all of its motion from this point.

The process of AutoKeying consists of: first, moving the time slider to tell C4D "when" to have something done and second, telling C4D what to do over that time. So, since we already have our first keyframe set at 0 frames, move your time slider to frame 30 (Figure 11.3). At 30 fps, this means we are one second into the animation. Now, within your view panel, move the cube to another position. (Figure 11.4). This tells C4D, "At frame 30 you should now be here."

Some things happen as soon as you release your mouse. First, a thin yellow line appears. This line shows the path of the movement. If you move the time slider back to frame 0 and click the Play Forward button, you'll see the cube move along this path. If you look closely at this path, you'll actually find that it has two yellow points at either end. These points are a visual spatial representation of a keyframe. What's really powerful about these keyframe points is that

FIGURE 11.3 *The first step of AutoKeying (after recording an initial keyframe to define point a) is to tell C4D how long it is to take to get from point a to point b.*

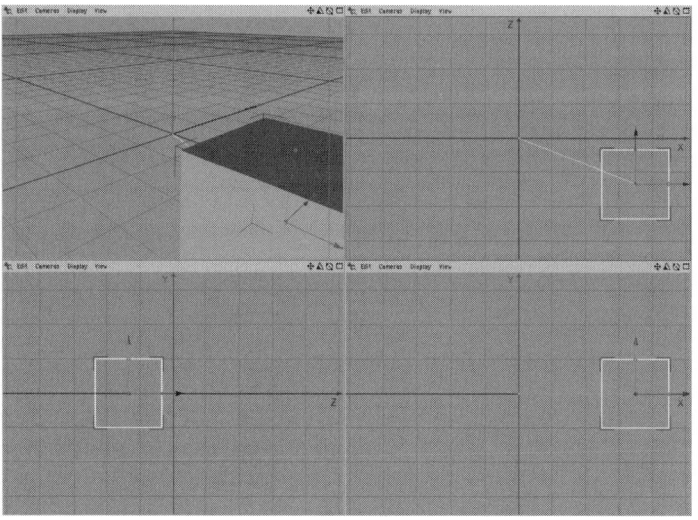

FIGURE 11.4 *The second step is to tell C4D where point b is.*

you can select them within the view panel and adjust the Bezier handles to change the path the cube takes to get from the first keyframe to the second (Figure 11.5).

Let's continue to animate this cube. Now move the time slider to frame 60. Move the cube into a new position. The animation path will be extended as C4D has just recorded a new position keyframe at frame 60. Repeat the process once more at frame 90, thus creating another position keyframe. Note that you can, at any time, select one of the keyframes on the animation path and change the path between keyframes (Figure 11.6).

Once you have these keyframes set, you can continue to edit this animation. If you move your time slider back to frame 0, 30, or 60, you can reposition the object and the keyframe will be rewritten. However, since you have AutoKeying active, if you miss frame 30 (say, for example, your time slider is on frame 29) and move your object, you all of a sudden have another keyframe at that frame 29, meaning that your object must make a big jump in the course of one frame. But, by the same token, if you find that you want to further define movement, you can just move your time slider to a frame between keyframes and reposition your object for a new keyframe, and thus record new information.

Now deactivate the Position track and activate the Rotation track. Again, move your time slider back to frame 0 and click the Record button to give C4D a starting point. Now let's say that we don't want the object to start to rotate until 45 frames into the animation. Move the time slider to frame 45 and click Record

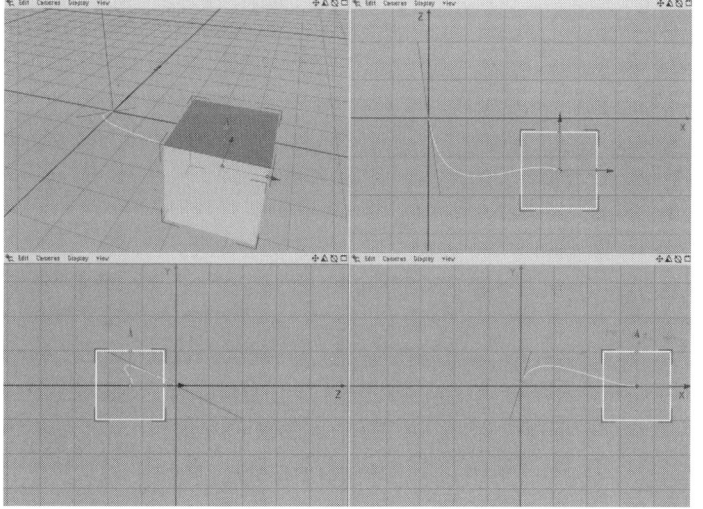

FIGURE 11.5 *The yellow line shows the animation path. The animation path also consists of visual representations of the keyframes. These keyframes can be selected and adjusted to change the shape of the animation path.*

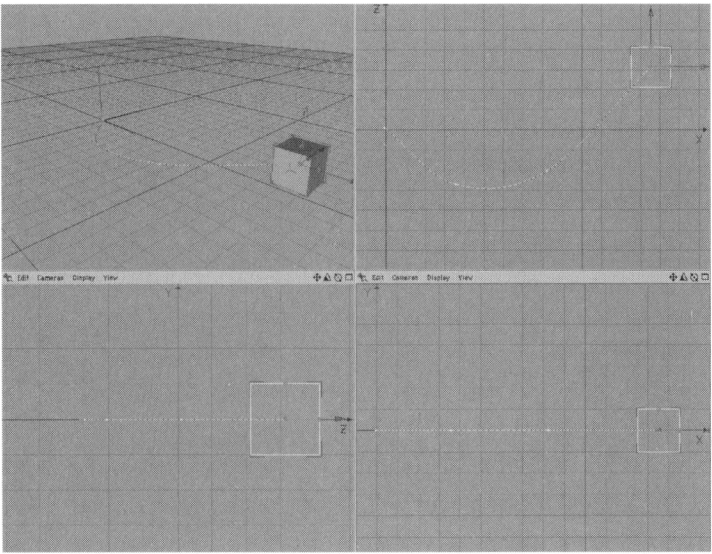

FIGURE *Continued AutoKeying.*
11.6

again. This gives it two keyframes that are identical to each other; so C4D says, "at frame 0 I'm rotated 0° and at frame 45 I'm rotated 45°, so no rotation between frames 0 and 45." You must click the Record button in this instance, since there was no change in the rotation and thus no auto-placed keyframe. Move the time slider to frame 90 and rotate the cube 90° by entering 90 in the H input field of the Coordinates Manager (Figure 11.7).

Play the animation and the cube will move along, and then at frame 45 it will start to turn and end up turned 90° by the time the time slider reaches frame 90. You could further add a Scale track and have the object change scale as it moved as well – try it. As an added bonus, give the Cube a fillet and animate the Parameter track and change the roundness of the fillet over time.

It's important to note that although we worked with each track (Position, Rotation, Scale, and Parameter) separately, you can record keyframes on multiple tracks at the same time. For instance, if, in a new file with a new cube, all four tracks were activated and you were to click the Record button, a starting keyframe would be set for all for tracks. Then as you moved the time slider to a new frame and made some changes to the object, C4D would automatically record a keyframe for all the things you changed – but not for tracks that did not change.

Although AutoKeying may seem like the end all, be all of animation, and while it certainly is the quickest and easiest way to create animation, it does

Chapter 11 Animation Basics

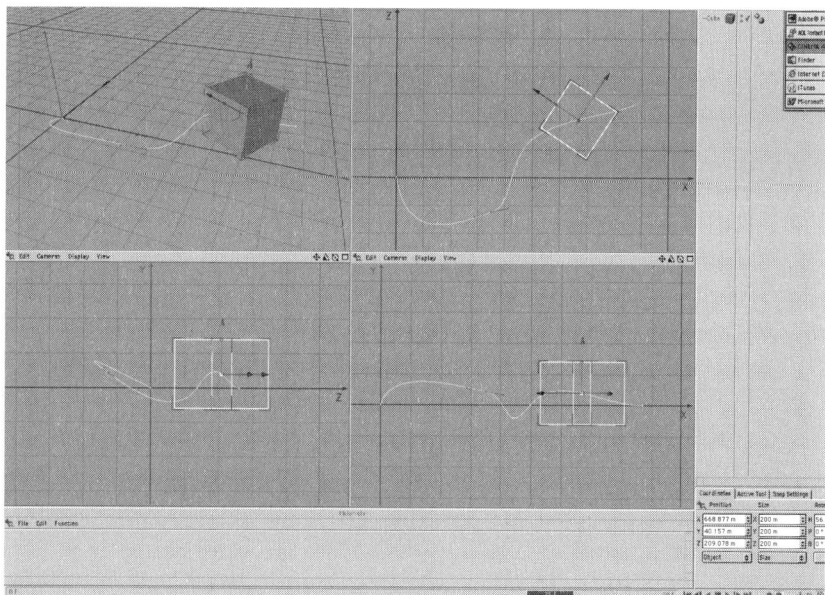

Figure 11.7 *Added rotation keyframe.*

create some problems when it comes to needing to make changes to your animation (which inevitably happens). Sometimes, you need to position objects to get a feel for a potential placement, but decide the time's not quite right or the position is not quite right. With AutoKeying activated, that "look" for potential has been recorded as a keyframe. Although an extra keyframe isn't the end of the world (it can be deleted later after all), if you're not very careful, you can end up with legions of keyframes you don't want or know where they came from. For complex animation sequences, you may want to consider using a more manual method.

Non-AutoKeying Animation

When AutoKeying is deactivated, the animation process is much the same. You can still choose which track or collection of tracks to record keyframes to, but you must remember to click the Record button every time you want to actually record that keyframe. This can be tricky if you're not in the habit of clicking that Record button, but once you get in the habit of clicking the Record button every time you want C4D to "remember" a new position, rotation, scale, or parameter this becomes a nice way to work.

TIMELINE

Still more manual than this is working within the Timeline. The Timeline is a separate window available by selecting Window>Timeline or by pressing SHIFT-F3 on your keyboard. The Timeline is an incredibly deep and powerful tool. Every generation of C4D has revealed a more and more powerful Timeline. The Timeline in C4D XL v6 has some special benefits in organizational capabilities.

When you first open the Timeline (Figure 11.8), you'll be presented with a new complex set of pull-down menus. Just under those pull-down menus are a collection of organizational tools in the top left, and the Powerslider and Timeline Ruler. The organizational tools can be used to group, lock, or hide objects as they appear down the left side of the Timeline. To assign an object to a group, just select the object and click one of the numbered boxes. The gray dot next to the object will change to the corresponding tag. You can then hide groups or lock them by clicking the eye or lock icons below the colored boxes. This works great as your projects become more complex and the list of objects becomes huge. The more objects you have, the more screen real estate rises in value. Being able to hide a large group of objects allows you to keep the Timeline small on your screen and keeps the relevant objects visible in the list.

The Powerslider is a tool to allow you to quickly zoom in on certain sections of your Timeline. The green rectangle in the Powerslider represents where (or when) in the animation the time slider is. This time slider can be moved here by click-dragging this green rectangle around. The two light gray rectangles show the range visible in the Timeline. If you move these rectangles closer together, the Timeline will be displaying fewer frames, and thus they will appear further apart. The long, dark gray bar that connects the two can also be click-

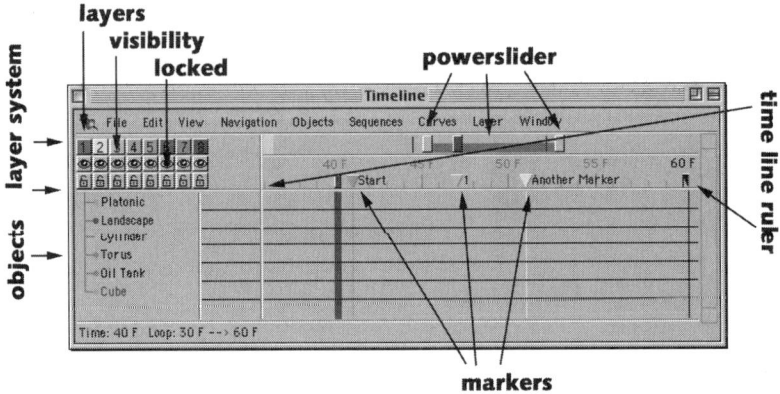

FIGURE *Timeline.*
11.8

dragged to scrub along the entire Timeline. There is a collection of tricks to manipulating this Powerslider to quickly maneuver through time. SHIFT-click-dragging either of the gray range rectangles expands or contracts the selection in both directions. Double-clicking on either of the gray range rectangles expand the range to the beginning or end of the available time.

The Timeline Ruler shows hash marks to visually define frames. The green rectangle is the time slider and can be scrubbed through time in your animation. You can place markers for your own reference to assist in planning the timing by CTRL/COMMAND-clicking along the ruler. By double-clicking the ruler you can change the name or layer color. Remove the marker by click-dragging the marker upward.

ANIMATING WITHIN THE TIMELINE

Now that we know how the Timeline is organized and how to move within it, we can look at how to animate in it. The largest space of the Timeline are the rows next to each of the objects. These rows are there to allow you to create tracks. Tracks, as we discussed above, include (among other things) the object's position, rotation, and scale. When you have a track activated within the Time Manager and you record a keyframe, a track is created here in the Timeline. A track will then contain sequences. A sequence is the bar that appears in the next section of the Timeline, that defines how long a collection of keyframes are (Figure 11.9).

You can select and move or delete keyframes, sequences or tracks. By CTRL/OPTION-click-dragging a track, sequence, or keyframe you can copy from object to object. Or, in the case of sequences and keyframes, you can

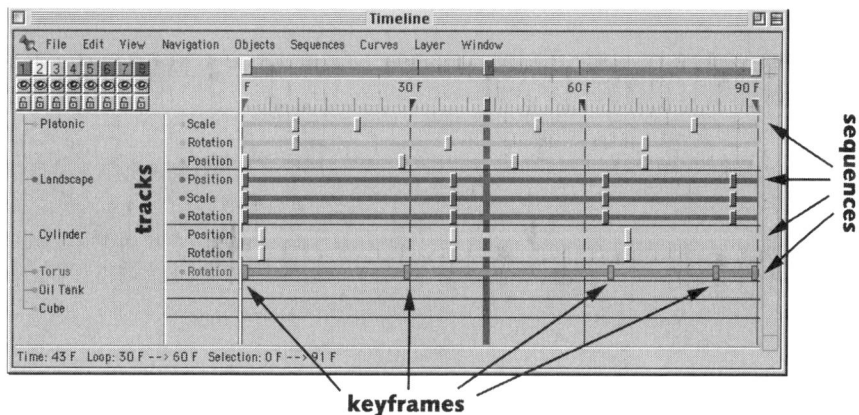

FIGURE *Tracks, sequences, keyframes.*
11.9

CTRL/OPTION-click-drag and copy a sequence later within the same track. Further, you can marquee around tracks or sequences which can then be moved, deleted, or copied.

There is actually a large collection of tracks that can be assigned to an object; many more than just the Position, Scale, Rotation, and Parameter tracks we've already discussed (Figure 11.10). To assign a track to an object, right-click (COMMAND-click on a Mac) on the target object and select New Track, then select the track you want from the resultant pop up menu. When you create a new track, there are no keyframes attached. To establish a keyframe on a track, CTRL/COMMAND-click anywhere on the track.

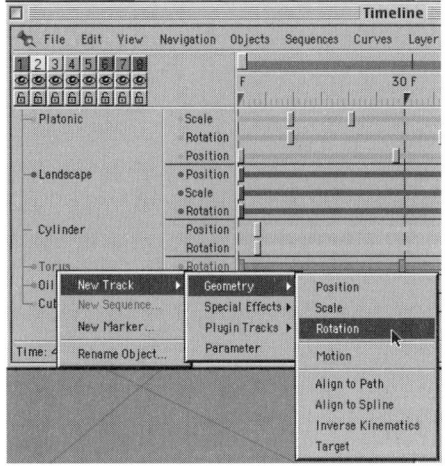

FIGURE 11.10 *Assigning a new track.*

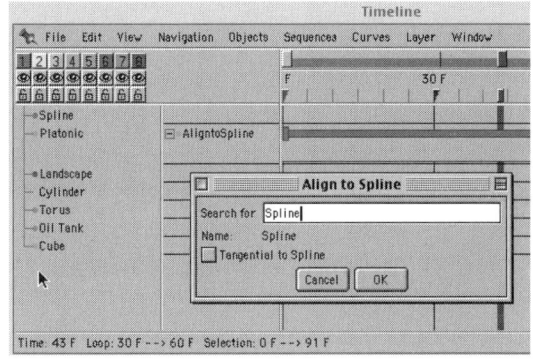

FIGURE 11.11 *When you create a keyframe for an Align to Spline track, C4D immediately asks for a spline to align to.*

Each track deals with keyframes slightly different. For instance, some tracks — like Align to Spline — immediately open a dialog box asking what spline you wish to align to (Figure 11.11). By expanding the track you can see what spline is assigned to each keyframe. Tracks such as Pulsate ask you to define how the object is to pulsate (Figure 11.12). Both of these tracks only need one keyframe for motion as long as the sequence runs. Still other tracks like a Texture track allow you to define how a material is applied to an object (Figure 11.13). If more than one keyframe is assigned, C4D gradually changes the texture from keyframe to keyframe. For a detailed description of each track and what it does, see page 563 in the manual. We will be looking at how to use several of these tracks over the course of the coming tutorials.

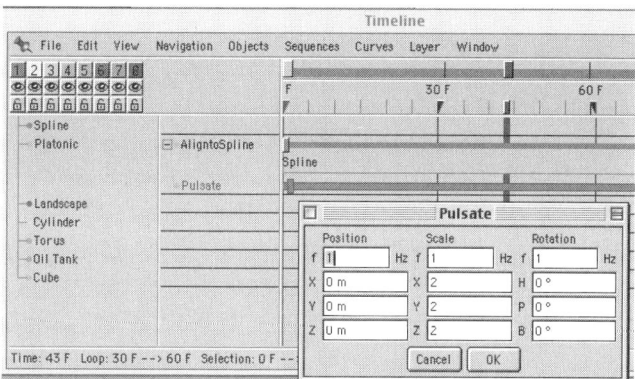

FIGURE 11.12 *The Pulsate track requires different settings upon creating a keyframe.*

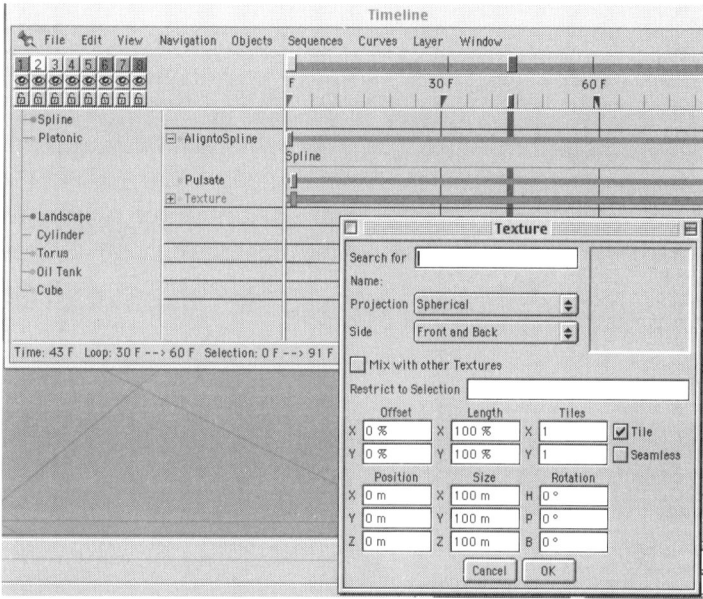

FIGURE 11.13 *Texture tracks allow for the alteration of texture over time.*

The best way to learn how to use the Timeline is to use it. To demonstrate we'll look at several tutorials in this chapter.

11.1 Animating a Bee's Wings

TUTORIAL

ON THE CD

Ultimately, we are going to be animating this little Bee flying through the Dining Room that we've modeled, textured, and lit in past tutorials (Figure 11.14). We'll animate his antennae moving and his legs twitching. For now, though, we'll just animate his wings. Take a minute to open this character off the CD (Bee.c4d) and take a look at how he's modeled. Simply put, he's a simple Hyper NURBS Object built from a Cube Primitive. As in tutorials past, only half of him really "exists" — the second half is the result of him being within an Symmetry Object (Figure 11.15). This will come in handy in more ways than one by the end of this tutorial.

Notice that besides the eyes, eyebrows, and wings, this character is all one mesh. The stripes were done by creating Selection sets, and then making sure that the materials were applied using Restrict to Selection. The bump was created with a simple Noise 2D shader; if you have BhodiNuts's *SLA*, you might play with creating more "fuzzy" surfaces. The wing material is actually mostly Fog.

As a simple exercise, let's make the little guy's wing flap. The wing's axis is already appropriately placed. We want to make sure that the wing flaps from where it attaches to the Bee's body. We'll want to make this wing rotate very fast, so it will rotate a long distance over a short period of frames. Select the wing within the Symmetry Object. Select Rotate Active Element and rotate the wing by the Z-axis handle. Notice that as you rotate the one wing, the "symmetried" copy rotates as well. This means that we only need to animate the one wing and the other will do its part automatically.

With the wing Object selected in the Object Manager, activate the Rotate track in the Time Manager and deactivate the other tracks. Make sure your time slider is at 0 frames, and rotate the wing 40° by entering this value in the B input field

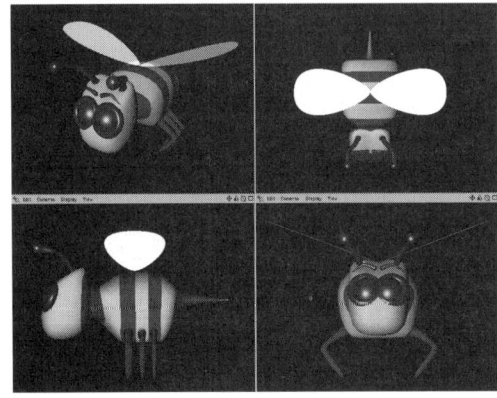

FIGURE 11.14 *Bee character.*

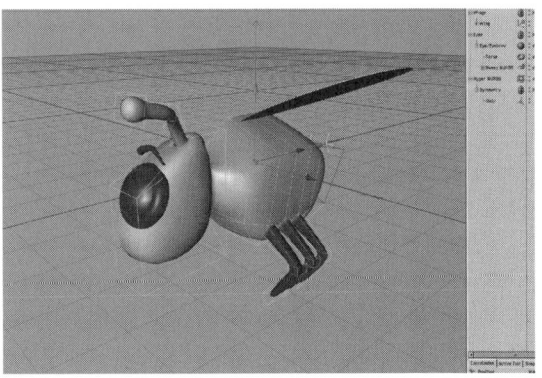

FIGURE 11.15 *Almost all of the Bee is part of a Symmetry Object.*

of the Coordinates Manager. Record a keyframe. Move your time slider to frame 5 and enter -40° in the B input field of the Coordinates Manager. Now we could animate the wings, moving back down to 40° and then back up to -40°, or we could simply loop this one motion.

Looping a series of keyframes is actually looping a sequence. Open your Timeline (Window>Timeline) and expand down until you can see the wing Object with its Rotation track. If your file was set to the default 90 frames, your Rotation track and sequence probably stretches out to fill all 90 frames, even though you only have keyframes at frames 0 and 5. The first thing we want to do is shorten this sequence so that it contains just enough length to contain the movement once. Double-click on the sequence (light gray bar upon which the keyframes sit) and in the resultant dialog box (Figure 11.16) have the sequence go from 0 to 10F. But why 10 frames when the motion we've done is only 5 frames? Well, in that same dialog box, you'll find the Loops collection of options. Within these Loops options are places you can tell C4D how many times or for how long to loop this sequence. At the bottom is a Soft option. This tells C4D to look ahead (or behind) and make a smooth transition from the last keyframe of the looped sequence to the first. So in order to have the wings rotate back down to the first keyframed position, we need to give C4D 5 additional frames to do it.

The Timeline should now appear like Figure 11.17. The light gray bar represents the original sequence, which contains our two keyframes. The dark gray bar indicates that this is playing a loop. You cannot place any keyframes on the looped section, but there is no need. If we need the wings to move faster, we can simply alter the two keyframes already placed, and the changes will go into effect through the entire loop.

Now, depending on the speed of your machine, click the Play Forward button in the Time Manager. You may notice that for 3 wing flaps a second, it seems to be moving quite slow. This is because as models become complex, C4D and your

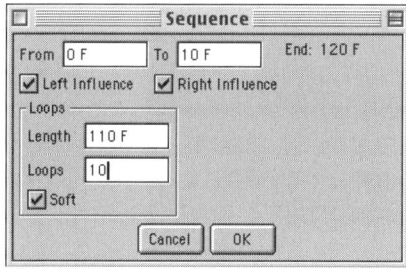

FIGURE 11.16 *Looping a sequence.*

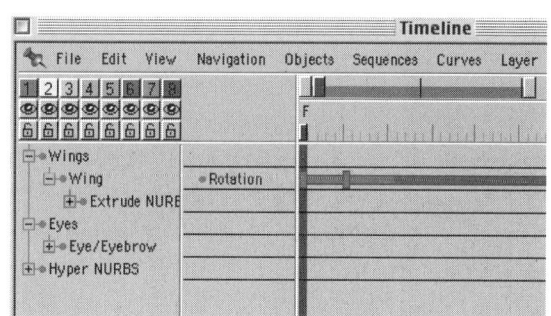

FIGURE 11.17 *A sequence and its looped visual representation.*

machine can't display the frames quickly enough to maintain the 30fps. So, there is a slowdown. This is often an issue of confusion for animators as they try and time their animations based solely on what the Editor shows them; this is usually a mistake. However, to render out a raytraced animation takes a great deal of time; and a project that is so big that it won't play back for the Time Manager is probably big enough to slow down C4D's Renderer at least a bit. The key is to do a rendering, but not have C4D calculate the raytraced version; rather, have it render the scene as you would see it in the Editor and put the frames together into a movie. This movie then would give you an accurate idea of the speed.

To create such a movie, you'll need to make some adjustments to the Rendering settings. Select the Edit Render Settings button (Figure 11.18) from the top command palette. Within these settings, adjust the General, Output, and Save tabs to match Figure 11.19. You are telling C4D to put each frame, as it would be shown in the Editor, together as a QuickTime movie and save the movie to your disk. Make sure that in the Output tab, you select a range that

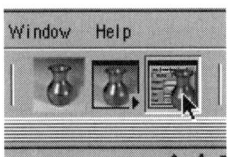

FIGURE 11.18 *The Edit Render Settings button.*

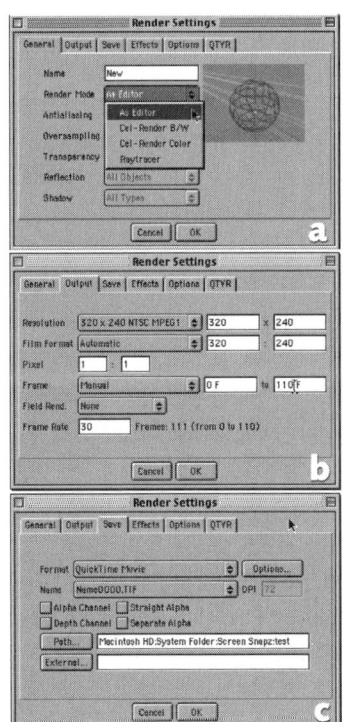

FIGURE 11.19 *To set up the Render Settings in order to create a quick rendered preview of your animation, match the settings to these.*

includes several loops to get true idea of the movement. Upon rendering (Figure 11.20), you can get an idea of the movement.

This movement isn't bad; however, we're going to want those wings to be moving so fast, they're a blur. We can set up Motion Blur settings (much more on this in Chapter 18), but that probably still won't do the trick unless we have an extremely high setting. The higher the Scene Motion Blur setting, the longer the animation takes to render. So, we'll add mass to these wings by making a couple of copies and offsetting the timing. Select the Symmetry Object that contains the wings in your Object Manager and copy and paste three copies (Figure 11.21).

But just copying and pasting the wings isn't going to make much difference, as they all have the same timing. To remedy this problem, we'll offset the looped sequences so that each wing is at slightly different places. The combination of multiple wings, even rendered with a low Motion Blur setting, will help develop a believable mass of wings. To offset the motion, simply grab the sequence and offset it by a few frames. However many frames you offset the sequence (backward in time is best), add that many frames to the Loops Length setting in the Sequence dialog box. Your Timeline should look something like Figure 11.22. Notice that we even have frames in the negative time direction – no problem, we can still just tell C4D to start rendering from 0. Figure 11.23 shows a still of what our wings look like.

Now that our Bee's wings are flapping, let's show it how to fly. We want to be able to move the entire Bee, wings and all, as one object. So group all of the Bee together and name it "Bee." Now, even though we have animation already occurring on the wings, when we make any Motion, Scale, or Rotation keyframes for

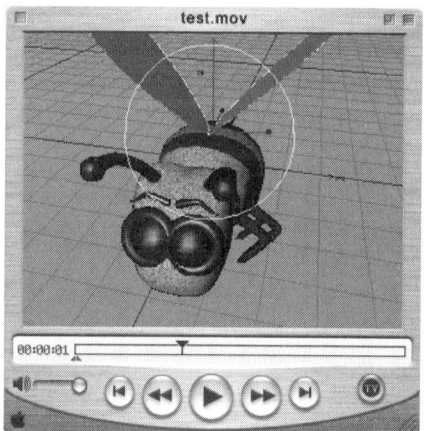

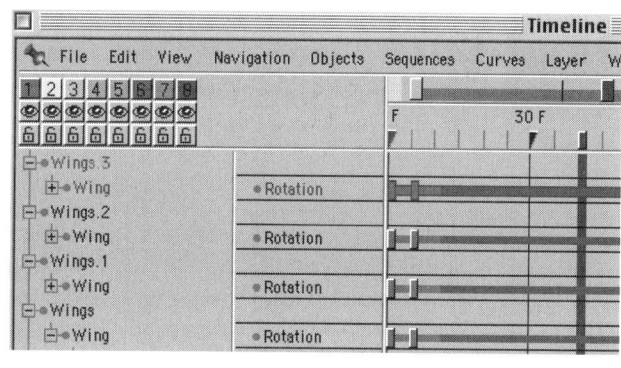

FIGURE 11.21 *Three versions of the same wings.*

FIGURE 11.20 *The output movie is a QuickTime file that can play the 30 fps to give you an accurate view of the timing.*

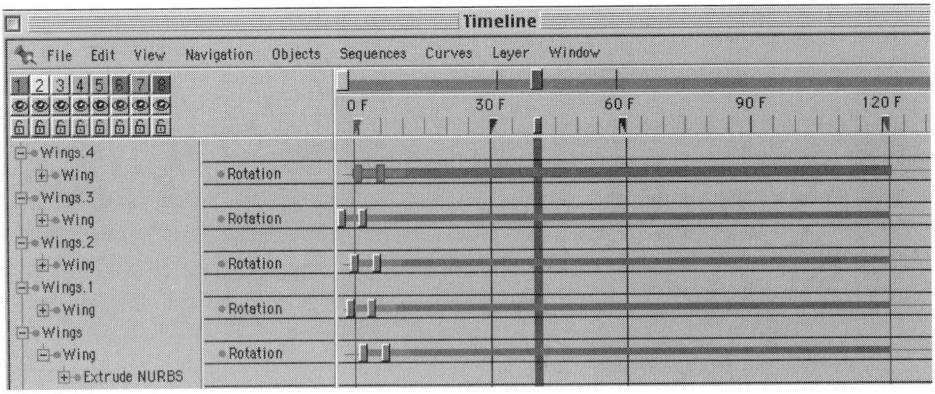

FIGURE **11.22** *Offset duplicates make each set of flapping wings just offset from the next.*

the Bee group, the wings will continue flapping and make the changes with the rest of the object.

We could just make the Bee fly in a straight line, but let's make an obstacle course to really test his wings. Figure 11.24 shows our Bee with a collection of Primitives laid out. One method to negotiating this course would be to carefully place keyframes at each point where the Bee should turn. However, there are some easier methods. Instead of working out each turn and keyframe, use a Draw Spline tool to draw a path that you want the Bee to follow (Figure 11.25) and name the spline "Bee Path."

Now within the Timeline, right-click (COMMAND-click) on the Bee Object and select New Track>Geometry>Align to Spline (Figure 11.26). This will create a new track for the group Bee. However, until there is a keyframe assigned to the track, it doesn't actually take effect. CTRL/COMMAND-click on frame 0 and enter "Bee Path" into the input field; make sure also to activate Tangential to Spline (Figure 11.27).

What this keyframe does is tell C4D that over the duration of the sequence, it is to take the Bee Object and move it along the Spline Bee Path. Tangential to Spline makes the object turn its heading as the spline curves; however, it does not make the object bank. Scrub the time slider in the Time Manager to see the results (Figure 11.28).

The Bee Object follows the spline alright, but it's following it backwards. This is because when an object aligns to a spline, it does so according to the object's Y-axis. For our Bee Object, the positive Y-axis is the back of the Bee. So to fix this, we need to rotate the Bee's object axis 180 degrees along its heading (H). Select the Object Axis tool, and select the Bee Object group from the Object Manager. Add 180 to whatever value is present in the H input field of the Coordinates Manager and scrub through the Time Manager again (Figure 11.29).

Chapter 11 Animation Basics

Figure 11.23 *The blurred result.*

Figure 11.24 *Obstacle course.*

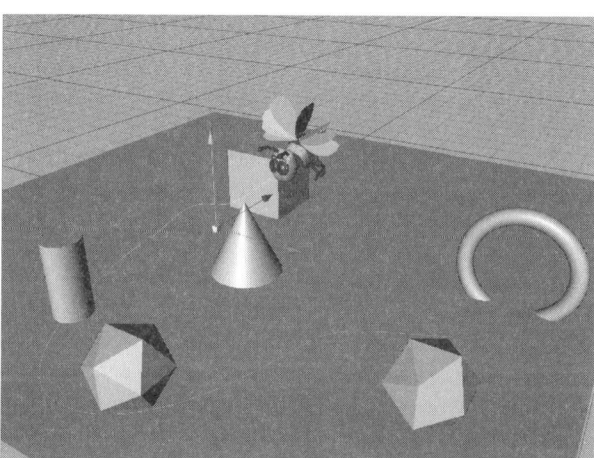

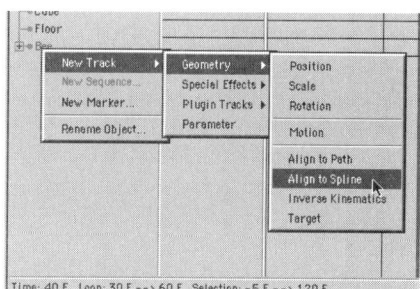

Figure 11.26 *Creating a new Align to Spline track.*

Figure 11.25 *With the Draw Bezier Spline tool, create the path that you'd like the Bee to follow. Make sure to look at the path from multiple angles to allow the Bee to go over some things and through the torus.*

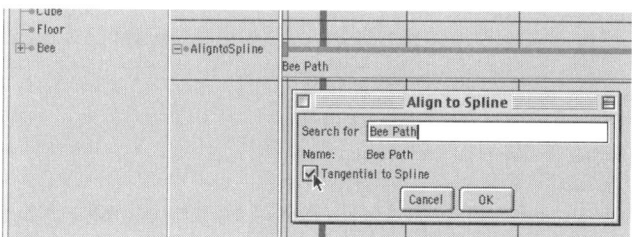

Figure 11.27 *Creating a keyframe to enable the Align to Spline track.*

Voila! Your Bee is following the complex path with the placement of one keyframe.

Align to Spline and Align to Path are two shortcuts to complex paths. However, they do present some problems. As an object aligns to a spline, it doesn't bank (rock side to side); therefore, to create good flying movement, you often need to go in and add additional Rotation keyframes to get the banking correct. The second problem is that you have very little control over the speed of the object within the sequence. You know how long it takes to get from the beginning of the spline to the end since that is defined by the length of the sequence, but what if you wanted the Bee to speed up over the box but slow down around the sphere? No go. If relative speeds are important, these are probably not the tracks for the job.

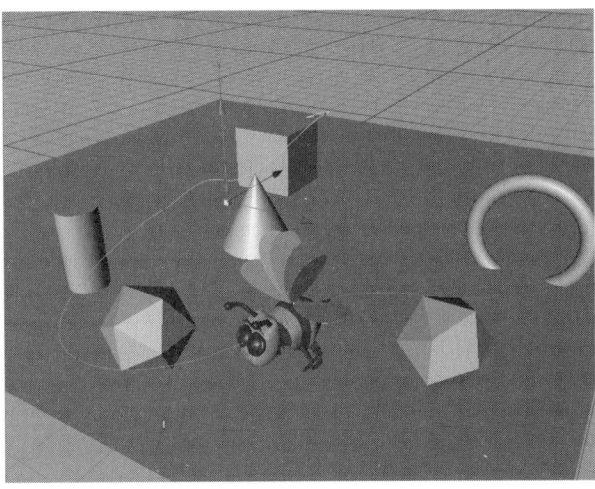

FIGURE 11.28 *Bee following the spline – but following it backwards.*

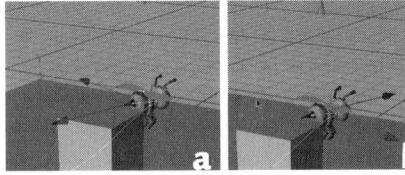

FIGURE 11.29 *Rotating the Bee's object axis so that it heads in the right direction.*

11.2 CAMERA ANIMATION

TUTORIAL

Now that we have the Bee flying, let's find an interesting way to capture that flight. Create a Camera Target Object and make sure that you are looking at the scene through that camera by choosing Cameras>Scene Camera>Camera within a view panel. The immediate result will probably be that you are not looking directly at anything of importance, since the Camera Target is placed at (0,0,0). Select the Camera Target in the Object Manager and move it so that it is inside the Bee (Figure 11.30).

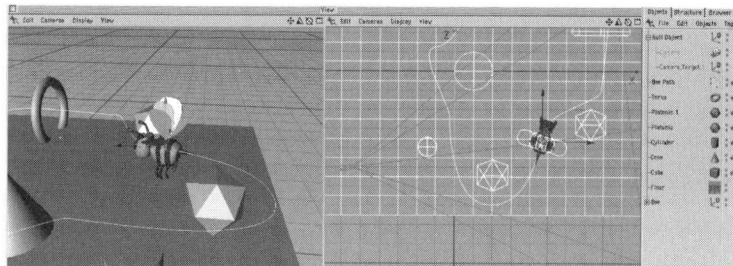

FIGURE 11.30 *If you want to look at the Bee, move the Camera Target Object within the Bee.*

Now, we want to make sure that the camera continues to look at the Bee as it flies through the course. Take the Camera Target out of the Null Object it is in and make it a child of the Bee group. As of now, where the Bee goes, the Camera Target goes. When the Camera Target moves, the camera points at it. The net result is that the camera stays focused on the Bee through all of its flight (Figure 11.31).

Now let's take it one step further and have the camera follow the Bee as it travels. There are actually a couple of ways to do this. One way is to move the camera into position behind the Bee, and then place the camera as a child of the Bee (Figure 11.32). However, using this method, the camera stays stiff and uninteresting in its pursuit. A more exciting method would be to have the camera follow the same path as the Bee, only just a few frames behind. To do this, we need to copy the Align to Spline track to the camera. CTRL/OPTION-click-drag this track to the Camera Object within the Timeline. If you left this as is, you would see the entire animation from *inside* the Bee as the camera would jump to the same location as the Bee. Click-drag the

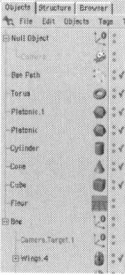

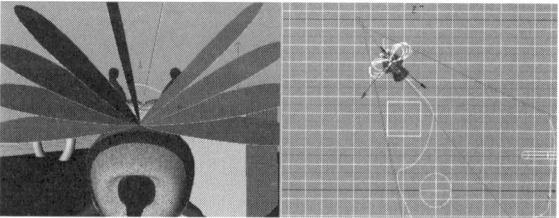

FIGURE 11.31 *After the Camera Target is within the Bee in the view panel, make it a child of the Bee Object in the Object Manager so that the camera will continually point at the Bee.*

FIGURE 11.32 *By moving the camera into position and then making the camera a child of the Bee Object, the camera acts as a mounted camera riding on the Bee's back.*

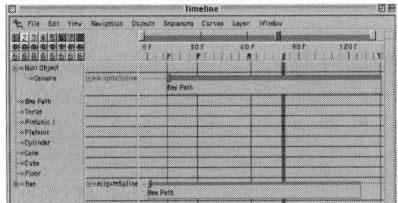

FIGURE 11.33 *By copying and offsetting the Align to Spline track to the camera, the camera has a life and path of its own as it flies in pursuit, while it stays pointed at the Camera Target which is inside the Bee.*

sequence for the Align to Spline track for the camera 10 frames later in the animation (Figure 11.33).

Now there are still some weird issues to this method. For instance, the animation starts inside of the Bee but quickly gets out of the Bee. To fix this, you would need to make a copy of Bee Path, name it something new, like "Camera Path," and alter the path's beginning and ending points to stay a bit behind Bee Path. Remember to change the keyframe for the camera from Bee Path to the newly created Camera Path.

This same technique could be used to animate our cute little Bee flying anywhere in our Dining Room. You could use combinations of following for a while with a short Align to Spline sequence, and then stay still to simply point at the Bee as it continues to move. The possibilities for this kind of motion are limitless.

11.3 ANIMATED FLYTHROUGH

TUTORIAL

Well this isn't as much a tutorial as it's a list of suggestions. For our Room, an animation following a Bee screaming through the space may be a little inappropriate. Architectural visualization is a hot market for 3D animators and mastering the flythrough is an important technique. A few suggestions to making good flythroughs.

- Keep the camera at a human height. Assume that the camera you're going to use in a flythrough is being manned by a person. Keep the camera about 6 feet off the ground.
- Keep the focal length "normal." It's easy to make your camera have a fisheye focal length in an attempt to allow the viewer to see more of the room. However, in the case of a flythrough, the user will get to see whatever it is you want him/her to see in due time. Fisheye views in flythroughs remove the viewer from the experience, as short focal lengths end up bending walls and other effects, thus creating a very surreal movie.

- Movement within the scene is good. No need for an intense amount of movement as it would distract from the intricate details you've included; however, the rustling of curtains, or the gentle opening of a door can help to add visual movement and interest to a scene.
- Don't worry about keeping it in real time. If you have any NLDVE package (Premiere, Quicktime Pro, Final Cut Pro, After Effects, etc…), consider making your flythrough a series of moves spliced together using gentle cross fades. The movie really doesn't need to be all one shot – although it could be. Oftentimes, the best solution is to create several sweeping clips without a lot of camera turns that show off the strong parts of the room.
- If you are keeping it as one long shot, keep the camera turns slow. Even though in real life we turn our heads quickly, we're not used to that sort of movement in animation. Most camera pans are slow, allowing the viewer to understand their location, to take in the scene, and to be acquainted with their surroundings. Too often, in 3D, the camera turns happen so quickly that it makes the viewer seasick and they really don't enjoy the viewing experience.
- Slow it down. At our university, one of the first assignments is an architectural flythrough. Almost without exception, the first draft turned in is much too fast. Timing is a tricky thing when you are not dealing with complex 3D scenes, but to make matters worse, learning to visually see on a Timeline how long a motion takes is not an easy thing. Converting frames to seconds and deciding how many seconds is a tricky process and typically is mastered only with practice. To really be able to enjoy and look at the architecture, there needs to be plenty of time to observe textures, movement, colors, reflections, and lighting. Too fast and all the viewer remembers was running through a room. Providing the pacing to allow the viewer to absorb all the information is critical. If you're just starting in animation and don't have a good handle on timing quite yet, almost always double your initial guess as to how long to make each move.

CHAPTER 12

Advanced Animation and Character Animation

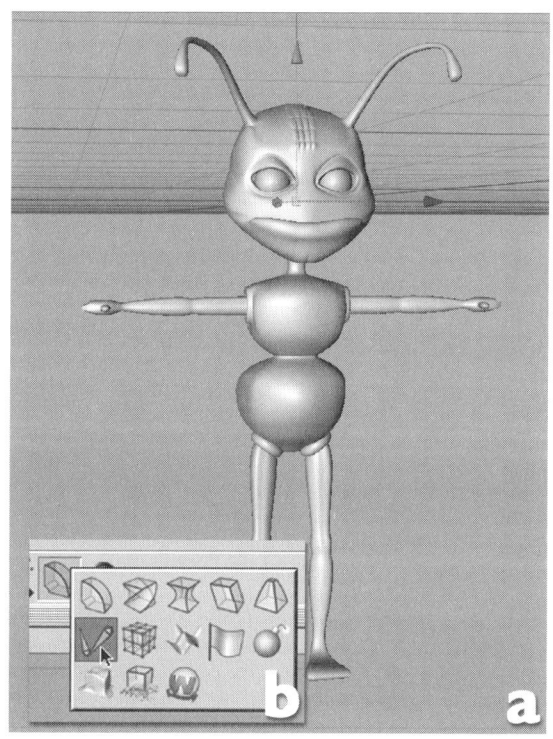

Character animation (CA) is one of the hottest areas of 3D animation today. Good character animators are hard to find, and the skills needed to bring a collection of polygons to life are hard won and long practiced before they are mastered. The specifics of the art of character animation are well beyond the scope of this volume; however, we can certainly look at how to use C4D's Character Animation tools to create basic character movement.

This chapter is a simplified presentation of a variety of ideas in character animation. None of these techniques are the end all, be all technique of CA, but they will assist you in getting started on the CA trail. The first simplified issue is the idea that most characters are either segmented, single mesh, or a combination of the two. A segmented character is a character that has a separate object for each body part. Figure 12.1 (a) shows a simple primitive-only segmented character that shows this idea of one object for the head, one for the neck, one for the torso, one for the shoulder, one for the upper arm, etc.... Figure 12.1 (b) shows a single mesh character in which the entire character (except perhaps the eyeballs) are part of one collection of polygons. There are advantages and disadvantages to both types of animated characters.

SEGMENTED CHARACTERS

There are several important aspects of creating segmented characters. The first is that each segment must have its axis of rotation placed in an appropriate location. Figure 12.1 (a) shows a segmented character created entirely with primitive forms; however, if they were left as primitives, they would each rotate around the center of the object, rather than at the joints where they should rotate

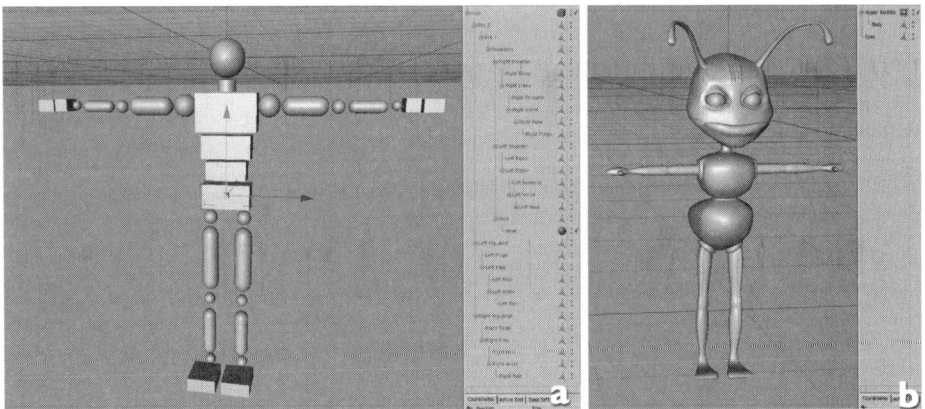

FIGURE 12.1 *(a) Segmented character with a different object for every part of the body. (b) Single mesh characters are characters in which the entire body is one collection of polygons and one object.*

(Figure 12.2). To solve this problem, remember that if a primitive is made editable, then the object axis can be moved into a more appropriate place.

The second is that organization is paramount. How each body part is organized in the hierarchy will make all the difference when it comes time to move the character. Most motion in our bodies is centered somewhere between the belly button and the crotch. Of course, different characters will have different center of gravities, but for most humanoid forms, the center of gravity is about the same. Now this is important, because if we know where the center of gravity for a form is, we know where the topmost object in the character's hierarchy should be. In the case of our segmented character introduced in Figure 12.1 (a), the Hip Object would be the parent-most object. Then, the Leg Objects below, and the Rib Objects above, would be on the same hierarchical level (Figure 12.3 a).

Remember that, even though you may have one sphere for an elbow and another shape for a forearm, the forearm will probably never rotate differently than the elbow. And so, having the forearm as a child of the elbow, as well as having the wrist at the end of the forearm a child of the same elbow, you can simplify the hierarchy. You can do the same things with the legs — group the hip joint and the thigh together. Figure 12.3 (b) shows a suggested organization for a segmented character.

With a hierarchy like that shown in Figure 12.3 (b), you're ready to pose and animate the segmented character. Notice that the first set of ribs is at the same hierarchical level as the legs. In essence, the hips start and everything radiates out from that object. Notice that things like the head and neck are children of

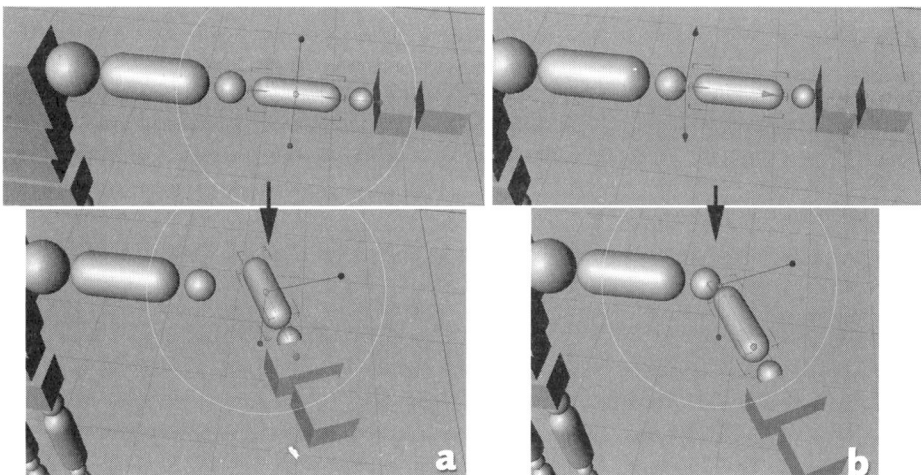

FIGURE 12.2 *The default object axis causes joints to rotate inappropriately (a). Only after you make primitives editable and use the Object Axis tool, can joints have an accurate rotation axis, and thus rotate appropriately (b).*

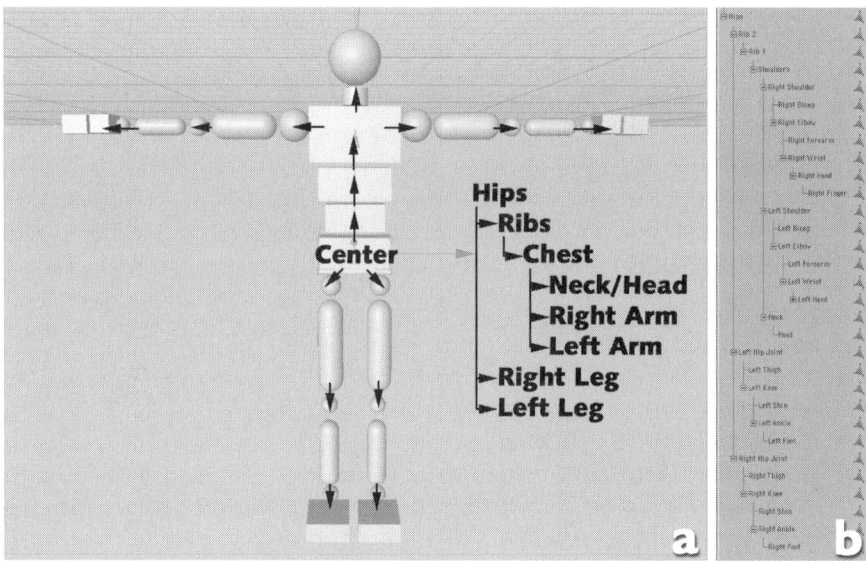

FIGURE 12.3 (a) Hierarchy organization of our segmented character. (b) General organization for a segmented character.

the shoulders. This sort of organization makes it so that when the shoulders turn, or the shoulder's parent object "Ribs" bends, then the head goes with them.

KINEMATICS

Most character animation (CA) can be broken down into two main methods of movement: Forward Kinematics (FK) and Inverse Kinematics (IK). Both are essentially methods of defining poses that are recorded as keyframes. The difference is essentially in whether you are posing by positioning objects from the parent down, or posing simply from the child up.

ON THE CD

Forward Kinematics (FK) is the method of animating by defining poses that the character is to hit over time, by rotating each joint into position starting from the parent-most object and ending with the child-most object. To see how FK works, open the Segmented Character file from the CD and start by rotating the segmented character's arms down to his sides (Figure 12.4 a). Now with the idea of FK being that poses are created from the parent down, we need to make sure that we're recording only Rotation keyframes. So make sure that all tracks are disabled but the Rotation keyframe. There are a couple of ways to record keyframes when you pose objects in FK. One method, which is really a shotgun-like method, is to activate the Hierarchy button within the track activation bank of tools in the Time Manager (Figure 12.4 b). What this does is record keyframes for all the children if a keyframe is recorded for a parent object. So, if you started with the right shoulder and moved the shoulder, then the forearm, and finally the hand into place, then selected the right shoulder object and clicked Record, a Rotation keyframe would be recorded for all objects that are children of the right shoulder in one fell swoop. This may seem like a smart way to work, but it makes for very robotic movement as all joints move with the same timing. In reality, movement is more complex. Often our forearm will begin moving before our bicep does, but it keeps moving as the bicep begins its rotation. As such, it's often a more tedious, but accurate method to record keyframes for each part of each joint separately. However, for this first exercise, let's simplify matters and turn the Hierarchy button on.

Once again, FK is essentially all about Rotation keyframes. FK is also about starting high on the hierarchy and moving down. To begin with, make sure that your time slider is at 0 frames, then select the Ribs 2 object and record a keyframe. This records a keyframe for the Ribs 2, Ribs 1, Shoulders, Neck, Right Shoulder (and arm), and Left Shoulder (and arm). Essentially, all the objects that are highlighted in red within the Object Manager when Ribs 2 is selected now have a Rotation keyframe at 0 frames. Now move the time slider to 15 frames, and using only the Rotate Active Element tool, rotate the Ribs 2 Object and each of its children into position as if it were grabbing the ball (Figure 12.5). Using the FK train of thought, rotate each object, then move to its child and rotate that

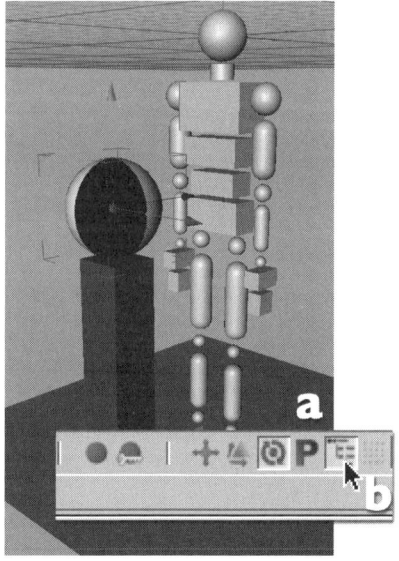

FIGURE **12.4** *(a) Starting pose of segmented character. (b) The Hierarchy On/Off button for recording.*

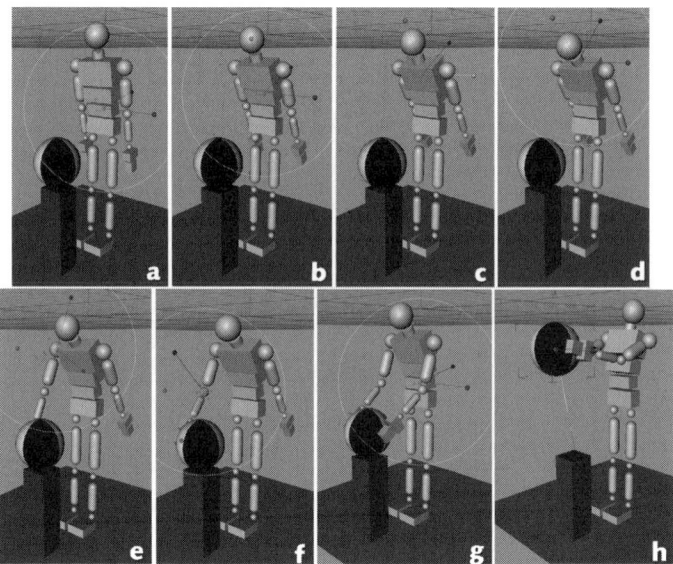

FIGURE 12.5   *FK is the process of rotating each object and then moving on to its child. Using the Hierarchy On tool, we can pose everything, and then by selecting the uppermost object (of the objects moved), one keyframe can be recorded all the way down the hierarchy.*

object. Now, select Ribs 2 and record a keyframe. It's very important that Ribs 2 is selected when you record this keyframe, or C4D "forgets" the new rotation of the other objects. Similarly, make sure that as you are rotating each of these joints that you do not use the Undo command. If you do, C4D forgets all changes made and reverts back to the last keyframe recorded. After this second keyframe is recorded, you can scrub from frame 0 to 15 and see the movement.

To have the character stand back up, simply move the time slider to frame 30 and repose the character erect again. Again, make sure that once the character is posed erect, you select the Ribs 2 Object and record a keyframe to record the new rotation for all the objects (Figure 12.5 h). The trickiest thing here is that the ball is not a child of the arm; therefore, its movement must be animated separately. For a simple lifting motion like this, a Position keyframe can be recorded at frame 15 to tell the ball to start there, and then another keyframe recorded at frame 30 with the ball repositioned up in the hand.

By using Rotation keyframes that are all recorded at the same point, we can reuse poses by copying and pasting keyframes. So if we wanted our segmented character to place the ball down again, we could select the keyframes set at frame 15 by marqueeing around them in the Timeline and CTRL/COMMAND-click-dragging them to frame 45. Make sure that you get the Position keyframe for the ball as well. Then, to have the character stand erect again with his arms at his sides, marquee around the keyframes at frame 0 and CTRL/COMMAND-click-drag these keyframes to frame 60. To get an idea of how the movement is, do a test As Editor rendering.

FK Walk

One of the trickiest parts of character animation is the complex issue of locomotion. Walks, runs, skips, hops — all are a diverse combination of flailing appendages and the building up and releasing of power. Creating a walk using Forward Kinematics is one of the simplest, most easily controlled, but least accurate, and most time-consuming, ways to move a character along. Using FK allows you to carefully define when and where each joint is rotated – this has benefits and drawbacks. The benefit is that you are always in complete control; the drawback is that this control is time-consuming, as you must define each little movement to get the movement to happen. The biggest drawback to FK walks is the "Scooby-Doo Effect." Remember those episodes of Scooby-Doo where the gang was walking along with the camera following along in profile? Since the characters were animated separately from the background, oftentimes the feet would slide along the ground when the two didn't match up. FK is a walk that walks in place. The feet don't plant into position, since they are simply rotating rather than moving. This makes animation easier in some ways, as you can always be looking at the same section of the model as you animate, but it becomes very tricky when you need to have the character move along at exactly the same pace as the feet are moving.

ON THE CD

Characters walk in cycles. From left footfall, to right footfall, to left footfall, and repeat. To analyze how to do a walk cycle, open the SegmentedCharacter-Walk.c4d file off the CD. This file has a good starting position for a walk cycle. We won't go too much into the physics of the walk, but notice that when the right foot is forward, then the shoulders counterrotate to keep the weight evenly distributed (Figure 12.6 a).

To start out with, we'll place some general keyframes to establish the skeleton of the movement. We'll do this by establishing right footfall, left foot raised, left footfall, right foot raised, and then right footfall again. Since we'll not only be animating the legs moving, but also the arms moving and a rough approximation of the weight shifting, make sure that you have the Hierarchy On button selected, then select the Hips Object and record a Rotation keyframe. Now that every object has a Rotation keyframe from which to start, you can begin the animation process.

For a rough start, let's place each of the keyframes we've talked about at 15 frame intervals. Move the time slider to frame 15, and rotate the left leg by starting at the hip joint and moving down to the ankle so that the ankle and foot is at the height of its path moving from the back to the front. Move the right leg that was in the front to directly beneath the body and very close to straight (although not completely). It turns out that our legs are hardly ever completely straight, especially when we walk. They are always involved in either bending in absorption of weight, or bending in anticipation of expanding to push our weight forward.

Reverse the Ribs 2, Ribs, and Shoulders to a 0 rotation, as at this point in the walk cycle, the body would be nearly straight forward. Continue to rotate the arms so that they are both even with the body. Select the Hips Object again and record a Rotation keyframe (Figure 12.6 b). Notice that the right leg will be through the floor — when we walk, we actually have quite a bit of up and down motion. But for now, we'll just animate the body's rotation as the character walks, and worry about the actual movement later.

Move the time slider to frame 30, and now move the left leg forward (again starting from the left hip joint and moving down as is the method of FK) so that it sits in a footfall position as if it has barely touched the ground. Move the right leg (starting from the right hip joint) back into position as if it is about to leave the ground. Remember on both legs to not neglect the ankles and the rotation that takes place there. Continue to rotate body parts with Ribs 2, Ribs 1, Shoulders, and both arms, so that the Left Shoulder is now behind the body with the Right Shoulder and arm in front to counterbalance the Left Leg. Again, select the Hips Object and record a Rotation keyframe (Figure 12.6 c).

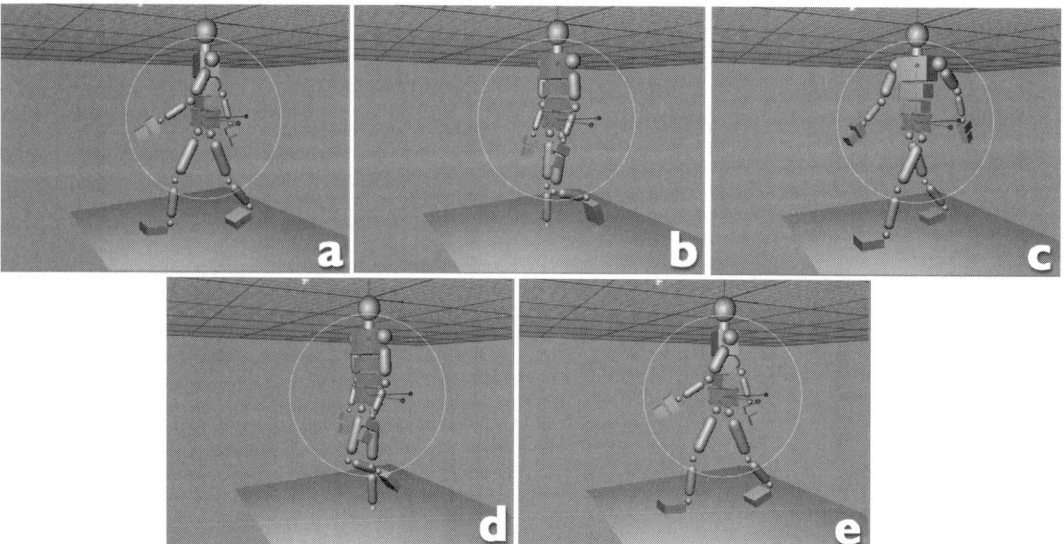

FIGURE 12.6 *(a) Starting right foot forward position. (b) Frame 15 is where the left foot has begun its move forward and the body has rotated to accommodate this new shift. (c) The left footfall keyframe at frame 30. (d) Right foot raised at frame 45. (e) Frame 60 is just a copy of frame 0.*

CHAPTER 12 ADVANCED ANIMATION AND CHARACTER ANIMATION

At frame 45, position all objects just opposite of frame 15; the Left Leg has moved below the body, as it is now the sole supporter of the weight, and the Right Leg has moved up in anticipation of its own footfall. The Shoulders and Ribs are square and the arms are at the side. Select the Hips Object and record a Rotation keyframe (Figure 12.6 d).

Frame 60 is back where we started. So, a quick solution would be to marquee around all the Rotation keyframes within the Timeline and CTRL/COMMAND-click-drag them to frame 60, thus completing the loop (Figure 12.6 e).

Do a quick rendering using As Editor in the General Rendering Settings to see what you've got. This isn't a bad start, but there are a few problems. The first is that even though the legs seem to be acting as though they are receiving weight, there is no up and down shift of weight. Further, the feet go through the floor.

To fix this, we'll record some Position keyframes for the Hips Object. Since all the rest of the objects are children of the Hips Object, we don't need to record Position keyframes all the way down the hierarchy, as when the Hips Object moves up and down, the rest of the body will go with it. So, activate the Position track button and deactivate the Hierarchy On/Off button in the Time Manager (Figure 12.7 a).

Again, for general illustration purposes, we'll record Position keyframes at our defined points of frames 0, 15, 30, 45 and 60. At frame 0, record a Position keyframe, as this is where we want to start (Frame 12.7 b). At frame 15, move the Hips Object (and thus the entire body) up so that the right foot is actually sitting atop the floor and record a keyframe (Figure 12.7 c). Simply copy the keyframe set at frame 0 to frame 30 in the Timeline so that the body is again sitting on the floor with the legs bent when they are both on the ground (Figure 12.7 d). Frame 45 should be approximately the same position vertically as frame 15, but you may want to manually position the Hips Object — just in case there is a bit of a difference, and record a keyframe (Figure 12.7 e). Since frame 60 is a copy of frame 0 in every other way, simply copy the keyframe from frame 0 to frame 60 with a CTRL/COMMAND-click-drag in the Timeline (Figure 12.7 f).

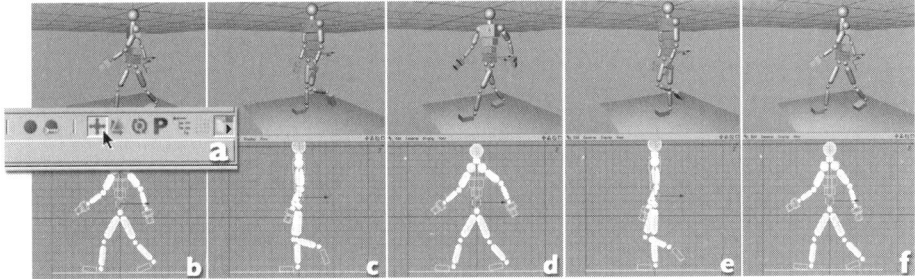

FIGURE 12.7 *(a) Time Manager settings in preparation of moving the body up and down to show weight. (b,c,d,e,f) Positioning the body so that the feet are on the floor during the up and down movement of the walk cycle.*

ON THE CD

Now there are still some problems. You may notice that around frames 20 and 50, the feet pass through the floor. To fix this, you'll just need to add a couple of Rotation keyframes in that area and rotate the ankle up a bit more to keep them from dragging through the floor. The results should appear something like the movie WalkingFKSegmented.mov on the CD. Also included on the CD is the file AnimWalkingSegdCharacter.c4d which is the animated version of the c4d file.

This, of course, is a fairly gross simplification of a walk cycle. There should still be vertical shifting in the shoulders and hips as weight is absorbed at each footfall. Further, there should be some secondary movement in the hands as they swing along their path. But this discussion is better left for another volume. Suffice it to say, this walk cycle is an illustration of FK techniques, not believable physics.

INVERSE KINEMATICS

IK works just the opposite of FK, in that instead of dealing with each object and moving down a hierarchy, you simply move (with the Move Active Element tool) the child-most object and the objects that are the parents to it rotate into place. There are actually several incarnations of the IK technique; or rather several different tools related to the idea of IK animation.

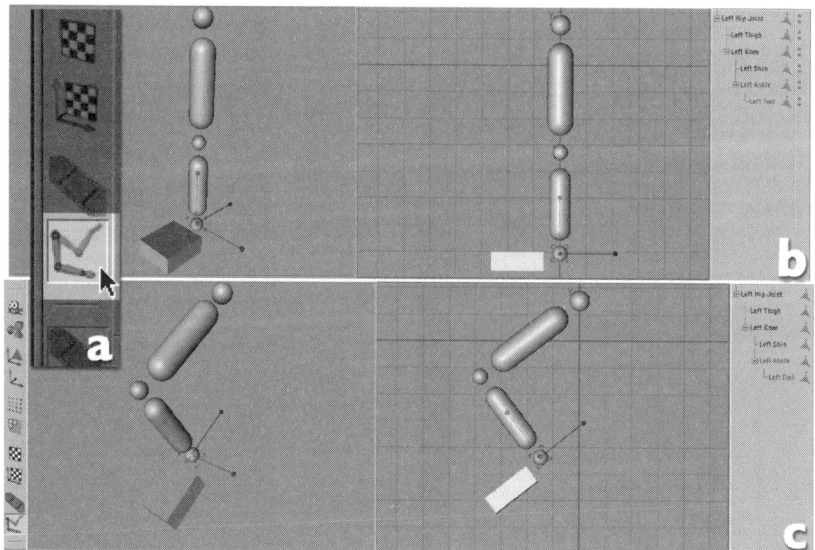

FIGURE 12.8 *(a) The Inverse Kinematics tool. (b and c) Using the Inverse Kinematics tool allows you to grab a child and move it to a position that the parent objects rotate to accommodate.*

CHAPTER 12 ADVANCED ANIMATION AND CHARACTER ANIMATION

The Use Inverse Kinematics tool (Figure 12.8 a) allows you to pose a group of objects, using the ideas behind IK. Figure 12.8 (b) shows just one leg of our segmented character. Using the Inverse Kinematics tool, the Left Ankle or Left Foot objects can be grabbed and as you click-drag either of these objects around, the objects above these in the hierarchy rotate to match (Figure 12.8 c).

The problem with just using this tool is that it isn't necessarily a very intuitive animation tool. To animate with this tool, you must record a Rotation keyframe for the entire IK chain (or objects involved in the IK function) by recording a Rotation keyframe to the parent-most object with Hierarchy On. Then move the time slider, use the Inverse Kinematics tool to repose the IK chain, (which feels very much like you are changing the position of the child object), but then select the parent-most object and record another Rotation keyframe to lock in the new rotation of each of the objects. Then, if you choose to edit this pose, you need to again record a Rotation keyframe over the old collection.

Luckily, there are some other methods that help make this work a little better. However, you need to spend a bit more time before hand "rigging" your model to use these IK tools.

IK EXPRESSIONS

C4D allows for the creation of expressions that allow you to create special relationships between objects. The Target Camera that we talked of earlier is actually a camera with a Target Expression that tells the camera to stay pointed at the Target Object. A Sun Object is actually a light with a Sun Expression applied. You can even create your own expressions through C4D's C.O.F.F.E.E. (see chapters 16). One of the most powerful expressions is the IK Expression.

In simplest terms, IK expressions are best applied to the child-most object in an IK chain. For a simple example, let's use the leg we've been posing above (minus the foot for now). To apply an IK expression, right-click (COMMAND-click on a Mac) an object and select New Expression>IK Expression from the resultant pop up menu (Figure 12.9 a). An input field will appear, asking what object you wish to use for a target; for now leave this blank and click OK. A new tag will appear next to the object indicating this new expression (Figure 12.9 b).

Note that this new IK expression doesn't have any power quite yet. For an IK expression to take hold, you must define a target object that you want the IK chain to point to. To continue with the simple illustration of the leg, we'll create a Null Object (Objects>Null Object). This Null Object has no geometry so it will never render, but C4D can recognize it as a target for an IK chain. Since it is to be the target, it's been renamed to "Left Leg Target". The position of this IK target is fairly important. IK chains will attempt to reach or point to their target. If the target is within the reach of the IK chain, the chain will bend to accommodate, but if it is beyond reach, the IK chain will extend and point at the

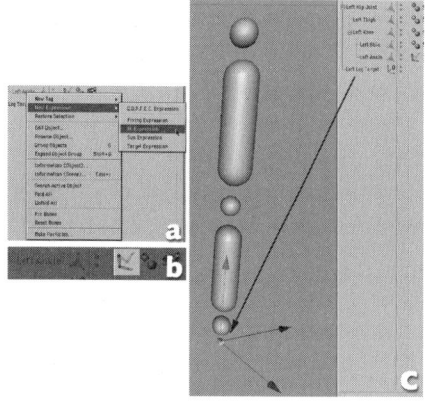

FIGURE 12.9 *(a and b) Applying a new IK expression and the resultant new tag. (c) Left Leg Target (a renamed Null Object) is positioned at the end of an IK chain.*

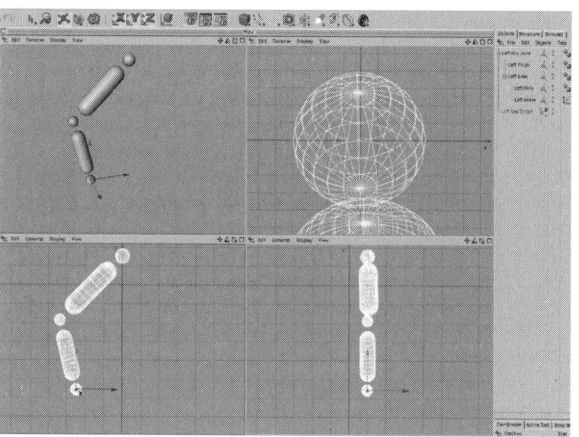

FIGURE 12.10 *With IK expressions, animation becomes a matter of adding Position keyframes for the IK target and all the rotation of the IK chain is automatically calculated.*

target. Figure 12.9 (c) shows the Left Leg Target set just beyond the reach of the leg IK chain; we'll look more at the position of IK targets a little later. Make sure to leave the IK target out of the leg hierarchy. We need the IK target to be independent.

Now all that needs to happen is to tell the IK chain to point at this target. Double-click the IK expression tag within the Object Manager. The input field that opens allows you to type the name of the IK target, which in this case would be "Left Leg Target." Notice that as you begin typing, C4D anticipates and looks for potential targets. Click OK as soon as C4D understands what the target is to be.

Now with this expression activated, using the Move Active Element tool, you can select the Left Leg Target and move it, and the IK chain of the leg will bend accordingly. Now, the beauty of this method is that all you need to do is record Position keyframes for the target, and the leg will rotate automatically with no added keyframes on the IK chain (Figure 12.10).

Since you are animating a target which has absolute position within 3D space, you can establish definite footfall locations. Rather than defining the rotation of the legs as we do in FK, you can define where the feet are supposed to fall, and how the feet are to travel and let C4D do all the rotating for you. We'll look more at this technique a little later in this chapter.

Additionally, you can work opposite of moving the IK target. With an IK expression established, you can move the IK chain and it will stay pointed at the IK target. So a dance where the character's feet stay planted is a simple matter of recording keyframes for the body and the feet stay planted as the knees bend.

CHAPTER 12   ADVANCED ANIMATION AND CHARACTER ANIMATION

Using FK, this would be a nightmare, as you would have to record Rotation keyframes for all the joints, plus Position keyframes for the body and take special care to make sure that the ends of the joints (namely the feet) end up in the same place.

MULTIPLE TARGET IK (MTIK)

Part of the real power behind this IK expression idea is that you aren't limited to only one target. With only one target, it becomes awkward to have the entire leg (including the right angle of the foot-ankle joint) point to one position. Usually, you want the thigh, knee, and shin part of a leg to point down at one target, but the foot to point forward at another. A powerful technique is to use more than one IK target. In the example shown in Figure 12.11, a new Null Object has been created and named "Left Foot Target." This new target will be used to define where the foot should point, so a new IK expression has been added to the Left Foot Object defining Left Foot Target as its IK target.

MTIK allows you to define over an animation period effective rotation of the foot. When we walk, the ankle hits the ground before the toe does, and leaves the ground before the toe as the foot leaves the ground. If the two targets are grouped, this group can be rotated to define exactly the rotation of the foot (Figure 12.12).

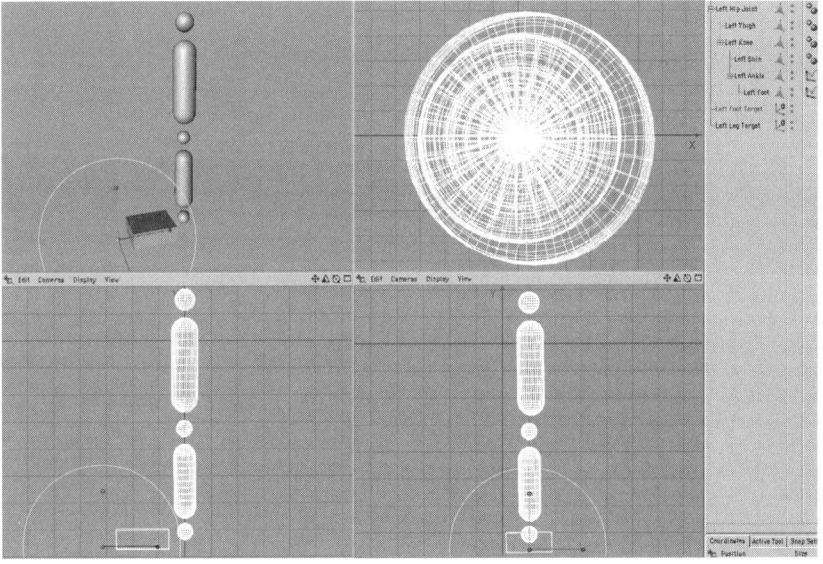

FIGURE 12.11   *Multiple Target IK allows for one target to define where the leg is to point, and another to define the direction of the foot.*

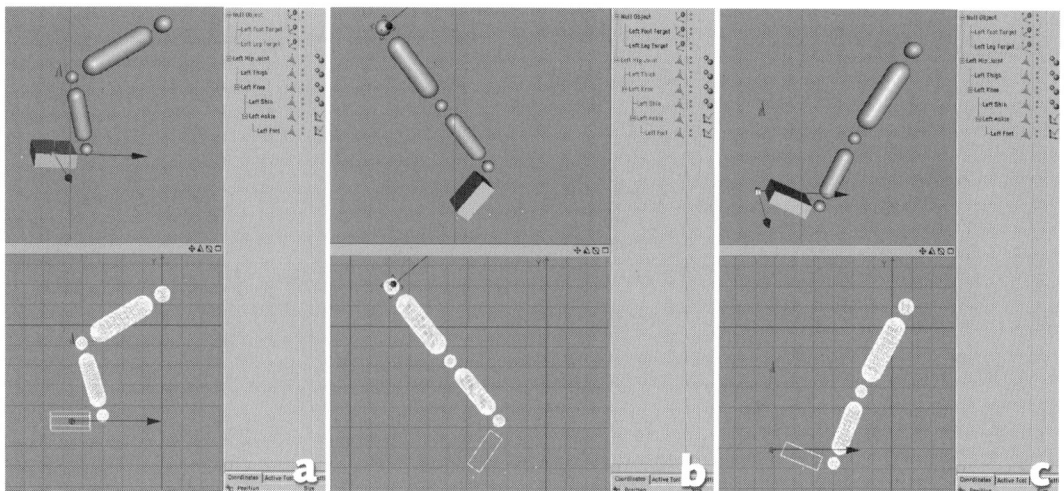

FIGURE 12.12 *With two targets defining the leg and foot, you can move the group of targets to affect the entire leg, or rotate the group to shift the angle of the ankle. Further, you can move each target independently to leave the toe on the ground or have the ankle hit the ground first.*

Some people even like to define a third target at the knee. Turns out that this is an excellent idea, in that you want to often be able to control the direction of your knees separately from the position of the feet. However, if your character is walking and not involved in very dynamic crouching movements, you may not need this extra control; it may just be in the way and require more tweaking than you want. Your mileage may vary, and the technique you find best will largely depend on the kind of movement you are attempting and the layout of your character. The general rule is that there are no rules, and that your IK rig may change for each character, as each character's needs will be unique.

IK TAGS

If you've been playing along with the techniques thus far, you may have noticed the painful looking result shown in Figure 12.13 (a) as you've moved your targets around. This happens because C4D simply knows it's to rotate the IK chain to meet the IK target; it does this the best it can with the information provided. By default C4D doesn't know that a knee joint oughtn't bend this way. However, we can tell C4D to recognize joints and recognize how these joints may bend.

To do this we need to add IK tags to objects. IK tags define a range of motion for an object or group of objects. But before you begin defining ranges, there are some things to prepare first. When you find ranges of motion, it's nice to have the objects set at 0°. To do this, first deactivate the IK expressions by turning off Expressions in the left collection of tools (Figure 12.13 b). This allows you the freedom to rotate objects around in very exploratory ways.

With expressions deactivated, objects "relax" into their neutral pose. For the leg we've been using to demonstrate the ideas of IK, this leaves the leg hanging straight down. By activating the Object Axis tool, we can zero-out (enter 0 in the H, P, and B input fields of the Coordinates Manager) for each joint. This gives us an easily defined neutral point of reference. For the leg we've been using, the Left Hip Joint, Left Knee, and Left Ankle should all receive this sort of treatment. Although this isn't absolutely necessary, it just allows for a clean and easy way to remember settings.

Now that all the joints are neutrally set, we can find the amount of movement we wish to allow each of these joints. You may want a piece of paper to jot down the values you discover. You can start wherever you like, but for illustration purposes, we'll start at the Left Hip Joint and move down. With the Left Hip Joint selected, use the Rotate Active Element tool and rotate the joint back into a position at the edge of the rotation range for a leg. This is largely subjective, even though there are physiological limits of a leg; however, with character animation there needs to be quite a range. Figure 12.14 (a) shows the leg rotated backwards about 45° in the P (Pitch) direction, which looks about right. You can see this value in the Coordinates Manager. Rotate the leg back so that you find a comfortable forward rotation, which in this case is –45° (Figure 12.14 b). This gives you the negative and positive ranges in the Pitch. Next, find the amount of rotation you want to allow the leg to rotate out. Figure 12.14 (c) shows a

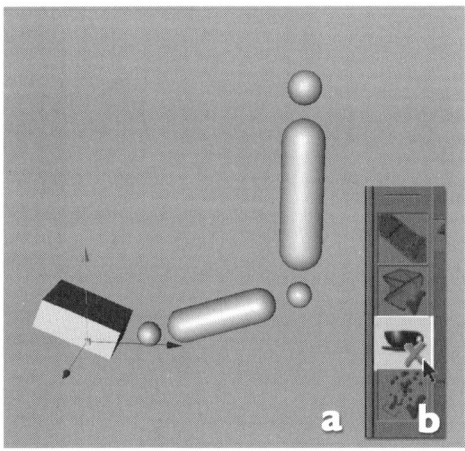

FIGURE 12.13 *(a) Painful result of rotating legs in the wrong directions. (b) Turning Expressions off allows you to explore range of motion when you create IK tags.*

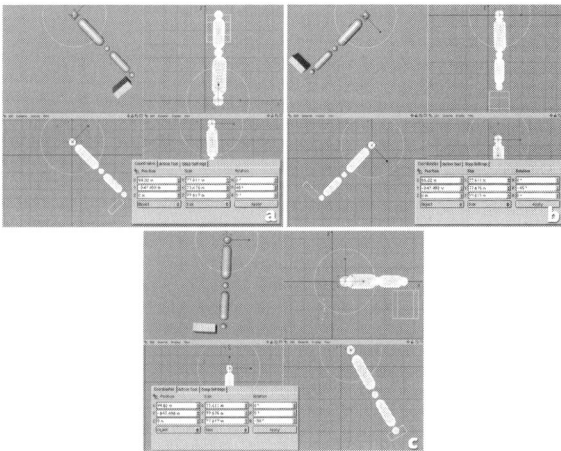

FIGURE 12.14 *Tentative range of motion for the Left Hip Joint.*

rotation of about –30° in B (Bank). Although not entirely accurate, we'll keep the leg from rotating inward to avoid worrying about the legs knocking together. So the range of the B would be from –30 to 0. To continue with our simplistic setup, we'll make the leg so that it cannot twist in its joint, so the H settings range should remain 0 to 0.

So how do we make use of this information? First, we need to add an IK tag to the Left Hip Joint telling C4D that we want to limit its movement within IK situations. To do this, right-click the Left Hip Joint Object within the Object Manager and choose New Tag>IK Tag from the resultant pop-up menu (Figure 12.15 a). Immediately, you'll be presented with a dialog box that allows you to activate the restraints (by clicking the boxes next to each H, P, and B settings) and enter the restraint angles you want to use for that object (Figure 12.15 b). Click OK when you've entered the values you've jotted down, and notice the new IK tag that appears next to the Left Hip Joint Object in the Object Manager.

Next we'll move down to the Left Knee, which has very limited movement. Only along the P value should the knee be allowed to rotate back; we'll generalize and allow 90° movement (thus, the range is 0 to 90). The other directions (H and B) will remain at 0. Again, add an IK tag — this time to the Left Knee — and activate restraints in all directions, making sure to zero-out all ranges but P, setting the values there from 0 to 90.

Continue with this method for the Left Ankle Object. Again, as a generalization, we'll leave the H and B values so that the ankle won't rotate at all, but allow –45° to 30° for the P setting (Figure 12.16). Enter these values in the Left Ankle IK tag, and you're set to go.

Now, reactivate Expressions in the left command palette, and when you move the IK targets around, no matter how you move them, the leg doesn't bend in any way it oughtn't.

FIGURE 12.15 *(a) Creating an IK tag. (b) The Inverse Kinematics tag and the settings needed for the Left Hip Joint.*

CHAPTER 12 ADVANCED ANIMATION AND CHARACTER ANIMATION

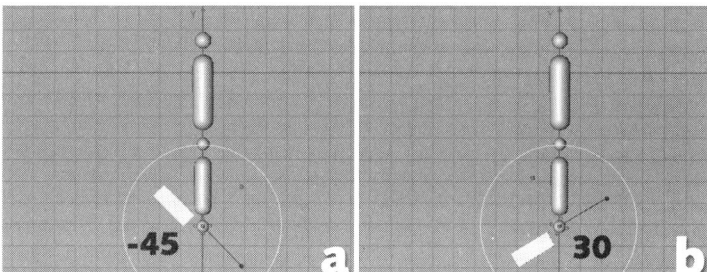

FIGURE 12.16 *Rotating range for the ankle joint.*

Repeat this process for the right leg, and your legs are prepared for IK animation, using IK targets and IK expressions.

In theory, an IK rig could be set up for the body and the arms. However, in most cases, you'll probably find that since the arms are rarely fixed to a surface, that FK works great for the upper body. On the other hand, if you're animating a gymnast, or the character is crawling, then establishing IK tags and IK expressions would be a good idea.

IK WALKS

Producing a walk in IK has some drawbacks. First, a walk cycle really isn't feasible, as you'll be establishing each footfall using the IK targets; but this does provide extra power in the ability to have your character walk over almost anything, from a bumpy terrain, to stepping over objects, to climbing stairs. Assuming that the IK setup is ready for your legs, a simple walk would proceed as follows:

ON THE CD

IKSegCharWalk.c4d is a file on the CD that includes the IK'd character doing a simple walk, and climbing stairs. To start with the walk, activate the Position track in the Time Manager; we'll be establishing Position keyframes for the Right and Left Leg Target as well as the Hips Object. The idea here is that we'll animate a simple version of the feet moving along, and animate the Hips (and thus the rest of the body) moving along with the feet.

INTERPOLATION ISSUES

Before we begin recording keyframes, though, it's important to talk about interpolation for a minute. Interpolation is the process of "filling in" information. In the case of animation, Soft Interpolation means that the frames that C4D places between the keyframes overshoot the keyframe a bit to allow for smooth movement before and after the keyframe. Most character animation is done in smooth arcs, so this would seem like an ideal method of filling in frames between keyframes. But, there are some problems.

For much of this animation, one leg's target or the other are going to remain in place or planted, while the other moves or takes a step. With the default Soft Interpolation, two keyframes placed over a period of time, but at the same position, produce a little loop in space (Figure 12.17). The result of this little loop is that the supposed planted foot (via the target) would be moving around when it should be staying still.

There are, however, other ways to define how C4D is going to fill the frames in between the keyframes you are to define. At the far right corner of the Time Manager is a button that when it is pressed, it allows you to define (among other things) the kind of interpolation you are going to use (Figure 12.18). Hard Interpolation creates linear travel between keyframes, while Soft Interpolation creates overshot rounded paths. But Medium Interpolation is just right. When there is distance between keyframes, Medium Interpolation creates soft, gentle paths; however, when there is no distance (only time) between keyframes, Medium Interpolation keeps the frames placed in the interim in place. This makes Medium Interpolation the perfect selection when you animate the legs through the leg targets.

Once you have Medium Interpolation selected, you can move on to recording Position keyframes for the leg targets with confidence.

Record a keyframe (Position) for the Right Leg Target; this tells the Right Legs Target that this is where its movement is to start. The process of the IK walk will entail keyframes for the leg targets at footfall, top of step, and footfall again. For

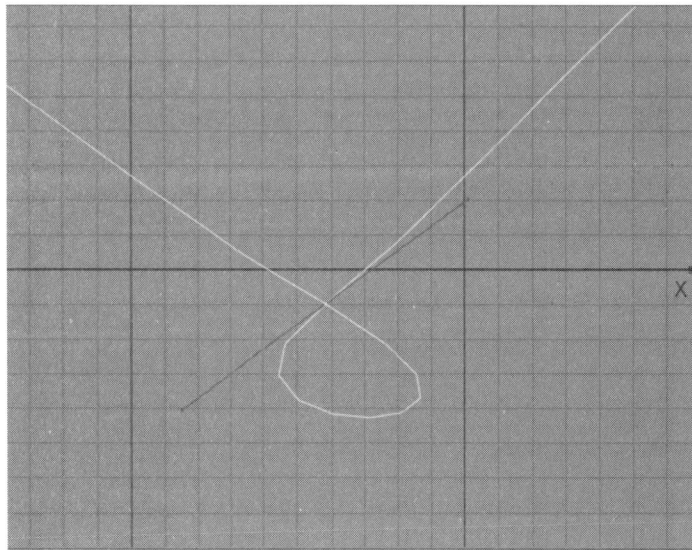

FIGURE 12.17 *Looped result of Soft Interpolation when two keyframes are placed in the same place over a period of time.*

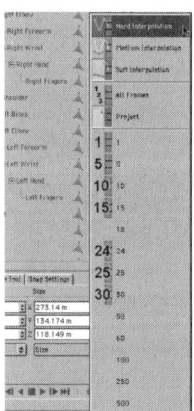

FIGURE 12.18 *You can change the Interpolation setting before recording keyframes within the Time Manager. Medium Interpolation is the setting you'll want to use for IK walking.*

CHAPTER 12   ADVANCED ANIMATION AND CHARACTER ANIMATION   357

a rough approximation, let's set each keyframe at 15 frames from the last. So move the time slider to frame 15 and move the Right Leg Target a bit forward and up (Figure 12.19 a); record a keyframe. While you are still at frame 15, select the Hips object and move the Hips forward a little bit so that the weight is centered over the midway of the two feet (Figure 12.19 b); record a keyframe. Now move the time slider to frame 30 and move the Right Leg Target to the floor again (Figure 12.19 c); record a keyframe. Select and move the Hips Object again so that it is midway between the two hips and down a bit as the weight of the body is distributed over a greater distance (Figure 12.19 d); record a keyframe.

Now while you are still at frame 30, select the Left Leg Target and record a keyframe. This tells the Left Leg Target that this is where its motion is to begin. Move the time slider to frame 45 and move the Left Leg Target to its top of step and record a keyframe (Figure 12.20 a). Move the Hips forward and upward to center the weight, and record another keyframe (Figure 12.20 b). Move the time slider to frame 60 and place the Left Leg Target on the floor and record a keyframe (Figure 12.20 c) and again record a keyframe with the Hips moved into position (Figure 12.20 d). Lastly, while you are still at frame 60, select the Right Leg Target and record a keyframe. This tells the Right Leg Target that since its last keyframe is at frame 30, it's not to move.

Repeat the process for the Right Leg Target by again placing a keyframe at the top of step (frame 75) and footfall (frame 90) while you continue to move the Hips along. Again, don't forget to place another keyframe at frame 90 for the Left Leg Target to let it know that it's supposed to have stayed put since the last keyframe.

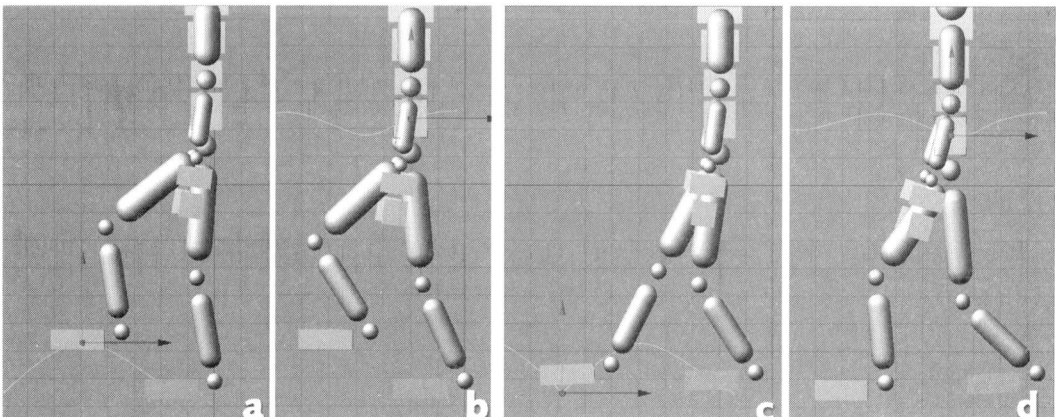

FIGURE 12.19   *(a and b) Record a keyframe of the Right Leg Target at its top of step, and record a keyframe for the Hips moving along to match. (c and d) Record a keyframe at frame 30 for the Right Leg Target footfall, and another keyframe for the Hips moving forward and down.*

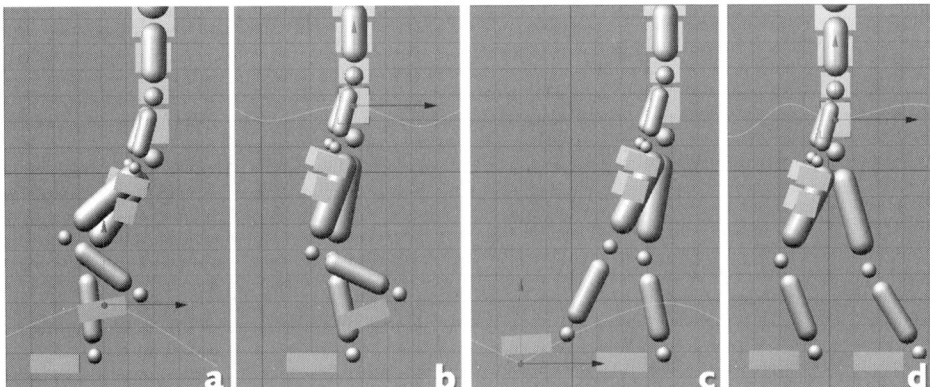

FIGURE 12.20 *(a and b) Begin animating the Left Leg Target by adding a keyframe at the top of step and another keyframe for the Hips at frame 45. (c and d) Continue the Left Leg Target's journey by recording a keyframe at frame 60 with the Left Leg Target on the ground, and another keyframe for the Hips to match the forward movement.*

The stairs are no big problem either when you use this method. Simply continue defining top of step and footfall keyframes for each foot as it moves up the stairs, making sure to keep one leg still while the other leg target moves. The placement of your top of step keyframe may take some adjusting to make sure that the feet don't travel through the steps (Figure 12.21).

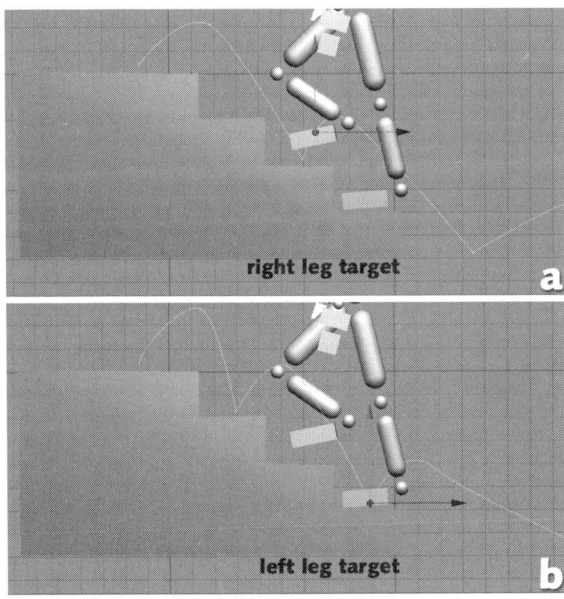

FIGURE 12.21 *Stairs are easily mounted using IK targets. Just make sure to over-emphasize the travel path so that the feet clear each step.*

After you have the foot placement correct and the motion of the lower body done, go back and insert Rotation keyframes (pose using FK) for the upper body — including the Ribs, Shoulders and Arms. Even with the upper body animated, upon rendering you'll find that this is still obviously a very generalized version of a walk. The feet should rotate more in anticipation of each step, the hips and shoulders should rotate vertically as the hips absorb the weight of the body, and a host of other touches are needed to make this walk clip truly believable. But, as an IK illustration, this overview is fairly complete. The fine-tuning is up to you.

BONES

FK and IK are great techniques, and are especially well illustrated in the segmented character shown above. However, most characters aren't actually designed as simple segmented primitives. As we've discussed earlier in the book, the most impressive forms are single mesh; that is, one solid (or hollow actually) collection of polygons.

Figure 12.22 (a) shows a single mesh character designed and built by Desiree Maher. Everything from the antennae to the tips of the toes are one collection of polygons. This model is nice, but is still lifeless until we can find ways to bring it to life. Within the top command palette are the Deformation tools. We've

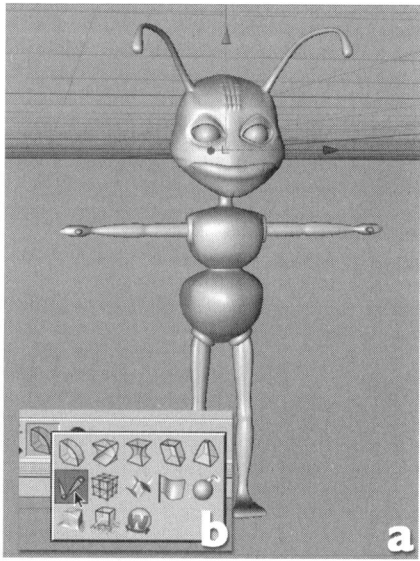

FIGURE 12.22 *(a) Single meshed character by Desiree Maher (b) Creating a Bone deformer.*

already looked at deformers like the Bend, Twist, and Taper. However, there is one deformer that is particularly powerful in this situation – the Bone (Figure 12.22 b).

Bones allow us to take a mesh of polygons and bend them. Imagine these virtual bones much like the bones in our own body. When the bone moves, the skin around the bones moves as well. The polygons of a mesh become the skin, as the bone deformers become the bones. For a quick illustration of the power of bones, see Figure 12.23 (a). This is a simple cube that has been extruded to form a stylized arm. Notice that the cube has been placed within a HyperNURBS object, and thus the low poly-count cube becomes a more organic, subdivided form. When a bone is created either through the button in the top command palette or by going to Objects>Deformation>Bone, a green object will appear in the scene (Figure 12.23 b, a). This bone contains several important parts. The first of course, is the bone's axis. This axis is where the bone rotates around, which can be rotated with the Rotate Active Element tool. The orange dot at the end of the bone serves a couple of functions. First, it defines where the bone ends. Second, you can click-drag this dot to lengthen the bone (Figure 12.23 c). This orange dot also becomes the "spawning" site for new bones which can be spawned by CTRL/COMMAND-click-dragging this orange dot (Figure 12.24 a). When you CTRL/COMMAND-click-drag this dot, the new bone grows out of the end of the original. Not only this, but the new bone is automatically placed as a child within the hierarchy shown in the Object Manager (Figure 12.23 c). You

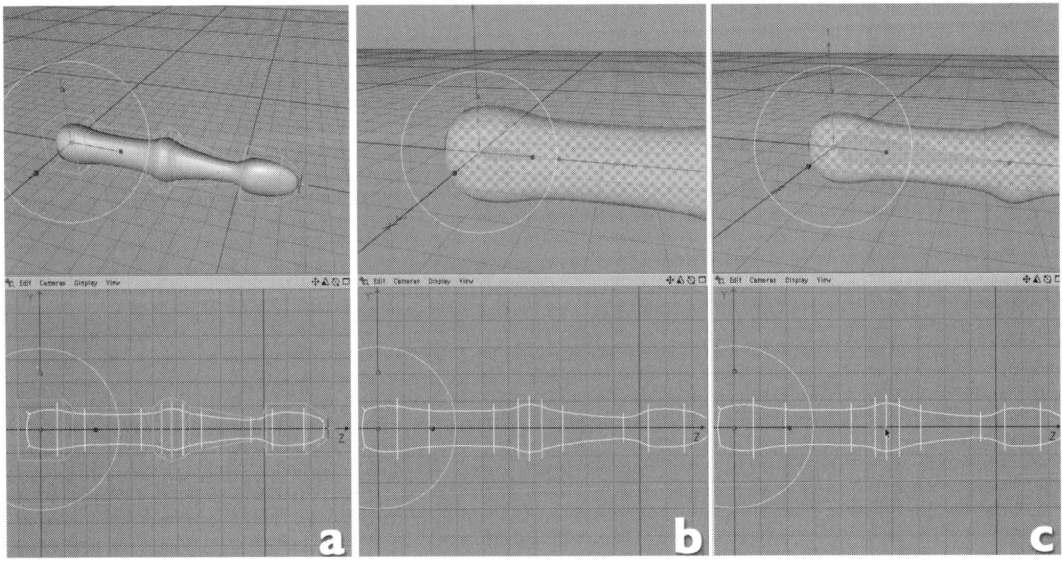

FIGURE 12.23 *(a) Subdivided arm. (b and c) Created bone with orange dot available for lengthening.*

can continue to "grow" bones out of old ones until you have the hierarchy and bone chain that you want (Figure 12.24 c).

Traditionally, it's best to create your bone structure within the mesh you want the bones to affect. However, just because they are placed within the same space doesn't mean these bones know to affect these polygons. In fact, if you were to rotate any of your bones as they sit now, the bone would move but the mesh would not be deformed. The hierarchical order in which bones exist is vital to letting the bones know what to exert influence on. The simplest way to do this is to place the bone chain as a child of the object they are to affect. However, this can get complicated as meshes become more complex. A more comprehensive method is to group the bones and the poly mesh into one new object (Figure 12.25 a). This sort of organization allows the bones to know that they are supposed to exert influence on any object or polygon that is also a child of the Null Object.

Now, even though the bones are within the Null Object, they must be activated and fixed to actually take effect. Activating a bone allows it to begin influencing polygons around it. You can activate a bone by clicking on the red X next to the bone, thus changing it to a green check. Fixing a bone tells the bone where its default position is to be. By right-clicking the Null Object and selecting Fix Bones from the pop-up menu, you can fix and activate the bones in one fell swoop. You will know that the bones have been activated — the red X that was previously beside the bones will change to a green check. Now, if you rotate a bone using the Rotate Active Element tool, it will deform the mesh with it (Figure 12.25 b).

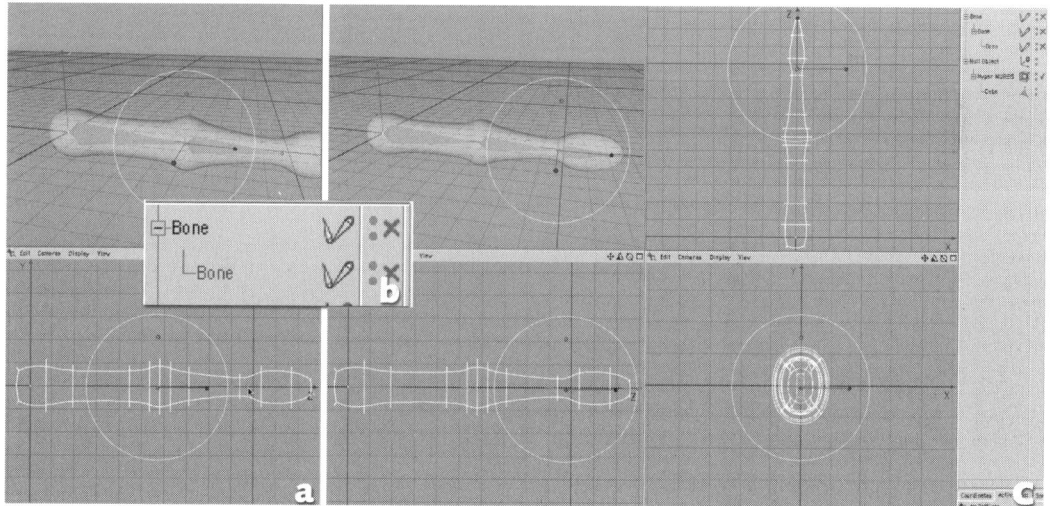

FIGURE 12.24 *(a) CTRL/COMMAND-click-dragging the orange dot at the end of a bone creates a new bone that is a child of the first. (b and c) Complete bone chain.*

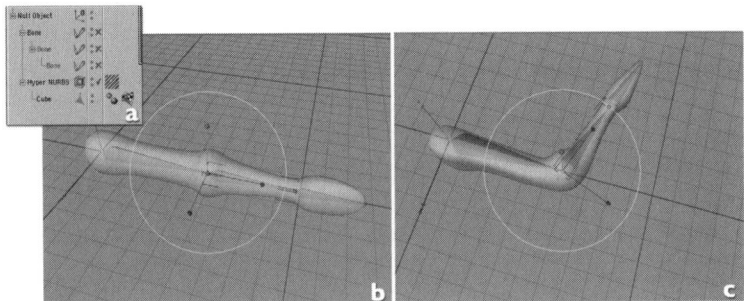

FIGURE 12.25 *(a) Organizing bones in the hierarchy is important. If you are going to have a large, complex mesh, it's best to group the bone and mesh together on the same level of the hierarchy. (b) Once the bones are activated, you can rotate a bone and the mesh will deform with it.*

But this isn't the end of the functionality of the bones. When you double-click the orange bone icon in the Object Manager, a dialog box will open, allowing you to adjust the settings of the bone (Figure 12.26 a). The Length input field obviously allows you to change the size of the bone. The Function field is an important area. There is a difference in how a limp noodle bends and how our elbow bends. 1/r^2 creates a very gentle bend (Figure 12.26 b). A higher value 1/r^8 or 1/r^10 creates a much crisper bend (Figure 12.26 b). Note that whatever Function setting you select for the top bone of a bone chain will be carried down to the children bones.

Think of polygons like pieces of metal. Think of bones as magnets. When bones are activated, their magnetism is turned on and they reach out for all metal objects (polygons) that are in the same hierarchy as they are. In simplest form (as in just the one arm), this works fine. However, what happens if the model is more complex? Let's say we have a creature with more than one arm (Figure 12.27 a). With these arms in the same Null Object group, the polygons of the added arms are also, by default, under the influence of the only set of bones present in Figure 12.27. Thus, when we rotate the bones inside the first arm, the other two arms show the effect (Figure 12.27 b).

When you activate the Limit Radius option within the Bone dialog box, you are beginning to define how strong these bone/magnets really are. When you activate the Limit Radius option, the Min. Radius and Max. Radius input fields become active. When these contain non-zero values, "capsules" will appear in the Editor showing where the influence of the bone starts, where it is at its strongest (inside the Min. Radius Capsule), and where the influence ends entirely (the Max. Radius Capsule) (Figure 12.28 a). These capsules can be changed within the Editor by click-dragging the orange control handles. When all the bones have limited radii, then when a bone is rotated, it will only affect

CHAPTER 12 ADVANCED ANIMATION AND CHARACTER ANIMATION

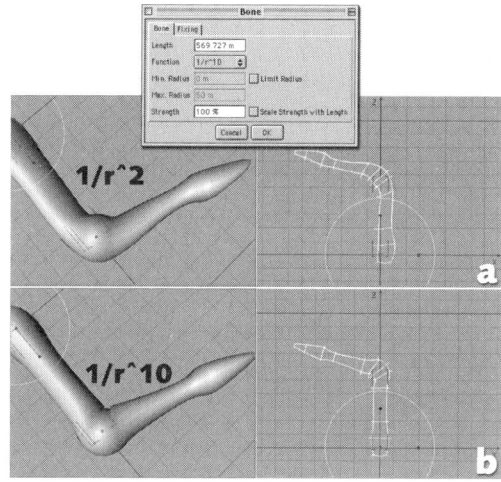

FIGURE 12.26 *(a) bone dialog box. (b) The Function setting is important in defining the style of the bend.*

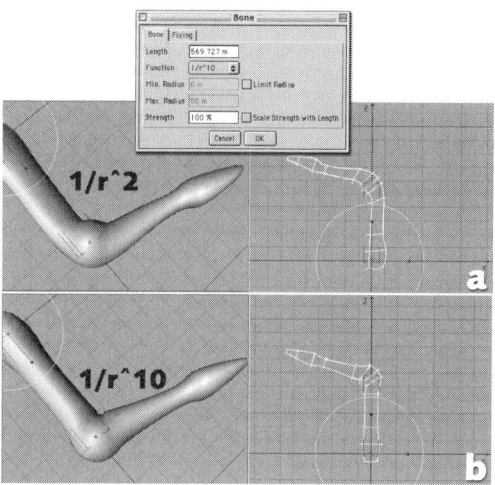

FIGURE 12.27 *By default, activated bones have influence over all polygons in a hierarchy.*

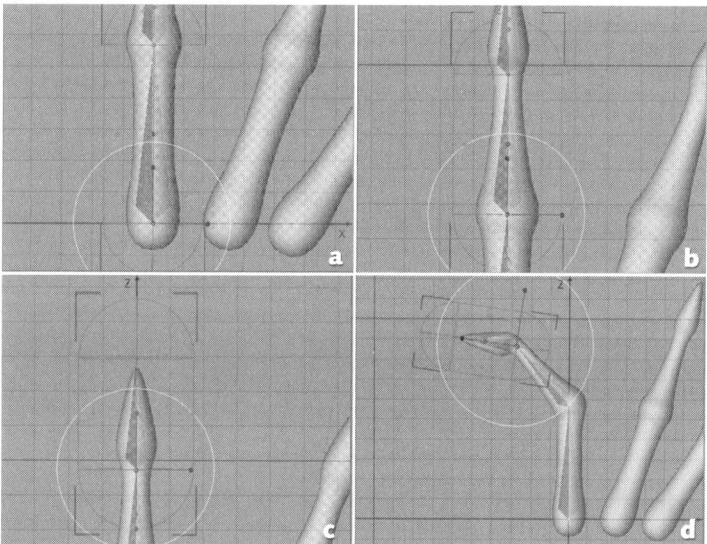

FIGURE 12.28 *Using the Limit Radius options allows you to roughly define the influence of a bone.*

the polygons that exist within its respected capsules. The influence will gradually decrease from the Min. Radius Capsule to the Max. Radius Capsule.

This is a very simple method of limiting the effect of a bone. Unfortunately, it isn't always the best method. For instance, if you had other areas of the model that were very close to the influenced areas, it would be difficult to get the capsules of influence large enough to affect the desired polys, but small enough to not drag other unwanted polys with it (Figure 12.29 a).

RESTRICTION TAGS

Luckily, new to version 6 in C4D are some much more powerful methods of restricting the influence of bones. Restriction tags are tags added to Bones that tell the bone exactly what collection of polygons or points they can influence. To add a Restriction tag, right-click (COMMAND-click) on a bone within the Object Manager and select New Tag>Restriction Tag. A dialog box will appear, asking you to define the Selection Set or Vertex Map set that you wish to restrict this bone to. For now, simply leave everything blank and click OK (Figure 12.29 b). You'll notice a new tag does indeed appear next to the bone which at any time can be double clicked giving you the dialog box just closed (Figure 12.29 c).

So what are these Selection Sets and Vertex Maps?

SELECTION SETS

Selection sets are data sets of either collections of polygons or points within a single mesh object. To create a selection set for an object, first select the object in the Object Manager. Then, in either Polygon Mode or Points Mode, select a group of polygons (or points) by using the Live Selection tool or by SHIFT-clicking.

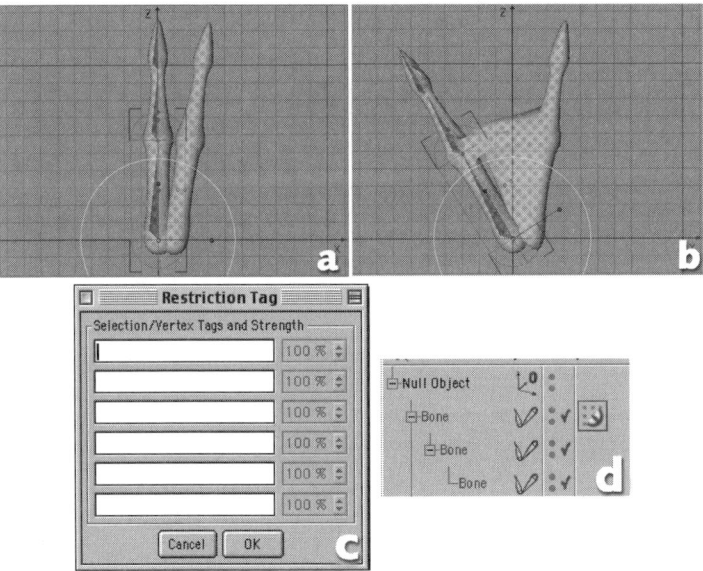

FIGURE 12.29 *(a) Some problems with the Min. and Max. Radius method occur when you deal with collections of polys that are close together. (b and c) Creating a Restriction tag allows you to define what Selection set or Vertex set to restrict the selection to.*

For instance, if we wanted to create a Selection set for the bicep of the HyperNURBS object that is our arm, we would select all the polygons of the Cube that makes the arm (Figure 12.30 a). Then, choose Selection>Set Selection. (Figure 12.30 b). Immediately, a new tag will appear next to the Cube object within the Object Manager (Figure 12.30 c). When you double-click this tag, you can name the Selection set (in this case "Bicep"), and there is a host of other options, such as allowing you to hide certain parts of the mesh you are dealing with (Figure 12.30 d).

In the case of this arm, as there are three bones, it would make sense to create Selection sets. When you make another Selection set, you must take special care of a few issues. To create the Forearm Selection set, we'd first select the polygons (Figure 12.31 a). But before you set this Selection set, you must make sure that the Bicep Selection set in the Object Manager is *not* selected. Do this by clicking on any of the other tags, or even by clicking on another object and coming back to the object that you are defining a Selection set for. The reason for this, is that if the Bicep Selection set is highlighted in the Object Manager when you choose Selection>Set Selection, the existing Bicep Selection set will be overwritten with this new collection of polygons. To create a new selection set, there must be no Selection set highlighted in the Object Manager when Selection>Set Selection is chosen.

Note that after you have named a Selection set, when you move your mouse over the Selection set in the Object Manager, the name of the Selection set will appear in the bottom left hand corner of the general interface, right above the Time Manager. Note also, that in the preceding steps we created polygon-based Selection sets, but we could have also created points-based Selection sets which would create a tag similar to Figure 12.31 (b).

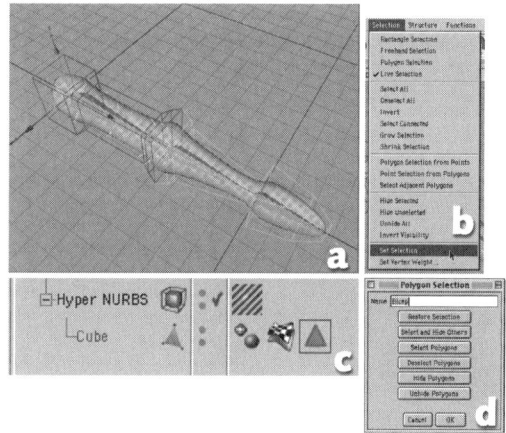

FIGURE *Creating and naming a Selection set.*

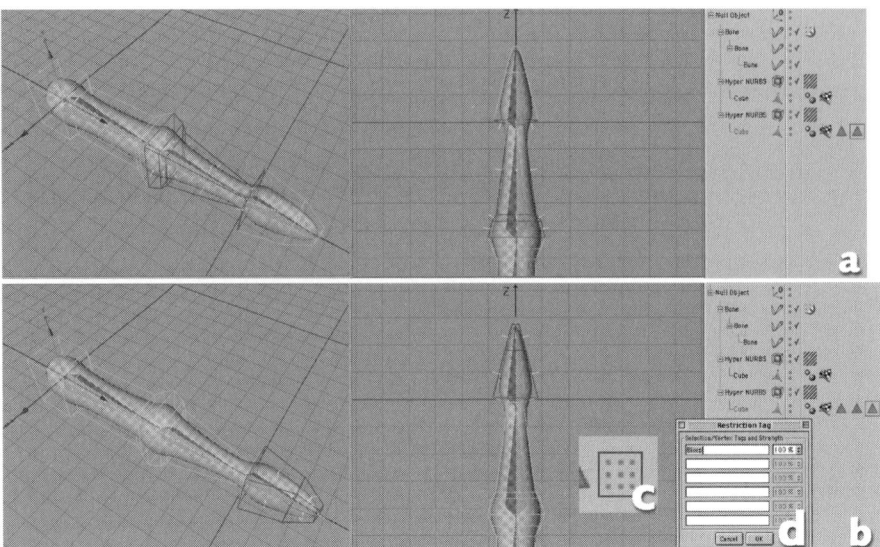

FIGURE 12.31 *(a) Two new Selection sets created for the arm — one for the Forearm and one for the hand. (b) Points-based Selection set. (c) Enter the name of the Selection set that corresponds to each bone within that bone's Restriction tag.*

Now to make use of these created Selection sets, double-click the Restriction tag for the bone and enter the name of the Selection set *exactly* (Figure 12.31). Take special care to use the exact same title. 90% of the time when students have problems, it comes from some slight typo in either the naming of the Selection set or in calling up that Selection set in the Restriction tag.

Now, with Selection sets created for the polygon mesh, and Restriction tags assigned to the appropriate bones, when the bones are rotated, only the desired polygons are affected, no matter how close other polys are to the bone chain. An important thing to note about this powerful function, is that with Hyper-NURBS Objects, you only need to select Selection sets for the cage (or low-poly version of the subdivided model); C4D takes care of the rest by performing the deformation act on all the subdivided polys within the HyperNURBS Object.

VERTEX MAPS

Vertex maps are similar to Selection Sets except that you are dealing primarily with the vertices of polys, and the ability to make gradated maps. To create a Vertex Map, use the Live Selection tool to select a group of points or polygons. With the Selection>Set Vertex Weight pull-down menu you create a new Vertex Map tag next to the object in the Objects Manager (Figure 12.32). Note also that your model will be suddenly presented in a yellow/red paradigm; the yellow being the active parts of the map, the red being the inactive sections.

CHAPTER 12 ADVANCED ANIMATION AND CHARACTER ANIMATION 367

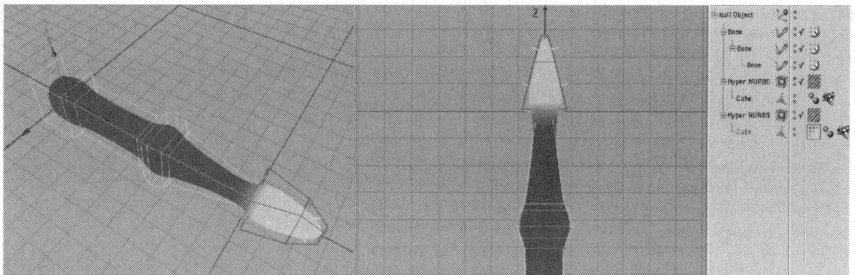

FIGURE 12.32 *Immediately after defining a Vertex map by using the pull-down menu (Selection>Set Vertex Weight), your model will show you where the Vertex map is. Yellow is heavy influence, red is none.*

The new Vertex Map tag, when it is clicked once within the Object Manager, will activate the Vertex map and you'll be able to see it and its effects with the yellow/red view in the Editor. If you double-click the tag, you can select a name for the Vertex map that can later be put in a bone's Restriction tag.

But there is much more to these Vertex maps. The Live Selection tool comes into heavy play in the establishment and alteration of Vertex maps. When a Vertex map is active (made active by clicking once on the Vertex map tag in the Object Manager), you can use the Live Selection tool to "paint" areas of the poly mesh to be more or less influenced. To do this, make sure that you are in Points mode (as you are going to be altering the vertices of the poly mesh). Next, activate your Live Selection tool and make sure to click the Active Tool tab under the Coordinates Manager in the bottom right of the default interface (Figure 12.33 a). Notice the section called Vertex Painting? By enabling this, you can choose to Set, Lighten, or Darken vertices as part of this Vertex map. When the mode is on "Set", whatever vertex you then paint over in the Editor will be set to completely yellow, as it assumes you wish to add this vertex to the active Vertex map. When you set the Vertex map to Lighten, the vertices you paint over will be made more yellow, depending on the Strength slider below; remember that the more yellow the area, the heavier the map, and thus the more it will be affected by bones restricted to that map. Conversely, when the mode is set to Darken, you can paint vertices more red, thus lessening the influence on this section of the mesh. Indeed, at 100% strength, you can paint points quickly to be immediately red, and thus a bone restricted to that Vertex map would have no influence at all on that point. The beauty of this is the ability to paint rows of vertices with progressively darker or lighter areas; thus making the map of influence have very gradual falloffs (Figure 12.33 b).

For areas like the shoulders and where the legs meet the hips, this sort of gradual transition is very important. Further in areas such as facial animation where skin stretches gradually over the face of the bone, this is absolutely

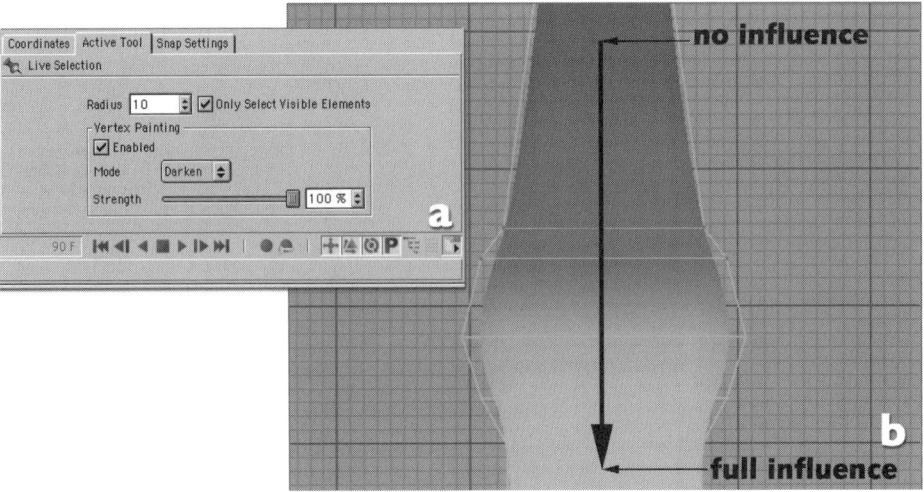

FIGURE 12.33 (a) *The Active Tool Manager for the Live Selection tool allows for the use of Vertex Painting. (b) By using Vertex Painting with progressively smaller Strengths settings, you can create very nice gradients of weight for the map.*

essential. In the next chapter, we'll look at ways to further exploit this powerful feature in both facial and full body animation.

This powerful idea of vertex painting is made even more powerful by its ability to quickly create several Vertex maps. Using our arm as an example, and assuming it has no Vertex maps assigned, observe the following way to quickly create all the maps needed.

With the Cube that makes the arm in the HyperNURBS object selected (Figure 12.34 a), and with Points Mode active (Figure 12.34 a), select the Live Selection tool and make sure that Vertex Painting is enabled (Figure 12.34 b). For simplicity, make sure the Mode is at Set and the Strength is set to 100%. Now, simply begin painting on the object in the Editor. Immediately, several things will happen. First, the object within the Editor will turn to red, except the vertices you are painting, which will turn the form yellow (Figure 12.34 c). Second, a new Vertex map tag will automatically appear next to the Cube in the Object Manager, indicating that a new Vertex map has been created (Figure 12.34 c). You can continue to paint with the Live Selection tool until your selection looks complete. You can take time now to create the even gradients of influence by changing the Live Selection tools mode to Darken or Lighten now, or you can always do it later. When you are done, double-click the Vertex map tag in the Object Manager and name it "Hand Vertex."

When you're happy with this Vertex map, click on any other object in the Object Manager to deactivate the first Hand Vertex map. Now click the Cube (that is the hand) again, which will display the hand normally again. Now start painting again where you want the next Vertex map to begin. Again, the same thing will happen; the Editor will show the same red/yellow paradigm showing where the Vertex map exists, and a new Vertex map tag will appear next to the Cube in the Object Manager as a new Vertex map has been created automatically. When you have the map like you want it, double-click the Vertex map tag and rename it "Forearm Vertex." Repeat the process for any other needed areas. To finish off, just make sure to enter the names of each of the Vertex maps into the Restriction tags for the related bones and remember to fix/activate the bones.

Pretty neat eh? This method of quickly and interactively creating Vertex maps that can be used in Restriction tags makes linking a collection of bones to a poly mesh a fairly quick and painless process. However, creating a collection of bones that move one arm is one thing, creating a rig that will work for an entire character is another. Stay tuned to the next chapter for details on creating rigs for entire characters.

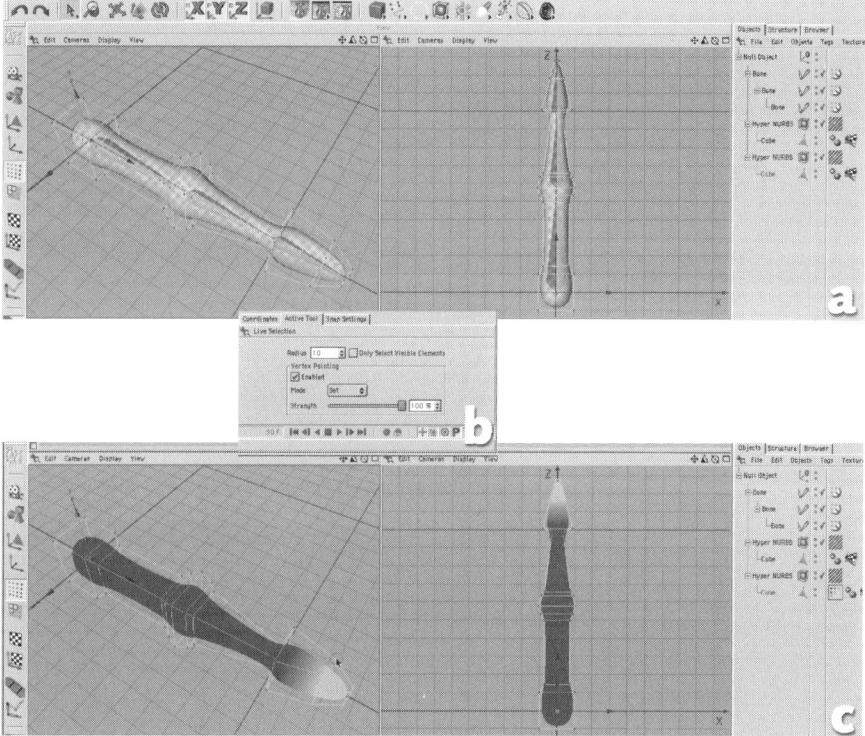

FIGURE 12.34 *Process of creating an interactive Vertex map by simply painting one into existence.*

CHAPTER 13
Character Animation in Action

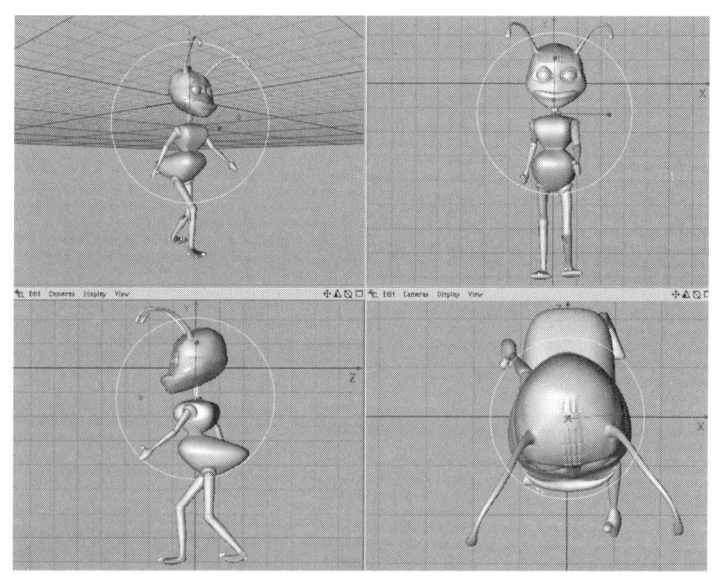

So far we've looked at how bones work. We've analyzed how bones can be attached to polygons to deform poly meshes. We've also taken a peek at IK techniques and FK uses. The culmination of all of these ideas is taking a complex single mesh character, laying bones within it, and then being able to rig those bones to create believable animation. In this chapter, we're going to look at rigging the character shown in Figure 13.1 so that the legs are available for IK, and the upper body is set for believable FK. Then, Chad Griffiths will show a trick or two about giving your character some simulated soft body dynamics. Finally, for the last tutorial, we'll look at some PLA and Bone tricks for enabling facial animation.

TUTORIAL

13.1 RIGGING THE ANT FOR ANIMATION

Figure 13.1 shows an ant modeled by Desiree Maher. This model is a fairly dense model, as is Desiree's modeling style; however, the density of points, in this case, will actually be an advantage in our illustration in how to "rig" the character for motion. A few things to notice about this model. First, every part of the model, except the eyes, is one solid polygon mesh. It wasn't always so, though; she built the character using the powerful tool of Symmetry. However, a "symmetried" model creates problems when it comes time to place bones, and move each arm and each leg independently. To meld the two sides of the symmetry together, the Symmetry Object was selected in the Object Manager, and Structure>Make Editable was selected (or the keyboard shortcut "C" was used). This makes the symmetried side one solid mesh with the original. So, although each model's organizational needs may be a little different (some models will actually work best if the hips down are one object, and the torso is another for example), for this tutorial, make sure that in your own model (if you are following this tutorial using a different model source) is one complete mesh; no two sides about it. If you'd like to follow along using this model, it is on the CD as AntbyDesireeMaher.c4d.

ON THE CD

The first step that we'll want to do is lay in the bones that will control this mesh. But, laying bones into a character can sometimes be frustrating as you're trying to find where the bones are in 3D space. A helpful tip is to create a temporary new material with the Transparency parameter activated and apply this material to the character. The result is a see-through character that will allow you to see inside to the bones.

As we discussed earlier, the center of gravity for bipedal creatures is somewhere between the crotch and the belly button. The hips are where the axis of most rotation occurs. So, for this ant, the first bone we'll create will be the Hip Bone. When a bone is first created, it is placed facing the negative Z direction with the axis of rotation sitting at (0,0,0). Since this places the bone sticking out of the back of the ant's head (Figure 13.1 a) we'll need to make some alterations. First, rotate the bone so that it is facing straight down and move the bone down into position so that the rotation point is set at where the chest section meets the hips (Figure 13.1 b). Then refine the rotation of this bone so that it is bent back in anticipation of bones emerging for the legs (Figure 13.1 c). Lastly, in the Object Manager, name this bone "Hip Bone."

This is going to be a relatively stable bone. It's going to be the solid foundation that the rest of the bone structure is built upon. When we build IK chains (as we will in a bit), we don't want this bone to go jerking around every time we move a foot target. As such, we want to anchor this bone down. To do this, we'll add an Anchor tag to the Hip Bone by right-clicking (COMMAND-clicking on a Mac) the Hip Bone and selecting Tag>New Tag from the resultant pop-up menu. A new Anchor tag will appear next to the Hip Bone.

To continue, we'll add the bones that connect the legs to the hip. To do this, CTRL/COMMAND-click-drag the orange dot at the end of the Hip Bone out, so that it reaches the place where the leg meets the body (Figure 13.2 a). We want another bone on the other side just like it, and we want to make sure that it is also a child of the Hip Bone. So, select the parent Hip Bone in the Object Manager again, and again CTRL/COMMAND-click-drag out a new bone (Figure 13.2 b). Label these Left Hip Joint and Right Hip Joint according to the ant's right and left sides. Add an Anchor tag to both of these bones as well, as they shouldn't be affected by IK functions.

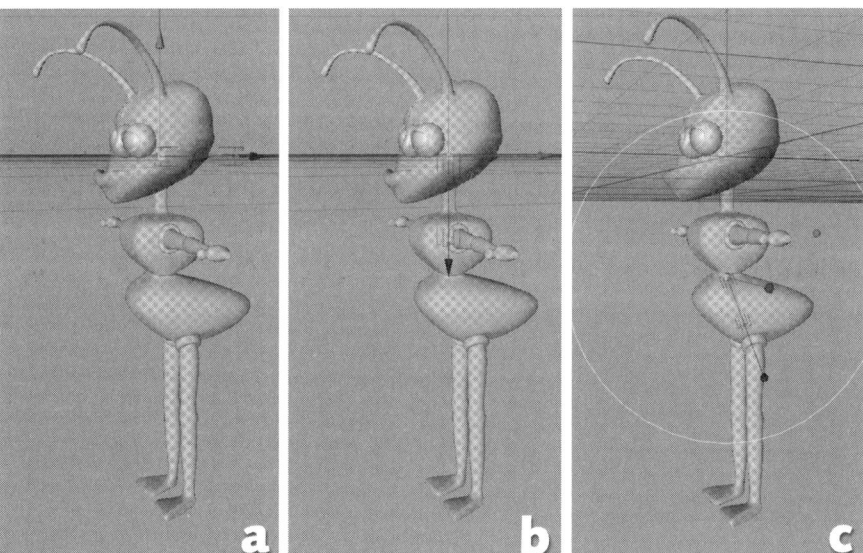

FIGURE 13.1 *Model by Desiree Maher. The model in preparation for animation is all one mesh placed with a Hyper NURBS form. Placing the Hip Bone.*

Now as we begin the legs, it's important to note that in some cases we would need the above collections of bones. One strategy to boning a character would be to simply start the Leg Bones and not worry about the Hip area bones. However, we want to be able to have some movement in the hips eventually, so we add the bones. If we never planned to deform the hip region, then these bones would be unnecessary.

Something you may have noticed as you were CTRL/COMMAND-click-dragging new bones into existence is that bones' angles are created and listed in the Coordinates Manager as being their angle to the previous bone. As we begin creating the legs, we need to keep this in mind, as eventually we're going to make the Leg Bones part of an IK chain, with IK tags restricting their movement. In the segmented character we looked at earlier, we could zero out the Segments axis; however, this can't be done with bones. To solve this problem, we'll make little Corrector Bones. Corrector Bones are bones that exist solely to create convenient angles for larger, more important bones. Create a Corrector Bone just like any other bone, but make it very, very small. Its angle is important, in that it must point in exactly the direction we want the rest of the leg to be (Figure 13.2). Now these bones are really small. They actually won't have any effect on any polygons directly. However, if the bones are indeed pointed exactly in the direction as the leg bones are to be created, it'll save you lots of headaches when it comes time to IK. Notice that in Figure 13.2 (c) there is a Corrector Bone for each leg. They are labeled Right Leg Corrector and Left Leg Corrector.

Now, with the Corrector Bones established, you can CTRL/COMMAND-click-drag the Thigh Bones into existence. Notice that since they are being created off the Corrector Bones, their angles are listed as H=0, P=0, and B=0 in the Coordinates Manager (Figure 13.2 c). Name them Left Thigh and Right Thigh.

As you're CTRL/COMMAND-click-dragging bones to create them, you may notice the tendency bones sometimes have of spinning around in unwanted angles. For our general Hip and Corrector Bones, it's not a problem if the bones get twisted around, but for the Thigh Bones, it's very important that the bones are straight in relation to the previous bone. So, after you've created each of these Thigh Bones, make sure that the Coordinates Manager reads 0 in H, P, and B. If not, make sure to zero these values out.

The Shin Bones are more of the same, just create the Shin Bone by CTRL/COMMAND-click-dragging out of the thighs. CTRL/COMMAND-click-drag down to where the Ankle would begin. Again, make sure that these Shin Bones are also at 0° in relation to the Thigh Bone (Figure 13.3 a). Name them Left Shin and Right Shin.

We'll create the bones for each foot as three bones. The first will be another Corrector Bone (again short, very tiny) with a Foot Bone and a Toe Bone branching off of that (Figure 13.3 b). Again, make sure to zero out the

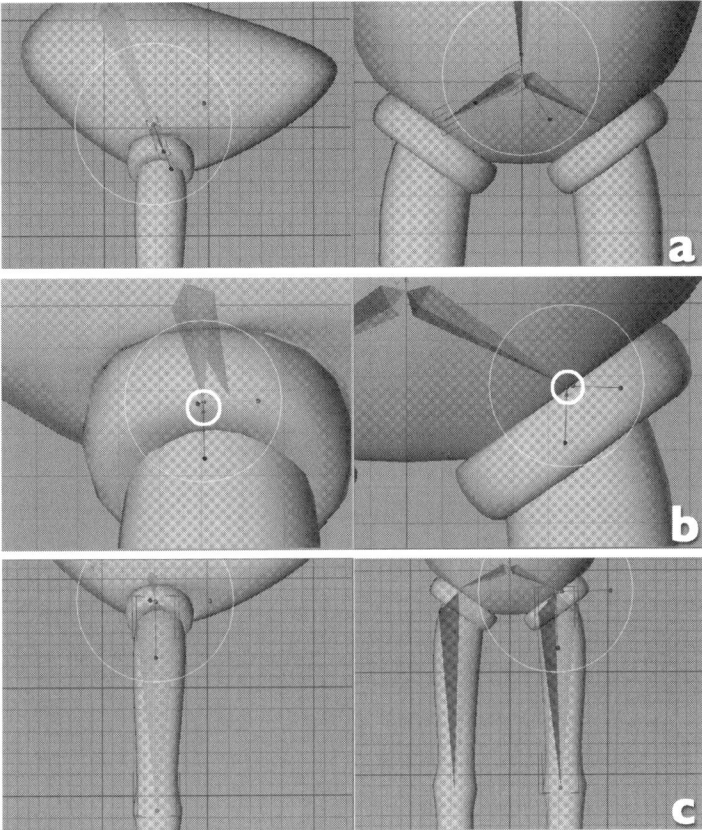

FIGURE 13.2 *(a) Linking the Hip Bone to the start of the legs. (b) Corrector Bones created to allow for easy-to-manipulate angles for the Leg Bones. (c) Thigh bones created as children of the Corrector Bones.*

rotations for the Foot and Toe bones. Rename these new bones Right Foot Corrector, Right Foot, Right Toe, Left Foot Corrector, Left Foot, Left Toe. Your Hierarchy for the bones thus far should look something like Figure 13.3 (c).

Now that we have the Bone Hierarchy set up, let's assign parts of the model to these bones. To do this, we'll create some Vertex maps so that we're sure to get a soft transition from the legs to the hip region. Change to Points mode and select the Ant Polymesh Object in the Object Manager. Now activate the Live Selection tool and enable Vertex Painting in the Active Tool Manager and for now, turn off the Only Select Visible Elements option. Now in a front view, begin painting one of the legs (Figure 13.4 a). Since you have the Only Select Visible Elements option turned off, you can be sure that you're painting through the object and getting the vertices on the back side as well. Paint all the way up the leg until you get a Vertex map similar to Figure 13.4 b). Double-click the Vertex map tag, and name this map Left Leg Vertex.

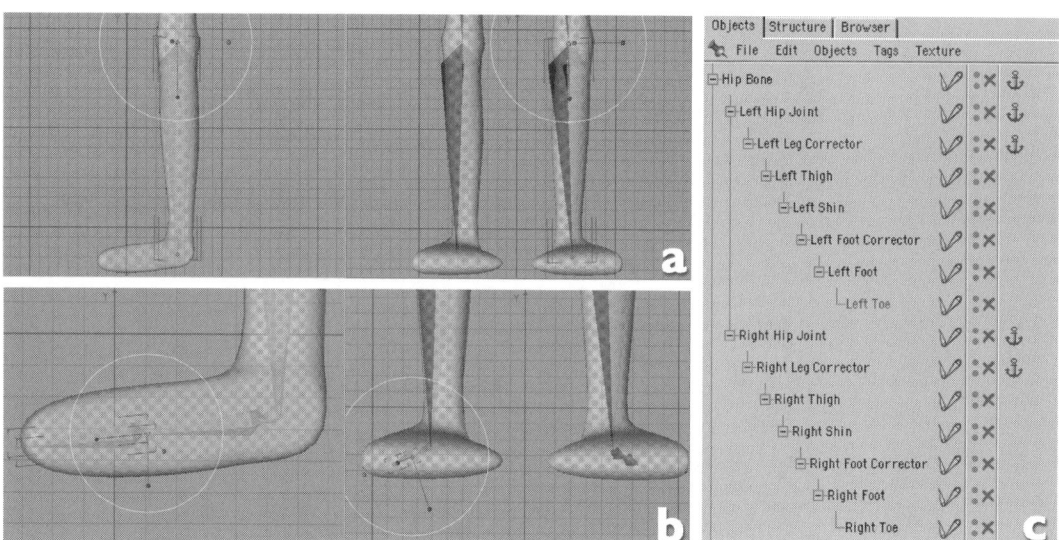

FIGURE 13.3 *(a) Creation of the Shin Bones. (b) New feet bones again using the idea of a corrector. (c) Hierarchy for our two legs and feet bones.*

Now click on any other object in the Object Manager and then again select the Ant Polymesh. Again, using the Live Selection tool, paint a new Vertex map and name this new map Right Leg Vertex (Figure 13.4 c).

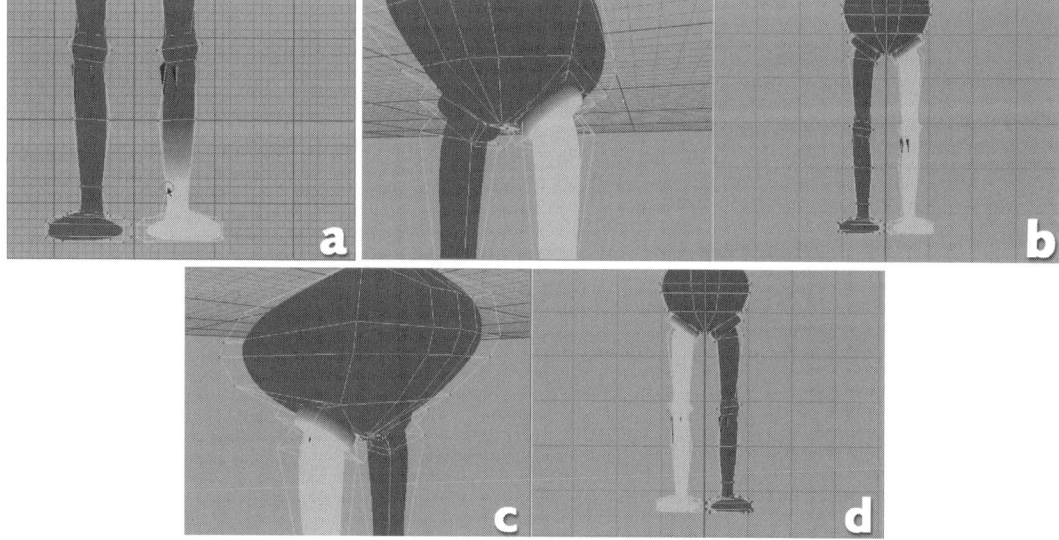

FIGURE 13.4 *(a and b) Creating the Left Leg Vertex map. (c and d) Creating the Right Leg Vertex map with the Live Selection tool.*

So now you've got a polymesh with two Vertex maps to match the two strings of bones. Some animators may want to create a Vertex map for each segment of the leg (one for the foot, one for the shin, etc....), but overall, this is typically not needed. We want to allow all these bones to quickly affect the entire leg; no need to do more work than necessary.

To get these bones to actually take effect, group the Hip Bone (and all its children) and the Ant Polymesh together by activating your Object Manager, pressing "G" on your keyboard, and marqueeing around these objects. Name this group "Ant." Don't worry about the spheres that make up the eyes for now.

Now before we activate the bones and fix them, let's first limit their effect. Right-click (COMMAND-click on a Mac) the Hip Bone and add a Restriction tag. At this point, we don't want the Hip Bone to actually have any effect on polygons, so leave the input fields blank and click OK. This is a great trick when you use bones as placeholders. Once you have this blank Restriction tag created, you can duplicate it by CTRL/COMMAND-click-dragging it to the Corrector Bones and the Hip Joint Bones (Figure 13.5 a).

Now, for the Left Thigh, add a Restriction tag, but enter Left Leg Vertex in the input field. Duplicate this tag to the Left Shin, Left Foot, and Left Toe Bones. For the Right Thigh, add a Restriction tag and enter Right Leg Vertex in the input field and again duplicate this Restriction tag to Right Shin, Right Foot, and Right Toe. At this point, every bone should have a Restriction tag assigned to it.

Now, select the group Ant. Right-click (COMMAND-click) and select Fix Bones from the pop-up menu. Click Yes at the pop-up option of whether or not to include sub-objects. All at once the positioning of the bones is fixed and the bones are activated. To test our work, select the Left Shin and using the Rotate Active Element tool, rotate the shin backward to see the deformation on the leg (Figure 13.5 b). To make this leg bend a little better, double-click the Hip Bone in the Object Manager and change the function to $1/r^8$ to make the bend a bit more sharp and prevent the Thigh from shifting when we're bending the Shin (Figure 13.5 c). Now rotate the Left Thigh to see how the Vertex map is allowing for a nice deformation of the joint where the Leg meets the Hip (Figure 13.5 d).

While we're working on the Legs, let's establish the IK scenario. Again, for illustration sake, we'll oversimplify the settings here, but you can adjust them as you'd like. First, let's define the range that we're going to allow these joints to have. To do this, we'll place IK tags for the Thighs, Shins, Foot, and Toes.

Let's start with the Left Thigh. The Left Hip Joint and Corrector above this joint have Anchor tags, so we don't need to add a IK Tag for those bones as they're already locked into place. With the Left Thigh selected, use the Active Element tool to rotate the Leg back as far as is feasible with the physiology of the ant. Take note in the Coordinates Manager what the settings are. In my case, when the Leg rotates back as far as looks right, the Pitch reads 60° (Figure 13.6 a). Upon rotating the thigh forward, the Pitch reads –80° (Figure 13.6 b).

To make use of this information, add an IK tag (right-click/COMMAND-click New Tag>IK Tag) to the Left Thigh. Activate restrictions for H, P, and B. For the H, let's allow a small range for the Legs to straddle, say –20° to 20°. In the P Minimal and Maximal input fields, we'll enter our discovered –80° and 60°. For the B, change the values from 0 to 0 as we don't want the Leg to twist in the socket at all. This is where those Corrector Bones are made worthwhile. The values are easy to remember, and it's easy to find these values. Plus, if we don't want movement in a particular direction all we have to do is enter 0 instead of trying to find at what angle the bone is sitting at rest (Figure 13.6 c).

Continue down to the Shin. Using the Rotate Active Element tool again, rotate the Shin to the limit that looks correct — in the version shown in Figure 13.7 this value is 135°. Of course, it shouldn't bend at all in the (-) direction or in H, or B. Add an IK Tag to the Left Shin and enter 0° to 135° in the P input fields and zero in the rest.

For the Left Foot Corrector, add an Anchor tag to keep it still within the chain. For the Left Foot and Left Toe, again find the range that is appropriate for the bones (it may not be appropriate in issues of the Pitch) and incorporate these values into IK tags added to each of these objects. Repeat this process for the

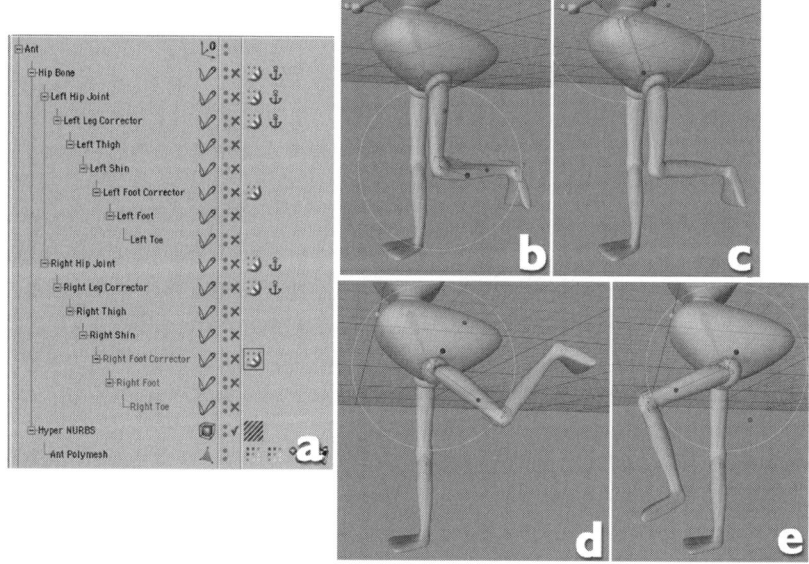

FIGURE 13.5 *(a) Blank Restriction tags for the bones that are placeholders or Connector Bones that oughtn't effect polygons. (b and c) If all's well, the Shin will bend and take the Leg with it. Some fine tuning is achieved when the function is set to 1/r^8 for the Hip Bone (and thus all the children bones). (d and e) Our Vertex maps have made for nice deformation in the hip joint area.*

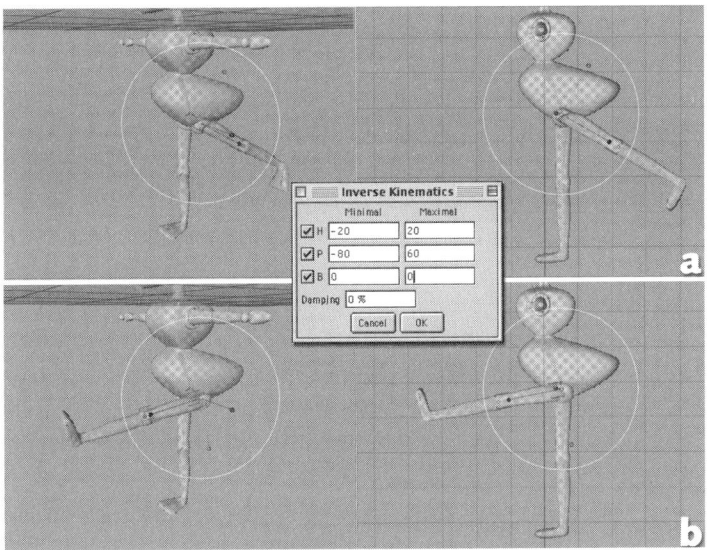

FIGURE 13.6 *(a and b) Rotating front and back and making note of what the Coordinates Manager says, gives us an idea of what the IK restrictions should be. (c) The Inverse Kinematics tag for Left Thigh.*

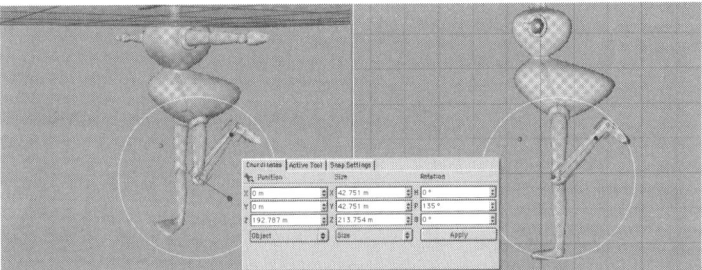

FIGURE 13.7 *Discovering the range for the shin/knee to be entered in the IK tag.*

collection of bones that make up the Right Leg. Make sure that you check the settings for each bone; as we did not spent a lot of time in carefully resetting the Corrector Bones, there might be positive values on the left leg where there are negative values for the right.

Now that the bones know how to behave, we need to give them a target to point at. Create a Null Object (Objects>Null Object) and rename it Left Leg Target. Place this Left Leg Target just below the heel of the Right Leg (Figure 13.8 a). Copy and paste this object and rename the newly pasted object Left Foot Target. Place this target just beyond the reach of the Toe (Figure 13.8 b).

Group these two targets together in the Object Manager and rename the group Left Target.

Repeat this process for the Right Leg, creating a new group of targets called Right Target. It's important that within the Object Manager, the Target Objects are outside the Hierarchy that the bones and polymesh are contained within. The Hierarchy thus far should look something like Figure 13.8 (c).

Now, all we need to do is tell our bone chains to become IK chains and point at our targets. We'll do this by creating IK Expressions. For the Left Leg, we want the Left Shin and the bones above it to point at the Left Leg Target, while the Left Toe upward to the Left Foot Corrector should point toward the Left Toe Target. So, create an IK Expression for the Left Shin (right-click/COMMAND-click New Expression>IK Expression) and enter Left Leg Target in the dialog box that pops up. Repeat the process for the Left Toe, only entering Left Toe Target as the object to search for. Repeat the process for the Right Shin and Right Toe.

In theory, now if you were to move the group Left Target, then the bones pointing at those targets would rotate to accommodate your movement. Unfortunately, sometimes the initial plans don't work quite right. Enter our arch nemesis – the Gimbal Lock.

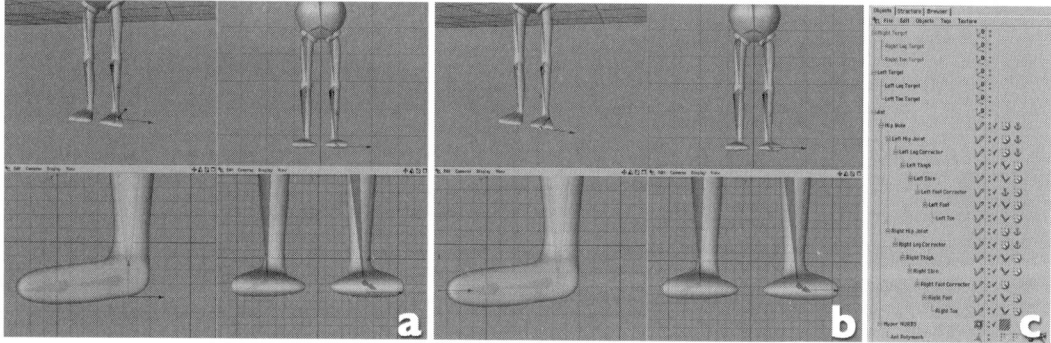

FIGURE 13.8 *(a) Use a Null Object as a target and place it just beyond the reach of the Leg. (b) To define the target direction of the Foot, make another Null Object and place it just beyond the reach of the Foot. (c) Hierarchy of newly created target forms.*

GIMBAL LOCK

When you create objects upright as we have been doing, and then rotating bones down into position, the bones "forget" an axis of rotation. The result is that when an IK chain is set up, when the targets are moved that are part of that chain, the bones "lock up." They don't bend like they ought to, because they've forgotten that they can. This Gimbal Lock is the bane of much of 3D and can be incredibly frustrating.

If you experience Gimbal Lock, luckily there are some solutions. Typically, in C4D if you only have two bones between an anchored element and an IK target, you are probably going to encounter Gimbal Lock if you've been working with your character upright. To solve the problem, we need to add one more object to the IK chain. There are several ways to do this. Some folks like to actually create another bone, a really small bone similar to our Corrector Bones, only this is a Gimbal Bone. Another solution is to use the Target Objects as this Gimbal Bone. Essentially, in this case, we already have Null Objects placed into position at the end of IK chains. If those Null Objects (in this case Right Leg Target, Right Toe Target, Left Leg Target and Left Toe Target) are copied and placed into the Hierarchy, they make a third Gimbal-breaking element in an IK chain.

So, for the moment, right-click on the Ant group and reset the bones. Delete the IK Expressions from the Left Shin, Left Toe, Right Shin and Right Toe, as these expressions will be assigned elsewhere. For the Left Leg, copy and paste the Left Target group. Rename the Left Leg Target and Left Toe Target to Left Leg Effector and Right Leg Effector. Don't move these effectors in digital space as they are already placed in the right place for our purposes; however, we do need to place them in the appropriate place of the Bone Hierarchy. Place the Left Leg Effector as a child to the Left Shin Bone. Place the Left Toe Effector as a child of the Left Toe Bone. Now these Effector Objects should contain the IK Expressions, linking them to Left Leg Target and Left Toe Target. Do the same for the Right Leg (Figure 13.9 a). Again, fix the bones.

Now Gimbal Lock doesn't always occur. Some folks like to prepare their bone chains from the beginning in anticipation of Gimbal Lock occurring. Some animators even prefer to build and IK their model lying down, and then rotate the entire boned model to stand upright when all the IK settings have been assigned. Others worry about Gimbal Lock when it happens and take steps like we described here to break the lock. It's all up to you.

BACK TO IK

So, now with Null Objects (our effectors) at the end of chains that are also in the same initial location as the targets they are pointing at, and with IK Expressions established, we can then grab our Target Objects (Left Target or Right Target) and move them; the Legs will bend to accommodate (Figure 13.9 b).

UPPER BODY AND FK

The upper body needn't have the same complex collection of IK Targets and Expressions. Most upper body movement is best done with FK. However, even with FK, we still need a collection of bones that can deform the polymesh and Vertex maps to define where those bones can have influence.

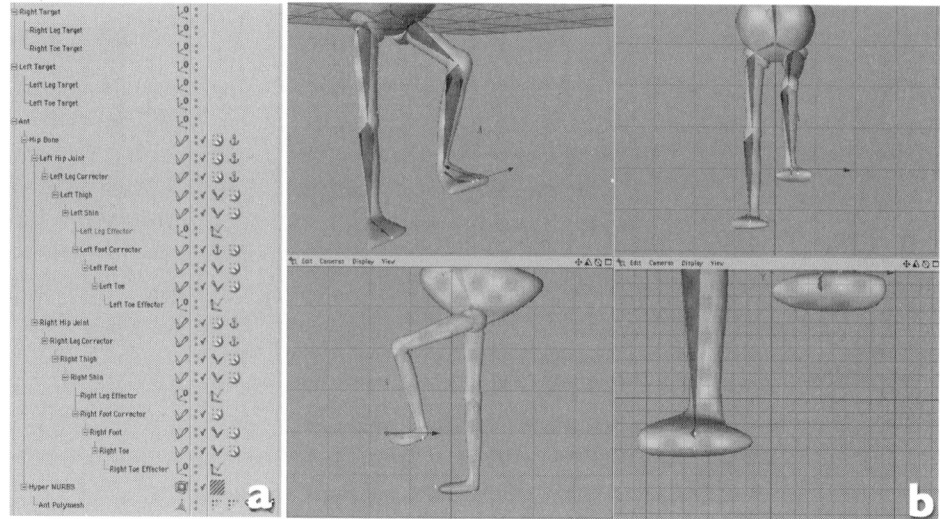

FIGURE 13.9 *(a) Fix Gimbal Lock by adding another element to the IK chain. In this case, making a copy of the targets, placing them in the appropriate hierarchical location, and assigning the IK Expression to them breaks the Gimbal Lock. (b) IK chains in action.*

Select the Ant Object and reset the bones in anticipation of new collections of bones. Create a new bone and rotate and position it so that it moves halfway up the chest (Figure 13.10 a) and rename it to Chest. This center Chest Bone will be the launching spot for both Arms and the Neck, so make sure that it intersects where the Arms connect to the torso and below the Neck.

Now, from this Chest Bone, CTRL/COMMAND-click-drag into existence several bones to make up the Arm. Make sure to make a Shoulder Bone that connects the Chest Bone to where the bones should actually emerge. The complexity of this bone chain is largely up to you. If you never plan to do much animating with the Hands, you don't need quite so many bones there (Figure 13.10 b). Name each bone according to its location.

Now select the Chest Bone again in the Object Manager and build another set of bones for the opposite Arm. Since it is built off the same Chest Bone, each of these Arms are at the same level of children of the Chest Bone. This means that if the Chest is rotated, both the Arms go with it (Figure 13.10 c). Label these bones appropriately.

Once again, select the Chest Bone in the Object Manager and build one new bone for the Neck and another for the Head. If you're really ambitious, you could build additional bones for the antennae; but we won't do that here. Your Hierarchy should look something like Figure 13.10 (d) at this point.

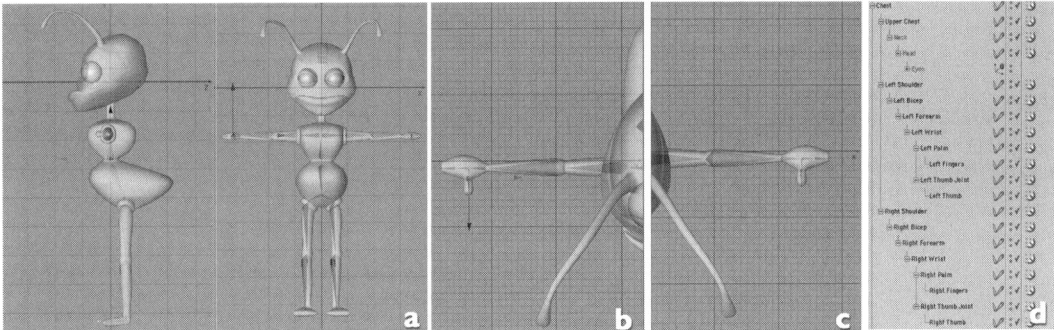

FIGURE 13.10 *(a) Getting started with the bones for the upper body. (b) Creating the Arm off the main Chest Bone. (c) Create the second Arm also off the Chest Bone. (d) Hierarchy organization of upper body bones.*

Now it's important that this upper body collection of bones end up as children of our main Hip Bone. So once you have all the bones aligned and placed appropriately, select the Chest Bone (which is the parent bone of all the upper body bones) and make it a child of the Hip Bone.

Next, we need to define what areas of the model we're going to allow these bones to affect. A good place to start is the Arms. Make a Vertex map for each Arm (Figure 13.11 a), one for the Chest, one for the Neck, and one for the Head (Figure 13.11 b). Remember to use the method of painting in a new Vertex map to make the process go quickly. This should give you seven Vertex maps in all: Head Vertex, Neck Vertex, Chest Vertex, Right Arm Vertex, Left Arm Vertex, Right Leg Vertex, and Left Leg Vertex.

When all the Vertex maps are created, right-click (COMMAND-click) the Ant Object (which should now contain all of your bones and the polymesh – but *not* the IK Targets for the Legs) and select Fix Bones. Now using the IK Targets, you can pose the legs, climb stairs, or whatever you'd like, and using FK, you can rotate the upper body bones into position to pose the gestures and movement of the Ant's upper body (Figure 13.12).

Whew! Pretty intense, eh? It takes a while to get a rig like this set up right. However, once it's set up, the animation ends up moving fairly smoothly. The better the rig is organized, the smoother your animation will go. A rough version of this tutorial's file can also be found on the CD called SingleMeshRigged.c4d.

ON THE CD

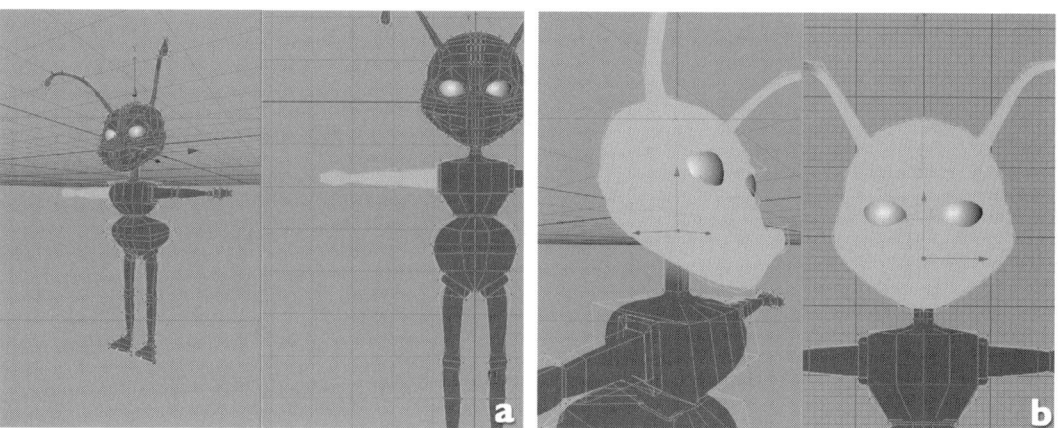

FIGURE 13.11 *(a) Create a Vertex map for each Arm. (b) Include Vertex maps for the Head and Neck.*

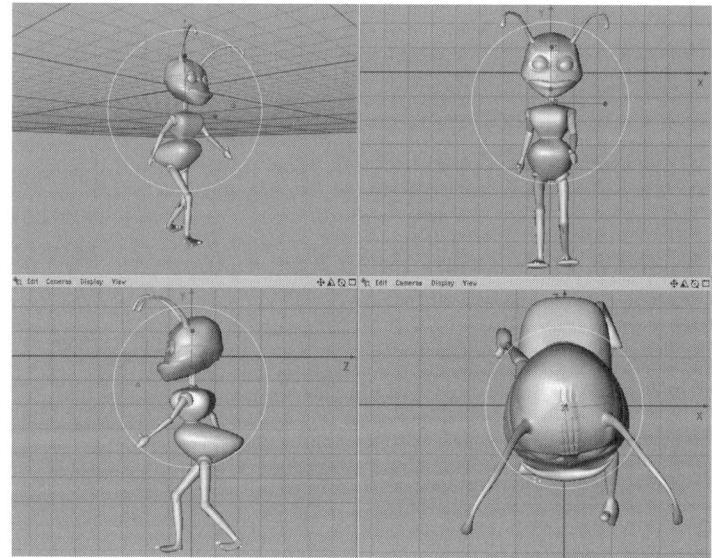

FIGURE 13.12 *IK with IK Targets for the lower body. FK with rotating bones for the upper body.*

13.2 SIMULATING SOFT BODY DYNAMICS
By Chad Griffiths

TUTORIAL Living creatures usually have masses of soft tissue in several parts of their bodies. When living creatures are in motion, gravity and inertia act upon these masses, sometimes rolling them about and causing jiggling. Imagine a summo wrestler running down the street and this principle will become evident. To be truly lifelike, a 3D character must also have a certain amount of jiggle when it moves. This tutorial demonstrates one way to simulate the effects of gravity and inertia on soft tissues.

We will begin with a basic skeleton structure and a round, heavy character model. The character will be animated in a run-cycle. The example model is a fat hippopotamus, but feel free to use any similarly husky character you choose.

To add to the illusion of weight to the character, the softer parts of his body will need to flop and jiggle as he runs. This means that we will need to have direct control over several areas of the model surface, such as the Belly and Cheeks. This can be achieved by inserting extra bones into the skeleton that will influence only the soft tissues of the body. In this tutorial, these bones will be referred to as Surface Bones. The bones of the regular skeleton — including the arms, legs, spine and head — will be called Structural Bones. But before we do any work with the skeleton, the surface must be specially prepared.

The entire body of the example character is a single Polygon Object. Since certain parts of the surface will need to be affected exclusively by certain bones, the Polygon Object will need to be divided into its major parts. For instance, the bones of the Left Leg will need to influence only the surface of the Left Leg, and have no influence on the Right Leg. The Belly will need to be distinct from the rest of the body, as will the Chest, Head, Arms, etc. We will do this by defining those parts as Polygon Selection sets. These are groups of surfaces in a Polygon Object that can be treated as distinct units while they remain a part of the whole. As an example, the surfaces that make up the head can be defined as a separate group from the rest of the body by making them a Polygon Selection set. Even though we will effectively be splitting the Skin into sections, the Polygon Object will remain intact.

The Polygon of the character's body is nested inside a HyperNURBS Object for smoothing. However, we will be dealing directly with the Polygon Cage throughout the animation process, so we can deactivate the HyperNURBS Object for a faster display. Click the green checkmark next to the HyperNURBS in the Object Manager to switch it off. You can toggle it back on at any time by simply clicking the red X.

To start dividing the surface into selections, highlight the object in the Object Manager for the body and switch to the Use Polygons tool (Figure 13.13 a). Begin with the Left Leg. Select all the surfaces that make up the Leg (Figure 13.13 b) and choose Selection>Set Selection. In the Object Manager you should now see a Selection set tag. Double-click the tag and enter an appropriate name for the Selection in the resulting dialog box. Repeat this process after choosing other surface areas to create additional Polygon Selections. When you finish one selection and move on to the next, make sure that the finished tag is not still highlighted with a red box. This would indicate that the finished tag is still selected. Unless you click to the side to deselect it before moving on, the next group of surfaces will be added to the currently highlighted tag instead of creating a new one. You will need to know the names of each Polygon Selection for future reference, so it might be a good idea to write them down. However, if you move the mouse pointer over a Selection tag, you will see its name in the feedback line of the GUI.

The example character is divided into the following parts: Head, Chest, Belly, Back, Tail, Left Arm, Right Arm, Left Leg, and Right Leg. You can reorder the icons by click-dragging to one side or the other. While you divide the body into selections, it will be easier to see what is left to define if you click the Hide Polygons button every time you name a new selection. (Figure 13.14 a) The surfaces of the selection will become temporarily invisible. This will also help by showing you if any surfaces were accidentally missed (Figure 13.14 b).

If you need to add any surfaces to a selection, select the Polygons that were missed, then Unhide and Select the Polygons of the incomplete selection by double-clicking the Selection tag and using the Unhide and Select buttons. With the tag still highlighted, choose Selection>Set Selection to add the new surfaces. Once the divisions for the whole Polygon are finished, unhide all the selections.

The next step in the process is to add the extra bones that will make the surface jiggle. This will be easier if you apply a Translucent texture to the model so that the bones will be visible beneath the Skin. Put a Transparency map on a material and assign it to the Polygon Object. You can temporarily remove the transparency by deleting the texture tag from the Object Manager. Apply the texture again to restore the transparency simply by click-dragging it from the Materials Manager to the Polygon Object.

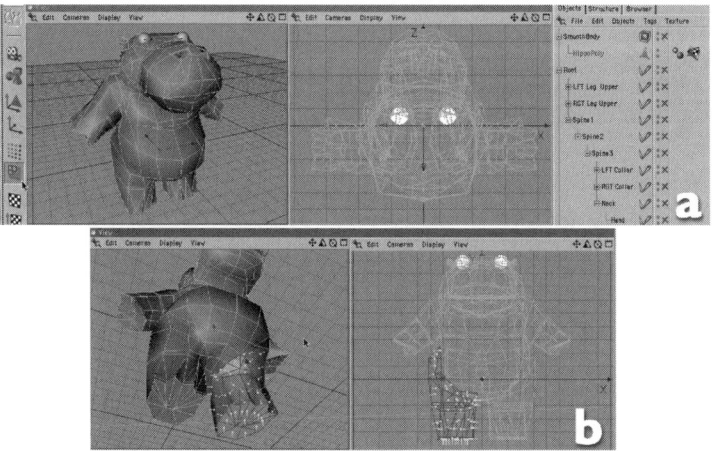

FIGURE 13.13 *(a) To begin splitting the model up, select the object in the Object Manager, then in Polygon mode, you're ready to start selecting polygons. (b) Once the polygons for a region are selected, create a Selection set for future access.*

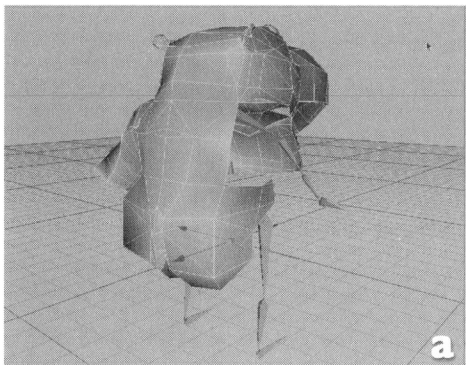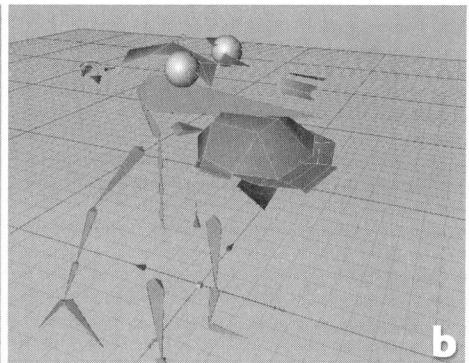

FIGURE 13.14 *(a) Hiding selection sets as you go assists in making sure you don't select Polygons twice. (b) As you select and hide, you can also find any Polygons you may have missed.*

The example character will need Surface Bones for the Belly, Posterior, Tail, Chest, Cheeks, Chin and Ears. (Figure 13.15). Of course, the list may vary depending on the specific anatomical considerations of different characters.

The Surface Bones will not need to line up with any joint in the structural skeleton. They can be placed in the IK Hierarchy as children bones by click-dragging them in the Object Manager to the appropriate parent bone. (Figure 13.16 a) All the Surface Bones must be inserted into the Hierarchy.

Two other objects of the example character will also need to be attached to the structural skeleton: the Eyes. Because the Eyes in this case are separate Polygon Objects, they will need to be attached to the Head Bone. They can be made to act as children in the IK Hierarchy by click-dragging their icons to the Structural Bone of the Head.

Once the IK chain is complete and the Bone Hierarchy is correct, we can apply and fix the bones to the skin. Drop the Skeleton Hierarchy into the Polygon Object (Figure 13.16 b). Select the top bone of the Hierarchy and choose Objects>Fix Bones from the pop-up menu of the Object Manager. When the

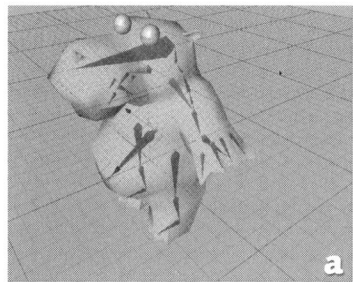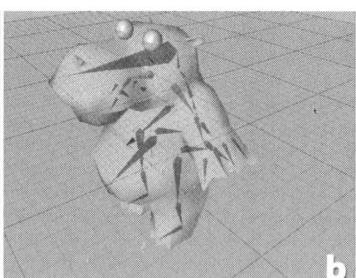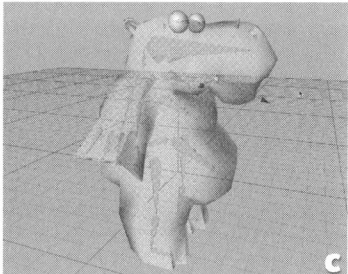

FIGURE 13.15 *Create various bones to allow for control over all the "jiggly" parts.*

message asking if you wish to include sub-objects appears, choose Yes. The skeleton is now attached, as indicated by the green checkmarks by the Bone icons in the Object Manager.

At this point, if you try rotating some of the bones, strange things happen. The bones' influence is too broad and needs to be restricted. This can be done by applying Restriction tags to the bones that refer to the Polygon Selection sets we defined earlier. A bone with a Restriction tag will only influence the surfaces of specified Polygon Selections.

With a bone selected, choose File>New Tag>Restriction Tag from the Object Manager. In the dialog box that appears, write the name of the selection to which the bone will be restricted. The percentage to the right can be changed, depending on how strong of an influence you want the bone to have. You can assign the bone to multiple selections with varying strengths. For example, the Left Leg may need to have some influence on the Belly and Back Surfaces in addition to its primary influence on the Leg Surface (Figure 13.16 c). After a Restriction tag is set, you can copy it to all the bones lower down in the Hierarchy by choosing Tags>Copy Tag to Children from the Object Manager.

The rotation of all the bones in the skeleton should now be tested to see if the skin deformations are satisfactory. It is a good idea to restrict all of the bones before testing the motion. If influence adjustments are necessary, you will not want to have interference from bones that have not yet been restricted. Pay close attention to the effects of the Surface Bones. The Belly, for instance, should waggle up and down as a full, rounded mass when you rotate its bone (Figure 13.17). The Cheeks should behave in a similar fashion while they blend

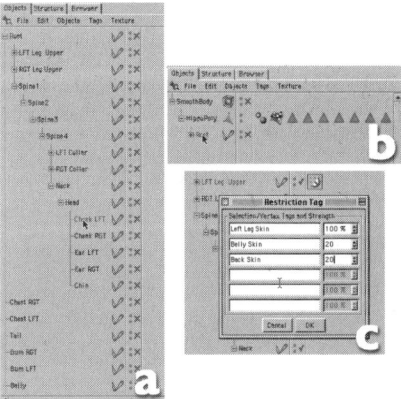

FIGURE 13.16 *(a) The Surface Bones don't need to physically connect to any other bones; however, it is important that they be contained within the Hierarchy of the Object Manager. (b) Place the Bone chain as a child of the Polygon Object so that C4D knows what polygons to allow these bones to affect once they are fixed and activated. (c) Restriction tags allow you to assign a bone to have effect on multiple Selection sets.*

naturally with the rest of the head. Fine adjustments will be needed in order to make it appear as if there are soft, fleshy masses of tissue beneath the Skin.

Additional functions for adjusting the influence effects of a bone can be found by double-clicking its icon in the Object Manager (Figure 13.18 a) With Surface Bones, turning the function on for Scale Strength with Length helps to make the influence more appropriate for soft tissues. You may also want to adjust the radius of influence for certain bones. Turn the Limit Radius function on after double-clicking the Bone icon. Enter a Minimum value of 10 and a Maximum value of 100. Two green wire cages will appear around the Bone in the Editor window (Figure 13.18 b). One represents the Minimum radius, the other represents the Maximum radius. The orange manipulator handles can be pulled out to interactively adjust both radii of influence.

If a Bone needs to be repositioned or set at a different starting Rotation, highlight the Bone in the Object Manager and select Objects>Reset Bones. This returns the bone to the Rotation values it had when it was initially fixed, then detaches it from the surface. After making the necessary changes, reactivate the bone by selecting Objects>Fix Bones.

Once the Rotations of all the bones have been tested and their influences adjusted, the character will be ready for animation. Start by using the Structural Bones to make the character run. We will add the animation of the Surface Bones after the rest of the body is moving appropriately. This animation will cycle, so it is only necessary to animate two steps of the run. One possible loop could be from Right Foot to Left Foot, then back to Right Foot.

When the run cycle is complete, go back in the Timeline and animate the Rotation of the Surface Bones to make the soft tissues jiggle. (Figure 13.19) The motion of the surface should be slightly offset from the structural motion so that the soft tissues roll around in reaction to the running. For instance, as the

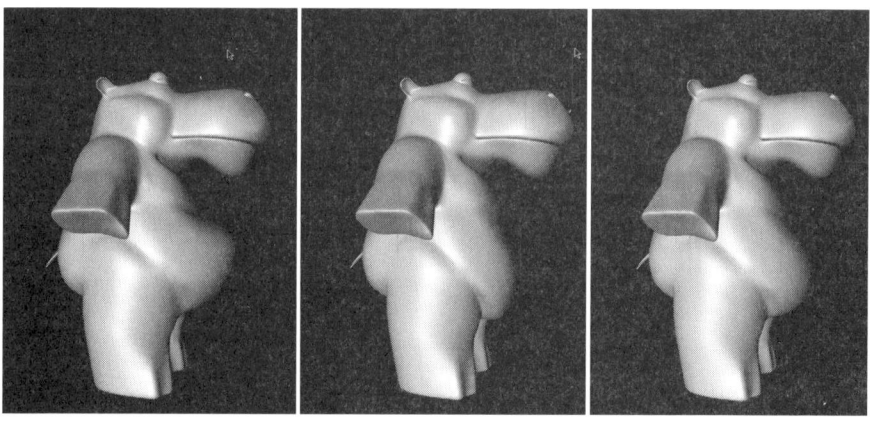

FIGURE *Jiggly sections need to move as rounded masses.*
13.17

character comes down on one Foot, the Belly should be lifted up after the body begins to drop (Figure 13.20 a). Upon impact, (Figure 13.20 b) there should be a short delay before the Belly drops to the bottom of its Rotation, (Figure 13.20 c) followed by a bouncing rebound. This same principle of overlapping the

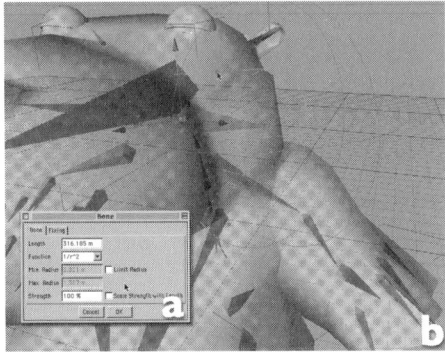

FIGURE 13.18 *(a) Further refinement can be achieved through alterations in the Bone dialog box. (b) For soft bodies, the capsules of influence can help define areas of falloff.*

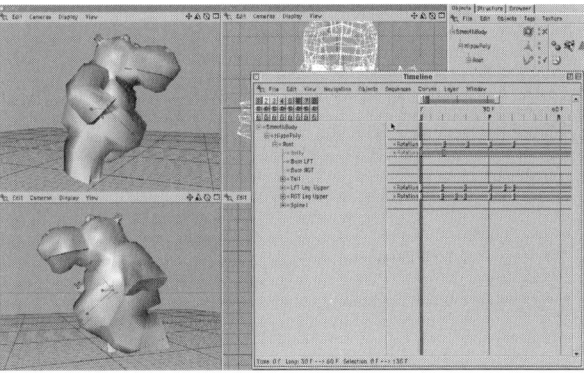

FIGURE 13.19 *Animate the soft bodies after the run is complete.*

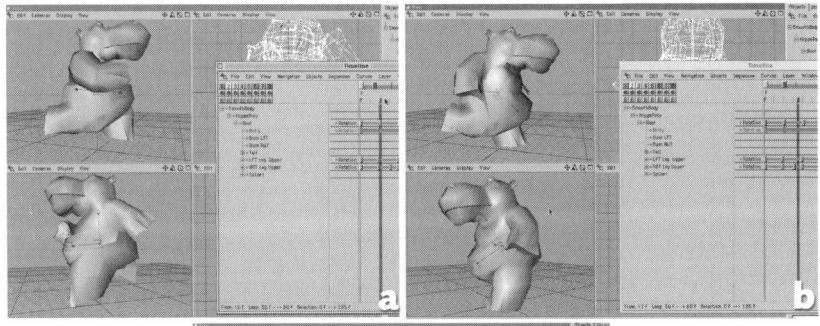

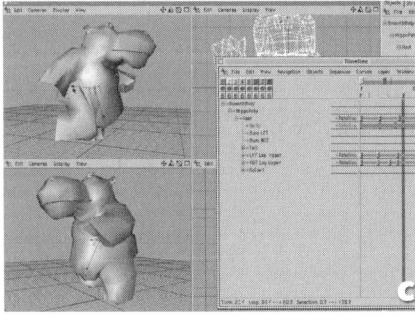

FIGURE 13.20 *The soft body animation in action.*

ON THE CD

motion of the surface with the motion of the structure will need to be applied to all the Surface Bones. The result will be a sense of weight and mass that will make your character animation far more dynamic.

Be sure to check out the examples of this technique on the CD.

TUTORIAL

13.3 STRATEGIES OF FACIAL ANIMATION

In this tutorial, we'll briefly discuss two methods of achieving animation within a facial region. None of these methods are the end all, be all of facial animation techniques; however, if all three of these are mastered, almost any model is animatable.

PLA (POINTS LEVEL ANIMATION)

The first method of facial animation we'll discuss is PLA. PLA stands for Points Level Animation. We've discussed briefly before the PLA track visible in the Time Manager (Figure 13.21 a). The idea behind PLA is that over time, you can actually animate the structure of an object by pushing and pulling the points that make it.

PLA isn't recording new positions or rotations of objects. It records states. Just like other forms of animation, in PLA you animate from pose to pose to create animation when C4D fills in the frames between your posed keyframes. For this illustration of PLA we'll use our trusty little Ant and animate the HyperNURBS Cage that forms the Ant.

So, to animate facial expressions, follow these steps. First, make sure the polymesh is selected in the Object Manager, as this is the object that the PLA track will actually be recorded to. To change the object on a Points level, you must be in Points mode so that you can see the points. Lastly, make sure that the PLA track is activated in the Time Manager. Record a PLA keyframe at frame 0 (Figure 13.21 b).

For this exercise, let's have our Ant smile and blink its eyes a couple of times. Move the time slider to frame 20. Now using the Move Active Element tool, select the points that create the mouth and position them in a grin (Figure 13.22). Record a PLA keyframe to lock in and record this new state.

As you are pushing and pulling points in defining this new state, remember that there already exists a keyframe at frame 0. So, resist the temptation to use the Undo command, as your model will undo back to the last known keyframe. To make the process a little less hazardous, record and rerecord the keyframe for the state you are working on. Pose the mouth, click the Record button, pose

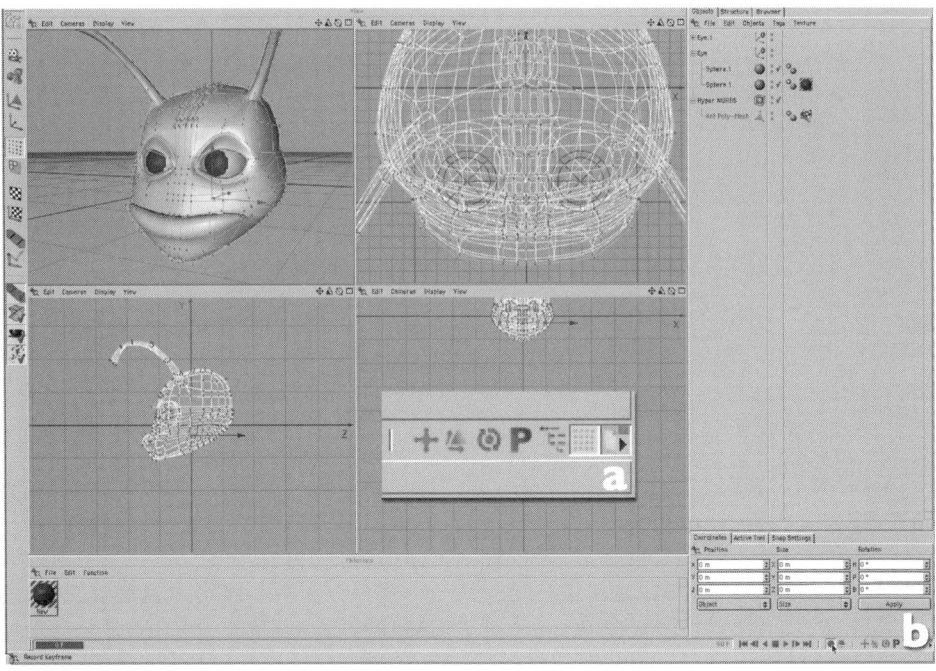

FIGURE 13.21 *(a) The Activate PLA Track button in the Time Manager. (b) Getting ready for PLA.*

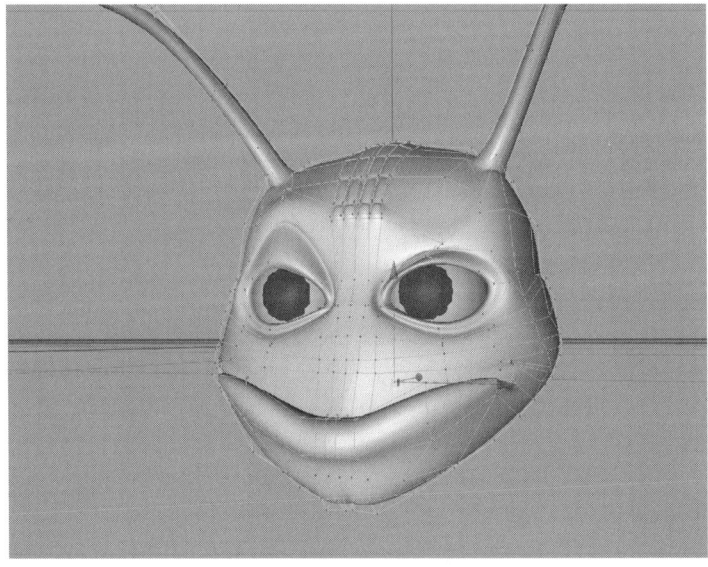

FIGURE 13.22 *Posing the face through points and recording the new state.*

the eye, click the Record button again, etc.... This way, if you need to click Undo, it undoes back to the last keyframe, which is the keyframe you're presently on.

Let's have the character hold this smirk for a second. To do this, we need to have two identical keyframes over a period of time. Move the time slider to frame 60 and record another keyframe. Since there have been no changes made, C4D now understands to hold this state from frame 20 to 60. To have our character relax back out of his smirk, we'll just copy the first PLA keyframe or state to a new position. Do this by CTRL/COMMAND-click-dragging and drop it where you want the character to not be smiling anymore. In this example, we've placed the copy of the first keyframe at frame 90.

Now for the blink, we'll create a short sequence that can be repeated. To do this, we'll first need more frames in our animation. The default 90 frames can be lengthened through the Edit>Project Settings pull-down menu within the Timeline. Here, you can tell the project to have more keyframes (200 in this case (Figure 13.23 a).

For our blink, we want the start of our new sequence to be identical to the end of the last. CTRL/COMMAND-click-drag the current PLA sequence further down the Timeline (Figure 13.23 b). Delete all the keyframes but the first in this new sequence, and shorten the sequence by double-clicking the sequence and entering new values (Figure 13.23 c). Make the new sequence about 10 frames long, starting at frame 105 and going to frame 115.

Now that we already have a keyframe with the eyes open, move the time slider to frame 110 and move the points of the eyelids so that they're closed and record a PLA keyframe (Figure 13.24 a). Duplicate the first keyframe of that sequence to frame 115 and your blink sequence is complete.

ON THE CD

Now that you have the short 10-frame sequence of the eyes opening and closing, you can CTRL/COMMAND-click-drag as many copies as you'd like. Sometimes you may want a double blink, while at others you want long breaks between the blinks (Figure 13.24 b). Take a look at BlinkingPLA.mov on the CD for the results. The file BlinkingPLA.c4d can also be found on the CD.

You can see that this is a nice, quick and dirty way to do facial animation. Some of its benefits include the ability to save various states or collections of motions that can be duplicated to other points in the animation. Some of the drawbacks are that it's nearly impossible to overlap animations easily. Let's say we wanted to make the Ant blink while he was in the process of smirking. We would have to go in and add keyframes in interim positions during the smirking sequence, thus effectively locking in every time we want to call up the smirking set of keyframes. The character will blink in the same way. This is because in PLA, C4D thinks of everything as one giant object. In the following section we'll look at ways to make C4D think of different parts of the face as different objects, thus allowing us to overlap movements as we need.

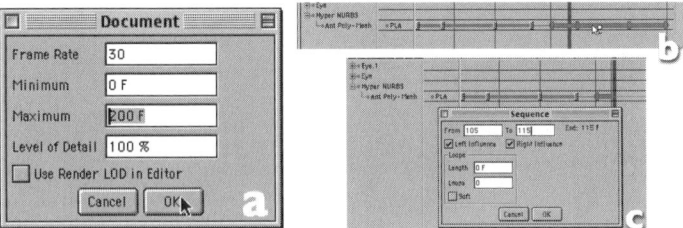

FIGURE 13.23 *(a) Giving ourselves more animating room. (b and c) Creating a new sequence for the eye blink.*

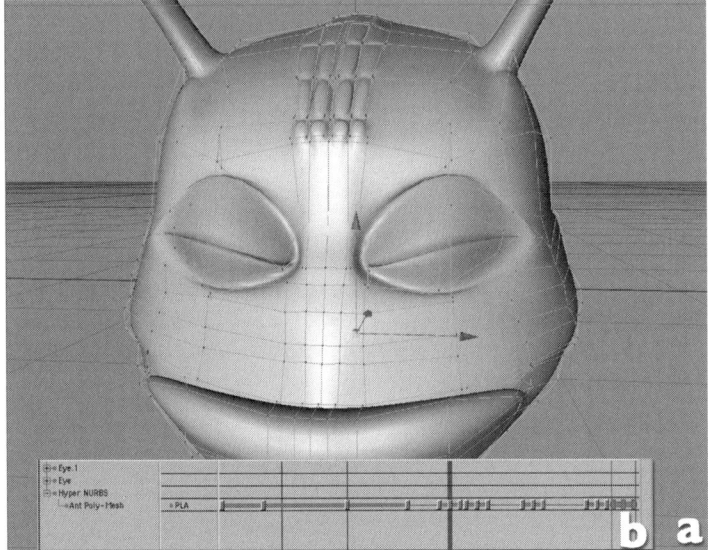

FIGURE 13.24 *(a) Creating the eyes closed state for a PLA keyframe. (b) Scattering the blink sequences.*

FACIAL BONING

The process of facial boning is the process of Vertex mapping mastery. If you can effectively set up your Vertex maps, you can then effectively assign bones to those maps. With bones attached to various parts of the face, you can animate each part differently. To demonstrate the idea of facial boning, we'll use a class project by Ya-Tsun Yang. It is also a HyperNURBS Object that she has built with the hair, eyes, and face all different objects (Figure 13.25 a). To work with this, we'll temporarily remove the texture for the face and replace it with a texture with transparency so we can see the bones we're working with. Also, we'll hide the eyes and hair (Figure 13.25 b).

CHAPTER 13 CHARACTER ANIMATION IN ACTION 395

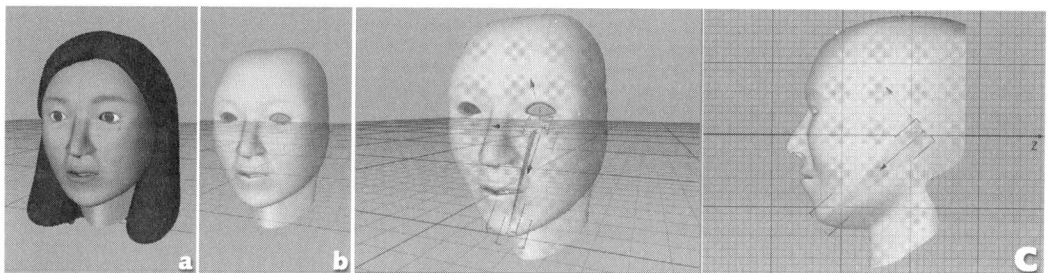

FIGURE (a and b) Starting form that we'll use facial boning to animate. (c) The Jaw Bone placed.
13.25

Let's start off with the biggest moving object, the jaw. Begin by creating one large bone set in the head to allow for the jaw to rotate in the appropriate way (Figure 13.25 c). This should have the center of rotation just in front of the ear. Often, it's easier to keep track of a bone if you actually extend it beyond the range of the Polygons. Try making sure the length of the Jaw Bone extends through the chin. Label this bone Jaw and also give it a Restriction tag listing Jaw Vertex as the vertex to restrict to.

Group all the objects in this scene together and select the new Null Object and fix bones. Now, we need to create the Jaw Vertex we told the Jaw Bone to look for. With facial animation, we'll want to have very gradual transitions from area of full influence to no influence. So, select the Polygon Object that is the Head, and activate Points mode. Select the Live Selection tool and in the Active Tool Manager, enable Vertex Painting with the mode at Set. Since this is a symmetrical model, turn off Only Select Visible Elements. Now, start the Vertex map out by selecting a very small group of vertices from a side view (so you select the points on the other side of the face as you go) that lay direction on the path that her real Jaw Bone would lie (Figure 13.26 a). This collection will be fully influenced by the virtual Jaw Bone in our scene.

Next, we want to start building out from this area of absolute influence. Set the mode to Lighten in the Active Tool Manager and pull the Strength down to 75%. Paint over the next row of vertices down from our initial selection (Figure 13.26 b). Reduce the Strength still more (to 40%) and select the next row down the Neck and paint up onto the Cheek (Figure 13.26 c). Remember that Vertex Painting is cumulative, so as you're painting these lesser areas of influence, be sure that you don't paint over again other vertices already defined – if you do, the Strength setting will be added to its previous setting.

Since our bone is already affixed, at any time you can select the Jaw Bone and rotate it to see the effects of our Vertex Painting (Figure 13.27).

Normally, you'll want to establish a bone or collection of bones for every major moving part. There should be a collection of bones and Vertex maps for

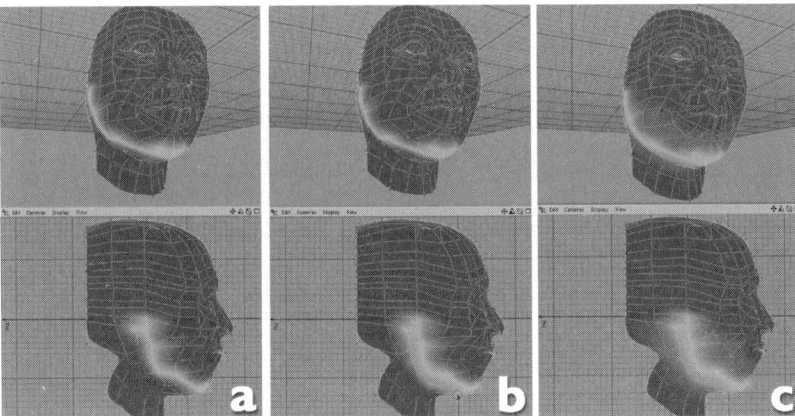

FIGURE 13.26 *(a) First selection for the Jaw Vertex map defines the area of absolute influence. (b) At 75%, begin selecting down the Neck by one row of vertices. (c) At 35%, keep working down the neck and begin working on the Cheeks as well.*

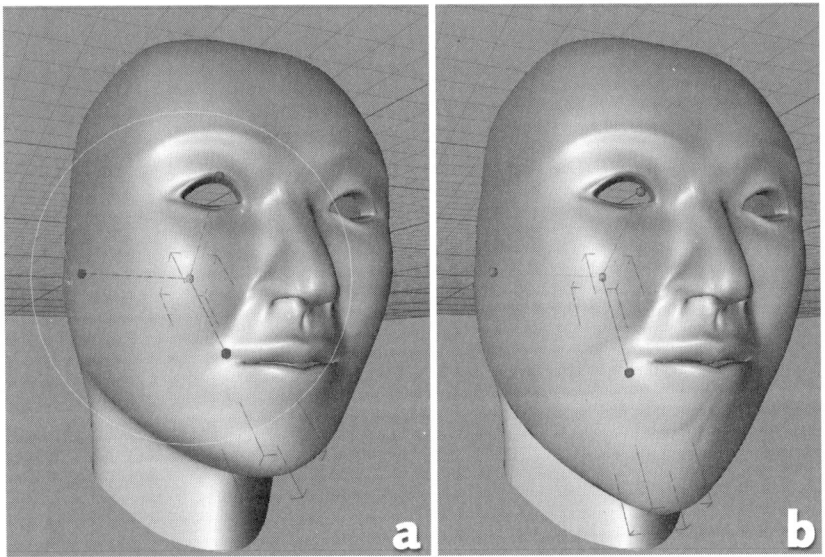

FIGURE 13.27 *Good start, the transition is working well on the Cheeks and under the Chin.*

the Jaw, Lower Lip, Top Lip, Left and Right Eyebrow, and Left and Right Eyelid. Figure 13.28 shows the Vertex map selected for the Bottom Lip (called Lower Lip Vertex). For this tutorial, we'll simply add this vertex to the Restriction tag for the Jaw Bone. However, for complex animations, you'll want to be able to move the Lips independently of the Jaw, and thus will create other collections of bones for those Lips.

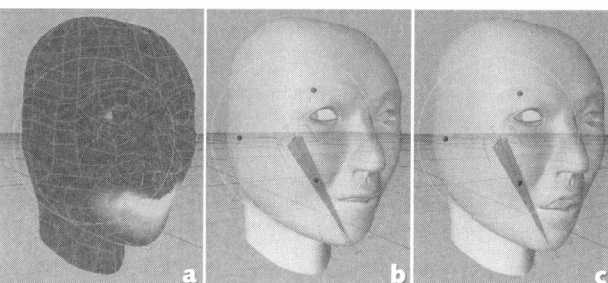

FIGURE 13.28 Lower Lip Vertex is also added to the Jaw Bone Restriction tag. So when the jaw drops, the bottom lip goes with it.

Repeat this step with each of the Eyelids by placing a bone with the center of Rotation back enough that the Rotation of the Eyelid takes it in a circular motion over the Eyeball. Make Right and Left Eyelid Vertex maps. Make sure that before you place them into the Null Object that contains your Polygon Object, that you first Reset Bones (Figure 13.29).

For more expressive parts of the body such as the Eyebrows, one bone probably just won't do it. You'll still only need one Vertex map per Eyebrow (Right Eyebrow Vertex and Left Eyebrow Vertex (Figure 13.30), but you'll want more control over these Eyebrows than one bone can provide.

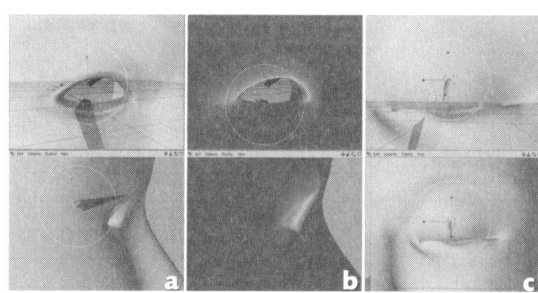

FIGURE 13.29 Eyelids can be opened and shut with Vertex maps assigned to bones that allow for a circular path of the Eyelid.

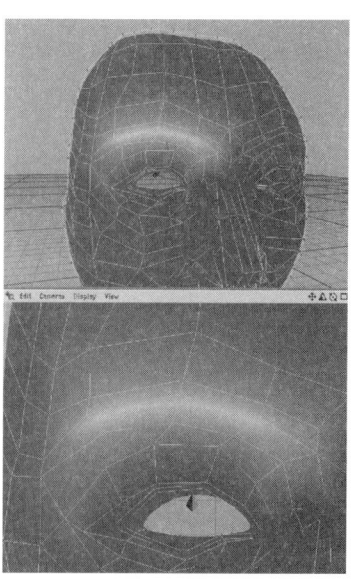

FIGURE 13.30 Vertex map for the Eyebrow.

There are a couple of different ways to manipulate an Eyebrow (these theories also apply to the Mouth, by the way). One is to create groups of bones (all with the same Restriction tag of the Eyebrow Vertex map) that act like levers behind the scene, raising and lowering the Vertex map assigned to it (Figure 13.31 a). With several bones making several layers, you then have several different control points from which to distort the Eyebrow (Figure 13.31 b).

The other method is much more akin to what we've used bones for before. In this method, you lay the bones (with Restriction tags restricting the bones' influence to the Eyebrow Vertex map) inside of the polymesh in roughly the same shape as muscles behind the Eyebrows. Once these bones have been fixed and activated, you can move them like a snake, thus deforming the Eyebrow in front of it (Figure 13.32).

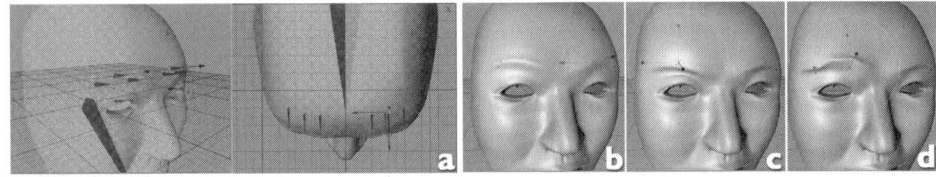

FIGURE 13.31 *(a) Eyebrow lever method; creating levers from bones behind the Eyebrows. (b) Some possibilities of the lever method.*

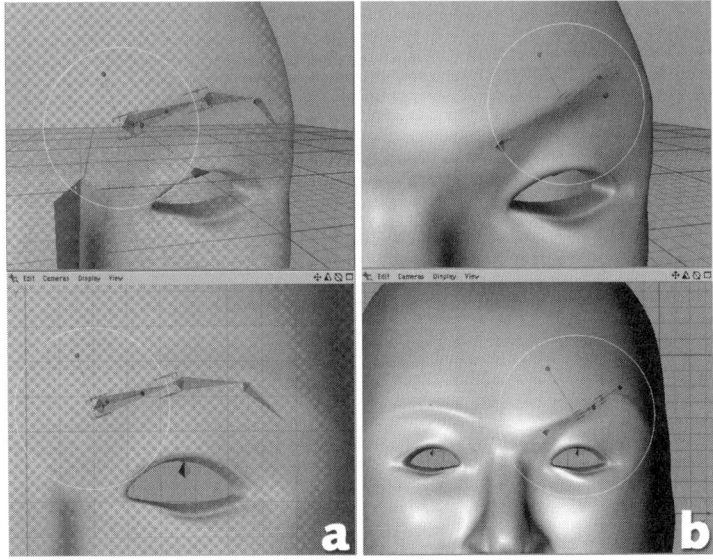

FIGURE 13.32 *Another method for the Eyebrows is to lay the bones within the Eyebrow for alteration.*

ON THE CD

Both methods have their strengths and weaknesses. In the file included on the CD are both scenarios so you can play with them and find what you like best.

One of the nice things about this bone method is that each of the bones can be moved or rotated independently of the others. So, you can have the Eyebrows raising as the Mouth opens, while the Eyelids start to close. Later if you want to start the Mouth opening while the Eyebrows move differently you can do so, as the animation between those collections of bones are separate.

Whew! We've looked at a lot of powerful, complex, but important concepts in this chapter. Character animation is tough and takes practice finding what techniques work for you, and what works for your model. Your techniques will probably even change from model to model, but being familiar with the ideas of a lot of techniques just puts that many more tools in your 3D toolbox to use when they are needed.

CHAPTER 14
Rendering

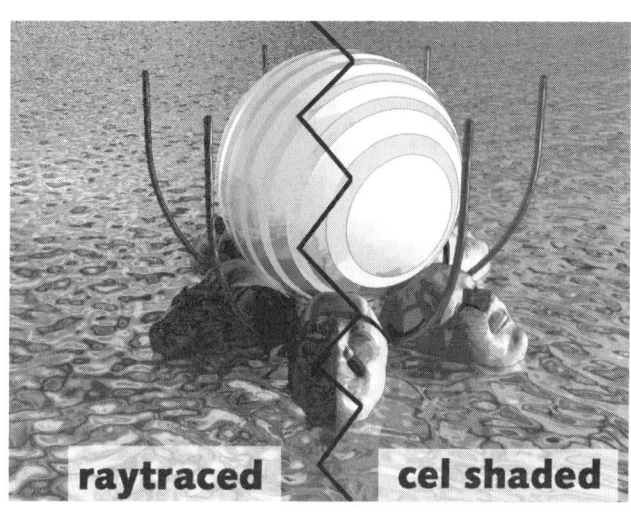

We've looked at modeling forms. We've looked at adding texture to these forms to create tactile looking surfaces. We've looked at how to bring those polygons to life through the ideas of animation. The last step of 3D animation (that takes place within a 3D application anyway) is rendering.

Rendering is the process of C4D taking all the modeling, texturing, lighting, and animation information, and "painting" it complete with shadows, highlights, reflections, etc... Through the course of the book, we've done several test renderings to get a quick idea of how our work has been looking. However, manipulating the Rendering settings is an art form in itself, and can present a good project at its best. Conversely, rendering is one of the slowest parts of most animation projects; so, mastering the art of the Rendering settings can save hours inrendering time, allowing you to move quicker on your project, and produce better projects through more in-depth revision.

RENDERING TOOLS

There are three main buttons allowing you to access the various rendering options. All three are located in the top command palette (Figure 14.1). To start with, we'll look at the Rendering Settings button (far right) as it determines how the other two tools will work.

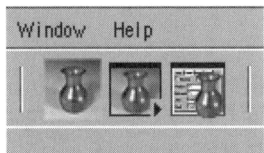

FIGURE 14.1 *The rendering tools of the top command palette.*

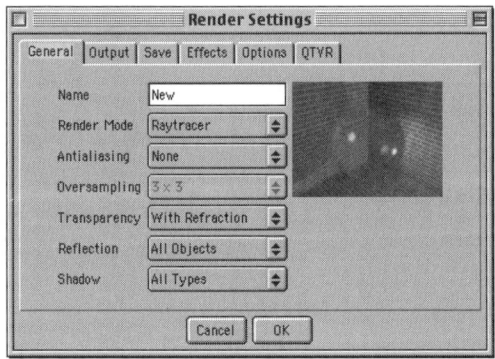

FIGURE 14.2 *General tab.*

Upon clicking the Rendering Settings button, a dialog box will appear that allows you to define how C4D will interpret the information you've given it thus far. The Rendering Settings is split up into six tabs in C4D XL v6. The first, the General tab (Figure 14.2) allows you to make general changes to how the scene is rendered. C4D can render in several modes, the default Raytracing is probably closest to real world situations (Figure 14.3 a). However, C4D can also render

Chapter 14 Rendering

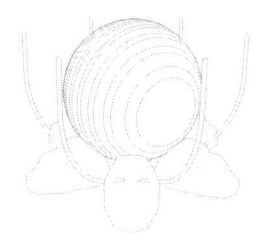

FIGURE 14.3 *(a) Raytraced rendering. (b) Cel-Render B&W. (c) Cel-Render Color.*

collection of frames "As Editor." This isn't usually of much use in still work, but in animation it's important, especially with complex scenes, to create quickly done renderings As Editor to get an idea of the true timing of your motion. Besides As Editor, C4D can alsorender in a couple of Cel renderings. Cel animation is the traditional animation most people think of with flat planes of color surrounded by black lines almost any Saturday morning cartoon is a cel animation. C4D does a Cel-Render B/W (Figure 14.3 b) and a Cel-Render Color (Figure 14.3 c) that attempt to mimic this look. Basically, these attempt to break down any gradient in color to smaller flat planes of color (or just lines in the case of Cel-Render B&W).

When C4D renders, it's dealing with a lot of information and a lot of calculations. Because of this, the Rendering Settings have been optimized to attempt to provide good quality in very little time. However, sometimes you may not need C4D to calculate all the things it looks for in the rendering process. Or perhaps the default quality just doesn't cut it, and you need C4D to spend a bit more time to provide a little more refined rendering There are several ways and places to decrease or increase the amount of issues C4D takes time to look at as it renders. You can tell C4D's Renderer to not worry about everything from reflections to shadows. You can tell C4D to be careful in how it handles edges or to just pound them out. Knowing when to ask C4D to do what will determine how much time you spend waiting for C4D to render. To analyze these possibilities, we'll look at a Rendering mode and how the different options can be altered or manipulated.

RAYTRACER OPTIONS

Right there on in the General tab is one of the quickest ways to raise the quality of Raytraced renderings. By default, C4D renders with no antialiasing, which often results in "jaggies" or roughly rendered edges even to smooth surfaces. This stair-like effect is referred to as aliasing. Figure 14.4 (a) shows a rendering done at the default, No Antialiasing setting. Notice the jaggies along the bent capsule shape. When any of the Antialiasing options are activated, C4D takes extra time to "Oversample" pixels as it renders. With this extra time comes more accurate and smoother renderings, but at a fairly healthy rendering cost. Antialiasing always slows rendering. However, when you work with still images or broadcast animation, some antialiasing can be necessary (Figure 14.4 b).

So the key is to know when to use what Antialiasing and what Oversampling settings. Although there are no rock solid rules, there are some general guidelines that you can count on. First, when you do first-run renderings even of stills, don't bother with the antialiasing — no need. For those first renderings, you want C4D to pound out the rendering giving you accurate color and composition, but not worrying about immaculate edges.

Antialiasing>Edge spends extra time oversampling the edges of objects. However, this Antialiasing setting does not bother with shadows and textures. For many scenes where the textures are secondary, or the shadows are not clearly seen, this is a perfect setting. Antialiasing>Edge with 3x3 Oversampling can produce a clean rendering that stands up well to most initial inspection by clients.

When you're looking for really clean renderings that make your shadows beautiful (if they are seen), and that keep your whole image clean, Antialiasing>Edge and Color is the choice for you. Typically this makes for a great final Rendering setting, as it makes the edges, shadows, and texture smooth and clean. Typically, Antialiasing>Edge and Color with 6x6 Oversampling creates nearly flawless renderings for still print based renderings. If you're dealing with broadcast, Antialiasing>Edge and Color with 3x3 works great.

Antialiasing>Always oversamples every single pixel in the rendering. To put it bluntly, this is hardly ever worth it. The rendering slowdown is so immense, I've never had a complex project that has been allowed to render at this setting — it simply renders too slow. Usually, Antialising>Edge and Color works great. Stay clear of Antialiasing>Always — unless you've got more time than you know what to do with.

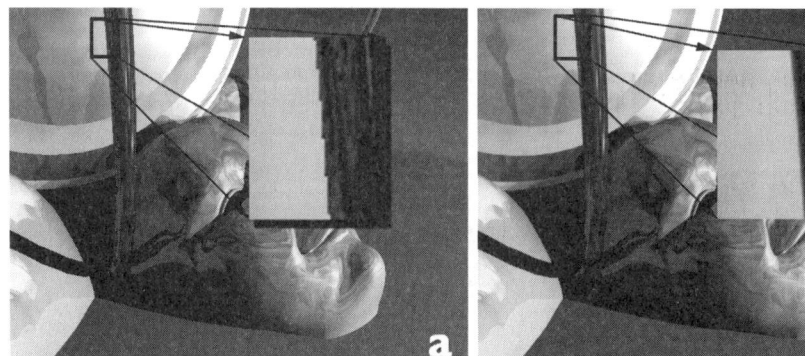

FIGURE 14.4 *(a) No Antialiasing and the resultant jaggies. (b) With Antialiasing activated, the image is rendered much smoother, but at a rendering cost.*

Transparency, Reflection, and Shadow

Still within the General tab are three options that can speed the rendering process. By default, raytraced images are rendered recognizing and showing objects' Transparency and Reflection properties. Also by default, the Raytracing Settings calculate Shadows. However, all of these options can be turned off. Figure 14.5 (a) shows the scene we've been working with with all of these turned on. Figure 14.5 (b) shows Transparency set to None. Suddenly all transparent, glass-like, or alpha parameterized objects become opaque. You can also use the raytracer to render transparency but not bother to calculate the bend of light as it passes through objects. The Transparency>No Refraction setting can give you a quick view and idea of transparent objects but still save time as the bent light isn't bothered with (Figure 14.5 c).

Similarly, Figure 14.6 (a) shows the scene (with Transparency activated again) but Reflection set to None. Figure 14.6 (b) shows the results of setting the Reflection to only worry about the Floor and Sky and not worrying about other objects in the scene.

FIGURE 14.5 *(a) Scene with all settings go. (b) Transparency>None means no transparent or alpha channels are calculated. (c) Transparency>No Refraction still shows transparent objects but doesn't bend the refractive light.*

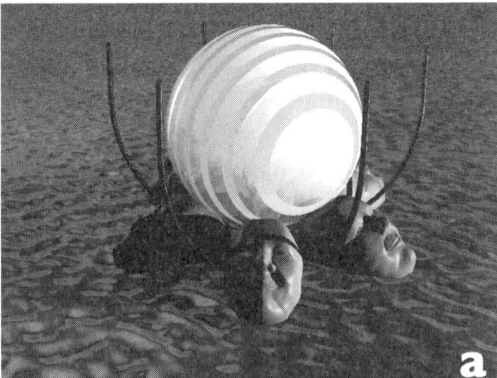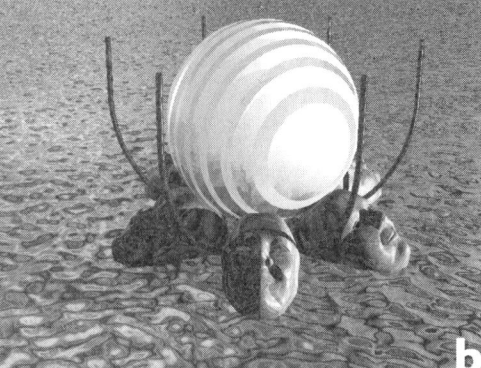

FIGURE 14.6 *(a) Reflection>None. (b) Reflection>Floor and Sky Only.*

RAYTRACING AND THE EFFECTS TAB

In the Effects tab is another collection of options that may be turned off to decrease rendering time. We've talked about the ability to do Depth of Field with cameras. We've talked of Glow parameters, Lens Effects, and the rendering hits caused by Volumetric lighting. However, sometimes when you are working within C4D, you don't want to have to go back in and manually turn each of these off for every light or camera to get a look at how your scene looks. In the Effects tab, you can deactivate the Depth of Field, Lens Effects, Glow Effects, or Volumetric Lighting to have C4D render without these. Make sure that if you turn these off for initial renderings, that you reactivate them for final renderings.

Level of Detail (LOD) was discussed a bit at the beginning of the book in helping to speed up how quickly the Editor would refresh. The lower the level of detail, the faster the refresh. Similarly, the lower the LOD setting within the Effects tab, the quicker the scene will render. Remember, though, that only certain objects support LOD; namely metaballs, primitives, and NURBS. If your scene is all polygon modeling based, adjusting the LOD setting does no good. Similarly, if you've established LOD tags (tags that allow you to define the LOD for individual objects) these tags will override any setting in the Effects tab.

Scene Motion Blur is really a nice effect. When you are watching a movie on your VCR/DVD player, try pressing the Pause button in the middle of some fast moving action. The result is a very blurred still image. This is because the lens is opening and closing so slow that there is considerable motion taking place between frames. The result is a blurred frame. Our eyes have come to expect this in film and television. In 3D animation, the lens captures every frame by default as a clean pristine image (Figure 14.7 a). By activating the Scene Motion Blur option, you can simulate the effects of real world cameras (Figure 14.7 b).

Scene Motion Blur comes with a price, though. In order to create the motion blur, C4D renders the frame several times (as defined by your setting in Scene Motion Blur) and then blends the frames together. It moves each frame slightly ahead of the last, which is what gives the blur. This is nice because everything (including shadows) are blurred, giving you a nice effect. The drawback is that if you are using 5 Times Scene Motion Blur, this means each frame must render five times; so your rendering time is automatically increased 5x. If you use higher blur (like 25 Times (Figure 14.7 c)), you get more blur, but 25x the rendering time. The only rendering benefit to this is that blurred scenes don't often need any antialiasing. So, if you're using Scene Motion Blur, you can typically turn off all Antialiasing options.

A decent alternative to Scene Motion Blur is the (by default activated) Object Motion Blur. This is only activated for objects that have a Motion Blur tag attached to them, created in the Object Manager by right-clicking (COMMAND-clicking) the object and selecting New Tag>Motion Blur Tag… from the pop-up menu. It is there that you can determine the percent of the Object Motion Blur. When C4D renders the scene when tags have Object Motion Blur attached, it blurs the objects in motion. This renders much more quickly than Scene Motion Blur, but doesn't take into account things like blurred shadows (Figure 14.7 d), or, if the camera is the fastest moving object and objects are still, there is no blur rendered.

Within the Effects tab is still the Filter option. These are filters that are applied to the rendering after it has been rendered. If you are doing still work, this is probably best left to Photoshop. If you are doing animation work, and don't want to work with After Effects, Premiere, or Final Cut to refine any pixel touch-up, see page 424 of the manual for descriptions of these filters.

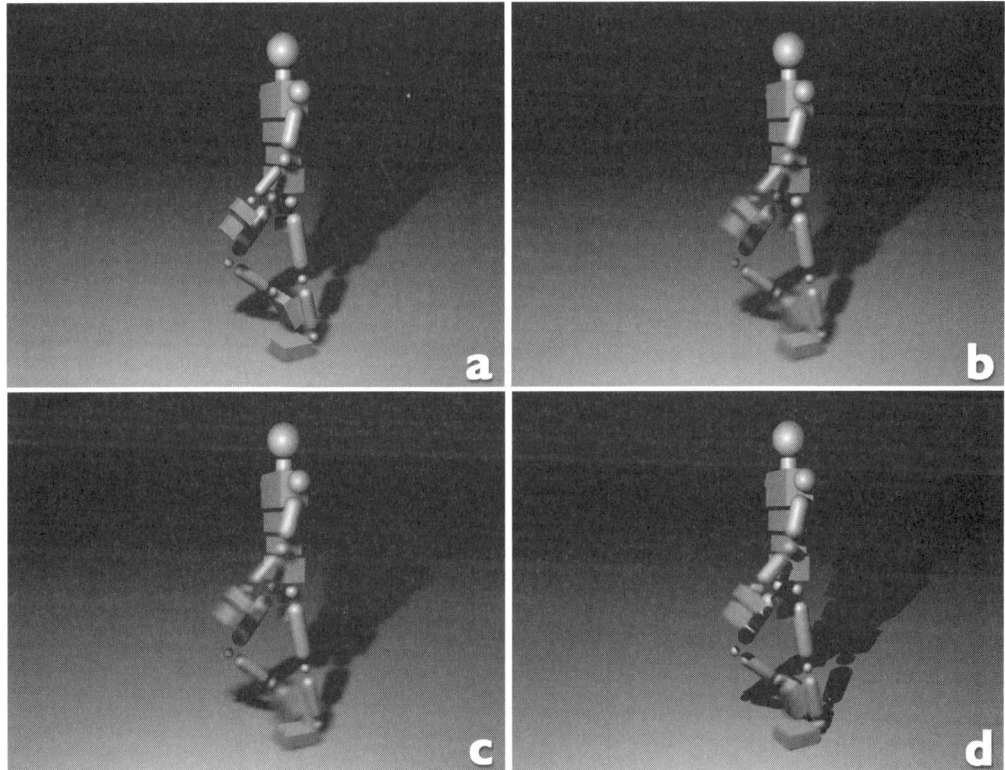

FIGURE 14.7 *(a) Regularly rendered frame with no motion blur. (b) Single frame rendered with 5 Times Scene Motion Blur. (c) Single frame rendered with 25 Times Scene Motion Blur. (d) Object Motion Blur; notice that the shadow remains crisp even though the hand and legs are blurred.*

RAYTRACING AND THE OPTIONS TAB

The Options tab provides further options for optimizing early renderings. You can choose here to have C4D render the Active Object Only to get a quick idea of a newly added object without having to manually hide all the other objects in a scene. You can choose to have C4D automatically render using the floodlight attached to the camera that we discussed in the Lighting chapter (Chapter 10) if there are no other lights in the scene using the Auto Light option. Conversely, you can turn this off if you didn't put any lights in the scene, and really want it to render without any lights (i.e. glowing eyeballs that are glowing through Luminance and Glow parameters). Within the Options tab, you can have C4D create a Log file that gives a report of the settings done for a particular rendering by activating the Log File option. You can also tell C4D whether to carry on rendering if it cannot find a texture as it begins rendering.

The next five input fields — Ray Depth, Refl. Depth, Shadow Depth, Threshold, and AA Softness — are all very specific ways of instructing C4D how closely to interpret your scene. Ray Depth has to do with how far each ray is allowed to travel through transparent or Alpha Parameterized objects. Figure 14.8 (a) shows the Editor view of several thin cubes with a texture defining the black parts as alpha'd. Figure 14.8 (b) shows what this scene should look like in theory. Figure 14.9 shows what happens at different Ray Depths settings.

Typically, the default setting of "6" is sufficient. However, in some situations, if you mysteriously find black regions rendering where the scene should be clear, you may need to adjust this setting. Remember that the deeper the rays needed to calculate, the longer the rendering time.

The Refl. Depth setting, stands for Reflection Depth. Basically, this is in reference to highly reflective objects that are close to each other or whose reflections

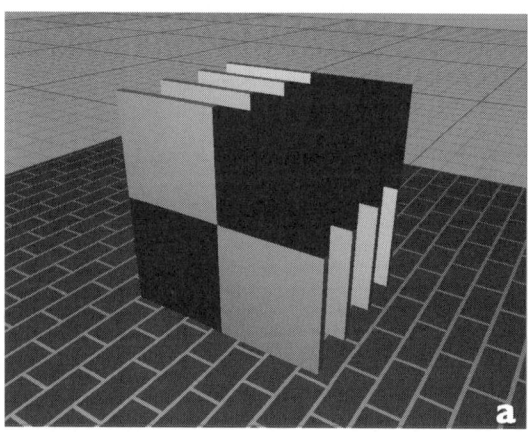 

FIGURE 14.8 *(a) Scene with multiple levels of objects using Alpha Channels. (b) How the scene ought to look.*

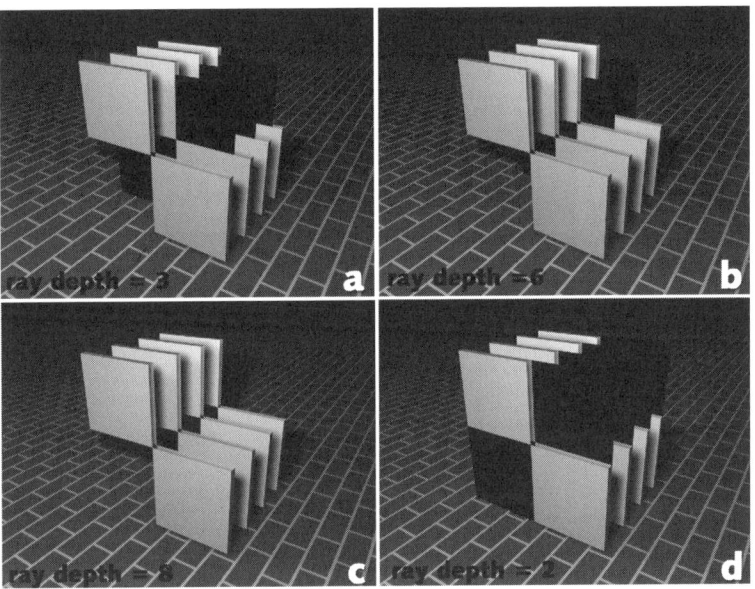

FIGURE 14.9   *How the scene looks at various Ray Depths settings.*

should be bouncing off each other. In theory, rays of light, or reflections, should continue indefinitely, or until they break down because of air or dust. However, infinite reflections can take infinitely long to render; besides the fact that too many reflections tend to muddy a scene and make it difficult to decipher. Figure 14.10 shows our scene with two mirrors on either sides of our forms that face each other. One mirror's reflection should be picked up by the other mirror, whose reflection should be bounced back again to the other mirror, etc… Figure 14.11 shows three settings for Refl. Depth and how the renderings appear. Notice that when Refl. Depth is 1, the mirror reflects the other mirror, but not the reflection of that other mirror. As the Refl. Depth increases, the number of times you can see the mirror's reflection's reflections increases. Also, as always, as the Refl. Depth increases and there is more to calculate, the rendering time increases.

The Shadow Depth input field goes hand in hand with the Refl. Depth setting. Notice in Figure 14.12 where the Shadow Depth is set to 1; none of the reflections show shadows. As the Shadow Depth is increased, the number of reflections revealing the shadows increase. More shadows to calculate, of course, means longer rendering time.

C4D is smart enough to know that light dissipates as it travels. The rays that it uses to raytrace dissipate as well. It turns out that with issues such as reflection, these rays spend a whole lot of time to create this nice effect. Essentially, for

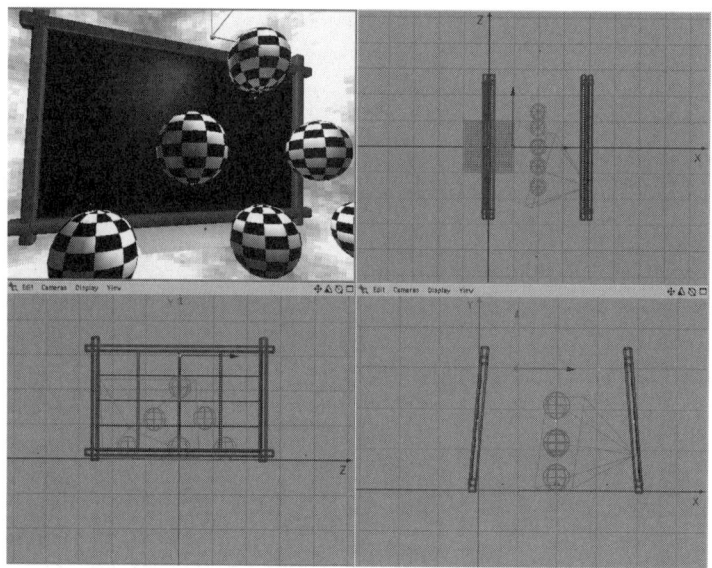

FIGURE 14.10 *Reflection Scene setup.*

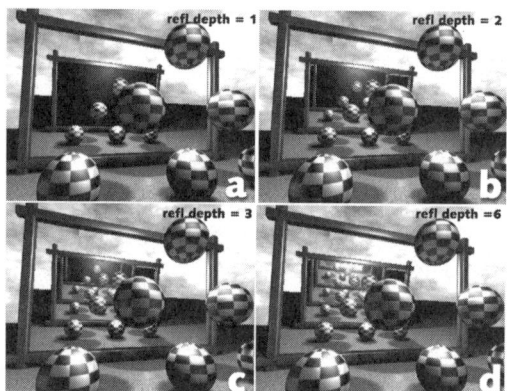

FIGURE 14.11 *Various Refl. Depth settings and their results.*

FIGURE 14.12 *Shadow Depth illustrations.*

most scenes, the reflections are a minor issue for the look as a whole. The Threshold setting tells C4D when to just stop worrying about a ray — once it drops below the percentage listed in this field, it stops the ray. Usually, the 15% listed by default works great; however, if your Reflection Parameter for a material is set below 15% (in cases where you want a very slight reflection), your scene will render with no reflection at all. To retain those very subtle reflections, decrease the Threshold value (Figure 14.13).

AA Softness deals with the antialiasing options. The higher this value, the "softer" your images will appear (Figure 14.14). If you need a crisp, non-muddied rendering, leave this value low. Lower values render more quickly. It's tough to tell the difference in black and white print, so be sure and check the image out on the CD, or do a couple of renderings yourself to see the image quality difference.

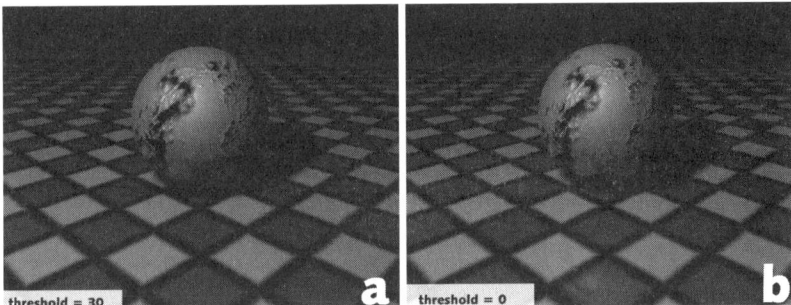

FIGURE 14.13 *Increased Threshold values result in faster rendering but less accurate reflections (a). Notice the subtle reflections in (b) on the tiled floor.*

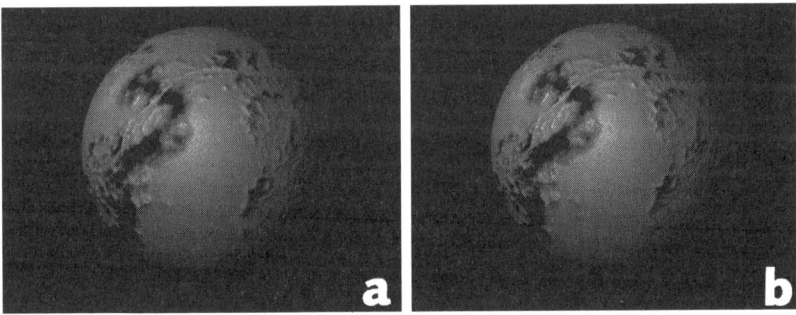

FIGURE 14.14 *The higher the AA Softness value, the "softer" the image looks. (a) AA Softness setting is at 100%, (b) AA Softness setting is at 10%.*

CEL RENDERING OPTIONS

The Cel Renderer attempts to make your renderings look like traditional animation. Sometimes in other programs this is called a toon shader. This method of rendering is slow. Further, in many cases, such as complex scenes, it's hard to see the real difference (Figure 14.15). Mostly in scenes with uncluttered textures and shapes, can Cel Rendering really show through (Figure 14.16).

ON THE CD

There are two kinds of Cel Renderers: Cel-Render B&W (black and white) (Figure 14.17 a) and Cel-Render Color (Figure 14.17 b) on the CD-ROM. Within these two Cel Rendering methods, many of the tabs within Render Settings are not applicable to Cel-Render options. But most work just the same. The place where the Cel-Renderer can be really optimized is in the Options tab. Within the Options tab exists a section especially for the Cel-Renderer. Notice that the other options within the Options tab can apply to Cel-Renderer too (i.e. Textures), but the Illumination, Outline, and Edges settings are specifically for the Cel-Renderer.

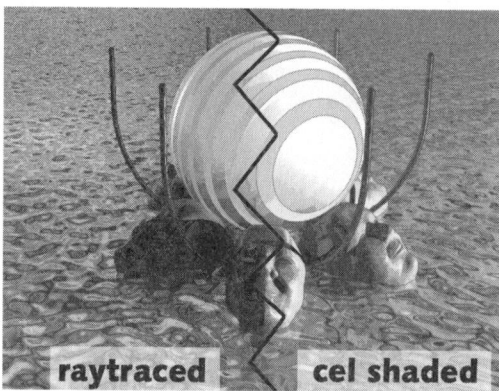

FIGURE 14.15 *Scenes with visually complex textures do not Cel Render much differently than traditional rendering.*

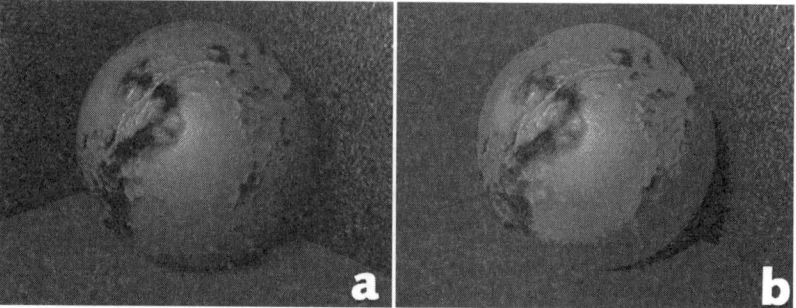

FIGURE 14.16 *With simpler forms, Cel Rendering can really come out.*

CHAPTER 14 RENDERING

The three options, Illumination, Outline and Edges are fairly self-explanatory. With all of them activated, the Cel-Renderer draws a line around each polygon in the scene (Figure 14.17 c). With Edges off, the Cel-Renderer draws its black line just around the outer end of each shape (Figure 14.17 d). With no Edges or Outline, the result is just planes of color (Figure 14.17 e). Finally, no illumination, outline, or edges, just draws absolutely flat planes of color without worrying about banding planes for visual modeling (Figure 14.17 f).

Overall, the Cel-Renderer isn't that effective for true cartoony looks. There are a couple of tutorials online that give some great alternatives though. If you have a project in which you need very cartoon-like renderings, please see:

Naam's very informative website.
http://www.xs4all.nl/~naam/cartoonrender.html
and Mike Ista's interesting use of SLA (*BhodiNut's Smells Like Almonds*)
http://allerleirauh.thomasson-project.cx/~mike/3d_frameset.html.

OUTPUT AND SAVE TABS

The Output tab allows you to define what size and how many frames C4D will render in the Picture Viewer. The settings here have no relevance when you use Render Active View, Render Region, or Render Active Object. But, when you render to Picture Viewer, C4D will reference the settings contained here. The Save tab allows you to define where the finished files are to be saved and in what format.

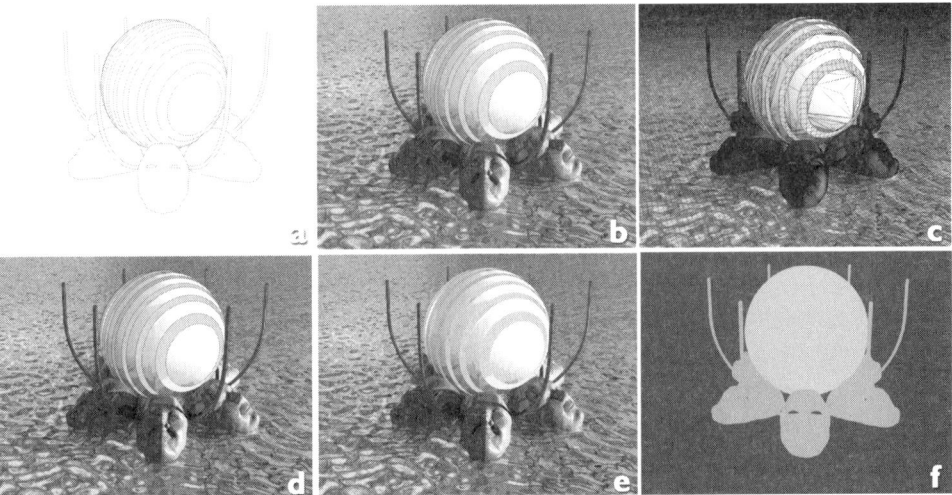

FIGURE 14.17 *(a) Cel-Render B&W. (b) Cel-Render Color on the CD-ROM. (c) Illumination, Outline, and Edges On. (d) Illumination and Outline on; Edges off. (e) Illumination on. Outline and Edges off. (f) Illumination, Outline and Edges off.*

When you render still images, you don't necessarily need to enter a Path in the Save tab, as you can select File>Export within the Picture Viewer. However, when you render animations, it's vitally important that you understand this tab.

When you render stills you can decide what file format to save the finished rendering in. However, when you are doing movies, unless you want huge collections of still images, make sure that the file format is changed to one of the Quicktime options or AVI options. Also, make sure that you define a location to save the movie to within the Path input field. If you don't, C4D could render the entire scene and you would not have anything to show for it, as C4D would not have known where to save the frames to.

The Alpha Channel and Depth Channel options here allow you to create renderings that make it easy to "drop out" the black background if there is one. Figure 14.18 shows a rendering in Photoshop and the channels that include the embedded information of where the rendered part ends and the black background begins. The Straight Alphas setting avoids dark seams that often happen with soft edged objects (smoke, volumetric light etc…). If Separate Alpha is checked, C4D creates a separate file that defines the Alpha Channel.

Often, if you are using one piece of animation within a larger project, mastering the Alpha Channel options can be very important. Most compositing programs recognize Alpha Channels, even embedded in animations that C4D produces. This makes it easy to grab a movie rendered in C4D and drop it into an AfterEffects project.

RUNNING THROUGH THE TABS

The important thing to remember when you render is that there are many options located in the different tabs. Before you send a big project to render for a final time, make sure you do a quick run through the tabs and make sure:

1) You're rendering using the right Renderer (Raytracer or Cel-Renderer).
2) You've got the *necessary* Antialiasing settings — don't activate Antialiasing until you're sure you're going to keep the rendering.
3) Check the Output tab to make sure that: a) You're rendering at the right size and b) If you're doing an animation, that you have the correct frames selected. It's a terrible feeling to come back from letting your computer render all weekend to find that it did indeed render frame 0, but that was all it rendered when you needed 500 frames of an animation done.
4) If you're dealing with animation, double-check that Format is set to Quicktime or AVI in the Save tab.

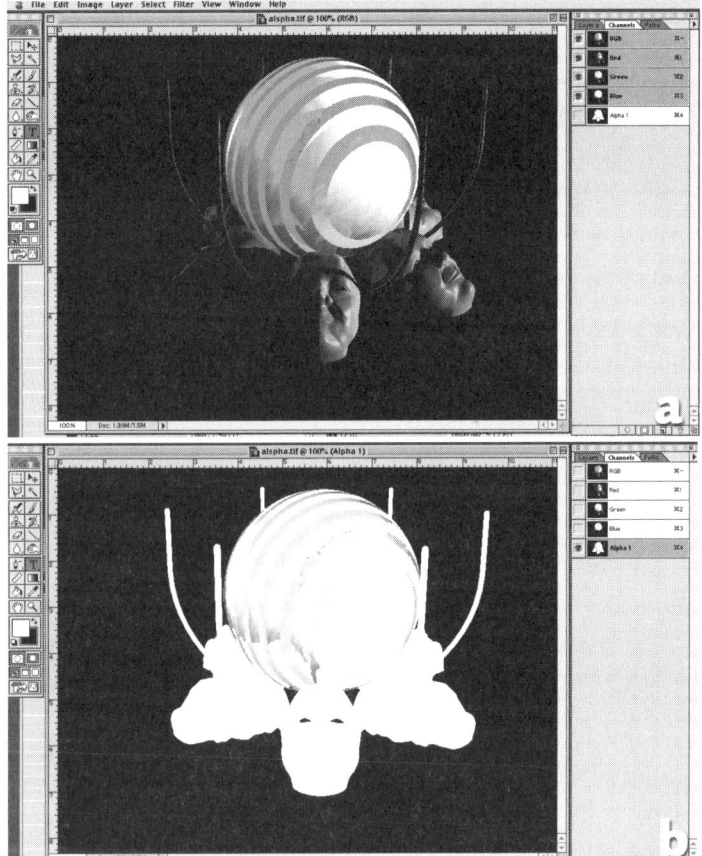

FIGURE 14.18 *Example of Alpha Channels. Notice the colored image, but the channels reveal that this file "knows" where the image ends, making new backgrounds easy to put in.*

5) Again, if you are dealing with animation, ensure that you are indeed saving the animation somewhere as defined by the Path in the Save tab, and that there is room on the disk you are saving it to. You can't suspend a rendering in C4D, so when you are rendering Quicktimes or AVIs, if you run out of room and the rendering stops, you've lost the entire rendering.

6) If you are still unsure about the animation, consider rendering to a series of .tiffs; if you are familiar with NLDVE programs, you can quickly drop this sequence in and render a Quicktime from the stills. The benefit of this is that if you need to adjust 30 frames in the middle of the animation, you only need to render those 30 frames again and drop them back into the NLDVE without having to rerender the entire project.

7) Whip through your Effects tab, to make sure all the effects you're using will actually render, and if you want Scene Motion Blur or Object Motion Blur — that it's activated.
8) Finally, take some good time to optimize your Options tab. Take series of small still test renderings to see if all of the "Depths" are appropriate.

TUTORIAL

14.1 C4D CEL-RENDERER AND FLASH

Using your 3D work on the web has been one of the Holy Grails of 3D-dom. Still, C4D doesn't work seamlessly with Flash or other vector-based web delivery methods. However, using the Cel-Renderer, there are some ways to get fairly good results. There are some restrictions to remember. First, in all cases, we are converting bit-mapped images to vector – and, a complex bit-mapped image converted into a complex vector doesn't save that much room. Second, even though you may animate and render Quicktime movies at 30fps, web animation typically is much lower than that to keep the downloads quick and the browsing experience snappy; so remember to keep the motion simple, as you'll probably end up with a project that is 12-20 fps. The best translation of animations takes place using the Cel-Renderer B&W, although we'll look at solutions to using Cel-Render Color.

The first thing to know is that since we need to convert the bit-mapped based projects into the Vector format that Flash likes so well, we'll need to have each frame of the animation separate. Even if we're doing a movie, we don't want to render to a Quicktime in the Save tab of Render Settings. If you are rendering a line animation (Cel-Render B&W) like in Figure 14.19 (a), render to TIFF, as we'll be using Adobe's Streamline to vectorize the frames. If you're dealing with a colored scene, render to JPEG as we'll be using Flash's built in Trace Bitmap function (Figure 14.19 b).

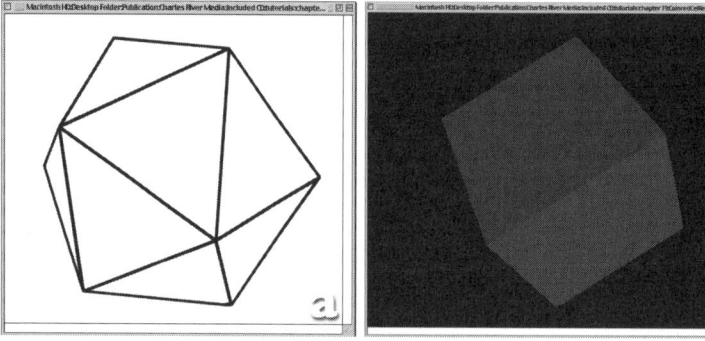

FIGURE 14.19 *(a) Cel-Render B&W, should usually be rendered as TIFFs. (b) Colored projects should be rendered as JPEGs.*

CHAPTER 14 RENDERING

The next important bit of information is that the process of tracing the bit-mapped based image into a vector-based image works best when there's lots of information for Flash or Streamline to work from. Render your images larger than you need them to finally be (usually around 800x600). The final vector-based frame that each bit-mapped frame will finally create, can be resized without penalty, but having clean bitmaps with lots of pixel information to start with helps the process immensely.

CEL-RENDERED B&W PROJECT

Let's start out with a line animation project. For this tutorial, a simple primitive form was created and Cel-Render B&W was selected. Also note that Edges was activated in the Options tab to allow for each edge of every polygon to be seen. Since we'll be using Streamline to batch convert all of the frames, the files were saved as TIFFs. C4D labels each TIFF numerically, which really is to our advantage when it comes time to import frames into Flash. For now, if you have Streamline, open it up.

The first thing we need to do is establish what settings work best. To do this, within Streamline, go to File>Open and open one frame (Figure 14.20 a).

The nice thing about Cel-Render B&W is that there is very little tweaking needed within Streamline. Select the Options>Color/B&W Setup....pull-down menu and change the Threshold setting to a lower value (Figure 14.20 b). To test how well this shift works, select File>Convert. The result should look something like Figure 14.21.

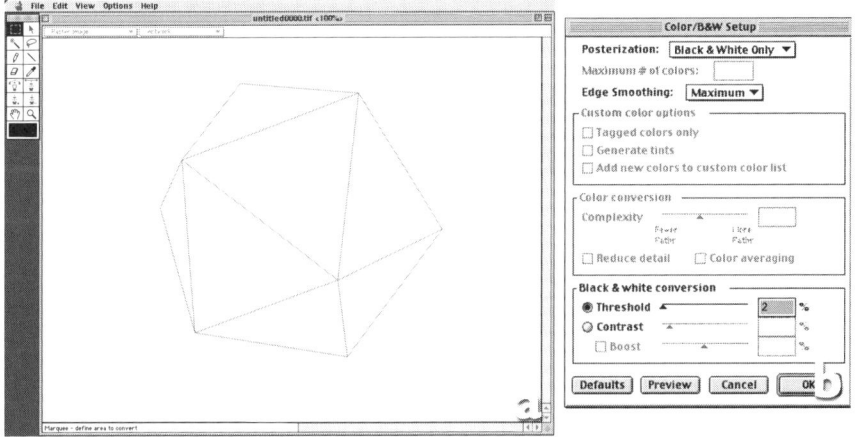

FIGURE 14.20 *(a) Opening Streamline documents. (b) Adjusting the Color/B&W Setup options to be more aggressive in finding lines.*

This adds a little bulk to the line animation, which is good. Now that you know that this works, we can tell Streamline to just convert an entire group of frames. To do this, go to File>Batch Select. Streamline will then ask you what frames to convert. Hopefully all your frames have been saved in one folder, so you can go to that folder and select Add All.

Then, after clicking OK, Streamline will ask you where to save the converted files and what format to save them in. Create a new folder to save these files to, and make sure that they are being saved as Illustrator EPS files. Streamline will then tear into the vertorizing process using the setting you had used for the test image. At the end of it all, you should have a folder filled with .eps files ready to be imported.

Within Flash, select File>Import. You only need to Add the first file (and, in fact, you want to make sure you only select the first file), because Flash will immediately recognize that this file is one in a sequence and ask you if you wish to import the rest of the files in the sequence. Of course, click Yes, and Flash will import all the frames and place each vectorized frame in a frame of the Flash file (Figure 14.22 a). Select Modify>Movie and click the Contents tool to resize the stage to the movie. Select File>Export Movie, and the exported .swf file will be small and quick. For the exercise contained on the CD, you can see that the resultant .swf file is only 20k.

ON THE CD

If you are planning to use an animation as a button or small visual element, make sure that you have selected Insert>New Symbol, and select Movie in the dialog box. This way, you can use the Movie symbol and drop it anywhere into your overall Flash movie and resize it to your heart's content.

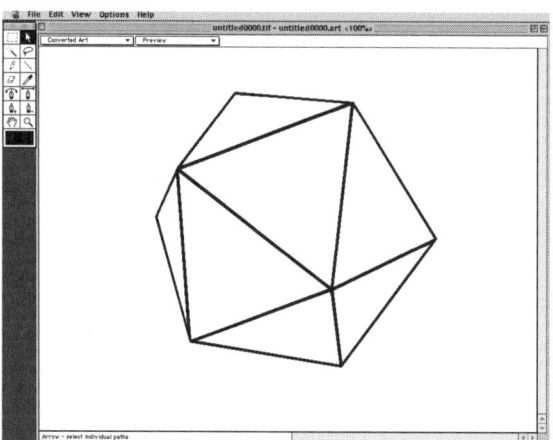

FIGURE *The "vectorized" test image.*
14.21

CHAPTER 14 RENDERING

CEL-RENDERED COLOR PROJECT

For colored Cel-Rendered projects, the process is a bit more labor intensive. Some folks can use Streamline to vectorize color images, but often complex images are hard to manage in Streamline. However, you might try Streamline first for your color projects as the batch process function is a very nice way to go.

If you can't get your project to work in Streamline, you can import the JPEG files directly into Flash. Again, simply use the File>Import pull-down menu and Add/Import only the first JPEG. Click Yes when Flash asks you if you wish to import the sequence of frames.

ON THE CD

What Flash then does is import the huge collection of bit-mapped images. Your Library will be full of these numerically labeled .jpgs. To vectorize these .jpgs, we'll use Flash's Trace Bitmap function (Modify>Trace Bitmap). Again, experiment with the first frame to get the best setting before continuing on to the others. For the tutorial included on the CD, the settings should be something like those shown in (Figure 14.22 b). The trick is to find the balance that produces the fewest paths, but maintains the best acceptable quality.

Here's the kicker: once you've found the right settings, you need to Trace Bitmap for every frame you've imported. Then, after that, you can further reduce the size of the project by Optimizing (Modify>Optimize). When all the frames have been vectorized, make sure to delete the .jpgs from your Library. Export the movie for the final effect. Remember, that if you do this process inside of a Movie symbol, it becomes easier to incorporate into other Flash projects or rescale.

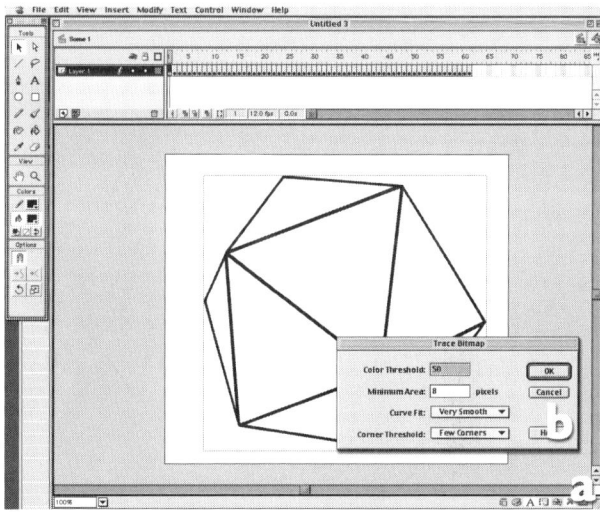

FIGURE 14.22 (a) Imported frames in Flash. (b) Settings for the Trace Bitmap function.

ON THE CD

On the CD, you'll find the C4D files that you can render out yourself to follow this tutorial. Also, find the final .swf files. Now these examples are very simple however, with a little massaging, you can create more dynamic Flash projects based on your 3D work.

CHAPTER 15
An Overview of 3D Real-Time Content Creation

By Ian Mankowski

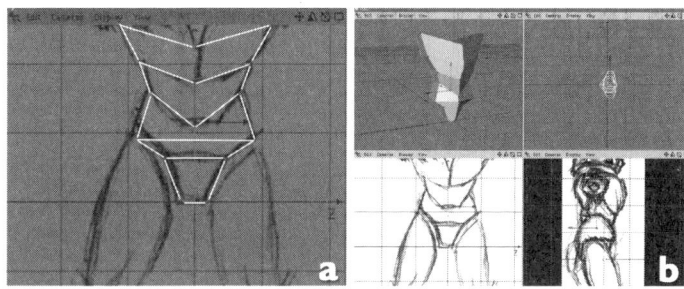

3D real-time content creation is a big word. In its technical definition, 3D real-time content creation can mean anything from small graphic demos that render models in real-time to test your graphic card's speed and power, to complex particle simulation on a car simulation deep within the confines of Ford or GM. To most of us, however, 3D real-time content creation is associated with games, and this is the association we will use throughout the next few sections.

Why Games?

Gaming is one of the most exciting fields of 3D animation, and the ability to interact with your personal creations is a very exciting opportunity for any 3D artist. From a more practical standpoint, game animation can provide job opportunities that are much more readily accessible than many big studio jobs (Figure 15.1).

Take a look at a PC Gamer, or an issue of Game Developer and thumb through the articles. Visit http://www.polycount.com. Take a look at their website and look at what program they're all using. 90% of the time, they're all using the 300 pound gorilla 3D Studio Max. Why? 3D Studio Max has a very powerful and expandable feature set that can give a game animator anything he could possibly need. 3D Studio Max has worked hard to promote themselves in this area as well, going so far as to offer a free version of their software, which they call gMax, to aid game content creation wannabes.

Cinema 4D for Gaming Content Creation

With 3D Studio Max as the reigning application, what's the point to learning to use Cinema 4D for game content creation? Well, believe it or not, C4D has some significant advantages to consider.

 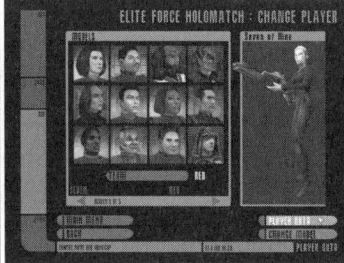 

FIGURE 15.1 (a) TM & ©2000 Paramount Pictures. All rights reserved. (b) Star Trek: Voyager and related marks are trademarks of Paramount Pictures. (c) and TM 2000 Activision, Inc. All rights reserved.

Chapter 15 An Overview of 3D Real-Time Content Creation

Cinema 4D is cross-platform compatible. This is its singular most important advantage. The ability to transfer your work seamlessly between Macintosh and PC workstations is invaluable, and its worth should not be underestimated. This is especially important to smaller game studios where you can't afford to be as picky as you may like to be in choosing your employees and what they will work with. Cinema 4D is also a very stable program. Stability is an important issue to any 3D field, and game developers are no exception.

These factors combine to make Cinema 4D a very real contender in the real-time content creation field. Although Cinema 4D may never make it quite as large as 3D Studio Max in the gaming field, it can become a very big player in the future, simply due to its cross platform compatibility. With BodyPaint, Cinema 4D's potential to become a 3D game creation heavyweight is only reinforced.

Sprite Animation vs. 3D Real-Time Content

Many games utilize Sprite Animation. Games such as Diablo 2, Escape Velocity, Baldur's Gate, and Myth 2, all utilize a Sprite-based Animation system. A Sprite-based Animation system is relatively similar to traditional 2D animation. Usually, in today's gaming world, a series of animated Sprites are created on a 3D program like Cinema 4D, and then rendered out as individual frames. Each frame is then imported into the game engine, and the game engine is instructed to run the animation as necessary. Sprite-based Animation is usually used when the player's view is static, meaning that you can only see the gaming world, characters, and buildings from one angle.

3D real-time content is currently the more popular game animation technique that is being used. This is mainly because real-time generated content can be dynamically viewed; that is, your viewing angle and distance perception of the gaming world and characters can change at any time in response to your actions. Games that embody this kind of animation include Quake 3 Arena, Unreal Tournament, WaterRace, and Star Trek: Elite Force (Figure 15.2).

Figure 15.2 *Screenshots of the game WaterRace (courtesy of French Touch SARL).*

Generally, in this form of game animation a model and animation is rendered in a 3D program; however, instead of rendering pictures of the animation to create the animation, the model and animation data is exported in a format that the game engine can understand. The game engine will then render the model in real-time on the monitor. Because of this the viewing angle can be changed in response to the player's actions, much in the same way that a Cinema 4D user can change their view of a model they're working on by simply using the Rotate tool.

In the next few sections, we will follow techniques for generating 3D real-time content, as in general, it's the more complicated to prepare for a game engine. Sprite Animation is simpler, in that it's a lot more like traditional 3D animation. Since you are rendering actual pictures that will be composited later in the game to form an animation, you have a lot more control over what the player will see. 3D real-time content, as you will see, is a very different world.

THE REQUIREMENTS OF 3D REAL-TIME CONTENT CREATION — WHAT YOU NEED TO KNOW

When it is compared to the rest of the 3D-animation world, 3D real-time content creation can appear horribly complex and overly simplistic at the same time. Many artists find that game content generation is less satisfying than creating animations for the big and little silver screens, due to the fact that in 3D animation, you have so little control. This is very important to realize. As a game animator, you have relatively little control over your final output. Unlike cinematic animation, you don't have control of your lighting, the setting your characters will be a part of, or any other number of details that are paramount when you are doing commercial animation. With this in mind, I'm going to compare and contrast game and commercial animation in the next few sections.

GAME ANIMATION IS A TEAM EFFORT

Even more so than commercial animation, game animation requires immense cooperation amongst the members of the game development group. A 3D artist can only control what the game will look like. Things such as how the player will interact with the game, what environments the character will be shown in, these are all matters that must be thoroughly discussed with the game programmers and designers to ensure that the game lives up to its original vision. Understand that while you can light a model in a certain way to achieve a certain impact on the viewer in commercial games, you'll very rarely be able to do such a thing in game animation. In a very real sense, games are not a medium for artists looking to present "perfectly," it is very much a world of good enough and compromises.

Chapter 15 An Overview of 3D Real-Time Content Creation

Game Animation Requirements

If you're a seasoned animator, the list of limitations I'm going to unfold before you that you'll have to adhere by may make you cry. You may find it depressing to try and be creative with so many limitations. Let me try and show you the silver lining on this before you go suicidal.

One of the greatest features of game animation is that because of all the limitations, your system can also be limited and yet produce good results. In typical cinematic creation, if you're a lone freelancer, you frequently have to fork over top dollar for a large hard drive, a gigabyte of RAM, and a bleedingly fast Thunderbird processor, or if you're on a Mac, an expensive dual 500 configuration.

While all of this is certainly nice to have, it is far from necessary on a gaming workstation. For animators on a budget, this is very important. A 20 gigabyte hard drive is sufficient, a fairly decent G3 or Pentium 2 processor will work, and 128 MB of RAM will be acceptable, if not the perfect situation. Now don't you feel better, knowing that you probably have a fine and dandy game animation workstation sitting on your desk? Enough happiness and good cheer, however — time to expose the darker side of game animation.

Game Animation Is About Limitations

A very important thing to realize is that game animation can be very limiting. If your past limitation in animation was that you had to revise your scene because your computer couldn't handle 126,000 lights in it, you're in for a whole new world. Real-time content is very limiting to work for in an artistic sense. Consider this; Pixar was able to devote a computer 8 hours to render one frame of animation for the movie, Toy Story 2. In game animation, however, you have to make a computer render 30+ frames of animation per second and make it look good enough so the game player doesn't lose his lunch all over the keyboard. Notice that I said render, not playback. Pretty much any computer can play back your gorgeous animation at 30 frames per second, rendering at 30 frames per second is a whole other ball game.

Modeling Limitations

Are you used to using 30,000 polygons + for objects and characters in your animations? In gaming animation, you may be instructed to work with a very limiting number of polygons, anywhere from 100-4,000. That's right, think you can make your 30,000 polygon + Starship Enterprise model look good with less than 1,000 polygons? Less then 500? The reason for this is that a game computer has to render an entire scene in real-time. Splash three or four characters on the screen, each with a 1,000 polygon count, and you can see that you'll very quickly have issues. As an experiment, try placing a few 500 polygon count objects in a Cinema 4D scene, take your Rotate tool and try rotating the scene — is the action still smooth? If it is, throw in a few more. Notice how quickly the rotation becomes jerky; as soon as it starts going jerky, we're throwing more at a computer than it can handle acceptably for game animation.

As computers get more powerful, the polygon limit increases. When 3D real-time content first exploded onto the gaming scene back in 1996 with Quake, the polygon range per character was 100-300 polygons. With the debut of Nvidia's Geforce3 we're starting to see some high polygon models in games. In a few years, perhaps processing speed will be enough that you can take your 30,000+ F-16 model and place it directly in a game. For now, however, you're going to have to realize that you'll have to learn to model using a very limited number of polygons.

It isn't really so bad actually. When you're in an explosive firefight with players around the world, characters flying around, guns blazing, with your computer rendering this firefight at 60 frames per second, the little details become unnoticeable. In animation, motion will always command the viewer's attention, and make the details blur into obscurity. In game animation, this effect is magnified a hundredfold, as there is so much action, and little time to pick out the details of a particular character or scene.

TEXTURING LIMITATIONS

For ultimate realism, you've created some gorgeous 4000x4000 texture maps, a bump map, a specular map, an alpha map, a displacement map, a reflective map etc., etc. Well, for the most part, you can chuck them. Games are advancing rapidly, but each texture map, each pixel means more CPU time. Today's CPUs aren't capable of displaying your model in all its photo-realistic glory. Most models will only need a few texture maps, and you'll have to cut down on their size. The gaming standard today seems to be 512x512 maps, though it's still a range in texture size, anywhere from 64x64 up to 1024x1024 is common. Some game engines also support bump mapping, alpha mapping, and reflective mapping as well. Texture maps are extremely important to game animation. Because the polygon count is so limiting, it is paramount that the texture successfully conveys all the detail that the model geometry could not.

ANIMATION LIMITATIONS

Animation limitation is subtler, but it's just as important. Somehow, you as a game animator have to convey a motion and action in the least number of frames possible. Each additional frame of animation means more CPU time, more RAM. So you've got to convey a lot of motion and visual candy, utilizing the least number of frames possible. There are several different game animation systems as well. The most basic is the frame animation system. Here, an animator creates a series of frames that represent an animation, perhaps a running animation. When the character runs on screen, the computer calls up the run animation data, and the character is rendered running on screen, frame by frame. This animation system, although simple to program and implement, has the problem of being RAM hungry. To load each individual frame into RAM means that if you have a large game, you're going to need a lot of RAM to play it.

A second animation system is the skeletal animation system. The concept is actually very simple. Instead of saving out frames of animation on a figure, you save out the bone animation information. Since all you have to save out is the bone information, instead of all 600 vertices at any given point in time on a model, you have significantly less data to worry about. This bone animation data is then imported into a game engine, where the game engine deforms a mesh in real-time. The advantage to this technique is that it is comparatively light in its RAM requirements. The bad news is that it is CPU intensive, as it has to calculate how the mesh will respond to the bone animation 30+ times a second.

There are all sorts of combo game systems as well. Some game engines support vertex based and skeletal based real-time interpolation animation systems. This means that you save the keyframes of an animation, either the mesh for vertex animation, or the bones structure of skeletal animation, and you let the game engine interpolate the frames in between.

A third animation system is rapidly gaining attention. This is real-time inverse kinematics. Here, skeletal animation is used, but it is also imported into the game engine with full inverse kinematics information intact. What this means for you is that a model can be made to animate differently every time. For example, in a typical game system, when player A shoots player B, and player B dies, the game engine calls up a string which displays a pre-built animation of player B dying. With a real-time IK animation system, the computer would calculate important factors, such as what player B was killed with, in what direction, and where in the body. It would then calculate how the body should react to this, all in real-time. If you've ever played a first person shooter before, you may have noticed that after a death animation, a character who was previously standing on a ledge is now collapsed on a ledge. Oftentimes, half of the character's body will be floating out in midair because the pre-built animation didn't take into account animations for dying on ledges. In a real-time IK system, the computer would calculate that the mass of the character's body would pull the body off the ledge and it would fall off once the character died. Each individual fall would be different, because the IK is calculated in real-time. If you're slightly confused, don't worry too much about it. Such an animation system is CPU intensive, and such an animation system is only found in games that are currently still in development.

Palette Limitations

Although palette limitations used to be a very important issue to game developing, it has declined rapidly in importance due to the fact that most current machines and graphic cards can handle a full 32 bit color palette. Be aware that some older graphic cards still only deal in a 16 bit palette — although this is not as limiting as the old 8 bit palette that many game animators had to work with back when 3D real-time game animation was first breaking onto the scene.

End User as the Defining Limitation

In games, the end user is the limitation that defines a game and how complex it is. To achieve a large enough mass market appeal, computer games have to be able to run on a wide variety of systems. Systems with different operating systems, with different resolutions, with different graphics cards, with different graphic APIs, with different input devices.... The list goes on and on. Generally, this information is not critical to a 3D animator, but it's a good idea to learn all of these limitations so you can better communicate with the programmer. What you do need to know is that the broader range of users you're trying to appeal to, the more limitations you're going to have to enact upon yourself. A prime example is the Voodoo line of graphics cards. If the end user is using a Voodoo 3 and older graphics card from 3Dfx, they'll only be able to play your game and animations in 16 bit color. Not only that, but they cannot display textures any bigger than 256x256. To ensure that they don't cut out such a large proportion of gamers, many game companies cut their 512x512 textures up into four 256x256 textures so the older Voodoo cards can handle it. It is critical that you and your programmer communicate on these issues, so you as a game animator know exactly how bad your work will look on a low end system, or if there are any limitations you need to know of. After all, it's not so much how good your animations look on a high end system, but how good they look on the lowest common denominator.

Modeling for Games

Modeling for games is much easier than modeling for many full scale animation projects, yet it is still a distinct challenge that prevents it from ever being a boring activity. On one hand, you're dealing with relatively simple meshes, so it's easy and quick to make changes to the model without becoming lost in all the geometry. On the other hand, because you're working under such a stringent polygon limitation, many artists find it hard to convey their ideas across such a limited workspace. In game animation, it is more important that you try and convey the general suggestion of a character/object, than try to actually model it exactly.

Setting Up the Workspace

Your workspace should have the following tools readily accessible:

- Add Point
- Align Normals
- Knife
- Optimize (selected)
- Untriangulate (selected)
- Weld (selected)
- Create Polygon
- Add empty polygon object
- Triangulate (selected)
- Move Selected Down Sequence
- Move Selected Up Sequence
- Mirror (selected)
- Extrude

In addition, it is strongly recommended that you make the Selection Info window a permanent fixture of your user interface. This will prove invaluable to you as you work to ensure that your models remain under the limit.

Defining the Poly-Count of your Model

There is no hard and fast mathematical rule for determining the poly-count of your model. Like typical animation, game animation requires that you use higher poly-count models for things that will be seen often and close up, and a lower poly-count for those items that will only be seen in the background, or only briefly.

Poly-count is also dependent upon the slowest computer the game can be played on. Many games, however, try to reach a broad market, so they will create models of several resolutions to cater to the needs of each individual gamer. These models are said to have a dynamic level of detail (LOD). Dynamic LOD can be done in two ways. It can be done automatically by the game engine. Superior game engines will input a game model and dynamically alter the polygon count of the model based on how far it is from the player's field of view, (FOV) and how powerful the end user computer is. Other game engines will accept both a high LOD model and a low LOD model that is created by the game animator. These two models will then be swapped back and forth, again, depending on the distance from the player's FOV and system specifications. The advantage of the second system with two LOD models is twofold. First, it is less CPU intensive, as it doesn't have to perform as many calculations per second. Secondly, it can look better; many dynamic LOD systems are poorly coded, and can make a model look pretty bad — this problem, however, can be offset if you have a top-notch programmer working on your development team.

So what poly-count should you shoot for when you are creating your model? Instead of answering the question directly, I think it may be of more benefit if I throw out some examples.

An Unreal Tournament player model is generally within the 500-700 polygon count range. A Quake 3 Arena player model is generally within the 800-1000 polygon count range. For my personal work, I establish the following ranges to work in. Note that these figures are just a starting point for a generic game engine. Once you discuss with the programmers exactly what the limitations are, and how the models will be optimized, you can establish a better working range for yourself.

- Character models (important characters) 700-800 polygons
- Character models (less important characters) 500-600 polygons
- Weapons 100-200 polygons
- Weapons in the character's hand (high LOD) 300-400 polygons
- Vehicles 400-500 polygons

But truly, there are too many variables you must factor in. The figures just given are not to be much more than a rough guide. You need to ask yourself a lot more questions than just how far away/important is this object to the game, and how powerful is the end user's computer? You've got to go into more aspects, such as how many of these objects will a person see at once? How many models will be on the screen at once? How long will a person interact with your model at any given time? It's obvious that if you're trying to depict a battlefield full of soldiers, you may have to restrict yourself to even lower poly-counts than what I've shown above. If character interaction is paramount above all else, and you'll be interacting with characters one on one, you'll need to consider upping the poly-count to make the player's gaming experience more exciting and visually stimulating.

STARTING YOUR CHARACTER

Draw. Pick up a pencil and draw. This can't be stressed enough. Because so many models will look similar due to their limited polygon counts, to bring out detail it is important that you sketch excessively to develop a full picture of your character. If you have a crystal clear image of your character from the start, you can clearly define him as an individual, instead of a slightly different looking face on a generic model. Do those character studies! Your two most important sketches will be the frontal shot and the profile shot of your character; take some time to line up the features in these sketches perfectly, as these will be your two most critical guides to modeling successfully. Use a scanner to bring these sketches into the computer so you can use them within Cinema 4D.

Seem like a lot of work already? It is, which is the main reason why you'll often see game animators in the field skipping over the sketching, or only touching upon it very briefly. Many games require dozens upon dozens of models, all textured and animated; and of course, these need to be done yesterday. A seasoned game artist will find corners to cut, shortcuts to utilize, all with the objective of getting an impossible task done before the shipping date. Even if you reach that level of competence where you can create stunning characters without concept sketches, ensure that you start your main vehicles and characters with sketches. Nothing hurts a game so bad as generic looking central characters. Remember, you are an individual — let your personal flavor shine through; do not strive for the stock model Library look. The gaming industry is already saturated with poorly defined and rendered games, the last thing the world wants to see is one more crappy game.

SETTING THE BACKGROUND VIEWS

Once you've got your sketches completed and scanned in, open them up in an image editing program, and get the width and height dimensions in pixels of each one of your sketches. Write these dimensions down. When you are done, open up Cinema 4D and set up your workspace to a 4-view workspace.

Select the Z-axis view panel for your profile view. You can tell it is your Z-axis view panel by the Z- and Y-axis lines that cross in this view. We're going to place our profile sketch in this view. Once you've selected this view panel, go to Edit>Configure Viewport. Go down to the Background options at the bottom of the dialog box. Check the checkbox, Show Picture, located directly beneath the Background subtitle. Below this checkbox is a button titled Path — click on it and navigate your computer's hard drive for your sketched profile. Click OK once you've found your image (Figure 15.3 a)

Back in the Configure Viewport dialog box, there are two boxes near the bottom that are labeled Horizontal Size and Vertical Size. Enter the corresponding values of your profile sketch that you recorded from the image editing program. This will ensure that your image is not stretched inappropriately in the view panel. Click OK when you are done. The Z-axis view panel should now display your profile sketch.

Move to your X-axis view panel. Repeat the steps above, utilizing your frontal view picture instead of your profile picture (Figure 15.3 b). If your picture happens to have its axis of symmetry offset from the Y-axis line like mine does, you can reopen the Configure Viewport dialog box and offset your image so its symmetry is realigned with the Y-axis. To the right of the Vertical Size and Horizontal Size input value boxes are another set of input value boxes entitled Horizontal Offset and Vertical Offset. Enter values to offset your image appropriately in your view panel (Figure 15.3 c).

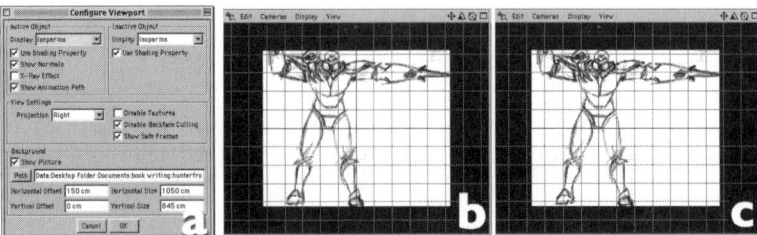

FIGURE 15.3 *(a) To get started, make sure you have your sketches appropriately entered and configured. Do this in the Configure Viewport dialog box (b) Inserting sketches into the front view. (c) If your inserted image is offset, you may need to adjust the position slightly within the Configure Viewport dialog box to put the center of the character at the center of digital space.*

When you are done, your X-axis view panel, (front) and Z-axis view panel, (profile) should now display your sketches. And if you wrote down your dimensions properly, these sketches should also line up. If you did a top view sketch, you can also repeat the above process for the top view.

BEGINNING YOUR MODEL

There are many ways to start your model; for this example, however, we're going to utilize the Box method to create our mesh. It's really quite simple. All you have to do is create a simple box shape and extrude it and manipulate its vertices to create your character.

From the Objects menu, create a simple Box Primitive, and scale it so it roughly fits inside our frontal and profile sketches, then move it into place. Remember that we're only going to model half our character, and use a Symmetry object to model the other half. We now have the central basis from which we'll base our character. However, a Box Primitive won't do us much good on its own, so we're going have to create an editable mesh from it. Select your cube and press "C" on the keyboard. This will create an editable mesh that we can perform extrusions from. Enter Polygon mode. Select the face that currently defines the axis of symmetry. Delete it — this will ensure that we don't have hidden polygons within our mesh when we build our model with the Symmetry tool (Figure 15.4 a). Now, let's create a Symmetry Object so it'll duplicate the other half of our work. From the Objects menu, create a Symmetry Object and drop the cube into it in the Object Manager. Your Hierarchy should look like Figure 15.4 (b).

We're now going to push and pull the vertices around so they match up with our frontal view sketch. To do this, we'll start out using the Live Selection tool. Make sure that you've unchecked the Only Select Visible Elements box in the Active Tool tab so that you select the vertices in the back as well

(Figure 15.5 a). Using the Live Selection tool, select the outside vertices and move them so they match up with the sketch (Figure 15.5 b).

Do not worry about fitting your mesh to the profile view at this time, although some artists conform the mesh to both the profile views and frontal views at the same time — I find that this method can become confusing, especially if the sketches are slightly out of alignment. For now, we'll just worry about conforming our mesh to our frontal view, then when we're done, we'll go back and rework the vertices to match up with the profile view.

EXTRUDING THE TORSO

Let's start by creating the rest of the pelvis. Enter Polygon mode and select the bottom polygon with your Live Selection tool (Figure 15.6 a). Make sure the Only Select Visible Elements checkbox is checked. Once it is selected, use the Extrude tool, or use the keyboard shortcut "D" to extrude the bottom face. Extrude it down till it reaches your next definition point on the pelvis (Figure 15.6 b). Don't move your points around just yet; continue to extrude to create the third definition line in our pelvis. Now, flip your view of the pelvis over to the top, select the top polygon, and extrude up — stopping where your frontal view sketch defines a major change in the shape of your character. When you have completed your extrusions for the torso, you should have a mesh that looks something like Figure 15.6 (c).

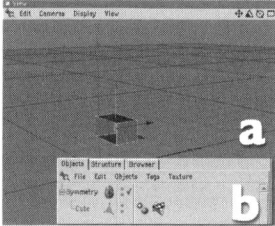

FIGURE 15.4 *(a) To prevent future seams when the object is within a Symmetry Object, select polygons that lie along the Symmetry Object's Y-axis and delete them. (b) Object Manager at this point in the process.*

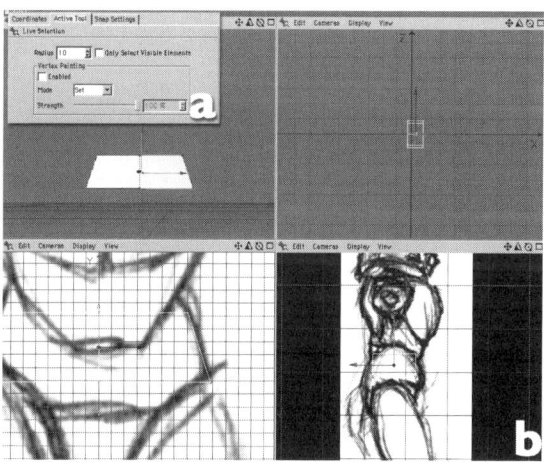

FIGURE 15.5 *(a) Make sure when you use the Live Selection tool to select both the points on the front and on the back of the object. (b) Move the points (vertices) to roughly match the hips of the character.*

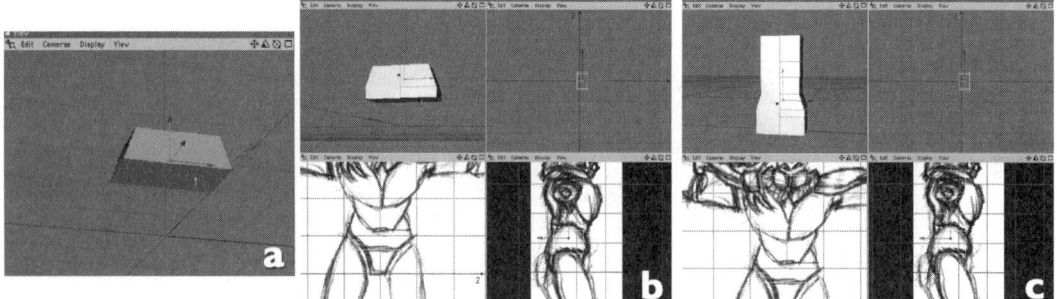

FIGURE 15.6 *(a) Use the Live Selection tool to select the polygon on the bottom of the pelvic region built thus far. (b) Extrude the poly down to the next definition point of the pelvis. (c) Start from the top of the pelvis and extrude needed segments upward.*

Now it's time to push and pull your vertices into place so they roughly match up with the frontal view of our character. Enter Points mode. Activate the Live Selection tool, make sure the Select Visible Elements checkbox is unchecked, and begin moving the points in the frontal view to conform to your front view sketch.

When you have moved all your points so they conform to your frontal view sketch, you should have a mesh that looks much like Figure 15.7 (a). Now, turn to your profile view, and push and pull your points in the same way you did with your frontal view, so your mesh will conform to your profile sketch. When it is complete, your torso will look something like Figure 15.7 (b).

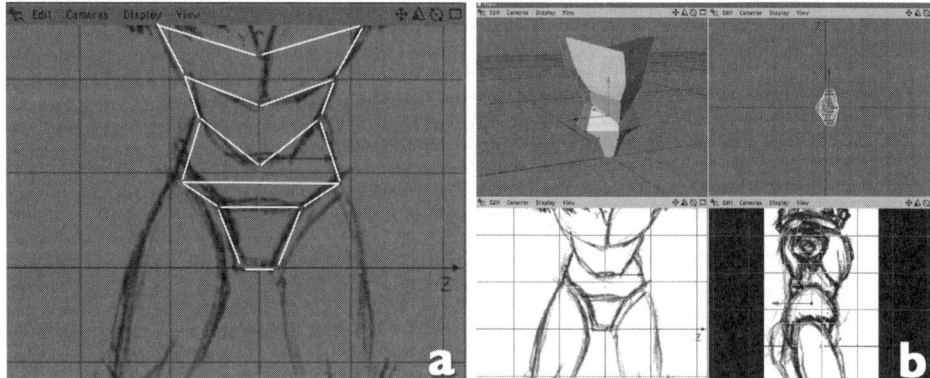

FIGURE 15.7 *(a) Match the front view completely. (b) Then switch to profile view and make additional adjustments.*

CREATING THE LEGS

To create the legs, you simply select the two polygons that form the sides of the pelvis bone, and extrude to your first frontal definition point. Make sure that you check the box, Preserve as Group, from within the Active Tool tab in the Coordinates Manager (Figure 15.8).

Rotate and move your polygons so further extrusions will extrude down the Y-axis. Right-click (COMMAND-click) in your view panel to bring up a pop-up menu. Select Edit Surface>Set Value. The Set Value dialog box appears. This will allow us to flatten our polygons along a certain axis. If we did not do this, our extrusions would deform and collapse upon themselves as we extruded. Set Value ensures that this does not happen. Make sure you flatten along the Y-axis by choosing the Center command from the pop-up menu (Figure 15.9 a). Follow the same procedure of extruding in your frontal view every time you reach a definition point where the shape of the mesh changes, just like you did with the torso. Figure 15.9 (b) illustrates what our thighs look like when we extrude them to conform to our definition points as defined in our frontal view.

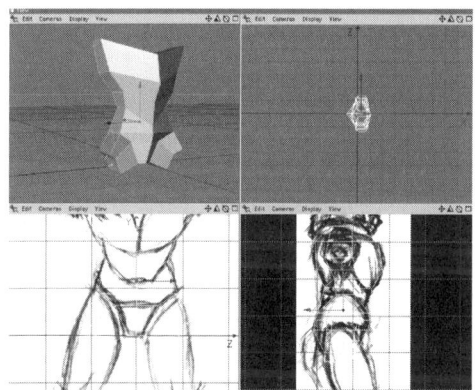

FIGURE 15.8 *Begin creating the legs by extruding out from the pelvis with Preserve as Group activated.*

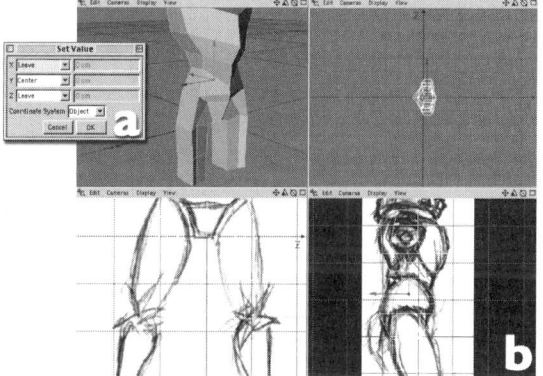

FIGURE 15.9 *(a) Ensure that the Y-axis is "flattened" using the Set Value command. (b) Thighs extruded to match reference sketch.*

Once you have done this basic extrusion, go back into Points mode like we did before with the torso and conform the points to the frontal sketch (Figure 15.10 a). Once that is completed, we now repeat the process with our profile sketch (Figure 15.10 b).

Once the thighs are completed, it's time to continue on down the shins. Follow the same procedure you used for the upper thighs.

1. Flatten.
2. Extrude to frontal definition points.
3. Conform vertices to frontal view.
4. Conform vertices to profile view.

With a little pushing and pulling, you should get something like Figure 15.10 (c).

Creating the Arms

To create the arms, we go back to the torso and select the uppermost polygon on the side of the body. Extrude it shortly, then flatten it using the Set Value command. However, since we are extruding along the Z-axis now, make sure that the Z-axis is set to Center, and the Y-axis is returned to Leave (Figure 15.11 a).

Now, extrude the arms out exactly the same way you did the legs. Figure 15.11 (b) illustrates what the arms look like when they are extruded according to our sketch's control points. Before we start moving vertices around, we need to do a little rotation so our arm looks a bit more organic. Because our arms currently consist of 4-sided polygons, and extrusions thereof, we need to alter their shape a bit to make them look more natural. Notice that from any angle, the arms look boxy, and inorganic. Quite simply they look too flat. We're going to solve this problem in a very simple way. Using the Select Polygon tool, select all of the polygons that compromise the arm, and rotate them using the

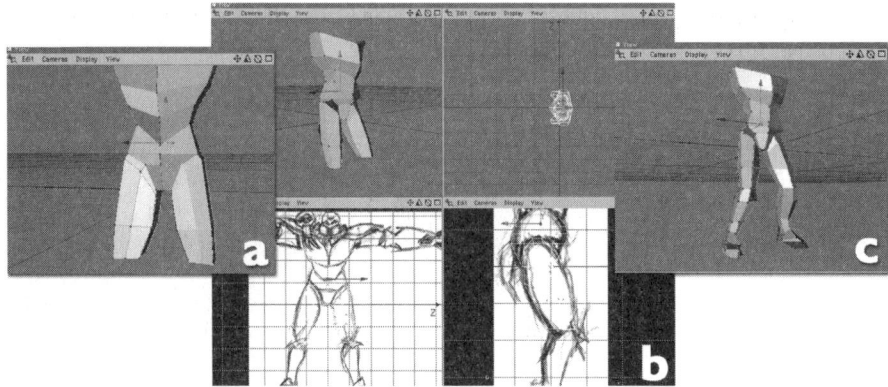

FIGURE 15.10 *(a) Refine torso through points manipulation. (b) Repeat fine tuning at Points Level from profile view. (c) Completed legs.*

Coordinates Manager. Rotate the selected polygons –45 degrees in the B input box (Figure 15.11 c).

It still looks inorganic and boxy; but it's a vast improvement over what we had before. To the human eye, a rhombus shape more closely resembles a round shape than a square, despite the fact that there is little difference besides perception.

Now, with the arm polygons rotated, push and pull those polygons to match up with your frontal sketch, then your profile sketch (Figure 15.11 d). For this model, the hands are in protective shields, and the greatest projection from the model are this creature's slashing spikes. In this case, I simply welded all of the vertices that compromised the last definition point to bring our mesh to a point.

SHOULDERS AND COLLARBONE AREA

We're rapidly approaching one of the most challenging aspects of low polygon modeling — that of the head. Before we can do that, however, we need to more accurately define this guy's shoulders and collarbone area.

Select the top polygon on the torso (Figure 15.12 a). Extrude this polygon with the Extrude tool, then immediately move it out so it hangs over the upper arm (Figure 15.12 b). Extrude again with the Extrude tool so we get the double shoulder armored look that our sketch depicts. Move it into position, and then

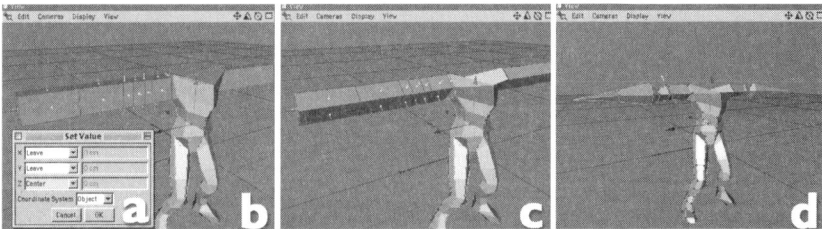

FIGURE 15.11 *(a) Flattening arms using the Set Value Command. (b) Extrude the arms outward; don't worry about reshaping yet. (c) Rotated polygons to add depth. (d) Refine the arms using sketches and point alterations to finish the arms.*

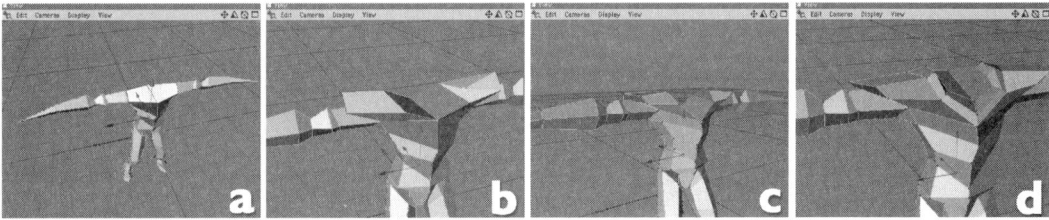

FIGURE 15.12 *(a) To refine shoulders and collarbone, first select the top polygon of the torso. (b) Manipulate the polygon to create an overhand shoulder pad over the upper arm. (c) Refining the shoulders on a Points Level. (d) Refining the collarbone area.*

refine the shoulders by pushing and pulling your vertices into place so they roughly match up with your sketch (Figure 15.12 c).

To create the collarbone area, we select the two polygons that define the upper inside of the armor. Once selected, we use two extrusions to define the area according to our sketches. Again, move those vertices around so they match up as well as possible with your sketch (Figure 15.12 d).

MODELING THE HEAD

The head is especially important to any game character, and it requires a different way of modeling. In a game, the part of a model that someone will look at most frequently is the head of a character; thus, it is important that the head be modeled with as much detail as possible, and be done with extra care. It must be modeled in a unique way because the pits and jags and other details that make up a face are too intricate to create merely with simple extrudes and point pushing like we've done with the rest of the body. Still, you must remember your poly-count limit, and do your best to adhere to it.

According to our sketch, our character really doesn't appear to have a neck. This is not entirely true; his neck just appears to be hidden because it is layered in a lot of armor and the helmet seems to obscure any other potential to see a neck. Normally, we would just create a character without a neck, and save ourselves several polygons. In this case, however, we have to create the neck, because the animations will require independent movement of the head. If we didn't create a neck, when we animated this character turning his head, his whole chest would deform with the turn, something we must avoid.

To create the head, select the neck polygon, (Figure 15.13 a) and scale it along the X-axis to make it resemble more of the start of the neck column instead of the entire top of the trunk. Next, extrude it up using the Extrude tool (Figure 15.13 b). Flatten it using the Set Value command so your future extrudes will extrude straight up; you may have to move the polygon somewhat so it doesn't overlap its symmetry. Once that is complete, it's time to begin the round shape that is the head — do an Extrude Inner on the selected polygon, but extrude it out. At the same time, move the polygon so it doesn't overlap with its symmetry. Finally, scale the polygon along the X-axis so it is slightly elongated (Figure 15.13 c).

Extrude up using the Extrude tool till you get to about eye level. Then extrude again till you reach the top of the head. Using the Scale tool to appropriately turn the head into a cone, and moving that cone so it mirrors properly along its axis of symmetry, we come up with the following (Figure 15.14 a).

CHAPTER 15 AN OVERVIEW OF 3D REAL-TIME CONTENT CREATION 439

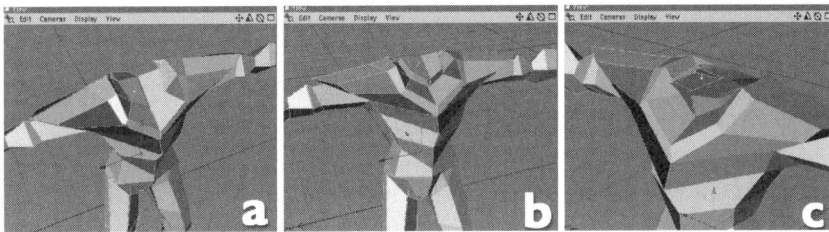

FIGURE 15.13 *(a) Build the neck by starting from polygons extant at the top of the shoulders. (b) Extrude a neck upward. (c) Elongate the neck making sure to not overlap symmetry.*

Using simple techniques like we did before, we Extrude Inner, scale, move, and rotate the front set of polygons so they somewhat resemble our character's faceplate/faceguard (Figure 15.14 b).

CREATING THE TAIL

Our character also has a curious tail coming out of his rear that is in need of modeling. This is done simply by selecting the lower polygon of the lower torso and extruding it out into the proper shape, using the Set As command if the polygon ever becomes unruly (Figure 15.15).

REFINING AND OPTIMIZING THE MESH

We've come a long way, and we now have our basic character, but we're still quite a way from being done.. For the most part though, the next step is just a lot of vertex pushing, pulling, deleting, and creating.

However, before we refine our mesh, let's clean up some really bad trouble spots. Most importantly, let's turn off the Symmetry Object in the Object Manager. To do this, simply click on the green checkmark beside the Symmetry Object. It will turn to a red x, and your character will no longer be symmetrical.

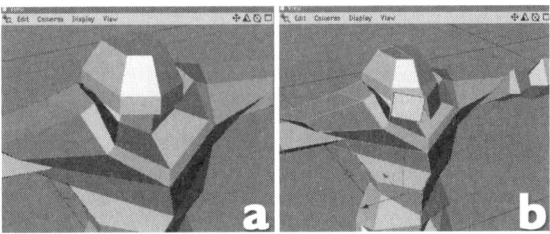

FIGURE 15.14 *(a) The beginning of the head modeled with simple extrusions. (b) Continuing extrusions creates the faceplate of the character.*

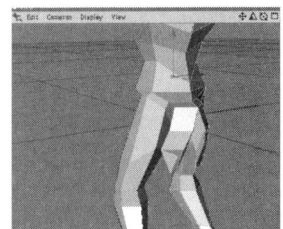

FIGURE 15.15 *Model the tail using continued extrusions.*

This allows you to see your axis of symmetry, and allows you to notice that there are several polygons that line your axis of symmetry. These polygons will never be seen, yet there they are, taking up precious polygon count. Remedy the situation by deleting those useless polygons that lie along your axis of symmetry. Once you've deleted the unwanted polygons, go ahead and turn your Symmetry Object back on by clicking on the red x till it changes to a green checkmark again.

Welcome to the World of Triangles

Game engines of today read model information in triangles, not quads. As a result, you're going to have to use the Triangulate command on your entire mesh before you start refining and optimizing your mesh. Using the Select All command, select your entire mesh, then use the Triangulate command (Figure 15.16 a).

Now would be a good time to check your poly-count to see how we're doing. As we can see, our mesh leapt up suddenly to 288 polygons, and we need to double that to account for the other side for the Symmetry Object. Suddenly, our mesh is close to 600 polygons. That leaves us with only about 100 polygons if we intend to stay within our goal of 700 polygons (Figure 15.16 b).

The Tools to Use

Using the Knife Tool

The Knife tool is very useful, adding extra points to sections of your mesh that do not have enough detail in themselves already. Use the Knife tool sparingly, however, as it can degrade your mesh pretty quickly if you're not careful. I strongly recommend you select the polygons you plan to cut with the Live Selection tool. This will ensure that you only cut and create points within the active selection; otherwise, you'll be startled to find later that you've got extra polygons and points all across your mesh, far from where you intended them. If you do make broad sweeping cuts with the Knife tool, be quick to weld the excess points that will crop up.

Welding Tool

This is another one of your Optimization friends, and you will learn to love it for what it does. When you delete points, you delete a polygon — and as a result you create a hole in your mesh. When you need to get rid of a point, see if it can be welded to any other point on your mesh — this will get rid of a troublesome

CHAPTER 15 AN OVERVIEW OF 3D REAL-TIME CONTENT CREATION 441

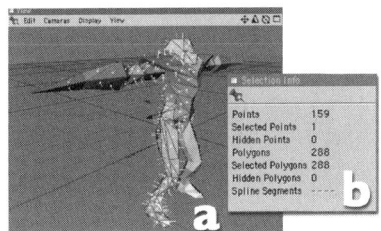

FIGURE 15.16 *(a) Triangulating the model before refinement. (b) Triangulating model suddenly increases poly-count dramatically. However, it is a necessary evil, as game engines only "see" triangles.*

point and polygon without creating holes in your mesh. Be careful, however, that you don't trap a poly line between two welded points. This will usually happen when you try to weld the opposite ends of quadrilateral polygons. Avoid doing this.

MOVE SELECTED UP, MOVE SELECTED DOWN SEQUENCE

These are curious, but very useful tools. Curious, because their main usage is for splines, not polymeshes. With splines, the Move Selected Up and Move Selected Down tools move the sequence of the points in a spline. So if you've got 3 points on your spline, a Move Selected Up sequence will make point 2 point 3; point 3 point 1; and point 1 point 2. This is useful, because when you loft splines and do other such things with them, Cinema 4D lofts according to their sequence, 1 to 1, 2 to 2 etc., etc. By using the Move Selected Up and Down tools, you change the sequence; and thus the entire shape of the object.

For game modeling, and polygon modeling in general, the Move Selected Up and Move Selected Down sequences perform a very timesaving feature, however. Figure 15.17 (a) shows the back of our character. His back is kind of funny; it seems to indent, where instead it should appear like a rounded plate, so it looks more like armor. You could delete the two selected polygons, and rebuild them in the opposite direction so you get the rounded feel, a convex look to the geometry. However, you can achieve the exact same thing by selecting the two polygons, and untriangulating them, make sure the Evaluate Angle checkbox is unchecked (Figure 15.17 b). Then use the Move Selected Up tool — this flips the orientation of the selected quad by moving the points around the polygon in the same fashion that it would with a spline. What's important, however, is that when you triangulate the selected quad again, the direction of your diagonal has changed, giving you a convex appearance (Figure 15.17 c).

This technique of flipping a polygon's orientation goes under the name "flipping edges" in the 3D Studio Max World, and it's great to be able to utilize the Cinema 4D equivalent, even if it is in a slightly obscure, roundabout way.

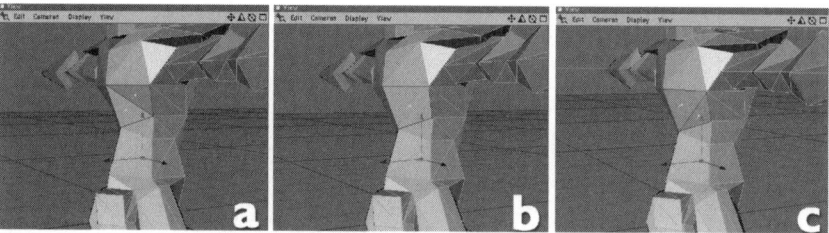

FIGURE 15.17 *(a) Present back of character with awkward indented modeling. (b) Untriangulate, making sure the Evaluate Angle Checkbox is unchecked. (c) Final convex appearance.*

REFINING THE MESH

The upper torso looks pretty good, but it doesn't look plated in layers like the sketch does. To remedy this, we do some good old point pushing, as well as deleting the polygons that make up the side breastplates, and creating entirely new ones that fit more true to our sketch. Don't get worked up with the details however; it is really easy to add more polygons than needed at this stage, and right now, you have the difficult task of adding more complexity to your mesh while at the same time simplifying it for gaming purposes.

Generally, that's all there really is: push and pull those points, cut and add polygons, delete polygons, etc., etc. A curious uniqueness to our model are the knee spikes. These are created by simply selecting the front knee polygons and individually extruding them, then welding the points of the extruded polygon together to create the spikes. Finally, the spikes are adjusted by moving their points into an aesthetically pleasing configuration.

When you are completely satisfied with your mesh, choose Selection>Select All to select your entire mesh and use the Triangulate Selected tool on it. This will ensure that you have no missing quad polygons floating around in your mesh.

The final mesh, weighing in at 654 polygons, is shown in Figure 15.18 (a). Ain't it cute? It's now time to get rid of our Symmetry Object so our entire character is a mesh, and we can animate the mesh independent of its mirror. In the Object Manager, select the Symmetry Object and press "C" on the keyboard to turn the Symmetry Object into an editable mesh (Figure 15.18 b). Your Object Manager will show that your Symmetry Object is now a Null Object. Beneath it in the Hierarchy, pull it out from under the Null Object, and delete the Null Object as it is of no more use to us.

If there are any asymmetrical parts of your character, now is the time to do them. For this mesh, we use this opportunity to create our character's shoulder cannon. Notice how cannon and character are not one surface. This was done for two reasons — the primary one being that if we were to extrude this cannon from the character mesh, the poly-count would be much higher than is acceptable. Secondly, we don't want the smoothing groups to smooth this in with the

CHAPTER 15 AN OVERVIEW OF 3D REAL-TIME CONTENT CREATION

FIGURE 15.18 *(a) Final modeled character. (b) Make your object one solid mesh (instead of a "symmetried" half) by pressing "C" on your keyboard to choose Make Editable.appearance.*

rest of the model, nor do we want it to bend and flex with the rest of the model. To do this, we create a simple cube and scale it so it is of the appropriate dimensions. To make the cube usable, we turn it into an editable mesh and place it above our character's shoulder. Create a Null Object and place the cube and the character within it in the Object Manager. From the Functions menu, choose Connect. The cube that will form our cannon and character mesh are now one mesh, which is exactly what we want. From there, it is a simple matter of extruding, cutting, and pushing polygons and points to realize our final shape.

The very last step is to select your entire mesh using Select All and run Optimize over it, getting rid of any excess points that may be floating in our mesh due to the Symmetry Object. If you did your modeling carefully, the Optimize tool will do nothing for you, but it's a wise thing to do, to ensure that your mesh is in tip top shape before you move on into animating.

TEXTURING

Texturing of a game model is critical to your model's success. When model poly-counts have to be kept so low, it is critical that the texture successfully expresses the details that the model geometry cannot.

This chapter will detail how to successfully texture your model in two different ways, one without the new Maxon 3D painting program BodyPaint, and the second one utilizing BodyPaint. Without BodyPaint, creating a texture template is a long, painful process that is almost as time-consuming as creating the model itself. With BodyPaint, however, the creation of a texture template is much less time-consuming and much less frustrating. We will cover both methods in depth to help the end user get the most control out of his texture mapping.

Ripping Apart the Mesh

Without BodyPaint, you must simply do what this neat program does manually, and you'll see after a while that you're doing a lot of manual labor. In the Object Manager, create a copy of your original mesh and delete the copied bones skeleton, as we will not be needing it. Hide your original mesh with bone skeleton by clicking on the gray dots in the Object Manager till they turn red. This will hide your original mesh from view (Figure 15.19 a).

Now, with our copied mesh, we need to start ripping it apart. Enter Polygon mode; using the Live Selection tool select sections of the mesh that should be one group and disconnect them from the rest of the mesh using the Disconnect tool. Make sure the Preserve Groups checkbox is checked when you do this. Once disconnected, use the Move tool to click-drag the group away from the rest of your mesh; place it somewhere where it's not in the way (Figure 15.19 b). Repeat this process, selecting logical groups of your mesh; groups like the torso, the arms, the legs, the tail, and separating them all from each other (Figure 15.19 c).

Matters of Critical Importance

Unless you like doing things over and over and over, ensure that you do not move any points on either your original mesh, or the mesh copy that you are

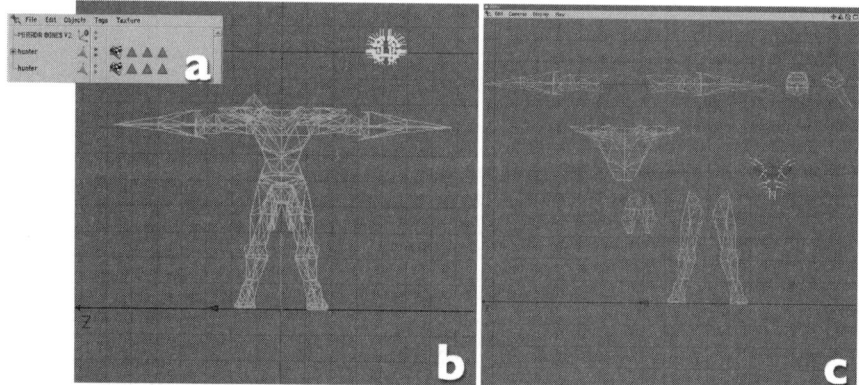

FIGURE 15.19 *(a) Hiding original mesh to be able to work unhindered on textures of new copied mesh. (b) Disconnect groups of polygons and move the new group away from the rest of the mesh. (c) Disconnected form ready to texture.*

ripping up. Even more importantly, do not add or delete any points from either mesh, as doing so will mess up the UVW synchronization between your ripped mesh and your original mesh.

Once separated, you need to start splitting the mesh groups down the Z-axis and moving them out appropriately. Do this by using the Live Selection tool and checking the Only Select Visible Elements checkbox. In the front view, paint over your selection group with the Live Selection tool, and disconnect your selection from the rest (Figure 15.20 a). You may have to CTRL/COMMAND-click to deselect any polygons from the back you may accidentally selected. Some parts of your mesh may be better disconnected from the mesh if you select them from the Y-axis. For instance, the shoulder guards and the soles of the boots would be better textured if you selected them as a group looking down the Y-axis instead of through the Z-axis. Once you have selected and disconnected those pieces, rotate them 90 degrees so they face the X-axis plane along with the rest of your mesh (Figure 15.20 b).

SPECIAL BITS

Remember that our texture map has to be 512x512 pixels. This means we've got to squeeze a ton of detail in an incredibly small area; to do this, we must make sure that we optimize our texture mesh template very, very carefully. This means that anything that will have the same texture map on it, should be left on top of each other so when you paint, the paint will apply itself to both meshes. In the case of the tail here (Figure 15.21 a), the front and back have not been split apart, in anticipation of the front and back looking exactly the same. Thus, if left the way it is, when you texture the front of the tail, you'll be simultaneously texturing the back, saving time and precious space. This technique is also good for any part of the mesh you anticipate having the same texture. Let's say that you're going to make the legs look identical to each other. You could over-

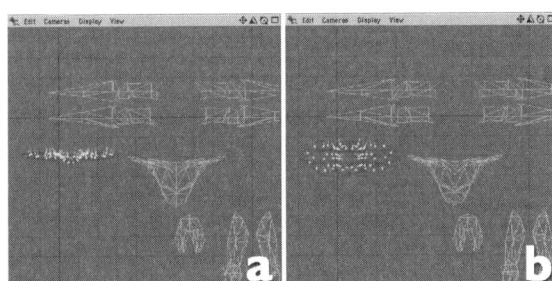

FIGURE 15.20 *(a) Using the Live Selection tool with Only Select Visible Elements activated, select frontal polygons and disconnect. (b) Rotate selected, disconnected pieces to face flat along the x plane.*

lay one leg on top of the other leg precisely in your front view panel; this would ensure that when you painted one leg, the other would be painted as well. A good example of this are the feet (Figure 15.21 b). The feet have been separated and rotated appropriately in this picture. Notice that the geometry is identical except for their orientation. The soles of the foot are usually low detailed areas on a mesh, because they are rarely looked at. Because of this, we can overlay the two meshes on top of each other. It'll be the rare person that will look close enough to notice that the soles are identical looking (Figure 15.21 c).

DISTORTING THE MESH

There's our mesh (Figure 15.22 a), all segmented for our texturing pleasure, but it's still a long way from being done. Take at look at the selected polygons that make up the side of the leg in the perspective view (Figure 15.22 b). When we examine those same polygons in the frontal view, which is making up our texturing template, we see a disturbing problem. If you were to paint in the frontal view of your mesh, you'd notice that very, very few pixels would depict the side of the leg (Figure 15.22 c).

This causes a problem called smearing, where one or two pixels has to define a large area on the mesh; this will make the texture look horrible, and must be avoided at all costs. To avoid this smearing we're going to select the vertices that make up the edge of these polygons, and move them along the Z-axis in our front view until we get some appreciable texturing space. Note that if we were

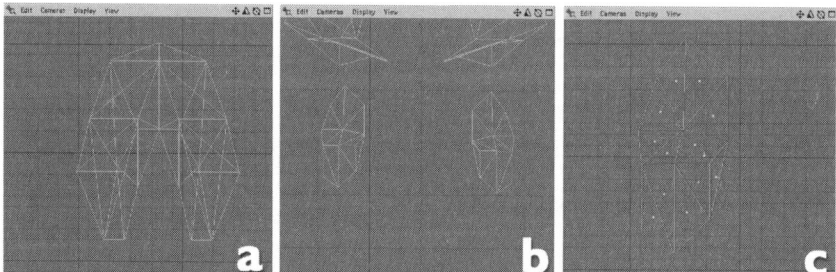

FIGURE 15.21 *(a) The flattened tail — the front and back will be textured the same. (b) The feet will be textured identically; so we don't need to have two copies of the polygonal feet as shown here. (c) We can place the meshes on top of each other to create identical feet and thus save space on our 512x512 texture map.*

Chapter 15 An Overview of 3D Real-Time Content Creation

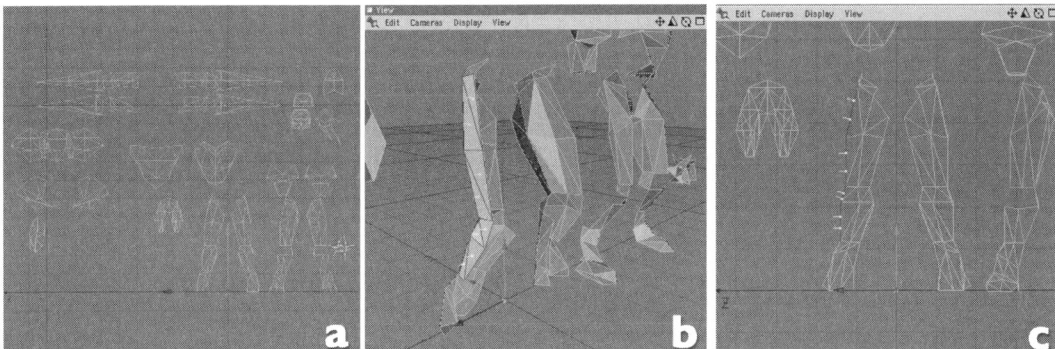

FIGURE 15.22 *(a) Properly segmented and disconnected polygon collection. (b) A close look at the legs in perspective view shows a distribution problem. (c) When we look at these polys from the front, we only see the edges; therefore, when we paint the texture there would be very few pixels defining what the side of the leg should look like.*

to paint from the back, to the sides, and finally the front of the legs, we'd get a seam in our texture going from the side to the front because the edges of those two mesh pieces aren't lined up; we're going to remedy this (Figure 15.23 a). Select the front leg mesh pieces, rotate them 180 degrees, and line them up next to the corresponding back mesh pieces (Figure 15.23 b). Now, enter Points mode, turn on Snap to Point, and move the vertices that make up the edges of the front and back pieces together, so that they share one continuous surface in the front view (Figure 15.23 c).

So now the side of your leg can be appropriately textured. All you have to do now is repeat this procedure on every other polygon that could smear like this throughout your mesh. Go ahead and get started, you might want to find a bookmark to hold your place while you work, it'll be a while. Don't worry, this book will still be here.

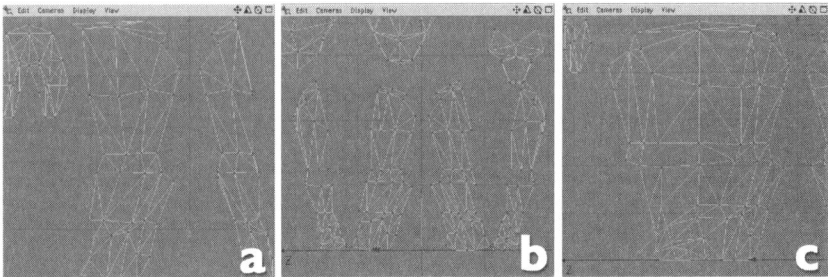

FIGURE 15.23 *(a) Because the edges of the meshes don't line up at this point, we would end up with seams in the texture map. (b) Line the front leg meshes up next to their matching back mesh. (c) Align the inner collection of vertices to make both the front and back share a collection of polygon edges.*

So you got it done, eh? All of the polygons that face the wrong planes have been rotated appropriately or stretched so that we can get some texture space in the frontal view, eh? Not only that, but you joined together all the mesh pieces that belong together, so now you won't get any nasty seams where you don't want them, right? Then perhaps your mesh template looks something like Figure 15.24 (a). Take a deep breath then, 'cause we're almost done.

SCALING AND OPTIMIZING THE TEXTURE AREA

The final step in this procedure is to place these mesh pieces appropriately, and scale them appropriately so that they utilize as much texture area as possible. Remember that we'll only be using 512x512 for the texture map of the character. Also remember that that the older Voodoo cards don't display textures bigger than 256x256. To get around this, we'll be using four 256x256 textures, which will make one big 512x512 texture. Notice in Figure 15.24 (b), the super grid defines four squares for us; well, if we imagine that each square is a 256x256 texture, we get one big 512x512 texture when we combine them all together. In essence we can allow the super grid to define where we place our mesh template on the texture.

Using your Selection and Move tools, move the sections of mesh around your screen until they fit nicely within the 2x2 super grid (Figure 15.24 b). However, notice that although we now fit within the 2x2 super grid, we're wasting a lot of space. Use the Scale and Rotation tools to make your mesh template fit better within the super grid. The idea is to make each mesh section as big as possible so you have more area to color; and thus, more detail that can be fitted onto your model.

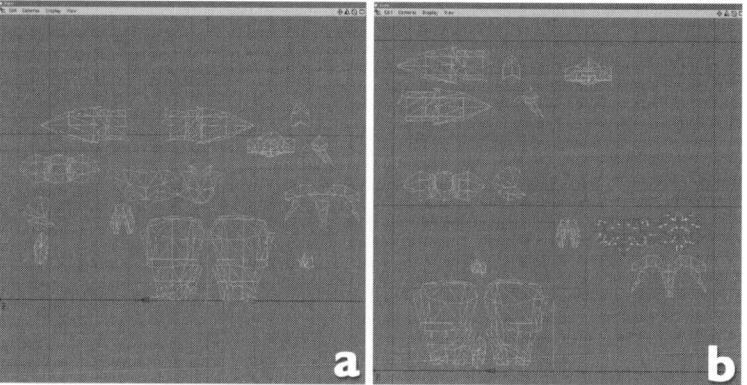

FIGURE 15.24 *(a) Correctly positioned polygons ready for texturing. (b) Move mesh collections to fit within a 2x2 super grid.*

How to Scale for Maximum Optimization

Although you want to scale your mesh as large as possible and still fit within the 2x2 supergrid, you need to rationalize what actually needs to be big, so it can retain a lot of detail. It makes no sense to blow up your foot really big, and sacrifice the size of the legs because of it, since you rarely see the bottom of the foot. Blow everything up as big as possible, but try and blow up the areas that should have more detail, and that the player will see most often; the face, chest, and legs for instance.

Grouping your Mesh

There is one other reason for splitting your 512x512 mesh into four 256x256 sections, besides the Voodoo card limitation. The reason for doing this is so we can swap changeable textures in with minimal strain on the computer. Suppose our game calls for three or four variants of this character we're creating, and the only difference lies in the facial features. If we put the facial texture map by itself on one 256x256 texture chunk, we would only need to tell the computer to switch out the facial texture piece, instead of the entire texture map which would take four times as much RAM and computing power, not to mention more work on your part as well. Group items that you may color or texture differently on the same mesh pieces so the game engine can swap them appropriately.

Creating UVW Coordinates

In the Materials Manager, create a new material, and apply it to your mesh template with Flat texture mapping. Use the Texture Axis tool to ensure that your texture is being mapped properly in the frontal mapping port; you may have to rotate it 90 degrees to get it to align properly. Notice that even though our texture is now correctly aligned, it does not cover our entire 2x2 supergrid (Figure 15.25 a). In the Object Manager, under the Texture menu, choose Fit to Region. Your mouse pointer changes to a crosshair. Draw a perfect square with it over your 2x2 super grid so it appropriately covers everything (Figure 15.25 b). Once you've done that, go back to the Texture menu and choose Generate UVW Coordinates. This tells Cinema 4D that the plane that you described will now be how this mesh is textured, no matter how the mesh is deformed. You now have your texture template. Take a screenshot of your working area, crop it appropriately so it matches the borders of your 2x2 supergrid, and bring it into Photoshop or a similar application for texturing.

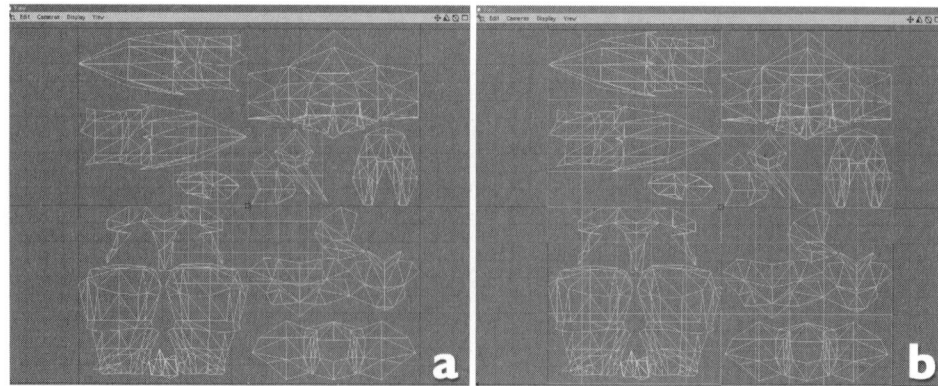

FIGURE 15.25 *(a) Upon first creating a texture and applying it using flat mapping, you may not have adequate coverage. (b) Use the Fit to Region function to adjust the size of your texture to match your 2x2 super grid.*

COPYING THE UVW COORDINATES

In the Object Manager, notice that your mesh template now has a small checkerboard-like icon next to it. These are your UVW coordinates. To make your original model display the same UVW coordinates and texture properly, simply CTRL/COMMAND-click on the UVW coordinates and apply them to your original mesh. Your texture will now work perfectly on the original mesh! Figure 15.26 (a) shows our original character, with UVW coordinates. We can tell that it works because we took a screen capture of our original mesh and applied it to our original character using UVW mapping. Notice how the lines that define this polygonal mesh all show up properly. Now all you have to do is take that screenshot, size it properly so it is 512x512 pixels, and start painting in Photoshop.

Once done in Photoshop, create a new material and use the image you just created as the image file. Apply it to your model using UVW mapping and voila! (Figure 15.26 b).

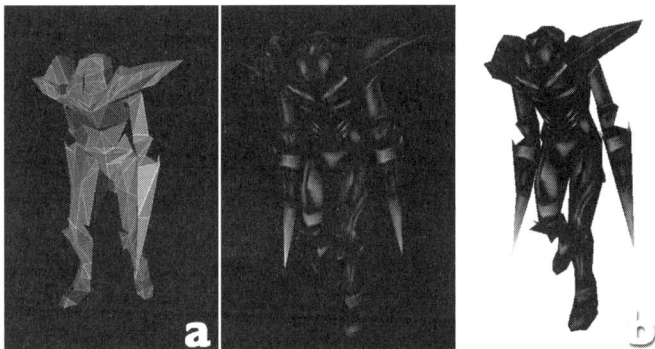

FIGURE 15.26 *(a) Original character, when we used the UVW coordinates established by the flattened mesh, properly aligns the texture. (b) After painting in Photoshop, apply texture using UVW Mapping and you have a textured game character.*

BODY PAINT

With BodyPaint 3D, things get a lot easier. One of the most significant advantages of using BodyPaint is the ability to revise and get instantaneous feedback and results. With the mesh ripping technique, you have to colorize in Photoshop, save the file, then import into Cinema 4D check to see how it looks. If there are problems, you must exit Cinema 4D, open the texture back up in Photoshop, make the changes, save, return to Cinema 4D, wash, rinse, repeat until the texture looks the way it needs to on your model. If you're really good, you'll only have to do this procedure once or twice, but if not… This process is so tedious, that many a game artist will shrug his shoulders and declare the texture, "good enough." With BodyPaint, you paint your texture, watching it update in real-time on your model. If something looks wrong, you can immediately change exactly what is needed without any additional trouble.

Another item that plagues modelers and texture artists, is that sometimes the UVW map wasn't laid out altogether too well, space is wasted, there isn't enough texture space, etc., etc. The procedure to change the UVW template is so time-consuming and mind numbingly dull that many artists will push though, accepting the inadequate UVW template as a necessary casualty. With BodyPaint, however, when a certain set of polygons is inadequately mapped, it is a simple matter of fixing it on the fly, allowing you to get the clearest, most precise texture map possible for your masterpiece.

But enough of that, let's figure out how to actually do this. Open up BodyPaint to reveal your model. As you can see, this is a really low polygon model so creating the UVW template shouldn't be too hard, especially with the aid of BodyPaint.

In BodyPaint's Texture window, go to File>New Texture. A new dialog box appears. Set the color to 50% gray. Since this is a small, low detailed model, we'll keep the texture size down as well. Set your width and height to 256x256 (Figure 15.27 a). Click OK. You should now get a gray square in your Texture window. Save this texture from the File menu. I recommend saving in Photoshop format. The format is supported 100%, and in my experience is more stable than the BodyPaint format.

Now, you've created the texture in BodyPaint, and saved it onto your hard drive. It's time to create a material that uses this new texture you've created. Go down to the Materials Manager, and select File>New Material. A new material appears; double-click on it to change its properties.

For the most part, leave these settings alone. In the Color Channel, there is a Texture option box. Click the Image button to bring up the texture you just saved. Click Refresh and close this window (Figure 15.27 b).

What you've done here is created a texture in BodyPaint, and then created a material that references this texture so you can use it appropriately. The last step is to apply this material to our model by dragging it onto your model. When you do this, a Texture dialog box will pop up. Leave all the settings at the default; however, ensure that the projection method is UVW. Click OK to exit this screen.

To begin our UVW template, enter Polygon mode and select your entire model. From the Texture window, select Functions>Start Interactive Mapping. This will bring up another Texture window. Set the projection setting to Flat and click OK.

Notice how in your main view panel a grid is superimposed on your model (Figure 15.28 a). This represents your texture. The default size looks appropriate for our circumstances. Go ahead and select Functions>Stop Interactive Mapping. Notice how in the Texture window, the UVW template accurately represents a map of a plane that is parallel with the side of the gun (Figure 15.28 b).

Although this is not a complete UVW template by any means, this is an excellent place to start. From this point you select parts of your model that resemble basic shapes. When no basic shapes work, use Flat mapping. For instance, on this model, there is a ring underneath the trigger and handle assembly that is cylindrical in shape. This is an excellent place to utilize Cylindrical mapping. To do this, select the ring only (Figure 15.29). Finding this difficult to do in the Texture view? Remember that your main view panel can also be used for selecting polygons; simply ensure that you're in Polygon mode, and rotate and zoom as necessary to get the exact selection of polygons necessary.

Again, select Start Interactive Mapping from the Functions menu. This time, however, set the Projection mode to Cylindrical. Your main view panel will look something like Figure 15.30 (a). Notice, however, that the superimposed

CHAPTER 15 AN OVERVIEW OF 3D REAL-TIME CONTENT CREATION 453

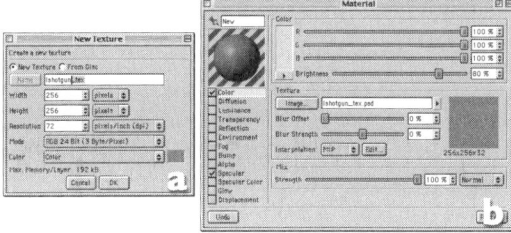

FIGURE 15.27 *(a) The New Texture dialog box within BodyPaint. Keep the texture size small as the object is small. (b) The Materials dialog box to make use of the new texture you're creating.*

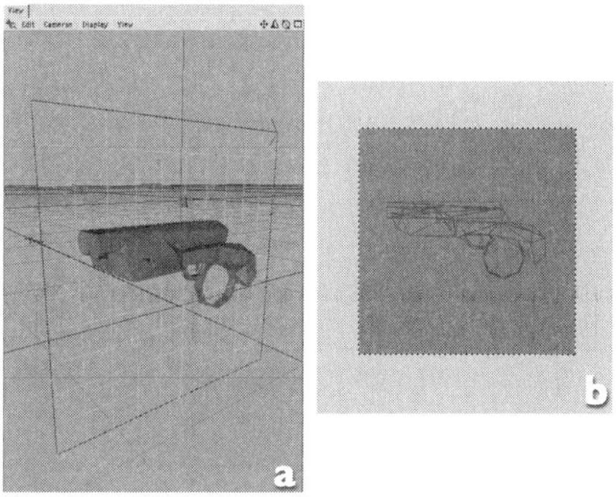

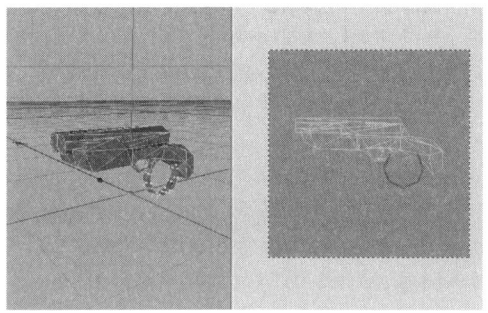

FIGURE 15.28 *(a) The grid shows the size of the texture in relationship to the model. (b) Within the Texture window, we can see the UVW template.*

FIGURE 15.29 *To select different mapping for other parts of the model, begin by selecting them in the main view panel in Polygon Mode.*

cylinder grid is perpendicular to the cylinder that our ring makes. To fix this, enter the Coordinates Manager and rotate it by typing 90 degrees in the Y rotation field. Click the Apply button to have your texture grid and the ring run parallel to each other (Figure 15.30 b). Stop interactive mapping for the changes to take effect in the Texture window (Figure 15.30 c).

Move this piece out of your way using the UV Move tool off to the corner/edge of the texture space. Select another section of your mesh and repeat the process. Be aware that interactive mapping isn't the only way to create a UVW template. For simple meshes where only a little stretching is needed to deliver more texture to a smaller space, simply select the necessary points or polygons and stretch them away from the main model by using the UVW Move tool (Figure 15.31 a).

Remember that when UVW template polygons overlap, those polygons will share that part of the texture. This is extremely useful for parts of your mode that are symmetrical. By texturing only one side, the texture is perfectly symmetrical and saves texture space, increasing the visual appeal of your model.

Once your mesh is nicely ripped so that every polygon that needs the texture space gets it, go ahead and resize your pieces appropriately so they fit nicely on your texture (Figure 15.31 b).

At this point you're ready for the fun part, actually texturing this bad boy.

To paint, make sure the Enable 3D Painting mode button is active, then in the Object Manager click on the Brushes tab. There are three main brushes we will be using: the Lighten brush, the Darken brush, and the Airbrush. Begin by using the plain old simple standard brush, and block in some color on your model. This should be the neutral tone of each part of the model. Remember that you can paint directly on your model as well, so you are afforded the highest possible accuracy in making your texture perfect.

Note to tablet users: If you wish to start painting with a tablet, go to Edit >General Settings. This brings up a new window. On the General tab, there are two checkboxes that will enable you to use your tablet successfully. By checking them you should be able to get rid of your tablet's tendency to throw your model off screen or scale it up and down obscenely.

So now that you have the basic color scheme done, it should look something like this (Figure 15.32 a). The next step is to define some rough details using the Darken and Lighten brushes (Figure 15.32 b). The Darken and Lighten tools work a bit differently than the other brushes, they're not really the dodge and burn tool from Photoshop. What they really are, are brushes that have a color that is saved to them — in the case of the Lighten brush, white, and for the Darken brush, black.

The important thing to realize is that you can change your Lighten and Darken colors if you wish. This is a boon and problem. Often when people work in BodyPaint, they will select the Eyedropper tool and acquire a color to use. If you still have the Lighten or Darken brush selected, it'll pick up that color and save it; then the next time you go back to use the Lighten brush, you'll be frustrated when it "lightens", using chroma blue. The rule to follow, is when you select a color with the Eyedropper tool, or whenever you change colors, make sure the Lighten and Darken brushes are not selected unless your purpose is to lighten and darken with something other than white and black.

Once you've done the rough pass, come in with your Darken and Lighten tool set down to a small size like 5 and the pressure down to about 5%. With these brushes, bring out your rough texture with fine details.

At this point, drop out of BodyPaint to go into Photoshop. I do this for most of my texture and coloring work, as I find Photoshop's Overlay layer feature invaluable. Remember that when you save out of Photoshop, that you must flatten all layers that contain unsupported layers in BodyPaint. As Overlay is not featured in BodyPaint, I have to flatten in Photoshop for it to work properly. Figure 15.33 shows the reimported texture in BodyPaint.

CHAPTER 15 AN OVERVIEW OF 3D REAL-TIME CONTENT CREATION 455

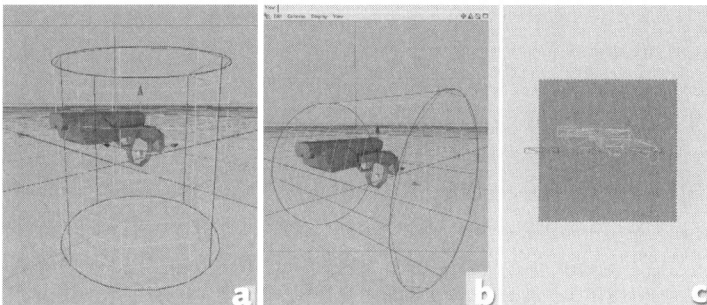

FIGURE 15.30 *(a) With just default cylindrical mapping set up, the mapping is inappropriately oriented to the rest of the gun. After rotating the texture within the Coordinates Manager (b), you can see the selected polygons in (c).*

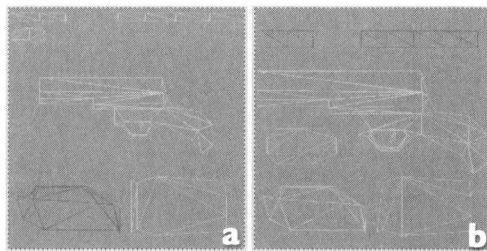

FIGURE 15.31 *(a) After selecting various sections and applying a more appropriate mapping technique, you are left with a UVW template that reveals different parts of the model. (b) To properly utilize all the texture space, resize the pieces to more effectively utilize the UVW template.*

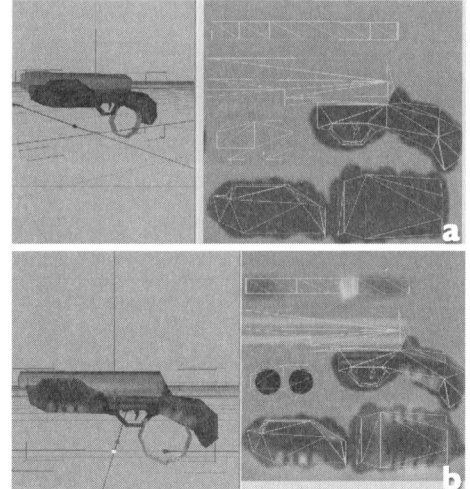

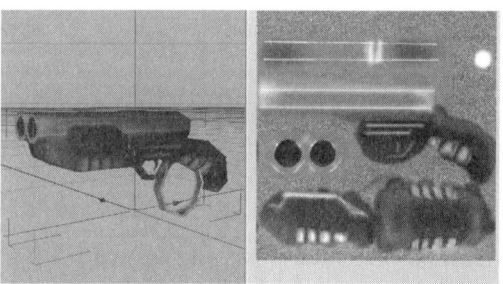

FIGURE 15.33 *You may find some Photoshop techniques more intuitive to your work flow. Make sure you flatten the image if you use techniques such as overlays before you reimport into BodyPaint.*

FIGURE 15.32 *(a) Using the standard brush, paint in general color fields. (b) Add detail with the Darken and Lighten brushes.*

Once back in BodyPaint, it's time to add some little text details. On the top command palette you have a Text tool. Select it, and in the Coordinates Manager, select the Active Tool tab. From here you can change the size, font, and content of the text. I create my text using black. To apply the text, click on the texture in the Texture window and click-drag to place it appropriately. This looks fine for printed text, but this should look like it's embossed in the metal, so apply your text again using white. Offset this from your original black text by a pixel or two, and suddenly you've got embossed/raised text (Figure 15.34).

From here it's final touchup; this texture looks kind of washed out. Using the Contrast and Brightness settings from the Texture window, in the Bitmap Filter window, adjust the brightness and contrast to help this model stand out better.

Finally, the texture is complete! Not too bad for 256x256 pixels and not using any bump maps or specular maps, eh (Figure 15.35)?

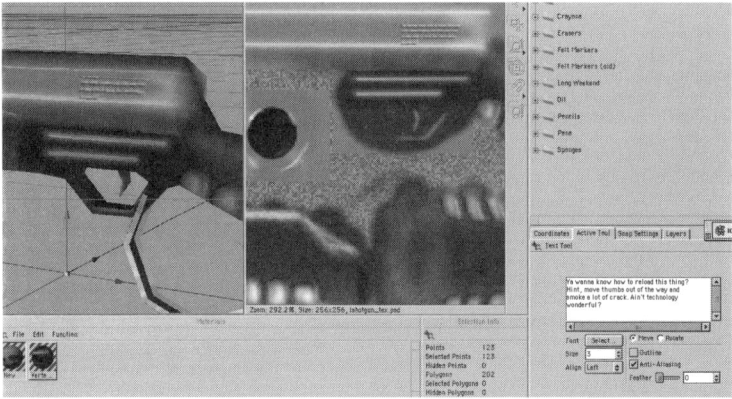

FIGURE 15.34 *Adding embossed text.*

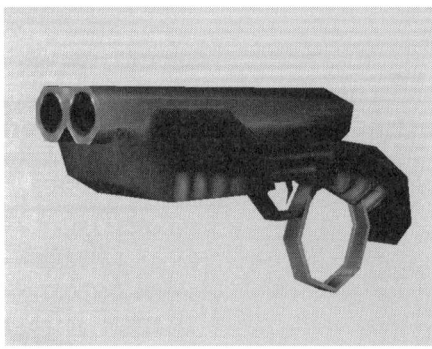

FIGURE 15.35 *The final product.*

CHAPTER 16

C.O.F.F.E.E.: A Comprehensive Introduction

By Donovan Keith

The goal of this chapter is to teach you how to write C.O.F.F.E.E. Expressions. Expressions allow you to automate many things that would be incredibly tedious or impossible to do otherwise. Imagine animating an object and automatically having 50 lights smoothly turn on and off based on the object's position in the scene. Have you ever wanted to make an object stick to a given point on an object? Well, it and many more things are possible through the use of C.O.F.F.E.E. Expressions. The process of creating expressions is quite simple after you learn how. C.O.F.F.E.E. Expressions are created by writing code in a programming language called "C.O.F.F.E.E.". Experience with programming languages like C++ and Java will help you understand what is going on in the following pages, but by no means is it necessary.

What is Programming?

Programming, in its simplest form, is the act of giving a computer instructions. Programming involves writing "code" (the instructions) in a programming language. A programming language is a language much like English, German, Spanish, and all the other written languages. Programming languages have their own vocabulary and grammar. You might wonder — why not just use a language like English to give the computer instructions. The main reason for not using a language like English is simple, English is a very "inexact" language. Most sentences can be interpreted in any number of ways; this doesn't lend itself well to computer instructions. Well, perhaps I have unwittingly misled you... there is an exact form of English, "Lawyer English". Because of the inaccuracies of spoken English and the incomprehensible nature of "Lawyer English," the pioneers of computing created programming languages. Programming languages range from low-level languages (assembly) to high-level languages (C++, JAVA, C.O.F.F.E.E, etc). The distinction between high and low level languages is mainly readability and power. High level languages allow the programmer to write code that can be easily understood, whereas low-level languages allow you to write code that is more closely related to the 1's and 0's that the CPU uses.

Getting Ready to Program

Before we can move on to the actual topic of C.O.F.F.E.E. programming, it is important that we have all the tools we will be using close at hand. To do this, we will need to customize the default Cinema4D interface. We will be using two things extensively: the Console Window and the Expressions Editor. Both the Console Window and the Expressions Editor will require a lot of space. In order

CHAPTER 16 C.O.F.F.E.E.: A COMPREHENSIVE INTRODUCTION

to make room for them, convert your main view panel to a tab (PushPin>Make Tab). Then open the Console Window window (Window>Console Window) and tab it to the View tab. Next, remove the Materials Manager from your interface (PushPin>Close). Now that we have finished setting up our interface, it would be a good idea to save it so that we can come back to it later. Go to Window>Layout>Save Layout As. Call the file "Programming".

HELLO WORLD

The first example in almost all programming texts is the "Hello World" program, why should we break from tradition?

Initial Setup:

1. Create a new scene file (File->New)
2. Make a Null Object (Objects->Null Object)
3. Select the Null Object and add an C.O.F.F.E.E. Expression Tag (File->New Expression->C.O.F.F.E.E. Expression)

A window called the "Expressions Editor" will appear. Tab this window to the View panel next to the Console Window.

Enter the following text into the Console Window (pay close attention to brackets and semi-colons):

```
main(doc,op)
{
        println("Hello World");

}
```

Once you have finished entering the text, click on the Execute button in the Expressions Editor. Now switch to the Console tab; you should have something like the following in the Console Window:

```
ReloadStart
{
}
ReloadEnd

Hello World
```

Congratulations! You have just completed your first C.O.F.F.E.E. Expression!

Now an Explanation:

The Hello World expression has almost no practical use; however, it is a very important first step towards understanding C.O.F.F.E.E. and programming in general.

The text "main(doc,op)" will be present in all of the expressions we will write. When Cinema4D executes an expression, this is where it starts. You should notice that there is a "{" just after "main(doc,op)"; this signifies the start of a block of code. The final "}" signifies the end of a block of code. These brackets control what Cinema4D executes first.

The line "println("Hello World");" is what tells Cinema4D to print "Hello World" in the Console Window. Try changing the text inside of the quotes to "Hello [your name]" and clicking the Execute button again.

If you feel a little lost or confused, don't worry. The following pages will explain in detail how and why everything works the way it does.

A Few Words About Commenting Your Code

Now that you have finished your first example, you probably want to move on to bigger and better things. However, before you do I would like to write a few words about commenting your code, a highly under-appreciated practice. As you write bigger and better expressions, they will become more and more complex, and as such they will become harder and harder to understand by just looking at them. This is where commenting comes into play. By commenting, I mean that you can "write notes in the margins," so to speak. There are two types of comments; each has its uses. The following is an example of commenting:

```
/*
Expression Name:    Hello World
Version:            1.0
Author:             Donovan Keith
Contact:            donovan_keith@hotmail.com

Description:        This expression prints the text inside of
                    println(""); to the Console Window.
                    It is utterly useless, however, I hope that you
                    enjoy using it as much as I enjoyed writing it.

Instructions:       Just copy this expression to any object and open
                    up the Console Window.
*/

main(doc,op)
{
        println("Hello World"); //Print the text "Hello World" to
                                the Console Window

}
```

Just copy the above code to the Expressions Editor and look at the Console Window. It should print the words "Hello World" just as in the last example. However, as you can plainly see, this is much longer than the previous example. This example adds the large block of text above "main(doc,op)" between the "/*" and the "*/", as well as the text following the "//". Everything inside of the "/*" and the "*/" is ignored by Cinema 4D. Cinema also ignores all text following "//" as long as it is on the same line. The "/*" and "*/" are best suited to large multi-line comments and the "//" style of comment is best suited to short descriptions of one to two lines of code.

I personally recommend that you comment once, at least every 5-10 lines of code using the "//" format. If there is a very complex operation that needs explaining, the "/* comment */" method should be used. It may be difficult to understand why you should "waste" so much of your time commenting; the reason can be quite simple. You may understand today, you may understand your code tomorrow, heck, you might even understand it two weeks from now. However, the real issue is whether or not you will be able to fully understand and remember the intricacies of an expression six months from now. Or even more important, will you be able to remember the last 400 lines of code you wrote for your current project? Commenting allows you to quickly get back "up to speed" in the smallest amount of time possible.

Variables

Variables are quite possibly the most important aspect of programming. A variable is a placeholder of sorts. It is a "thing" that allows you to store a value in it.

For Example:

variable X = 5
X + 2 = 7

Now what happens when we change the value of X?
X = 20
X + 2 = 22

The trick is to substitute the value of X with the variable X in the formula X + 2. Using the above trick:
X = 5
X + 2 = 7
5 + 2 = 7

So as you can see, the basic concept of variables is quite simple. When you program in C.O.F.F.E.E., it is very easy to create and manipulate variables. Try putting the following text in the Expressions Editor:

```
main(doc,op)
{
        var X = "Hello World"; // Create a new variable named "X" give
                                it a starting value of "Hello World"

        println(X); // Print the value of X ("Hello World") to the
                      Console Window.

}
```

Click the Execute button and you should see that once again the text "Hello World" is printed to the Console Window.

Now an Explanation:

The text "var X" is what is called a variable declaration. "var" tells Cinema4D to create a new variable. "X" is the variable's name. You can use almost any characters in a variable name except for special characters like: !, @, #, $, %, ^, &, *. You also can't have spaces in variable names; however, a good alternative to a space is an underscore "_".

```
" = "Hello World" " sets the value of the variable "X" to "Hello
World".
```

"println(X);" prints the value of the variable X to the Console Window. The semicolon at the end of the line should be placed at the end of every C.O.F.F.E.E. statement.

Another Example:

```
main(doc,op)
{
        var X = 5; // Create a new variable "X" and set its initial
                    value to 5

        println(X); // Print the numeric contents of "X" to Console
                     Window

}
```

This example prints the number "5" to the Console Window.

Another Example:

```
main(doc,op)
{
        var X = 4; // Create a new variable "X", set its initial value
                      to 4
        var Y = X + 7; // Create a new variable "Y", set it to the
                         value of "X" (4) plus 7
        println(Y); // Print the contents of "Y" to the Console Window

}
```

This expression is more complex than any of the previous examples. In this example, there are two variables present, X and Y. However, when you apply our previous variable principles to this example it becomes quite simple indeed:

Step One (Replace X with the value of X):

```
main(doc,op)
{

        var X = 4;
        var Y = (4) + 7;
        println(Y);
}
```

Step Two (Replace Y with the value of Y):

```
main(doc,op)
{

        var X = 4;
        var Y = (4) + 7;
        println(11);
}
```

That wasn't so hard was it?

VARIABLE TYPES

In C.O.F.F.E.E., variables are said to have different types. The type of a variable is based on its contents. We will mainly be working with three types of variables: integers, floating points, and strings. Integers are standard counting numbers. Integers are usually used for counting how many times something has happened. You probably know floating points as decimal numbers. Floating points are mainly used for storing positions of objects and all other things that require a high degree of accuracy. Strings are variables that store alpha-numeric data. Strings are commonly used for storage of user input, like the names of Target Objects.

Examples of Integers:
-27, -12, -3, 0, 1, 2, 5, 7, 9

Examples of Floating Points:
-27.3, -18.72, 0.0, 2.45, 3.141592

Examples of Strings:
"Target", "067zA", "@#$%^", "Enter Your Name: "

When you declare a variable, you do not need to specify its type, it will be defined by its initial value. However, you must be careful that you set the initial value to something representative of its intended variable type. For example, 50.0 / 100.0 is equal to 0.5. However, 50 / 100 is NOT equal to 0.5, it is actually equal to 0. This is because both 50 and 100 are integers and do not support decimals.

There are three more variable types that are slightly more complex but aren't used as frequently. These are booleans, vectors, and arrays. A boolean has one of two values: TRUE or FALSE. "TRUE" is stored as: 1 in a boolean, and "FALSE" is stored as: 0. A vector can represent a position, scale, rotation, translation, or anything else you can think of that needs an X, Y, and Z component. An array is a variable that allows you to store a "list" of variables. The following are examples of the three variable types in action:

An example of Booleans:

```
main(doc,op)
{
        var TrueOrFalse = TRUE; //Create a new var "TrueOrFalse"
        println("True Or False?");
        println(TrueOrFalse); //Prints 1 to the Console Window because
                              "TrueOrFalse" is true
}
```

Chapter 16 C.O.F.F.E.E.: A Comprehensive Introduction

In the last example, a variable called "TrueOrFalse" was created and given the starting value of "TRUE". From this point on, C.O.F.F.E.E. sees TrueOrFalse as being a boolean variable. The next line prints the question "True Or False?" to the Console Window. The final line prints the value of TrueOrFalse to the Console Window. You should see that it actually prints "1" instead of the "TRUE" that you might expect. This is because C.O.F.F.E.E. stores TRUE as 1 and it stores FALSE as 0.

An example of Vectors:

```
main(doc,op)
{
        //Create a new vector called "position"
        var position = vector(-200.0, 300.0, 440.0); //Set X = -200,
                                                     Y = 300, and
                                                     Z = 440

        println("Position-X");
        println(position.x);

        println("Position-Y");
        println(position.y);

        println("Position-Z");
        println(position.z);
}
```

In this example, a new vector called "position" is created. You should note that the format for creating a vector is this:

```
var variable_name = vector(xValue,yValue,zValue);
```

Take the time to remember this format, as it will be used quite frequently. The next line of code prints the "Position-X" to the Console Window. The line after this prints the value of xValue (as in the above format) to the Console Window (in this case the value of xValue is -200). You should see that accessing the xValue is quite different than accessing the value of a "normal" variable; it is achieved by placing an ".x" after the name of the vector (in this case "position"). The format for accessing the yValue and zValue is the same as accessing the xValue except that you replace the "x" following the period with the relevant letter.

An example of Arrays:

```
main(doc,op)
{
        var EmployeeNames = new(array,3); //Create a new array with 3
                                                          members
        EmployeeNames[0] = "Bob"; //C.O.F.F.E.E. starts counting @ 0
        EmployeeNames[1] = "Jane";
        EmployeeNames[2] = "Fred"; //2 is actually the 3rd entry

        println("Employee Names:");
        println(EmployeeNames[0]);
        println(EmployeeNames[1]);
        println(EmployeeNames[2]);
}
```

In the above expression, a variable called "EmployeeNames" is created. The value assigned to it is "new(array,3)"; this tells C.O.F.F.E.E. to allocate three "slots" in a list for EmployeeNames' use. If you needed a list with 23 items, you would write "new(array,23)" which translates to: Set the variable type to "array" and create 23 slots in the list. To access the different items in an array, you use the format "ArrayName[itemNumber]". The line "EmployeeNames[0] = "Bob";" tells C.O.F.F.E.E. to set the value of the first item to "Bob". Note that the first item in an array is accessed with the itemNumber (actually called an "index") of 0 rather than 1. The same format is used to stuff "Jane" and "Fred" into the two remaining slots. "println(EmployeeNames[0]);" prints the contents of the first item to the Console Window. Keep in mind that you can place any value in an array; you aren't limited to strings.

You should now have a pretty good understanding of the various variable types and what they do. If you are having trouble understanding any sections, reread them and pay close attention to the examples. If you still don't understand a specific variable type, don't worry — things will become clearer as this chapter progresses.

NUMERICAL OPERATIONS

Having a good understanding of C.O.F.F.E.E.'s mathematical operators is a very important part of programming expressions. Below is a table listing of some of C.O.F.F.E.E.'s most useful mathematical operators.

    *   Multiply
    /   Divide
    %   Remainder
    +   Add
    -    Subtract or Negative

CHAPTER 16   C.O.F.F.E.E.: A COMPREHENSIVE INTRODUCTION

Each of the operators are listed in order of operation. To clarify: Multiplication is performed first, then division is performed, then the remainder operation is performed, then addition is performed, then subtraction is performed. However, it is possible to "override" C.O.F.F.E.E.'s built-in order of operations. This is done by placing a given operation in parentheses.

Examples:
3 + 5 * 8 = 43
In this example, 5 is multiplied by 8, then 3 is added.

(3 + 5) * 8 = 64
In this example, the result of "3 + 5" is multiplied by 8. "3 + 5" is performed first because it is in parentheses.

((3 + 5) * 8) * 4 = 256
In this example, 3 is added to 5, then the result of that operation (8) is multiplied by 8. Then the result of the past two operations (64) is multiplied by 4.

Code Example:

```
main(doc,op)
{
        println("3 + 5 * 8 = "); //Print the equation to the Console
                                    Window
        println(3 + 5 * 8); //Print the result of the equation to the
                               Console Window

        println("(3 + 5) * 8 = "); //Print the equation to the Console
                                      Window
        println((3 + 5) * 8); //Print the result of the equation to the
                                 Console Window

        println("((3 + 5) * 8) * 4 = "); //Print the equation to the
                                            Console Window
        println(((3 + 5) * 8) * 4); //Print the result of the equation
                                       to the Console Window
}
```

LOGICAL OPERATIONS

C.O.F.F.E.E. has a number of logical operators that can control the execution of certain segments of code. Below is a table listing some of C.O.F.F.E.E.'s most useful logical operators.

==	equality; true if the value on the left is equal to the value on the right
!=	inequality; true if the value on the left is not equal to the value on the right
>, <	greater than, less than; true if the value on the left is greater/less than the value on the right
>=, <=	greater than, less than or equal to, less than or equal to; true if the value on the left is greater/less than or equal to the value on the right
&&	AND; true if both left and right are true
||	OR; true if both left or right are true
!	NOT; true if its argument is false

Each of these operators is extremely important; you will probably use at least one of them in every expression you write. The following are some examples of each operator.

Equality Examples:

3 == 5	FALSE
5 == 5	TRUE

Inequality Examples:

3 != 5	TRUE
5 != 5	FALSE

Greater/Less Than Examples:

3 > 5	FALSE
5 > 5	FALSE
3 < 5	TRUE
5 < 5	FALSE

Greater/Less Than Or Equal To Examples:

3 >= 5	FALSE
5 >= 5	TRUE
3 <= 5	TRUE
5 <= 5	TRUE

AND Examples:

(3 == 5) && (3 == 5)	FALSE
(3 == 5) && (5 == 5)	FALSE
(5 == 5) && (5 == 5)	TRUE

OR Examples:

```
(3 == 5) || (3 == 5)        FALSE
(3 == 5) || (5 == 5)        TRUE
(5 == 5) || (5 == 5)        TRUE
```

NOT Examples:

```
!(3 == 5)   TRUE
!(5 == 5)   FALSE
```

CONDITIONALS

Conditionals allow a programmer to control whether or not a block of code is executed based on whether or not a given condition is met. There are two conditionals, the if/else condition and the switch/case conditional.

If/Else Conditional Example:

```
main(doc,op)
{
        if(3 == 5) // If 3 is equal to 5 do what's in the "{}"s
        {
                println("3 is equal to 5");
        }

        else // If 3 is not equal to 5 do what's in the "{}"s
        {
                println("3 is not equal to 5");
        }
}
```

If the statement in the parentheses following "if" is true, the code inside the following {}'s is executed. However, if the statement in the parentheses is false, the code inside of the {}'s following "else" is executed. Keep in mind that you aren't required to include the "else {}".

Switch/Case Example:

```
main(doc,op)
{
        var X = 0; // Set the value of X to 0

        switch(X) // Use X as the value for the switch statement
```

```
        {
                case 0:  //If X == 0
                println("X is equal to 0");
                break;

                case 1:  //If X == 1
                println("X is equal to 1");
                break;

                case 2:  //If X == 3 or X == 3
                case 3:
                println("X is equal to 2 or 3");
                break;
        }
}
```

Switch/case conditionals take the value in the parentheses following "switch" and compare it with each of the values following each of the cases. If a match is found, all of the following code is executed until a "break" or "}" is reached. In this example, the input for the switch/case conditional is X. X is equal to 0, so the code "println("X is equal to 0");" is executed. If the value of X is equal to either 2 or 3, the following code is executed "println("X is equal to 2 or 3");". To make things slightly more clear, the following example has the same result as the above example, except it is constructed out of if/else statements.

Switch/Case Example Rewritten As If/Else Example:

```
main(doc,op)
{
        var X = 0;

        if(X == 0)
        {
                println("X is equal to 0");
        }

        if(X == 1)
        {
                println("X is equal to 1");
        }

        if(X == 2 || X == 3)
        {
                println("X is equal to 2 or 3");
        }
}
```

Chapter 16 C.O.F.F.E.E.: A Comprehensive Introduction

In situations where you need to compare a variable with more than two cases, a switch/case conditional should be used. For all other situations, the if/else conditional is the best for the job. Why not just use if/else conditionals for everything, you ask? The main reason is that switch/case statements can be far more efficient than if/else statements when you are dealing with a large number of comparisons. Making your code as efficient as possible allows Cinema 4D to execute it faster, thus speeding up Editor redraw and rendering speeds.

It is also possible to "nest" conditionals. By this I mean that you can place a conditional inside of a conditional. This can make your code more efficient, as well as easier to read. Nested conditionals are often used to get to a given result in the least number of steps possible.

Nested Conditionals Example:

```
/*

        Expression Name:        User Input Switch/Case Example

        Description:            Takes the values of motion and axis and
                                prints the relevant case to the Console
                                Window

*/

main(doc,op)
{
        var motion = 0; // 0 = Position, 1 = Scale, 2 = Rotation
        var axis = 0; // 0 = X, 1 = Y, 2 = Z

        //Switch based on the user-selected motion
        switch(motion)
        {
                //Position
                case 0:
                println("The Motion is: Position");
                switch(axis)
                {
                        case 0: //X-Position
                        println("The axis is: X");
                        break;

                        case 1: //Y-Position
                        println("The axis is: Y");
                        break;
```

```
                case 2: //Z-Position
                println("The axis is: Z");
                break;
        }
        break;

        //Scale
        case 1:
        println("The Motion is: Scale");
        switch(axis)
        {
                case 0: //X-Scale
                println("The axis is: X");
                break;

                case 1: //Y-Scale
                println("The axis is: Y");
                break;

                case 2: //Z-Scale
                println("The axis is: Z");
                break;
        }
        break;

        //Rotation
        case 2:
        println("The Motion is: Rotation");
        switch(axis)
        {
                case 0: //X-Rotation
                println("The axis is: X");
                break;

                case 1: //Y-Rotation
                println("The axis is: Y");
                break;

                case 2: //Z-Rotation
                println("The axis is: Z");
                break;
        }
        break;
    }
}
```

The above expression will print which motion and axis the user has selected. The user selects the motion and axis by setting the value of two variables ("motion" and "axis") to either 0, 1, or 2. A switch/case conditional then decides which case to go to, based on the value of "motion". At each of the cases, the relevant motion is printed to the Console Window. After the println() is completed, another switch/case conditional decides which case to switch to, based on the value of "axis". Each of the cases prints the relevant axis to the Console Window. I must note that this is not the most efficient way to go about printing the corresponding motion and axis to the Console Window. If you just wanted to print the motion and axis to the Console Window, you could just have two conditionals directly follow each other (the first would be for motion and the second would be for axis). However, this arrangement of switch/case statements allows you to perform a specific operation based on any one of the nine different motion/axis combinations that the user can select.

Looping

Often one needs to do the same thing over and over and over again. This can become quite tedious if you are doing it enough times (imagine having 50 println()'s). Luckily, most modern programming languages allow for something called "looping"; C.O.F.F.E.E. is no exception. A "loop" executes a block of code repeatedly until a given condition is met. There are two main types of loops, the "while loop" and the "for loop". In a while loop, a block of code is repeatedly executed as long as a given logical expression remains true.

While Loop Example:

```
main(doc,op)
{
        var x = 0;

        while( x <= 50 )  //Do the following while x is less than or equal to 50
        {
                println(x);
                x = x + 1;
        }
}
```

Something like the following should be printed to the Console Window with the numbers 0 to 50:

```
0
1
2
3
4
5
...
```

In the above example, a variable "x" is created, and given the initial value of 0. Then a while loop is created, and the code in the loop is repeatedly executed until the logical expression in the parentheses is false (x <= 50). In this case, the value of x is printed to the Console Window, and the 1 is added to the value of x. The fact that 1 is added to x every loop is very important; if it didn't happen, the loop would never end and the computer would hange. A non-ending loop is called an "infinite loop" and should be avoided at all costs. The for loop helps to prevent infinite loops.

For Loop Example:

```
main(doc,op)
{
        var x;

        for( x = 0; x <= 50; x = x + 1 )
        {
                println(x);
        }
}
```

The result of this for loop should be the same as the previous example (the numbers 0-50 should be printed to the Console Window). In fact, if you look at the code closely enough, you can see that it is almost exactly the same as the above example, except that certain parts have been "rearranged".

For Loop Prototype:

```
main(doc,op)
{
        var x;

        for( set x's initial value; a logical expression; an operation
            performed on x )
        {
```

CHAPTER 16 C.O.F.F.E.E.: A COMPREHENSIVE INTRODUCTION

```
            do something;
        }
}
```

A for loop makes it more difficult to forget to increment a variable; this can be quite useful. Thus, for loops are most useful when you are dealing with numerical increments/decrements, and while loops are best suited to loops in which you need the utmost control over the variable that is changing over every loop. Loops are also very useful for filling arrays.

Loop to Fill Array Example:

```
main(doc,op)
{
        var max_number = 50;
        var counting_numbers = new(array,max_number);
        var i = 0; //declare counting variable

        for(i=0; i<max_number; i = i + 1)
        {
                counting_numbers[i] = i;
        }

        println(counting_numbers[3]);
}
```

Although this particular expression has no practical purpose, the concepts learned here directly apply to working with arrays of points and polygons.

FUNCTIONS

As you probably know, expressions can get extremely long and hard to understand. "Functions" allow you to break your code up into smaller chunks that you can use any time you need. You have actually been using a function for quite some time now, the function is "println()". The function takes an input value (usually a string) and prints it to the Console Window. The following expression should give you a better understanding of functions:

Function that Returns a Result Example:

```
AbsoluteValue(x) //Create a new function "AbsoluteValue()" with x as an
input
{
        if( x < 0 ) //If x is less than 0 convert it to a positive
        number
        {
                x = -(x);
        }

        return x;
}

main(doc,op)
{
        var X = -12;
        println("Before:"); //Before
        println(X);

        println("After:");
        println( AbsoluteValue(X) ); /* Call Absolute value and print
                                its result to the Console Window. */
}
```

The first part of this expression creates the AbsoluteValue() function. The "x" inside of the parentheses directly following "AbsoluteValue" is called an "input variable". This variable can be used from that point on inside of the function. The code inside of the "{}"s following "AbsoluteValue(x)" takes the input value, x, and then finds its absolute value. "return x;" returns the value of x to wherever the function is called (by called I mean "executed"). The rest of the expression is mostly self-explanatory. Try using different values for X inside of the "main" part of the expression. Try replacing "X" with some other variable name; there should be no change in the result of the function.

There are two kinds of functions: functions that return a result, and functions that don't return a result. The previous example showed a function that returned a result, the next is a function that doesn't return a result.

CHAPTER 16 C.O.F.F.E.E.: A COMPREHENSIVE INTRODUCTION

Function that Doesn't Return a Result Example:

```
AbsoluteValue(x) //Create a new function "AbsoluteValue()" with x as an
input
{
        println("Before:"); //Before
        println(x);

        if( x < 0 ) //If x is less than 0 convert it to a positive
        number
        {
            x = -(x);
        }

        println("After:");
        println( AbsoluteValue(x) );
}

main(doc,op)
{
        var X = -12;
        AbsoluteValue(X);
}
```

The result of this expression should be the same as the previous example. There is one important difference in the two. In the first example, the AbsoluteValue was called and then its returned value was stuffed into a println(). In this example, all of the println()'s are performed in the AbsoluteValue function. This example makes it easier for one to do a series of println()'s very easily; however, it makes it impossible to do any further manipulation of the absolute value of X after the function is called. So, when you need to do something repeatedly and don't need to further manipulate the result, you should use functions that don't return values. However, if you need to manipulate the result of a function, you should use functions that return values.

A Brief Overview Of OOP

So far, the expressions that have been covered have no practical purpose, mainly due to the fact that we have been limited to using the "prinln()" function. After this section, you will be able to manipulate objects and their various parameters. The thing that will allow us to do this is OOP or Object Oriented Programming. At best, this will be a brief overview; if you need or want more information, there are many books dedicated to OOP Theory. OOP is based on two things: objects and classes. In the most general sense, a class is a category of "thing" and an object is a specific "thing". For example, a bicycle is a class, but a Cannondale R600 is an object. All members of a class must share the same properties; for example all bikes have two wheels, a drive chain, and a seat.

Bicycle Class Example:

```
//Define a class called "Bicycle"
class Bicycle
{
        //Public Variables
        public:
        var speed; //Speed in Miles Per Hour
        var braking; // 1 = yes or 0 = no
        var accelerating; // 1 = yes or 0 = no

        //Public Functions
        Bicycle(); //Function that sets initial values
        GetBrand(); //Function returns brand
        GetModel(); //Function returns model

        //Private Variables
        private:
        var brand;
        var model;
}

//Set initial value for all new bicycles
Bicycle::Bicycle()
{
        brand = "";
        model = "";
        speed = 0.0; //[float] All bikes start @ 0 mph
        braking = 0; //[int] Brakes are not on
        accelerating = 0; //[int] Bike is not accelerating
}
```

Chapter 16 C.O.F.F.E.E.: A Comprehensive Introduction

```
Bicycle::GetBrand() { return brand; } //allows one to view "brand" from
outside the class
Bicycle::GetModel() { return model; } //allows one to view "model" from
outside the class
```

The above defines a new class named "Bicycle". All variables and functions of a class are either "public" or "private". Public variables and functions can be accessed from anywhere in an expression. Private variables and functions can only be accessed from within the class. Everything after "public:" but before "private:" is a public variable or function. Everything following "private:" is a private variable or function. So speed, braking, accelerating, Bicycle(), GetBrand() and GetModel() are all public and can be accessed from anywhere in the expression. However, brand and model are private and can only be accessed from within the class. You might wonder, why make the distinction between private and public? Well the main reason is, it prevents one from doing something that shouldn't be done (like changing the brand of a bicycle after it has been manufactured). The speed, braking, and acceleration of a bike are all implicitly defined by the bicycle itself, whereas brand and model are explicitly defined. So, it only makes sense that one can modify speed, braking and acceleration of a bicycle, but one can't change its brand or model.

After the initial class definition, all of the functions that are members of the class are defined. When you define a function, you have to indicate the class it belongs to, using the following format "ClassName::FunctionName(){ function contents }". The first function is called the constructor, it is called every time a new object based on the class is created. The constructor has the same name as the class, in this case, the constructor is the "Bicycle()" function. The job of the constructor is to set the initial values for all the variables. So, when you first create a bike, it has no brand or model and all other values are set to 0.

To see a an example of how to create objects based on classes and access their members (members of a class are its public variables and functions), just copy the class definition code from above to the Expressions Editor and paste the following code at the bottom of the expression:

```
main(doc,op)
{
        //Create a new Bicycle, store it in variable "bike"
        var bike = new(Bicycle);
        
        //Print the Brand and Model Info
        println(bike->GetBrand());
        println(bike->GetModel());
```

```
//Print the speed
println("Speed:");
println(bike->speed);

//If the bike is accelerating...
if(bike->accelerating == 1)
{
        println("The bike is currently accelerating");
}
else
{
        println("The bike is not currently accelerating");
}

//If the bike is braking...
if(bike->braking == 1)
{
        println("The bike is currently braking");
}
else
{
        println("The bike is not currently braking");
}
}
```

The above code has two very important things in it that haven't been explained before. The first is the creation of an object based on a class. This is done with "var bike = new(Bicycle);". This is much like the creation of any other variable except that instead of a numerical or text value, it is set to "new(Bicycle)". This code creates a new object based on the "Bicycle" class — the procedure is the same as this for the creation of all other objects. The second important thing is that the members of the "bike" object are accessed. This is done with an arrow like this "->". For example, to access the speed of "bike" you would write "bike->speed".

OOP becomes most useful when you create hierarchies of classes. For example, a "superclass" (think of class relationships in terms of parent/child relationships) of bicycle would be "vehicle". A "subclass" of bicycle would be "mountain bike" or "triathlon bike". By creating hierarchies of classes, a lot of possibilities are opened up. To see a an example of how class hierarchies work, just copy the "Bicycle" class definition code from above to the Expressions Editor and paste the following code at the bottom of the expression:

Chapter 16 C.O.F.F.E.E.: A Comprehensive Introduction

```
//Define a class called "MountainBike"
class MountainBike : Bicycle
{
      public:
      var Gear1;
      var Gear2;

      MountainBike(); //Constructor Function
      GetBrakeType();

      private:
      var BrakeType;
}

MountainBike::MountainBike()
{
      super(); //Include all the variables and functions from
               superclasses
      Gear1 = 1; //1,2 or 3
      Gear2 = 1; //1-9
      BrakeType = 0; //0 = Cantilever, 1 = L-Brake, 2 = Disk Brake
}

MountainBike::GetBrakeType()
{
      return BrakeType;
}

main(doc,op)
{

      var MB = new(MountainBike);

      //Access one of the members of "MountainBike"
      println("Brake Type: ");
      println(MB->GetBrakeType());

      //Access one of the members of MountainBike's superclass
      println("Speed: ");
      println(MB->speed);
}
```

The MountainBike Class declares 3 variables: Gear1, Gear2, and BrakeType. However, you can still access speed, braking, accelerating, brand, and model. This is because MountainBike is a subclass of Bicycle. The line "class Mountain-

Bike : Bicycle" creates a class called "MountainBike", the " : Bicycle" indicates that it is a subclass of Bicycle. Because MountainBike is a subclass of Bicycle, MountainBike "inherits" all of the variables and functions that were members of the "Bicycle" class. If you want to initialize the values of the variables from a subclass's superclass, you must call the "super()" function. The super() function calls the constructor of the superclass (in this case "Bicycle()") and as such should be placed in the first line of any subclass's constructor.

PREDEFINED CLASSES

C.O.F.F.E.E. includes many predefined classes — by this I mean there are ways to manipulate object and document properties like position scale and rotation built into C.O.F.F.E.E.. The classes you will be using most are "BaseObject", "BaseDocument", and "BaseContainer". The following is a condensed version of the "BaseObject" class definition.

BaseObject Class Definition:

```
class BaseObject : BaseList4D
{
public:

  [BaseContainer] GetContainer(); //Returns Container
  [bool] SetContainer([BaseContainer] bc); //Sets objects container

  [BaseDocument] GetDocument(); //Gets the document the object is in

  [string] GetName(); //Gets the name of the object
  [bool] SetName([string] name); //Sets the name of the object

  [vector] GetPosition(); //Returns the object's local position
  [vector] GetScale(); //Returns the object's local scale
  [vector] GetRotation(); //Returns the object's local rotation in
          terms of Radians

  [bool] SetPosition([vector] p); //Sets local position to "p"
  [bool] SetScale([vector] s); //Sets local scale to "s"
  [bool] SetRotation([vector] r); //Sets local rotation to "r"

}
```

Chapter 16 C.O.F.F.E.E.: A Comprehensive Introduction

This class definition looks slightly different than the others we have covered so far. This is mainly because of the "[]"s before all variables and functions. The "[]"s tell you the type of variable is after it, or the type of variable the function will return.

BaseObject Class Example:

```
main(doc,op)
{
        var op_pos = op->GetPosition(); //Get op's position and stuff
                                          it in this variable
        println(op_pos);

        var op_rot = op_pos * (PI/180.0); //Convert the position to
                                            Radians
        op->SetRotation(op_rot); //Set op's rotation to op_rot
}
```

The first line of this expression creates a new variable "op_pos" (short for op_position) and sets its value to the op's current position, which is accessed with "op->GetPosition()". The next line prints the value of op_pos to the Console Window. The line after that declares a new variable and sets its value to "op_pos * (PI/180.0);". By multiplying op_pos by (PI/180) we are converting from degrees (if the object is at 180,180,180 the object will rotate 180 degrees on all axis) to Radians, which is the measurement that C.O.F.F.E.E. stores rotations in. The last line sets op's rotation to "op_rot". "op" is actually the object that the expression tag is on, so try moving it. You should see it rotate. If you look in the Coordinates Manager H will be equal to X, P will be equal to Y, and B will be equal to Z.

The following is a very condensed version of the BaseDocument class.

BaseDocument Class Example:

```
class BaseDocument : BaseList2D
{
public:

  [BaseObject] GetFirstObject(); //Get the first object in the Object
                                   Manager
  [BaseMaterial] GetFirstMaterial(); //Get the first material in the
                                       Materials Manager

  [int] GetFps(); //Get the doc's Frames Per Second
```

```
    [bool] SetFps([int] fps); //Set the doc's Frames Per Second

    [BaseTime] GetTime(); //Get the current document time
    [bool] SetTime([BaseTime] t); //Set the current document time

    [BaseObject] FindObject([Marker,string] o); //Find the object with a
name equal to the value of "o"
}
```

The BaseDocument class includes many important functions; however, it is likely that "FindObject()" is the most crucial to expressions. The following is an example of using both the BaseDocument class and the BaseObject class.

BaseDocument and BaseObject Classes Example:

```
main(doc,op)
{
        var target_name = "target"; //Type in the name of the target
                                       object
        var multiple = 0.5; //Multiply the target's position by this

        var target = doc->FindObject(target_name); //Find the object
        if(!target)
        {
                println("No target object!"); //alert the user
                return; //Stop executing!!
        }

        var target_pos = target->GetPosition(); //Get the target's
                                                   rotation
        target_pos = target_pos * multiple; //Multiply the position by
                                               "multiple"

        op->SetPosition(target_pos); //Set op's pos to that of
                                        target*multiple
}
```

Create two objects in Cinema 4D; name one of them "target". Place the above expression on the object that is NOT named "target". Move the target object; you should see the other object center itself between "target" and the world origin. Now onto the explanation of why it works.

Why This Expression Works:

"var target = doc->FindObject(target_name);" tells Cinema 4D to find an object with a name equal to the value of target_name inside of the current document (doc). The conditional following the creation of target tests to see if target actually exists in the current document. If doc can't find the object whose name is the same as the value of target_name, the contents of the conditional are executed. "return;" essentially prevents the function "Main(doc,op)" from executing further. The rest of the code is simply a modified version of the previous example explaining the BaseObject class.

The BaseContainer class is what most, if not all, object properties are stored in. For example, the radius of a sphere is actually stored in a container. The following is a condensed version of the BaseContainer class.

BaseContainer Class Example:

```
class BaseContainer
{

public:

  [bool] SetData([int] id, [any type] data); // Set's the data @ the id
                                                    to "data"

  [int] GetInt([int] id, [[int] preset = 0]); // Convert the data to an
                                                  integer and return it
  [float] GetFloat([int] id, [[float] preset = 0.0]); //Convert the
                                                  data to a float and return it
  [vector] GetVector([int] id, [[vector] preset = vector(0.0)]);
     //Convert the data to a vector and return it
  [string] GetString([int] id, [[string] preset = ""]); //Convert the
                                                  data to a string and return it

}
```

The BaseContainer class stores data based on id's. All parametric objects in Cinema 4D have a number of predefined id's that can be accessed through the BaseContainer class. The following example sets the radius of a sphere based on the position of a target object.

Setting the Radius of Sphere Based on Target Object Position:

```
main(doc,op)
{
        var target_name = "target";
        var target = doc->FindObject(target_name); //Find the target
        if(!target) { return; } //If target doesn't exist, return

        var target_pos = target->GetPosition();
        var op_pos = op->GetPosition();

        var distance = vlen(target_pos - op_pos); //Measure the
                                        distance between target and op

        var op_container = op->GetContainer(); //Retrieve op's
                                                            container
        op_container->SetData(PRIM_SPHERE_RAD,distance); //Set op's
                                                    radius to distance
        op->SetContainer(op_container); //Set op's container to
                                                       "op_container"
}
```

In order to set up a scene to test this expression, do this:

1. Add a Sphere Primitive to the scene.
2. Add another Sphere Primitive to the scene and make it smaller than the first (by adjusting the radius with the orange dot).
3. Name the new Sphere "target".
4. Add the above expression to the first Sphere and click Execute.
5. Move the Sphere called "target." Now move the other Sphere.

As you move the target Sphere, the first Sphere's radius should change so that it reaches the target object.

Now the Explanation:

The line "var distance = vlen(target_pos - op_pos);" declares a new variable "distance" and sets it to the length of the vector (target_pos - op_pos). The vlen() function is one of C.O.F.F.E.E.'s predefined mathematical functions; it calculates the length of a vector. "(target_pos - op_pos)" is a mathematical representation of how you could get from op's position to target's position. However, this isn't important right now because the purpose of this expression is to demonstrate the use of the BaseContainer class. "op_container = op->Get-Container();" retrieves op's container. "op_container->SetData(PRIM_SPHERE_

RAD,distance);" sets op_container's data at the "PRIM_SPHERE_RAD" ID to "distance". Which translates to: this line of code sets the Sphere's radius to "distance". "op->SetContainer(op_container);" sets op's container to "op_container", thus updating the object's radius.

PROGRAMMING EXERCISES

This section will attempt to give you a greater understanding of how to write expressions from scratch. There are three main stages to programming any expression: describe what you want the expression to do in great detail, devise a series of simple steps to reach that goal, program each step and link them together. As you can see, most programming expressions doesn't even involve programming! The rest of this section will go over how to approach various useful expressions.

EXERCISE 1: COPY ROTATION

What You Want It To Do:
The expression should set an object's rotation to that of a target object. The expression should allow for parameters like axis activation, and rotation scaling.

Small Steps:
1. Retrieve the user input:
   -Target Name
   -Scalar
   -H activated?
   -P activated?
   -B activated?
2. Find the target object.
3. Retrieve its rotation values.
4. Multiply by the scalar value.
5. Retrieve the object's rotation
6. Set the object's rotation based on which axis are activated.

The Expression:

Step 1. Retrieve User Input:

```
main(doc,op)
{

//********* User Input ****************\\

var target_name = "target";
var scale_factor = 0.5;
var hActive = TRUE;
var pActive = TRUE;
var bActive = TRUE;


//***************************************\\
```

Step 2. Find the The final product.Target Object:

```
var target = doc->FindObject(target_name);
if(!target) { return; }
```

Step 3. Retrieve its Rotation Values:

```
var target_rot = target->GetRotation();
```

Step 4. Multiply by the Scalar Value:

```
target_rot = target_rot*scale_factor;
```

Step 5. Retrieve the Object's Rotation:

```
var op_rot = op->GetRotation();
```

Step 6. Set the Object's Rotation Based on Which Axes are Activated:

```
if(hActive == TRUE) { op_rot.x = target_rot.x; }
if(pActive == TRUE) { op_rot.y = target_rot.y; }
if(bActive == TRUE) { op_rot.z = target_rot.z; }
op->SetRotation(op_rot);
```

Finished. The Complete Expression:

```
main(doc,op)
{
        //********* User Input *****************\\

        var target_name = "target";
        var scale_factor = 0.5;
        var hActive = TRUE;
        var pActive = TRUE;
        var bActive = TRUE;

        //***************************************\\

        var target = doc->FindObject(target_name);
        if(!target) { return; }

        var target_rot = target->GetRotation();
        target_rot = target_rot*scale_factor;

        var op_rot = op->GetRotation();

        if(hActive == TRUE) { op_rot.x = target_rot.x; }
        if(pActive == TRUE) { op_rot.y = target_rot.y; }
        if(bActive == TRUE) { op_rot.z = target_rot.z; }
        op->SetRotation(op_rot);

}
```

EXERCISE 2: BOUNCING BALL

What You Want It To Do:
The expression automatically applies squash and stretch to a ball, based on how close to the ground it is. It should also keep the ball above a given height so that it does not pass through the floor.

Small Steps:
1. Retrieve the user input.
2. Retrieve the ball's position.
3. Retrieve the floor's position.
4. Calculate the vertical difference between the two.

5. Ensure the object is above the minimum height.
6. Retrieve the ball's radius.
7. See if the distance is less than the object's radius.
8. If not, set the object's scale to 1,1,1.
9. If yes, Calculate the width and height of the ball based on its position relative to the floor (ensure there is no division by 0).
10. Set the ball's width and height to the calculated values.

The Expression:

Step 1. Retrieve the User Input:

```
main(doc,op)
{
var min_height = 5;
var floor_obj = doc->FindObject("Floor");
if(!floor_obj) { return; }
```

Step 2 & 3. Retrieve op_pos and floor_pos:

```
var op_pos = op->GetPosition();
var floor_pos = floor_obj->GetPosition();
```

Step 4. Calculate the Vertical Difference Between the Two:

```
var vertical_difference = op_pos.y - floor_pos.y;
```

Step 5. Ensure the Object is Above the Minimum Height:

```
if(vertical_difference < min_height)
{
        op->SetPosition(vector(op_pos.x,floor_pos.y +
        min_height,op_pos.z));
        vertical_difference = min_height;
}
```

Step 6. Retrieve the Ball's Radius:

```
var op_container = op->GetContainer();
var radius = op_container->GetFloat(PRIM_SPHERE_RAD);
```

Step 7. See If the Distance Is Less than the Object's Radius:

```
if( vertical_difference < radius )
{
        var height = 1 * (vertical_difference / radius); //Step 9
        var width = sqrt(1 / height); //Step 9
        op->SetScale(vector(width,height,width)); //Step 10
}
```

Step 8. If Not, Set the Object's Scale to 1,1,1:

```
else
{
 op->SetScale(vector(1,1,1));
}
```

Finished. The Complete Expression:

```
main(doc,op)
{
        var min_height = 5;
        var floor_obj = doc->FindObject("Floor");
        if(!floor_obj) { return; }

        var op_pos = op->GetPosition();
        var floor_pos = floor_obj->GetPosition();
        var vertical_difference = op_pos.y - floor_pos.y;

        if(vertical_difference < min_height)
        {
                op->SetPosition(vector(op_pos.x,floor_pos.y +
                min_height,op_pos.z));
                vertical_difference = min_height;
        }

        var op_container = op->GetContainer();
        var radius = op_container->GetFloat(PRIM_SPHERE_RAD);

        if( vertical_difference < radius )
        {
                var height = 1 * (vertical_difference / radius);
                var width = sqrt(1 / height);
                op->SetScale(vector(width,height,width));
        }
```

```
    else
    {
     op->SetScale(vector(1,1,1));
    }

}
```

To Use This Expression:

1. Create a new document.
2. Add a floor object.
3. Add a Sphere.
4. Place this expression on the Sphere. Ensure that "floor_obj" is searching for the floor object.
5. Move the Sphere up and down; you should see it squash and stretch as it impacts with the floor.

Try the next two exercises on your own.

EXERCISE 3: IN THE MIDDLE

What You Want It To Do:
Have an object stay in the middle of two objects. The user should be able to enter both object names, and specify whether or not an axis is activated.

EXERCISE 4: AUTO DOF

What You Want It To Do:
Have a camera automatically adjust DOF settings based on the distance it is from a target object.

You will need the following container ID's to complete the exercise.

CAMERAOBJECT_DEPTHTYPE [int] Depth of field type (see dialog box)
CAMERAOBJECT_DEPTHFRONT [float] Front focus
CAMERAOBJECT_DEPTHMIDDLE [float] Sharpness
CAMERAOBJECT_DEPTHBACK [float] Rear focus

CHAPTER 16 C.O.F.F.E.E.: A COMPREHENSIVE INTRODUCTION

WHERE TO GO FROM HERE

C.O.F.F.E.E. is a very deep programming language; it has more intricacies than could ever be covered in a single chapter. Because of this, I have written this section. With any luck you now have a strong foundation in C.O.F.F.E.E. programming — it is now up to you to use the various resources out there for learning and writing C.O.F.F.E.E..

THE C.O.F.F.E.E. SDK:

In order for you to go onto anything more than simple expressions, you will need to reference the C.O.F.F.E.E. SDK. It has a full listing of all of C.O.F.F.E.E.'s predefined classes, variables and functions. To download the SDK, please visit: www.plugincafe.com

GENERAL PROGRAMMING BOOKS:

There are many books already out there on programming that are applicable to C.O.F.F.E.E. (although not directly). A trip to your local used/discount bookstore might be a good investment of your time. Look for books on OOP, Programming Theory, Graphics Algorithms, or programming languages like C++. Most of these books will help give you a stronger base in the how's and why's of programming.

PLUGINCAFE:

Maxon has provided its users with an extremely useful place called "PluginCafe" (www.plugincafe.com). There, you can post your expressions, download others, or even ask seasoned programmers questions on the C.O.F.F.E.E. support forum. They also have a tutorials section where you can pick up pieces of information.

CHAPTER 17
Learning from the Masters

So who's using C4D? Well, the demographics are broad. There are C4D users worldwide; some using it as a hobby, others making a living off of their C4D knowledge and artistic prowess. Included here are three brief interviews with some of the best, and some of the most high profile C4D users.

SIMON WICKER

DIGITAL MATTE PAINTER, MILLFILM

So please tell us a little bit about yourself. Where are you from?
Simon Wicker, age 32, born, educated and working in London, England.

Where do you work? What kinds of projects do you do there?
Currently I am working as a digital matte painter at Millfilm, which is a company based in London. We provide visual effects services for feature films. A digital matte painter creates set extensions that will fill out a live action plate. Generally this will be some kind of digital environment that needs to be re-created (either because the set would be too costly to build or doesn't actually exist anymore).

What are some notable projects you've worked on in the past?
I guess (what with the Oscars) the one everyone will know is *Gladiator*. Millfilm provided the visual effects for the film, recreating first century Rome for director Ridley Scott.

I produced about 8 matte paintings of the city of Rome that were used as backdrops for the live-action. I used a combination of 2D and 3D elements to

FIGURE 17.1 *© 2001 Copyright Simon Wicker.*

build up a layered scene that was then composited using Discreet Logic's *inferno* system.

Currently I have just finished some work on Brian Helgeland's *A Knights Tale*, creating several backdrops of medieval London.

ART BACKGROUND

What artistic/technical training do you have?
Well I studied graphic design for three years at a great college here in London called Ravensbourne. I always thought that design was going to be my life long vocation as working in films was something that "other" people did. Being a designer seemed more real world and practical at the time (Figure 17.2).

Have you any official 3D training?
No.

How'd you get started in 3D?
I'd been working at the Mill (Millfilm's sister company) for four years as a Mac operator and was getting bored of doing type setting for television commercials. I wondered whether there was something else that would interest me and gradually I came to think that being a matte painter would actually be a fun vocation to have (I have always been interested in the kind of work that Syd Mead did with *Blade Runner*, creating these believable but wholly invented environments). Working with 3D became an integral part of my work as a matte painter.

FIGURE © *2001 Copyright Simon Wicker.*
17.2

What parts of 3D really excite you?

Modeling and surfacing something. For whatever reason. I just love pulling polygons around and have this fanatical idea that if I keep hacking away at a design I will eventually be able to create the ideal mesh. Also I love photography, and getting reference images for my models is a great way to get away from the computer screen and back out into the real world.

Also I find that there is something magical about building something on the computer and then rendering an image of this imaginary space.

What parts of 3D turn you off?

Hmm. Tricky question. Nothing really turns me off, but I always hate it when a piece of software doesn't work in exactly the way I expect it to. I get frustrated very easily when things get more complicated than they should be. I guess this was one reason why I hassled the guys at Maxon to let me become a beta tester for them.

What do you feel are the necessary skills to have to enjoy a career in animation?

Well for the sort of thing I do it would definitely be a love of architectural space!

Matte painting is very much about building a plausible environment. For that you have to have a sense of proportion and scale so that the live action will fit correctly with the synthetic background. This whole "architectural" way of looking at things will inform the way you model and render an environment. Also the light has to be absolutely spot on - lighting a huge great building is very different than lighting a character.

Finally a love of all things fanciful doesn't go amiss (Figure 17.3)!

C4D

How did you discover C4D?

Well I've only ever worked on a Macintosh so when I was looking for a 3D application to use the choice (at that time) was between XL, Lightwave and EI. I chose XL because it was the most Mac-like and stable app around at that time.

What things work well for you in it?

I find the Cinema GUI is easy to get to grips with and the application imposes a logical workflow on what I do. I like the integration between the whole modeling/surfacing/animating part of things.

I can create test models very quickly and I can tweak the settings easily without getting too involved in the mechanics of what I am doing. also, XL is solid as a rock which is nice!

FIGURE © 2001 Simon Wicker
17.3

What things would you like to see changed?
Hmm. Most of what I do involves scenes set outdoors so I have always wished we had the ability to simulate real world effects more (true arete style water, a sky generator, snow simulation, weathering effects, that kind of thing).

Rumor has it, some Gladiator shots were done using C4D as a tool. Could you tell us a bit more about this.
Yes. I used XL to create buildings and elements that were brought into Photoshop and layered up with photographs of Roman style buildings we shot around London and Malta (where they did the live action shoot). These then formed the backbone of my matte paintings. I should add that when you see the coliseum that was created in Softimage and then rendered using radiosity information created in Lightscape by the wonderful 3D department here at Millfilm - the images I worked on tended to be the long shots where the whole vista of the city is revealed.

My favorite matte painting I worked on was probably the end shot of the film where the camera pulls up over the top of the coliseum revealing an unfeasibly grandiose roman city in the background.

WORKFLOW

Do you do more animation or still work?
Well all of the matte paintings I did for *Gladiator* were stills that were then given a post move in the compositing stage on the *Inferno*. This is good as you can

always take the final render and tweak things in Photoshop (painting bits out and suchlike) if things are not perfectly perfect.

However I was pleased that the latest matte painting I did for *A Knights Tale* was a big helicopter shot flying over a jousting arena. It was nice to deal with the complexities of an animation - it took about 10 days to render the whole sequence using the three dual processor Macs that I had available to me (Figure 17.4).

What is your typical workflow in developing projects?

Mmm. It depends. Sometimes we will be given very detailed production paintings for a shot created by the film's art department. In this case we can get straight on to creating the final shot, modelling, texturing and photographing to match what we have been given.

Other times we will simply be shown the live-action plate and then told to stick a city in the background. For this I will need to make lots of design sketches and test renders to create something that looks good (and the director approves) before building and rendering everything before the deadline runs out.

Ridley Scott was a great director to work with. When he came round to look at the shots we were working on he would make these tiny little thumbnail sketches showing us exactly the kind of image he was looking for. It cut out a lot of guesswork in the planning stages and let you home in on his vision of Rome as a living city.

I guess much of what I do relies on spending time beforehand doing lots of research and going out getting reference images. Then it is a lot easier to come up with a plausible design for a matte painting.

FIGURE *© 2001 Simon Wicker*
17.4

CHAPTER 17 LEARNING FROM THE MASTERS

If someone were hoping to work in the same industry as you are, what kinds of preparation would you suggest?

Well if I knew what the preparation needed to get on in matte painting was it certainly wouldn't have taken such a long and convoluted path getting where I am now!

I think the only advice I can give is get a good college education (as you can't beat the experience), and then try and get straight into your chosen industry by hook or by crook, even if you initially only get taken on in a peripheral position like a runner or technical assistant.

©2001 Simon Wicker.

PHIL CAPTAIN 3D MCNALLY

ILM ANIMATOR AND AWARD WINNING ANIMATOR OF PUMP-ACTION

Captain, tell us a bit about your artistic background? What sort of training (artistic or otherwise) do you have?

For extra details have a look at the gallery at...

http://.www.captain.3d.com

I followed a creative education from Art foundation through a BA in 3D Design and finally a Master of Art degree in Furniture Design from the Royal College of Art (RCA) in London. While at the RCA in 1991, as well as being introduced to computer aided design, I had taken a one-day Holography course and this had sparked my interest in Stereo (3D) Photography which continued throughout the course and formed some of my first freelance work after graduation.

My partner Deepa who was a Graphic Design graduate from the RCA changed my direction when she bought our first computer - Apple Mac 6100/60. Excited more by the thought of unlimited games of Maelstrom, I found myself spending more and more time at the machine.

We spent the next 5 years on a variety of freelance projects, for example, completing over 100 posters for The Body Shop as well as modeling furniture in 3D software for stereo output. I also developed an interactive, stereo, montage installation for the Tokyo Metropolitan Museum of Photography called Captain 3D's Space Station. The final piece of work before Pump-Action was a 3D animation for the Royal National Lifeboat Institute in the UK and showed how a capsized boat could right itself in a rolling sea. You can see this piece and other early work in my gallery at...

http://.www.captain.3d.com/gallery/html/freelance/rnli.htm

FIGURE © *2000 Phil McNally.*
17.5

Have you any formal 3D training?
No, Just the C4D tutorial manual and all those great tips from the forum.

What got you interested in 3D?
I actually consciously avoided it at college as I did not like the whole technical drawing side of design. My first experience of computer modeling was with Modelshop and Swivel 3D back in 1991. That was enough to put me off for years. But in 1996 I was asked by a medical company about producing some graphs in Stereo and I knew I could do it in a 3D modeling package. So reluctantly I started the project on my friends machine using Strata Studio Pro 1.75. It did not take long until I was seduced by those raytraced reflections which looked even more amazing in Stereo.

http://www.captain3d.com/gallery/html/freelance/cpr.htm
http://.www.captain3d.com/stereo/gallery/c/_/_/_/_/html/stereo.html

Who were your original 3D inspirations? How about recently?
I can remember being amazed at school by early computer generated sequences of a paper airplane floating around a room being followed by the camera under chairs etc. It was probably only wire frame or flat shading but this new form of imaging excited me even though I never thought I would be involved with that techy computer stuff.

Tron came out soon after. More recently of course Toy Story 2. I saw it projected digitally at the Odeon Leicester Square - London - Fantastic entertainment.

C4D

How'd you get involved in C4D? What attracted you to it?
After the success of the Medical graphs and a spinning logo or two I was asked by a friend if I could teach him 3D if he got an Arts Council grant. It would pay me to teach him. I was surprised when he actually got it and then I realized I had to get my own software to run on my own machine. I was all ready to go with Strata when they released version 2 and the complaints about its bugs were

so loud on various email lists that I was put off. By chance the first version of Cinema 4D for Mac and PC had just come out (May 1997) and got a rave review in MacFormat about stability and rendering speed. I must have been one of the first to buy it as it cost me £800 and XL hadn't been invented yet.

What do you feel its strengths are?
Maxon the company, stability and ease of learning.

What about its weaknesses?
I don't really know. I tend to work within it, with what I have got and don't get too stressed about what could be there.

SUCCESS OF "PUMP-ACTION"

Most people involved with C4D have heard of the phenomenal success of "Pump-Action." What are the latest accolades it's achieved?
Winning Media Masters is the latest and maybe the last prize for Pump-Action. I am coming to the end of the list of festivals still to be judged.
What is the biggest success it garnished?
My personal favorite was to get into the Electronic Theatre at Siggraph 2000 and to actually be there and see it projected on a 60ft screen in front of a huge and enthusiastic audience. There were only 41 films selected from around 650 entries and about 10 of the finalists were from major studios.
http://www.captain3d.com/pump/pump/studio/html/siggraph/siget.htm

Do you think it has anything to do with your present employment?
I think it is the other way round as my job offer from ILM came through after Siggraph. In fact my interview was at the show in New Orleans and all the staff asking me questions had seen it on the big screen the night before. What could have been better?

How long did you work on it?
From scribbling down my first thoughts to backing up the finished movie was 14 months and a total of 3800 hrs or 17.5 hours work per finished screen second. The thing I did not realize at the time was that I would spend a further 6 months on festival entries, writing press articles, creating the website, visiting shows and general promotion before getting the first job interviews. I am writing this on 12/5/00. I started Pump-Action on 11/25/97 and I still haven't started work as I am waiting for my visa (Figure 17.6).

FIGURE © 2000 Phil McNally.
17.6

FIGURE © 2001 Phil McNally.
17.7

Did you have a job as you were doing it?

No I decided to quit all my freelance work in order to concentrate full time on the project although I only expected it to take 6 months when I stopped earning money.

What sorts of hardware/software did you use to create it?

All 3D work was produced in Cinema 4D XL 5.3 and all audio was recorded into Premiere. Photoshop was used extensively for textures and After Effects was put to use for motion blur, final output and a bit of depth of field.

All of this was running on a B/W G3 400Mhz with 512 MB ram and 107 GIG of storage. I have two more G3 400's and an 8200 which serves the files to CinemaNet for rendering. I found that this setup was rendering slightly quicker than I could produce the next scenes so that was perfect until I finished the creative work. For the final push on rendering I borrowed 2 more G3's from my friends Andy Green and Colin Wilson and added two new iMacs to make a 7 machine team and a very warm room even though it was January.

How did you get "Pump-Action" seen?

With months of work. Deepa and I struggled through 100+ festival forms and websites finally mailing out 70 packs around the world. By the time we had sent the selection vhs, and later if you are lucky, the screening Beta SP along with the entry fees, it worked out at around $50 per festival. I made sure I included a full press pack with each one containing printed text and a CD of high res images ready for CMYK printing plus the text again on file so they had the basis of a story. Having things to hand often made the difference when magazines were curious. Websites like iFilm and Animation Express were also important in the whole process of keeping it available and my own site provided lots of extra info and contact details.

For more on entering festivals...
http://www.designfreak.com/freakzine/3/10/article.asp

Where did you show it?
You really want the list? It has now screened at 50 festivals.
  OK they are all here...
  http://www.captain3d.com/pump/index.htm

You produced a tape with Naam. How did that fit into the exposure strategy?
The tape was more for the C4D community to find out what was involved in making our two films. The project was funded mainly by HiSoft, the UK distributors of Cinema4D, but also myself, Naam and Maxon USA covered expenses. It is a good tape which still needs to sell more to break even.

MODELING

In "Pump-Action" what were your primary modeling tools? Why?
I used NURBS (not hyperNURBS) for the characters because it was more intuitive to model in the first place seeing the profile change live as the splines were adjusted, but also they allowed me to set a low poly editor view to keep things moving while I animated and a very high poly render setting for those fine details like the wrinkles (Figure 17.7).

Did you create all your textures from scratch? Did you use any stock textures?
Apart from the odd brick or wood grain base everything was built from scratch in Photoshop. I did shoot a lot of my own photographic reference material with a digital camera which formed the basis of almost every final texture.

I loved the face and chest of Vic Vinyl. Did you just scan in marker sketches? Tell us more about that great texture/character choice.
That idea was straight from my design background. Vic is supposed to be a prototype of a new inflatable character that Inflatable Engineering is making. He is still a work in progress. The designers did not even have enough orange and blue vinyl to finish him off and while they were testing him out they thought it would be funny to give him some extra hand drawn features.

  For convenience I actually used Painter's digital marker pens for those files.

Lighting

I thought the lighting was superb in "Pump-Action." What sorts of previsualization techniques did you use?

I don't consider myself a lighting person and I certainly don't have confidence in how to set up what I need, but I do have a good eye for what isn't working so I just keep going until I am happy. Part of the reason for taking on the whole Reservoir Dogs idea was that I could borrow all the lighting and set design which those experts had set up (Figure 17.8).

How many lights did you use?
48.

You mentioned negative lights in your video. Would you please expand on that?
Yes, there are a few negative lights to help with shadows. They are small visible lights that fill areas with darkness. Not all of my lights cast shadows and those that did were mainly soft. This meant that areas in between boxes or Vic's legs were lighter than they should have been. These black lights gave the effect that I wanted.

There were great shadows everywhere. Did you plan those shadows or build them as you went?
It was easier than that. I copied the shadows from the set of Reservoir Dog's. I liked the atmosphere that the strong diagonal lines created and it gave me a working model to emulate. It still took a lot of personal judgement to get the right balance and all object lighting had to be my own work.

In some shots, the character's shadows became very important in the scene. Were there any tricks to accurately communicating that?
Not really. It is how it looks. Shadows cast by lights. No texture tricks although they might have been better in some cases.

Did you organize the outdoor lighting scheme differently than the indoor? How?
The front door shot has minimal lighting, just an omni on the left and two spots on the right. One spot had the leaf pattern.

CHAPTER 17 LEARNING FROM THE MASTERS

FIGURE © *2001 Phil McNally.*
17.8

How'd you do those great shadows of leaves fluttering in the breeze in the opening scene?

It was a simple solution in the end. I videoed the moving leaves of a real tree silhouetted against the sky, then converted the captured movie to black and white using After Effects. This movie was imported into the transparency channel of a new C4D texture and that was applied to the spotlight.

CHARACTER ANIMATION

Did you find the character animation enjoyable in "Pump-Action?"

No not the actual keyframing. But I found the results so exciting I kept coming back for more. I also found the motion analysis very interesting as well. Sitting there going over and over the same action with your own arms trying to understand the mechanics of something you do instinctively. I used video extensively for this recording myself repeating the action and picking out which shoots I liked and then re-recording to refine the action.

http://www.captain3d.com/pump/pump/studio/html/movies/dive.htm
http://www.captain3d.com/pump/pump/studio/html/movies/balloons.htm

Did you use FK and IK? Or primarily one or the other?

I used FK most of the time as I preferred the control of working each limb section individually. IK was used on Balloon Boy's legs and the arm that rests on the box. It was essential in order to lock the feet and hand in position as the body move around them.

You mentioned and showed an interesting bone technique on your video, where you created feeler or influence bones that were the children of what we'd consider the skeleton of the character. Could you expand on that a bit? I was very impressed with the joints and how the plastic seemed to "bunch." How'd you do that?

The folds in the vinyl were created with the so called 'limitations' of version 5.3's bone system. I set up one skeleton that defined the joints of each limb but these bones had no influence over the mesh. Their strength was zero. The folds were handled by what I called influence bones, which I positioned where ever I wanted to distort the mesh. They did not have to conform to the skeleton layout. As long as they were made child objects of the skeleton bones, they moved in unison with the animation of the limbs. Each of the influence bones had a radius of influence set to control a specific area of the mesh. I don't think the new vertex mapping in XL6 would have been any use in this situation.

Pump-Action had very nice anticipation/action/reaction. Where'd you learn those skills?

Simply from recording myself performing the actions live and noting what was good and what was bad. Having identified what I like, I would do it all again trying to expand the good bits. Eventually I would have a 'take' that I liked and could use for frame by frame analysis. I never actually rotoscoped the animation but sometimes counted movie frames to get the overall pacing of an action.

CAMERA WORK

I thought the cinematography style and pacing was one of the nicest aspects of "Pump-Action." Was it based upon any particular work?

Not consciously. I had used my video camera to make some personal documentaries and have shot stereo stills for years so that probably helped my eye for composition. The dance sequence borrowed heavily again from Reservoir Dogs but the rest came out of my preparation work where Deepa and I had performed the whole story live and I had edited it as we went. This gave an excellent opportunity to experiment with shots.

There was such a nice easing in and easing out of much of the camera movement. How'd you do that?

I struggled with this for quite a while on the door shot the first one I did with a slow track. I thought it could easily be done with a 2 point S curve in time control using path mode, but I could never get the start and finish delicate enough until I added 2 more points near the beginning and end to really limit the take-off angle. Once I was happy with the pace of the camera move I saved the curve, then imported it into the direction track so the two matched each other. Once I had cracked it, it was easy on the other shots (Figure 17.9).

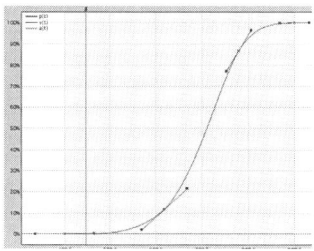

FIGURE 17.9 *Added points along curve for more gentle easing in and out.*

FIGURE 17.10 *© 2000 Phil McNally.*

If you could do the entire "Pump-Action" saga again (from pre-vis, to production, to promotion) would you do anything differently?
Ah. Good one...Overall I would not mind doing it the same way next time but I would be more careful about spending a whole afternoon making a texture for an object that does not get a close up etc. That comes down to a tight storyboard,. I thought I did have it under control but looking back, the storyboard could have been worked over and over to really have the film finished before I started constructing. Maybe it would have been useful to have screenings of the storyboards to friends to see if they laugh or where the pace is too slow.

Actual construction, I am happy with.

What were the most important things you learned through your 3D career up to this point?
Pump-Action really is my 3D career even though I had produced a variety of smaller projects beforehand. The learning curve really took off when I started this short and I recommend it to everyone who really wants to get it there. There is no better way of learning than having to get on with it in a real project. One thing I have learned is that progress only takes place through hard work. There is no point looking for the magic button. This was never clearer than when returning to Pump-Action after a day away to find it had not progressed a single frame in my absence.

Do you have any Words o' Wisdom for folks hoping to follow in your footsteps?

I did a talk at Computer Arts Live in London and called it... 'Stop wishing, Start working.' I really think sometimes that the only thing that stops people getting from where they are now to where they want to be is the fact that they never set off on the path towards the goal. Too busy, can't afford to, not fair, etc.

It took me 14 months to make Pump-Action - an insignificant but fun 4 mins of animation. To many it sounds crazy, but for me it has literally taken me from wishing and dreaming in my bedroom studio to the start of a whole new life in a world that I previously only glimpsed at through 'The making of...' TV specials (Figure 17.10).

Is 14 months a high price? Well think back to where you where 14 months ago and ask yourself how much has changed using your current plan. I was stuck for quite a few years until I finally had enough.

Speech over...
©2001 Phil McNally.

Alec Syme

Freelance 3D Illustrator (www.flukestudio.com)

Background

Rumor has it, you started out as an airbrush artist. Tell me more?

Yea, back in the mid eighties I picked up an Associate's degree in commercial art. I learned airbrushing there. I went right from school to being freelance. I didn't make much money but had lots of free time. I later took an illustration position at Studio West (a small illustration shop). I was lucky to work with some old school masters. I grew a lot. In '93 I bought my first computer. (A smokin' Quadra 650.)

What formal art training do you have?

I went to Minneapolis College of Art and Design for a couple years before the commercial art school and one year at Ball State University in Muncie, Indiana, of all places, before that.

Do you have any official 3D training?

Ummm... No. I'm self taught.

FIGURE 17.11 © 2001 Alec Syme.

FIGURE 17.12 © 2001 Alec Syme.

What do you currently make your living doing?
3D animation and illustration.

What percentage of your paid work is 3D?
All of it.

What got you started in 3D?
After buying the Quadra, I bought a game called MYST and was blown away with the graphics. On the CD was a sort of short "Making of" section. It showed these two guys using Strata on Quadras. I bought it soon thereafter and really got into it.

What parts of 3D appeal to you?
I guess I like the final results. Also, the methodic technical side appealed as well. It's good mind food (Figure 17.11 and 17.12).

C4D

How'd you discover C4D?
I was using Strata and Electric Image and a few other modelers back in '97. I got a hold of a demo of C4D somewhere and started playing around. I loaded a huge skeleton model that was choking the other software, was amazed at the speed of the screen redraw and the rendering. I bought it right away. Soon I was using it for everything. I sold EI and my copies of the other programs languished. I loved the object oriented nature of C4D. Not to mention everything actually worked.

What do you like about it?
Workflow and speed. I can really fly in Cinema. There's about a thousand other things, but those are the big ones.

What things don't work well for you?
Can't think of too much. If I have a problem with something I call Jason at Maxon. He's the all-knowing Cinema tech guru.

Do you do more illustration or animation with C4D?
I'm doing more and more animation these days. I started off transposing my airbrush skills to the computer and focused on print. It's leaning the other way now.

I loved your "Jack" project. Could you tell me more about the story behind the concept, and the process you used to create it?
Hmmm...I got a call from Paul Babb at Maxon. They needed a cool image to promote the new huge release of version 6. (I was a beta tester at this point). The image needed to be attention grabbing and show off some of the new features. HyperNURBS was a big feature so I thought I'd focus on that. A nice face model was in order. I bounced ideas around with Paul, and we came up with a mask sort of image. Then, as per chance, I got an email from someone who wanted me to illustrate a Jack-in-the-box image for some online gaming thing. I didn't take the job but it got me thinking about a Jack-in-the-box. It just sort of progressed from there. Paul was a very easy client. He just kept saying "just make it cool." He left it pretty much up to me (Figure 17.13).

WORKFLOW

When you are doing illustration work, how does your workflow run?
I usually get a really crappy sketch and have a long talk with the art director. Then I start modeling whatever it is and get some basic lights and textures in the scene. I'll do a low-rez render and bring it into Photoshop and sort of mess it up with filters. 3D renderings are too perfect for the first comp. I can't let the client focus on details. Then I'll get input and do another comp or two before nailing everything down.

Chapter 17 Learning from the Masters

Is this significantly different than when you're doing animation? Please explain.

Animation needs a lot more up front work in the form of storyboards, quick test renders and lots more planning.

Employment

Do you find 3D work very profitable?

Yes, I can do a lot more work (than traditional) and it always pays better.

Could you give a short list of your clientele?

3M, Cargill, Coca-Cola, Dayton Hudson, Discover Magazine, Dow, Ericsson, Federal Express, First Union Bank, Formica, Gatorade, General Mills, GTE, K-Mart, Harley Davidson, Lexus, Lucent Technologies, Merck Pharmaceuticals, Minnesota Lottery, Motorola, National Car, National Geographic Magazine, Nestle, Nordic Track, Norwest Banks, Paramount (Figure 17.14), Pillsbury, Regis Hair Care Products, Reliastar, Starbucks, SW Bell, Target Stores, Volvo, Wam!Net.

How do you drum up business? Do they come to you or do you pound the pavement?

I have a killer sales rep here in Minneapolis, and two others in different parts of the country. I let them bring the work to me.

Figure 17.13 © 2001 Alec Syme.

Figure 17.14 © 2001 Alec Syme.

What are your ultimate career goals?

My ultimate goal is to have a studio with a hand full (perhaps more) of employees. This is actually about to happen. I'm partnering with Jeff Johnson and forming a new company. Jeff and I have been working together for a few years now with separate businesses.

If someone was hoping to do what you do (follow in your footsteps), what advice would you offer?

Work on regular old art skills as much as you can. Very valuable. Study real world lighting situations and explore creative problem solving. There's always many ways to get a result you're after. Work on the portfolio or demo real whenever you get a chance (Figure 17.15 and 17.16).

©2001 Alec Syme.

FIGURE 17.15 © *2001 Alec Syme.*

FIGURE 17.16 © *2001 Alec Syme.*

CHAPTER 17 LEARNING FROM THE MASTERS   515

INSPIRATION GALLERY

Luckily, there are quite a few very talented artists besides those listed above doing incredible work with C4D. Unluckily, we don't have room to include interviews with all of them. However, here are some samples of some of the best out there. Note, all images are copyrighted and are owned by the artists.

ON THE CD

NOTE: Be sure to check these images and other renderings and movies on the included CD. The colors are worth the time.

ANDREAS CALMBACH

FIGURE © Copyright Andreas Calmbach 2001.
17.17

CHRISTIAN RAMBOW

FIGURE © Copyright Christian Rambow 2001.
17.18

DAVE TAYLOR

FIGURE 17.19 © *Copyright Taylor Imaging 2001.*

DEAN BAKER

FIGURE 17.20 © *Copyright Dean Baker 2001.*

Chapter 17 Learning from the Masters

Gareth Lockett

Figure 17.21 © *Copyright Gareth Lockett 2001.*

Gray Ginther

Figure 17.22 © *Copyright Gray Ginther 2001.*

JANINE PAUKE

FIGURE 17.23 © *Copyright Janine Pauke 2001.*

LAURENT HEIDERSCHEID

FIGURE 17.24 *Laurent Heiderscheid, NiceLTD.com. © Copyright Nicosia Creative Expresso, 2001.*

Chapter 17 Learning from the Masters

FIGURE 17.25 *Laurent Heiderscheid, NiceLTD.com. © Copyright Nicosia Creative Expresso, 2001.*

MARTIN KAY

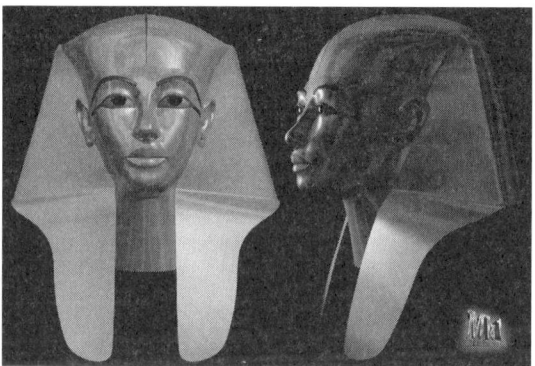

FIGURE 17.26 *© Copyright Martin Kay, 2001.*

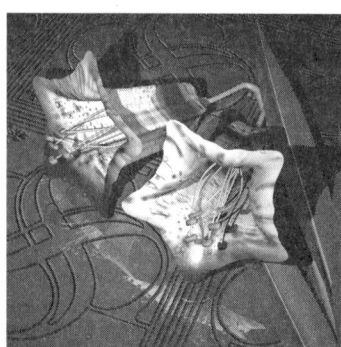

FIGURE 17.27 *© Copyright Martin Kay, 2001.*

Mark Mathieson

FIGURE 17.28 © *Copyright Mark Mathieson, 2001.*

Michael Ambjörn

FIGURE 17.29 © *Copyright Michael Ambjörn, 2001.*

MICHAEL VANCE

FIGURE 17.30 © Copyright Michael Vance, 2001. Mvpny.com

NEIL VAUGHAN

FIGURE 17.31 © Copyright Neil Vaughan, 2001.

FIGURE 17.32 © *Copyright Neil Vaughan, 2001.*

ONUR PEKDEMIR

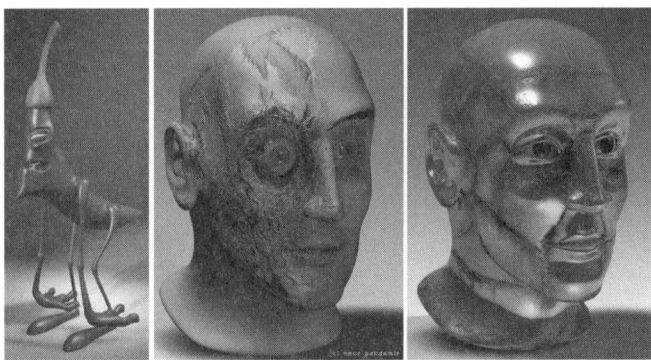

FIGURE 17.33 © *Copyright Onur Pekdemir, 2001.*

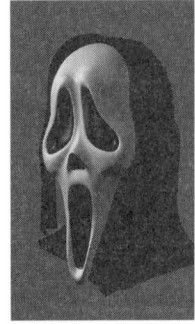
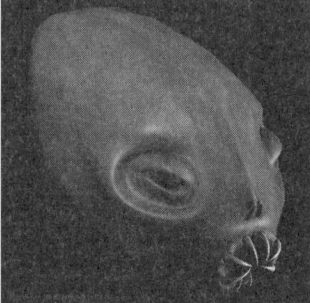

FIGURE 17.34 © *Copyright Onur Pekdemir, 2001.*

Chapter 17 Learning from the Masters

Jérôme Pastorello

Figure 17.35 © EUROSPORT/Jérôme Pastorello.

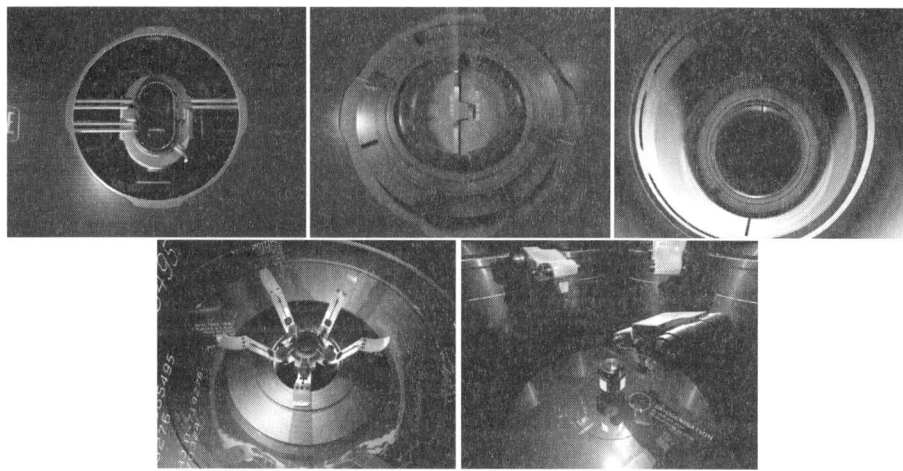

Figure 17.36 © 13eme RUE/UNIVERSAL STUDIOS channels France/Jérôme Pastorello.

Philip Nicholson

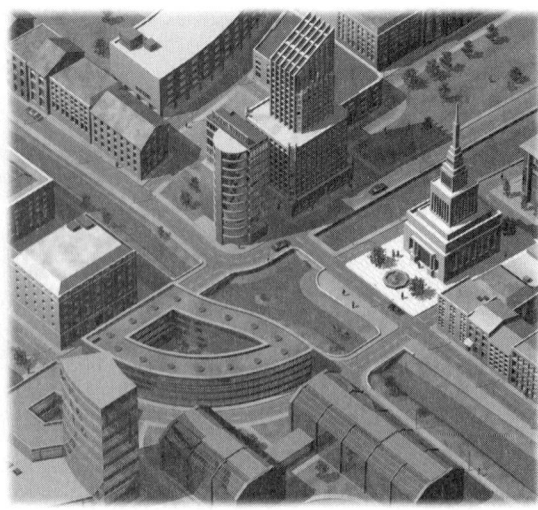

FIGURE 17.37 © *Copyright Philip Nicholson, 2001.*

FIGURE 17.38 © *Copyright Philip Nicholson, 2001.*

CHAPTER 17 LEARNING FROM THE MASTERS

RAI

FIGURE 17.39 © Copyright Rai, 2001.

ROBERT BOEHM

FIGURE 17.40 © Copyright Robert Boehm, 2001.

SIMON KNOWLES

FIGURE 17.41 © Copyright Simon Knowles (digitalart@ndirect.com), 2001.

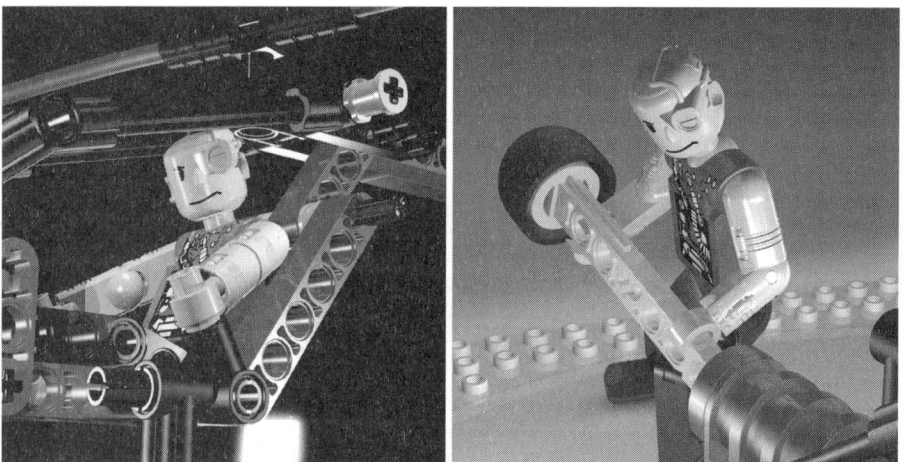

FIGURE 17.42 © Copyright Simon Knowles (digitalart@ndirect.com), 2001.

Chapter 17 Learning from the Masters 527

Steve Townrow

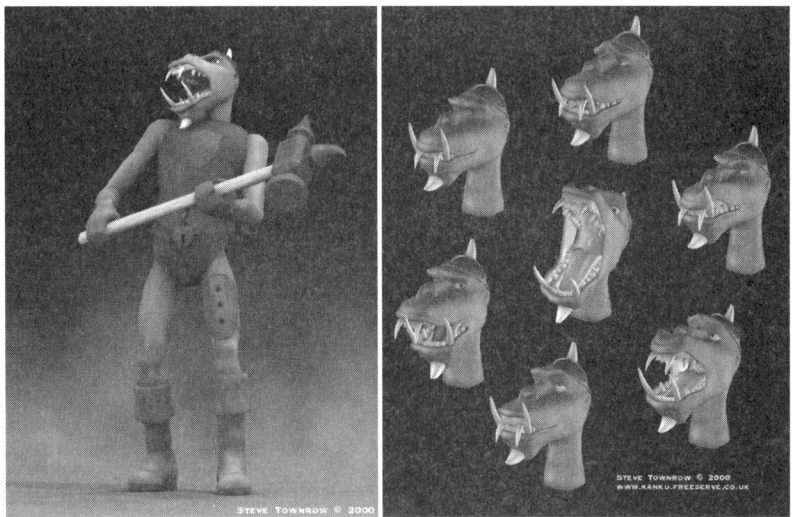

Figure 17.43 © *Copyright Steve Townrow, 2001.*

Suon-Oon Lim

Figure 17.44 © *Copyright Suon-Oon Lim, 2001.*

FIGURE 17.45 © *Copyright Suon-Oon Lim, 2001.*

APPENDIX A
About the CD-ROM

THE CD-ROM THAT ACCOMPANIES THIS BOOK IS DIVIDED INTO FOUR MAIN SECTIONS:

1) All images contained from within the book are contained in full color on the CD. In the areas of texture and lighting, full color images are especially important to see in order to understand some of the more subtle points. As you go along in the book and find an area that you want more visual clues, please refer to these color versions. In addition, the work of some very talented 3D artists are included in this volume and their work can most fully be enjoyed through the full color versions contained here.

2) Included with certain chapters are supplemental PDF chapters meant to add extra dimension to some particularly detail-oriented chapters. Cinema4D XL is such a multi-dimensional program that everything that needs to be said couldn't fit in this one book. In fact some important information originally intended for these pages wouldn't fit. However, rest assured, if you are a beginning C4D user and need some extra hints and tricks, please make sure you take a look at the supplemental chapters included here on the CD.

3) Some chapters include very in-depth tutorials exploring key concepts in C4DXL. Often, simply reading about the tutorial doesn't do the trick. To alleviate this difficulty, included on the CD are several of the tutorial C4D files that can be opened with C4DXL v6 or v7. These files will give you the opportunity to further dissect the projects and see how the certain techniques are actually put together.

4) A full demo of C4D and Bodypaint v7 is also included for both Mac and PC. Although this version is save disabled, it is fully functional and will allow you to experiment with all aspects of C4D.

Index

(0,0,0) point, 21, 33
2D shaders, 234
3D real-time content, 423
3D real-time content creation, 422
3D shaders, 233
3D Studio Max, 422
A Subtract B setting, 111
AA Softness and renderings, 411
absolute value, 476
acceleration, 17
accessing buried managers, 2
Action Safe, 16
active object, 43
Active Object Only setting and renderings, 408
active view, 15, 22
Add Points tool, 89
adding commands, 8–9
adding points in empty space, 199
adding surfaces to a selection, 386
adjusting influence effects of a bone, 389
Akima Spline Curve, 70
aliasing, 403
Align to Spline track, 326
All Commands option, 10
All-Views mode, 22
Alpha Channel and rendering, 414
altering points, 73
anchoring a bone, 373
animated flythrough, 336
animation
  defined, 318
  editing path of movement, 321
  illusion of movement, 318
  Parameter track, 322
  path of movement, 320
  Position track, 319
  Powerslider, 324
  recording on multiple tracks simultaneously, 322
  reusing poses by copying and pasting, 344
  Rotation track, 321
  Scale track, 322
  time slider, 318
  Timeline Ruler, 324
animation of run cycle, 389
animation system
  real-time inverse kinematics, 427
animation without AutoKeying, 323

antialiasing, 403
  edge, 404
  edge and color, 404
  rendering speed, 404
Antialiasing Always setting
  rendering speed, 404
applying texture, 239
Array Object, 296
arrays, 105–110, 464
As Editor rendering, 403
assigning a new track, 326
assigning keyboard shortcuts, 10
Auto Light and renderings, 408
AutoKeying, 319
  time slider, 320
axes, 16
  defined, 20
banking, 332, 334
beveled text, 78
Bezier handles, 69
Bezier NURBS object
  using, 102
Bezier Spline Curve, 69
blank Restriction tags, 377
BodyPaint, 451–456
  3D painting, 454
  adding text details, 456
  advantages over mesh ripping
    technique, 451
  cautions about Eyedropper tool, 454
  contrast and brightness, 456
  creating a UVW template, 451
  creating material to reference
    texture, 452
  Darken and Lighten brushes, 454
  in conjunction with Photoshop, 454
bone hierarchy, 375
bones, 359–364
  anchoring, 373
  axis, 360
  connecting, 373
  fixing, 361

fixing position, 377
Function setting, 362
grouped with poly mesh, 361
grouping, 377
lengthening, 360
Limit Radius option, 362
restriction tags, 364
rotation and mesh deformation, 361
spawning, 360
viewing by creating see-through
  character, 372
Boolean Objects, 110–116
booleans, 464
bounced light, 300
  Soft Shadows setting, 301
Bridge tool, 89, 151
  pausing, 200
B-Spline Curve, 69
building bump to augment material,
  261
bump map, 170
Bump parameter, 240
  Strength setting, 240
C.O.F.F.E.E. programming
  absolute value, 476
  bouncing ball, 489–492
  code commenting, 461
  conditionals, 469–473
  copy rotation, 487–489
  endless loops, 474
  functions, 475–477
  infinite loops, 474
  logical operators, 467–469
  nesting conditionals, 471
  numerical operations, 466–467
  order of operations, 467
  overriding order of operations, 467
  predefined classes, 482–487
  variable declaration, 462
  variable naming, 462
  variable types, 463–466

INDEX

C.O.F.F.E.E. programming
    variables, 461–466
  arrays, 464
  booleans, 464
  floating points, 464
  integers, 464
  strings, 464
  vectors, 464
C.O.F.F.E.E. SDK, 493
C4D
  translucency, 290
C4D cross-platform compatibility, 423
C4D image files
  formats, 236
  search path, 236
  storing, 236
C4D vs. 3D Studio Max, 422
cage
  density, 121
cage creation
  Point Cage Creation method, 88
  Primitive Cage method, 88
cage modeling, 83
calculating IK restrictions, 377
Camera Move tool, 20
Camera Move vs. Camera Scale, 21
Camera Scale tool, 21
Camera Target Object, 334
candle flame
  Color, Luminance, and
    Transparency parameters, 305
candlelight
  Gradient setting, 305
  soft shadows, 306
canned texture, 233
Caps, 61, 78
Cast Shadows option, 294
Cel animation, 403
Cel Rendering
  speed, 412
Cel renderings, 403

Cel-Render
  web delivery, 416–420
Cel-Render B&W, 412
Cel-Render B/W, 403
Cel-Render Color, 403, 412
Cel-Rendered B&W project, 417–418
Cel-Rendered color project, 418–420
Cel-Renderer
  Illumination, Outline, and Edges
    settings, 412
center of digital space, 33
changing keyboard shortcuts, 10
character animation
  arm position, 346
  leg position, 346
  limiting movement, 354
character model
  cheeks, 188
  chin, 186
  ear, 187
  ear position, 189
  eye socket, 185
  eyebrows, 189
  eyelids, 185
  lips, 187
  mouth, 186
  nose, 186
  sketching, 183
  subdivisions, 183
characters
  overlapping surfaces, 266
children of objects, 51
cinematic animation
  system requirements, 425
Circle Plane Primitives
  active view and placement, 67
  rotating vs. changing plane, 67
Circle Spline Primitives, 66
  creating ellipses, 66
  creating rings, 66
  Plane setting, 67

classes
  predefined, 482–487
closing splines, 72
code commenting, 461
code defined, 458
Color parameter, 235–237
  activating, 239
  importing an image, 235
  mixing color and texture information, 237
Color parameters
  sliders, 235
Color Picker dialog box, 17
colored scene rendering, 416
combining eyelid/eye files, 210
combo game systems, 427
command appearance, 13
Command Manager, 8
  activating, 8–9
  command organization, 9
command palette
  nested shapes, 38
command palettes, 6–17
  creating new, 8
  defined, 2
  docking, 7
  purpose, 6
  scrolling, 2
  undocking, 7
commands, 6
conditionals, 469–473
Configure Viewport dialog box, 197
connecting bones, 373
Console Window, 458
Constrain Contour setting, 81
converting grayscale bump map to Specular map, 262
Coordinates Manager
  mathematical formulae, 48
  object placement, 43
  sizing, 42
  Snap Settings, 46

copying animation sequence, 393
copying objects, 44
copying tracks, sequences, or keyframes, 325
copying UVW coordinates, 450
corner pieces, 33
corrector bones, 374
cranial skeleton, 193
Create Poly tool, 199
Create Polygons tool, 89
creating a polygon, 26
creating primitives, 38
creating splines, 65
creating very curvilinear forms, 69
cube
  parameter editing, 36
  segments, 36
  separate surfaces, 37
Cube Primitive, 42
Cubic Curve, 70
curves, 27
default interface, 1
default object axis, 52
defining a new state, 391
defining where bones have influence, 381
Deformation Objects, 56–61
  geometry, 57
  Limited option, 58
  Unlimited option, 58
  Within the Box option, 58
deleting keyboard shortcuts, 10
deleting splines, 69
deleting tracks, sequences, or keyframes, 326
Depth Channel and rendering, 414
depth of field in renderings, 406
Details tab, 78
Diffusion channel, 245
directional handles, 49
disabling Symmetry Object, 141
disabling the symmetry object, 125

INDEX

Disconnect function, 154
Distant Light setting, 300
  shadows, 314
dividing polygon object into major parts, 385
dividing surface into selections, 385
docked managers, 3
downloading images
  making seamless, 246
Draw Freehand Spline, 68
dropping a point from a selection, 73
Dutch tilt camera rotation, 21
dynamic LOD, 429
Edges and Cel-Renderer, 413
Edit Palettes, 9
Edit Rendering Settings button, 256
Editor
  object visibility, 54
ellipses, 66
empty spline, 65
Enable Snapping, 45
endless loops, 474
Euclidean Geometry Model, 19
expressions
  purpose, 349, 458
Expressions Editor, 458
Extrude Inner
  car window modeling, 129
Extrude Inner tool, 92
Extrude NURBS, 77
  Y Movement setting, 96
  Z Movement setting, 96
Extrude tool, 91
extruding a profile, 77
extrusion
  car body modeling, 124
  Start and End Steps settings, 83
extrusions
  Cap settings, 78
  Maximum Angle setting, 92
  Offset setting, 92
  Preserve Groups setting, 91
  rounding, 78
  Variance setting, 92
extrusions
  Regular Subdivision option, 82
face model
  anatomy, 193–194
  aqueous humor, 203
  Bevel tool to create a small hump for eye, 208
  blocking light behind pupil, 201
  bridging points of eye polys, 206
  building area around eyes, 210–213
  building area around the eyes, 210
  building the ears, 224–229
  building the eyelids, 205–209
  building the eyes, 200–204
  building the mouth, 217–219
  building the nose, 216
  cornea refraction, 203
  creating eyelid depth, 208
  drawing background color, 197
  drawing reference polygons, 196
  eye shape, 194
  facial expressions, 194
  facial musculature, 194
  feature alignment in Photoshop, 196
  filling in forehead, chin, and cheeks, 222–224
  filling in the eye, 207
  filling in the face, 219–221
  folds of eye, 212
  hand drawings, 195
  hierarchy for creating, 205
  iris, 194
  lacrimal caruncle of eye, 205
  Lathe NURBS object/Globe Spline object for eye, 201
  Lathe NURBS object/Iris Spline object, 201
  lips outline, 217

Null Object and other eye objects, 202
photographs, 196
placement of eye components, 210
placing points for eyelids, 205
rearranging points along Z-axis for eye, 206
reference image scaling, 198
reference images, 195
references, 195
skull, 193
soft tissues, 194
superior palbebral sulcus, 210
views, 195
Y-axis placement problem for eye, 212
facial boning, 393–399
facial musculature, 194
  orbicularis oculi, 194
  orbicularis oris, 194
  phonation, 194
facial recognition, 192
facial skeleton, 193
field of view, 429
file size
  eye renderings, 203
Fillet option, 54
fillets, 37
filters and renderings, 407
Fit to Region, 449
FK, 342
  hierarchy, 342
  recording keyframe automatically for children objects, 342
  robotic movement, 343
  upper body movement, 381
FK walking, 345
FK/IK body movement, 383
Flash
  importing JPEG files, 419
  Trace Bitmap function, 419
  web delivery, 416–420

flat scenes, 239
flipping edges, 441
flipping UVs, 280
floating points, 464
folded tools, 38
folding commands, 13
Forward Kinematics, 342
FOV, 429
frame animation system, 426
Free Selection tool, 74
functions, 475–477
game animation
  ability to run on variety of systems, 428
  axis of symmetry, 440
  background views, 431
  deleting unnecessary polygons, 440
  flipping edges, 441
  Knife tool, 440
  limiting number of polygons, 425
  mass market appeal, 428
  matching vertices to sketch, 433
  number of frames, 426
  optimization, 440
  palette limitations, 428
  rendering and playback time, 425
  sketching and scanning, 430
  system requirements, 425
  texture limitations, 426
  texturing, 443
  triangulation, 440
  untriangulating, 441
  Welding tool, 440
game modeling
  dynamic level of detail, 429
  player's field of view, 429
  poly-count requirements, 429–430
game modeling workspace requirements, 428–429
General Settings dialog box, 14
Generate UVW Coordinates, 449
generators, 64

INDEX

geometry, 50
  moving, scaling, rotating object axis, 53
Gimbal Bone, 381
Gimbal Lock, 380–381
global illumination, 310
globe of eye, 194
Glow Editor tab, 306
glow effects and renderings, 406
Glow parameter, 291
gMax software, 422
Grid Points setting, 102
grouping, 99
  parent-child, 51
grouping bones, 377
grouping groups, 52
grouping objects, 50
grouping targets, 351
hard interpolation, 356
hardware-driven OpenGL acceleration, 17
head model
  basic shape, 176
  creating Face object, 176
  deleting polygons, 179
  ears, 181
  Extrude Inner and Extrude for nostril, 179
  Extrude Inners for mouth, 179
  extruding polygons for nose, 177
  eye cavity, 180
  inner areas of ear, 181
  Inner Extruded eyes, 180
  knife cuts, 177
  knife cuts for mouth, 179
  lips, 180
  oral cavity of mouth, 180
  Sphere Primitive for eye, 181
hiding objects, 54
hiding selection sets, 386
Hierarchy button, 342

Hierarchy tool, 319
high poly-count objects, 59
hip bone
  creating and rotating, 373
Hole Inwards setting, 81
hollow extrusion, 78
hotkeys, 12
Hull Inwards setting, 78
human perception of faces, 192
Hyper NURBS
  Extrude Inner/Extrude child manipulation, 94
  segment distance and rounding, 86
HyperNurbs, 83–94
HyperNURBS modeling
  avoiding triangulation of control cage, 123
HyperNURBS used as parent objects, 120
IK, 342
  hierarchy, 348
IK expressions, 349–351
  deactivating to define range of motion, 353
  defining a target object, 349
  moving chain without losing target reference, 350
  multiple targets, 352
  pointing chain to target, 350
  position of target, 349
IK Expressions for bones, 380
IK tags, 352–355
  defining range of motion, 352
  limiting movement, 354
  restraint angles, 354
IK tags for bones, 378
IK Targets for bones, 379
IK walking, 355
  medium interpolation, 356
  stairs, 358
IK/FK body movement, 383

Illumination and Cel-Renderer, 413
image maps
  bad seams, 237
  seamless, 239
importing files in Flash, 418
importing JPEG files into Flash, 419
infinite loops, 474
instances, 105
integers, 464
interactive mapping, 266
  stopping, 269
interpolation, 31, 66
  splines, 71
interpolation problems in animation, 355–359
interpolation types, 356
Inverse Kinematics, 342
iris, 194
jiggling
  gravity and inertia, 384
jiggly sections
  moving as rounded masses, 388
joining points, 151
keyboard shortcuts, 10–12
  assigning, 10
  changing, 10
  Current input field, 10
  deleting, 10
  hotkeys, 12
  operating system, 12
keyframe
  AutoKeying, 319
  recording, 318
keyframes, 318
  defining tracks, 319
  Hierarchy tool, 319
knife cuts
  creating a car, 122
knife cuts to subdivide meshes, 128
Knife tool, 92
  Restrict to Selection, 94

Lathe NURBS object
  using, 100
layering bones, 398
Layers Manager, 267
layout files, 14
layouts
  customizing, 18
  loading, 17
  resetting, 19
  saving, 17
  saving as default, 17
Lens Effect tab, 306
lens effects and renderings, 406
level of detail and renderings, 406
light array, 296
lighting
  area lights, 298
  bounced light, 298
  Brightness setting, 295
  candle flame, 305
  candlesticks, 304
  Cast Shadows option, 294
  ceiling and floors, 293
  computer speed, 290
  daytime, 299
  direct vs. reflected, 310
  Falloff setting, 296
  full intensity and overexposed areas, 295
  Glow parameter, 291
  Inner Distance setting, 297
  instance, 294, 312
  Luminance parameter, 291
  nighttime, 291
  Outer Distance setting, 297
  Render tags, 293
  shadows, 293
  skydome, 310
  softening shadows, 298
  target expression, 310
Limit Radius function, 389

INDEX

Limited option, 58
line animation rendering, 416
linear interpolation, 109
Live Selection tool, 73
loading layouts, 17
loading materials, 248
LOD
  dynamic, 429
LOD setting and renderings, 406
LOD tags, 406
Loft NURBS object, 106
Log file of renderings, 408
logical operators, 467–469
Loop option, 109
looping, 473–475
  Soft option, 329
looping a sequence, 329
looping series of keyframes, 329
looping time, 329
low poly-count objects, 59
Luminance parameter, 254, 291
Magnet tool, 186
main window, 2
making bones visible beneath
    skin, 386
managers
  buried, 2
  defined, 2
  docked, 3
  moving, 4
  nested, 2
  resizing, 3
  undocking, 4
master animator, 318
material
  creating new, 239
material tag, 235
materials
  applying, 234
  Bump parameter, 240
  Color parameter, 235, 237
  copying, 239
  defined, 232
  editing parameters, 232
  parameters, 232
  parent-child relationships, 242
  projection method, 249
  Reflection parameter, 242
  Specular parameter, 235
  test rendering, 239
  transparency, 242
  using a grid as a guide, 254
Materials Editor, 232
  preview sphere for color, 235
  Refresh button, 235
Materials Manager, 232
  preview sphere for material, 235
materials parameters
  Color section, 233
  texture maps, 233
  Texture section, 233
mathematical formulae, 48
Maximum Angle setting, 92
medium interpolation, 356
Menu Manager, 13
merging files, 210
Metal mode, 244
modeling
  plane axes, 184
Move Active Element, 43
Move Selected Up, Move Selected
    Down Sequence, 441
moving extruded polygons, 165
moving managers, 3
moving tracks, sequences, or
    keyframes, 326
MTIK, 351–352
negative time direction, 331
nesting commands, 13
nesting conditionals, 471
new palettes, 7
NLDVE package, 337

non-linear interpolation, 109
non-round vertices, 75
Null Object, 50
  geometry, 50
  moving, 51
  renaming, 51
  resizing, 51
  rotating, 51
numerical operations, 466–467
NURBS, 28–31, 64
  geometry, 28
  purpose, 64
  rendering, 64
  splines, 31
NURBS tools, 28–31
  Bezier, 76
  Extrude, 76
  Hyper NURBS, 76
  Lathe, 76
  Loft, 76
  Sweep, 76
object axes, 98
object axis, 52
  moving, 53
  rotating, 53
  scaling, 53
Object Axis tool
  movable parts, 173
object axis vs. world axis, 47
Object Manager
  defined, 34
  material tag, 235
Object Motion Blur and
    renderings, 406
object oriented programming,
    477–482
Object tool, 52
objects
  children, 51
  geometry, 50
  hiding, 54
  make editable, 38
  parents, 50
  renaming, 35
  visibility, 54
Offset setting, 92
offsetting motion, 331
Only Select Visible Elements
    option, 132
OOP, 477–482
  accessing members of an
    object, 480
  classes, 478
  constructor function, 479
  creating object based on class, 480
  objects, 478
  private variables and functions, 479
  public variables and functions, 479
OOPS
  hierarchies of classes, 480
OpenGL, 17
Optimize command, 122
order of operations, 467
Output tab, 256
Output tab and rendering in Picture
    Viewer, 413
overriding order of operations, 467
oversampling, 404
overwriting Selection tags, 278
painting over grids, 257
palettes
  creating, 6
panning speed, 337
Parallel Light Object, 300
  brightness, 300
  Hard Shadows setting, 300
  Inner Distance setting, 300
  Volumetric setting, 300
parallel lighting
  speeding up computer, 301
parameter handle, 46
Parameter track, 322
parametric handles, 34

INDEX

Parametric primitives
  altering parameters, 36
parent object, 50
perspective, 22
Photoshop
  converting image to grayscale, 261
  layers, 257
  Offset filter for image maps, 237
  Rubber Stamp tool for image maps, 238
  using Airbrush to build up color gradually, 257
  Wrap Around option for image maps, 237
Photoshop work, 257–264
Picture Viewer, 16
  Output tab, 413
  Save tab, 413
Pin pull-down menu, 6
PLA, 319, 391–393
placing primitives, 38
planes
  editing parameters to create a car model, 122
  used to create a car model, 122
planes and planar drawing, 121
planning the geometry of a model, 120
Play Forward button, 320
PluginCafe, 493
Point Cage Creation method, 88
Point Light Object, 307
points, 26–28
  altering, 73
  Editor, 26
  moving independently of other points in spline, 75
  order and direction, 200
  Renderer, 26
  rotating independently of other points in spline, 75
  scaling independently of other points in spline, 75
  vertex, 26
Points Level Animation, 319, 391–393
Points mode, 26–28
poly-count, 28
  screen redraw time, 28
polygon deletion
  closing a gap seamlessly, 145
polygon editing, 122
polygon extrusion
  Maximum Angle setting, 142
Polygon Primitive, 42
polygon selection sets, 385
Polygon Selection tool, 74
polygon thickening
  copy, paste, reverse, extrude method, 167
polygons
  cage, 83
  creating curved shapes, 26
  creating with Bridge tool, 89
  deleting, 122
  Extrude Inner tool, 92
  Extrude tool, 91
  Knife tool, 92
  normals placement for car model panels, 140
  number of sides, 199
  sharing points, 26
  solid surfaces, 26
  spherical shape, 28
  splitting, 137–139
  subdividing and rounding, 84
  subdivision, 83
  three-dimensional, 26
  vertices, 26
polygons and points, 26–28
Position track, 319
Powerslider, 324
  maneuvering quickly through time, 325

precautions before rendering, 416
predefined classes
  predefined, 482–487
Preserve Groups option, 154
Preserve Groups setting, 91
Primitive Cage method, 88
primitive control handle, 55
primitives, 31–38
  creating, 32–33
  mathematical nature, 32
  parametric, 32
  placing, 38
  rounding, 37
programming
  C4D interface changes, 459
  for loops vs. while loops, 475
programming books, 493
programming defined, 458
Projection command, 150
Pulsate track, 326
QTVR Object movie, 256
Quantize tab, 46
quick rendering, 17
Radiosity, 296
Ray Depth and renderings, 408
Raytracing, 84, 256, 403–411
  AA Softness, 411
  Active Object Only setting, 408
  Auto Light option, 408
  default rendering mode, 402
  depth of field, 406
  Effects tab, 406–407
  Filter option, 407
  glow effects, 406
  lens effects, 406
  Level of Detail setting, 406
  LOD, 406
  Object Motion Blur setting, 406
  Options tab, 407–411
  Ray Depth option, 408
  Refl. Depth setting, 408
  Reflection option, 405

refraction, 405
Scene Motion Blur effect, 406
Shadow Depth, 409
Shadows, 405
Threshold setting, 411
Transparency option, 405
volumetric lighting, 406
Real Time Texture Mapping, 17
recording keyframes, 318
recording only Rotation
  keyframes, 342
Rectangle Selection tool, 74
Redo, 32
redocking windows, 4
reference image files
  pixel dimension and offset, 197
reference images
  displaying in C4D, 197
Refl. Depth setting and
  renderings, 408
reflected light, 301
Reflection channel, 242
reflection in renderings, 405
refraction in renderings, 405
Refresh Active View Only, 15
Regular Subdivision option, 82
renaming objects, 35, 44
Render Active View button, 239
Render in Picture Viewer button, 236
Render Safe, 15
Render Tag, 293
rendering
  Alpha Channel, 414
  Cel, 403
  defined, 402
  Depth Channel, 414
  items to check beforehand, 416
  Raytracing, 403–411
  Separate Alpha setting, 414
  Straight Alphas setting, 414
rendering a movie without
  raytracing, 330

INDEX

Rendering Settings button, 402
rendering time
  scene motion blur, 406
renderings
  Log file, 408
resetting layouts, 19
resetting Rotation values of bones, 389
resizing windows, 3
Restriction tags copied to multiple selection sets, 388
Reverse Normals command, 141
rings, 66
Rotate Active Element, 44
Rotate Camera tool, 21
Rotation track, 321
rounding, 78
  connected polygons, 86
  Constrain Contour setting, 81
  Hole Inwards setting, 81
  Hull Inwards setting, 78
  Separate Surfaces option, 86
Rounding settings, 83
RTTM, 17
run cycle, 385
Save tab and rendering in Picture Viewer, 413
saving layout, 14, 17
Scale Axis, 16
Scale Strength with Length, 389
Scale track, 322
scaling, 42
  when to use blowups, 449
scene motion blur
  rendering time, 406
Scene Motion Blur and renderings, 406
Scene Motion Blur setting, 331
screen redraw
  object visibility, 54
screen redraw time, 28

segemented characters
  axis of rotation, 340
segment distance and rounding, 86
segmented characters
  center of gravity, 341
  defined, 340
  defining poses, 342
  hierarchy organization, 341
  rotating and the Undo command, 344
selecting multiple points, 73
selection sets
  creating and naming, 365
Selection SetsSelection Sets, 364–366
selection tags, 266
Selection tools, 73
Semi-Transparent Axis, 16
Separate Alpha and rendering, 414
Separate Surfaces option, 86
Set Value command, 145
shaders, 233–239
  defined, 233
Shadow Depth and renderings, 409
shadows in renderings, 405
Show Picture option, 197
single mesh characters, 340, 359–364
skeletal animation system, 427
skull, 193
skydome, 310
  Distant Light setting, 314
  grouping lights, 312
  instance, 312
  rotation of light group, 312
slope
  car cab modeling, 125
smearing, 446
Smooth Shift function, 140
smoothing tag, 209
Snap Settings, 45–49
  Coordinates Manager, 46
  Edge, 46

Quantize tab, 46
Radius, 46
Type, 45
soft interpolation, 355
  loops, 356
soft tissues, 194
software-driven OpenGL
    acceleration, 17
solid extrusion, 78
Specular parameter
  adjusting, 240
Spherical projection, 255
Spline Creation tools, 65
Spline Curves, 68–72
  Akima Spline Curve, 70
  Bezier Spline Curve, 69
  B-Spline Curve, 69
  Cubic Curve, 70
  Draw Freehand Spline, 68
Spline Primitives, 65
  altering parameters, 65
spline projection, 150
  number of segments, 150
splines, 31, 64–66
  closing, 72
  construction objects, 65
  creating, 65
  deleting, 69
  described, 65
  drawing view, 76
  editing, 70
  empty, 65
  geometry, 31
  interpolation, 31, 66, 71
  mode after creating, 69
  moving after creating, 69
  nature of line between points, 65
  non-linear interpolation, 109
  placement order of copied
      splines, 108
  points, 65
  renaming, 71

splines and perspective view, 76
splitting, 137–139
Sprite Animation, 423
Straight Alphas and rendering, 414
Streamline
  frame conversion, 418
strings, 464
subdivision
  HyperNURBS, 83
subdivision modeling, 82
surface bones and structural
    bones, 385
surface bones in IK hierarchy, 387
Sweep NURBS object
  using, 101
symmetried modeling problems, 372
tabs, 6
tangent handles, 75
Tangential to Spline, 332
Taper Deformation, 57
target expressions, 202
targeting the eyes
  procedures, 204
texture
  applying, 239
  bunched at poles, 255
  scaling, rotating, and moving, 268
Texture Axis tool, 203
Texture input channel, 235
texture scaling, 248
Texture tag, 248
Texture tag dialog box, 203
Texture track, 326
texture/materials, 232
textures
  Flat and Cubic, 249
texturing the eye
  purpose, 203
texturing the globe
  bump map, 203
  color map, 203
  specular highlights, 203

INDEX

transparency map, 203
texturing the iris
  bump map, 203
  color map, 203
  specular highlights, 204
texturing without BodyPaint, 443–450
  cautions, 444
  conserving space, 445
  copying UVW coordinates, 450
  creating UVW coordinates, 449
  distorting the mesh, 446
  grouping the mesh, 449
  optimizing mesh template, 445
  ripping apart a copy of the mesh, 444
  scaling and optimizing grid, 448
  smearing, 446
thickness
  adjusting, 139–167
three-dimensional shapes, 28
Threshold setting and renderings, 411
Time Manager tool palette, 318
time slider, 318
Timeline, 324–327
  organizational tools, 324
  zooming, 324
Timeline Ruler, 324, 325
Title Safe, 16
Toggle Active View tool, 21
toon shader, 412
Torus Object, 61
tracks
  sequences, 325
transparency, 242
transparency in renderings, 405
Transparency map, 386
transverse profile of eye, 194
triangulation, 123
Turbulence, 240
Twist Deformation Object, 60
Undo, 32
Undo Depth, 32

undocking, 4, 7
unfolding commands, 13
Unlimited option, 58
Unused Points checkbox, 122
upper body movement, 381
Use Inverse Kinematics tool, 349
Use Object Axis tool, 52
Use World Coordinate System, 49
UV Uniform Scale tool, 269
UVs
  correcting overlapping, 284
UVW mapping, 249
UVW projection problems, 255
variable declaration, 462
variable naming, 462
variable types, 463–466
variables, 461–466
Variance settings, 92
vectorizing in Streamline, 417
vectorizing jpgs, 419
vectors, 464
vertex, 26
vertex mapping, 393–399
vertex maps, 366–369
  active and inactive sections, 366
  matching sets of bones, 377
  Set, Lighten, Darken settings, 367
  Strength slider, 367
vertex painting, 367
view panel
  axes, 20
view panels, 19–23
Views tab
  Color, 17
  OpenGL, 17
  Views section, 14–16
Visibility setting
  overriding, 54
volumetric light, 300
volumetric lighting and renderings, 406
walk cycle, 345

web delivery, 416–420
web resources for textures, 246
Weld Points Tolerance setting, 213
Welding tool, 440
Wireframe mode, 58
  segments, 36

Within the Box, 58
X-, Y-, Z- axis lock/unlock, 49
X-Ray setting, 102
zoom, 54
zooming on Timeline, 324

GRAPHICS RESOURCE CLUB

A complete graphics reference library and resource center right at your fingertips!

With the **Graphics Resource Club** (http://www.graphicsresourceclub.com) from Charles River Media you have access to best-selling graphics books and new, hands-on tutorials every month.

For Just $99 you get over $700 worth of product!

A New Online Book Each Month (12/year) ($600 Retail Value)
- All files in PDF for easy viewing and downloading
- Books are selected from our best-selling graphics titles

3 New, Online Monthly Tutorials (36/year)
- All files in PDF format
- 3 New tutorials each month that can be downloaded or viewed online covering modeling, animation, and digital effects using leading programs including LightWave, 3D Studio Max, Maya, EI, Poser, Bryce, Carrara, Illustrator, Rhino, and more. All tutorials written by best-selling authors. Plus we have "bonus" months that include extra tutorials!

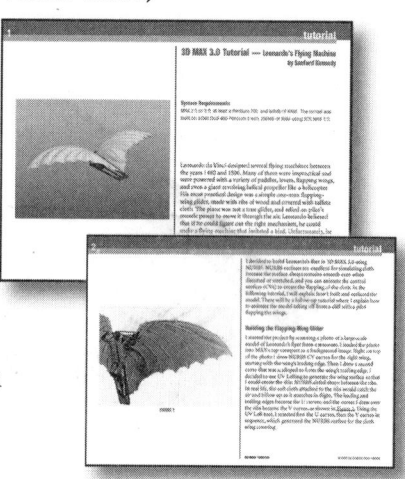

Monthly Newsletter written by Shamms Mortier
- Covers industry news, product information, and useful tips and ideas

One PRINTED book per year – Free shipping ($54.95 value)
- Selected from our best-selling titles

Visit the site and find out how to sign up!
http://www.graphicsresourceclub.com